Continuing Library Education

as viewed in relation to Other Continuing Professional Education Movements

By
Elizabeth W. Stone

Published By
American Society for Information Science
1974

The opinions expressed by contributors to publications of the American Society for Information Science do not necessarily reflect the position or official policy of the American Society for Information Science.

Partial support for the preparation of this volume was provided by the ERIC Clearinghouse on Library and Information Sciences, formerly operated by the American Society for Information Science for the National Institute of Education.

Library of Congress Catalog Card Number: 74-21737
ISBN: 0-87715-108-3
Printed in the United States of America

CONTINUING LIBRARY EDUCATION AS VIEWED IN RELATION TO
OTHER CONTINUING PROFESSIONAL EDUCATION MOVEMENTS.

TABLE OF CONTENTS

LIST OF FIGURES

LIST OF TABLES

CONTINUING LIBRARY EDUCATION AS VIEWED IN RELATION

TO OTHER CONTINUING PROFESSIONAL EDUCATION

MOVEMENTS

I. PURPOSE AND SCOPE

This review attempts to show the present status of continuing library education
in its major aspects and relate each aspect to other continuing professional
education movements. It highlights the roles of relevant groups within professions with responsibility for continuing education, their interface with each
other, and their relationship to the individual professional. As recent research in the field of adult learning concludes that education for adults must
be planned and implemented to meet their particular needs and criteria for
learning, sources are also included which deal with the nature of the adult
learner and the modes of learning adapted to his needs.

A bibliography is like other reference tools. It is easier to use if the intent
of the author is known. This bibliography presents a great quantity of literature from many professions. This broad viewpoint is used in the hope that
librarians will find new insights by looking at continuing education activities
in other professions. Librarians are becoming increasingly concerned with
continuing education, and it was the hope of this reviewer to bring new aspects
to their attention by examining the work of other professions, some of which,
like medicine and engineering, have been active in this area for many years.

This objective has influenced the form of the bibliography and accounts for
the fact that it contains abstracts, resumes, annotations, and quite a number
of fairly long quotations. If a particular   work contains material that
might shed new light on continuing education or suggest new approaches, it
is described in some detail. For example, the five papers presented by
leaders in continuing education in the professions of architecture (R-39),
banking (C-10), engineering (M-30), education (L-27), and ministry (G-10)
are presented at length as they are to be found no place else in the literature
and they were prepared especially for the Mini-Workshop on Continuing
Library Education sponsored by the Continuing Library Education Committee
of the Association of American Library Schools. (See Appendix A.) For
other works a title may be sufficient to suggest content or a certain technique
or method.

Only in recent years has there appeared any volume of literature on continuing education, although some eminent early professional leaders such as
Flexner and Osler believed (and demonstrated by their lives) that physicians
should be life-long students and that the profession should be supportive to
such a life style   (H-33). Only in the past year or two has library literature
begun to consider the question in any depth. In 1962 a survey revealed that
a million professional persons (excluding teachers) were involved in formal
or independent study related to professional development and since that time
there has been an enormous increase of university, professional,association
and employer involvement in continuing education in all its aspects (G-134).
With that has come expanded research and development.

In some ways this review of the literature was frustrating. First, the
term "continuing education" is a broad one. Some professions define it very
loosely; others hold it within very narrow boundaries. The differences and
problems of definition will be dealt with in the text. But any material that
deals with fundamental concepts that explain a profession's approach to
continuing education has been included. This includes some basic and frequently quoted studies that help explain the success of continuing education
programs in a variety of professions.

Second, the material which is so plentiful in describing continuing education
in many professions, is not so abundant in the field of library science. This
is frustrating since the library is the vantage point for this study.

Third, there is the difficult question of how far back one should go in discussing activities called continuing education. The solution is a haphazard
selection varying according to the particular topics and the time that a
particular profession began to involve itself with continuing education. The
goal was to go back far enough to describe the state of library education
and to compare it as it exists today with other fields. This was always done
in the hope that it might inspire librarians to greater activity and perhaps
show them paths they might follow -- or avoid.

4

II. CONTINUING EDUCATION: CONCEPTS AND RELATIONSHIPS

Definitions and Scope of Continuing Education

Even the slightest examination of the literature of professional continuing education will reveal immediately that "continuing education" has many meanings. Questions of definition arise whenever position papers are written, questionnaires distributed, funding proposals prepared. And such questions consume an unwarranted amount of time on any agenda. For some groups the term excludes formal education for a degree or specialty training leading to certification; whereas other groups give a much broader interpretation. In the Guidelines Statement written by the Staff Development Committee of the ALA Library Administration Division as set forth in Library Trends (A-41,98) it was defined as "referring to all activities and efforts by the individual to upgrade his knowledge, abilities, competencies or understanding in his field or specialization." In the 1972 position paper on continuing education adopted by the Association of American Library Schools (A-77) Houle's statement was used: "Continuing Education might be defined as any kind of learning or teaching which extends or builds upon previous experience in the same general realm of knowledge and whose specific goals are not intended to terminate all study in that realm. It implies that the learner has studied some related body of content previously and is carrying on the process further; it implies that the programs depend upon his having done so; and it implies that he proposes to continue such learning in the future." (H-38)

The section on Continuing Education in the Library Education and Manpower Statement, adopted by the Council of the American Library Association, June 30, 1970, (A-42) states: "Continuing education opportunities include both formal and informal learning situations, and need not be limited to library subjects or the offerings of library schools." In the next section it specifies: "The 'continuing education' which leads to eligibility for Senior Librarian or Specialist positions may take any of the forms suggested directly above so long as the additional education and experience are relevant to the responsibilities of the assignment."

In searching for a definition everyone will not be in complete agreement. But as Houle (H-38) points out, common terms cannot be used without careful definition, for "they have come to mean so many things that now they mean little or nothing at all. All that can be done is to mark out a point of view and a method of approach that offer as large an area of common agreement as possible and that allow the maximum scope for creative thought and action."

5

The following are examples from other groups or individuals who have struggled with the problem of definition:

The Committee on Goals of Engineering Education of the American Society for Engineering Education (A-56) views engineering education beyond the first degree as serving many purposes. The engineers define purpose as the individual student's goal, not the method used to accomplish the goal. Four purposes are identified by the engineers:

1) Upgrading a person's education (work toward a graduate degree);
2) Updating a person's education (make his education comparable to that of a person receiving like degree at present time);
3) Diversification to new fields (person may seek some formal education in another field, but not necessarily at higher degree level);
4) Broadening a person's education (adding new perspective to his own field, such as inclusion of financial, political, and social factors).

Another characteristic of continuing education as noted in the Goals of Engin-Engineering Education report is that it usually refers to training which better equips a person for his contemporary work, for the job he has now, or aspires to in the near future.

A few pages later the Committee states (A-56:430):

The objective of continuing engineering studies is the specific enhancement of the competence of the individual as a practicing engineer, rather than the attainment of an additional academic degree. This dimension of engineering education must expand and achieve new levels of effectiveness. It differs from the traditional academic ladder of successive degree levels in formal education. It might well be termed the career ladder a sequence of more individualized studies pursued at various times outside of degree programs and selected principally for the independent purpose of career extension and stimulation.

The Committee illustrated its "dual ladder" concept with a diagram as illustrated in Fig. 1. This diagram shows on the left that the academic institutions alone are responsible for the degree ladder, but are partners with industry, government and the engineering societies in the broader "career ladder" activities.

The Committee viewed "continuing education" as primarily including items 2, 3, and 4--updating, diversifying, and broadening. It viewed

6

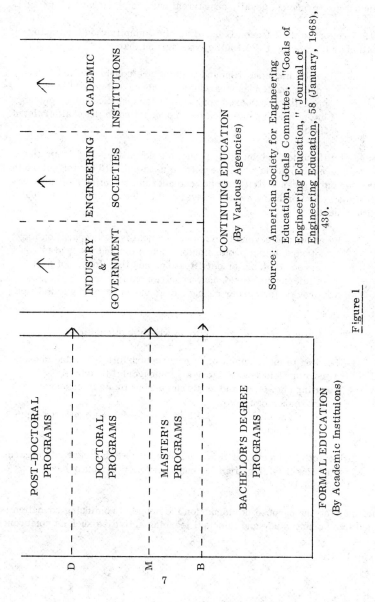

POST-DOCTORAL
PROGRAMS

DOCTORAL
PROGRAMS

MASTER'S
PROGRAMS

BACHELOR'S DEGREE
PROGRAMS

FORMAL EDUCATION
(By Academic Instituions)

INDUSTRY
&
GOVERNMENT

ENGINEERING
SOCIETIES

ACADEMIC
INSTITUTIONS

CONTINUING EDUCATION
(By Various Agencies)

Source: American Society for Engineering
Education, Goals Committee. "Goals of
Engineering Education," Journal of
Engineering Education, 58 (January, 1968),
430.

Figure 1

The Dual Roles of Formal and Continuing Education

advanced degree education as chiefly concerned with item 1--upgrading.
"Another feature of advanced-degree education is that it usually is preparatory,
and is undertaken prior to embarking on a career at a new and higher level
of performance. By contrast, continuing studies involve a more or less
continuous performance, usually concurrent with employment" (A-56:408).

In a 1967 report to the Surgeon General by his Committee on Continuing
Education and Training (U-20:196), it was agreed that:

> Continuing education and training are considered to be those
> educational endeavors which are above and beyond those
> normally considered appropriate for qualification or entrance
> into a health profession or an occupation in the health related
> fields.

Because of difficulties arising in applying this definition, the Committee
developed several criteria which were to be used collectively for determining
whether or not a given activity can be considered as continuing education
and training. The primary criteria developed by the Committee are that all
activities must:

-- Be above and beyond basic, core or qualifying preparation for
   entrance into a profession or occupation and not lead to
   degree, diploma or certification, and therefore, not part
   of internship, residencey requirements.
-- Not provide for career change, e.g. nurse becoming a dietition,
   etc.

The activity must meet the criteria where applicable:

-- Leading to the assumption of new responsibilities in the chosen
   career field (supervisory and managerial training).
-- Updating knowledge and skills in current fields of endeavor
   (refresher courses).
-- Updating knowledge and skills in a different but basically related
   health field.

If the activity meets the above criteria, it is to be included, regardless of how it is classified for budgetary or other purposes.
(U-20:196-197).

Sometimes for the purpose of discussion the scope of continuing education is
divided into formal study and informal learning activities such as conferences,

workshops, professional meetings, reading, writing, editing, consultation, etc. (S-72). This concept is illustrated in Fig. 2. "Professional librarian" is defined in this chart, and used in the present paper, as all librarians, administrators, and other specialists in public, school, academic and special libraries, library associations, and government agencies with responsibility in the field of librarianship, who have received a Master's degree in Library Science. Nattress (N-17) believes that "Continuing education... should be goal oriented rather than activity oriented, that is, the objectives should be clearly stated in behavioral terms before any activity is planned. The activity should be appropriate to the objectives. Therefore, continuing education is a process whereby a person who has completed his formal education is provided with a means for meeting his needs for further personal development. The learning, or how well the objectives are met, must be evaluated." This approach is shown in Fig. 3.

Nattress (N-17:44) explains his definition in the following manner:

> Applying this model to the problems of continuing education, it becomes evident that the role of the educator must be more than that of an educational agent or a facilitator of learning prescribed subject matter. The educator must be willing and able to interact with the student in each segment of the model. For example, the educator must be sensitive to pressures and tensions within and between individuals in order to help them set reasonable short- and long-range objectives. This, in fact, may be viewed as his primary role, for, as Mager has said, "If you give each learner a copy of /the/ objectives, you may not have to do much else (M-25)."

This discussion of definition has been presented in the hope that concepts presented may be of help to some groups struggling with a definition that will meet their needs. For the purpose of this paper, wide in its scope, continuing education is broadly defined as given by Houle (H-38), and, as stated in the Library Education and Manpower Statement of ALA (A-42), includes "both formal and informal learning situations, and need not be limited to library subjects or the offerings of library schools," but it is limited to education or training which better equips a person for his contemporary work, for the job he has now, or aspires to in the near future.

Technological Obsolescence

A central concept and concern in discussing continuing education is that of obsolescence, stemming from the accelerated growth and expansion of knowledge and technology. In order to maintain their job effectiveness, all professionals need to acquire new knowledge after receiving their last degree.

DEFINITION CHART

To show the relationship of key terms as used in this study the following chart is presented to
help you in filling out the questionnaire.

PROFESSIONAL DEVELOPMENT; PROFESSIONAL GROWTH; CONTINUING EDUCATION

In this study these three terms refer to all activities and efforts by the individual to upgrade his knowledge, abilities, competencies, and understanding in his field of work or
specialization so that he can become a more effective professional and be able to handle
responsibilities of greater scope and accountability. This study is chiefly concerned with
factors that may be associated with librarians' motivation to develop professionally through
formal education and professional improvement activities.

FORMAL STUDY; FORMAL EDUCATION

Formal course work or training as a fully
registered student:
--in credit or non-credit courses;
--in a degree program or a non-degree
  program;
--in library science or
--in special subject areas related to your
  work, such as data processing, systems
  analysis, budgeting, story-telling,
  history--any area that contributes to
  your professional growth;
--after your MSLS degree.

PROFESSIONAL IMPROVEMENT ACTIVITY

All your activities and efforts, with the exception of formal course work, which may
contribute to your professional growth, such as:
--attending conferences, short courses, workshops, professional meetings;
--reading, writing and editing of professional
  literature;
--consultation, teaching, speaking to groups;
--participation in in-service (on-the-job)
  training programs;
--membership in informal study groups inside or outside your library;
--recruitment activities;
--research, etc.

PROFESSIONAL LIBRARIAN

In this study, the term professional librarian includes:
--all librarians, administrators, and other specialists
--in public, school, academic, and special libraries,
  library associations, and government agencies
--with responsibility in the field of librarianship
--who have received a Master's Degree in Library Science.
In this questionnaire, the MALS, MLS, MS in LS. and
other degree designations are all, for the sake of brevity,
usually referred to as MSLS.

Figure 2

Source: Elizabeth W. Stone. "A Study of Some Factors Related to the
Professional Development of Librarians." Unpublished
Doctoral dissertation, American University, 1968, p. 435.
10

MODEL of Process of Continuing Education

Direct relationships ___
Feedback
relationships - - -

Pressures & Tensions	Objectives	Subject Matter
External and internal states that influence the individual to change	That which learners will be able to do at the end of an educational experience that they could not do before.	Content which is directly related to the objectives that determine what is appropriate in the learning experience.

Application	Readiness to Change	Learning Experience
Doing things in the real world that demonstrate the value of what has been learned and the consequence of what has not been learned.	A professional's commitment to keep on learning, willingness to accept new ideas and to modify behavior.	Presentation of subject matter to learners through educational methods and techniques appropriate for the subject matter.

Criterion Performance	Evaluation	Mastery
External standards set by law or authoritarian bodies against which behavior is measured.	Measurement of the amount and direction of change in the learner and therefore of how well the objectives have been met.	Achieving skills and knowledge related to professional competence; personal perception of knowledge and skills gained.

Note: The model may be entered at any point. The point of entry should ideally be the point of exit. It is desirable but not essential to move through each segment at least once between entry and exit. Movement through the model is usually clockwise.

Figure 3

Source: LeRoy William Nattress. "Continuing Education for the Professions in the United States." Convergence, 3 (no. 4, 1970), p. 43.

11

In fact the degrees themselves are in part obsolescent because the knowledge represented by the degree is itself partly obsolescent, as is so aptly expressed by Shera (S-24) in his article, "The Self-Destructing Diploma."

A large part of the literature uses the term "technological obsolescence." Often undefined, in an individual it is generally taken to mean "a deficiency of knowledge such that he approaches problems with viewpoints, theories, and techniques less effective than others currently used in his field of specialization (C-24:5).

There are several types of obsolescent persons. One is the person who has not kept up with new knowledge and techniques in his field. His competence has aged in the face of the knowledge explosion, and makes him obsolescent as compared both to new graduates and to his colleagues who keep up and apply new findings. A second type of obsolescent person is the one who is over specialized, who has only kept up with his very narrow field of specialization, in which he has probably been working for years; he has lost contact with broader changes. He has become so overspecialized that he cannot effectively undertake new work in his own or in closely related fields, and cannot apply relevant new knowledge from them to his own particular specialty. A third type of obsolescent person is the one who moves out of one career into another that may not be very closely related. He is obsolescent in his own specialty because his training is no longer closely integrated with his work.

Although there are different degrees of technical obsolescence and it does not affect all people the same way, the majority of people seem to recognize it as a threat to their job competence, or even to their employability. There is evidence in the literature that the degree of the threat varies. One study in librarianship (S-72:149-52, 156) demonstrates the anxiety that technology can bring. The respondents, middle and upper-level librarians, showed the greatest demand for courses in automation, even though few of them were in libraries that were automated at the time and no immediate plans for automation. It was shown statistically that having automated activities in the respondent's library and wanting to take a course in library automation were unrelated. The high demand seemed to be caused by the anxiety feelings the respondents had, fearful that they might need automation in their jobs in the future. In the other sections of this study, it was shown statistically that there was a high correlation between the other courses the respondents wanted to take and their present job needs.

A striking case of the differences in employability of those who do and those who do not keep up to date through continuing education is reported in the literature (C-24:7). The background of 125 engineers, all laid off at one time by a large division of a major corporation showed that there was only one constant variable among the layoffs--not one had taken any form of extracurricular education in the last six years.

The problem of obsolescence is complicated by the fact that it is not only a matter of the individual overcoming his own obsolescence, but, as pointed out in the Continuing Education for R and D Careers Report (C-24:8), it is a matter of "changes taking place in knowledge itself as a source of problems experienced by individuals, rather than stressing inaction on the part of individual professionals."

Largely as a result of the public's blaming the engineers after Sputnik for not having accomplished as much as the Russians, changes were made in the engineering school curriculum. The Joint Advisory Committee on Continuing Engineering Studies (C-30:25) concluded:

> There is now a significant difference between the preparation of recent engineering graduates and their counterparts of a decade or more ago. Large numbers of earlier graduates possess engineering experience which is no longer applicable and lack currently essential theoretical background. On the other hand, recent graduates possess much more sophistication technically, but still need instruction to be able to apply this knowledge effectively. For both of these groups, comprehensive systems of continuing engineering studies covering the spectrum from fundamental knowledge to engineering application are essential.

To guard against obsolescence and the harm that it could cause to the individual as well as to the profession generally, the Goals Committee of the Joint Advisory Committee undertook to plan for the future in terms of a lifetime of continuing study as part of every engineer's normal career (A-56). This is one of the chief goals of the engineering profession at the moment. "When this goal is achieved, 'overcoming' obsolescence will give way to 'preventing' obsolescence -- which is in turn synonomous with 'keeping up to date' with new knowledge and maintaining useful skills and knowledges (C-24:10-11)."

As knowledge in every discipline advances, the public, aware of the social and economic role of information, has a right to expect library service to be performed that will meet clients needs in the most efficient manner possible. However, Bundy and Wasserman (B-39:9-10) maintain that most librarians resist the idea that the most important commodity of modern times is information in myriad forms, and their continuing reliance on the book, combined with their lack of specialized knowledge in subject areas, have resulted in their failure to satisfy the newly-emerging demands from clients. They raise the question whether or not librarianship will be able to institute changes and transform itself in a manner demanded by current pressures in society. Klempner (K-17:729) believes a major factor contributing to this inability of librarians to meet newly-emerging user demands is the lack of continuing education for librarians.

Patterns of Professionalization

Houle (H-31) suggests that before any feasible comparisons can be undertaken between professional attempts at continuing education, it is necessary to consider the root question of the definition of a profession and to a consideration of whether all professions use the same basic way of work, or whether their services conform to different patterns. In reviewing the literature in this area, this reviewer feels that Houle's solution to this problem is the one that offers the most helpful approach to this problem in relation to the development of continuing education programs, therefore he is quoted at some length in this section. He takes the position that much of the difficulty would be resolved if a profession were not defined as a vocation in which a fixed level of achievement or certain standards have been or have to be attained, but rather as an ideal state toward which many occupational groups are striving. Houle (H-31) suggests 13 such aims that such a group might seek:

1.   To master the rudiments of fundamental and complex bodies of knowledge and theory that have been derived for theoretical and descriptive rather than practical reasons.

2.   To use these bodies of knowledge to deal with a category of specific problems and concerns that arise in the vital practical affairs of mankind.

3.   To create a body of knowledge and technique that is broadly concerned with the nature, history, dimensions, and processes of its field of practical application.

4.   To transmit this body of knowledge and technique to all recognized practitioners both before they enter service and throughout their careers.

5.   To test the capacity of individual practitioners to perform their duties at an acceptable level of accomplishment and license those who are qualified to do so.

6.   To maintain associations that will advance and protect the interests of practitioners and maintain their standards of performance.

7.   To secure legal recognition of the special rights and privileges of the vocation.

8.   To foster the general public's awareness of itself as an entity

14

by a broadly conceived public relations program explaining the functions of the professionalizing group and its position on relevant issues.

9.   To establish a tradition of ethical practice, sometimes reinforced by a formal code or by legislation.

10.   To establish and enforce penalties for those who fail to act in terms of accepted standards of practice.

11.   To establish formal relationships between the profession's practitioners and the people who use their services.

12.   To establish formal relationships between the profession's practitioners and those of allied occupations.

13.   To nurture a subculture for the members of the profession, with lore, folkways, mores, traditions, role differentiations and relationships, variations in authority and power, meaningful and random clusterings of people, and other social attributes.

Since the landmark statement by Flexner in 1915   (F-10) there has never been any complete agreement on which indicators are infallible. New ones are constantly being suggested by various professions, and it is unlikely that there ever will be any agreement. A strong case can be made, however, for Houle's position that a "dynamic concept of professionalization, based on discovery, growth and innovation" offers the educator concerned with continuing education the best base line on which to build. Such an approach also gives, as Houle notes, the educator a position of advantage because his expertise is seen as a way of enhancing and speeding up the process of professionalization. He can be of service both within and without the profession.

Houle (H-31) presents another factor which is essential before embarking on any comparison of the continuing education efforts of the various professions. Different professions have different patterns of work and what might be the best or ideal method for one group might not be the most effective for another. Therefore to avoid distortion, it is necessary to recognize that service provided by professionals follows several different patterns; each group has its own dominant way of working, though of course there are many individual exceptions. Houle has identified three basic patterns:

THE ENTREPRENEURIAL OCCUPATIONS, in which "the practitioner organizes, operates, and assumes the risk for his own work,

15

either alone or in partnership with colleagues. He offers direct service to his clients as they need it. The professionalizing groups in which this pattern is dominant include accounting, architecture, dentistry, law, medicine, and "optometry."

THE COLLECTIVE OCCUPATIONS, in which "the practitioner performs his service in an institution that has employed him. Sometimes his clients are the members of an association, as is true with most Protestant and Jewish ministries. Sometimes his clients are members of the general public or of some special public. Among the professionalizing occupations predominantly using this latter form of service are engineering, forestry, journalism, librarianship, nursing, pharmacy, social work, and teaching. The practitioners who follow this pattern sometimes work alone, but more often they are associated with a group of colleagues in either their own vocation or in others allied to it."

THE HIERARCHICAL OCCUPATIONS, in which " the practitioners also work within an institutional framework but their expertise lies not in giving of direct service but in their capacity to operate an ordered structure of authority and to initiate or to enforce the policies that best foster and maintain this structure. Among the professionalizing groups that characteristically follow this pattern are the armed services (air force, army, coast guard, marines, navy) business administration, and the Roman Catholic clergy. In some of these cases -- most notably the armed services and the Roman Catholic clergy --there is, for practical purposes, only one employer. If the practitioner leaves the employ of the sole possible user of his services, he leaves the profession. In other cases, alternative employers exist and the individual often gains advancement by moving from one to another."

Using this classification as presented by Houle, it becomes clear that the independence of action is the greatest in the entrepreneurial group, and is present in varying degrees in the other two classifications. The expertise of the individual professional gives him a quality that distinguishes him from others employed in the same institution.

The knowledge of these basic patterns has implications for the development of continuing education programs. Not only do they make the task of comparison much more difficult, but the educational practices used are influenced by these basic differences in patterns. The educator concerned with continuing education cannot make his greatest contribution unless he understands the nature of the work environment of the professional group that he is serving.

16

Analyses such as the foregoing are valuable and necessary for the educator with responsibility for planning and programming continuing professional activities, but the individual professional needs a definition as a guide to daily practice. The School Library Manpower Project (S-9:44) identified professionalism as a major competency area for the education of school library media specialists, and provided this definition:

> Professionalism is the conduct of qualified people who share responsibilities for rendering a service; for engaging in continued study; and for maintaining high standards of achievement and practice within the principles, structure and content of a body of knowledge.

Eight behavioral objectives are set for this area of competency by the Project (S-9:44-45), one of which deals specifically with continuing education:

> To engage in continuous study for professional growth including the study of current information and trends affecting message design and system analysis and contribution to the creation of such processes.

Another source for a simple working definition is the Position Paper on Teacher Education and Professional Standards published by the National Commission on Teacher Education and Professional Standards (P-26:2). It states:

> Teaching is a profession to the degree that its members are professional. A person who qualifies as a professional in any field:
>
> -- Is a liberally educated person.
>
> -- Possesses a body of specialized skills and knowledges essential to the performance of his job.
>
> -- Makes rational judgments and acts accordingly; accepts responsibility for the consequences of his judgments and actions.
>
> -- Believes in his service to society.
>
> -- Assumes responsibility with his colleagues in developing and enforcing standards and abides by these standards in his own practice.

17

-- Seeks new knowledge and skill in order to improve his practice.

Relative Stages of Development of Continuing Education in the Professions.

Nattress (N-17:44) in his comparative study of continuing education for the professions in the United States, finds that there are represented in the country today three stages of development in continuing education programs. He cites the clergy as exemplary of a profession in which continuing education is just beginning to be recognized as necessary for proficient practice. He cites law as an example of the second stage in which continuing education has been joined to formal pre-service education into a continuum where one blends into the other. It is a continuous process -- not something just added on. From his study he feels that medicine is the profession which today most approximates the ultimate criterion by which effectiveness can be measured. In medicine there is a broad approach designed to be available to each individual. Its overriding goal is to reduce the morbidity and mortality of the total population. In making comparisons it should be noted that two of these fall within the single classification of Entrepreneurial Occupations as classified by Houle and noted earlier.

Stage 1 as exemplified by the Clergy

Nattress (N-17:45)explains his description of the clergy as the least developed by stating that only recently has the clergy been awakened to new roles it can play in our rapidly changing society. This includes the concept of the "church without walls" -- taking clerical services to the people rather than waiting for the people to come to the church. Up until this time universities have made the most continual impact by offering a variety of courses in the hope that individual clergy would find courses and programs to meet their needs. It is true that little attention was paid either to the objectives of the individual or to the objectives of the experience being offered. In addition, many programs were viewed by participants either as a repeat of what they had had in their basic training in seminary, or as being of a "faddish" nature. The clergy stated that they preferred their own methods of continuing education -- namely self study, as other methods lacked continuity, were not meeting their real needs and were too expensive.

There are, however, signs of corrective actions being taken. Nattress (N-17:45) cites the 1970 creation of a Voluntary Committee for Continuing Professional Education of the Clergy which lists 12 personal objectives for members that would result in better service to congregations.

18

Gamble (G-12) reported the founding of another group concerned with continuing education of the ministry, SACEM (Society for the Advancement of Continuing Education for Ministry). This group is not restricted to an ordained clerical group; rather, it is a resource for helping the people of the churches, Protestant, Catholic, Jewish, to find the resources for life-long learning that will enable them to become more competent for life whether they are mechanical engineers, clergymen, or people engaged in other forms of ministry. This group is oriented toward the person of the learner as well as updating information. Gamble pointed out that the group has only 300 members, and that their task was heightened because the members are people for whom continuing education is a "second assignment." Of the 300 theological seminaries in the United States, only 10 have persons who have continuing education as a primary assignment.

Another recent gain was the launching in 1968 of the ecumenical Academy for Parish Clergy (U-2:74-75), with the help of a $75,000 grant from the Lilly Foundation. Open to all interested parish clergymen, this organization exists to:

1) Motivate parish clergy to lifelong learning.
2) Motivate congregations to encourage their pastors in their continuing education endeavors.
3) Motivate colleges, universities, hospitals and other training agencies to make provision for continuing education of ministers (U-2:74).

For a membership fee of $25 annually, any pastor may become an active participant, but membership requires a strict study discipline: two weeks out of every year spent in Academy-approved study, and involvement in regionally-based research projects related to the work of his own church. Failure to maintain the discipline will result in loss of membership after three years and one who has dropped out will not be allowed to rejoin. It is intentionally designed to make it a mark of achievement and competence to be known as a member. The Academy's basic strategy for continuing education is to focus on the actual sites where the ministry can serve people's needs best -- the "classroom" for continuing education becomes the "field" (U-2:75).

The United Presbyterian Church of the United States of America took a major step forward in the appointment of a Temporary Commission on Continuing Education. This group has issued a major position paper for the Church which is in the process of study by the denomination in preparation for implementation. This Commission found its work, as well as a special

19

survey it commissioned Gamble to do on continuing education for ministry, hampered throughout by the lack of any universally acceptable definition of continuing education. Gamble, for example, had to settle for including program data on the basis of whatever the respondent's own definition might be (U-2:96).

The Commission has defined "Continuing Education" as commencing when formal, preparatory education for the professional ministry is completed and as pertaining most immediately to the full-time professional employee of the church, ordained or unordained. The Commission also concluded that programming for continuing education must not be isolated from an understanding of developments in the training process associated with the basic period of ministerial formation, namely, formal theological education. The Commission stated that it foresaw many ways in which a continuing education program will mutually strengthen both institutions, to the common benefit of the whole Church (U-2:77-79).

The Commission's report recommends a structure for ongoing programs to center in the establishment of a Cooperative Agency on Continuing Education for Ministry, and details the function and emphases it recommends for such an agency in considerable detail (U-2:79). It also recommends that structural arrangements be made to aid ministers' participation in continuing education programs (U-2:91).

In reviewing the present condition in the ministry, Nattress (N-17:45) concludes that "continuing education for the clergy is coming into existence" and that a great deal of change can be anticipated in terms of content, methods, and techniques.

The Commission on Continuing Education of the Presbyterian Church (U-2:95) viewed the over-all continuing education situation in the ministry this way:

> The present open market lacks any semblance of order or of underlying educational philosophy. It has come into being. . .because most of the programming in the field has been designed and administered by church agencies that are chartered to perform other functions. Their interest in continuing education, therefore, is not their primary reason for being; they have neither the time and resources nor the motivation to develop the field seriously and in sufficient scope. Their interest in continuing education, however, is genuine. Increasingly they are establishing new staff positions and program units to develop their continuing education

enterprises, so the variety and calibre of these offerings seem
to be increasing all the time. Yet the overall field remains
unattended and becomes increasingly confusing.

Gamble, in speaking to librarians at the Association of American Library
Schools' workshop in January, 1973, identified the continuing education
activity in the ministry as being a "side-line operation," representing a
small commitment in terms of dollars and personnel, but an area of
excitement as frontier developments were now happening which give signs
for encouragement (G-12).

Stage 2 as Exemplified by the Legal Profession

The group that Nattress identified as being in the second stage of
development regarding continuing professional education was the legal profession. According to Nattress, "the limitations of formal legal education
due to time and the scope of the field are recognized, and formal education
has been joined with continuing education in a continuous process" (N-17:44).
In spite of having the constant motivation of a judge and jury continually
evaluating how much a lawyer is benefiting from continuing educational experiences, the legal profession recognized that with the proliferation of
legal materials and institutions, action should be taken at a national level.
In 1947 the Committee on Legal Education and Admissions to the Bar of the
American Bar Association recommended that the American Law Institute,
in cooperation with the American Bar Association, assume the task of
providing continuing legal education (N-17:46).

Since 1965, the Institute has published each year the Catalog of Continuing
Legal Education Programs and Publications in the United States, which
today has about 1000 entries. Many of the programs listed, however, have
the same weaknesses as current offerings in the field of ministry -- they
repeat pre-service courses and give little attention to the formulation of
objectives related to the continuing education needs of lawyers. A unique
feature of the continuing education in law is that a large proportion of the
programs are carried on outside law schools through institutes sponsored by
the American Bar Association (N-17:46). A parallel is found in banking
in which the continuing education effort is carried out by the American
Institute of Banking, sponsored by the American Banking Association
(C-10).

At the 1969 Galaxy Conference on Adult Education, Paul Wolkin, Director
of the Joint Committee on Continuing Legal Education of the American Law
Institute, reported on two new formats in continuing legal education:

1) two-day travelling seminars; 2) production of cassette recordings of meetings sponsored by law associations.

Nattress (N-17:47) sums up the basic characteristics of the middle level of continuing professional education: "... continuing legal education, in a formal sense, is heavily content and activity oriented. There is great reliance, however, on the reality that the practice of law is in itself a continuing education activity. In addition, most discussants of continuing legal education emphasize the point that legal education and continuing legal education are both part of the same process " (N-17:47). Also it should be explained that it is organized at a national level and designed to serve all interested lawyers.

Stage 3 as Exemplified by the Medical Profession

In the Nattress ranking of stages of development relative to continuing professional education, he states: "In medicine, there is an ultimate criterion by which effectiveness can be measured, and a broadly based activity approach to reduce morbidity and mortality in the population has been attempted" (N-17:44).

Nattress (N-17:47) gives part of the credit for this top ranking of the medical profession in the area of continuing education to the federal government which, through the passage of Public Law 89-239 and other legislation in 1965, has made possible a great amount of experimentation and innovation in the development of new programs (especially in the area of institutes and workshops) and in modes of learning fully utilizing the new technology, that has not characterized other professions. However, all of the credit for the advanced stage, comparatively speaking, of continuing education in the medical profession cannot go to the federal government because of funds they have made available for experimentation and implementation of new programs. In 1962 the Joint Study in Continuing Medical Education was organized as a result of widespread recognition of the need for coordination and leadership in the continuing education of the physician. In 1961 the American Medical Association invited other major medical organizations to send representatives to a meeting "to consider the formation, under the sponsorship of major medical organizations, of a national agency to further continuing medical education" (D-29:676).

In 1962, this Joint Study Committee in Continuing Medical Education presented its report, entitled "Lifetime Learning for Physicians," written by Dryer (D-28). This "landmark" statement clearly states the objective for the continuing medical education study: "A conceptual and practical blue-print for the provision of equal, coordinated, educational opportunities throughout the country for those physicians who need, want, and will continue their lifetime postgraduate learning" (D-28:ix-x).

It proposes that this "university without walls" for continuing medical education be implemented through an organization that "should have the function and independence of a university but need not have the physical plant, resident faculty, and resident student body which a university ordinarily has. Its functions should be those of teaching, research, development, and coordination in continuing medical education" (D-29:678). Community, professional and personal criteria were established that such an organization should meet. The necessity of a wide use of the available new technology in implementing such a program is emphasized as an imperative if the objective is to be achieved (D-28, D-29). Though the full-blown plan and its accompanying proposals for action have not yet been fully formalized, the document has served a valuable purpose by acting as a baseline for program development. One of the characteristics of many of the programs developed has been the setting of realistic objectives and the evaluation of programs on the basis of these objectives.

The Stage of Continuing Library Education

Where does librarianship fit within this three-stage classification scheme? It would seem on the basis of evidence reflected in the literature that it could only qualify for stage one. In fact, many of the types of weak-nesses, present type of activities, and high hopes for the future closely parallel those described under the clergy efforts.

Rothstein (R-42:2226-2227) analyzed the trouble in librarianship: "...continuing professional education is essentially a peripheral activity within librarianship. It is the central responsibility of no agency within our field and it has no organization to see to its planning and rational development. Everyone is interested in the baby but no one looks after it."

Lorenz (L-25),Gaver (G-20), Monroe (M-60), Shera (S-24), and Zachert (Z-1) are among the many who have noted much activity but many weaknesses. For example, Stevenson (S-58:284, 280) states:

> There is much concern and a considerable amount of activity,
> but it needs focus and direction, coordination and cooperation,
> to gain the best results from the time and energy expended...There
> is a plethora of conferences, workshops, institutes, and short courses

23

offered by library schools, state extension agencies, and library associations. But again they offer no pattern of progression; they do not build one on the other; there is little or no coordination between these informal learning experiences or with formal education.

There has been little attention to structure either from the point of view of society's needs or from the point of the individual practitioner's needs. Lorenz (L-25:8) stated a thesis which is still not developed, but only developing in librarianship:

My thesis . . . is that society has a right to look to the various professions and to their professional associations for effective planning and action in developing opportunities for continuing education at local, regional, and national levels; the efforts toward systematic development of full-scale programs of continuing education to meet the needs of library personnel at all levels and in all types of libraries have been insufficient, indeed. Programs of continuing library education have been, to say the least, hit or miss.

In spite of the weaknesses brought out in these quotations, there have been some positive steps taken. Shera (S-24:5-6) takes an optimistic view of the current situation:

It is important to emphasize, however, that the role of continuing education is being increasingly recognized, and at the Detroit convention of the ALA, the Council of the Association approved as association policy a statement on library education and manpower that emphasized the desireability of both formal and informal programs (A-42). The following year Dr. Margaret Monroe, then president of the Association of American Library Schools, appointed a study committee under the chairmanship of Dr. Elizabeth W. Stone to investigate the role that AALS should be playing in this area of educational activity and the report of that committee has just appeared in the official journal of the association (A-79). Librarians, thus, like other professionals, are becoming increasingly aware of the need for a variety of learning experiences that extends or builds upon previous experience in the same general area of knowledge and the specific goals of which are not intended to terminate all study in that area . . . One should also note that efforts are now underway to promote

an interest in continuing education on the part of the
National Commission for Libraries.

For accuracy of the record, it should be noted that the Journal of Education
for Librarianship did not publish the full AALS Position Paper (A-77) referred
to in the quotation by Shera, although this was requested by the Committee.
Rather, it published a three-page summary of the report (A-79) and reactions
of the chairman of the Committee to the presentation of the document that was
made at the January, 1972 annual meeting of the association (S-78). It should
also be added that in an effort to broaden the concern for continuing education
and to have a viable medium of communication, the AALS Standing Committee
on Continuing Library Education has been building a network of those concerned
about continuing library education in library schools, library associations,
and state library agencies. Committee membership, as it existed in the fall
of 1972, is listed in the Journal of Education for Librarianship (A-78).

At the regional level, "A Plan for Developing a Regional Program of Continuing
Education for Library Personnel in the Western States" (L-14) provides a
helpful model for similar development elsewhere. Its stated objective is
"to develop a regional organizational structure for initiating and continuing
long-range coordinated programming of educational activities for library personnel in the WI CHE states" (L-14:14). It outlines the stages of development
for the plan and specifies exact program tasks for each (L-14:14-32).

Currently, the Southwestern Library Interstate Cooperative Endeavor (SLICE)
(S-46), a project of the Southwestern Library Association, is engaged in a
project called "Continuing Education for Librarians in the Southwest" (CELS).
Initial activity of the CELS project was a U.S.O.E.-funded conference in New
Orleans emphasizing library planning and evaluation. CELS is now engaged
in a needs survey to be used as a data base for planning, programming and
evaluation activities.

At the state level, two reports stand out as having special value. One, edited
by Guy Garrison and entitled Changing Role of State Library Consultants,
made six recommendations relating to the education of state library personnel
and all have implications for continuing library education as well as for the
upgrading of state library consultants. The six recommendations are listed
under the bibliographical citation for this work, G-17.

The second significant report, entitled Education of State Library Personnel,
(H-19), has implications for continuing education far beyond the group for
which it was specifically designed, namely State Library Agency Professional

Personnel. In fact most of the report can be applied equally well to all levels of library personnel and in all types of libraries. The report grew out of a charge by the (then) American Association of State Libraries and the Library Education Division to their Interdivisional Committee on Education of State Library Personnel. Its stated objectives were:

1) To assess the needs of professional personnel performing functions unique to state library agencies, with emphasis on the consultant and administrative-supervisory personnel;
2) To recommend means and methods of designing educational programs to meet these education needs;
3) To recommend a structure for carrying out this programming (H-19:i).

The emphasis throughout the report is on "continuing education," whether formal or informal. In order to accomplish the goals described, the Committee emphasized the need for cooperation with other agencies and institutions, especially graduate schools in the fields of librarianship, communications, and related disciplines; professional associations; and regional and national agencies in higher education. The report is valuable from a number of viewpoints: one of these is that specific means of implementation for the stated objectives are detailed through the suggestion of two immediate steps for implementation, and one long-range plan for later consideration. The report also recommends a National Advisory and Action Committee for Continuing Education of State Library Personnel, with a suggested composition of eleven members, meeting twice yearly. Selected conclusions and recommendations from the report are included in the bibliographical section of this report.

At both the state and local levels there have been many activities, many made possible by federal funding, which in themselves have been successful, but as pointed out by Shera ". . . they suffer from a lack of coordination and a unified formalized structure that would establish them firmly as an important part of the practicing librarian's professional life" (S-24:6). He continues, however, that the avenue to progress is here: "To think constructively, rather than to engage in emotional polemics or sentimentalizing about continuing education, one should first inquire into the environment in which it flourishes" (S-24:6). This advice is in keeping with the positive note in which observers of the efforts in the ministry look to the immediate future for the strengthening of plans, structures, programs. These conditions referred to by Shera are reviewed in the text of this paper in Chapter II.

26

National Organizations Involved in Continuing Education for the Professions
Nattress (N-17:49) calls attention to two national organizations with concern
for and involvement in continuing education for professions: The Adult
Education Association (AEA) of the U.S.A. which formed a Section on Continuing Education for the Professions in 1966, and the National University
Extension Association (NUEA) which formed a similar section in 1969.
Generally, the AEA (A-11) has focused attention on the problems of the
learner and the NUEA on the problems in relation to the administration of
continuing education programs. To date, the professions have not used
either of these national associations to any great extent as a means for interface with other groups. Instead, all the professions seem to be moving
"separately down the same path" at different rates of speed. Houle (H-37)
has pointed out the wastefulness of such an approach and urges inter-professional cooperation in which each of the professions would drop the assumption
that each of their processes is wholly unique. Houle believes that such
inter-professional efforts would lead to important and healthy consequences
for our society. Examples of such cooperation are on the whole lacking.
One notable exception was the National Institute of Mental Health Conference
on "Continuing Education: Agent of Change" (U-20) which made a determined
effort to include participants which cut across disciplines and professions
as well as to represent citizens served by continuing education programs in
the health sciences.

James E. Allen (A-14), speaking at the 1969 Galaxy Conference on Adult and
Continuing Education, saw the creation of local and national lifelong learning
councils as a way of gaining the cooperation of a vast array of community,
educational, and cultural endeavors, all focused on improving continuing
education.

Implementation of Continuing Education Within the Professions
The over-all rationale that has been developed over the last few years for
implementing continuing education within a profession is reflected in the
literature and can be summarized as follows:

The individual carries the basic responsibility for his own development and
for keeping up-to-date (G-16:12), but others share in this responsibility. The
employing institution has the responsibility for opportunities and for a work
environment, or climate, that encourages and stimulates the individual to
keep up-to-date. The professional societies and universities are expected to
help by providing the opportunities from which the individual can select those
related to his needs. Generally, employers and professional societies, more
than universities, have shared the responsibility for making the individual more

27

aware of his needs and in helping him to meet those needs. The existence of such a division of roles is apparent in most professional continuing education literature.

These roles, expressing the distribution of responsibilities, are also either specified or implied in the official statements of groups relative to continuing education. Examples are the "Goals of Engineering Education" statement by the American Society for Engineering Education (A-56); the "Landmark Statement from the American Nurses' Association on Continuing Education" (A-52); the "Report" of the Temporary Commission on Continuing Education of the United Presbyterian Church (U-2); the statement of the Joint Study Committee in Continuing Medical Education, "Lifetime Learning for Physicians: Principles, Practices, Proposals" (D-28); and the "Position Paper on the Role of the Association of American Library Schools in Continuing Library Education" (A-77).

Such "official reports," "position papers," and "landmark statements" by authoritative bodies in a profession are, indeed, one of the main ways of gaining a consensus on the roles that are to be played by relevant and concerned agencies within a profession.

The federal and state governments also recognize responsibilities in the area of continuing education. An example is the Government Employees Training Act, which in 1958 ordered federal managers to establish training programs. This Act (U-12) says: ". . .it is necessary and desirable in the public interest that self-education, self-improvement, and self-training . . .be implemented by Government-sponsored programs." In effect, the Act placed the basic responsibility for his own development on the initiative of the individual. If the individual wants to learn, opportunities are at hand to help him. When an individual is motivated he can obtain guidance and help from management.

The Continuing Education for R and D Careers. . .Study (C-24) additionally quotes Chalmer G. Kirkbride as he pointed out that some professions and industries are accepting a larger share of responsibility for continuing education of employees than they have in the past.

> In the past, it was commonly accepted that the employee
> has the entire responsilbity for keeping himself up-to-date.
> Several factors are now causing important changes in the
> thinking, however. First of all, the problem of keeping
> up-to-date has increased by several orders of magnitude in
> the last two decades. Secondly, the increasing costs . . .to
> to support a technical man supplies the company with a

> strong economic incentive. . . Then, too, employees
> are encouraged to plan an increasing role in community
> affairs, thus reducing the time available for continuing
> education (C-24:12).

Just as companies generally are beginning to re-evaluate their positions on
their role in continuing education, the American Library Association in its
"Library Education and Manpower Statement" of 1970 recognized that the
employing library has a mutual responsibility for the individual's continuing
education.

> Library administrators must accept responsibility for
> providing support and opportunities (in the form of
> leaves, sabbaticals, and released time) for the con-
> tinuing education of their staffs (A-42:8).

These roles are also reflected in the answers to surveys made of the individual
members of the profession. For example, in librarianship a recent study of
a cross section of different types of libraries examined what the practicing
librarians felt should be the roles of seven relevant groups in relation to
continuing library education (S-72:170-196). In a study of university libraries,
Kaser (K-4:71) found that, despite all the new talk about continuing education,
". . .few libraries actually seem to be doing much about it in any organized
or concerted way," as revealed by the amount actually budgeted for continuing
education.

In succeeding chapters the roles of these various agencies in relation to continuing education are dealt with in greater detail.

Conclusion

The lack of any universally acceptable definition of continuing education, as
revealed in the literature, is a stumbling block that has slowed down action
in many professions. Some professions take a broad definition that includes
advanced degree-seeking (beyond the first professional degree) and management and communication training, and incorporates all activities and efforts,
formal and informal, by the individual to upgrade his knowledge, abilities,
competencies, and understanding in his field of work or specialization so
that he can become a more effective professional and be able to handle responsibilities of greater scope and accountability. This review accepts this
broad definition, but many official statements or professions are much nar-
rower and eliminate such activities as advanced degree-seeking, management
and communication training, and any training not focused on the subject

specialty in which the individual is immediately engaged in his work situation.

The concept of continuing education which emerges from an examination of the literature is heavily influenced by current concern for overcoming obsolescence (catching up) and preventing obsolescence (keeping up-to-date). With the accelerated growth of knowledge and technology since World War II, the "durability span" of the first professional degree in all fields has decreased to a point that, in theory at least, continuing professional education is universally considered a necessity for preventing extensive obsolescence during the career of any professional.

This is reflected in the statement by Kreitlow (K-37) in which he prophesies that the time will come when continuing education and retraining are the positive alternative to unemployment. He envisions the time when the adult response to questions about his employment will elicit but three alternative responses: 1) "I have a job;" 2) "I'm in retraining;" 3) "I'm retired." (K-37:4). Within such a framework he says there can be no unemployment. "It is then that the narrow walls of thinking about education must crumble" (K-37:4), and there will no longer exist the myth about higher education being a terminal educational goal.

As the literature reveals, that there has never been any complete agreement on the infallible indicators that distinguish a profession from an occupation, the position is accepted in which professionalism is thought of as an ideal state toward which many occupational groups are striving. Such a position gives the continuing professional educator an advantage because his expertise is seen as a way of enhancing and speeding up the process of professionalization.

In making comparisons between the professions regarding the methods and practices used, it is necessary to keep in mind different patterns of work. What might be best or ideal methods for one group might not be most effective for another. Therefore, in order to avoid distortion, the classification of of the occupations by Houle into three basic patterns has been accepted: the entrepreneurial occupations, the collective occupations, and the hierarchical occupations. The educator concerned with continuing education cannot make his greatest contribution unless he understands the nature of the work environment of the professional group he is serving.

A helpful definition of professionalism for the practicing librarian has been supplied by the School Library Manpower Project: "Professionalism is the conduct of qualified people who share responsibilities for rendering a service; for engaging in continuing study; and for maintaining high standards of achievement and practice within the principles, structure, and content of a body of knowledge" (S-9:44).

In making comparisons between the professions it is also important to realize that different professions are in different stages of development. Roughly three stages are in evidence today: 1) the stage (exemplified by the ministry) in which continuing education is just beginning to be recognized as necessary for proficient practice, 2) the stage (exemplified by the legal profession) in which continuing education has been joined to formal pre-service education to form a continuum where one leads naturally into the other and is not thought of as something that may or may not be added on, 3) the stage (exemplified by the medical profession) in which the stated goal is the availability of continuing education to every professional who wishes it, made possible by full use of new technology; a stage in which identification and management of the conditions of learning are considered in relation to continuing education programs; a stage in which behavioral objectives are identified for programs, in which criteria have been established, and in which evaluation procedures are systematically integrated into the whole programming and planning process. Based on a summary survey of continuing education librarianship, the profession seems to be in a developing condition which would most accurately place it in the stage one category.

The literature shows a rather simplistic approach to the problems of continuing education by assigning roles to the associations, the employing agencies, the academic institutions, government agencies, the individual himself and various interface relationships among these. In spite of the great and ever-increasing quantity of literature in the field of continuing professional education, there are indications that statements of intent and conviction exceed, by a considerable amount, records of actual implementation of continuing education concepts.

III. FACTORS AFFECTING THE DESIGN
OF A CONTINUING EDUCATION SYSTEM

Systems Approach to Continuing Education

> We will have to reorient our thinking so as to look upon education
> as a life-long process for the continuing development of the individual.
> In planning the education program, we will have to learn to consider
> the whole person -- not merely one or two aspects of his existence.
> In short, we will have to adopt a systems approach to education.

This statement by Greenwood (G-42:4) of the Brookings Institute is followed
by a criticism of the education profession for not preparing individuals for a
multi-disciplinary approach to problem solving, for not preparing individuals
to give appropriate consideration to all of the significant elements and relationships in a situation. He believes a choice must be made between fragmented
failure or systemic progress. Greenwood summarizes his position as follows
(G-42:5):

> The systems approach is a new departure in applying both new con-
> cepts and established techniques and knowledge to the analysis and
> solution of problems. The emphases in the systems approach are
> on interrelatedness -- the inter-relatedness of the elements and pro-
> cesses within a sub-system, the inter-relatedness of sub-systems,
> the inter-relatedness of systems with their environment -- and on
> the holistic viewpoint, the recognition that the whole is something
> more than or different from the mere sum of its parts.

Although Greenwood (G-42:5) admits that the systems approach might be characterized as only a bundle of concepts with varying degrees of clarity and definition, he feels that even so it has very significant advantages over traditional
methods. So many in fact, that he concludes: "The managers of today and of
the future -- in industry, government, and education -- must be prepared to
apply the systems approach or perish."

Adelson (A-10) in taking a broad perspective of the systems approach, states
that it is able to produce "demonstrably good" or defensible solutions which
may take many forms and which may use many different techniques. Basically
the systems approach is a creative process which includes arrangements for all
appropriate sources to make relevant contributions. In the literature dealing
with the systems approach there can be found one group of authors dealing

32

chiefly with the approach as applied to educational systems and learning systems and another group of authors dealing mainly with the approach as applied to training systems within an organizational framework. In this section, authors are mentioned in the former category; authors writing specifically on training systems in organizations are discussed in the chapter on "Continuing Education and the Work Environment."

Cook (C-31-C-35) believes that the systems concept should be used widely throughout education. He employs the systems philosophy idea of William D. Hitt, who describes the characteristics as "a problem being considered in its broadest context; placing emphasis on the functional relations between the variables in the system; investigation of the interactions between the variables along with their main effects; and placing emphasis on the study of models which are developed to represent the actual system" (C-32:3). Cook believes the systems concept has had and will continue to have an impact on the field of education, and urges that the approach be implemented, but with the greater emphasis being given to "the development and understanding of processes and the creation of attitudes favorable to their use" (C-32:9-10). He summarizes the specific applications of systems philosophy in the field of education as being in 1) instructional systems, 2) project management systems, 3) management information systems which establish a "data base" which can be used for long-range planning, 4) planning-programming-budgeting systems, and 5) operations research (C-32:5-8).

Knezevich (K-19) presents a brief, but comprehensive, explanation of the "systems approach," its demands on an organization, and its implications for a systems-oriented administrator. The educational enterprise is conceptualized as a unified systematic vehicle for translating resources in the form of money and people into outcomes or outputs related to the goals of society. The school system is viewed as a conversion system made up of seven interrelated sub-systems, which he identifies as: a goals- and priorities-setting sub-system, a resources sub-system, a control sub-system, a client service sub-system, an educational manpower sub-system, an environment relations sub-system, and a student manpower reentry and retraining sub-system. A model showing the school as a conversion system and its related systems is discussed. Two other dimensions of the systems approach, PERT (Program Evaluation and Review Techniques) and PPBS (Planning, Programming, Budgeting System), are described as major tools that can be used by the systems-oriented administrator.

> There must be literally a systems effort to move beyond the confusion and limited awareness of systems approach in school administration that presently characterize the state of the art. It must be a task-force effort of local school administrators

acting in concert with specialized representatives of institutions of higher learning, federal agenices and professional societies. (K-19:84).

In the last few years there has been a rapidly increasing focus on the application of the systems approach and management planning techniques to educational planning. For example, Operation PEP (S-93) has a collection of 21 reports presented at a symposium which served as a culminating activity for training 100 California educators. Systems and management concepts, as they apply to educational planning, are discussed. Another group of significant articles is that found in the May, 1965, Audiovisual Instruction. The whole issue is devoted to the examination of the "systems approach" to education. Some of those writing on the systems approach to education listed in the present bibliography are Cook (C-31-C-35), Knezevich (K-19, K-20), O'Toole (O-14), Pfeiffer (P-16), Ripley (R-25) who advocates PERT as a management tool for educators, Ryans (R-46), Schalock and Hale (S-2), Smith (S-41-S-43), Stolurow (S-66), and Taft (T-1).

An early statement in a professional journal on the value of considering an educational system as a system was presented by Foecke (F-12) in the Journal of Engineering Education in 1967. He began by offering a definition: "an educational system is a self-correcting activity in which a deliberate attempt is made to establish the conditions which seem most suitable, in the light of the relevant factors, for assisting one or more learners in achieving desired learning objectives" (F-12:117). He distinguishes between "education" and "learning" as follows:

> Learning is a very natural activity of the human organism;
> it is the almost inevitable by-product of all human experience. Learning goes on continuously and inescapably,
> whether planned or unplanned, smoothly or erratically,
> consciously or otherwise. Education enters the picture
> only when there is a deliberate intervention in this
> natural activity--in order to direct it efficiently toward
> certain chosen goals.

> So, learning can occur without the presence of any educational activity; indeed, considering all of the things learned
> in a lifetime, most learning is probably of that kind. Furthermore, although education is an effort to set the stage
> for certain learning to occur, because so little is really
> known about the nature of the learning process, the "stage"
> will sometimes be ineffective and therefore educational
> activity can take place without learning (at least not the
> kind intended) (F-12:117).

34

Foecke continues:

>Next, the definition makes it clear that no educational system
>can exist without at least one learner. It may seem that an
>educational system with one learner might be such a special
>case as to deserve exclusion, but this is merely because
>most people think only in terms of elaborately organized
>systems of formal education. The definition applies to any
>educational undertaking, which inclues not only the many com-
>mon instances of a one-to-one teacher/pupil ratio to be found
>outside of formal education (home, sports, music, etc.) but
>also the even more abundant cases of self-education. Indeed,
>one might contend that all elaborate formal education is large-
>ly for the purpose of preparing people to engage in self-
>education, to be independent, life-long, deliberate learners
>(F-12:117).

Foecke emphasizes the fact that all learners differ in their intellectual ability,
motivation, health, vulnerability to "outside demands," previous experience,
education, etc. Therefore, contrary to much educational practice, the educational system "could hardly be expected to function optimally without a thorough
knowledge of the characteristics of the learners (F-12:117).

"Next, the definition of an educational system shows the necessity of directing
the learning activity toward the achievement of certain desired learning objectives" (F-12:117). Foecke makes a distinction between knowing which objectives are possible and deciding which are desirable. "Of all the things which
a given individual could learn, which are the things he should learn? Clearly
this kind of choice process involves a value system--something which guides
a decision among competing 'goods,' among various possibilities all more or
less good in themselves" (F-12:118). After posing the question of who should
do the choosing, he concludes that "organized education" should give "to the
maturing learner an increasing role in establishing objectives" (F-12:118).

Foecke lists several factors which should influence the educational design:
1) substantive knowledge of principles regarding human learning, motivation,
and behavior, 2) a set of resources--inanimate (equipment, technology, etc.)
and human (especially teachers), 3) constraints (time, funding, etc.).

In addition to considering the ingredients which enter into the development of
an educational design or plan, it is also necessary to consider the design process which Foecke likens to an engineering design, "except that it is much
more difficult and frustrating by virtue of the less fully developed state of the
underlying sciences and because of the vastly increased number of interacting

variables" (F-12:118). The educational designer is called upon to "map out a 'program' of learning experiences--not only to select among various possible kinds of learning situations . . . but also to decide generally upon day-to-day activities . . ." (F-12:118). The next element is the execution of the strategy. The plan does not need to include a teacher, but it usually does in formal systems of education. "When a teacher is involved, still another fundamentally different kind of activity is involved--the art of facilitating student learning . . . it is the task of the 'learning facilitator' to guide the process in such a way as to most effectively achieve the objectives." (F-12:118). And finally this leads to still another kind of activity--the assessment of the achievements of the learners, or in engineering parlance, "instrumenting the system and interpreting the data."

The roles of a teacher in such a system are basically different. These roles are: learning facilitator, performance evaluator, objective selector, and strategy developer. Foecke points out that most teachers "genuinely desire to be effective, but they handicap themselves if they fail to reflect upon the nature of teaching sufficiently to discern that it is more than one undifferentiated activity, that it is really a constellation of fundamentally distinct roles with entirely different requirements for effectiveness" (F-12:120). This leads him to the conclusion that educational research and development are necessary in order to identify all the educational roles that a teacher must perform and how they may best be accomplished.

The Commission on Instructional Technology's Report to the President and the Congress of the United States (U-14:5) defines instructional technology as "a systematic way of designing, carrying out, and evaluating the total process of learning and teaching in terms of specific objectives, based on research in human learning and communication, and employing a combination of human and non-human resources to bring about more effective instruction."

A learning system has been defined as a structured sequence of instructional events organized to accomplish a given purpose. As presented by Ofiesh (O-6:34), the concept is specifically delineated by the following boundaries:

1. A learning system emphasizes the importance of the individual learner. Instructional material is presented to him in accordance with his needs, starting at his current state of development and carrying him to the desired performance level.

2. The final criterion for the effectiveness of a learning system is the performance of the learner. Therefore the system is tested, revised, and retested until it meets the desired specifications.

36

3. A learning system is based not upon loosely stated "objectives" but upon a specific and detailed description of what the learner is expected to do after training, and of the conditions under which he is expected to perform.

4. In developing a learning system, the techniques and instructional media most suited to the training problem are selected. Economic as well as technical considerations are carefully weighed.

According to Ofiesh (O-5:763), "the 'systems approach to education,' in brief, involves the specification of behavioral objectives, the assessment of student repertoires, the development of instructional strategies, the testing and revising of instructional units (validation), and finally packaging and administering a validated learning system." Such an approach, Ofiesh maintains, results in the development of learning experiences for the individual which are designed to meet his needs and learning modes. "The learning experiences, however, are designed to produce the behaviors specified; in other words, the specified behavioral objectives are the constant in the system" (O-5:763).

Gagne (G-3) sums up the concept of an educational system as an arrangement of people and conditions whose purpose is to bring about learning. He discusses five areas of decisions which affect the function of an educational system: learning objectives, the structure of knowledge to be learned, motivation, conditions for learning, and the transferability of knowledge and assessment.

Conditions for Adult Learning

The Commission on Instructional Technology (U-14:79)reported that the first and
most farreaching reason that instructional technology has not been more widely
accepted and used is the lack of a practical understanding about the process of
human learning. In The Modern Practice of Adult Education: Andragogy versus
Pedagogy (K-22:39), Knowles' premise is that the adult educator must be
aware of certain basic factors about adult learning that are quite different from
the learning patterns of the young. He specifies four of these assumptions:

> As a person matures, 1) his self-concept moves from one of being
> a dependent personality toward one of being a self-directing human
> being; 2) he accumulates a growing reservoir of experience that
> becomes an increasing resource for learning; 3) his readiness to
> learn becomes oriented increasingly to the developmental tasks of
> his social roles; and 4) his time perspective changes from one
> of postponed application of knowledge to immediacy of application,
> and accordingly his orientation toward learning shifts from one of
> subject-centeredness to one of problem-centeredness.

One of the most forceful statements on the importance of continuing library
educators knowing how adults learn is to be found in Zachert (Z-1:42):

> Library science education has traditionally conceived of its students
> as children. Inherited curricula and teaching methods reflect this
> orientation, which has not yet been seriously challenged either at
> the level of basic professional education or at the level of continuing
> education. The most pregnant generalization from adult learning
> research is that adults learn differently than children, the inescapable
> conclusion is that education for adults must be planned and implemented
> differently than education for children. Acceptance of this generaliza-
> tion augurs for change.
>
> The ultimate success or failure of the efforts for continuing education
> may well rest not on how perceptively the planners and the teachers
> understand the great perplexing problems of librarianship, but on
> their perception of how adults learn. Administrators also have a
> share in the responsibility. As a group they have been slow to accept
> the relationship between motivation and participation in continuing
> education, and slow to provide the requisite motivation. To me the
> almost total lack of perception about how adults learn is the greatest
> single flaw in continuing education today, pervading the ranks of
> planners, teachers, and library administrators alike. It is because

of this lack of perception that I am postulating a new role for
learners. Instead of the inert, childlike posture of the past, I am
suggesting a dynamic role, at once purposive, aggressive, and self-
fulfilling. It is a role that will move the cause and the reality of
continuing education for librarians forward. I see this role as purposive because it is a preventative against future shock. I see it also
as potentially aggressive, marked by the initiative and driving force
so often lacking in prior continuing education efforts, and as self-
fulfilling, for the learners as they participate in the process will be
the beneficiaries. I see the role of the learner as essentially an
individual one, though recognizing that much of the vital force I
predict from it will devolve from its corporate thrust.

Zachert (Z-1:52) sums up the findings of recent research about adult learning
and explores their implications for continuing library education under three
kinds of differences: physiological, psychological, and social. Preceding this
perceptive and selective analysis she emerges with the profile of the adult
learner (Z-1:49); the profile of the role of the adult learner (Z-1:50); and the
"configuration of the complementary learning situation" (Z-1:51); and briefly
touches on the role of the teacher (Z-1:52).

Hiatt (H-19:25-26) in Education of State Library Personnel identifies 5 characteristics of the adult learner and gives ten principles concerning adult learning
that have implications for designing continuing education programs. The
"Guidelines to the Development of Human Resources in Libraries" (A-41:110)
specify that the design of the staff development program must be based on the
nature of the adult as a learner and specify four factors to consider in relation
to the adult as a learner.

In the continuing education literature of each profession, planners and leaders
of continuing professional education programs are urged to take into account
the way in which adults learn. A few examples will serve to illustrate this
universal condition.

Professor Howard McCluskey (I-4:27-28) stresses three differences between
adult learning and childhood learning in planning continuing education programs
for public administration:

1) The Time Dimension: Few adults have access to the large blocks
   of time that are available to young people. Instead, the adult must
   look to few and scattered periods such as evenings, weekends,
   vacation or released time from regular obligations. The adult's
   use of time is competitive. When engaged in learning, some other
   activity must give way.

2) Authority Relationships: The authority of the teacher of the young
is established by law and reinforced by many factors. In adult
education, the superiority possessed by the teacher is based only
on the competence with which he performs his instructional tasks.
The fact that both students and teachers are adults has significant
implications for the climate of interaction in the learning process.
It suggests the desirability of shared responsibility for the success
of learning in which the teacher helps the learner to learn and the
learner helps the teacher to teach.

3) Reality Potentials: For the young, schooling is largely preparatory
for a world of experience yet to come. For adults, learning arises
from and becomes part of the here-and-now world of life itself.
There is often a one-to-one relation between the item learned and
the presence of that item in daily work experience. In no other
area of education is the ratio of input to impact potentially so
favorable and impressive.

In continuing nursing education there are many references to the principles of learning as bases for program design. For example, Training and
Continuing Education: A Handbook for Health Care Institutions (H-30:87-92)
lists eight principles and gives a substantial annotated bibliography on sources
used in deriving their principles.

1) Learning depends on motivation.
2) Learning depends upon a capacity to learn.
3) Learning depends upon past and current experience.
4) Learning depends upon active involvement of the learner.
5) Learning is enhanced by problem solving.
6) Learning effectiveness is dependent upon feedback.
7) Learning is enhanced by an informal atmosphere and the freedom
to make mistakes.
8) Learning is augmented by novelty, variety, and challenge.

Stein (S-55) also lists eight concepts of adult learning which have particular
application to continuing education. These are summarized in the annotated
bibliography.

A frequently quoted source which deals not only with the characteristics of
adult learners, but also with the whole teaching-learning process in a comprehensive manner is the U. S. Department of Agriculture Faculty Handbook
Part II: Improving Teaching (U-15). Another helpful source, because it is
specifically geared to the learning process as applied to short-term learning
situations, is the paper by McKeachie (M-15). One emphasis he makes more
strongly than many authors is the importance of curiosity in the learning process.

Learning Needs--Basis for Programming

"Learning Needs--Basis for Programming" is the title of the second chapter in the Training and Continuing Education developed by the Hospital Continuing Education Project under a grant from the Kellogg Foundation (H-30:7). The chapter starts immediately with this statement: "There is no more important element in the whole process of personnel development than adequate determination of employee learning needs. . .an educational program that does not make sense to the employees will not succeed, for they cannot be expected to respond enthusiastically unless they see a reasonable relationship between the activity or program and their own needs."

The chapter defines "learning need" as meaning "a lack of knowledge, skill, or attitude that prevents an employee from giving a satisfactory job performance, or that interferes with his potential for assuming greater responsibilities. In all cases, therefore, existence of a need means that present performance should be changed in some way. In all cases, also, change must come through new learning. The term 'learning needs' is therefore an accurate designation for all those lacks that can be identified. It should be kept in mind that learning is not limited to acquiring information, but but includes acquiring new or greater skill, or a new point of view or attitude" (H-30:7).

"Continuing Education Needs: The View From the Field" (I-4:25) is the second chapter in Continuing Continuing Education for Public Service: A Design for Action for Education and Training for the Public Service, published by the Institute for Local Self-Government, Berkeley. Immediately, the question is asked: "What does the Public Service Want?" and lists the needs of those surveyed in the public service that will have to be met if the program is to be successful, and points out that it should be recognized that: "participation in continuing education. . .is a highly personalized intentional endeavor. The satisfaction of this intention becomes a principle objective of the learning situation. Learning unrelated to experience and interaction, or not perceived to be so related. . .is likely to be the cause of profound disappointment, discouragement, frustration, and a negative outlook on future offerings." (I-4:27).

Dr. Thomas G. Webster (U-20:37), in speaking at the National Conference on Continuing Education in Mental Health on "Continuing Education: Agent of Change," stated that a top priority for developing continuing education projects at the National Institute of Mental Health was to develop programs targeted to the needs of a specific group of trainees, rather than offering isolated courses for whomever might be recruited. "Program development implies gathering of data to assess needs and priorities and the ongoing impact of the program of the future. . .Program development also implies joint planning by trainers and trainees. . . "

41

In the survey of "Continuing Education for R and D Careers," (C-24:52), it was stated that "it should always be kept in mind that any continuing education activity . . . is relative to a particular area of knowledge needed on the job . . ."

Similarly, in a survey by Stone (S-72:122) of a cross section of different types of librarians, it was found that the sources of encouragement (motivating factors) that led the librarians to engage in continuing education activities (both formal and informal) were chiefly content factors related to the work process. That is to say, they were continuing education activities that met his job-related needs.

These are but a few of many examples to demonstrate that it is generally accepted today that human beings are goal-seeking, need-meeting organisms (Maslow, M-33; McGregor, M-12) and that this factor should have top priority in planning continuing education programs if enrollees are to be expected in most professional continuing education programs. Enrollment is entirely an optional matter left up to the individual's decision whether it is worth his while to attend. Knowles (U-20:202) expressed it this way: "Learning is one option available to them (human beings) in achieving goals and meeting needs, and they will choose this option when they perceive it to be effective for these purposes. Implication for inservice education: Learning will be most effective when the employees have diagnosed their own needs and forumulated their own goals for learning."

A frequently cited Management Program that makes use of this principle with great effectiveness is the "Williamsburg Program" conducted by the Graduate School of the U.S. Department of Agriculture (I-4: 42-43) in three phases over a month. The first is a two-day diagnostic and planning meeting in Washington, D.C. during which time the needs of the participants are identified and analyzed as a basis for program and course content. This takes about two weeks. Then there follows a second phase at the Williamsburg Lodge which is an intensive six-day workshop tailored to the needs of those attending. The program concludes with a two-day, follow-up session in Washington where members assess the practical application of ideas gained from the program. The basic course "Management Development Program for Government Executives" has been given more than forty times, but each time the course is structured differently as indicated in the two-day diagnostic session which precedes it. In addition to the course being based on the needs of the participants each time and their involvement in planning the course, it also takes into account another important factor in planning continuing education programs, that is recognition of the personalized criteria of the participants.

Meeting the Personalized Criteria of the Professional

Dryer (D-28:50) states that any continuing professional education programming of the physician will run the expensive risk of becoming an inefficient bureaucratic clockwork unless it meets highly personalized criteria:. . .1) personal satisfaction; 2) freedom of choice; 3) continuity; 4) accessibility; 5) convenience.

The first criteria, personal satisfaction, refers to the point made in the preceding paragraphs, namely that the primary requirement for the physician's participation in a continuing education program is meeting his personal needs. "Any educational plan will have to make sense to him on his own terms." This criteria assumes that learning is essentially an individual, personal achievement.

The second, freedom of choice, provides for diversity of offerings. It is based on the assumptions that: 1) ideal motivation consists of personal standards of excellence; and 2) education mo st beneficially occurs separately from regulation (D-28:93). The physician should have the right to choose any or all of the available curriculum.

The third, continuity, refers to the fact that the continuing education program should take the form of an organized, sequential curriculum, comprehensive in scope and that this curriculum should be continuously available. "If a national body could, in a practical way, combine the benefits of continuity with the freedom of choice available in diversity, then a physician could choose any combination most beneficial to himself" (D-28:57).

Writing on the fourth criteria, accessibility, Dryer states: "No doctor or his patient should be penalized because of his distance from an organized center of learning--or if the distance is small, the price in lost time exacted by traffic congestion" (D-28:59). "Television offers the best opportunity to give doctors everywhere equal access to the best teachers and centers of instruction in the country. By itself, the vicarious experience of television viewing will hardly be more than partial learning--but in tandem with other more personal, more active, more participative methods of learning, television can go to work effectively tomorrow " (D-28:60).

Convenience, the fifth criteria, could be supplied, according to Dryer (D-28:79), by building a curriculum of integrated teaching materials--" the book, the magnetic sound tape recording, film, box of slides, the CPC protocol, and so on-- could reach him by mail, in advance, to help provide him with every opportunity to widen his understanding of whatever he wanted to learn at a pace and place chosen by himself. "

43

After detailing the five criteria, Dryer reaffirms the case for his central thesis (D-28:85), that only a national planning body can provide all of these criteria.

> Our specific primary objective is an apparently simple insistence upon pivoting the entire plan on the needs of the physician as a lifetime student. . . Only a national assembly of educational partners possessing multi-disciplinary knowledge and skills can give seriously attended voice, everywhere, to the belief that vocational information and instrumentation must remain tools in our society, and never become masters of that delicate cognitive cobweb spun from personal values, goals, and understanding which together create the only true education. Such a national assembly can provide national access, everywhere, to practical expressions of the concept that the fulcrum of lifetime learning is poised only within the individual minds of freely choosing men and women.

Dryer relates four of these criteria, freedom of choice, continuity, accessibility, and convenience, to the first, meeting the physicians' need for knowledge to better serve the patient. Caution needs to be used if the first criteria -- professional need -- is not sufficiently provided for in planning continuing education activities.

Thus, Stone (S-72:201-206) found that generally the reasons a librarian engages in continuing education activities are different from, and not merely opposite to, the reasons which deter him from participating; and factors that deal with the content of the continuing education opportunity which can be related to the librarian's actual job are the most influential in motivating participation. These highly motivating factors tend to give the librarian a feeling of growth in job competence. It was found that the deterring forces were primarily associated with extrinsic conditions, such as lack of time, inconvenience of location, requirements, costs, low accessibility. The point here that is important for the planner of continued education activities is that even though all these contextual factors are splendidly provided for, they alone will not influence librarians to a high level of participation. That is to say, no matter how well packaged the course, or how good the video-tape or convenient the location, or how convenient the timing, these environmental-related factors are, they in themselves will not motivate librarians to a high level of participation; only content related to job-related needs will provide high participation. However, it is important for the continuing educator to provide for the context, (environmental factors), for if they are unsatisfactory or not present, they tend to discourage participation, regardless of the excellence of the content or will influence participants to drop out of programs. Generally, this evidence supports the conclusion reached by Herzberg (H-15) and his associates relative to satisfiers and dissatisfiers in the job situation.

Examples of successful programs which take personalized criteria into account along with need-oriented content, abound in the literature. Three examples follow.

The University of Southern California has developed The Intensive Semester-- public administration courses administered on an intensive basis. "Students enrolling in these courses are required to do six weeks of studying and reading in <u>advance</u>. Books, periodicals and other reading materials are sent to the student. These constitute the course reading and complete coverage of the reading is expected before the student comes to class. Classes are then held for a solid week. From one Saturday morning through the next Saturday night at least 40 hours of classwork is scheduled. Sessions are held mornings, afternoons and some evenings. During the first meeting of the class, an examination is given covering the reading assignments which were completed prior to coming to the campus. Students who do not pass this test lose their place in the class and "fail" the course. At the end of the intensive week, students are assigned a term paper or research project which must be completed within six weeks of the end of the week of classroom work. A final class convening is held at the end of that time for discussion of papers and final evaluation of course accomplishments. This session usually runs about ten hours." The format provides an opportunity for study without long periods away from the job (I-4:35-36).

Another example of meeting personalized criteria is the Open University concept. On November 9, 1970, the <u>New York Times</u> praised the idea:

Taken seriously, the degree earned without direct class attendance on campus could lead to a major reform movement. Out of the establishment of an Open University with the sole purpose of providing instruction and supervision for the external students might come greater speed toward that revolution in instructional methods that has been blocked by institutional conservatism.

An example that involves several of these personalized criteria are the monthly cassettes, prepared under the supervision of Dr. Rose (R-39), Director of Continuing Education for the American Institute of Architects. The cassette which comes out once a month is called "The Review of Architectural Periodicals" (RAP). Each month, 50 journals and newsletters are culled for information that could affect an architect in his office. Priority items are ranked by importance of the subject, based on a needs analysis of AIA members; articles are condensed and put on an hour tape by professional actors and actresses and mailed to subscribers.

The Learning Needs Analysis

Speaking to the attendees at the AALS mini-workshop on Continuing Professional Education, Dr. Rose (R-39), Director of Continuing Education of the
American Institute of Architects, admonished the librarians to focus on
the needs of practicing librarians before building programs or designing
organizational structures. "It is a free enterprise continuing education
system. At this point in time there is no requirement for an architect to
engage in continuing education." He went on to point out that when he started
at AIA, he was given $8,000 seed money and the very first thing he did was
to spend $1,000 for a continuing education needs survey by mass mailing
the AIA membership. One of the chief products he obtained from the survey
was a priority rating of the subjects in which the AIA members were chiefly
interested. He now discusses the subjects for coverage in his cassette series
based on the rank order information from the questioning.

Training and Continuing Education: A Handbook for Health Care Institutions of
the Hospital Continuing Education Project (H-30: 15-34) devotes a chapter to
the methods by which a needs analysis may be conducted, including observing
and listening, interviews, skill inventories, surveys, questionnaires, slip
technique, exit interviews, postemployment questionnaires. The National
Institute of Mental Health bibliography on Training Methodology: Part II
(U-23:25-34) has nine pages of annotated bibliography on conducting a needs
analysis. Kortendick and Stone include a bibliography on "interviewing
techniques" (K-31: 473-475) and a section on "questionnaire sources" which
includes references to sample questionnaires of merit (K-31: 448-494).

Gagne (G-5) in a now "classic" paper made the assumption that total performance can be analyzed into a set of component tasks that are relatively distinct
from each other and that proficiency of task components is what determines
total performance. In summing up his thesis that task analysis has everything
to do with training, he states: "If I were faced with the problem of improving
training, I should not look for much help from the well-known learning principles
like reinforcement, distribution of practice, response familiarity, and so on.
I should look instead at the technique of task analysis, and at the principles of
component task achievement, intratask transfer, and the sequence of subtask
learning to find those ideas of greatest usefulness in the design of effective
training " (G-5: 90). To Gagne, the most important thing is "what is to be
learned"; learning principles are accorded a secondary position . Gagne (G-5: 88)
suggests a series of three psychological principles useful in analyzing training
problems:

1) Any human task may be analyzed into a set of component tasks which are quite distinct from each other in terms of the experimental operations needed to produce them.
2) These task components are mediators of the final task performance; that is, their presence insures positive transfer to a final performance, and their absence reduces such transfer to near zero.
3) The basic principles of training design consist of: a) identifying the component tasks of a final performance; b) insuring that each of these component tasks is fully achieved; and c) arranging the total learning situation in a sequence which will insure optimal mediational effects from one component to another (G-5:88).

Although Gagne states these principles are not in opposition to the traditional principles of learning, such as reinforcement, familiarity, etc., he does state that they are "in complete opposition to the... assumption 'the best way to learn a task if to practice the task '" (G-5:88). After these questions have been answered, attention can be given to other matters, such as specific techniques.

Kortendick and Stone (K-31) used the task analysis approach in designing their questionnaire. The rationale was that in order to have courses and/or curriculum meet the needs of librarians in their work situations, it was deemed necessary to find out what the librarians in the population actually do in their present positions. They took the view, supported by considerable research evidence, that the aspect of course and curriculum development that should receive primary attention is the development of well-defined job-relevant objectives based on what the individual needs to know to perform his job. Accordingly, a task inventory or outline of major duties of librarians was prepared, using appropriate methods of job analysis and adapting techniques worked out by earlier researchers, such as Corson (C-42), Curnow (C-51), and others listed in the Kortendick and Stone bibliography on "Job Inventories" (K-31:495-498).

Another study in librarianship, The School Library Manpower Project (S-9), also used the task analysis as an activity leading to the development of new definitions of school library media personnel and the identification of roles presently performed by a wide variety of staff positions in school library media centers. This led to the publication of School Library Personnel: Task Analysis Survey. A Task Analysis Committee was appointed to analyze the tasks performed by school library media personnel. In carrying out this function, the Committee had to determine what tasks should be performed by a variety of school library media personnel in a building level school library media center to meet the personnel requirements of the 1969 Standards for School Media Programs. The study of these tasks resulted in many tasks and responsibilities

being assigned upward or downward to other school library media positions
in order to effect a more meaningful approach to the development of occupational definitions.

In the NIMH Bibliography, Training Methodology: Part II (U-23), eleven
annotated listings are given on job and task analysis. The series of needs
analyses by Dubin and his associates (D-31, D-39) provide an array of studies
on the continuing education needs of various professions, such as: managers
and supervisors, hospital personnel, engineers. For example, the study on
the educational needs of city managers (D-31) contains the full questionnaires,
answer sheets, complete results, and bibliographies used in the study. These
provide an excellent model to study in the designing of surveys of educational
needs.

Determining Objectives

Knowles (U-20:204) states that objectives for education programs are derived
from three sources of needs and interest: 1) the individual, as perceived by
him; 2) the sponsoring institution, as perceived by its leaders; and 3) society,
as perceived by the relevant professions. "Adult education always starts with
the self-diagnosed needs and interests of the learners, but artistically nego-
tiates for the inclusion of those of the institution and society."

The Continuing Education Handbook of Hospital and Health Care Institutions
distinguishes learning needs from objectives in this manner: "Learning needs,
which relate to deficiencies in the learners, should be distinguished from
'learning objectives' which relate to what is to be learned. Learning objectives are statements of what the employee should know, or should demonstrate
that he is able to do, as a result of the learning experience." (H-30:8)

One of the chief emphases in the literature today centers on the importance
and methods of setting learning objectives and the determination of whether or
not objectives have been reached. Some of the most frequently referred to
authors cited in the area of determining objectives are: Bloom (B-17); Gagne
(G-1, G-2); Granger (G-40); Guba (G-46); Melching (M-40); Krathwohl (K-34);
Mager (M-24, M-25); Off (O-4); Smith (S-41, S-42, S-43). Others are listed
in the NIMH Training Methodology: Part II bibliography (U-23).

In the literature on objectives three terms are used which are important in
the measurement of learning: behavior, terminal behavior, and criterion.
"All learning results in some degree of behavioral change. We conclude that
someone has learned an idea or a task when his behavior changes. 'Behavior'
in this sense, is used to mean any relevant, observable activity displayed by
the learner. It is fundamental that the results of learning be observable;
otherwise progress toward objectives could not be determined" (H-30:36).

In setting objectives, it is of particular concern what behavior the learner is able to show at the end of the learning experience. In order to describe terminal behavior (what the learner will be doing) Mager (M-25) suggests: 1) identifying and naming the over-all behavior act; 2) designing the important conditions under which the behavior is to occur; 3) determining the criterion of acceptable performance. Mager recommends that a separate statement be written for each objective. "The more statements you have, the better chance you have of making clear your intent."

Summarized briefly, operational goals are observable and objectively measureable. They state explicitly and percisely what the student should be able to do and under what circumstances. They do not use such non-objective terms as "appreciate" or "understanding." Mager (M-25:53) considers the formulation and statement of objectives so important that he insists: "If you give each learner a copy of the objectives, you may not have to do much else."

The term "criterion" is used to mean a standard or test by which terminal behavior can be evaluated. "A criterion is a measuring stick that tells how well the learner is expected to do something after instruction has been completed. Establishing criteria with which to measure or appraise terminal behavior is fundamental to evaluation of results " (H-30:36).

Ofiesh (K-33) stresses the importance of establishing behavioral objectives before a student enters the program as indicated in Figure 4. He also emphasizes the necessity of knowing where the student is when he enters the program in order to ascertain if he has the necessary entry skills to profit from the program and to complete it successfully. In developing continuing education programs, Ofiesh also stresses the importance of understanding the implications of Gagne's hierarchy of learning, which he illustrated by the diagram shown in Figure 5.

In summary, "learning is concerned with observable behavior, particularly with the 'terminal behavior' shown at the end of the learning experience, which is to be evaluated with reference to criteria that state how employees are expected to perform " (H-30:36). Criteria should state specifically how and under what conditions the participant is expected to perform. That is to say, objectives should describe just what the instructor or evaluator should be able to observe in the participant's performance when the objective has been reached.

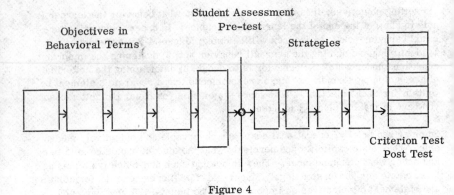

Figure 4

Diagram Illustrating Ofiesh's Emphasis on the Establishment of Behavioral
Objectives Before a Student Enters an Educational Program

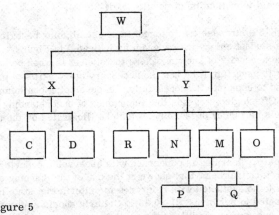

Figure 5

Diagram Illustrating Gagne's Hierarchy of Learning Theory

Thus, competencies X and Y are both necessary for the student to learn concept
W; C and D are necessary to learn X; R, N, M, and O are necessary to learn
concept Y; P and Q are necessary to learn concept M. However, it is not necessary for the student to learn X before he learns Y; as they are not dependent on
each other, the student should be free to enter at either point.

Evaluation

A review of the literature on continuing education from all professions leads
to the conclusion that one of the weakest features of continuing education programs is lack of evaluation. Continuing Education for R & D Careers (C-24:
160) emphasizes that this has not only been true of programs offered, but
also of newer methods of instruction used, including the use of television.
That study challenges the universities to take the lead in evaluating the
modes and methods of learning in continuing education programs because of
their knowledge and expertise in the area of evaluation in relation to other
educational programs. In relating the need for evaluation of adult education
programs to library science, Thiede (T-8:93) states:

> Libraries and library schools have been as dilatory as most of the
> rest of adult education in committing resources of money, staff,
> and mind to the problems of evaluation. We have all been service-
> oriented and pressed to greater service demands than the resources
> provided would support. However, if we wish to have evidence
> and not just faith that we are a vital force in the education of the
> people, then we must evaluate....As a sympathetic colleague from
> a related field, let me assure those in library science that there
> is not a great deal of help to be had elsewhere in terms of specific
> methods; you must set yourself down in the middle of the problem
> and start chipping away.

For examples of evaluation studies that may help librarians in the "chipping
away" process, Thiede suggests referring to the "Adult Education" issues of
the Review of Educational Research for June, 1959 and June, 1965, and the
summer issues of Adult Education, "Reasearch and Investigations in Adult
Education, " in the last several years.

Guba and Stufflebeam (G-46:13) point out that one of the most difficult problems
in evaluation has been "a lack of adequate conceptualizations regarding the
nature of educational evaluation in the context of the emergent programs of
educational change." They discuss six theoretical problems which they feel
must be solved before meaningful evaluation methodology can be developed.
These are:

1. Inadequacies of present definitions of educational evaluation.
2. A lack of understanding of the different educational settings
   within which evaluation must be conducted.

51

3. A lack of understanding of generalizable information requirements which educational evaluation studies must meet.
4. The lack of a valid structure for the generalizable parts
   of evaluation design.
5. The lack of concepts needed to organize and operate
   evaluation systems.
6. The lack of an appropriate set of criteria for judging the
   worth of evaluation strategies, designs, instruments,
   reports, etc.

In response to these problems Guba and Stufflebeam propose some conceptualizations which they feel should undergird the evaluation process. They suggest a model designed to answer questions posed by decision-makers
(G-46:16). They also offer a definition (G-46:15): "Evaluation is the process
of obtaining and providing useful information for making educational
decisions." Guba and Stufflebeam (G-46:26) also offer a valuable service in
distinguishing four types of evaluation: context, input, process, and product
(forming the acronym CIPP).

Context evaluation services planning decisions, which determine objectives;
Input evaluation services structuring decisions, which determine procedural
   designs for achieving objectives;
Process evaluation services implementing decisions, which determine the
   executive of chosen designs; and
Product evaluation services recycling decisions, which determine whether
   to continue, terminate, or modify a project.

Thomson (T-9) provides a helpful diagram of the CIPP model (see figure 6)
which shows that evaluation is a systematic and continuing process and that
each type of evaluation includes three basic steps as outlines by Stufflebeam
(T-9:25). These steps include "the delineating of questions to be answered
and information to be obtained, the obtaining of relevant information, and the
providing of information to decision-makers for their use to make decisions
and thereby improve ongoing programs." He summarizes how decision types
are served by the four kinds of evaluation (T-9:25-26):

Context evaluation provides information about needs, problems,
and opportunities in order to identify objectives. Input evaluation
provides information about the strengths and weaknesses of
alternative strategies for achieving given objectives. Process
evaluation provides information about the strengths and weaknesses
of a strategy during implementation, so that either the strategy

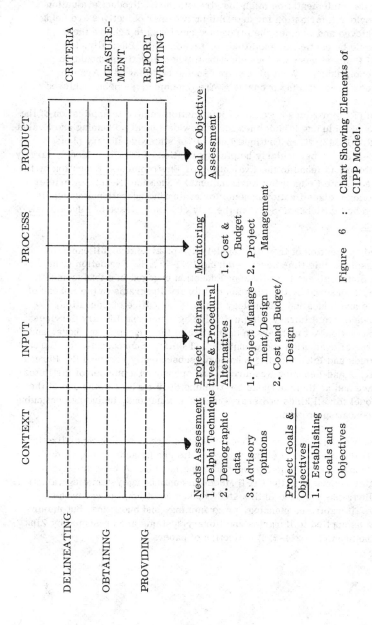

Figure 6 : Chart Showing Elements of CIPP Model.

Source: David D. Thomson, Planning and Evaluation for Statewide Library Development: New Directions. (Columbus, The Ohio State University Evaluation Center, 1972), p. xv.

53

or its implementation might be strengthened. Product evaluation provides information for determining whether objectives are being achieved and whether the procedure employed to achieve them should be continued, modified, or terminated. Basically, the CIPP Model answers four questions: What objectives should be accomplished? What procedures should be followed? Are the procedures working properly? Are the objectives being achieved?

Thomson (T-9) provides a wealth of information related to application of the CIPP Model including "Guidelines for Statewide Library Planning and Evaluation"(T-9:231-242); "Ten Critique Letters" of statewide library plans (T-9:243-273). A particularly helpful application of the CIPP Model, largely in chart form, is found in the Evaluation for Environmental Education by the New Jersey State Council for Environmental Education (N-18). A briefer model giving a classification scheme for evaluating educational change is presented by Stufflebeam (S-97) in the July 30, 1968, issue of Educational Technology.

Study and application of the CIPP Model have particular significance for librarianship at this time because during 1971-72, the Evaluation Center of the Ohio State University College of Education engaged in a twelve-month program, sponsored by the Division of Library Programs in the Bureau of Libraries and Education Technology in the U. S Office of Education, "to train heads of state library administrative agencies and Library Services and Construction Act planners in each state in the concepts, methods, and procedures of evaluation and planning " (T-9:ix). Subsequently the Bureau of Libraries and Educational Technology (subsequently renamed the Bureau of Libraries and Learning Resources) has sponsored a number of institutes which have had as their purpose the training of librarians in the use of the CIPP Model for all kinds of library-related evaluations, including continuing library education programs.

For those who have not had the benefit of exposure to the conceptualizations of the CIPP Model, many of the same results can be achieved through the use of planning, programming and budgeting models. A chief difference is the greater emphasis in the CIPP Model on continuous systematic evaluation. The bibliography included in this study makes no attempt to cover the extensive literature on planning, programming, and budgeting, but major concepts as applied to libraries and library systems are presented by Zink in the Thomson (T-9:211-215) collection of papers.

Another helpful source specifically designed for the evaluation of staff development and continuing education programs for library personnel is provided by Conroy (C-52:25-32). Five guidelines are suggested for evaluation, each followed by a number of criteria and suggestions for meeting the guideline.

Thiede (T-8: 89)   makes this important observation regarding the value of objectives:

> The most common difficulty in evaluation as well as in curriculum (i.e., program) building in adult education is failure to arrive at objectives agreed upon, understood, and accepted by leader and learner.... While it is possible (although not desirable) to build   programs on the basis of content, methods, and resources available, it is not possible to evaluate such a program on any other basis than a client "happiness index." We frequently build programs based on intriguing methods we have seen or used or on persons known to be available and "dynamic speakers." In these cases objectives must then be inferred and are not available for use in evaluation. An evaluator develops statements of objectives only with patient, painstaking work with the instructor(s) of the program. These objectives are derived by instructors from societal need, learner need, organizational goals, subject matter, and learning theory.

Excellent materials on determining objectives are available, but only a selected few of these are included in the present bibliography. For example, Bloom (B-17) and Krathwohl (K-34) are used extensively as sources for indicating the range and sequence of possible objectives in cognitive and affective areas. Mager (M-24; M-25) is used widely as a source for writing instructional objectives.

Hudspeth (T-9:168-170) emphasizes the necessity of translating goals into objectives which can be observed and measured. He defines a specific objective as "something which can be counted, seen, or felt." Specific objectives are a necessary condition for effective evaluation.

One of the areas related to evaluation of continuing education on which there seems to be greater emphasis in the literature than in many other areas is the evaluation of effective teaching. For example, the October, 1967, issue of the Journal of Engineering Education contains articles by Foecke (F-12);

Kraybill (K-35; K-36); Lancaster (L-1); Dabney and Williamson (D-1).
Kraybill (K-36) describes the contribution of the Committee for Young Engineering Teachers, established within the American Society for Engineering Education in 1950, in improving the teaching of engineering instructors.

An example of a packaged evaluation kit for teachers and students is that provided by Cavalier (C-11) as an instructor performance inventory for courses sponsored by the American Institute of Bankers. As it is a self-evaluating tool, it offers no threat to instructors. Cavalier (C-10) has found that it is widely used with beneficial results. Reemers and Manual (R-15) present a rating scale for instruction which can be used for student ratings and as a self-rating instrument for the teacher, who is charged to respond to the instrument "as he perceived himself." Greenfield and Page (G-41) completed a survey to discover the use of educational methodology in continuing engineering studies and concluded that interest was high, but little was being done. They found that computer-assisted instruction, closed-circuit TV, programmed instruction, and the electrowriter were all being used but there was little or no evaluation of their effectiveness as teaching methods. Faegre (F-1) presents an analysis and evaluation of present and future media needs in higher education generally.

Two examples of evaluation of specific continuing education programs in library science are provided by Allen (A-15) and Conroy (C-52).

Thiede (T-8) emphasizes an evaluative concept that is often overlooked when he states that each learning experience should make the participant more independent. "This demands that as a part of each learning experience, the adult be helped to diagnose his educational need, plan the learning experience, and evaluate his progress" (T-8:92). A special report of the Adult Education Association (I-9) indicates: "In adult education, methods of evaluation must exemplify that sense of freedom which characterizes the learning process itself . . . Methods of evaluation should be internal, not imposed from without. Adult learners, in short, must also learn how to evaluate their own success or failure."

One of the major trends predicted by Luke (L-27) was that in all continuing education activity there is going to be an increased emphasis on accountability. Stufflebeam (T-9:24-33) provides a helpful article on the relevance of the CIPP Evaluation Model for educational accountability. He defines accountability as "the ability to account for past actions in relationship to the decisions which precipitated the actions, the wisdom of those decisions, the extent to which they were adequately and efficiently implemented, and the value of their effects" (T-9:26). He shows the relation between evaluation and accountability, in relation to the CIPP Model, in chart form (see Figure 7). He indicates the main decision served by the CIPP Model in the first row of the matrix while the second row identifies the main accountability needs that are served by each evaluation type.

It is pointed out in the May, 1971 issue of Evaluation and Measurement News-letter that demands for accountability have led to performance contracting by private corporations engaging in educational activities for profit, "an incursion into the traditional educational structure." The Newsletter states: "Accounta-bility demands results, good results. It seeks to determine desired accomplish-ments according to prescribed standards. It assumes an empirical and a more systematic approach to examining the results of the educational process and to scrutinizing the components of the process: pupil abilities, teacher-training, teaching methods, and materials. . . Unless leaders in education show con-cern and take the initiative not only in developing new educational programs but in evaluating those programs, they run the risk of having groups outside the school determine the direction of education" (E-6:1).

Three educational journals have recently devoted complete issues to accounta-bility, its analysis, and tentative solutions -- the December, 1970 issue of Phi Delta Kappan, the January, 1971 issue of Educational Technology, and the May, 1971 issue of the Evaluation and Measurement Newsletter (published by the Ontario Institute for Studies in Education).

Based on a review of the literature relative to evaluation, it would seem that the following recommendations would constitute important conditions for the effectiveness of continuing professional education programs:

1. Evaluation must be a systematic and continuing part of continuing education studies and programs. One model that would seem particularly helpful in this respect is the CIPP Evaluation Model developed by the Ohio State University Evaluation Center.

2. Because of their resources and expertise, universities should take the lead in developing standards and evalu-ative criteria for continuing education formats and modes of instruction.

57

EVALUATION TYPES

(USERS)

	CONTEXT	INPUT	PROCESS	PRODUCT
DECISION-MAKING	Objectives	Solution strategy Procedural design	Implementation	Termination, continuation, modification, or installation
ACCOUNTABILITY	Record of objectives and bases for their choice	Record of chosen strategy and design and reasons for their choice	Record of the actual process	Record of attainments and recycling decisions

Figure 7 : The Relevance of the CIPP Model to Decision-Making and Accountability

Source: David D. Thomson, Planning and Evaluation for Statewide Library Development: New Directions. (Columbus: The Ohio State University Evaluation Center, 1972), p. 27.

58

3. Those responsible for continuing education programs should be able to account for past actions by answering questions concerning both the ends and the means of their programs.

4. Continuing education programs should make provision for self-evaluation by each participant in terms of his particular goals and objectives.

In short, no longer can the continued existence of continuing library education programs be their principal defense.

Recognition for Continuing Education

Generally, participants in continuing education activities have received little or no recognition for their initiative. There is no universally accepted means of measuring non-credit activity. Some feel that the absence of a system to give recognition has tended to weaken the concept of education as a life-long process. It has also been pointed out that the lack of documented evidence has made it difficult to secure an adequate funding base for continuing education consistent with commitment and needs.

Some educators point to the fact that lack of recognition has meant the lack of a strong motivating factor on the part of individuals to participate in continuing education activities. According to Maslow (M-34:45-46), the egotistic needs of man--need for self-esteem and esteem from others--are very strong motivators. Maslow divides esteem needs into two categories: needs for achievement, adequacy, mastery, and competence; and needs for reputation, prestige, status, recognition, and appreciation. Thus, it is concluded that the desire for recognition will motivate people to participate in continuing education if there is some type of reward structure.

Barrett (B-3), in a recent study of research and development personnel, concluded that the reward structure in terms of promotions, recognition, and professional reputation was seen as an important determinant of self-development efforts. "If organization members do not perceive a link between their development activities and the organization's reward system, the probability of active efforts to update knowledge and skills is lessened" (B-3:12).

In order to stimulate greater participation in continuing education activities, employing organizations and professional associations are experimenting in devising ways to give recognition and rewards. Some of these are considered.

Engineering

The Committee on Recognition of Continuing Engineering Studies was appointed by the Engineer's Council for Professional Development (ECPD) because it was felt a new approach was needed to stimulate the participation of engineers in continuing education courses in order to improve their effectiveness as employee and their own satisfaction as professionals. The new approach decided upon was a well-organized recognition system in addition to the academic degree system of education (J-6).

The ECPD believed a well-organized recognition system was needed to enable:

60

1) The engineer to demonstrate and measure his continued efforts for maintenance of professional and managerial competence and for further training in preparation for greater future responsibilities,

2) The engineer and his employer to better evaluate the relative merits of different available courses or educational programs,

3) New employers to assess the value of continuing engineering studies by job applicants, and

4) The continuing engineering education faculties to facilitate their planning of courses and educational programs for engineers (J-6:20).

ECPD takes the position that "it should seek to stimulate individual engineers to participate in continuing engineering studies by certifying the completion of registered courses which are directed toward the career objectives of an individual whether largely technical, managerial, social-cultural or mixed" (J-6:20).

The report describes the system in detail. A few of the more salient features are summarized here. The system is based on 1) a mechanism to evaluate and record continuing engineering studies and courses in accordance with course evaluation criteria, and 2) a system of accumulation of credit and the evaluation of the composite for recognition by awarding national Achievement Certificates.

Criteria were established in the areas of content, extent, instructional competence, student performance, and sponsorship. For the award of an Achievement Certificate, criteria were established on the basis of units of study. For example, an ECPD certificate will be awarded upon the accumulation of a minimum of 20 units of study together with the submission of a short essay outlining the plan of the student in his pursuit of continuing education, and the way he considers the 20 units to fit into his plan. Additional certificates will be granted for each additional 20 units of study recognized by ECPD and accompanied by the essay. Course certificates will be issued in triplicate, the original and one copy to be given to the student by the organization conducting the course. The third copy will be sent to ECPD headquarters. When the student has collected at least 20 units of relevant study, he shall send in his certified copies for each course, toegether with his essay, to ECPD headquarters. The essay shall be read to determine whether the student has given proper consideration to an integrated program of continuing education in selecting his courses. When the ECPD considers that the selection has been too random or opportunistic, additional

61

units beyond the 20 submitted may be required before a certificate is issued. A time limit will be established beyond which credits will become obsolete.

Banking

The American Institute of Banking's recognition system is based on the awarding of three levels of certificates (C-10). The BASIC CERTIFICATE consists of 15 units of work. The STANDARD CERTIFICATE is an additional 21 credits; the ADVANCED CERTIFICATE is 30 additional credits. By the time the student has earned an ADVANCED CERTIFICATE, he has 66 credits of AIB work. At present, the Institute is issuing 300 Advanced Certificates per year as opposed to about 5,000 Basic Certificates.

In addition, the AIB has another certificate called GENERAL CERTIFICATE which consists of 36 credits. Here the student can apply any credits offered in the national program, whereas in the other three, the number of credits in each area of study (Foundations in Banking, Banking Functions, Management and Supervision, Communication, and General Elective) are specified. A more detailed description of the system is presented in Chapter IV.

Medicine

At its Clinical Convention in December, 1968, the American Medical Association House of Delegates established the Physician's Recognition Award for participation in continuing education (P-18).

The award was first offered during 1969. It was based on the continuing medical education activities carried out by physicians during the three-year period beginning July 1, 1966 and ending June 30, 1969. Over 16,000 physicians applied for the Award at this first offering, and about 75% of the applicants were found to be qualified. . . (P-18:1).

The purpose of the Physician's Recognition Award is to accord recognition to physicians who participate regularly in continuing medical education and to encourage other physicians to engage in this important activity. The AMA strongly believes that all physicians should continue their education on a regular basis throughout their professional careers.

Since a lifetime of learning is an obligation of those in our profession, the Award is planned in such a way that a physician engaged in any field or fields of medicine can qualify for the Award (P-18:2).

The Award is granted for a minimum total of 150 credit hours of continuing medical education that are earned over a continuous three-year qualifying period. At the end of the three-year period, a physician who has met the requirements receives a certificate that is valid for three years. During the three years that his certificate is valid, it is expected that a physician will be earning the credits to qualify for another Award when his certificate expires.

Of the 150 credit hours needed to qualify for the Award, a minimum of 60 credit hours must come from any combination of Required Education categories. Required Education includes activities in six categories: 1) Internship-Residency (or Fellowship), 2) Education for an Advanced Degree (other than the M.D.), 3) Research in Lieu of Training (given only for full-time medical research), 4) Continuing Medical Education Courses, 5) Teaching, and 6) Papers or Publications.

In addition to Required Education categories, there are four Elective Education categories from which the remaining 90 credit hours may come: 1) Scientific Medical Meetings: Local (credit given on an hour-for-hour basis with a 50 credit hours limit), 2) Scientific Medical Meetings: State, Regional, National or International (also had a 50 credit hours limit), 3) Scientific Exhibits (10 hour limit, and 4) Additional Teaching.

In order to earn their 60 credit hours of Required Education activities, it is assumed that most practicing physicians will use Category 4 of Required Education--Continuing Medical Education Courses. The Journal of the American Medical Assoication carries the lists of courses creditable toward the Award.

There is a non-refundable application fee of $5.00 which partially pays for the cost of review and the handling and mailing services.

Nursing

Meng (M-41) describes in the November-December, 1971 issue of The Journal of Continuing Education in Nursing how one professional organization sought to encourage continuing education and give recognition to the continuing learner. The plan for Recognition for Continuing Education is based on "recognition points" which may be acquired under three categories of continuing education: 1) short-term courses or programs; 2) independent and informal study (2-5 recognition points for every one hour of presentation; limit of 15 points per publication of scholarly article); 3) formal academic study relevant to nursing or fulfilling a requirement for a degree (1 semester credit = 15 points; audit of courses = 1/3 the recognition points of a course taken for credit). Each member of the association is encouraged to strive for the acquisition of 50 recognition points in each 2-year period. Recognition will be given in the following ways: 1) a certificate for each person achieving 50 points in the 2-year period; 2) a letter of recognition to the individual's employer. A Continuing Education Approval Committee determines criteria for approving continuing education activities, approves activities for recognition points, and approves applications from members for these recognition points. Sample application forms for receiving points toward certificates are included in the article.

One of the seemingly most promising developments toward a nationally-accepted continuing education measure is "the continuing education unit" concept. In its January-February, 1973 issue, the Journal of Continuing Education in Nursing published a "Landmark Statement" from the organizing group for the American Nurses' Association Council on Continuing Education.

Conscious of the need in the nursing profession for a means to quantify and record the involvement of nurses in continuing education, the American Nurses' Association (ANA) Commission on Nursing Education endorsed the use of the continuing education unit (c e u) in December, 1971. "The Commission views the c e u as a means of recognizing individual nurses' participation in non-credit continuing education activities in nursing" (A-51:28). For the past four years, the ANA has worked with a group of associations interested in the feasibility of a uniform unit of measurement for continuing education and has been jointly engaged in a process of development, field testing, and refining of such a unit. The associations providing the major thrust have been the National University Extension Association, the American Association of Collegiate Registrars and Admission Officers, the U. S. Civil Service Commission, and the U. S. Office of Education.

The Continuing Education Unit (c e u) is defined as follows: Ten contact hours of participation in an organized continuing education experience under responsible sponsorship, capable direction and qualified instruction.

The use of the c e u is specified. Included in the system are classes, lectures, workshops, symposia, institutes, short courses, organized independent study, etc. Types of study ordinarily not awarded continuing education units are:

1) Any program carrying academic credit,
2) Programs leading to high school equivalency certificates or diplomas,
3) Organizational orientation training programs,
4) Short duration programs only casually related to any specific upgrading purpose or goal.

Activities carried on outside of organized channels without sponsorship or instruction do not lend themselves to uniform measurement and, therefore, useful as they may be to the individual, are outside the program. Examples of activities not included are: selective and general reading, exposure to the communications media, travel, films, discussion groups, attendance at meetings, organizational and committee membership, community and social activities.

The ANA endorses the concept of continuing education for registered nurses as one means by which nurses can maintain competence and meet standards of practice developed by the profession. In its Guidelines for Certification, ANA has defined the term "certification" as " ' recognition of excellence in clinical practice.' To meet the requirements for certification, the individual practitioner will have to submit data to indicate currency of knowledge, among other criteria. Evidence of c e u for courses attended would be one valid source of such data" (A-51:30).

The statement concludes: "The acceptance of the continuing education unit is just one example of finally arriving at a suitable means of recognizing and rewarding individual and institutional efforts in the pursuit of conitnuing education" (A-51:31).

Industry

An appealing concept of recognition is provided by the 'Bank Account' Policy for Continuing Education of the Research and Engineering Division of the Kimberly-Clark Corporation.

First introduced in 1965, the plan was designed as a way of establishing an organizational environment which would encourage scientists, engineers, and technicians to maintain and extend knowledge in their own and related disciplines. Its overall purpose is to provide an opportunity for each person to carry out development activities which contribute to the individual need for personal and professional growth and to the Division need for more effective performance results. A recent addition to the program is the Academic Residence Fellowship program which provides for sabbatical study and research. This addition supplies an opportunity for "in-depth" self-renewal and more intensive industry-academic interface and communication.

Basic principles of the program provide time and money allowances in the "bank account." Recognizing that development of any individual is accomplished primarily through his own initiative and motivation, the company "can only provide the climate and opportunities which encourage individuals to develop to their full potential" (K-13:5). Besides performance level (established by a results oriented evaluation), such other factors as potential for growth, probable placements or assignments, years of possible use, and record on earlier development opportunities are used to determine allowances for individual use. Each individual applying for "bank account" allowances must have participated, with the help and advice of his immediate supervisor, in the formulation of a plan that states his objectives for development. Allowances may be applied to tuition fees, registration costs, travel, memberships, meetings, books or other material for independent study, etc. If an employee is awarded an Academic Residence Fellowship (summer or semester), the company will pay salary, tuition, and residence costs not covered by bank account allowances.

Ministry

The Commission on Continuing Education of the United Presbyterian Church (U-2) recommended the formation of a Cooperative Agency on Continuing Education for Ministry. In turn, it recommended that the Cooperative Agency give immediate attention to the design and implementation of programs to serve ministers in their first five years of professional work. One program recommendation was the establishment of a recognition system. "The key aspect of this program would be that those who meet standards for effective participation in the five-year educational program would be designated "Fellows in Ministry" (U-2:85). Those wishing to receive this designation'would be examined on their written reports of several completed projects of ministry, on their knowledge of literature relevant for the practice of ministry, on their ability to plan ministries, to deal with difficult problems that commonly arise in ministry, and to evaluate their own ministries and those of others " (U-2:85).

66

Just as this program would be voluntary, the fact of a man's entering upon it and the findings of his examinations would be confidential. Under no circumstances would these records, or reports of their contents, be available to persons or agencies other than the examining committees and the candidates themselves. There must be no possibility that the contents of these records could enter into consideration of a candidate's career within the Church. The administering agency, however, would publish the names of those designated as Fellows in Ministry (U-2:85).

The report states that it does not see the application of the "Fellows in Ministry" incentive as only applying to younger ministers, but that it would be equally applicable to those in later career stages. Standards and conditions similar to those described earlier might pertain in the later career periods, and the designation "Fellows in Ministry" for experienced pastors might have specific reference to specialized competence acquired in fields of individual preference.

Another type of recognition is provided by the new ecumenical "Academy for Parish Clergy" (U-2:74). In this case, it is sustained membership itself that supplies the recognition factor. Any pastor may become an active participant in the program of the Academy, but membership requires commitment to a strict study discipline: two weeks out of every year spent in Academy-approved study, and involvement in regionally-based research projects related to the work of his own church. Failure to maintain the discipline will result in loss of membership. One who has dropped out will not be allowed to return. It is anticipated that after the Academy becomes established, the standards will gradually be tightened. It is intentionally designed to make it a mark of achievement and competence to be known as a member.

Summary

These examples of recognition plans for continuing education represent several different models. The engineering and banking examples are based totally on courses taken in order to be awarded a certificate. The Physician's Recognition Award plan states that it is expected that most doctors will build up their points by taking continuing medical education courses, but nine other options are offered, including teaching, publishing, attending professional meetings, producing an exhibit, and working for an advanced degree. The plan of the North Dakota Nurses' Association for recognition of continuing education gives recognition points under three headings: short-term courses or programs, independent and informal study that leads to some type of presentation or publication, and formal academic study. The c e u excludes any program carrying academic credit, inservice programs in organizations, and short-term programs not related to any specific upgrading purpose or goal.

The "bank-account" system of the Kimberly Clark Corporation has a different orientation. In that program, the recognition and the reward are in the provision of time and funds for continuation activities, including tuition fees, registration costs, travel, living expenses, books and resources for independent study, society memberships, meeting costs, etc. The criteria for authorizing use of the allowance is the degree to which such use helps the individual meet his development needs.

Two variant forms are illustrated by examples from the ministry. The Presbyterian format of "Fellows in Ministry" has the added factor of examination based on written papers and written appraisals submitted by those familiar with the candidate's work. The Academy for Parish Clergy is centered around the fact that membership in the group shows certain criteria and membership itself is the recognition.

Today within library science there is no generally recognized recognition plan sponsored by any of the professional associations. Interest has been shown in exploring the possibilities, however, and at present there is a committee of the Public Library Assoication, a division of the American Library Association, investigating what other professions are doing in this area.

Conditions Under Which Continuing Library Education Has Flourished

This chapter has surveyed some factors that, from a review of the literature, seem to be important in the design of continuing professional education programs. They are: using a systems approach; providing conditions
favorable to the adult learner; using identified learning needs as a basis
of programming; taking account of the motivational factors which encourage participation in continuing education activities; determining specific
objectives; providing for continuous evaluation; giving some type of recognition to the individual for participation in continuing education.

From his observations and experience, Shera (S-24) has
identified ten conditions under which continuing library education has
flourished:

1. in periods of crisis, change, and professional stress;
2. in formats which emphasize interdisciplinary approaches by
   those outside of librarianship -- "the degree of 'outside'
   participation offered";
3. in patterns which are cumulative, "each building upon and
   being more advanced than that which precedes it";
4. in programming that demands more than passive listening --
   "ideally exercises, reports, even tests or examinations,
   should be required to give the participants a goal toward
   which to work and a sense of accomplishment when the
   program is ended";
5. in allocation of time for participants to talk informally with
   staff and other program participants;
6. in cooperative planning and implementation involving the
   libraries, the library schools, the state library and the state
   library association ("with the state library in the strongest
   position to assume leadership");
7. in application of the system concept;
8. in demanding sacrifices on the part of all involved -- participants and the employing library;
9. in providing adequate financing; and
10. in recognizing that continuing education is an integrated
    whole, not a cluster of sporadic and isolated instances --
    "the state library, the state library association, and the
    libraries of the state must stop playing around the edges of
    the problem."

Another way to review the factors which influence the continuing education process is to present a model which makes it easy to visualize the relationships which compose the system. Cohen and Dubin (C-18:4-6) present such a model in Figure 8, showing how the multiple factors which could enhance the updating may be displayed at once. Figure 8 presents the authors conceptualization of such a model.

> The input to this system is the individual. Professional updating involves such factors as environment, psychological factors and motivation. Box W in the system represents the past formal education of the professional. Continuing into the main system, Box P represents the effects of supervision on possible updating. Next is Box A and t_a, which are outside influences of the system caused by management policies. $I = B + K + D + E + F$ represents various approaches to updating practices which a professional can undergo. In this case, the professional can go through any combination of I simultaneously or one at a time.
>
> Boxes G and H represent the positive effects of peer groups and/or self achievement as a result of the updating process. This is shown as feedback in this system.
>
> If no positive feedback occurs due to peer groups and/or self achievement, the system can have a cycling effect back to the main system via the third feedback loop, e.

The final output of this continuing education system model is either an updated or non-updated individual. A strength of this particular model is that it incorporates educational, environmental, psychological, and motivational factors, from the systems viewpoint. Also it can be used for both individuals and groups of professionals. In the text (C-18:9-11), the authors also demonstrate mathematically how it may be determined which variables are most influential in the updating process, thereby making the model useable as a decision making tool.

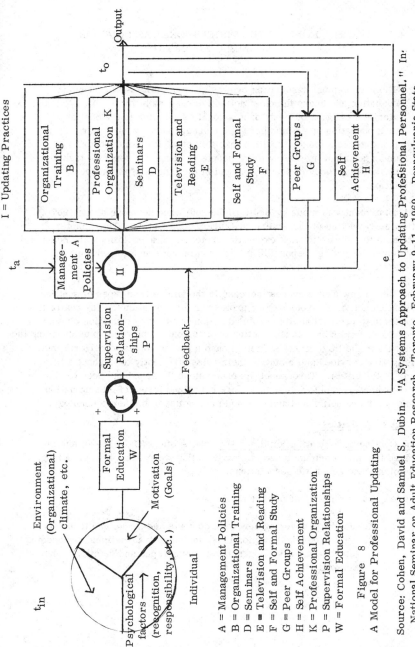

t_{in}

Environment
(Organizational)
climate, etc.

Motivation
(Goals)

Psychological
factors
(recognition,
responsibility, etc.)

Individual

Formal
Education
W

t_a

Management A
Policies

Supervision
Relation-
ships
P

II

I

Feedback

e

I = Updating Practices

t_o

Output

Organizational
Training
B

Professional
Organization K

Seminars
D

Television and
Reading
E

Self and Formal
Study
F

Peer Groups
G

Self
Achievement
H

A = Management Policies
B = Organizational Training
D = Seminars
E = Television and Reading
F = Self and Formal Study
G = Peer Groups
H = Self Achievement
K = Professional Organization
P = Supervision Relationships
W = Formal Education

Figure 8
A Model for Professional Updating

Source: Cohen, David and Samuel S. Dubin. "A Systems Approach to Updating Professional Personnel." In: National Seminar on Adult Education Research, Toronto, February 9-11, 1969. Pennsylvania State University, February, 1969, p. 5. (ED 025 718). (C-18)

71

IV. THE ROLE OF THE PROFESSIONAL ASSOCIATION
IN CONTINUING EDUCATION

> The professional association crowns all other efforts at continuing
> education and bears the chief collective responsibility for it . . . . a
> manifest function of every professional association is the contin-
> uing education of its membership; indeed, scarcely any other
> function has a longer tradition than this one. It is, moreover,
> undertaken not merely by a few people working at a separate task but
> by the whole body of people engaged in the affairs of the assoc-
> iation.

This statement was made by Houle (H-36:266) when he spoke at the 1967
Midwinter meeting of the American Library Association. This chapter
attempts to indicate to what extent the professional associations are bearing
the "chief collective responsibility" for continuing education within their
professions.

The 1960's saw a tremendous increase in the number and types of continuing
education activities sponsored by professional associations. The realization
has come to profession after profession that preservice education plus an
occasional trip to an annual meeting or a regional conference plus scanning the
journals in the field cannot suffice to enable professionals to perform their
distinctive services and maintain their roles efficiently throughout a lifetime (H-36:259). Throughout the professions the trend has been to plan,
to coordinate, and to implement more organized forms of dissemination
based on more definite structures and making use of the new technology.

Types of Activities

The Continuing Education for R and D Careers study (C-24:18-20) summarizes the most common types of activities that were found in engineering,
chemical, and scientific associations.

    A. Dissemination of Information

        1. Journals covering new developments knowledge and techniques
        2. Other technical publications, including transactions, proceedings,
           abstracts and bibliographies, monographs and detailed technical
           information.

3. Non-technical publications containing news both of general interest and specifically pertaining to continuing education, as well as technical areas of broad interest. Chemical and Engineering News is a good example of this type of publication.

4. Annual meetings including both the traditional presentation of papers and discussions and the newer formats of short course, review and state-of-the-art papers as part of the meeting.

B. Planning, Coordinating and Implementing Specific Continuing Education Activities Aimed at Updating and Keeping Up to Date to Overcome or Prevent Obsolescence.

1. Guides for local chapters or sections for planning continuing education activities from inception to implementation.

2. Specific instructional materials or recommendations for where they can be obtained.

3. Speaker-lecture tours and touring short courses.

4. Surveys of members to determine their needs, interests, and attitudes regarding continuing education. The society is a mechanism for quickly and readily obtaining information of new developments as well because of the dispersion of its membership geographically.

5. Cooperative efforts with other societies, universities, and employers in solving problems and meeting the needs in continuing education.

These nine activities as reported in this engineering study are typical of educational activities in the broadest sense as sponsored by the majority of professional associations. Generally, they make available specific information of new developments and often provide special instruction in the form of intensive workshops or seminars either before or after annual meetings of the associations. Three of the most common modes of continuing education are attending meetings, short workshops or courses, and reading literature. The professional associations traditionally sponsor the first two, and by their publications are responsible for a large amount of the literature. In addition, some professions have developed cooperative structures by which the professional societies within a given profession can further develop programs and activities. One example is the Engineers Joint Council for Professional Development, made up of nine leading engineering societies. In 1965 they established a permanent Committee on

Continuing Education with a full-time director (C-24:20).

Houle (H-36:261) points out that generally the professional associations have come to the realization that "Lifelong learning cannot be achieved simply by increasing pages of print or the frequency of meeting   A broad object-ive must be analyzed into specific goals and the means to reach them must be perfected and adopted.   Precisely, this process is now occurring in con-tinuing professional education.   Out of the fresh but vast experience of the several professions, a basic structure of concerns is emerging."

In the professional association, this concern is shown by experimentation with many additional forms of activity.   Examples of some of the new ways in which professional associations are developing new approaches follow, featuring the five professions which reported on activities at the national level during the mini-workshop presented by the Continuing Library Educa-tion Committee of the Association of American Library Schools at the annual meeting of the Association in Washington, D.C. in January, 1973.

Examples of Programming in Various Professional Associations

Architecture

The structure established by each professional association or associations is of particular interest to those concerned with building new programming patterns.   Rose (R-39) in his presentation to the librarians spent quite a bit of time describing the structure he had built up in the American Institute of Architects (AIA),   stating: "I think that the structure might be something that you may wish to relate to in terms of developing continuing education in your own profession."

The whole continuing education effort at AIA is divided into divisions: the behavioral division and the information division.

The behavioral division deals with skills, how to do things, "process--verb-oriented and action-oriented activities."   Within the behavioral division, several activities are in operation:

1) Architectural Training Laboratories -- These are short, compact, one, two, three and one half day training programs, offered to limited size groups.   These were developed at the national level and are made

available to groups all over the country. Nationally, the AIA Washington continuing education office handles the original development, the scheduling, charges, and registrations. These are chiefly attended by high-level employees of architectural firms. During each lab, the participants are asked how much they will start changing when they get back home to the office on Monday morning. To make training programs available for employees who cannot take time away from their work, a series of local labs, using local resources, in a program with a format that occurs during lunch hours, evenings, or other no-conflict times, have been developed.

2) <u>Architectural Service Centers</u>--Some kinds of services that an architect supplies require equipment that can be shared through a consortium. A group of architects can keep such expensive equipment busy, while none can afford it alone.

3) <u>Game Seminars</u>--These seminars are like the training labs, but they are correspondence oriented. However, they are not like usual correspondence courses, because they are essentially training laboratories in which a lot of mini-lab techniques are used in the program. Usually, a whole firm or a group of three to six can take the course and by the end of the course, the participant has had an actual opportunity to put a deal together with his investors ; his loan and everything is assembled step by step.

<u>The information division</u> is concerned with the kinds of things that are necessary "to plug into the process side in order to bring the whole thing together. "

1) <u>Monthly cassettes</u>-- A cassette comes out once a month that is called "The Review of Architectural Periodicals" (RAP). Each month 50 journals and newsletters are reviewed. "If the information can effect an architect in his office, we flag it; we rank order the items on priority of importance for the subject (established by means of a needs analysis from the field); we condense it--usually only about a fourth of the flagged information can go into the hour tape. This is a digest of the hottest items found that month. "

2) <u>In-depth subject cassettes</u>-- These are information programs based on cassettes which go in depth on a subject. The cassette is supplemented by written matter (like numbers or statistics), or slides.

3) Computerized reference service -- This is a computerized system
   of inventorying all the programs at universities and other associations that could have relevance to what architects want. The listing
   is catogorized in two ways: 1) live programs that must be attended;
   and 2) packaged courses that can be done at home.

4) AIA AIDS -- AIDS, standing for Architects Information Disseminating
   Service, is planned for starting operation in the summer of 1973.
   "We have centralized the development of a professional data bank,
   but decentralized the distribution by use of the telephone. Architects
   will be able to call from anywhere in the country toll free. In this
   system, the question will be to create information; in the other
   systems, some one will buy a cassette because he has an interest
   in that information, but he may not apply that right away. In this
   system, he has a specific problem to deal with; he calls to get
   some verbal information, and something in the mail in a day or two.

Each of the programs in each of the two divisions has three components:

1) Knowledge or content of the subject--some resource that has information.

2) Expertiße in a medium--the cassettes, for example are not live tapes,
   but have been processed ahead of time, been sent through production
   writers that look at it from a listening viewpoint, and use professional
   actors, actresses and sound crews to make the final productions

3) Mechanics--smooth operations and delivery. A smooth distribution
   system is essential if anything is going to happen.

Within these two domains: behavior and information, there is a constant
search for different ways to engage people. People at different levels
like to be engaged in a certain way. People have certain habits, and styles
of learning that must be engaged in different ways. "I am alwasy looking for
opportunities that are diverse to meet the needs of different people based on
their context and background. The subjects that could occur may be the same,
but the media contact can be made in a variety of ways."

Rose considers the subject content all important in the development of the
AIA continuing education program. A simple marketing procedure is used.
"We look at the basic components within the profession, and do sampling
with a large array of subjects . We generated about 140 subjects from
which a person could express no interest to high interest in stages. We
could break that down into areas of the country and by person. Anything
that we do follows the priorities of subjects that we discovered."

The whole program is based on the fact that continuing education is a free
enterprise system. "There is no requirement for an architect to engage
in continuing education at this point in time, although some laws are coming
into effect that may require continuing education for re-registration. This
is similar to your driver training re-testing. It looks like it will take the
form of many hours of professional development activities a year. Thusly,
now I am having to find out what kinds of real problems they do have, and
how they really do feel, and what ways I can viably make contact with them."

For every program produced, there is an evaluation system. On the information programs only one device is used--how do the participants feel about
it. This information is solicited through various questions in order to get
feedback. On the behavior change porgrams, there are two evaluations:
1) one is administered immediately after the program; 2) the second is
administered in three to six months to measure actual change.

As AIA is a trade association, the salary of the national director of continuing
education is paid for by dues--anything beyond that is from fees for services
rendered. Publicity is handled through the use of flyers, both for the cassettes
and the training labs.

In summary, the whole program has been built on a needs analysis of the
members of AIA. The program structure, as outlined here, was built and
has reached its present status in just one year. The first year $8,000 was
budgeted for programming. Now there is nothing budgeted as all the services
are paying for themselves. Continuing Education is one way of answering
the member's query, "What's my association doing for me?"

The continuing education program of the American Institute of Architects has
beenreviewed in this much detail because it is a demonstration of what
can be accomplished nationally, using the new technology with a minimum
investment on the part of the association's dues in the program, in one brief
year. Programs feature content which is related to expressed need--what

surveys of librarians say that they wish also. The programming is available wherever the architect may be in the United States; he does not have to go anywhere to take advantage of it. A variety of formats are available to appeal to the learning patterns and motivation patterns of different types of people.

Engineering

Marlowe (M-30),representing the American Society of Mechanical Engineers
at the AALS mini-workshop on professional continuing education, explained
that there are in the United States today about 750,000 people who can
legitimately call themselves engineers. Most are industrially employed.
"We have never been able to develop a centralized engineering profession.
In fact, we are very decentralized; there are about a dozen large professional societies. There are about 12 societies with over 20,000 members,
and about 120 smaller societies. In order to actively practice in engineering, a person must belong to more than one."

In order to get various societies to work together cooperatively, the profession has resorted to federations for different purposes. For example, the
Engineers' Council for Professional Development (ECAD) is chiefly concerned with accreditation of engineering curricula, but it also has other
committees, such as the Student Development Committee, the Development
of Young Engineers Committee, the Ethics Committee and the Committee on
Recognition (E-5). Its Board of Directors is made up of 13 different participating bodies and affiliates (E-5). The Engineers Joint Council is concerned
with wages and salary surveys (M-30). The American Society for Engineering
Education (ASEE) is concerned with the promotion of engineering education
in its many phases. Dougherty (D-51:1020) in his history of the Society
states that "probably the most intense effort has been a study of an adequate,
desirable, and feasible course of study. Report after report has been made,
and the end is not yet in sight."

In 1964 a cooperative effort by the American Society for Engineering Education, the Engineers Council for Professional Development, the Engineers
Joint Council, and the National Society of Professional Engineers led to the
publication of a joint report, Continuing Engineering Studies (C-30).
Dougherty (D-51:1029) comments on the report: "Continuing Engineering
Studies shows that much is being done, but much more is needed to keep the
practitioner in step with changes which are constantly taking place. Continuing education has always been a key weapon of those who succeed and now it
has become the necessity of those who will keep up with the pack. Engineering is a learning profession as well as a learned one."

Marlowe (M-30) reported that in spite of these efforts, "We have no centralization in continuing education. Nevertheless, continuing education is
the principle reason for the professional engineering societies. I need go
back no more than ten years and it would have been accurate to say that
continuing education was their only reason for existence."

Individually, each of the engineering societies is devoting much of its time and resources to continuing technical education. This is done on a national and even on an international scale. For example, Marlowe (M-30) explained: "I attended in Lima a meeting of the Union of Engineering Societies of North, Central, and South America. Twenty-six countries were represented at that meeting. Continuing education of the professional engineer was one of the principal topics on the agenda."

The individual engineering societies depend heavily on regional and sectional organization. In the mechanical engineers, there are eleven regions and 95 local sections.

Most of these local sections are based on a large city; principally these will be cities in which large industries are located since they form the focus of large enough groups of engineers to support a local section. These continuing education programs are financed by dues and by sales of educational materials.

The types of programs issued today take advantage of the new technology. Marlowe (M-30) brought with him a cassette lecture on air pollution. The cassette states that a background about the Master of Science level in any field of engineering or science should be adequate preparation. This particular course consisted of twelve lectures over eight and one-half hours, a notebook of all the slides, one reprint volume, and one reference volume. Total cost for this packaged program: $165.00.

Speaking on the self-taught materials available for study, Marlowe (M-30) explained that all societies print journals (for example, the Journal of the American Society of Electrical Engineers). These journals are all available to members as part of the dues payment and each issue will print seven to eight articles a month on modern technology. A major emphasis is on "pre-prints" which are issued by the hundreds about new technical material, usually four to six pages offset print. These cost from 75¢ to $1.00. The journals also contain abstracts of papers, and members can write in for the papers they wish. With the dues to the society, each member is entitled to a certain number of abstracts free, for each one over the basic number there is a charge. Marlowe also emphasized the importance to engineers of the advertising in the journals. "Not only is it a way to support the journals, but they are also heavily read for new information. Particularly if you want to know about equipment." He also pointed out that a totally free form of education results from the efforts of salesmen. "Everyone who is active in engineering spends a certain portion of his day talking to salesmen to find the latest equipment. I have had practicing engineers tell me that fifty per cent of their input for new information comes from salesmen."

In the future, Marlowe predicted enormous changes in the continuing education field. In addition to continuation of the journals, pre-prints and audio tapes already being used, he saw greatly increased use of what has already been started in "in-plant TV courses. Already in many states there are networks where a university course is transmitted by microwave to a local large employer and the employees take time from work to take the course. Participants have an audio connection with the instructor so that they can ask questions."

With the advent of Cable TV, Marlowe (M-30) predicted that such programming will take an enormous jump upward since as many as 400 channels may be available. "The opportunity for home and plant study will be greatly expanded; even beyond the advent of TV cassettes. Already on the market, they are fairly expensive, but bound to come down in price over the next ten years. This will blow the whole area of continuing education wide open."

Marlowe (M-30) reported that most of the group oriented continuing education efforts are used by the younger members of the profession, people 45 and under. "When someone graduates at 23 from the university, he is almost continually registered in a short course or some form of continuing education. The reason for the drop in educational participation seems to be that about 40-45 per cent, about half of the engineers, go into management, and then cease the technical practice of engineering. As managers they all undergo crash courses in the management skills that their technical careers did not prepare them for, but this is not supplied by the engineering societies themselves."

Speaking on motivation for continuing education, Marlowe (M-30) explained:

> In engineering it is very simple; it is a matter of professional life or death. We have a term called technical obsolescence, and this means simply that technology has proceeded at a rate that the individual has not kept up; in a very short time, sometimes only ten to fifteen years, he becomes useless to his employers. In a ten year cycle about half of what you know has become obsolete and needs to be replaced by new material. This makes our continuing education problem one of great difficulty and great timeliness.... If the program is not adequate or the person does not make the effort for **continuing education,** then he will soon find himself unable to secure employment.

Marlowe (M-30) explained that engineers have been quite successful in establishing that the continuing education of the engineer is one of the costs of doing business. Most of the engineering continuing education programs are financed either in the form of the employer directly running the educational program or subsidizing the individual who embarks on it.

We now have, in draft circulation, a cooperatively developed (between the Engineers Joint Council and major employers) a Standard Condition of Engineering Employment. This statement will be given to every graduate of an engineering school. The candidate can look down this form and decide if the company is offering conditions of work that students should regard as acceptable. A principle of that statement is provision of continuing education time and funds. This has taken us almost 25 years to do. There was a time when the individual was burdened with this cost himself. For the employer this is a pretax cost, which is very different from the post-tax cost to the individual.

Marlowe (M-30) explained that although continuing education is a company overhead and the employer is eager to cut overhead, at the same time, when the employer is in a tough competitive situation he wants his best engineering done, so that his line of products will command more than its share of the market. "The other thing is that continuing education has come, in the last 15 years, as a condition of employment. When a recruiter comes to campus now, the young candidate, especially the good one, will not ask what the retirement system is, rather he will say, 'What is the opportunity for continuing education?'"

In summary, there are a number of concepts from the engineering profession that would seem to hold potential for consideration in librarianship:

1) That continuing education is the principal reason for professional societies.

2) That regional and local organizations of societies consider continuing education programming their chief function.

3) That continuing education efforts should make use of the new technology; that formats such as pre-prints, cassette tapes, cassette based packaged programs, talk-back TV programs, and Cable TV are modes of continuing education that need to be exploited.

4) That programming be based on the free enterprise principle of marketing; that surveys be taken to determine needs and on the basis of priorities, programs are offered; if the program goes it is supported, if not, it is dropped.

5) That a "Standard Condition of Employment" be used by employers guaranteeing that provision of continuing education time and funds will be provided by the employing institution.

Banking

Cavalier (C-10), Director of Continuing Education for the American Institute of Banking, made the presentation for the banking industry at the AALS mini-workshop on professional continuing education. He explained that the American Institute of Banking (AIB) is one of the largest divisions of the American Bankers Association (ABA) which is a trade association made up of 13,000 member commercial banks in the United States. The AIB, unlike the ABA, has individual memberships. There are now about 240,000 bankers who are members of the Institute, roughly 25% of the total bank population of just over a million. At the national office in Washington, there are about 40 staff people in the AIB offices.

A great deal of success of the AIB over its 73-year-old history lies in its elaborate organizational structure. Each year it enrolls about 120,000 bankers in courses which are conducted in 375 chapters over the United States. At the next lower level, in addition to the formal chapter structure, there are an additional 200 "study groups." According to Cavalier (C-10), "every community in the land, regardless of size or density has some form of AIB study group." The local chapters and the study groups are the major instruments of continuing education.

In addition to group programming, the AIB conducts a successful correspondence program which reaches about 2,000 new enrollments each year. Currently, there are about 6,000 enrolled. In answer to a question about the way in which uniformity was ensured in the correspondence courses, Cavalier (C-10) responded:

> There is no way to guarantee uniformity in these programs. We develop the courses at the national level, and most chapters will use those courses. However, recently we have instituted a new policy whereby chapters can construct their own local courses. This makes uniformity impossible. But in locally constructed courses, the chapter is required, if they want national credit, to submit to us an application in which they indicate the specifications of the course, the qualifications of the instructors, etc. If it meets with our minimum standards, it gets approval for national credit.

One of the most unique features of the Institute is that all of the various types of study groups at each level are conducted on a volunteer basis by bankers themselves. Each chapter has its own organization with elected officers. The total structure is voluntary; it is the volunteer effort that makes the whole continuing education effort work.

There is local structure to support all the continuing education work. The elected chapter officers carry out the program. For these offices, there is competition so that those who wish to aspire to offices usually are around the chapter as students and then as teachers and become well known. At the national level, there is an Executive Council to which any local member may aspire as an officer. The nation is divided into 12 population-based districts.

The reviewer was recently invited to a special dinner honoring all those who had participated in the AIB continuing education programs during the last year in the greater Washington area. There were approximately 900 there, all paid for by their employing institutions. It served as an occasion to honor them for their continuing education endeavors. The cost of the dinner was borne by the employing banks of the participants in the Institute. About six months later, the reviewer was informed that another special dinner would be held--this time to award certificates and give awards for outstanding academic accomplishments. As explained at the annual dinner and by Cavalier (C-10), the Institute and its activities are supported entirely by the banking industry. Tuition for the individual courses ranges from $10 to $50 per semester per participant; in practically every instance, this tuition is paid by the bank employer.

With such a volunteer system, a major problem, according to Cavalier, is that of quality control. This problem is offset nationally through the development of as much information as a leader might need to conduct the course. Every textbook is provided with an instructor's manual which breaks the course into units. "We supply the instructors with specimen examination items."

Cavalier (C-10) brought samples of the texts and other materials produced at the national level to the AALS mini-workshop. One group of materials was entitled "Learning Methods Laboratory: Design and Operation" (A-29). The focus here was on the importance of establishing learning objectives, establishment of qualitative standards, measurement of performance, evaluation of results, and submission of credentials to the National office. The term "laboratory" is used to describe a national experimental approach to the development of new learning methods and techniques. In order to participate in the Laboratory, the chapter must submit an application listing course specifications. If selected for implementation, the chapter must submit an evaluation report after the completion of the laboratory. Nine procedural steps are described for the conduct of the laboratory.

84

Cavalier (C-11) has produced an <u>Instructor Performance Inventory</u> (IPI) which helps the volunteer instructors in the American Institute of Banking to understand and improve their teaching performance. It is not a method of faculty rating or evaluation; rather it is a technique to be used voluntarily by the instructor for his own self-development. The form consists of three parts. The first part deals with the treatment of material in class; the second part concerns teaching method and technique; part three offers material on student-instructor relations. The IPI Instructor's form is paralleled by the IPI Student's form, in which the students evaluate the teacher's performance. The IPI for the instructor and the IPI for the student contain the same items. A third booklet is the instructor's score sheet providing the necessary forms for the teacher to compare his self-evaluation of his own teaching with that of his students. These inventory booklets are handsomely printed and packaged.

Another source to help the volunteer teachers is Cavalier's (C-12) booklet entitled <u>Toward Becoming a Better Teacher</u>. It is designed to upgrade the quality of the teaching. It covers methods and techniques of effective teaching, the psychology of communication, motivation, and student-instructor relations. It seeks to serve the same purpose as the Department of Agriculture's Faculty Handbook (U-15) but is in a much more compact form.

The national curriculum now includes 35 courses, with 17 in the planning stage. These courses fall into five content areas: 1) Foundations of Banking; 2) Banking Functions; 3) Management and Supervision; 4) Communication Courses; 5) General electives (designed for the student who wishes to carry courses from colleges which may be evaluated for AIB credit).

The Institute has also an elaborately worked out certificate program:

1) the BASIC CERTIFICATE consists of 15 credits of work.
2) the STANDARD CERTIFICATE, which is an additional 21 credits.
3) the ADVANCED CERTIFICATE, which is 30 additional credits.
4) the GENERAL CERTIFICATE, which consists of 36 credits, in which the student can apply any of the credits taken in any of the functional areas.

This means that the student who earns the advanced certificate has 66 credits of AIB work. Each year, about 300 advanced certificates are issued as opposed to 5000 basic certificates.

Up until three years ago, the Institute had no relations with any colleges. Now there are 133 formal operating cooperative programs between AIB chapters and local colleges. Cavalier (C-10) explained that this local letter of agreement is reviewed by the national office and becomes a matter of record. As a result, the AIB is no longer serving bankers only. "At the present time on the drawing boards is an attempt to coordinate all of these college relations into a national consortium. It is our view that the AIB can serve as a catalyst with the community college for the purposes of a national relationship, whereby there would be reciprocal credit among the schools."

The AIB organization has a policy making body, the Executive Council, who are bankers. The total AIB is divided into 12 districts and each district has an executive coucilman who is on the national board. In addition, three elected officers (past president, president , and president-elect) serve with those 12 on the executive council. In addition, there are five staff officers who report to the AIB executive council.

The Institute has formulated a structure for determining educational needs. It is called "determining training and education needs." Cavalier explained :

> It is a kind of questionnaire and it is predicated on a meeting between chapter officials and bank officials where they go through questions, and as a result of this process, come up with some idea of education and training needs. It has not been a very successful operation for us. At the local level, needs analysis is very difficult to accomplish. On the other hand, through the ABA organization we have a very valuable input, because in developing our curriculum we will lean on the various functional divisions of the ABA. For example, now we are working on a textbook in real estate finance. The outline of that book was developed by the real estate finance committee of the ABA. My responsibility will be to locate authors and get the project going, but it is the responsibility of the commiittee to review the outline and the content of the book. The Training Committee also provides input to us as a technical advisor, suggesting to us new kinds of materials and programs that we should develop. We also have a National Educational Advisory Board which consists of six university professors who are acquainted with AIB programs and work with us periodically in educational systems and methods.

In summary, there are a number of concepts from the American Institute of Banking that would seem to hold potential for consideration in librarianship:

1) That the whole nation is structured so that some type of continuing education study group is available in every community.
2) That quality control for packaged or textual materials be produced at a national level, using the greatest expertise available.
3) That honor be bestowed on those participating in continuing education programs in some fashion.
4) That the principle of volunteer leadership be explored in depth.
5) That thorough consideration be given to the concept of an Instructor Performance Inventory coupled with the use of a student form.
6) That consideration be given to the preparation of faculty manuals for the use of all those engaged in continuing education programs.
7) That means be found by which employers would provide for continuing education opportunities through provision of time and funds.

Education

Luke (L-27) represented the Division of Instruction and Professional Development of the National Education Association (NEA) at the AALS mini-workshop on professional continuing education. He emphasized the fact that the concepts of inservice education had changed radically in the last few years. Increasingly, the emphasis is on learning functions instead of teaching processes; this is effecting inservice education.

Part of the change, according to Luke, has come as a "demonstrated lack of confidence in public education now. Just as public education was blamed for the fact that we didn't get Sputnik into the air first, so now the fact that students can graduate from high school without being able to read, write, or figure is being blamed on the educational system. As a result of this, new forces have come in which may be called accountability."

This emphasis on accountability will have far reaching effects, just in itself. Luke (L-27) explained:

> What this boils down to is that states are going to set up certain standards as to what youngsters should attain as a group, and measure the youngsters at some point to see if they meet that standard. The teacher will be held accountable for a variance in that scale. Naturally, some of these things have had a turn around effect on some of the teachers so that they are busy in state legislatures seeking means to get increased control over their own licensure and over their own inservice education. By and large, I think engineers and architects have their professional standards set for entry in the profession and exit from it by engineers and/or architects. In the teaching profession, teachers have been pretty largely excluded from the licensing boards. These boards are usually appointed by politicians so that in no state in the country are teachers in the majority on the professional standards boards. Basically, this is still in the hands of the institutions of higher education and the "public."

Another change that relates to inservice education "has been increased emphasis on competency, rather than on serving time, or meeting requirements. This trend shows in competency-based teacher education." According to Luke (L-27) this is bringing about a major change in inservice education. "Recognition of achievement is going to be based on demonstrable skills, rather than on clock hours in classes."

Finally, boards of education over the past few years have
been moving increasingly into the field of inservice education.
Previously, it was almost entirely at the institutions of
higher education. Teachers were told that a raise in salary
or new educational skills had to be acquired in other places
and institutions. Now boards of education themselves are
setting up inservice education programs. The reasons
that these boards are doing such programs are precisely
the same reasons that business likes to train its own
people. The superintendents and boards have pressures
on them from Congress, state legislature, and everywhere. In response to these pressures, the boards are
offering their own programs of inservice education.

Luke (L-27) outlined what all of these changes and conditions mean so far as
the position of NEA in the field of continuing professional development.

Differing from many other professional groups, teachers dues
will not be used for inservice professional development, rather
dues will be used to put pressure on boards of education and
colleges of education to provide some kind of inservice education that is relevant. It is the position of NEA that the teacher's
professional association does not have the responsibility for providing a good inservice education program that meets teacher
needs. So we are helping teachers to negotiate not only for
salaries and working conditions, but also for inservice education programs that are useful and effective.

In other words, the staff of NEA (as well as those of similar organizations),
is going to become increasingly involved in a consultative role in the process
of planning what inservice education programs ought to do.

Secondly, the NEA is working to develop "teacher centers." The basic idea
of a teacher center is an inservice educational development process, which
involves a wide range of learning experiences. It can be classes at a university, it can be local school classes with released time, it can be teachers
working together setting kinds of demonstration programs. This process
is to be surrounded with systematic learning experiences, including constant
evaluation. One of the key issues that NEA is concerned with is the governance
of the teacher center--that it be made up of teachers, and that they have available to them as authentic a needs assessment program as possible. Who they
hire for their director should be open to their choice.

Edelfelt, in writing on "renewal centers," insists that such centers "cannot succeed if they are not by the teacher, of the teacher and with the teacher. Teachers are tired of being done to, of having innovation imposed, of being led or pushed into in-service training... Encouragement of intrinsic motivation for professional development has too seldom been fostered for American teachers. The time is right to emphasize intrinsic motivation, and this must begin with teachers working on their own problems, indicating their own needs" (E-2:124).

Edelfelt outlines the type of guidelines that should be provided for in a renewal center:

1) The staff should include everyone from teacher aide to senior professor, and governance of the center should be the right and responsibility of those who use it.

2) Teachers should work individually, but also in groups, to study and solve problems.

3) Study and research should be an integral part of the usual school operation.

4) The community (parents and laymen) should be deeply involved.

5) Many community agencies and institutions should work with the school.

6) Adequate money and the readiness to gamble with new and different ideas should be evident. (E-2:125).

Another aspect of the present in-service effort is a needs assessment program. The NEA wants the local associations to work collaboratively with students, faculty and administration so that needs will represent a comprehensive picture of the situation. Local associations are trying to find the kinds of procedures for need identification that take into account all the kinds of influences that work on teachers. Another aspect of the consultive role of NEA will be at the needs assessment level.

The concept of the teaching center or the renewal center is related to a fairly new concept in the education profession--the differentiating of teaching roles. This concept is covered in the annotated bibliography in several publications, including The Teacher and His Staff (T-7) and Remaking the World of the Career Teacher (N-10).

Edelfelt (E-1:2) argues:

> It is time to reorganize schools and to differentiate staff roles
> so that personnel can be deployed in ways which will make
> optimum use of interests, abilities, and commitments and af-
> ford teachers greater control over their own professional inter-
> ests. And it is time to establish a variety of categories of
> teaching personnel, with career or senior teachers as the
> leadership corps of the teaching segment of the profession.

Jordan (T-7:27) predicts that the conversion to differentiating teaching roles will
produce great gains for continuing professional development.

> The business operation of the enterprise could then be managed
> by somebody who is trained in business operations. Information
> on the latest innovations in education could be piped into every
> school where a professional member of the staff would have an
> official responsibility for discussing with other appropriate staff
> members ways and means of making use of them.

> Ongoing in-service education programs for all personnel could
> become a regular part of the school's operation, probably in
> collaboration with institutions of higher learning . . .

As things now stand, most teachers are expected to assume such a heavy work-
load that it is unrealistic, if not impossible, for them to devote the time and
energy to continuing inservice education that ideally they should be engaged in.

At first consideration, it may seem that there are not as many concepts from
the education profession as from some of the other professional continuing
education programs memtioned in this paper. But considering the fact that
most of the trends memtioned in the Luke (L-27) paper also have bearing on
library education and that school media specialists are a part of the differentiated
teaching roles concept, a number of ideas presented here would also seem to
hold potential for consideration in librarianship:

1) That the differentiated professional role concept has implications for
   libraries of all types, not just school media centers, as evidenced by
   the Booz, Allen and Hamilton (B-24) study of the organization and
   staffing of the libraries of Columbia University, and therefore has
   implications for the type of continuing education programs that are
   developed.

91

2) That increased emphasis on competencies calls for a re-examination of the type of continuing education programming offered by the professional associations.

3) That serious consideration needs to be given to whether the position should be taken that professional association dues should be used to support professional development activities themselves, or whether association funds should be used by staff members of associations to play a consultative role in helping other responsible groups plan for continuing education programs.

4) That librarians become involved in the planning and implementation of the "teacher center" concept.

5) That the professional association has a responsibility for promoting the practice that costs of professional development should be borne by the hiring organization, not as a fringe benefit, but rather as an essential for a professional.

6) That professionals become skilled in ways and means of showing accountability for the stewardship of resources assigned to them.

Nursing

The nursing profession is distinguished by the number of "landmark statements" that have been issued by its various professional associations. A few of these are cited here.

In 1962 the American Hospital Association (AHA) issued the "Statement on Functions of a Hospital Department of Nursing Service." One of the functions listed was: "To provide and implement a program of continuing education for all nursing personnel (A-33:32)."

In 1968 the American Hospital Association (A-33) approved a "Statement on the Role and Responsibility of the Hospital for Inservice Education." This document stated that it was essential that each hospital have an inservice program of staff education, with one individual specifically responsible for it. Other criteria suggested were: 1) the framework within which the program is organized delineates lines of administrative control, establishes inter- and intra-departmental relationships, and provides mechanisms for planning and decision making; 2) functions of staff assigned to the program are delineated; 3) objectives of the program are defined; 4) program content is planned on the basis of an analysis of employee and hospital needs; 5) the program is oriented to group instruction and enhances, but does not replace, educational activities that are the responsibility of the supervisory staff; 6) a system of evaluation of the program is established; 7) an adequate budget is provided; 8) appropriate classroom, conference and office facilities are provided; 9) appropriate audiovisual equipment and teaching aids are provided; 10) appropriate library facilities and materials are provided, and 11) policies are established concerning attendance, scheduling and follow-up.

In 1970 the American Nurses' Association (ANA) issued (A-52) "Landmark Statement on Continuation Education." Some quotes from this document will indicate the breadth of its scope:

> In these newer types of continuation education programs, educators are departing from traditional, formal classroom techniques and are experimenting with the use of such media of mass communication as movies, two-way radio and television programs, kinescopes, and audio and video tapes. They are recognizing, too, that such programs can serve an important purpose in interpreting results of research and in bridging the gap between experts and general practitioners in the several nursing fields. The need for interdisciplinary conferences which focus on broad problems and contemporary issues of concern to related professional groups,

as well as to voluntary and governmental agencies, is also receiving attention.... (A-52:21).

It is also being recognized that adult learners -- experienced practitioners -- differ in many respects from the young student: they bring capabilities, interests, motivations, experiences, and needs which can be built upon. Continuation education programs are therefore increasingly directed to the acquisition not only of new knowledge and skills but also of new values, of greater self-awareness and sensitivity to others, and of greater understanding of group behavior (A-52:21).

Today, the majority of continuation education programs in nursing are designed to ensure deep involvement of students in their own learning and in the development of new perspectives on themselves, their practice, and the role of nursing in present-day society.... Nurses are assisted not only in increasing their knowledge of facts and principles derived from natural, social, and behavioral sciences, but also in applying this enhanced knowledge in patient care settings (A-52:22).

No nurse is deprived of opportunity for continued growth if she takes advantage of sources readily available to her: the professional literature; the institutes, conferences, and meetings sponsored by her professional organization and by allied health groups; the resources for study inherent in her own practice; and the inservice education programs within her employment situation (A-52:22)

Paralleling the information the nurse can gain through the literature is the equally important information to be derived from attending the meetings and institutes sponsored by units of her professional organization and by other health associations. Such meetings have value for the nurse over and above the specific information provided: that of stimulation and of interchange with members of her own and allied professions. Through such meetings, the nurse becomes an active participant, rather than a passive observer of the changes that are taking place within her profession (A-52:23).

None of the foregoing professional and educational activities, however, will accomplish the purpose for which they are intended until they bring about changes within the patient care setting. Continuing education is not directed to the acquisition of knowledge for the sake of knowledge alone; it is, rather, concerned with the utilization of that knowledge in nursing practice (A-52:23-24).

Thus, still another form of continuing education is the nurse's individual and systematic study of her own practice. A critical analysis of the activities which comprise her work is possible for every nurse...Keeping a work diary, identifying a nursing problem, speculating on possible approaches and solutions, collecting more information, and arriving at conclusions and decisions for future action: these are all procedures which make for a continued renewal of nursing practice, and for more challenge and satisfaction within that practice.   The important thing is that the nurse go beyond the knowledge and skills that she acquired in her basic program and that she continue to look at, to analyze, and refresh her own practice (A-52:24).

The nurse may find valuable assistance and support in this ongoing process of self-evaluation through the inservice education program offered by her employing agency or institution. This will be especially true if the program has been carefully designed to foster the continuing education of particular groups of nurses... (A-52:24).

The objective of continuing education in nursing is to add constantly to one's nursing knowledge and competence so that neither becomes obsolete. Any one of the several types of continuing education opportunities described here represents a valid and fruitful means to that end. Furthermore, the categories are not mutually exclusive. The last one, in particular -- independent learning -- cuts across all the others and is essential for any nurse concerned with the quality of nursing care she provides (A-52:25).

Also in 1970 the American Nurses' Association joined with the American Academy of Pediatrics and issued a "Landmark Statement" entitled "Guidelines on Short-Term Continuing Education Programs for Pediatric Nurse Associates (A-50)." This statement was heralded by the President of the ANA as an action representing "an historic national effort by medicine and nursing to work together to improve the delivery of health care service. "

The two associations, recognizing that innovative methods were needed to utilize professional skills more fully, created a Pediatric Nurse Associate program to enable nurses, both in practice and reentering practice, to update and expand their knowledge and skills. The document consists of guidelines and concepts for short-term continuing education courses for Pediatric Nurse Associates (PNA).

The goals of the program were broken down into 11 behavioral objectives.
Planning between the two associations was also to involve district and state
nurses' associations, nursing and medical schools. "Active participation
should be sought from consumer groups, since their orientation to the
changing roles of physicians and nurses will determine the effective utilization
of these professionals to a significant extent" (A-50:37).

Other guidelines spelled out specifics of services and facilities, faculty, course
content, admission of students and length of the program. In connection with
the evaluation of the program, it was stated that each program should conduct
ongoing evaluation of graduates to include: 1) adequacy of care rendered, 2)
acceptance of expanded role by self, pediatrician and recipients of care, and
3) productivity measures and cost effectiveness analysis (A-50:40).

In 1971 a "Landmark Statement" was issued announcing a bill, passed by the
Assembly of the California Legislature, which proposed an addition to the
Business and Professions Code relating to health occupations. This bill
represents a history-making attempt to legislate for continuing education.

The bill provides for the establishment of a Council on Continuing Education
for the Health Occupations, consisting of a director, who serves as the chairman of the Council, and four additional members appointed by the director:
one administrator of a licensed hospital, one registered nurse, one licensed
vocational nurse, and one public member.

The duties of the Council are to "establish standards for the continuing education . . . which will assure reasonable currency of knowledge as a basis for
safe practice . . ." The standards "shall be established in a manner to assure
that a variety of alternatives is available. . ." incluing, but not limited to,
academic studies, inservice education, institutes, seminars, lectures, conferences, workshops, extension studies, and home-study programs (L-4:29).

The last "Landmark Statement" was released in the January-February, 1973
issue of the Journal of Continuing Education in Nursing and is entitled "The
Continuing Education Unit." Prepared jointly by the American Nurses'
Association (A-51) and the Council on Continuing Education, it defines the
Continuing Education Unit (c e u) as: "ten contact hours of participation in an
organized continuing education experience under responsible sponsorship,
capable direction and qualified instruction." (A-51:29). This document is
discussed in the section on "Recognition, Certification, and Awards."

In 1970, Lysaught (L-29), director of the National Commission for the Study of Nursing and Nursing Education, stated that the three documents issued by the Commission "describe one of the broadest examinations ever conducted by any profession." From its intensive study the Commission identified continuing education as one of "the most salient problems" in all of the nursing profession. Because of the "chaos and lack of articulation" of these programs, the Commission stated as its primary recommendation in nursing education that:

> Each state have, or create, a master planning committee that
> will take nursing under its purview, such committee to include
> representatives of nursing, education, other health professions,
> and the public, to recommend specific guidelines, means for
> implementation, and deadlines to ensure that nursing education
> is positioned in the mainstream of American educational
> patterns . . . (L-29:6).

The state master planning committee for nursing education was asked to identif one or more institutions to be responsible for regional coverage of continuing education programs for nurses within that area. It recommended that continuing education programs be jointly planned and conducted by interdisciplinary teams.

The basic philosophy of the Commission's action program for continuing education is summarized as follows:

1. Continuing education should be an essential element on the agenda
   of the master planning committee -- on an equal plane with preparatory and advanced education.
2. There must be designated responsibility for the planning and accomplishment of the program. . . The institutions of higher learning
   and the interstate commissions for higher education must become
   more involved and must be given responsibility and support in far
   greater measure for the lifelong growth of professional learning.
3. Continuing education should be run on congruent and interdisciplinary
   bases.

The Commission further recommended that:

> Health care facilities, including hospitals, nursing homes, and other
> institutions, either individually or collectively through joint councils,
> provide professional training and staffs to supervise and conduct

inservice training and provide released time, facilities, and organizational support for the presentation of inservice nursing education as well as that for other occupations (L-29:9).

This recommendation had three important elements:

1. Through cooperative and joint approaches, better means can be built, rather than being bound by the limited funding and human resources of one institution.
2. Professional inservice faculty must be available for students.
3. Adequte time and conditions must be provided for these educational efforts or else they will be shunned by those for whom they were intended to provide opportunities.

The Commission also stated that ". . . not until statewide and regional plans are recast into specific charges of responsibility, and not until support for continuing education is viewed as an integral and equally important segment of the total educational process, will we truly be able to offer the needed opportunities for professional and individual growth that the health care needs of the nation demand" (L-29:10).

Lysaught concluded his paper by placing final responsibility for development on the individual nurse.

Only the nurse can, in the last analysis, make nursing an unambiguous profession. The National Commission, the master planning committees, the joint practice boards, the growth of support bodies, all these can place tools at nursing's disposal. But in a world in which knowledge is the surest power, nursing will ultimately choose to wield power or to cast it away. Continuing education is an integral portion of the long path upward for nursing (L-29:10).

An idea of the type of role played by professional associations relative to continuing education is gained from Spector's (S-47) review of what the American Nurses' Association has done in this area.

Spector explains that in addition to conferences, workshops and publications, which are clearly visible, a continuing effort is made behind the scenes to encourage the development of continuing education programs and to make it possible for the profession to determine the standards of its education and practice. Thus all of the organization's structural units are involved in continuing education. The array of activities carried on by the association, as reported by Spector, can be summarized as follows:

1. A Coordinator of Continuing Education was appointed in 1970 to unify and strengthen the Association's total activity concerning the continuing professional growth and development of nurses (S-47:41).

2. One of the functions listed in the ANA's by-laws in 1896 was "to provide for the continuing professional development of practitioners" (S-47:41).

3. Through the years the chief efforts for increasing and updating professional knowledge and skill have been: short-term courses, inservice programs, professional conferences, workshops, and seminars (S-47:42).

4. While the ANA's concerns are practice, teaching, administration, and research, the highest priority has been placed on increased competence through practice (S-47:42).

5. A Study Committee on the Functions of ANA in its final report in 1966 stressed the provision of continuing education for practitioners at the national, state, and district levels (S-47:42).

6. In order to provide a structural arrangement in which practitioners in all clinical areas might find their needs met, Practice Divisions were formed. in ANA, all of which had continuing education as their chief concern. These six divisions (Mental Health, Community Health, Geriatric, Maternal and Child Health, Medical-Surgical, and Psychiatric) were made responsible for including clinical and scientific sessions at conventions, institutes and other meetings, for providing forums for reporting and discussing research findings, and for otherwise disseminating information to improve practice (S-47:42).

7. Since 1962, all conferences have featured the presentation of "clinical papers." Criteria were set for the presentation of clinical sessions, as well as for the clinical papers themselves. A clinical paper was described as one "which describes a clinical problem and provides implications or suggestions for the improvement of nursing practice which can be shared with other practitioners." The wide distribution of the definition of a clinical paper and the "Guidelines for Submission

of Clinical Papers" had a far-reaching effect in stimulating nursing studies. The Guidelines were also adopted by other groups outside the ANA, such as state and regional nurses' associations. Clinical papers have been published in nursing publications and used by groups such as graduate university programs. In 1970 a total of 225 clinical papers were submitted. The number of clinical sessions held at conventions also increased. Also in 1970, clinical programs were conducted in the morning and afternoon on three days and included ten clinical sessions and seven debate programs (S-47:42-43).

8. Clinical debates were initiated at the 1968 ANA convention as a means of stimulating examination of different or opposing views on issues in nursing practice. The debates have been made available on audiotapes and been widely used by individuals and district nurses' associations as a basis for local programs (S-47:43).

9. Other programs at conventions have included Nursing Problem Clinics and a transoceanic telephone conference between the United Kingdom and the United States (S-47:43).

10. Regional Clinical Conferences conducted by ANA have followed essentially the same format as conventional clinical sessions. Held for three days each in two cities, with the program the same in each city, the clinical conferences' average attendance has been 950 (S-47:43).

11. In addition to convention programs, there have been major conferences on special topics, cosponsored with groups such as the American Heart Association. These specialized conventions have drawn nurses from as many as 40 states and had attendance over 500 (S-47:43).

12. Evaluation of clinical programs has been ongoing; plans for each year are made only after careful evaluation of past performance. Concern that practitioners were not being reached led to a survey of attendees which showed that the majority attending conferences were teachers and administrators. This knowledge led to ways of facilitating attendance by practitioners. This included registration on a daily basis and publicity emphasizing the relevance of sessions for practitioners (S-47:43).

100

13. Another innovation, starting in 1969, was the preparation of "Guidelines for Speakers," prepared by the ANA Public Relations staff to assist clinical speakers in making the presentation of their papers more interesting (S-47:44).

14. ANA has encouraged inservice education as an avenue of furthering continuing education. The position of ANA on inservice education is indicated in the following:

> Inherent in all of ANA's statements concerning inservice education is the basic premise that health agencies should conduct ongoing programs to assure that the agency staff is competent to meet the needs of the clients served by the agency. Another premise is that the purpose of the health agency's educational programs is to provide for orientation of new employees and the acquisition of new knowledge and skills required for the clients of that agency. Basic educational preparation of all health workers, including nursing assistants, is held to be the responsibility of educational rather than service institutions (S-47:44).

15. ANA has played a significant role in promotion of legislation for public health funds for nursing education, both for graduate education and for continuing education of graduate nurses (S-47:44).

16. ANA maintains working relationships with a large number of national health organizations and joins with them in providing continuing education programs and in developing guidelines for programs. ANA is actively concerned with programs developed by other groups for education of health workers, and, if indicated, issues a position statement in relation to such programs and encourages individual practitioners to participate in such programs (S-47:44).

17. "The major consideration in continuing education at ANA is to perform those leadership functions that can best be done by the national organization in a way that complements and does not duplicate state and district nurses' associations' functions" (S-47:44).

18. A chief concern of continuing education for nurses at present is to assist nurses in preparing for an expanding role. "It is the responsibility of the national organization to set forth guidelines and policies regarding the transfer of medical functions to nursing and the preparation necessary for nurses to assume these tasks and incorporate them into the body of nursing practice" (S-47:45).

19. ANA is working on developing standards for continuing education and ways of assuring that the number of continuing education opportunities for nurses increases (S-47:45).

20. ANA keeps constant contact with its 54 state and territorial nurses' associations and the 870 district associations, thus providing "a vital communication network through which the association can plan, coordinate, and implement its continuing programs" (S-47:45).

Another activity of the professional association in nursing should be noted. In 1970, the American Nurses' Association initiated the publication of the Journal of Continuing Education in Nursing (J-9), which serves as one central place where all continuing education ideas, reports, and activities are collected for the whole profession. Its stated objectives are:

1. To bring together a body of literature pertinent to continuing education in nursing.
2. To scan the horizon for developing trends, in education and in health care, which will have impact on continuing education in nursing.
3. To report program designs and educational approaches which have proved effective in meeting some of the learning needs of the nurse practitioner and those significant others under nursing supervision who assist in providing care to patients.
4. To present experimental and innovative approaches which offer new and more promising routes to the adult nurse learner.
5. To explore problem areas of major concern to those in continuing education.
6. To offer an additional outlet for those who are motivated to write and add to the developing theory, methodology, and body of information relating to continuing education in nursing.

Editorials are on major topics such as the importance of uniform structuring for all types of continuing education. Editor Hutchison (H-45:6), in the second issue of the Journal, invited readers to take a long, hard look at structure--the structure of all the relevant groups responsible for continuing education in nursing. "Those in the field have a responsibility to thoroughly examine the accrued experience and contribute their knowledge so that structure does in fact enable, facilitate, support and encourage the vital function of continuing education in nursing" (H-45:7).

The January-February, 1973 issue of the Journal contains a report by Pluckhan, Peltier and Spicher (P-22) describing how one state--Kansas-- has been working on the structuring problem. In this case, it is being solved through a Coordinating Committee on Continuing Education which is using an interdisciplinary and interagency approach. To date, the chief document produced by the group has been "Guidelines for Continuing Education Programs for Nurses in Kansas." These guidelines are comprehensive in coverage and as they could serve as a model for others, they are listed below:

1. Program content should be readily identifiable as being concerned with the improvement of nursing care.
2. Programs should be planned based on the expressed needs of potential participants, needs identified for the staff by employers and supervisors, needs of the professional nurse which he may not be aware of but may reduce his ability to provide effective health care services.
3. Statewide needs of practicing nurses in all types of health care agencies and all nursing specialties should be considered in program planning.
4. Consumers, as active members of the health team, should be considered in program planning to help them gain knowledge of health practices and understanding and acceptance of the changing role of the professional nurse.
5. Resource personnel should be qualified to present the material assigned.
6. Program objectives should be developed for each conference, continuing education course or workshop and corresponding tools be utilized to evaluate the program. (One- to two-week post-conference evaluation by the conferee and employer is also suggested.)
7. Principles and theories used in program development should be geared to the adult learner.
8. When a team approach to health care is presented, efforts should be made to have members of corresponding health disciplines represented in the audience as well as on the program.

9. Consideration should be given to previously scheduled programs to prevent unnecessary duplication of content in the same geographical area and overlapping of dates.

10. Program planners should be encouraged to consider their offering in relation to [association recognition systems]. Advertisement of the program should include the number of C. E. U. s [continuing education units] accepted. Contact hours for the programs should be stipulated on the program and/or on a certificate of attendance (P-22:24-26).

Another publication that is intended to be a continuing education aid for nurses is Nursing Update, inaugurated in 1970. It provides the nurse-reader with practical and up-to-date clinical and nursing information. Designed for quick reading and ready reference, special features include: "express stops" (marginal summaries of articles), resource files (lists of supplementary reading), pre-punching for easy 3-hole notebook filing.

In summary, there are a number of concepts from professional associations in nursing, but especially the American Nurses' Association, that would seem to hold potential for consideration in librarianship:

1. That there be one central publication in the profession in which everything regarding continuing education would be published, including official statements by associations on continuing education opportunities and papers about developments relative to continuing education in the professional's field of activity.

2. That "landmark" and position papers as adopted by associations within the profession be printed, not just in summary form, but in full and given visibility for the benefit of the whole profession.

3. That consideration be given to the construction and publication of recognition and reward systems.

4. That guidelines and standards for continuing education programs be specified.

5. That new programs have objectives stated in behavioral terms.

6. That associations join together in studying and providing continuing education opportunities.

7. That the National Commission on Library and Information Science be urged to set continuing education as a top priority for its consideration.

8. That consideration be given to systematic structuring for continuing education, such as a master planning committee for continuing education for each state.

104

9. That papers be published pointing out that the role the individual practitioner plays in continuing education is the most important one, regardless of the position of the profession as a whole.
10. That professional associations state in their by-laws and/or other official publications that continuing education is one of the, if not the chief concern of the association.
11. That an interdisciplinary emphasis be made throughout the development of continuing education programs.
12. That an inter-professional cooperation characterize the planning and implementation of continuing education programs.

Public Accountants

In many respects the American Institute of Certified Public Accountants (A-35) serves the same functions for its members as the American Institue of Bankers provides for its members.

The Professional Development Division of the American Institue of Certified Public Accountants plans continuing education programs one year in advance and prints these in a booklet for all members. Basically, it plans six types of programs using a wide assortment of educational methods in various combinations: seminars, courses, workshops, lecture programs, training programs (including a basic and advanced staff training program) and individual study materials (not designed to serve as a substitute for active participation in professional development programs). The 1971 booklet listed 63 programs, which represented nearly a 50% change in material from that offered in 1970.

The Institute assumes the principal responsibility for the development of materials and overall administration of the programs; it is the state societies who assume the responsibility of offering the programs throughout the nation.

Believing that on-the-job training cannot solve the staff training problem alone, the Institute has developed a four-level Staff Training Program. The first two levels offer comprehensive practical training in the broad areas of general practice, with emphasis on those kinds of work which the staff man is expected to perform during his first two years in practice. Beginning with the third level, the Staff Training Program branches out into the three principal areas of specialization in accounting--accounting and auditing, taxation, and management advisory services. Each of these three specialized areas is covered in two successive levels of increasing complexity.

Evaluation services are provided for in all of the staff training programs. Participants are evaluated by their discussion leaders. These evaluations are sent to the participants' firms. Objective evaluation of Levels I and II concludes with a comprehensive examination. The raw score on the final examination, along with the discussion leader's evaluation, is sent to the participants' firms. In addition, during the late fall the sponsoring firms receive a rating, reported in percentiles, which gives each person's score in relation to those of all participants who attended the program during the year.

106

Chemistry

In 1972 the editor of the Chemical and Engineering News, published by the American Chemical Society (ACS), took a stand for compulsory continuing education (M-8:1).

> We must formalize continuing education programs, making their availability compulsory with employee participation voluntary. Adult education programs, continuing education such as that sponsored by ACS, company-sponsored training are all fine as far as they go, but they don't go far enough. Under a compulsory system, organizations would be required to set up   definite and formal programs whereby employees could devote a given portion of their time acquiring new knowledge. Cost could be handled much the same as depreciation allowances for capital equipment. After all, we've worked out a system that compensates for equipment obsolescence, we've established another to compensate raw material suppliers for depletion -- how about our most precious raw material, human talent?
>
> As it is, our base education trains people for 12 or 16 or more years, then turns them out and says: OK, you're on your own.   Then we line up a whole system against them. It's a gross mismatch. Our educational system is too geared to a lifetime cycle. But more and more people are obsolescing well within their lifetimes. They need after-service.

In the same issue, President-Elect of ACS Nixon (N-21:23) announced an aggressive program for more professionalism which he proposed should be funded by a $10 assessment against all members during the year. The proposed assessment could raise about $1 million in one year. By professionalism, Nixon explained that he meant more direct involvement by ACS in the employer-employee relationship. The basic objective of ACS in Nixon's view should be to act more directly in the support of its members -- "establishing and maintaining a high-level dynamic, economic, and professional environment in which they can work productively in not only their own but also their employers' and the public's interest" (N-21:23).

In the same issue of Chemical and Engineering News (p. 22) there is a full column advertisement for tape cassettes from ACS meetings with the note that they are for half-day sessions and include materials. If the individual prefers open reels to cassettes this is also possible according to the ad. In 1965 the American Chemical Society made news when it put together short courses that were repeated in various parts of the country (A-5;A-6).

Psychology

The American Psychological Association made a major contribution in the areas of research related to continuing education in its Project on Scientific Information Exchange in Psychology (A-53). The project's chief objective was to describe the scientific information exchange environment of the scientific psychologist. Most of the studies centered on channels of communication in psychology, including journals, conventions, the distribution and use of reports prior to publication, and informal face-to-face communications.

The plans and objectives of the project are described in the introduction as follows (A-53:I, 1):

> Four general processes can be identified in any successful
> system of scientific information exchange: the origination
> of information, its transmission, its storage, and its use.
> There appear to be three roles in the system: the source,
> the user, and information conveyance devices that have
> both transmission and storage functions. In an effort
> to develop a description of the scientific information-exchange
> environment in psychology, the initial problem attacked
> was the identification of the persons and institutions
> associated with these three roles and the determination
> of the scope of their responsibilities in fulfilling them.
> The second step was that of developing a description of
> the time characteristics of each process and of the "filter-
> ing" that determines the amount and type of information
> which will be available to the user.... The third step was
> that of examining the storage properties, when present, of
> various information conveyances.... Finally the user was
> studied -- his access to the information he needs . . . and
> the way in which he uses it.

Seventeen different studies are presented in the two volume report. The population used in the studies was the American Psychological Association's (APA) 21,000 members. Out of this number it was found that only about 2,000 psychologists were extremely active in scientific communication within psychology, and on the whole they were members of APA (A-53: I, 6).

They furnish most of the research material that requires or
warrants information exchange activities in psychology, and
their efforts keep psychology going as a basic science (i.e., they
regularly publish journal articles and make formal presentations
at annual meetings; they are the producers of books on
psychological subjects; they are the holders of the major federal
research grants and often serve as monitors or advisors on other
federal grants or programs; and, also, the body governing professional psychology are generally contained within this group).

It was found relative to journal publication that content published this month
would have been started 30 or 36 months previously. From start on publication until some 18 months later the work reaches a stage at which a
rather complete report can be made. The first reports are informal and
usually take place within the producer's own institution. Next a
formal oral report may be made at a small, special interest group. The
next step is the author's writing up the final form of the report. During
this time the author may make a report for reasonably large audiences at
a national or regional meeting. The information found on the dissemination
of material presented at national conventions is interesting (A-53 I,8):

About one in five articles is reported to national meetings....
The contents of a single paper are rarely reported both to
national and regional meetings. When such reports occur, they
are usually separated by a year and follow some modification
in contents. In the case of work reported to the APA annual
convention, the first public announcement is made in the form
of a listing of the title and abstract in the published program distributed to all APA members prior to the convention. Although
the convention presentation could be heard by up to 3,000
attendants at regional, and up to 10,000 attendants at national
meetings, the number attending a particular paper session rarely
exceeds 100.

About a year prior to journal publication the distribution of preprints starts.
This is the first wide distribution of the report. It was found that approximately 40% of the authors distribute preprints. The purpose is to provide
immediate dissemination of the information and avoid the communication
lag. On the average, copy is submitted to a journal 9 months before its
actual publication. If a manuscript is rejected, publication is probably
pushed back at least a year. After going through all this process it was
determined, in the project, that the audience for most articles in journals
is exceedingly small. It was estimated that most articles would be read
by about 200 readers. After journal publication a large percentage of the

authors distribute reprints. Finally about 15 months after publication an article may appear in Psychological Abstracts or the Annual Review of Psychology (A-53:I, 8-9).

One of the patterns to be seen by studying dissemination of research papers was the small portion which go through public channels, as opposed to those with restricted audiences. And the public access comes late, when the material is relatively old. Hans Peter Luhn, a leader in the field of information retrieval, is quoted, after studying this data, as saying that "the contemporary information-retrieval approach was like sending stale bread to China via air express" (A-53:I, 9).

Other studies in the project dealt with the user. It was found that programmed events such as papers, symposia, and speeches are the most important sources of scientific information at meetings.

Information exchange of ideas through discussion seemed to be one of the most effective ways of disseminating ideas during conferences, especially if there is a concentration of active researchers at the meetings. The project, based on this and other findings, concluded:

> Considering, now, both the processes of dissemination and the
> behavior of the active user, it seems clear that while information
> retrieval services mainly wait for "public" information (i.e., from
> or in archival sources), the scientist who wants contemporary
> findings to plan research or to interpret his own findings does not.
> During the various stages leading to journal publication of work, he
> is involved in trying to discover every means of obtaining informa-
> tion on new, on-going, or recently completed work relevant to his
> own. He does not seem willing to wait to discover this in a journal
> or a secondary source; rather he seems to use journals to catch
> what he has missed in his efforts to gather information during the
> past couple of years. If he actually finds a particularly interesting
> source in a journal, he often attempts to contact the author to learn
> what he is presently doing and to establish a colleague relationship
> so that, henceforth, he may receive information prior to journal
> publication (A-53:I, 10).

From the description of the 17 separate studies in the total project, many techniques and methods are used which would be useful in other professions interested in studying the communication patterns within their professions. Questionnaires and interview schedules are included.

Library Science

The record of what various professional associations are doing in the area of continuing education has been presented. What has been the record of library associations relative to continuing education ? If a librarian were invited to speak at a mini-workshop such as the AALS held in January, 1973, what could he have reported on the topics that were assigned to the five professional educators that spoke at that time ? These were:

    a)   Function, objectives, and scope of their programs
    b)   Guides and criteria established for program development
    c)   Clientele served (professional and/or others)
    d)   Organizational structure (regional, state, etc.)
    e)   Sources of funding
    f)   Program formats (workshops, correspondence, cassettes, etc.)
    g)   Methods of distribution
    h)   Personnel (faculty)
    i)   Guides and criteria developed for evaluation methods
    j)   Rewards or recognition given to individuals for participating in continuing education programs
    k)   Programs and prospects for the future.

In an attempt to get answers to some of these questions the Continuing Library Education Committee of the Association of American Library Schools (AALS) mailed, in August, 1972, questionnaires to twenty-six library associations. (See Appendix B for the questionnaire used). This total included the thirteen divisions of the American Library Association.

By December, in spite of follow-up letters, only six associations had sent back the completed questionnaire. A summary of the data requested is presented in Appendix C. In reviewing the data it should be realized that the response of six out of 26 represents only a 23% return by the library associations. Therefore, the report is only a sampling of what is being done, and not a comprehensive survey of all twenty-six library associations to which the questionnaire was sent. It does raise the question, however, of whether those who did not respond were not doing a great deal and therefore did not wish to return the report.

The six associations which responded were: the American Association of Law Libraries; Reference and Adult Services Division of ALA, Resources and Technical Services Division of ALA, the Association of Jewish Libraries, the Medical Library Association, and the Special Libraries Association.

From the results received it is apparent that the most frequent type of activity has been the workshop, the seminar, and the pre- or post-conference institute. There was little activity reported showing library associations cooperating with other library associations or other professional groups, employing libraries, or with library schools.

There was also no report from the six associations of the development of packaged printed programs, and only one group reported the development of cassettes for distribution. In the publication field, the activities were carried on by all the groups -- bibliographies, articles in official journals. There was a lack, however, of books published specifically for continuing education programs, or of programmed texts. There was no mention of circulation of pre-prints but this question was not specifically asked. There was no reported use of talk-back TV or of the development of tutorial centers; only one association reported any programming in Cable TV. One group reported the use of clinics.

The only association which reported any research projects was the Medical Library Association, which reported two projects, one on the continuing education needs of medical librarians and the other, closely related, on the continuing education needs for medical librarianship.

No group reported that it had held an annual conference with its chief focus on continuing education.

In answer to the question, "What are the continuing education objectives and concerns of your association ?" the following responses were given:

1. a. To upgrade the library service our members can offer in their libraries, by developing new skills and upgrading existing skills.
   b. To design and implement a total plan for continuing education for all levels of health science library personnel.

2. To "stimulate the continuing professional growth of library personnel presently and potentially engaged in public service."

3. Provide continuing education opportunities through programs and publications to librarians working in the field of acquisitions, cataloging, and the development and coordination of the country's library resources.

4. To offer professional training and guidance to librarians, professional and otherwise, in small, often isolated, libraries.

5. The association's major concern is to continue to hold seminars at the annual conferences. Seminars should be of interest to all groups of special librarians interested in updating and alerting new and old libraries to new techniques in the profession.

6. Continuing education of presently employed law librarians who are employed both at advanced and intermediate levels of professional responsibility.

Three of the associations responded that continuing education was a "high priority" in relation to other objectives of the association. A fourth stated that it was "important." Another responded that the objectives of the association were not ranked, and another that it was a matter of budget.

The six reporting associations indicated that the Education Committee and/or the Board of Directors, on the basis of input from committees or individuals, decide on the continuing education programs that will be developed and implemented.

In answer to the question on how needs are determined, two of the associations said that questionnaires and surveys were used. One stated that need was determined through analysis of journal articles, letters to the editor of the association's publication, and information from conversations. The others seemed to rely on decisions by the Board of Directors and/or the Committee on Continuing Education.

The associations provide continuing education programming for all members who are accepted into the association. Generally membership seemed to be open to all practitioners who wished to join.

In answer to a question concerning structuring, it appears that the major thrust is accomplished by the continuing education programs presented as pre- or post-sessions to the annual meeting of the association. Content varies according to needs of the various divisions of the association. It also appears that programs are presented at state and regional levels as well as nationally, but not on a systematically worked out basis. Such programs seem to be left to the initiative of the local group with a variety of local patterns emerging. For example, one association might combine with others in an area for an all-day workshop, or various interest groups might join in an area to present a program.

113

Two stable structuring patterns were reported. The Medical Library Association reported that twenty courses are available. These may be sponsored by any regional medical library, regional medical program, regional medical group, or any other interested group on a local, state, or regional basis. The American Association of Law Librarians reported four rotating Continuing Education Institutes offering four special subject area curricula, held at pre-conventions since 1964. These are planned to meet the needs of presently employed law librarians who are employed both at advanced and intermediate levels of professional responsibility.

Two associations reported that continuing education programs were funded totally by registration fees. Three others reported funding by a varying combination of registration fees, dues, and grants.

The chief method of distribution of materials developed seems to be through packages of materials prepared to be given out at the time of pre- or post-conference sessions, through the publications of the associations, or through proceedings of institutes which are published afterwards.

In answer to the question as to how leaders are identified or chosen to develop programs, the most frequent pattern seemed to be by the Continuing Education Committee and/or by the Board of Directors.

The two chief means of evaluation reported were reaction evaluation sheets from the members attending the programs, and review and evaluation by the planning committee or executive committee responsible for implementation of the programs. Only one of the associations reported that specific evaluative criteria had been established by the association.

In the area of recognition, two associations stated that certificates were given for participation in programs. Another stated that a certificate of attendance was going to be offered from now on.

Three of the associations reported that one specific person or group had responsibility in the area of continuing education. In each case this was the Chairman of a committee with responsibility for continuing education. This individual generally seemed to have the same responsibilities in all three associations, namely: directing and coordinating continuing education activities; surveying and evaluating programs developed; advising and providing guidelines and standards for programs throughout the association. Only one of the associations reported a full time director with a subsidiary staff, the Medical Library Association. The other positions were held by volunteers. The associations reported that background, training, and experience were qualifications for the position, but none reported any specific training or orientation being given to those responsible for continuing education activities.

In regard to clearinghouse functions, the chief one (reported by three associations) was for bibliographies. One association stated that it was a clearinghouse for cassettes.

The following response was received regarding support through continuing education in the area of management and administration:

Training in administrative and management concepts for middle
managers -- 2 associations reported in the affirmative
Training in administrative concepts and practices for top
administrators -- 1 association reported in the affirmative
Training for first line supervisors for the role as a developer
of human resources assigned to individual -- 1 association
answered in the affirmative
Training key personnel to optimally utilize nonprofessionals --
1 association answered in the affirmative

The following response was received regarding support for continuing education program development:

Training for continuing education program development --
2 associations answered in the affirmative
Provision of consultation in continuing education program development
for groups in association wishing to plan continuing education
programs -- 2 associations answered in the affirmative

Three associations reported that they provided training which had as its chief objective updating the practitioner in his or her subject specialty.

Two associations stated that they established experimental programs intended to discover new methods and solutions to persistent problems in the field. Four indicated that their associations search for new and effective educational techniques and modes in order to maximize the content presented in continuing education programs.

This concludes the summary of information that was obtained through a questionnaire sent to 26 library associations during the fall of 1972 and which was answered by six associations only.

A position statement on continuing education was made by the Activities Committee on New Directions for ALA (A-38). This document stated forcefully the Subcommittee on Manpower's position that "commitment to the continuing education of the profession must be made by the individual librarian, by the managers of libraries, and by the professional association--especially the ALA" (A-38:42). Credit was given to the Association for "its extensive conference programming, publishing activity, and task-oriented committees"-- all of which "combine to make the Association by far the most active agency for library personnel development in the world, " but it pointed out that ALA could do much more than in the past to support continuing education (A-38:42). "Accusations of Association non-interest are justified only in the sense that it has not in the past seen fit to bring together all of its activities concerned with continuing education under a single administrative oversight, so as to give them uniform organization, coordination, and direction" (A-38:42). The Subcommittee stated that such a move seemed now to be called for and cited the following ways in which the ALA could do more than it had done for the continuing education and professional growth of its members:

1) sponsor a wide range of seminars and workshops, perhaps mounted regionally but outside of the annual conference, on issues of current or topical concern to librarians; the recent MARC II workshops and occasional joint programs with the regional associations might serve as prototypes;

2) prepare packaged multi-media programs for professional updating that can be lent or rented to local libraries and to library agencies for use by their personnel;

3) design and produce programmed instructional courses for sale to librarians who wish to improve the currency of their expertise or gain new professional skills or understanding; both these recommendations would seem to be natural extensions of ALA's existing publishing program;

4) gain much wider promulgation than there has been in the past of the work done by ALA's clearinghous e for opportunities outside of ALA for the continuing education and professional growth of librarians;

5) lend consultative and advisory, perhaps even support, services to local libraries and library agencies wishing to develop continuing education programs of their own;

6)   coordinate, articulate, and rationalize all ALA activities
concerned with the professional upgrading of librarians.

Although covered by what has already been said above, one
particular aspect of post-professional training is so needful of
attention that in the eyes of the Committee it deserves special
mention in this report. That is the need for management training for librarians who find themselves assigned to positions of
administrative responsibility. It is patently false to assume
that a good librarian will necessarily be a good manager, yet
hierarchical promotion in many libraries appears to rely
heavily upon this criterion. It appears essential that special
effort be expended by the ALA to help facilitate the transition
of good librarians into good managers when their duties and
responsibilities call for it (A-38:43).

Certainly particular notice should be given to the workshops sponsored by
the Information Science and Automation Division (ISAD) of ALA, mentioned
under item one in the preceding list. Starting with the one-day meetings
on automation and systems analysis at the 1969 annual conference of ALA
in Atlantic City, the Division has maintained a steady record, particularly
with its MARC II workshops, in taking continuing education opportunities to
librarians in many sections of the United States. The 1969 format used by
ISAD at Atlantic City served as the model on which the Staff Development
Committee built its programming, which is described in the next section.

The statement of the Activities Committee on New Directions for ALA regarding the critical need for management training for librarians is borne
out by many listings in the bibliography (for example, Booz, Allen, and
Hamilton, B-24 ; Ginzberg and Brown, G-25 ; Harlow, H-5 ; Kortendick and
Stone, K-31; Stone, S-72). A significant contribution toward improving this
situation is being made through the recent establishment of the Management
Studies Office of the Association of Research Libraries. Although designed
to serve the members of that Association, its publications can have an
important influence on continuing library education efforts in the area of
administration and management for all librarians. In addition to its publication program (see items A-81 - A-86, B-24, and W-13 in the bibliography),
the office conducts an ongoing research and development program which prepares special studies related to basic issues and problems of university
library management, such as a paper on Library Policies (W-13), and the
Library Management Review and Analysis Program (A-81). For member
libraries the Office will also conduct library management conference programs and provide library management consultation.

117

The efforts of two other groups will be reported briefly. One is the Staff Development Committee of the Personnel Section of the Library Administration Division (LAD) of ALA. The LAD did not return the questionnaire, but the activity of the Staff Development Committee is available through the files of that Committee. The other is the Association of American Library Schools' Committee on Continuing Education, which sent out the questionnaire.

At the January, 1970 meeting of the Staff Development Committee of the Personnel Section of LAD, two major avenues of approach in the area of continuing education were decided upon by the Committee members. One was the use of an all-day mini-workshop concept on the opening day of the ALA annual conference, and the other was the publication of a Library Trends issue on Personnel Development and Continuing Education.

The first concept was built on three assumptions:

1) That the American Library Association has a role in personnel development and, as our leading professional body, it should emphatically foster continuing education of its membership.

2) That continuing personnel development is an important commitment librarianship must face today;

3) That in librarianship we are a long way from realizing the potential represented by the human resources now employed in libraries (S-74:1).

The first micro-workshop was held the first day of the 1970 ALA Conference in Detroit. Papers relating to staff development and continuing education were presented under the umbrella title: "New Directions in Staff Development: Moving from Ideas to Action"(S-74). A copy of the program is presented in Appendix D.

During the workshop, 200 plus participants filled out evaluation sheets which provided important feedback for planning future workshops. (See Appendix E). Analysis of the questionnaires submitted by the participants showed that there was a distinct preference for having a day's Micro-Workshop concentrate in one area of staff development in greater depth, rather than cover several areas in survey fashion. In rank order, the four specific areas that were rated highest by the conferees for future continuing education workshops were: 1) employee motivation; 2) participatory management; 3) training techniques and educational methods for staff development programs; and 4) management by objectives as an approach to staff development.

Based on this data, the second Staff Development Workshop was held at the 1971 ALA Conference in Dallas on "Motivation," and a third workshop was held in 1972 at the annual ALA Conference in Chicago on "Educational Technology as an Aid to Staff Development." The reason that the second choice -- "Participatory Management" - - was not scheduled for 1971 or 1972 was that there was a strong emphasis on this subject during the 1970 Workshop.

It should be noted that the first workshop in Detroit was entirely conceived, planned and implemented through the initiative of the Staff Development Committee with minimal support from LAD. The ALA Conference Office cooperated by assigning a place on the printed schedule for the Workshop and by providing free-flowing coffee during the day, and needed audio-visual equipment. The Committee members themselves, through their own resources, produced the packaged handouts distributed at the Workshop (programs, motivation bibliography, write-ups on the volunteer program leaders, evaluation sheets, film information, etc.); sent the mailings to registrants with pre-conference bibliographies prepared by leaders; sent a pre-workshop paper by Marchant to set the stage for the emphasis on participatory management. In other words the Committee had the objective of demonstrating that such a program featuring staff development and continuing education was a felt need of the ALA membership and that it would be supported by attendees. The Detroit Workshop was a notable success and since that time, the Library Administration Division has budgeted funds for the support of the Staff Development opening day mini-workshops.

The participants at the first mini-workshop, by means of an evaluation sheet (See Appendix E.)   ranked other possible activities in which the Staff Development Committee might engage as follows:

1) To bring to practicing librarians the best articles related to staff development in related disciplines (abstracts);

   --This suggestion was implemented by the Committee's publishing for limited distribution "Clips and Quotes on Staff Development for Librarians."

2) To prepare guidelines to help the individual library manager improve and expand his grasp of staff development and continuing education;

   --This suggestion was implemented by the Committee's publishing "Guidelines to the Development of Human Resources in Libraries," and "Developing a Model for Continuing Education and Personnel Development in Libraries,"

119

in the July, 1971, issue of <u>Library Trends</u> (S-79).

3) To provide guidance, counsel, or programming in the area of staff development for state and regional library programs.

--The Committee submitted a proposal to secure funding to do this on a nationwide request basis, but it was not funded.

The second main activity of the Staff DevelopmentCommittee was the publication of the July, 1971, <u>Library Trends</u> issue entitled "Personnel Development and Continuing Education in Libraries"(S-79). The Committee prepared two of the contributions for the issue -- the guidelines and the model noted above -- and selected the qualified leaders who contributed the other articles to the issue. The subjects covered in the issue (S-79: 1-2),as decided by the Staff Development Committee, are "Personnel Planning for a Library Manpower System," "Employee Motivation," "Participative Management as Related to Personnel Development." "Personnel Evaluation as an Impetus to Growth," "The Training Subsystem," "Social Interaction Skills," "Developing a Model for Continuing Education and Personnel Development in Libraries," "Guidelines to the Development of Human Resources in Libraries: Rationale, Policies, Programs and Recommendations," "The Educational Third Dimension: I Continuing Education to Meet the Personalized Criteria of Librarians," "The Educational Third Dimension: II Programs for Continuing Library Education," "The Educational Third Dimension: III Toward the Development of a National Program of Continuing Education for Library Personnel."

The recent efforts of the Association of American Library Schools in the area of continuing library education are dealt with in the section below.

In the fall of 1968, President-Elect Kortendick of AALS wrote a proposal, later funded by the Council on Library Resources, to hold a conference in Bethesda, Maryland, for the purpose of identifying needed research in library and information science. Other conveners of the conference, in addition to Father Kortendick who served as chairman, were Kurt Cylke, the acting Chief of the Library and Information Sciences Research Branch of the U.S.O.E., and Foster Mohrhardt of the Council on Library Resources. As a result of the conference, Harold Borko (B-47) was engaged as principal investigator to carry out the objectives set by the conferees. The objectives were:

1) To describe and summarize the content of existing programs being offered in librarianship and information science.
2) To identify problems and needs in library and information science

120

education, and to indicate the data and the research that would
be required to resolve these problems.

3) To coordinate the various research suggestions and to list them
in order of priority.

One of the areas covered in the Borko report was "Research Needs in the
Field of Continuing Education for Librarians, " by Kortendick (K-30:197-233).
The specific research proposals suggested in the area of continuing library
education were:

1) Feasibility Study of a National Program of Continuing Education
for Librarians (K-30:205).

2) A National Survey of Continuing Education Needs of Librarians:
A Study of Educational Needs, Job Dimensions, and Professional
and Personal Characteristics (K-30:206).

3) Motivational Factors Related to Participation in Continuing
Education Activities (K-30:207).

4) Development of a Model for Continuing Education and Staff
Development in Libraries (K-30: 208).

5) Development of a Comprehensive Model for Managing and Evaluating Short-Term Institutes and Workshops for the Continuing
Education of Librarians (K-30:209).

6) Communication and Research Information Exchange in Library
Science (K-30:210).

7) The Development of Model Packaged Programs of Study in
Selected Defined Areas Pertinent to the Needs of In-Service
Librarians for Updating and Expanding their Knowledge of
Advances in the Field (K-30:212).

8) Evaluation of the Potential Capabilities of Various Media for
Use in the Continuing Education of Librarians: A Feasibili ty
Study (K-30:213).

9) Toward Closer Reciprocal Relationships between Library Science
Professors and Practicing Library Administrators: An
Exploratory Study (K-30:214).

10) Postgraduate Internships and Trainee Programs in Librarianship:
An Evaluation of Existing Programs and a Proposal for Develop-
ment of the Internship Concept in Continuing Education for
Librarians (K-30:215)

11) A Study of Attitudes and Responses to Participation of Mid-Career
Librarians in Community Affairs as Stimulators and Effectors in
Continuing Professional Growth (K-30:216).

In 1970, President Monroe appointed an ad hoc committee to write a position paper on the "Role of AALS in Continuing Library Education" (A-77). Appendices F and G). The following year, at the 1971 Annual Meeting of AALS, the position paper was presented to the membership and was used as a point of departure for the program meetings which concentrated on continuing education. During this conference, the Executive Board of AALS voted to establish a Standing Committee on Continuing Library Education. This committee, as appointed by President Slavens, consisted of the members who had served on the ad hoc committee plus others who had indicated a particular interest in this area of activity of the Association.

The activities of this Standing Committee on Continuing Library Education are outlined in a report published in the Fall 1972 issue of the Journal of Education for Librarianship (A-78). (See also Appendix H, 1972 Report).

One of the charges of the Committee was to build a library continuing education network made up of representatives from the library schools and library associations. The list of these liaison representatives from the schools and associations, as it existed in October, 1972, is printed in this issue of the Journal. At present the network is being enlarged to include representatives from library schools not yet accredited by ALA and representatives of state library systems and state and regional library associations.

A second activity engaged in by the Committee was the planning and presenting of a mini-workshop on continuing education as practiced at a national level by a representative group of professional associations. This workshop, referred to at numerous places in this paper, was held during the 1973 Annual Meeting of the Association.

A third activity of the Committee was to write, and to urge 26 other library associations to write, to the members of the National Commission on Libraries and Information Science, urging them to select continuing library education as one of their top priorities for attention and action. The AALS Committee, therefore, was encouraged when the Commission granted on June 29, 1973, a 9 month contract for a Continuing Education Study for the purpose of receiving recommendations, based on research, for a nationwide program of continuing education for personnel in the library and information science fields. In January, 1972, the AALS Board allotted $2000 to the Committee on Continuing Library Education to carry forward its work for 1973. In the Spring of 1973, the Committee drew up a tentative position paper on Continuing Library Education for the purose of submission to other relevant groups to see if agreement could be reached on such a statement so that a landmark statement might be arrived at which would be endorsed by all relevant associations and could then be published. (See Appendix J). This paper was, in turn, submitted to the Educatiom l Task Force of the Council of National Library Associations in June 1973 for reaction from member associations by January, 1974.

This concludes the section in this chapter on activities by associations relative to action in the area of continuing library education. It would also seem appropriate to give a sampling of reactions of practicing librarians concerning their recommendations to professional associations in the area of continuing education. A few of these are presented next.

Stone (S-72:176-178) found that practicing librarians believed that library associations needed, first and foremost, to upgrade the content of their activities. To sense the conviction with which content was emphasized, four replies are quoted:

> Concentrate on solid content -- not inspirational speeches.
>
> Am getting weary of so-called professional associations which have degenerated into social groups or duplication of the type of activity I can get better in other similar groups in the community.
>
> Let a professional meeting be just that, a professional meeting.
>
> Don't be afraid to evaluate! Send out forms to members for evaluation of meetings and ask for their suggestions.

Next to content, the practicing librarians were desirous of deeper involvement in the affairs of the association; this was especially lacking, they felt, in regard to new members of the association (S-72:177-179):

> Have the guts to permit broader participation by promising non-tried people.
>
> Do not stifle new members. They have the energy and enthusiasm to carry through the problems that the old pros claim as their birthright and rarely achieve.... make new members feel welcome.... I think most members feel as though they are on the outside looking in.

The third most frequent category of recommendations urged professional associations to take continuing education opportunities to where the librarians are geographically located. They recommended that programs of worth-while content travel (S-72:180).

Suggestions to local, state, and regional associations, and to national professional associations are also offered in "Guidelines to the Development of Human Resources in Libraries" in the July, 1971, issue of Library Trends (A-41:114-15).

In addition to the national association activities mentioned in this chapter, there are many excellent programs sponsored by state and regional library associations, which are mentioned in Chapter II. Taken together, this sampling of activities indicated clearly that there is interest in and concern for program development in the area of continuing library education. It also shows that there is a need, as stated in the AALS position paper (A-77:14), for joint action and planning by relevant groups to "outline a conceptual and practical blueprint for the provision of equal, coordinated, continuing library educational opportunities throughout the United States and Canada for those librarians who need, and are willing to continue, their lifetime of postgraduate learning." It would also seem to imply that serious attention should be directed to the suggestion spelled out in some detail in Appendix A to the Position Paper (A-77:18-32) that provision should be made for some type of national planning and structure to create prototypes and advise and coordinate the type of functions deemed necessary to further continuing library education.

Conclusion

In planning for the future, it would seem that those concerned with improving the quality and quantity of continuing library education should pay serious attention to what has been and is being accomplished in other professions. Several suggestions are made on the basis of the data presented pertaining to activities sponsored by these professional associations at the end of each section of this chapter. Some of these that would seem to merit special attention are highlighted here. They are listed randomly; no attempt has been made to indicate any priority or ranking order.

1. Focus on what the chief continuing educational needs are within the profession, and then design organizational structures that will produce new skills and new information to meet those needs.

2. Establish a recognition system for continuing education. Consideration should be given to using the "continuing education unit' as recently adopted by the American Nursing Association. Seek a variety of ways of honoring those who lead and those who participate in continuing education endeavors.

3. Experiment with a training laboratory concept in which people can, through simulation, try library practices without commitment.

In a laboratory situation, one can experiment with ways of doing something, and if it works, the individual will be more willing to go back home and try it.

4. Encourage groups from the same library to attend continuing education experiences. A single individual who has been turned on by a continuing education experience finds it very frustrating to go back and find out that no one else understands what he is talking about.

5. Develop a computerized system, similar to that described by the American Institute of Architects, for inventorying all live programs (those that must be attended) and packaged courses that could have relevance to what librarians want, so that this information would be continuously available and up to date for every librarian in every location. Until a computerized system is worked out, this clearinghouse type of listing for live and packaged programs should be published regularly. Excellent examples can be found in Chemical Engineering News, published by the American Chemical Society, and in the American Dental Association's publication, Continuing Education.

6. Local, state, and regional professional associations which are not now active in continuing education should review their programs to determine what more they could be doing. Reaction from practicing librarians gives the impression that in many communities local chapters often primarily fulfill social functions or make continuing education a once-in-a-while activity. National associations should provide materials and guidelines to local chapters interested in intensifying their continuing education activities.

7. Consider ways of increasing the number of preprints and of review articles and papers. There does not seem to be much emphasis placed on publication of original research findings. This type of publication should be balanced with comprehensive statements of emerging trends in theory and practice, based on application of research findings covering a wide range of topics and including trends and practices in other disciplines that have application to library and information science.

8. Issue a regular publication, jointly financed and sponsored by the various professional associations, featuring continuing education, which would cover what all of the associations are doing and have to offer. Excellent examples can be found in the Journal of Continuing Education in Nursing, published bimonthly, and in the American Dental Association's quarterly, Continuing Education.

9. Experiment with types of correspondence opportunities, using packaged materials or games, but differing from usual correspondence courses because individuals using the materials in one location are urged to take the courses together and use mini-lab techniques as practiced by the American Institute of Architects.

10. Issue a cassette a month which would review not only information from library science and information science, but information from related disciplines that can affect the practicing librarian and the library which he or she serves. Coverage of subjects would be proportionate to needs expressed by practicing librarians based on survey techniques.

11. Prepare for distribution on demand in-depth subject cassettes which would be supplemented with written material, slides, graphs, charts, etc. The preparation of these would be governed by current needs expressed by practicing librarians based on survey techniques. An example might be the library and its use of CATV, or the Library and Revenue Sharing.

12. Give consideration to four components in all planning and programming for continuing education: 1) content that is job-oriented; 2) constant search for modes that meet the personalized criteria of individual librarians; 3) expertise used in preparation of the medium; 4) smooth and continuing distribution system.

13. Develop a dissemination of information service for librarians, similar to the AIA AIDS program. This would constitute the development of a professional data bank, which would offer decentralized distribution of information by use of the telephone. This reference service for librarians would contain data on such topics as: the latest information on networks and their availability; legialation; employment information; etc.

126

14. Use marketing techniques for production and distribution of materials and services. If these are based on real needs from the field, they can be self-supporting as demonstrated by other professional groups in their production of materials.

15. Exploit the new technology in continuing education programming; formats such as pre-prints, cassette tapes, cassette-based packaged programs, talk-back TV programs, and Cable TV need to be used more widely.

16. Develop a "Standard Condition of Employment" based on the statement in the ALA Library Education and Manpower Policy Statement (A-42), to be used by employers guaranteeing that time and funds for continuing education will be provided by the employing institution. An excellent example can be found in the engineering profession.

17. Build quality control into materials and programs produced through the use of ongoing user evaluations and through a national review structure consisting of experts drawn from different professional associations, as well as from library schools and from practitioners in the field.

18. Develop a comprehensive model for managing and evaluating short-term institutes and workshops.

19. Re-examine the type of continuing education programming offered by other professional associations in terms of the increased emphasis on competencies demanded by the public and in accordance with current insistence on accountability.

20. Formulate guidelines and position papers endorsed jointly by the various library associations. Examples from nursing, medicine and banking suggest the types of such statements that would prove useful: "Landmark Statement on Continuing Education, " "Guidelines for Continuing Education Programming, " "Evaluative Model for Managing and Evaluating Short-Term Institutes and Workshops, " "Recognition System for Continuing Education, " etc. The statements that are adopted should be printed in full and given visibility for the benefit of the whole profession.

21. Establish a master planning committee for continuing education in each state and region.

22. Appoint one individual to be responsible for coordinating continuing education programming within each association and with other relevant groups outside the association.

23. Engage in inter-disciplinary and inter-professional cooperation in the planning and implementation of continuing education programs, as well as joint planning among the various professional associations within the profession.

128

V. CONTINUING EDUCATION AND THE WORK ENVIRONMENT

Some Observations on Current Practices

"Continuing education" and "technical obsolescence" are probably the
two most common subjects in industrial education circles. It is becoming increasingly obvious that the former is not a panacea for the
latter. While there seems to be a great deal of concern over the trend
toward earlier obsolescence of our work force, it is not clear that anyone has found a successful process for assuring the continuing development and effective utilization of a person's capability throughout his
working career.

These are the opening sentences of an article by Lassiter and others (L-8:114) describing the Sandia Laboratories' experiment with an individualized continuing professional development program based on recent research findings. The authors
continue by pointing out that up to this time the greatest emphasis on "continuing
education" has been on short courses, advanced degree programs, formal courses,
or variations of a traditional education type. However, based on recent research,
the company came to wonder if courses alone were the answer (L-8:114). New research is showing that courses alone are not an effective remedy to the problems
of aging and obsolescence (Dalton and Thompson, D-2). Landis (L-3:   in a
study of 1146 engineers in 12 major companies concluded that "...most engineers
are not interested in continuing education; they are interested in doing their current job better. They will respond to training rather than to education, and they
will demand an almost immediate payoff in terms of recognition or salary."
Barrett (B-3) concluded that just to provide courses for employees is to invite
obsolescence. The need, he found was to gain individual commitment for professional growth by means of participation in a plan for self development. Out of the
143 research and development people in the study, roughly 75% "expressed the
lesire to spend more time on training and development activities, but fewer than
one-half of the respondents --44% -- actually expected to have sufficient time for
self development (B-3:10)." This conflict between need for professional growth
and the pressure of time was so strong that there seemed to have to be a "payoff"
in terms of a reward structure or recognition system for individuals to put forth
substantial efforts in the area of professional development. "If organization
members do not perceive a link between their development activities and the organization's reward system, the probability of active efforts to update knowledge
and skills is lessened" (B-3:12). Another factor related to continuing education
came from Barrett's study. He reported that 70% of the respondents reported
a desire for more freedom to pursue their own interests in selecting new
projects to work on. Assuming that new projects chosen would require at
least some professional development, it would seem to hold that more freedom

in the selection of topics would prove a stimulus toward engaging in continuing professional education activities.

In 1972, the Office of University Library Management Studies of the Association of Research Libraries (A-87: 4)   reported on a survey based on 55 of its member libraries concerning current practices in staff development. The surveyors (Webster and Putnam) looked at three categories included in the area of staff development: 1) training programs to upgrade or secure skills required to perform defined job responsibilities, 2) supervisory and management development programs sponsored by or participated in by the organization, and 3) opportunities offered by the library for the individual to secure additional subject and professional knowledge. The study concluded:

> Everyone likes the idea of staff development, but very few
> are providing concentrated organizational support. The pre-
> vailing philosophy generally is that it is the individual's
> responsibility for developing himself. Again, this has worked in
> the past, but in many instances the uncoordinated efforts at
> individual self-development do not produce the staff capabilities
> necessary for the library to maintain its performance, or, for
> this matter, meet the challenges of the future (A-87:4-5).

The surveyors found that even if an individual was motivated to engage in continuing education there were many obstacles in his way, such as: restrictions on travel funds, no remission of fees for course work, restrictions on the nature and types of course work that can be done, and little advice in counselling the individual on continuing education that would relate to his individual career goals.

In 1971, Kaser (K-4:71) stated that it seemed reasonable to assert that the current level of concern and interest in continuing library education was "vastly higher than it has ever been in the past. Conferences and workshops on staff development, articles in the library press, and speeches on the subject virtually abound, creating an impression that untold manlives of time are being devoted to it in the nation's libraries and library schools."

Based on a questionnaire sent to 69 public and 76 academic libraries, he concluded, however, that in spite of all the new talk about continuing education, "few libraries actually seem to be doing much about it in any organized or concerted way " (K-4:71).

This chapter considers continuing education in relation to employer philosophies, programs and practices, and to some of the influences on continuing
education in the work place. The general pattern of the presentation will
be that discussion will refer to other professions and then compare this
data with related literature in library science.

Management Philosophy

Companies such as Sandia (L-8:116-117) and Texas Instruments (R-30:99-
100) are basing their continuing education programs on several basic assumptions prevalent in much of the behavioral science literature today. The
"Guidelines to the Development of Human Resources in Libraries" (A-41)
are also based upon these several assumptions about human and organizational
behavior. One of these assumptions is that most individuals have a natural
inclination toward growth and development (Maslow, M-34; McGregor, M-12;
McClelland, M-2, M-3, M-4; Herzberg, and others, H-14, H-15, H-16).

In Chapter 14 of The Human Side of Enterprise, McGregor (M-12:190-206)
delineates what this assumption would mean when applied to the staff development program of an organization. McGregor's philosophy as applied to
staff development goes far beyond the "manufacturing approach" which relies chiefly on mechanical approaches in which the employee is a "passive
agent being rotated or sent to school or promoted, or otherwise manipulated."
He develops an environmental framework in which the individual will "grow
to what he is capable of becoming." He emphasizes throughout the uniqueness of each individual in terms of his capacities, his interests and goals,
his talents. The old manufacturing approach, he points out, does many
things "to him and for him, but generally with the tacit assumption that what
is good for the organization is good for him"(M-12:191-92). He examines
some of the environmental conditions that affect staff development and the
motivation to participate in continuing education, including the philosophies,
programs, and practices of the organization; the behavior of the immediate
supervisor; the role of the management development staff. He sums it all
up in this way (M-12:191):

> In the last analysis the individual must develop himself, and he
> will do so optimally only in terms of what he sees as meaningful
> and valuable. If he becomes an active party to the decisions
> that are made about his development, he is likely to make the
> most of the opportunities that are presented.

In addition to the assumption about individual behavior, another assumption
being made relates to organizational behavior. That is that jobs can be so
organized and enriched, that the nature of the work will provide individual
motivation for growth and development (Herzberg and others, H-14, H-15,
H-16 ; Gomersall and Myers, G-30; Myers, M-75, M-76; Ford, F-13).
This assumption was first developed by Herzberg, and later reinforced by
Myers, based on research at the Texas Instruments Company. In sum,
this theory states that employees are motivated positively by challenging
jobs which provide achievement, growth, advancement, recognition, and
enjoyment of the work itself -- factors related to the content of the work
itself. Employees are affected negatively by such environmental factors as
wages, supervisor relations, working conditions, fringe benefits, etc. --
factors related to the context of the job situation. An employee tends to
ignore or pay minimal attention to negative context factors when he finds
his job a motivating one, but he finds these context factors strongly dis-
satisfying when, as Myers (M-76) states it, the employee's "opportunities
for meaningful achievement are eliminated." Roche and MacKinnon (R-30:
99) describe the "meaningful work" program which was designed to "vitalize
the factors which motivate the worker positively and quash the factors
which demotivate him."

Two research studies in Library Science that have used Herzberg's
motivation-hygiene (maintenance) theory as a basis for their investigations
are those by Stone (S-72) and Colley (C-21). Stone found, as outlined in
Chapter II, that, in general, the reasons that the librarians in the sample
participated in professional development activities differed from, and were
not merely opposite to, the reasons they did not participate in such activities.
The librarians engaged in continuing education activities for reasons that
were concerned primarily with the content of the opportunity and its relation
to the work process; the librarians did not participate in activities for reasons
that dealt primarily with factors that were peripheral to the content, or with
contextual elements. The encouraging (positive) factors that rated highest
were quality of the opportunity offered, exposure to new and creative ideas,
and opportunity to use new knowledge in the job situation. Deterring
(negative) factors were time, location, inferior quality of the development
opportunity, and lack of support in their continuing education activities from
their supervisors.

Colley (C-21) took a "cross-bearing" over a period of time of the work expectations of employees of the Manchester (England) Public Library. He
found that top-ranking expectations of employees in the work place were:
1) to have an interesting job, 2) to experience a feeling of achievement, 3)
to be on good terms with colleagues, 4) to have chances of promotion and

growth, and 5) to receive full appreciation of work done (C-21:350). All but one
of these (to be on good terms with colleagues) arise from job content and are related to Herzberg's satisfiers (motivators); i.e., if these expectations are
fulfilled there is job satisfaction, motivation to work, and motivation for continuing education. Colley concludes:

> Today's manager is not content to train for increased efficiency
> or increased production. He appreciates that the greatest
> resource he has is the untapped potential of the individual men
> and women who constitute his work force. His training programme
> is designed to release this potential and is designed with the
> objectives, the needs of the individual employee in mind. With
> this reorientation there is no barrier to the achievement of the
> objectives of the organization (C-21:350).

A third assumption is that the continuing professional development program of an
organization should be conceptualized as a sub-system of the total organizational
system. Current writers in this area (Likert, L-18; Crawford, C-44; Odiorne,
O-1) point out that three areas of consideration that are often not considered
relative to staff development in an organization are important: 1) the relationship
between the system of management and the content of the development programs;
2) the internal consistency of the content of management development courses, and
3) the congruence of the methods used in the programs with the management style
of the organization. In other words, it is not enough to determine training needs
from the individuals in an organization. The goals of the entire organization must
first be examined to see if the training needs that are identified by individuals are
in keeping with the goals of the organization. If they are not, many problems and
frustrations arise when the philosophy and methods used in the area of staff development are incongruent with other components of the library's management
system. For example, if a library, or any other organization, in which the style
of management is authoritative, develops a continuing education program based on
the concepts of participative management, it will tend to be disfunctional to both.
The systems approach emphasized that the goals and objectives of the organization,
the organizational structure, the policies and procedures, the management activities, and the selection process all must be compatible with training and continuing education practices. Likert (L-18:125) warns that a system which does not
have such total integration will fail to benefit from a training program which is
democratic in its structure and the results may even be harmful.

Another characteristic of the systems approach which has an influence on
training efforts of the organization is the concept that training has no beginning and end once specific objectives have been met. Odiorne (O-1) points

133

out the necessity of borrowing from the cybernetics model of the communication theorist. In other words, training should be viewed as a continuous process. As discussed under the CIPP evaluation model in Chapter III, there should be an ongoing evaluation system which will continuously feed back information on how the training process can be improved. Training is viewed as a continuously recycling process which will provide self correction as it proceeds. Likert (L-18) also emphasizes the importance of time in the evaluation process. In other words, it is the sum total of changes that occur over a substantial period of time that is the true measurement, not measurement at any one particular time.

Campbell (C-3:269) helpfully sums up the systems approach as it applies to training in the following manner:

> Such an approach goes beyond merely recognizing that it is the line's ultimate responsibility to train, with the training staff acting in a consultative capacity. It implies that the training function is a subsystem within a larger system and that while it has its own inputs and outputs, these overlap and interact with the inputs and outputs of the entire organization. Pushed to its logical extreme, this means that the time a manager spends in a training session must be demonstrated to be worth more in terms of the organization's goals than a similar period of time spent on some other activity (e.g., working). While it may be impossible to demonstrate such things in dollars and cents terms, the admonition of the systems approach to consider as carefully as possible all the points in the organization where training activity interacts with other programs must be heeded.

Kaser notes that the American library community appears to be "increasingly aware of the need for attention to the continuing education of staff and that substantial resources are being put to the purpose. It is as yet, however, seldom thought of as a subsystem of the total library system" (K-4:76-77). The Lees (L-13) present a personnel development plan using a systems approach in the July, 1971 issue of Library Trends.

Before leaving a consideration of theory as related to practices, perhaps a word of definition is in order regarding the terms "training" and "development," which often seem to be given different meanings. Training often seems to imply something specific and factual, while development seems to imply a more general approach to broader topics such as human resource development, decision making, or similar areas. The terms are used interchangeably in this paper and the following general characteristics as stated by Campbell (C-3:233) are accepted:

134

1) Management training and development is, first of all, a learning experience.
2) It is planned by the organization.
3) It occurs after the individual has joined the organization.
4) It is intended to further the organization's goals.

The survey of staff development by the Office of University Library Management Studies, ARL (A-87:4), found that it was difficult to examine staff development practices in libraries due, partially at least, to the confusion in defining terms. For the purposes of that survey three categories of activities were included in staff development: 1) training programs to upgrade or secure skills required to perform defined job responsibilities, 2) supervisory and management development programs sponsored or participated in by the organization, and 3) opportunities offered by the library for the individual to secure additional subject and professional knowledge. Of these three components the survey (A-87:6) found that the greatest interest was in inservice training, but the majority of libraries surveyed did not have the resources to develop their own inservice training programs. "The university does not provide the money and no one on the staff is a specialist at developing, testing or implementing such a program." It was found, however, that there was a general consensus that inservice training programs would be very useful. Topics receiving the highest priority as subjects to be covered in such programs were: human relations and communications for supervisors, principles of academic library management, and overviews of library operations for nonprofessionals. "Eleven libraries of the fifty-five surveyed [reported that they had] taken some steps toward inservice training programs. In each case these programs have gained the cooperation of either the University Personnel Training Office or the Business School or both, as the library went about setting up and conducting the training effort" (A-87:6).

In this section some of the basic assumptions about individual organizations which are pertinent to professional development as presented in recent behavioral science and library literature have been reviewed. These were: 1) most individuals have a natural inclination toward growth and development; 2) jobs can be enriched to accommodate the development of the individual; 3) the importance of a systems approach in training and development programs (training and development are here used as synonomous terms). In the next section continuing education is considered in relation to employer concepts and programs.

135

Employer Concepts and Programs

The Joint Advisory Committee report on Continuing Engineering Studies
(C-30:45-48) made several recommendations which are pertinent in this
connection.

1) Industry must take the initiative and responsibility in defining
a continuing studies program, recognizing it as a management
tool that can be used to attain company objectives.

2) A continuing engineering studies program must have a sufficient
number of alternatives in order for each engineer to select and
integrate what is useful and needed by him.

3) Programs of continuing engineering studies should be established
with definite objectives. (JAC Report #9).

This JAC report (C-30) states that the organization's movtive in supporting continuing education is not altruistic, but to keep the "technical manpower
force as closely coordinated as possible to a rapidly changing technical
world."

In the National Science Foundation study entitled "Continuing Education for
R&D Careers"(C-24), several items regarding employer concepts and programs in the area of continuing education seem particularly relevant:

The three key points of top management philosophy concerning continuing
education seemed to be :

1) Management accepts the responsibility to provide at least some
opportunities...

2) Management expects ...employees to take advantage of these and
other opportunities to keep themselves up to date, particularly
in their own fields of specialization.

3) Management accepts only limited responsibility for motivating
the individual (C-24:43).

Managements which provide opportunities in continuing education generally
believed that those who were unmotivated to the extent of not taking advantage
of the continuing education programs offered should be "on the shelf and
forgotten (C-24:30). Programs are offered, but the initiative to partake

is left to the individual (C-24:30, 43).

The study identified five management objectives which continuing education activities could help the individual attain:

1) To achieve specialization or acquire capability in particular disciplines, new fields, or techniques.

2) To permit individuals to make progress in their assignment by acquiring knowledge needed as a basis for progress.

3. To provide refresher and updating opportunities for those who need them in order tomaintain them at a high level of work performance.

4) To reorient in mid-career a select few of the senior and pro-ductive research people who need and desire a revitalizing and refresher experience such as that provided by a full-time leave.

5. To encourage keeping up to date by ensuring that scientists and engineers have sufficient opportunity to develop and enhance their professional stature by attending meetings, publishing papers, and holding offices in learned societies, all for the purpose of keeping in touch with the wider world of science and engineering outside the laboratory (C-24:32).

It should be noted that these management objectives are not founded on the needs of individuals; they are directed to the work force as a whole. Whereas the individual employee are primarily concerned with their own continuing education needs and helping themselves in the performance of their own jobs and their own careers, management is concerned with continuing education because of its relation to accomplishing the organization's mission (C-24: 29-30).

Programs are designed to fit the five objectives listed above and consist chiefly of various combinations of different modes of education. Three modes of continuing education support provided by employers in the study were almost universal. The ones used by most employers were: paying the ex-penses to professional meetings, giving tuition refunds, and having in-lab lectures to keep people up-to-date. Outside short courses, in-lab courses and sabbatical leaves were less uniformly available (C-24:32-34).

The managers participating in the survey indicated that the employing organization expected to pay all costs of some modes and part of others. Employers thought everything on location should be paid for; short courses at universities from 50% to 90% (C-24:40). It was found that there were no accurate records kept regarding continuing education activities which show the number or type of personnel engaged in continuing education. Generally there was no effective means of evaluation to measure or determine the benefits either to the organization or to the individual . There were generally no cost records kept (C-24:36, 44).

Nine of the 17 organizations in the study used continuing education committees to consider needs, costs, and program development. They ranged in size from 3 to 15 and usually included various levels of personnel as well as representation from top management. Some only had members from the professional employees. These committees were found to meet regularly, but not necessarily frequently; their function is to recommend specific courses of action to top management. Almost all questions concerning the advisability of engaging in some continuing education activity are referred to this committee. It was found that such committees generally performed a valuable service (C-24:34-35).

Some organizations also found out about needs by using questionnaires or interviews regularly. Of the six laboratories using survey techniques to determine continuing education needs, four also had professional development committees. One of the 17 organizations reported a determination of continuing education needs tied in with the performance appraisal system. It was reported as follows (C-24:35):

> Performance appraisals are reviewed by the training staff to see what the supervisor and employee have agreed on. There is a 60 to 90 day follow-up on new personnel or new promotions or new assignments to see if training is needed. It is done each time an assignment changes. A form goes to the supervisor and asks him what the employee needs. It must be completed by the supervisor. The initiative of the employee is great. The employees here know they can get training if they want it. This has created a change in climate in which an employee can seek whatever training he needs.

Although this study did not consider degree-seeking within the scope of "continuing education," it was noted that degree-seeking by some members in an organization tended to have some serious side-effects. Chief among these was the fact that those not seeking degrees became anxious and wondered whether their time might not be spent to better advantage in acquiring

138

credentials rather than in pursuit of the knowledge they needed for their job. As a result of the prevalence of this attitude, the study recommended that "employers who sponsor degree-seeking programs . . . should also take steps to reassure those employees who do not seek degrees that it is job performance, not the possession of an advanced degree, which is critical to their careers" (C-24:42). The survey raised the question as to what was indeed more advantageous to the mission of the organization, degree-seeking or continuing education. It was recommended that the interrelationship between degree-seeking programs and continuing education programs be investigated to determine the impact of one on the other and to analyze the priorities which should be established for each relative to any one employer's total educational needs.

Supervisory Influence on Continuing Education

The Continuing Education for R&D Careers (C-24:132-135) study made a significant contribution in identifying three different types of supervisors, each of which exhibits different levels in the quality of supervision so far as continuing education is concerned. The study categorized three types: 1) the administrator type; 2) the innovator type; and 3) the inactive type.

The administrator type is characterized as the person who does what he can to motivate subordinates to avail themselves of continuing education opportunities which he thinks are worthwhile. Generally he views continuing education as just one of many ways of implementing the objectives of the organization. He accepts the continuing education that is provided by the organization but does not see his role of generating continuing education activities (C-24:132-33).

The innovator type interprets his role as one of creating new opportunities in addition to existing ones; he tries to provide novel and interesting ways for the subordinate to participate in continuing education activities. The innovator is a stimulating element in the working environment who is much more sensitive to the needs of employees for continuing education than the administrator type. He sees and makes use of the wider resources available in the community beyond those offered in the organization. He will work hard to see that workshops, courses, or seminars are created because he believes that these are ways of keeping up with new knowledge in "easily digestible and accessible forms"(C-24:133-34).

139

The inactive type is characterized by the study as being basically passive and noncommittal. He believes that continuing education and self-development are the responsibility of the individual employee outside of the work environment. He does not feel it his responsibility to stimulate participation in continuing education activities nor to initiate and devise any type of continuing education activities for employees. He makes pious statements about the value of continuing education, but he sees his role as a laissez-faire one in which his involvement is minimal or non-existent (C-24:134).

The study states that these three kinds of supervisors say and do entirely different things about continuing education in relation to their subordinates; they play entirely different roles "in arousing in subordinates the curiosity, enthusiasm, and energy needed to tolerate the inconveniences and the efforts demanded by substantial involvement in continuing education"(C-24:135).

Obviously, as is emphasized in the study, the innovators are the most productive in stimulating employees to continuing education activities. It is suggested that top administrators would be well advised to encourage and help supervisors adopt the "innovator" approach in dealing with subordinates regarding continuing education. If supervisors were aware of the differences between the innovator, the administrator, and the inactive types, it is argued that it might make a considerable difference to the supervisors "in conceptualizing their roles and responsibilities in influencing subordinates to continuing education"(C-24:135).

An important finding brought out by the study which reinforces the importance of the type of supervision is quoted (C-24:135):

> ...motivation is not a constant element inside a single person; it emerges as a dimension of the interactions of persons with each other and with the environment they share -- including, very importantly, the meanings, activities, goals, and needs embedded in that shared environment as well as all those brought to the situation by the participating persons.

As might be expected, it was found that each of the three types of supervisor deals in a different way with the "unmotivated man." An employee that the innovator might consider one needing special stimulation the inactive supervisor might regard as quite adequate as he is. An inactive supervisor who thinks it is useless to get men interested in new knowledge will probably collect around him a different type of audience than the one who continually talks, plans and undertakes activities designed to show his subordinates the excitements and benefits of new knowledge. The innovator seemed to be the only type who could relate the potentialities of continuing education experience

140

directly to the work of the employee. The innovator "regards continuing education less as an instrument for substantial changes in field or level of income than as a means for having livelier and more rewarding experiences in the normal pursuit of a professional career"(C-24:137).

Subordinates' View of Supervisory Influence Toward Continuing Education

When employees have been interviewed, they present a different picture of supervisor influences toward continuing education than do the supervisors themselves.

Dubin and Marlow found that a large number of employees believed their supervisors' attitudes toward continuing education were noncommittal (D-39:76):

> Approximately one-third (34%) or 688 engineers believed that their immediate supervisors encouraged them to actively pursue further education or training. However, 64 percent, or 1,313 engineers, felt that their supervisors took a non-committal attitude, and 2 percent, or 38 engineers, believed that their supervisors actually discouraged them from taking educational or training courses.

Continuing Education for R & D Careers (C-24:140) also stated that a substantial portion of employees reported that supervisors were noncommittal toward continuing education. It was found that attitudes of supervisors and the actualities of the job itself were more important influences toward participation in continuing education than the policies of the organization. Policies tended to give permission rather than encouragement. In fact, 23 percent of the scientists and 36 percent of the engineers said that organizational policy had no effect on their continuing education. Formal policy seems to be helpful in two ways: it can provide resources and facilities for continuing education activities and it can be stimulating when combined with encouraging supervision.

The employees interviewed indicated that there should be a wide selection of alternatives available for continuing education. There was "not enough reason to conclude that any one mode should be available to one set of professionals and not to another" (C-24:148).

In Library Science, as in engineering, there was opposition shown toward continuing education on the part of supervisors and administrators. Stone (S-72:54) found that 23% of the librarian-respondents sensed opposition from their supervisors or administration relative to professional improvement activities. Opposition was felt by 43% of the respondents from their supervisors relative to formal course work.

This noncommittal and/or negative attitude was reported by Dubin and his associates in a number of occupations. In the Dubin study (D-33:298) of managers and supervisors in local governments it was found that:

> Forty-six per cent of the managers and 40 per cent of the supervisors reported that their immediate superior was noncommittal toward their further education and training. Superiors should take a greater interest in the professional development of their employees.

Similarly, in Dubin's (D-32) study of managerial and supervisory educational needs of business and industry in Pennsylvania, it was found that a large number of management personnel believed their superiors' attitudes toward their further education was noncommittal.

Based on this type of reaction, each of the studies cited recommends that top management make it explicit that one of the functions of a supervisory position is to show concern for and to review each employee's plans for self-development. Additionally, Continuing Education for R&D Careers (C-24:149) recommends that "conscious recognition of what the 'innovator" type of supervisor is and does will help clarify what management can demand and expect of supervision."

Stolz (S67:142) reports that in companies where staff development is the most successful, all executives are responsible for developing their immediate subordinates and for seeing that these subordinates, in turn, recognize their responsibility to develop those reporting to them. ". . . each individual's development plan is unique -- based on study of his own needs by his superiors . . . The nub of the problem is still appraisal, but appraisal becomes a continuous, cumulative process."

McGregor states that the relationship between the employee and his immediate supervisor is critical and is probably the "most important influence affecting managerial development" (M-12:199). He cites an example in this regard which is possible without cost in any organization and which, in light of research findings presented in this chapter and others in this study, seems so important, at least to this reviewer, that it is quoted (M-12:203-204):

> A staff group in a large company made a concentrated attempt several years ago to follow the "manufacturing" approach to management development by creating an elaborate formal program. . . After some time, this group became aware that the desired purposes

were not being achieved . . . and there was rather generally a passive resistance to the whole field of management development . . . This group decided to start again using an entirely different approach. This   involved just one activity: annual meetings of the president of the company with each of his immediate subordinates, individually, in which the subordinate reported in detail to the president on his activities and accomplishments in creating an environment conducive to the growth of his subordinates. Each individual reporting to him, and each individual at the second level below him, were discussed with the president in detail. The emphasis was on what the manager was doing to make it possible for his subordinates to further their own self-development. The president made it clear -- not only in words, but also in action -- that he held his own subordinates accountable for this managerial function, and that how well they fulfilled the responsibilities in these respects would make a substantial difference in their own rewards and punishments.

This emphasis on the accountability of supervisors for the development of those reporting to them made a substantial difference throughout the whole organization. Each supervisor was encouraged to develop his own methods for presenting his analysis to the president and his own ways of working with his subordinates. The management development staff stood ready to give the supervisors help and guidance when they were called upon by them.

This experience coupled with years of experience and observation led McGregor to state that, in his opinion, "There is almost no relationship between the amount of formal programming and machinery of management development and the actual achievement of the organization in this respect" (M-12:204). This leads McGregor to his conclusion that "there is probably no single activity which will do more to create an environment conducive to managerial growth than the 'target setting' approach. . ." (M-12:205). In essence, target setting is an application of the concept of management by objectives, and McGregor describes how this might be actually done in a work situation in Chapter V (M-12:61-76) and follows this with a critique of the typical kind of performance appraisal in Chapter VI (M-12:77-89). Others who agree with McGregor that the target setting type of appraisal interview can be a great aid in staff development include DeProspe (D-12), Drucker (D-25), Odiorne (O-2), Dalton (D-2), and Surace (S-88).

Campbell (C-3:62-67) reviews recent research and literature in this area and concludes that McGregor's writing on a management by objectives approach to performance appraisal has had a significant impact.   Surveys

143

show that although performance appraisal via a trait appraisal still predominates, more and more organizations are moving toward a management by objectives approach and that it is apparent this trend will continue.

Participation in Decision Making

The Report of the Committee on Continuing Education and Professional Growth of the Cornell University Libraries (C-39:9) joins the process of continuing education with participation in decision-making:

> Over the past ten years, there has been an increasingly dynamic involvement of the library staff in the decision-making process within the library. Perhaps this is the most important educational development of the period, since it brings to the attention of each participating staff member the complex and concrete problems of real decision. This process began gradually....During the past year, the process of joining continuing education with participation in decision-making has continuing at a sharply accelerated rate. And indeed it appears that education without responsibility for decisions is hopelessly abstract, while decision-making without continuing education is inevitably inadequately informed.

Marchant (M-26; M-27) has also focused attention on the relationship between participation in decision-making and continuing education. The "Guidelines to the Development of Human Resources in Libraries"(A-41: 104-105) states in this connection:

> The chief administrator is responsible for the nature of institutional decision-making. Recent research and experience in organizational development indicate that leadership toward participative decision-making is important to staff development. Participation in decision-making by those to be affected by the outcomes of those decisions either as a group or individually provides for both motivation and continuous learning experiences. At each level in the library's organizational hierarchy there is an opportunity for the supervisor to use his work group to identify problems, to cast them into opportunities for improvement, and to work for solutions to those problems that confront them. In this way fulfillment of organizational objectives proceeds hand in hand with personal motivation and fulfillment of the employee as well as his growth in both personal and organizational terms. The principle of group decision-making does not take from the supervisor the responsibility for the quality of all decisions made by his work group and their implementation. Since he is accountable

144

for the decisions and results of his work group, personnel
development becomes an important concern to him.

Stone (S-72:171) found that the librarians sampled did not want library leaders
to decide what continuing programs were needed and establish them. Rather,
the librarians wanted to be consulted and involved in the planning, decision-
making, and implementing of continuing education programs.

Climate for Learning

Monroe (M-60) asserts that continuing education needs of librarians can be met
only in an organization which continuously maintains a climate for learning.
Elements in maintaining such a climate, as mentioned by Monroe, are 1) administration of libraries built on a concept of a professional group practice in
which librarians would find stimulation for continuing learning inherent; 2)
the professional learner sharing in the plan for his own learning; 3) the potential
of research activity as a method of continuing learning by the professional
practitioner is recognized.

Such a climate will aid in achieving what Monroe identifies as the first task
of continuing education -- reducing the resistance to change. Such a conceptualization fits into Bennis' view of leadership: "an active method for producing
conditions where people and ideas and resources can be seeded, cultivated,
and integrated to optimum effectiveness and growth" (B-9:19). Stone (S-72:172-
173) found that in making recommendations to administrators regarding their
responsibility in the area of continuing education, participant librarians gave
top priority to maintaining a climate conducive to professional growth. Emphasis
on the importance of organizational climate is an important condition if continuing
education efforts in an organization are to be effective. This point is made
throughout the literature dealing with professional growth. For example,
Miller asserts that for the engineer to be deeply involved in continuing education
he "must feel assured that he will have opportunities to use his talents and
skills to the maximum extent of his willingness and ability . . ." (M-58:1113).
He also insists that there must be provision of a "dual" ladder or pathway of
advancement provided by the organization. That is to say, there must be provision for progression by both administrative and technical (specialized)
channels. In a perceptive article on the "new organization man," Hanan suggests three minimal requirements for an organization if it is to accommodate
the needs of this "new organization man": 1) personal involvement--provide
new ways for getting employees involved; 2) collaborative leadership--empha-
sizing the joint exercise of authority and innovative approaches to goal-setting
achievement; 3) self-fulfillment options--"centering on the invigoration of
individual rights within the corporate framework and on the setting up of fast-
track recognition for excellence" (H-3:131).

Stone (S-72:212) found that practicing librarians sampled thought administrators were fostering organizational conditions which were often minimal for continuing education. The respondents described the type of leader who could best stimulate them to participate in continuing education in these terms:

> He should be approachable, open-minded, sensitive, and as concerned about the individual's goals as the library's objectives and have the ability to relate personal goals to library goals. They wanted management to keep them informed on all library matters, to recognize their performance, to encourage innovation, to be willing to accept mistakes and to let them take risks, and to expect a high level of performance from each individual librarian. They wanted to work under the supervision of administrators who were capable of organizing clear and efficient work systems.

In essence the respondents in the study were describing the type of developmental leadership that recent behavioral research has shown furthers the professional growth of employees. The respondents also stressed the positive influence of administrators who themselves participated in continuing education activities. In the opinion of the respondents, administrators should both create an atmosphere within the library hospitable to professional growth, and suggest various possibilities for continuing education outside the library.

Employer Programming

Continuing Education for R & D Careers (C-24:14-15) summarizes concepts related to employer programming for continuing education as it exists in engineering. Generally these same concepts (as stated in the next three paragraphs) would seem to apply in other types of organizations.

Those employing organizations which think in terms of mutual responsibility with the individual for providing continuing education opportunities, think in terms of 1) opportunities for continuing education which will directly benefit the organization and the individual, and 2) costs. The nature of the support that is given in terms of costs and time allotments is based on both organizational and individual needs. To avoid serious frustrations, the content, philosophy, and methods used for continuing education programs are in keeping with the goals of the organization. As a nearly continuous exposure is often necessary to keep the individual upgraded, continuing education is viewed as a continuous process.

146

An important aspect of employer programming for continuing education is structuring the job and the work environment so that the individual has time to keep himself up to date, or to catch up, if needed. Different kinds of education require different blocks of time. As a result, many writers on continuing education are calling for a rethinking of the job format to include time to keep up to date, not only in the particular area of the individual's job assignment, but in broader areas where new developments relate to the individual's original training and/or special interests.

While there are numerous examples in the literature of ways individual organizations provide programming for continuing education, it appears that a substantial number of employers do not support continuing education to any great extent. Reasons given for non-participation include lack of time, pressure of work, lack of resources.

Two persuasive statements presenting the case for employers making the effort to program for continuing education are those by Dubois (D-40) and Margaret Mead (M-36). Dubois maintains that once education and training have been distinguished (see Chapter II for his distinction), there are three reasons for justifying an organization's educating, and not merely training, its employees (D-40:1):

> First, when a business is considered as a component of the whole American economy, a continuing rise in employees' educational levels so demonstrably serves the national interest that employee education appears to be merely cooperating with the inevitable.

> In addition, those local communities to which an enterprise pays property taxes and from which it draws employees respond in important ways to visible programs of employee education. Finally, the education, as distinguished from the training, of employees may reasonably be considered an offset to labor turnover costs which, for a number of largely invisible causes, are higher than they might be.

> The complete case for employee education thus includes reasons of public policy, of community relations, and of payback. The second and third of these may in a few years impel more individual enterprises to adopt programs of education for their employees. If enough firms are so moved, there is little doubt that the implications of the first reason will add powerfully to the well-documented effect which rising levels of education have had for more than a generation on the Gross National Product.

147

Dubois (D-40:6, 10) believes that increasingly the task of educating Americans is going to be "recognized as a task of educating employed adults" and that organizations in the public interest have a responsibility for taking a leading role in this task. Commenting on his third reason -- an offset to turnover costs -- for employer sponsorship of continuing education, he demonstrates how relatively small savings in turnover can support substantial programs of employee education (D-40:10-14). He asserts that with an employee-education program the following can be expected (D-40:13-14):

> Lower turnover on all jobs. Employees sense that more personal attention is available to them whether they seek it or not.

> Lower recruitment costs for unneeded new professionals hired to fill urgently needed semiprofessional jobs. Present employees will be developed in advance of need to fill these semiprofessional jobs. [Relative to this factor he develops the argument that an organization that develops its own technicians to fill technician assignments will avoid the costs of recruiting professionals to do the work of aides and this will save an ongoing expense of paying higher wages to professionals who are misassigned.]

> Lower external recruitment costs. The company becomes basically a more attractive place to work.

> Lower recruitment costs for jobs filled from within.... Internal turnover may save the employer more costly external turnover.

> Lower turnover and recruitment costs for scarce professionals ...It is specially significant that the employee-education program's power is greatest for the very class of employee whom it costs most to attract in any other way.

Margaret Mead (M-36) makes a strong case for continuing education in the work place throughout adulthood by pointing out that it is an obsolete fiction to hold to the old concept that most people can complete all the formal education they will ever need before their productive work life starts. In this connection she states one of the most vivid truths of our time in relation to change (M-36:34): "No one will live all his life in the world into which he was born, and no one will die in the world in which he worked in his maturity." As she observes that in our society only business has started to think of human obsolescence as a capital investment, she

148

views business organizations as the appropriate agency in society to lead the way in dealing with obsolescence of the variety of skills that constitute human capital.

Summary and Conclusions

This section recapitulates some of the concepts presented in this chapter that seem to merit the special attention of those planning for continuing education in the work environment of the library. These suggestions are listed randomly; no attempt has been made to list any priority or ranking order. It would appear that such considerations and specifications are important, as it has been pointed out that few libraries are actually doing much about continuing education in any organized fashion.

1. Administrators should take the initiative and responsibility for defining and providing support opportunities for the continuing education of their staffs.

2. The continuing education and/or professional development program of the library should be conceptualized as a sub-system of the total organizational system.

3. Administrators should recognize the need for establishing a long range educational program with definite objectives to parallel long-range library goals. There is evidence that continuing education on an if-and-when basis is not sufficient to cope with the requirements of a library actively responding to societal changes.

4. Continuing education programs require strong support and encouragement by supervisory personnel. Top administration should make it explicit that one of the functions of supervision is stimulating subordinates to continuing education and reviewing with them their plans for development. Conscious recognition of what an "innovator" type of supervisor is and does relative to continuing education helps make plain what top administrators can expect of supervisors.

5. A philosophy should predominate in which it is assumed: 1) that most individuals have a natural inclination toward growth and development and that the individual will accept his share of responsibility for development; 2) that each person is considered an unique individual and his or her special talents are recognized, encouraged to develop, and utilized, 3) that each individual is allowed to identify his personal career goals and match those against the library's goals, and 4) that management's function is to supply the opportunity, guidance, and stimulation.

6. Continuing education programs require the personal motivation of the individual employee. There is evidence that for an individual to be personally motivated toward continuing education, he must see the results of the learning as being related and necessary to the performance of his job.

7. Individual jobs should be organized and enriched so that the nature of the work will provide individual motivation for growth and development.

8. Policy statements should recognize updating personnel as part of the daily work.

9. Employee appraisal should be recognized as closely related to development. To serve as a motivating factor toward continuing education, there is evidence that appraisal needs to be a continuous, cumulative process, using a management by objectives approach.

10. An active continuing education committee, representing the views and needs of all levels of the organization, should be established. The function of such a committee is to initiate, review, and recommend action programs in continuing education. The committee should also suggest priorities based on the conduct and evaluation of "reviews of need" in the work force as related to organizational goals and needs. A professional development committee can create and sustain enthusiasm for continuing education because its very existence demonstrates the administration's support and reliance on continuing education as a professional development technique.

11. It should be recognized that individual and group needs are so varied that short courses, degree programs, formal courses, institutes, etc. will not meet all continuing education needs. The organization should provide a sufficient number of alternatives in order for each professional to select and integrate what is useful and needed by him. (Some alternative modes of continuing education are outlined in Chapter VII.)

12. Deterring environmental factors relating to continuing education, such as lack of time, inconvenient location, poor working conditions, should be eliminated insofar as possible.

13. Ways and means should be developed to overcome the physical and psychological barriers of individuals participating in continuing education opportunities outside the work place. Management should set

150

up in some central place in the library where information on outside continuing education is collected, kept up to date, and made easily available to those considering or in need of outside continuing education opportunities.

14.   A system should be operative which periodically and systemically evaluates the need for continuing education opportunities.

15.   An ongoing evaluation system should continuously feed back information on ways and means by which the continuing education program can be improved.

16.   Management should maintain an accurate record-keeping system which reflects the number and types of personnel engaged in employer-sponsored modes of continuing education and the cost per participant. Ways should be found to measure and assess the modes of continuing education in terms of their value to the organization and to the individual.

17.   Participation in decision making should be viewed as one way of stimulating employees toward engaging in continuing education opportunities. According to Monroe (M-60:278) "there is no better educator than the exercise of responsibility nor is there a better prod to continuing formal education."

18.   The organization should continuously maintain a climate for learning. Elements in such a climate include: 1) the concept of professional group practice should pervade the library in which stimulation for continuing learning is inherent; 2) the learner shares in the plan for his learning; 3) research as a method of continuing learning is recognized; 4) a developmental style of leadership exists throughout the organization.

VI. ROLE OF THE ACADEMIC INSTITUTION
IN CONTINUING EDUCATION

Role and Problems of the Academic Institution in Professional Education

Before focusing on the role of the academic institution in continuing education as reflected in the literature, it is perhaps important to note the key
position that the academic institution holds relative to professionalism as
a whole. Mosher (M-72:35-38) states the case clearly as it applies to the
public service, and it would seem that his statements would be true
generally for other professions as well.

> Over the long pull, the most dominating impact upon the profes-
> sional public services will be that of the universities -- their
> professional schools, their departments in the physical and
> social sciences which produce professionals, and their faculties
> in general. Higher education...produces the bulk of future pro-
> fessionals. By their images, and by their impressions upon
> undergraduates, the schools have a great influence upon what
> kinds of young people -- of what quality, what interests, what
> values -- opt for what fields. It is clear too that they influence
> the choices of students among employers -- whether government
> or other....By their curricula, their faculties, their teaching,
> they define the content of each different specialism and the expecta-
> tions and aspirations of the students in each....My impression is
> that in most fields accreditation and high academic standing
> (grade point average) are more important to governmental
> employers than professional licenses. Where registration has
> been provided in only a few states or in none or all -- such as
> social work, or city planning, or librarianship -- accreditation
> and grades become almost the sole criteria. . . Where government
> employers have any significant choice among candidates for
> jobs in the recognized professions, their reliance is placed
> upon (1) whether they come from accredited schools, (2) their
> grade point averages, (3) the recommendations of professors.
> All three are of course academic determinants.

Mosher goes on to point out that this reliance on the academic institution
for the choice of professionals, the content of their work and their competencies, and their values will continue. "But the educational process
through which the professionals are produced and later refreshed (in continuing education programs) can be studied and changed" (M-72:38).

152

Mosher points out that professional education has become the largest part of higher education, yet there has been so little concern about the problems of professional education. Mosher (M-72:66) identifies four of these problems as being of particular relevance:

-- Intra-professional fission -- to what extent and at what stage should sub-specialization be recognized or encouraged in the education process?

-- Professional boundaries and the spillover of problems -- to what extent should professional education invade the zones beyond the traditional boundaries of the profession? More broadly, how should educators define the content of the profession?

-- Obsolescence -- how should professional educators cope with the accelerating growth of knowledge relevant to the individual professions? How should it be accommodated in the pre-career programs? How much emphasis should be given to continuing education?

-- Organization and management -- to what extent and at what stage should professional education recognize and prepare students for managerial responsibilities which a great many of them will subsequently assume?

To these he adds four other types of problems faced by the professional school. The first is the pull on the campus to pull away from pure vocationalism and emphasize the sciences and theoretical concepts. This leads to complaints from practitioners who say that academic institutions are producing "researchers rather than practitioners and that the graduates must then go through what amounts to an apprentice program to learn the real substance of professional practice" (M-72:68).

The second of these problems is the "ambivalent stance and relationships of professional schools at the universities." On the campus there seems to be the general attitude that training for professions "is of a lower order of human activity than the search for truth itself." In turn the professionals on the campus are critical of the humanists and "pure" scientists "because of their alleged ignoring of real problems in the world today, because of their confinement to narrow disciplinary specializations" (M-72:68-69).

153

The professional schools are like Janus: they face on one side their professions and the organizations which hire their graduates; on the other, they face the rest of the university, its standards, aspirations, regulations and personnel (including students). They are at the university but not completely in it or of it. The position is a difficult one and often a delicate one. But it is also a strategic one which can be...of great value, both to the rest of the university and to the society outside. The professional school provides a linkage between an important and esteemed occupational sector of the society and the knowledge "factories." It can bring to the appropriate places in the university the information derived from experience and problems from the real world which may direct and provide material for research and study by both scientists and humanists. And, conversely, it may translate the ideas and the findings of the academicians into terms that are usable in professional practice. It is one of our principal mechanisms for putting new concepts and new knowledge to work. (M-72:69-70).

Whether or not this process is effective depends to a large degree on which barriers are broken down -- the degree or interface the university has with the practicing profession. This leads to the third problem identified by Mosher (M-72:70):

...the communications between the professional schools and the professions themselves, and the impacts and the constraints they have upon one another. To what extent are the emerging problems and needs of professionals in the working world communicated back to the schools? And to what extent are they tooled into the curricula?

It also raises questions about the constraints put on the schools by the professions in the development of their programs -- by accreditation requirements for the schools, by employing agencies.

The final problem identified by Mosher (M-72:71) is the attention that is or should be given by the professional school to "the larger social context within which professionals work..."

The Role of the Academic Institution in Continuing Education

Because academic institutions are the specialists in preparing for the professions, are the gatekeepers for those entering the professions, and

154

set the standards of quality and dimensions of student performance (as pointed out in the foregoing paragraphs), colleges and universities occupy a central place in continuing education. The literature is full of what should be done by the colleges and universities in the field of continuing education.

The Carnegie Foundation (C-8), in 1967, in emphasizing the urgency of continuing education on the part of academic institutions and its broad scope, defined it in these terms:

> It has to do with the out-reach of a university to society at large, with extending the resources of the campus to individuals and groups who are not part of the regular academic community, and with bringing an academic institution's special competence to bear on the solution of society's problems.

Continuing Continuing Education for the Public Service (I-4), prepared for the University of California, was designed to motivate the University to take action in the area of continuing education. It presents a strong case, citing many educational and national leaders, for the University's providing a full range of continuing education opportunities for practitioners. The whole first chapter presents arguments on why it is the duty of the university to take responsibility for continuing education and emphasizing that taking on this additional role "would not dilute the University's nature as an institution of higher education or scholarship and scientific inquiry." The argument (I-4:5) continues:

> An expanded role is not suggested in the belief that the University is an agency of immediate social change or an urban redevelopment agency. It is primarily and must continue to remain an educational institution governed by academic values. It is primarily an institution for teaching in the broadest sense of the word, of disseminating and interpreting knowledge. However, there is no reason why the recipients of such dissemination and interpretation should be limited to persons seeking resident bachelor's or advanced degrees. The University should take as "students" any group of people or any individual willing to learn and capable of inquiry. In that spirit, it "...must develop special-education and extension programs matched to the problems and needs...of the tough problems...which are the essential ingredients of modern education in an urban setting."

The report not only makes the case for the necessity of the University providing continuing education for practitioners, but it places equal emphasis

155

on the advantages that will come to the University by providing an opportunity "for academicians to be intimate with the marketplace through the
mingling process inherent in a program of continuing education"(I-4:11).
It states (I-4:8-9):

> Continuing continuing education for the public service will be
> good for the University. It will benefit teaching, give greater
> pertinence and liveliness to campus life and win allies for the
> University. We strongly believe that a properly conceived and
> competently administered program will result in a stronger
> and more relevant learning-teaching-research process for the
> University and its faculty and bring it information and knowledge
> at least equal in importance to that which it imparts to
> practitioners.

The report makes the point that the special emphasis of a University
is to do things that other institutions cannot do (I-4:11-12).

> It [the University] should be ready to move forward along new
> lines in continuing education -- to experiment, to generate and
> try out original ideas and approaches in instruction, research
> and public service....Continuing education provides an un-
> paralleled opportunity to feed ideas into the system through its
> most "influentials" that will in time result in the modification
> and adjustment of the system to its environment.

The report (I-4:12) also points out that the university is uniquely suited to
take a leadership role in continuing education because it can provide interdisciplinary programs.

The Continuing Education for R&D Careers report (C-24:16-17) points out
that the demand for well-planned and broadly-gauged continuing education
programs is increasing and that they are sometimes recommended as a
mandatory role for the university of equal importance with undergraduate
and graduate training. It lists specific issues that are often spelled out
regarding continuing education and the role the university should be
assuming:

1. Defining the needs to be met.
2. Credit versus non-credit, and, related to this, maintaining
   academic standards versus the practical approach.
3. Obtaining a degree versus enhancement of professional
   competence.

156

4. Who will teach: regular faculty, qualified outsiders, or extension and night-school faculty.

5. Lack of involvement of regular faculty, and even hostility on the part of some of them, to continuing education programs.

In the literature, the general opinion seems to be that although the university may have to play the major role in continuing education, it is not a role that it should play alone. Rather, there should be cooperative interrelationships between universities and employers; together they share in the responsibility for continuing education. The phrase "university-employer interface" refers to this type of purposeful interaction (C-24:15-16). Commenting on the nature and importance of this interface,Brisco (as quoted in the <u>Continuing Education for R&D Careers</u>, C-24:17) stated:

> ...Continuing education should be a major reponsibility of the academic community, complementing regular degree programs in much the same way as research now complements instructional activities. Industry, on the other hand, "must reassess the nature of its support." Understanding between these two major segments of society must increase. If industry and the university were to resolve all specific issues, there would be little to deter the development of continuing engineering education.

These examples, representing but a few of many available in the literature, serve to illustrate the role that universities generally should be playing in continuing education. There seems to be a tendency, as specifically stated in engineering and public service literature, to dissassociate advanced degree seeking from anti-obsolescence continuing education activities. There are many suggestions of what should be done that is not being done. There is the implication that faculties are often indifferent or even actively resistant to continuing education activities. There is increasing emphasis on the nature of and the need for interface, regarding continuing education, that should exist between the university and the employing institution.

The Role of the Academic Institution in Continuing Library Education

The question arises: Is the role of the universities in relation to continuing library education generally the same, as reflected in the literature, as that regarding other professions? The answer would seem to be that there has been less emphasis put on either the need or the offering of opportunities than in other professions.   The basic issues and problems are quite similar.

157

Harrison (H-6) points out that until recently doctoral study has provided the only opportunity for advanced work, and this opportunity has only been offered by a small number of institutions.

According to the February, 1973 listing by ALA (A-90), nineteen schools offer the doctoral degree. Eyman's Checklist of Dissertation Titles for Doctorates Granted by Library Schools (E-8:vi) shows a total of 469 Ph.D.'s had been awarded through December, 1972.

Those elaborating on the doctorate in library science include Danton (D-6), Marco (M-28), Swank (S-89) and Dalton (D-4). The Spring, 1968 issue of the Journal of Education for Librarianship, in a section entitled "Reflections on the Doctoral Program . . .", featured descriptive presentations by library educators (Monroe, Held, Rawski, Swanson and Winger, Goldhor, Rufsvold and McMullen, Harlow, and Boaz).

Two doctoral degrees are offered: the Ph.D. and the Doctor of Library Science. The distinction between the two is not clear-cut, as brought out in a statement by Swank (S-89:16-17):

> Our confusion of theory with practice is best illustrated by the
> present fuzziness of distinctions between the Ph. D. in library
> science and the Doctor of Library Science degrees. In principle
> the distinction is clear. The Ph.D. is a research degree; it is
> preparation for a career of teaching and research, as in other
> academic fields. The D.L.S., like the M.D. and the Ed.D.,
> is preparation for high responsibility in the practice of the
> profession. The distinction is real in medicine, is less so in
> education, and almost disappears in librarianship. Some library
> schools offer the research degree, others the professional
> degree, . . . all without any significant difference. Both are
> interpreted uniformly as training for research, in that both
> culminate in dissertations; yet a professional, service-
> oriented, master's degree is required for admission; and the
> future careers of most graduates are in practice.

Both Harrison (H-6) and Dalton (D-3, D-4) point out that for the practitioner who does not wish to pursue a doctoral program, the main opportunity offered is via the post-Master's or advanced study certificate programs. According to the February, 1973 listing by the Association of American Library Schools entitled "Graduate Library School Programs Accredited by the American Library Association," nineteen of the 58 accredited schools in the United States and Canada offer a post-Master's specialist or certificate

program. These programs are not accredited by ALA. Studies by
Fryden (F-23) and Danton (D-5) found certain weaknesses in the sixth-year
programs as they existed when they made their surveys. Danton (D-5) found
that the wide variation in title and scope of programs was a weakness.

> There are, in fact, almost as many different designations as
> there are awards, fourteen in all. This seems a distinctly
> disadvantageous situation. Who, even in the library profession,
> is likely to be aware of all of these different titles, and to
> recognize that, despite their varied phraseology, they represent
> the same amount, and frequently the same kind, of advanced
> professional education? . . . It would seem highly desirable that
> the Association of American Library Schools, and, perhaps, the
> C.O.A., attempt to secure agreement among the accredited
> schools on a single certificate title, or, at most, upon not more
> than two or three titles. It would also seem desirable that
> the schools which give no award do so (D-5:35-36).

Danton noted that this specialist program, comparable to those in library
science, exists in numerous other fields. He cites as an example the conference held by the American Association of State Colleges and Universities
on "The Specialist Degree" in 1969, in which it was stated (D-5:38):

> Specialist degree programs are intended for those preparing
> for positions which call for a higher level of study than the
> Master's degree but not the emphasis on research required
> for the Doctor's degree. A major object of such programs
> is to strengthen an individual's area of specialization. . . .
> Specialist degree programs are functionally oriented toward
> the student's professional objectives.

Based on his findings from the 20 schools offering a sixth-year program at
the time of his study, Danton makes observations and recommendations,
including the following (D-5:73, 80):

> -- The basic concept of the sixth-year program is sound;
>   the idea should be encouraged and supported.
> -- A large majority of the programs will continue and
>   probably improve qualitatively and expand quantitatively.
> -- A majority of the programs are functioning reasonably
>   well to excellently.
> -- Most programs can be and a few need to be improved in
>   one or more respects.

-- A year or two of professional experience should be
   generally required for admission.
-- The schools offering programs should spell out clearly
   and in detail the nature of their programs, what they en-
   tail, what a student may expect to secure by enrolling,
   and what will be expected of him.
-- The schools should upgrade the educational attainment of
   their faculties to the end that, except under unusual and
   carefully evaluated circumstances, students at the sixth-
   year level will not be taught by instructors holding no
   degree higher than the B.L.S./M.L.S.

Harrison (H-6) and Dalton (D-4) agree with Danton (D-5) that the basic
concept is sound. Harrison sees two purposes for these "intermediate"
programs: 1) they afford an opportunity for some sort of specialization
not now provided at the basic master's level; and 2) they afford the practicing librarian who has been in the field for a while an opportunity for updating. Harrison opts for "advanced certificate" programs with specialization as their prime objectives, as this would serve the needs of librarians
in the field who are returning for refresher work in a special area. He
concludes:

> It seems, therefore, that there is a strong case for "advanced
> study in librarianship," quite apart from doctoral study (with
> "research" as a necessary concomitant). It may be the only
> solution to the problem of specialization. It surely has a
> tremendous potential in "continuing" and professional education.
> It will only play its proper part, however, if its real purposes
> are determined beforehand, if it is coordinated with the basic
> programs, and if the schools recognize that they must have
> adequate resources in terms of faculty, materials and accommoda-
> tions before they decide to embark upon such programs. In the
> United States there are ominous signs of advanced non-doctoral
> programs becoming the poor relation within the household....

Dalton identifies the most pressing problem facing American librarianship
as upgrading our "advanced study" programs to the stage where they will
be able to produce and provide places for those who are "prepared to commit
themselves deeply to the job of sifting, reviewing, and synthesizing
information, i.e., to handling information with sophistication and meaning"
as described in the Weinberg Report (S-15) and in Overhage's (O-16)
article in the February 17, 1967, issue of Science. Dalton (D-4:327) concludes:

160

Our advanced study programs are, of course, not very far
advanced. When they are, they will produce and provide
places for the kind of people described above. These people
are available and will be available in increasing numbers.
We have before us a job of selective recruiting at a high level.
We have done very little of this kind of recruiting and it will
not be easy to persuade the people we need most. But we
know we need them, even if our vision of the promised land
we are offering them is still a little cloudy.

Here lies the most pressing problem facing American librarianship today.

As a result of their survey of a cross-section of federal librarians,
Kortendick and Stone (K-31) recommended that the library school-based
post-Master's program should be recognized as the primary method
for upgrading and updating the profession. This was based on the character of the educational needs found in their study. They make recommendations on the form (K-31:286-292) and content (K-31:292-307) of
this type of program.

In addition to post-Master's programs using traditional course formats,
the library schools have been actively engaged in holding workshops, short
courses and institutes, and conferences. The extent to which these are
being used at the present time is partially   indicated in a later section of
this chapter. Over-all the extent of such offerings can be surmised by
studying the lists of continuing education opportunities in librarianship
which were initiated in 1964 by Reed (R-5, R-6, R-8) and published by the
U. S. Office of Education; and, since 1967-68 have been published by the
American Library Association (A-43; A-46; A-47; A-48) in varying forms,
the latest of which is issuance in American Libraries (A-44).

In spite of the efforts of the library schools in providing sixth-year post-
Master's programs and workshops, short courses, institutes, and conferences, the participation in these programs by practicing librarians has
not been great. For example, in   Kortendick and Stone (K-31:283) it is
reported that only 15% of the 365 librarians indicated that they had taken
six credit hours or more since receiving their MLS degree; 28% had taken
a workshop and/or less than six credit hours; and 57% had taken no formal
course or workshop of any kind.

161

In spite of their previous lack of participation, 70 per cent of the respondents indicated that they needed and would take courses in a workshop format; 51% checked that they would take a course later; 33% said they were interested in a one-year post-MLS program. If respondents indicate a need for updating and upgrading -- 49% said that they lacked courses that would have been of use to them on their jobs; 22% stated that because of deficiencies in training they were not performing duties in their jobs which they felt were required -- the question arises: Why has there been so little participation in continuing education activities as provided by the schools?

Indications of lack of support in the Kortendick and Stone study (K-31:282) cluster around such practical considerations of content not directly related to job needs, lack of financial support and leaves of absence, poor accessibility, and inflexible scheduling.

In a survey of a cross section of all types of librarians, Stone (S-72:180-184) reported that MLS practicing librarians felt that library schools were not giving enough serious thought to their roles in continuing education. There was a consensus that the schools should continually adapt the curriculum to behavioral, societal, and technological advances and provide courses needed by the participants in their present jobs. They felt whatever was offered should be: interdisciplinary in its scope; flexible and not bound by insistence upon credits or advanced degrees; accessible to all regardless of geographic location. Generally the plea was knowledge for the sake of doing a better job. The following responses were typical (S-72:183):

-- Find the real needs of alumni and then concentrate on those, not proliferate courses and workshops that are of dubious value.
-- It's EDUCATION, not CREDITS, that is important.
-- I wrote for four library-school catalogs recently and found only one course that a professional person who had been in the field for some time would have been interested in.

In summary it seems that the same problems that face other professions are present in continuing library education, only to a greater degree. Some of the chief issues around which problems arise are: 1) failure to identify needs to be met; 2) failure to present content related to identified needs; 3) failure to be flexible in dealing with the credit versus non-credit approach; 4) failure to make programs offered easily accessible and/or convenient to practicing librarians; 5) failure to accept continuing education as a major responsibility of the library school. There is little evidence

162

of active interface between library schools and libraries toward building purposive interrelations in order to jointly solve continuing library education problems.

The Place of Continuing Education in Academic Activities

Continuing Education for R&D Careers (C-24:150) sought academic points of view on continuing education from 71 academic persons in 24 schools by means of face-to-face interviews. As those interviewed included Vice Presidents, Deans and Associate Deans, Directors of Centers for Continuing Education, as well as Department Chairman in scientific fields, it would seem that the data obtained concerning the place of continuing education in academic activities would be fairly representative of continuing education in academic institutions generally. Therefore, the findings presented in this study in this regard are presented in some detail. In order to determine if these same opinions regarding the place of continuing education in academic institutions were shared by library science faculties, many of the same questions were posed to the representatives of the Continuing Library Education Network (Appendix K) by means of a mail questionnaire. The results of that survey are reported in the next section.

The R and D careers study (C-24:151) found that in general, the academic institutions conceived their primary function to be training students for degrees and generating new knowledge through research. Both were found to have priority over continuing education. All but five of the 24 schools admitted non-degree students to regular university credit courses. It was generally felt, however, that no modification should be made in the courses to meet the needs and objectives of continuing education as that would tend to weaken the standards of the degree-seeking programs. The study found that just admitting students to regular courses required nothing extra of the university and was therefore considered as a minimal level of continuing education activity for the college or university.

The study considered schools "active" relative to continuing education if they offered short intensive courses, in-lab courses, seminars, symposia, and non-credit courses specifically designed for practitioners who wanted to continue their education. Out of the 24 schools in the study, 12 were considered active by this standard. Usually the decision by the schools not to educate at an active level had been made by the faculty based on the reasoning that it was wisest not to dilute the main objectives -- degree granting and research.

163

It was found that in the active schools degree granting and research were still primary, but continuing education had a "respectable second place." (C-24:157).

Both "active" and "inactive" schools found it unsatisfactory to offer credit courses in the work place. The reasons given for this were: 1) students were not the same; 2) management tends to be less selective about who is admitted; 3) faculty inevitably change their standards of student performance when meeting off campus; 4) enrollments tend to be disappointing, leading academicians to say that employers have not adequately defined their needs. These and other reasons have resulted in colleges and universities concentrating their continuing education efforts in non-credit courses on campus (C-24:158).

The study (C-24:159) also found that different standards prevailed in non-credit courses on the campus.

> Non-credit courses...do not typically demand any specific
> level of student achievement: grades are not given, credit
> is not given, and whether or not the student learns only he
> himself can judge. "Success" seems to mean capacity enroll-
> ment, expressions of satisfaction from the students (and possibly
> also from their employers), and impressions of faculty that
> the non-credit course did, indeed, convey at least some learning
> to some of the student s.

It is realistic to think that different standards should exist for non-credit courses, but as pointed out in the study, there are few, if any, standards being applied at present to various modes of non-credit continuing education. This lack becomes greater as new educational techniques such as tele-lecture, electro-writer, and other audio-visual media are developed and a decision has to be made whether or not they are suitable and effective for continuing education purposes. "Without evidence on the effective-ness of present teaching methods in non-credit courses, it cannot be determined if newer instructional aids contribute or fail to contribute to continuing education"(C-24:159).

Another area in which the university should assume leadership, according to the R & D study, is in meeting the standards of quality for short intensive courses and for non-credit courses of longer duration.

However, the study concluded that colleges and universities cannot be expected to supply all the effort in continuing education.

Rather, continuing education . . . should be a <u>collaborative</u> effort
between universities training professionals, the societies which
represent their interests, their employers, and the professional
person himself. What the university faculty can contribute to
this collaborative effort is not only their knowledge and experience
with teaching but also their knowledge and experience in experimenting with, studying, and evaluating the modes and methods
of learning (C-24:160).

One of the main failures brought out by the R and D study was "a failure to
distinguish the need for advanced degrees from refresher, upgrading, and
diversification objectives of continuing education" (C-24:162). They found that
university credit courses were still being relied upon to satisfy both objectives, but that other modes of continuing education are necessary to
provide an adequate range of opportunities for practitioners. According to
the R & D study (C-24:162), "distinguishing degree-seeking from continuing education objectives is essential to clarifying needs in continuing
education. "

The academicians interviewed in the study insisted that more released
time from work activities will have to be given by employers if continuing
education efforts are to be successful. Ideally the university and the
employer should collaborate on a long-range basis in the planning for continuing education. On the basis of those interviewed, it was found that four
conditions must exist in order for academic institutions to enter into
collaborative continuing education arrangements with employing institutions
(C-24:165-66):

1.   Adequate <u>financing</u>, generally by the employer....
      Continuing education activities must be fully supported,
      not subsidized by the university.

2.   Academic <u>merit</u>, which means that the continuing education
      activity involves a learning experience which faculty regard
      as worthwhile to the student and which results in benefits
      to his employer through his increased competence on the job.

3.   Mutual <u>benefit</u>, that is, the university faculty must regard
      the continuing education activity as consistent with their
      image as educators and as providing some kind of feedback
      and teaching experience of benefit to them as teachers.
      They must also have the freedom to prepare and present
      themselves and their material in a way consistent with their
      standards and values.

4. Adequate staffing with persons who, in the opinion of the university faculty, are qualified to teach continuing education courses. However,   persons need not all be university-connected people, providing academic credit   not involved.

A topic that received a great deal of attention in the R & D study (C-24:166) was the matter of financing. Money given by employers for continuing education is regarded as "soft"money in that no   long-range commitment is usually made to the university; to make long-range plans involving the employment of faculty, it is necessary to have money available on a continuing basis. This is one reason why short-term courses are so popular -- no long-range commitment is involved and the courses are priced to pay for themselves. The study (C-24:167) suggests that all schools cannot afford to serve all continuing education needs and that diversity should be encouraged in two directions: 1) programs designed for general consumption such as short-term courses and 2) specific collaborative arrangements between individual employers and universities.

In summary, the R & D study (C-24:167-168) concluded that one of the most basic changes that will have to take place before continuing education receives the emphasis that it needs is

... to incorporate into the university reward system acknowledgement that continuing education is a respectable and reputable career line for academic faculty. At present, the interviews with academicians imply an underlying assumption that such activities are somehow second-rate and do not merit, or at least do not receive, the same rewards of prestige and promotion which accrue to faculty who do research, publish, and teach degree-seeking students. In other words, the place of continuing education in academic efforts at present is contingent on individual faculty members sacrificing the rewards of the academic system or squeezing continuing education efforts into the myriad of other activities demanded of them. This is one side of the coin.

The other is the general down-grading of non-credit activities in the spectrum of university teaching relative to courses in the regular cucricula. Yet there is general agreement that continuing education must be non-credit (for the most part) in order to develop formats which are more flexible than university credit courses in meeting individual's needs.

166

Specific recommendations are made in the R & D study concerning the place of continuing education in academic activities (C-24:168-69):

> Further research is needed on what standards should be applied to non-credit course work modes of continuing education along with investigation of the amount and quality of learning actually taking place in these modes . . .

> Universities and colleges should accept leadership in developing, evaluating, and experimenting with, new methods of instruction in order to explore their potential usefulness in the field of continuing education.

> Employers must be prepared to increase the amount of released time of employees to engage in continuing education in order to take advantage of appropriate modes of continuing education which are available only or primarily at times other than evenings and weekends. In the opinion of some experienced academicians, effective new options in continuing education may require one day a week, one weekend a month, or other time periods away from work at a university. While released time is a matter of employer policy, its relevance to university efforts is such that without it universities are effectively stymied in experimenting with varying-size blocks of time.

The study also recommends, as noted earlier, diversity in continuing education efforts on the part of the schools. This diversity should be encouraged in two ways: 1) programming activities for practitioners generally, and 2) development of collaborative relationships with specific employers which will mutually benefit the school and the employer. Special emphasis is placed in these collaborative arrangements on the need for long-range planning. This is coupled with the need for long-range financial support of universities by employers if universities are to commit themselves heavily to continuing education programming.

And finally the R & D Study recommends "that the search for new and different educational techniques and modes be continued in order to maximize the alternatives available" to practitioners (C-24:169).

The Place of Continuing Education in ALA Accredited Library Schools and their Parent Institutions

Next, attention is given to answers to a questionnaire developed by the AALS Standing Committee on Continuing Library Education and sent to the 57 accredited library schools as of August, 1972 by this reviewer (S-76), as part of the work of the AALS Standing Committee on Continuing Library Education (See Appendix L for full statistical tabulation of the questionnaire used). There was a considerable amount of unevenness in the replies returned; some forms were filled out in great detail, others were minimally answered. In reading the results of the survey it needs to be borne in mind that the findings represent only 56% of the library schools to whom the questionnaire was sent, and that there was a wide variation in the amount of data reported. Therefore the report can be taken only as an indication of the current status of continuing education as it exists in the accredited library schools, not as a definitive picture of the total continuing education philosophy and activities in library schools today.

Out of the 32 reporting schools, 26 indicated that they offered formal courses for credit to practitioners interested in continuing education. Some schools indicated that their offering formal courses simply meant that they admitted non-degree students to regular university credit courses. The data collected did not make it possible to tell how many of the formal courses were designed solely for practitioners at the post-Master's level.

According to the R & D Study criteria (schools offering modes other than formal courses for credit), 30 of the 32 schools would fall in the "active" category as they sponsored various modes of continuing education in addition to formal courses -- workshops, seminars, institutes, or conferences. The least popular mode was the non-credit course, with only seven schools reporting activity in this mode. This lack of use of the non-credit course would seem to imply a lack of experiementation in developing formats which are more flexible than university credit courses in meeting the individual's needs in continuing education.

Taking all the modes together, the highest concentration of single offerings was in 1) multi-media, 2) school/media librarianship, and 3) administration and management. When the 200 different offerings were divided into high categories or fields, the highest number of offerings were in 1) types of librarianship, 2) user services, and 3) administration.

One of the major criticisms by the R & D Study of continuing education programs sponsored by colleges and universities was the fact that there was no diversification of objectives between degree programs and continuing education programs. Out of the 32 reporting library schools, two schools submitted tentative policy statements which showed that separate continuing education objectives had been established; three other schools stated that committees had been formed to work

168

out comprehensive statements; another school reported that the library school was cooperating with the total university in working out a policy statement which would include a statement of philosophy and objectives for the whole university, including the development of standards. On the whole, the other statements were rather vague or informal. Typical statements were "nebulous, not defined" or "objectives have never been made explicit." The specific item mentioned most often (by 7 of the schools) was "meeting the needs of alumni and librarians by providing further study."

The decision to engage in continuing education or not to engage in continuing education was most frequently made by the faculty collectively, by faculty committees, or individual faculty action. This is important to note because it would seem to indicate that it offered the opportunity for schools to be innovative and experimental in their approaches, whereas the format, procedures, policies relative to advanced degree programs are generally firmly fixed by the university and are not subject to much variation. It also points up the fact that certain evaluative standards are necessary to insure quality programs.

The discontinuance of programs also seems to be left mainly to the school and faculty action. This decision is influenced, of course, by the enrollment since tuition is the main way of financing continuing education programs. The next most often mentioned means of financing programs was outside (including federal) grants. Five schools said that there was some provision for continuing education activities in the department's budget. Only one school mentioned the type of financing particularly recommended by the R & D Study, namely long-range financial support by employers. The one instance of this mentioned was a state Department of Libraries.

The R & D Study also found that one of the greatest impediments to the development of continuing education in academic institutions was the underlying assumption in the university reward system that continuing education activities are somehow second-rate; consequently, faculty members do not receive the same rewards or prestige as do those engaged in teaching degree students, publishing, or doing research. In relation to this problem, ten of the 32 library schools replied that there was nothing in the reward structure for recognizing participation in continuing education activities. Eleven comments were made indicating that continuing education activity was taken into consideration when salaries, promotions, etc. were being determined; nine comments indicated that lack of participation would be held against the faculty member, and implied that such participation was expected.

The respondents to the questionnaire were asked to react to the conclusions that were reached in the R & D Study regarding status of continuing education on

169

university campuses. The results are summarized in Appendix L, Table XVII. On the campuses in which the 32 participating library schools are located there seemed to be a more appreciative attitude evident toward continuing education activities than in 1969 when the R & D Study was made. However, the respondents did indicate that "Faculty members have to squeeze continuing education efforts into the myriad of other activities demanded of them." There also seemed to be a lack of long-range planning for continuing education in collaborative arrangements with professional associations, employing institutions, or other professional groups. This was more pronounced, according to the respondents, for the universities as a whole than for the library schools themselves. Generally, the replies received seem to indicate that continuing education has greater status and recognition in library science than in other places on the campus.

Taking the overall responses to the questionnaire there seemed to be a lack of emphasis on collaborative arrangements in continuing education activities between the schools and the library employers. On the basis of answers, one condition exists which is important in producing the spirit and attitude of cooperation which makes specific continuing education activities easier to establish in the future. This condition is the use of faculty in continuing education efforts off-campus.

Exchange of personnel was reported as taking the form of working with local library systems (4 schools listed); serving as consultant for workshops and special continuing education projects outside the university (2 schools listed); faculty involved with state library association on continuing education activities (6 schools listed); making surveys (3 schools); serving as consultant to director of state continuing education program (2 schools listed).

One form of collaboration is "released time" on the part of the employer. Released time generally refers to hours off the job, away from work, spent at the university on a regular recurring basis. One respondent wrote concerning the importance of this type of interface between the university and the employer:

> The major problem in regard to continuing education for librarians is the fact that librarians have little, if any, incentive to continue their education. Unlike teachers, they seldom receive salary increases because they have taken additional courses. Libraries must not only provide salary increases, but they must also give librarians time off to take additional courses. Libraries as well as the librarians benefit from programs of continuing education.

170

Another type of collaboration emphasized by Houle (H-37) and Allen (A-14) is between the professions. There were questions in the survey dealing with the interface with other professional groups on the campus. Eighteen of the 32 schools responding indicated that they discussed continuing education with those in other professional programs on campus. Eight said they did not, three said they did sometimes. Thirteen said they attended planning sessions of other professional groups on campus; eleven said they did not; 2 indicated they did "to some extent"' and two others said they did "rarely, not regularly."

On campus there seemed to be a mutual effort to keep the different schools aware of what was being done in continuing education. This effort was carried on through distribution of newsletters, extension bulletins, and other publications. Twenty-four schools said they were aware of what other professionally-oriented groups were doing on campus in the area of continuing education and two additional schools answered "somewhat" to this question.

The question relative to interface with other professional groups on campus asked in what ways library school personnel interacted or thought it would be beneficial to interact with other professional continuing education programs on campus. The activity that was mentioned the most often in this regard was participation in a campus continuing education advisory council. Mentioned next most frequently was increased awareness, pooling of resources, additional concern for bigger total program. Four respondents, however, indicated that they could not see benefit from campus interaction; they thought it better to interact with the profession. In this regard one school stated, "Each college 'does its own thing' -- little related to our interests."

Houle (H-37) recommends that members of each profession should not act as though they alone had any need of continuing education and should drop the assumption that their processes and needs are wholly unique. Such inter-professional efforts, also advocated by Allen (A-14), would, according to Houle, lead to important consequences for our society. It would seem that the campus would offer an excellent opportunity to start such cooperation, and that the time is ripe for innovation in this type of cooperative programming in continuing education.

In library literature there has been some criticism of the fact that the faculty members themselves should be participating in continuing education (Martin, M-31). In answer to the question whether there were any specific requirements regarding the continuing education of faculty members, the largest response, listed 21 times, was "No."

For examples of continuing education activities for faculty members on the art of effective teaching in another profession, engineering, the reader is referred

171

to articles cited in the bibliography by the Committee on Measurement of Teaching of the Association of Engineering Education (A-80), Dabney (D-1), Foecke (F-12), Kraybill (K-35: K-36); Lancaster (L-1). An interesting group in engineering that Kraybill (K-36) states has been particularly instrumental in improving teaching in that profession is the Committee for Young Engineering Teachers. Since its founding in 1950, this group has sponsored an array of activities designed to improve teaching including: the design of effective evaluation practices; design of teaching objectives; workshops before annual meetings; inservice training programs sponsored in cooperation with Colleges of Education; and perhaps most impressive a series of summer institutes on effective teaching.

The final question stated that higher education design patterns are in the process of transition today on a nationwide scale. It asked: "On your campus, do you observe indications of a change in role or a trend toward loosening up in the offering of continuing education opportunities to professional groups or individuals?" Only three schools stated that no drastic changes were seen. The variations of the other affirmative answers are presented in Table XVIII of Appendix L.

One respondent mentioned a problem relative to more continuing education which is probably widespread:

> We can offer 1-2 day institutes, workshops, clinics, etc., as we see it. The administration favors them.....But where, oh, where, do you get typists, artists, stamp stickers, ticket designers, address finders, etc., etc., in a fully loaded semester? These facilities or aids do not exist in any great number -- and they are vital. We can find experts or do the program ourselves. It is everything else that kills the desire.

In spite of this handicap, it seems clear that except in a very few instances the respondents were in agreement that on their campuses there were observable indications of a change in role or a tendency toward loosening up in the offering of continuing education opportunities to professional groups or individuals.

Conclusion

Based on the material presented in this chapter, it would seem that the universities should consider the following suggestions regarding continuing library education:

1. A clear distinction should probably be made between the objectives for doctoral study which is oriented toward research and the objectives of "advanced specialist" and other continuing education programs, which are functionally oriented toward

172

the participant's professional objectives, even as has
been done in other professions, such as engineering
(See Chapter II, Figure 1, "The Dual Roles of Formal
and Continuing Education").

2. Closer relationships should be developed with libraries
    and professional associations so that continuing education
    needs may be more clearly defined.

3. In addition to offering programs to practicing librarians
    on campus, collaborative arrangements should be worked
    out with libraries. On their side, libraries should provide
    released time to employees to participate in university-
    sponsored programs.

4. Continuing education should be given equal status with degree
    programs and research oriented activity.

5. The reward system in the university should include recognition
    for continuing library education activity on a par with degree
    and research oriented programs.

6. Research should be sponsored in the following areas:

    a. The standards that should be applied to continuing education
       programs, especially non-credit programs.
    b. The relative efficiency of different modes of continuing
       education, especially non-credit programs.
    c. The effectiveness of new instructional methods as they can
       be applied to continuing education, especially television,
       Cable TV, programmed instruction.
    d. The factors involved in motivating librarians to participate
       in continuing education.

173

VII. THE MODES OF CONTINUING EDUCATION

This chapter highlights some of the extensive literature on three grouped modes of continuing education and two specialized modes. The grouped modes are: 1) course work and related modes; 2) interaction modes; and 3) self teaching modes. The specialized modes are the continuing education center concept and the staff college.

The Continuing Continuing Education for the Public Service report (I-4:34-35) points out some of the criticisms of the various formats of continuing education. "There is widespread dissatisfaction with present methodologies. There were also frequent censorious comments concerning the instructional techniques which now characterize continuing education." The report goes on to state that those administrators offering training programs utilizing the most modern concepts and instructional techniques are most critical of those programs which rely on the simple lecture method as the main means of instruction. The report (I-4:45) cites Frank Sherwood, Executive Director of the Federal Executive Institute, as stating that most continuing education has been conducted:

> . . . exactly like a high school class. An expert is put at the head
> of the room, expected to convey his information to the less informed,
> and to take responsibility for the transmission process. The
> vehicle of communication is typically a lecture -- generally judged
> the worst possible way to get across information. . . . this
> traditional approach to learning reinforces behaviors that I be-
> lieve are antithetical to effective performance in an organization . . .
> [continuing education] ought to emphasize the assumption of
> responsibility for the learning, the implications of inter-dependency,
> the ambiguity of data as it applies to a given situation; and, the
> requirements for efficiency in the adult learning process.

Frequently mentioned shortcomings found in a review of continuing education listed   by the report (I-4:45-56) are "a failure to (a) provide an inter-disciplinary curriculum, (b) incorporate the latest conceptual insights and methodological approaches such as systems analysis, (c) tap the special expertise of the practitioner and (d) uninspiring formats and presentations of material."

The Continuing Continuing Education for the Public Service report (I-4:34-35) also emphasizes:

> An unshakeable conclusion from the field is the unanimous rejection of residence on the campus for extended periods of time. This universal opinion stems from a variety of reasons.... The Institute concludes that the belief is so strongly and prevalently held, that the University must accept this as a constraint within which to mold its continuing education programs. . .

The Institute proceeds to recommend (I-4:35) that models should be studied and replicated which both satisfy the academic desire for excellence and recognize the inability of the practitioner to leave work for extended periods of residence on campus.

Course Work Modes of Continuing Education

University Credit Courses Designed for the Degree-Seeking Student

The literature seems to indicate that the most common form of continuing education engaged in by all kinds of professional practitioners seeking continuing education is the university credit course designed for the degree-seeking student. These courses, offered by a college or university, are identical to those offered to degree-seeking students and the practitioner is participating in classes with the degree-seeking students. Because they are part of degree programs, these courses meet the requirements of academic standards. Students, whether or not they are seeking degrees, must meet admissions requirements before registering. These courses assign grades based on examinations or other requirements as a measure of student performance.

Because university credit courses have developed standards and adhere to them, they set a norm by which other course work modes are measured. The R & D study (C-24:63) found that practitioners tend to judge the effectiveness of other course work modes by comparing them to university credit courses.

In the AALS Continuing Education Survey (S-76), referred to in the last chapter, it was found that 26 of the 32 reporting schools admitted non-degree students to regular university credit courses.

175

The chief advantages in the university credit course as a mode of continuing education would seem to be that learning is presented in a logical and systematic fashion and that greater discipline is placed on the continuing student than in any other mode.

The R & D Study (C-24:66-69) points out some serious disadvantages, however, chief of which are:

    1)   The university credit course is not apt to have much emphasis on the frontiers of new knowledge, but rather   concentration is on background and basic materials.

    2)   They present physical barriers, such as travel time and scheduling problems, as the majority are scheduled during daytime hours.

    3)   There is a social-psychological barrier of being in credit classes with younger students because the practitioner feels he may not be able to show up well because of not having studied recently, and not having background information that all the others in the class may have.

    4)   The continuing education student may not have the prerequisites demanded of the degree-seeking student. If he obtains a waiver he is then inadequately prepared to do the same standard of work.

In conclusion it would seem that the regular university credit courses have many disadvantages for the continuing education students. Ways need to be found to overcome the physical and psychological barriers involved.

University Credit Courses Designed for the Continuing Education Student

A variant of the university credit courses designed for degree-seeking students is the university credit course designed for practitioners at the post-master's level. In library science, examples of this type of course are found at The Catholic University of America where three courses are offered which were based on a study of job dimensions and needs of practicing librarians at the middle- and upper-level positions (K-31). They are in automation of library processes, the development of human resources in libraries, and the administration of the special library. The advantages of such specially designed courses are:

    1.   Students are learning together with other practitioners and feel freer to enter into discussions and participate in other instructional modes on an equal basis with other practitioners, who have also been out of school for a while but have the same basic background of training.

2. Because content is built on basic fundamentals already mastered, there is more opportunity to experiment with newer and varied teaching methods such as simulation, case studies, games, etc. And, as a matter of fact, practicing librarians indicated that they expect such courses to use new methods of instruction (K-31:201).

3. They can be scheduled at a time that is convenient for working librarians.

4. As credit is given and classes are held within the university, the same standards of performance can be required both from teachers and students as for degree-seeking students.

5. Credit given for these courses may be applied toward a specialist certificate.

The chief disadvantages would seem to be: 1) giving enough time to promotion of such courses so that enough students will be found to enroll to enable the university to at least break even on the courses and be willing to continue to offer them, and 2) travel time for those not located close to a university offering such opportunities.

The credit course designed especially for the practicing librarian at the post-MLS level would seem to be especially valuable as a continuing education mode and one that should be offered at all library schools concerned with continuing education.

The number of these courses offered by library schools specifically designed to meet the needs of practitioners and offered exclusively to them (as opposed to degree-seeking students) is not known, but indications are that they are few in number.

Non-Credit, Employer-Sponsored Courses
This reviewer was not able to locate any statistics indicating the number of or evaluation of non-credit courses sponsored by employing libraries. This is a form of continuing education, however, that is used in other professions with varying degrees of success. The R & D Study (C-24: 69-77) summarizes the advantages and disadvantages of the non-credit course offered by employers.

The perceived advantages of the non-credit employer-sponsored courses are:

177

1.   Courses can be oriented and directly applicable to the needs of the work situation.

2.   Because all students are in the same work situation and share a common background, discussion of problems in class are more meaningful.

3.   They are convenient to take -- present no travel problems.

4.   They do not present the same social and physiological barriers to older employees that enrolling in a university course does. They are with colleagues who recognize and respect their position and experience and give deference to it in the class situation.

5.   They need not conform to arbitrary time periods, such as quarters or semesters.

6.   They are usually taught by practitioners who are more familiar with actual on-the-job learning needs.

7.   They appear to be an excellent mode for meeting the refresher and updating objectives of continuing education.

The disadvantages would seem to center around the following factors:

1.   Less content is usually covered in the same amount of time than in university credit courses.

2.   Standards are not so high and student performance is less demanding.

3.   Most employees have no long-range planned or systematic system for continuing education.

4.   The students and the teachers tend to be of a homogeneous nature and this tends to narrow the training received and lessen the enrichment from other disciplines.

5.   If many programs are offered, it tends to exclude the perceived necessity for other forms of continuing education.

6.   The employees can't count on systematic scheduling. Many courses seem to be one-shot offerings which are seldom, if ever, repeated.

7.   There is a lack of regular evaluation.

In summary, non-credit employer-sponsored courses seem to hold particular
value to meet the refresher and updating needs of practitioners if reasonable
standards are set and continuing effort is given to their planning and evaluation. Many criticisms have been made of the courses for not being demanding enough (C-24:86).

Short Intensive Courses
Short intensive courses, usually sponsored by academic institutions
or professional societies, require full-time study. Usually they are non-
credit, but if university sponsored can offer credit. Usually participants
are away from home and away from work. Courses can vary in duration from
a few days to six weeks, or can be spread over a longer period of time by
having short periods of intensive study interspersed with periods of independent
study by the participant at home. They are used for refresher and updating
purposes as well as for new advances in the state of the art.

As summarized by the R & D Study, these courses have the following
characteristics (C-24:77-78):

1.   The individual registrant is free from the demands of his work,
and, if away from home, from family and civic responsibilities also.

2.   The course consists of lectures interspersed with discussions
...supplemented by reading materials from which assignments are
commonly given.

3.   Fairly rigid schedules are maintained, and typically there is
somewhat more subject matter planned than can be comfortably
fitted into the time allowed. That is, these courses are fast-paced.

4.   There are usually no examinations, grades, or other
measures of student performance.

5.   Certificates of completion are given to registrants
who complete the course.

6.   These courses are relatively expensive per man for the
employer, because of the fee and the loss of productive work time.

There seems to be a trend toward developing a wide variety of formats for
the short intensive course, with great experimentation in differing time

periods. Some suggested models that are academically sound, but vary from traditional patterns, are reviewed in the Continuing Continuing Education . . . report (I-4:35-43). One pattern that seems to be growing in popularity is the short course meeting periodically rather than concentrating all of the course work in one block of time.

One shortcoming of many short courses is the difficulty in obtaining enough accurate detailed information about the courses for the individual to be able to ascertain in advance whether the course will be capable of meeting his needs. A systematic examination of 125 brochures about short courses reported in the R & D Study (C-24:83-84) revealed the same type of characteristics that are found in the examination of many library science short courses, namely: 1) the course is described in general terms only; 2) the description is apt to be one or two paragraphs at most; 3) there is usually no statement of desirable prerequisites; 4) there is no indication of advance preparation that would be advantageous in taking the course; 5) there is a lack of any statement of continuing education objectives -- whether the course is for updating, presenting new knowledge, etc.

Another shortcoming sometimes cited is that such courses are so intensive in their format that there is not enough time to absorb all the material and less is learned than when the course is spread out over a longer period of time. One solution to this might well be the suggestion of required prerequisites which would make the absorption of material easier in spite of the concentrated format of presentation.

Certainly, a major recommendation regarding short courses would be the maintenance of a central clearinghouse which would be able to supply information on these courses well in advance of the time of their being offered. In chemistry, this type of listing in found in Chemical and Engineering News, published by the American Chemical Society; in dentistry, it is provided by the American Dental Association's quarterly, Continuing Education, both of which members receive on a regular basis.

Interaction Modes of Continuing Education

This section presents comments on four interaction modes of continuing education which have in common the fact that they have some degree of interaction among colleagues and they are chiefly used as a process of keeping up to date on new developments as they take place. These modes are particularly valuable in providing the motivation and stimulation which sustain intellectual interest in the job situation and to those engaged in research it is an invaluable way of learning of new developments before they are reflected in the literature.

In considering the value of interaction modes of continuing education, one needs to keep in mind the definition that is accepted for continuing education. If it is limited to enhancement of job competence -- to what relates to the present job or to work anticipated in the short term future -- much that is learned from interaction may be of general value or useful at some future date, but not specifically job related.

On the basis of 205 interviews, the Continuing Education for R & D Careers report (C24:91) presents a chart which specifies five specific objectives of interaction modes of continuing education: further study, understanding, applications, decisions, keeping current, as presented in Table 1 . All of these uses of interaction are able to save time for the individual. They also tend to provide stimulation to the individual in his job situation by providing new ideas and concepts as well as giving a sense of security that the participant is in the mainstream of developments in his field of work.

Attending Professional Meetings

Generally throughout the continuing education literature it is stated that an important means of keeping up to date is attendance at professional meetings; that one of the main objectives of professional associations is to keep attendees informed on recent and current developments. Houle (H-36 and quoted in Chapter IV), speaking to the Midwinter Conference of Librarians in 1967, asserted:

> The professional association crowns all other efforts at continuing education and bears the chief collective responsibility for it.... a manifest function of every professional association is the continuing education of its membership; indeed, scarcely any other function is more manifest and has a longer tradition than this one. (H-36:266)

The most detailed analysis of the value of conventions relative to their use as a source of information, their part in the function of dissemination of information, the type of information exchange at meetings, and the type of material disseminated at a large scientific meeting were found in Volume 1 of The American Psychological Association's Project on Scientific Information (A:53, Vol. 1). The four papers in this volume relative to conventions and their relation to information exchange in psychology provide excellent models for similar studies that might be undertaken by other professional associations, including library and information science conventions. For each paper the survey instruments that were used are appended.

TABLE 1

THE OBJECTIVES OF INTERACTION WITH COLLEAGUES

Objective	Information Given by Colleague Consulted	Function Served for Receiver Colleague
Further Study	Points out best or most pertinent sources of information	Saves having to examine other available sources for himself
Understanding	Gives instruction in pertinent knowledge needed to approach a problem or understand research results	Saves becoming expert in the field in which instruction is received
Applications	Gives information on which approaches have been tried by others and with what results	Saves having to test out possibly unfruitful approaches to his problem
Decisions	Gives opinion on one best approach to use; several colleagues can give confirmation of best approach through consensus	Saves having to test out other possible approaches through literature or direct experimentation
Keeping Current	Gives information on current status of own research and of that of others known to him	Saves waiting for publication; is immediately related to own work for guidance and for future reference as needed

Source: Continuing Education for R & D Careers. Washington, D.C.:
National Science Foundation, 1969 , p. 91.

One of the chief advantages of the professional association meetings is the opportunity that it provides for interaction on an informal face-to-face basis between others with the same interests. This value, however, is related to and largely dependent upon the scope and content of the programs presented. A 1967 study of MLS practicing librarians (Stone S-72:177-79) found that there was a strong expression from the respondents that library associations were not maximizing the benefits that might be derived from the professional association meeting because of (1) lack of meetings in which content holds a continuing education potential, (2) content that is presented in not of top quality, (3) lack of planned opportunities to discuss with colleagues ideas presented, (4) lack of systematic evaluation of programs presented, and (5) apparent lack of using feedback from programs presented in planning for future meetings.

Interviews with R & D personnel (C-24:95) led to the conclusion that attendance at professional meetings was not supported by employers "solely, and perhaps not even primarily" because of a desire to provide continuing education opportunities, but rather seemed to be a "reward" which goes with employment as a professional and tends to increase the stature of the individual attendee and add prestige to the organizations sending a large delegation to association meetings. From observation and informal interviews, this reviewer believes that the same conditions prevail generally in librarianship. These cannot be considered as continuing education objectives.

Invited Conferences

Invited conferences bring together "experts" in a given area for the express purpose of talking over their latest research results and problems being currently investigated in the field. Characteristics of such conferences are identified in the R&D Study (C-24:94) as:

1. Sponsorship by a special interest organization such as a laboratory, a government or government agency, a university, a professional society, or some combination of sponsors;
2. A limited audience, whose members are themselves specialized in the topic of the conference; an invitation is a badge of being recognized as an expert in the field;
3. A limited scope restricted to one specialized topic or field of research; and
4. Papers which are presented for discussion as much as for information; considerable time is allotted for exploration of ideas through discussion.

The invited conference is considered such an important means of continuing education in the R&D Study (C-24:95) that it was reported that all employers in the survey were willing to support the employee by giving him time to go and payment for transportation expenses. Uniformly invited conferences seem to have high value for continuing education of professionals. A major weakness is that the potential in a given profession is such that the number covered is small -- less than seven per cent of the interviewees in the R&D sample.

Although the "invited conference" meets the requirements for meeting continuing education objectives, this reviewer did not find evidences of its use as a means of continuing education in librarianship.

In-House Lectures and Seminars

Formal lectures followed by discussion period from the audience (usually referred to in the literature as lectures and/or seminars) constitute a mode of continuing education that is frequently sponsored by employers for professionals. The R&D Study (C-24:101) reports that in-house lectures are primarily valuable for keeping people up to date with the state of the art. One of the advantages of the in-house lecture is that it is a means of bringing all levels of employees into contact with leaders in the profession outside the employing institution.

The feeling that great use might be made of in-house lectures and seminars in libraries was reflected in the following comments which were received in a survey of all types of librarians by Stone (S-72:175):

> Staff meetings: should be conducted on a plane of growth...
> should make a difference...staff should be involved in the
> planning and discussion...means of keeping staff abreast
> of changes in profession...groups as a whole should
> determine which ideas will be incorporated into the library
> program.

Another respondent urged that:

> Some method should be devised so that staff members could
> get together for free exchange of ideas and to keep up to date.
> In-house seminars for dialogue among all interested staff
> members.

184

Although individual libraries report the use of in-house lectures by those from
without, particularly as programs for staff association meetings, no statistics
were located to indicate the extent of the use of in-house lectures and seminars
by employing libraries or any systematic evaluation of their effectiveness as a
mode of continuing education.

Leaves with Pay

Leaves with pay, because of their long-term nature, have the potential
of serving as a major avenue for continuing education. Corson and Paul (C-42:
155-57) maintain that there is an urgent need for the individual to develop in his
career by "stepping out" from his job after six to eight years and again later
after twelve to twenty years in order to replace old knowledge and old skills
with new. These authors argue that detachment from the customary environment
is a necessary condition for rigorous stocktaking of what an individual has learned
and underpinning of their personal philosophy in relation to their job.

The R& D Study (C-24:104) identifies two major types of leave with pay which were
granted by the agencies in that study:

1. Sabbatical leaves, which enable mature researchers to break away
    at some point in mid-career and expose themselves to the stimula-
    t ing and broadening effects of an altered environment. These
    leaves are primarily for refreshing and updating and may involve
    diversification into new fields which are extensions of past research
    interest.
2. Educational leaves which are used to facilitate work toward a
    degree, such as fulfillment of course requirements and/or prepara-
    tion of a dissertation. These leaves are primarily for upgrading
    and not for continuing education purposes of refreshing, updating,
    or keeping up to date. [Degree-seeking activities are not considered
    as continuing education as the term is defined in the R&D Study.]

The Library Education and Manpower Statement (A-42) says specifically that
library administrators are responsible for providing support for continuing education in the form of leaves, sabbaticals, and related time for their staffs. In spite
of this affirmation, there is little evidence of wide use of sabbatical leaves, which
enable a career person to leave the work place at some mid-point in their career
to engage in a planned program of study or to engage in research. Similarly, the
R&D Study (C-24:104-105) found that sabbatical leaves with pay were the least
used mode of continuing education, yet the management and personnel interviewed
regarded sabbatical leaves as "the most comprehensive way of obtaining in-depth

updating and refreshing in a field specialization" as well as "an excellent way of obtaining diversification into new fields of interest."

The R&D Study (C-24:105-107) stated that the most significant factor about management policies on sabbatical leaves with pay was that they are not written and there were no fixed rules for eligibility. Applicants had to seek leave for themselves and justify how the leave would help them in the on-the-job situation. Reasons for lack of written policies were found to be:

1. Leaves with pay are the most expensive mode of continuing education per man....
2. ...a man going on leave causes...loss of his productive work effort...
3. The number of persons supported on leaves is quite small....
4. By contrast, in both industry and government, more than twice as many people are supported on educational leaves to seek a degree than are supported on sabbatical leaves....
5. Also by contrast, management policies on educational leaves are generally written and formalized with rules governing eligibility and other matters....
6. Management is very selective about who goes on sabbatical leave....
7. Top managers also state that they rarely actively solicit personnel to go on leave.

In summary, it can be said that sabbatical leaves with pay not only help professionals keep up to date, but provide a revitalization and stimulation that is probably unequalled by most other forms of continuing education. However, the costs and the loss of production of the employee in his place of employment lead to the conclusion that it will probably never be a heavily used mode, except perhaps in the academic institution where the professional librarian has achieved faculty status, and the pattern is already firmly established. The mode would seem particularly suited to combine with the leave with pay in the staff college concept, which will be discussed as a separate mode later in this chapter. For a particular application of leaves with pay tied into a recognition system, see an account in Chapter III of the "Bank Account" Policy for Continuing Education as implemented by the Kimberly-Clark Corporation.

Self-Teaching Modes of Continuing Education

The seven modes of continuing education presented in this section -- oral communication, reading the literature, teaching, invisible colleges, papers and publications, research, and home study --rely chiefly on the initiative of the individual and his own motivation. They are not employer-centered.

Oral Communication

The most detailed record of oral dissemination of information was found in the two volumes of The American Psychological Association's Project on Scientific Information Exchange in Psychology (A-53). A random sample of 78 psychologists kept detailed logs of their scientific information activities during a two-week period. Relative to the oral dissemination of information it was reported (A-53, Vol. I:12-13):

> One of the most striking aspects of this log study is the prevalence of informal symposia, colloquia, seminars, research conferences and meetings for the purpose of information exchange. Of special interest is the "information man" who attends a large number of these, spending a good part of his time in travel and then in imparting the information gained from such sources to his research staff, his colleagues, and the students whose research he directs. He becomes, apparently, a kind of walking encyclopedia of methodology and current findings, and a 'directory' as well, who can refer his associates to those with relevant research currently underway. Nearly every minute of his working day, which often extends well into the night, is spent in discussion -- communicating the results of his own research, or that of his colleagues and students, to others and receiving the same kind of information from them. Back at his 'home base', the information he has gained places him in the role of consultant and advisor.

It was found that over 25% of the sample were identified as "information men" as described in the foregoing quotation from the report. Their role was found to be a vital one in the informal exchange of information, consuming so much of their time that less and less time was being used for their own research activities.

Reading the Literature

One of the most obvious modes of continuing education is the reading of journals, report literature, and books. In a study of all types of librarians (S-72:135) reading professional literature in library science and subject specialities was seen as the most important mode of continuing education.

In the R&D Study (C-24:114-122) it was found that 85 per cent of the participants ranked reading the literature as either first or second in importance in keeping

No other single means of continuing education was believed to be as important, even though the respondents found that the quantity of material now published made it an exceedingly frustrating task. It was found that the average amount of hours spent per week on work-related reading was about ten hours either on the job or at home. Because of time limitations the participants reported they were making considerable use of short-cuts to the literature: abstracts, indexes, bibliographies, information retrieval output, documentation centers, recent textbooks, and review papers. They expressed a need for more review papers.

With the heavy emphasis placed on reading in the R&D Study, it was natural to find that the library was an important resource to the engineers and scientists participating in the study. The study reported (C-24:122):

> Although 98 per cent of the scientists and engineers report that
> they make some use of the library, the extent of use depends on
> how the individual views it as an up-to-date resource, the
> amount of time he has available for its use, as well as his own
> motivation and interest, and the distance it is from his place of work.

The study concluded that the library was not only an important resource for reading activity, but it provided a source of motivation to the employees by providing short-cuts to the literature and cutting down on the amount of material that had to be personally inspected.

In the American Psychological Association's Project on Scientific Information Exchange in Psychology (A-53, Vol. 1: 14), it was found that the 78 participants in the study spent a median of seven hours per week reading for the acquisition of information. The reading patterns showed wide variation, however, and varied from zero to fifty hours. It was interesting to note that three of the eight non-readers were the "information man" type identified above in the oral interaction section, who spent their time acquiring information by attending meetings and conferences and spreading the information to those with whom they came in contact.

A study of MLS librarians (S-72:69;197-198) found that respondents read an average of 3.5 library journals regularly, while one non-library professional journal was read regularly. The median number of books read in librarianship was between two and three; the median of books read in areas of subject specialization was four. Twenty five per cent had read no books at all in librarianship during the year preceding the study and 22 per cent had read no books in the area of their subject specialization. Fifty eight per cent did not read non-library professional journals regularly. Although it is not justifiable to draw specific conclusions for the whole profession from this one sample, it is obvious that librarians were not nearly as active in reading the literature relating to their work as were those reported on in the R&D study and in the study of psychologists mentioned above.

In an earlier study Bundy (B-40:418) commented on the lack of interest in non-library professional journals when she surveyed public library administrators' opinions of professional periodicals:

> As people whose business is the dissemination of information, one
> might have expected librarians to make more use of printed infor-
> mation from other fields. One suggestion afforded by this study
> is that the library periodicals might help to broaden the view of the
> library administrator by calling his attention to outside literature
> which has applications to librarianship -- and library schools
> might do more to introduce students to the literature in these areas.

A suggestion afforded by the present study is that librarians might provide services to librarians the same as for other professionals, rather than expect that because an individual is a librarian he has time to ferret out all information for himself. Librarians need time-saving methods in their continuing education efforts just as other professionals do.

Invisible Colleges

De Solla Price and Beaver (D-14), in American Psychologist, have identified the invisible college as a loosely knit group of people who meet together, correspond with each other, read papers to each other, circulate reprints, and generally stimulate one another through mixed collaboration and competition. Other names by which these groups can be identified in the literature are "journal clubs" and "grass roots seminars."

The R&D Study (C-24:125) reported that when the study was planned and the questionnaire designed no provision was made for this mode of continuing education,

189

but their existence became apparent during the course of the interviews. Twenty out of the 205 men interviewed reported that they had participated in such a group. From the interviews, the study defined the groups as follows:

> Journal clubs are voluntary, informal associations of small groups of scientists organized without higher-level management initiative or support, but may include working supervisors one or two levels up from the bench. The purpose of the journal club is to split up the literature on a topic, have each member read some of it, and report to the others in summary form. Other similar associations for the purpose of discussing research problems of mutual interest (and perhaps also the relevant literature) are informally referred to as "seminars" by some of the people interviewed.

The R&D Study (C-24:126) gave an example of the way in which these informal groups served as an instructional and communication medium:

> We have a journal club that meets right here in this room, and each person covers something from the literature. It's half an hour every two eeeks. We are aware of other things and other people's interest in that way. It's voluntary. Mostly the young ones want to have these. A few of the old-timers come, but quite a few don't care to come and participate.

In the same report (C-24:126) is quoted the answer one respondent gave to why he started such a club:

> Professionalism in my group is virtually non-existent. I think that one of the reasons we don't have any professionalism of attitude is the lack of professional and interpersonal interaction. You just don't have any. This is a mistake. It's only through discussion with other people that I start getting interested, and it makes tomorrow a day worth looking forward to.

In his remarks on continuing education to librarians assembled for the 1967 Midwinter meeting of the American Library Association, Houle (H-36:265) stated that "these groups exert an extraordinary importance, not only on their own participants but also on other alert people who aspire to membership."

In the study by Stone (S-72:79-80), out of 138 MLS librarians queried, 31 informal study groups were reported. Of those in which type of membership was identified, 9 consisted of fellow members in a library association, 4 were made up of fellow employees in the work place, and 15 were composed of librarians in the same geographical area with similar interests, regardless of association, employment, or other group affiliations. All of those reporting membership in such groups had a high Professional Index Score, as defined in that study.

All reports indicate that such informal groups have a high potential as an effective means for continuing education. It would seem that management and individual professionals who are concerned about continuing education should take the initiative in finding ways and means to stimulate the formation of such groups. It would also seem that many library committees might use this mode by means of correspondence to make their assignments more meaningful and productive.

Teaching

The best summary of the use of teaching as a means of continuing education was found in the R&D Study (C-24:127). It was reported that teaching was a very effective means of continuing education because:

1. Preparation for teaching requires knowing the current state of the art and how it is being taught by others, and this involves extensive reading of the literature and textbooks.
2. Teaching requires logical organization of material and a broad view of its applicability, thus serving a refresher and updating purpose.
3. Review serves to reveal relationships in a different light than they appeared when the teacher previously studied the subject.

None of the top managers in the R&D Study (C-24:128) consistently promoted teaching as a mode of continuing education, but recognized that it served the following purposes:

1. It reflects favorably on quality of the laboratory staff members when they are accepted to teach at nearby universities.
2. It contributes to the knowledge which the university faculty has about the laboratory and the quality of its personnel, creating a potential for cooperative relationships -- for example, in arranging dissertation work to be done in-lab rather than on campus by laboratory staff who are students.

On the negative side there was indication that some managers felt that their employees were hired to do research and that teaching was a diversion from their main function -- research for the organization.

191

An indication of the value of teaching as a mode of continuing education is evidenced in "The Physician's Recognition Award for Participation in Continuing Medical Education." Of the 150 credit hours needed to qualify for an award, it is possible to earn 90 by teaching -- none of the other categories carry as high a potential (P-18).

Regardless of how effective teaching is as a mode of continuing education for the individual practitioner, it has to be realized that it is a format that will be available only to a limited number of professionals.

Papers and Publication

The American Medical Association, in its "Physician's Recognition Award for Participation in Continuing Medical Education," allows ten credit hours for each scientific paper or publication. To receive credit a paper must be presented to a medical society or an organization whose membership is restricted to physicians; a publication must appear in a recognized medical or medically-related scientific journal. "Book reviews, medical editorials, and medical editing are not creditable." An indication of the importance attached to this form of continuing education is that it is one of the six (out of ten) Required Education categories from which a minimum of 60 credit hours (out of 100 total) must come for acceptance for a certificate.

The American Psychological Association's Project on Scientific Information Exchange in Psychology (A-53, Vol. 1:14-15) found that of the 78 persons who kept logs over a two week period of their activity, 60 were "writers." The most frequent type of writing (47 out of 60) was that of research papers prepared for journal publication or for a contracting agency or sponsoring organization. This study also showed that those who were writing for publication were in frequent and extensive correspondence with others about the research in which they were involved. "The cooperation and promptness of replies to requests for current information through correspondence within this sample was amazing." The investigators felt as a result of their survey that such an interchange was "usual and the result of their intense interest in, and preoccupation with, their research and with the general subject matter of psychology." A follow-up study requested exact information on material received and sent on the day that the questionnaire was answered. The results are reported in Table II. and confirmed the extent to which the psychologists were indeed trying to meet their information needs by writing to colleagues in other places.

Although the production of papers or publications would seem to be a mode of continuing education of value to the individual participant, 53 per cent of those

TABLE   2

Record of Amount and Kind of Correspondence Sent and Received
on a Single Day by 69 Psychologists in a Study Concerning
the Exchange of Information

The Table indicates the extent to which information needs were being met
by writing to colleagues in other places.

Mail Received	Percentage of Sample Receiving on a Given Day
Reprints	40%
Requests for reprints	51
Pre-publications copies	20
Inquiries concerning published work	10
Correspondence related to a general scientific issue	31
	N=69

Mail Sent	Percentage of Sample Sending on a Given Day
Reprints	40%
Requests for reprints	10
Pre-publication copies	20
Inquiries concerning published work	7
Correspondence related to a general scientific issue	35
	N=69

Source: "Scientific Activity and Information Problems of Selected
Psychologists: A Preliminary Survey," in The American
Psychological Association's Project on Scientific Informa-
tion Exchange in Psychology, Vol. I. Washington, D.C.:
American Psychological Association, 1963, p. 18.

surveyed in a sampling of all types of libraries (S-72:197) had not published any articles or delivered any papers at professional meetings during the past five years; 92% of the total sample had not published a book either in library science or in their area of specialization. The writing of papers and/or publications would seem to be one way in which the individual librarian could enhance his own professional development. Publications and papers presented in a scientific manner, and making materials produced visible to as wide a reading audience as possible, is suggested as one way by which the profession as a whole might also be upgraded.

Research

Research is also a category for which credits are given by the American Medical Association in its "Physician's Recognition Award for Participation in Continuing Medical Education" (P-18:4). It should be noted, however, that such credit is only allowed for each year spent in full-time medical research.

Although the respondents in the Stone survey (S-72:215) stated that research was an important means of continuing education for individual librarians -- that for those who engaged in research professional growth would follow automatically -- when they ranked (S-72:136) 37 different professional growth activities, it was found that there was considerable difference between the rankings of different types of librarians. Academic and special librarians ranked research 11th as a mode of continuing education, while the public librarians rated it 27th and the school librarians 33rd. Overall, 77.5 per cent of the total sample had not engaged in any research projects since receiving the MLS degree (S-72:197). No one in the study had engaged in more than two research projects since receiving his degree.

It could be concluded that the profession does not sufficiently honor or recognize those who engage in research to make the effort seem worthwhile. Bundy and Wasserman (B-39) have pointed up an essential difference between librarianship and some of the more scholarly disciplines. In the former, "prestige in the professional society typically comes from office holding and work for the organization, while in a scholarly discipline, prestige more usually follows upon academic productivity as reflected in the form of articles and monographs" (B-39:22).

Respondents in the Stone survey (S-72:215) who had engaged in research and published were generally dissatisfied with their career progress to date. There were no statistical correlation between career advancement and publication or research.

The respondents offered suggestions for stimulating such research activity. For example, they stressed making the results of research more visible to the profession at large in the belief that this would promote scholarly work, serve as a means of continuing education both for the producer and the consumer of the product, and at the same time would add stature to librarianship. The consensus was that research as a means of continuing education should be encouraged by both the employing library and library associations.

Home Study

The most comprehensive single article found on new concepts of home study as a mode for continuing professional education was one by Rebel (R-4) of the University of Tubingen, West Germany, entitled "The Necessity of Further Education in the Professions and Home Study as a Means of Realization." The comments in this section are based almost entirely on this presentation.

Rebel proposed that the way for educational systems to get out of the dilemma of lagging behind what is expected of them and of having too much expected of them in the way of new tasks is to find new forms for displaying knowledge and information. His solution—home study. He points out that the most striking difference between new teaching methods and use of new media in education, and the more conventional forms of teaching is the withdrawal of the teacher or lecturer, on whose knowledge learning success is largely dependent. "The teacher is replaced in modern teaching methods by a team of experts, who share what have been the functions of the teacher."

Rebel puts forward the thesis that home study provides a type of teaching that is independent of the number of pupils; that allows the greatest measure of individual teaching; that can be adapted, because of its great flexibility, to the most varied tasks and curricula; and that offers real chances for the "realization of the concept of an education and opportunities to learn that may last a lifetime." He points out that home study could not fulfill great expectations if it were identical with correspondence courses of the past. He emphasizes that home study is vastly different from older correspondence courses, which were not essentially different in their structure from the direct methods of teaching.

Rebel indicates the essential characteristics of modern home study as follows:

1. The teachers and the students are permanently separated. (This can be solved temporarily only when special arrangements are made for study groups, seminars, etc.)

2. The assignment of various people, who provide information to bridge the wide distance and to stimulate the student's capacities by the use of the various sense organs in the media compound.

3. Methods follow methodical objectives. It is based on a previously conducted analysis of the aims of learning, of the groups of addresses and of the steps of learning that follow one another logically.

4. It is charaterized by "methodics" used to foster studies, study instruction and control -- which makes it different from study taken purely on one's own. These means include correcting service, tests, reports on experiences, consultation service, annotated bibliographies, graphic presentations of study materials -- all of which facilitate learning.

5. Dependence on cooperation with educational agencies, such as adult education centers, and with organizations that have technical apparatus, libraries, and technical knowledge at their disposal. "To integrate home study into the education system, media centers should be established throughout the country, where films, videotapes, other audiovisual materials, books, scripts, and so on are available."

Rebel estimates that in the field of university home study about 2.35 million students are studying in 15 countries surveyed. Of this number, engineers, teachers, managers, and economists form the largest groups. Of those studying in Germany, 80 per cent wished to improve their professional qualifications. "Consequently, the hope that home study can give to overcoming problems of professional mobility is decisive."

As an example of the development of home study at the university level, he cites the German Institute for Home Study at the University of Tubingen, which has the following objectives: (1) the development of home study for teachers as a model for further educational study; (2) working out of models for home study courses into basic, accumulative, and contact study; (3) research tasks in the field of didactics and methodics of home study; and (4) coordination of the various attempts at introducing home study in the Federal Republic of Germany.

Generally home study follows a basic pattern: course coverage extends over two years; study letters and other teaching materials are sent monthly or more often; direct courses form fixed parts of every program; the possibility of organizing voluntary study groups for participants living in the same area are explored; radio, TV, films, tapes, records, and programmed course sections are put into

196

the media compound; at the end of the course the successful participants receive either a certificate or register to take examinations before state boards.

Along with the development of the home study concept the author sees the necessity for building media centers which would serve the following purposes: (1) be pools for machines, books, or printed materials, audio visual media, teaching programs, experiment kits, and for building up a documentation; (2) serve as laboratory centers where experiments and practical work are undertaken and all practical skills are taught; (3) be crystallization points for work and study groups; (4) possibly take over the task of advising and guiding people interested in the educational programs, including test centers open to all who want to be informed on their own interests and the possibilities for study.

In conclusion, Rebel states that "for the first time in the history of mankind, they [modern technologically-oriented teaching methods] make possible a planned, directed, and systematic program of further education for everyone for their entire life. Scientific investigations have disposed of the old idea that learning is limited to childhood and youth and that the adult is less suited to learning. . . . Because of this, learning takes on real meaning for the existence of every adult. Nevertheless there is one necessary prerequisite. The adult must be in a position to determine his own learning tempo and to fit the learning process into his own routine. This means that the most suitably planned learning process is the one that allows for a high percentage of individualization. Home study, in its modern form, can fulfill these demands better than conventional methods of teaching."

Mathison (M-35) in a review article on "Correspondence Study in Multimedia Learning Systems," asserts:

> In a conceptual sense a multimedia learning system is crudely analogous to that of "team teaching." The similarity is that each member of the team (whether the teacher, the student, or particular medium utilized) participates in a way that is both appropriate to the medium and designed to maximize the potential of each, to develop the conditions most conducive to learning (M-35:1).

The rapid upsurge in the use of "correspondence education" is, in part, explained by Charles Wedemeyer (W-15), who points out that this mode has pioneered in two important aspects:

1. in proving that learning does not have to conform to place-time
   limitations imposed by teachers and institutions, and
2. in making opportunity to learn available by self-selection, not
   by institutional, economic, geographic, or class determinants.

Mathison (M-35) reviews three examples of institutional responses to opportunities possible by the use of multimedia learning systems: the Open University in Great Britain, the AIM experiment at the University of Wisconsin, and the New York State College Proficiency Examination Program.

In summary, because of these and other attributes, home study can and will undoubtedly play an increasingly important and dynamic role in continuing professional education, especially when linked with other independent study methods made possible through use of new technology.

Continuing Education Center Concept

Increasingly in the literature there is reference to various types of centers, highly media oriented, where professional and non-professionals, and citizens generally, could go to continue their education. Rebel (R-4) argues:

> Media centers should be established throughout the country, where films, videotapes, other audiovisual materials, books, scripts, and so on are available.

Speaking to the librarians assembled for the Mini-workshop on Continuing Education as it exists in other professions, Luke (L-27) explained that:

> The basic function of the teacher center is to secure full time staff and separate facilities to support a wide range of teacher professional development activities which are based on the teaching staffs' own assessment of their professional development needs.

Whatever specific processes are evolved, the center should be surrounded with systematically organized learning experiences, including constant evaluation.

The NEA is encouraging local education associations to stimulate the investment by boards of education in the rapidly emerging program concept of Teacher Centers.

Luke (L-27) envisions the role of NEA as that of performing a consultative role to local education associations in the processes that must be followed in influencing boards of education to offer more-- and more effective -- in-service programs.

Edelfelt (E-2) pictures the renewal center (or teacher center) in a setting adjacent to schools where the education of teachers takes place simultaneously with the education of children. He argues that "renewal centers for teachers cannot succeed if they are not by the teacher, of the teacher, and with the teacher. Teachers are tired of being done to, of having innovation imposed, of being led or pushed into in-service training." He therefore argues that teacher centers must provide for the teachers a central role in the governance of such centers. He suggests the following guidelines (E-2:124-25):

1. The staff should include everyone from teacher aide to senior professor, and governance of the center should be the right and responsibility of those who use it.

2. Teachers should work individually, but also in groups, to study and solve problems.
3. Study and research should be an integral part of the usual school operation.
4. The community (parents and laymen) should be deeply involved.
5. Many community agencies and institutions should work with the school.
6. Adequate money and the readiness to gamble with new and different ideas should be evident.

One of the innovative proposals presented for discussion in the NEA publication Remaking the World of the Career Teacher (N-10:127-131) was the establishment of Instructional Laboratory Centers (ILC's) designed to promote professional education and facilitate the development of specialized careers in education. It was envisioned that the center could serve in the following ways:

1. Teachers would attend for two or three weeks, "during which time they would receive intensive instruction in the selection and utilization of new materials and technology most appropriate for the attainment of specific curricula objectives."
2. The flexible facilities of the ILC also would "enhance the conduct of experimental projects involving teaching teams, small group instruction, and various types of subprofessionals..."
3. The ILC..."would provide the perfect setting in which to introduce new administrators to the demands of careers in administration."
4. ..."an ILC would facilitate a cross-fertilization of ideas which in turn would enhance the competency of individual educators and communicate to outsiders a sense of the complexity of an increasingly scientific profession. "

The Staff College

Using as a model an adaptation of Henri Fayol's matrix showing the substantive knowledge and the understandings needed by an employee at various levels in an organization, Corson (C-41) insists that the individual rising in an organization not only needs an ever-expanding grasp of the substantive field in which he specialized during his formal education, but an overlay made up of: 1) an acquaintanceship with the environment surrounding the organization; and 2) administrative and executive skills and processes. To obtain this "overlay" Corson saw an urgent need for the individual taking a rigorous stocktaking after six to eight years, and again after 12 to 20 years (C-42:155). He suggests that "to refresh their spirits, to make more flexible their reasoning processes, as well as to acquaint themselves with the new that should replace the obsolete in what they earlier learned," they should be able to detach themselves from the day to day environment and receive the stimulation that comes from seeing new faces and places (C-42:156-157). He comments that a first-rate university can do this, "but only if it recognizes the individual's own need and does not force him into a rigid program reflecting the faculty's conception of a public executive's needs, or into courses and seminars designed for the training of Ph. D. candidates in teaching and research" (C-42:157). He notes an additional solution--the Staff College--but cautions that it "must be so structured as to provide the detachment, stimulation and individual opportunity . . ." (C-42:157).

The Continuing Continuing Education for Public Service report (I-4:56) states that the educational goal of a staff college should be to "prepare each student to exercise responsible, imaginative and informed leadership as a key administrator and one who will influence the development of ... policy. It should enable him to relate the program for which he is or will be responsible to ... ultimate community goals and values. The program design should enable the student to break from the confines of parochial specialization." In this report it is also stressed that the staff college should not only make provision for those who might be able to come for full time uninterrupted study, for longer periods, but should also provide short seminars three to six weeks in duration. This report presents a complete proposal for the establishment of a staff college, including philosophy, curriculum guidelines, budget, physical facilities, and governance, which could be used as a helpful model to those planning to develop a staff college.

Other models to be considered include: the Federal Executive Institute, opened in Charlottesville, Virginia, in October, 1968, supported fully by the Civil Service Commission as part of its training and development program, and featuring 8-week programs plus some intensive one-week programs; the Brookings Institution programs of short duration held at Williamsburg; programs developed by the Veterans Administration and other agencies which provide development programs meeting one or two nights a week and spaced over 12 to 18 months.

Conclusion

It would seem that all of the modes of continuing education presented in this chapter warrant attention as formats that hold some promise of effectiveness as means of continuing education. Some would seem to have a much greater potential than others. It should also be added that there are many variations of the modes which have not been touched upon in this review but also hold promise. Some of the modes presented here could be used to greater advantage if they were combined with appropriate technology, which is a rich new resource for continuing education. As stated in Continuing Continuing Education for the Public Service (I-4:86):

> Those who are seriously interested in presenting continuing education in a format that will entice and interest the practitioner must think in terms of something other than traditional seminars or stand-up lectures. Continuing education has not kept pace with the potent means of communication which modern society has found indispensable.

As this review is especially concerned with the development of continuing education for librarians, who increasingly are using modern communications devices in the institutions they serve, it is imperative that continuing education for this professional group be within the framework of the new technology.

In speaking of the use of instructional technology and its applications for continuing education and as noted in the comprehensive report transmitted to to Congress in March, 1970, by the Commission on Instructional Technology, it should be borne in mind that ". . .instructional technology goes beyond any particular medium or device" (U-14:19).

The report defined it as follows:

> ...instructional technology is more than the sum of its parts. It is a systematic way of designing, carrying out, and evaluating the total process of learning and teaching in terms of specific objectives, based on research in human learning and communication, and employing a combination of human and nonhuman resources to bring about more effective instruction. The widespread acceptance and application of this broad definition belongs to the future (U-14:19).

202

Types of instructional technology illustrative of new approaches which can be drawn upon in designing continuing education programs include programmed instruction, simulation and games management, role-playing, laboratory method, in-basket exercises, incident-process technique, problem analysis technique, modern audio visuals, and adaptations of statistical decision theory.

VIII. SUMMARY AND CONCLUSIONS

The Question of Definitions

From an examination of the literature on continuing education, it is apparent that there is no clearcut definition of continuing education that is generally accepted by all professions. This is a stumbling block that has slowed the development of continuing education in many professions. Four characteristics seem to be prevalent or gaining general acceptance, however:

1. Continuing education consists of those activities which are above and beyond basic or core preparations normally considered necessary or appropriate qualifications for entrance into a profession or occupation.

2. Continuing education is a process of keeping up to date, or lifelong learning, which will prevent obsolescence.

3. Continuing education better equips a person for his contemporary work, for the job he now has or aspires to in the near future. It emphasizes the enhancement of professional competence, rather than the pursuit of advanced degrees.

3. Continuing education is the concern of and should involve shared responsibility and cooperative interface between (1) the individual practitioner, (2) academic institutions, (3) employing institutions, and (4) professional associations.

Specific criteria in relation to these basic assumptions differ from profession to profession. For example, many people regard themselves as involved in continuing education when they are taking part-time university credit courses leading to a degree, but in engineering this type of study is excluded from the scope of continuing education. It is considered an upgrading effort on the part of the individual by means of which he is raising the level of his formal capabilities.

The general recommendation that is suggested here is that any study set forth clearly its definition and be consistent in the use of terms, otherwise failures of communication about what is meant will weaken the over-all results. One means of achieving clarity is to follow the general definition of continuing education with specific criteria which activities must meet.

A further difficulty presented by the literature is lack of clear distinction between the terms "training" and "continuing education." Often they are linked together in a way that implies that they are synonymous. Although both involve learning experiences for the individual, the focus or over-all objective is generally conceived to be distinct. Training is intended as a means of furthering the organization's goals; it occurs after the individual has joined the organization, and is planned by the organization.

Continuing education takes as its base the individual, and assumes that the individual carries the basic responsibility for his own development and for keeping up-to-date, but also encompasses the concern, shared responsibility, cooperation, and interaction of at least three relevant groups -- the employer, the academic institution, and the professional association. Each of these groups has its own motivations which determine the amount of responsibility it is willing to assume and the amount and degree of interface in which it is willing to participate. As a consequence, each fulfills a different role in continuing education.

The employing institution has the responsibility for providing opportunities for continuing education and for providing an environment that encourages and stimulates the individual to keep up-to-date. The professional associations and academic institutions are expected to help by providing the opportunities from which the individual can select those best suited to his needs. Generally employers and professional societies, more than universities, have shared responsibility for making the individual more aware of his needs and in helping him to meet those needs. Professional associations have also made a special contribution by issuing landmark or position papers on continuing education; such statements are one of the main ways of gaining a consensus on the roles that are to be played by relevant and concerned agencies within a profession.

The literature also shows that there has never been any complete agreement on the infallible indicators that distinguish a profession from an occupation. It is suggested that a constructive approach is that proposed by Houle, in which a profession is thought of as an ideal state toward which many occupational groups are striving, rather than setting forth fixed criteria that must be attained. Such a position gives the continuing professional educator an advantage because his expertise is viewed as a way of enhancing and speeding up the process of professionalization.

In making comparisons between the professions regarding the methods and practices used, it is essential to keep in mind different patterns of work. What might be best or ideal for one group may not be effective for another. Therefore, to avoid distortion, the classification of the occupations into three basic patterns, as suggested by Houle, is suggested: the entrepreneurial occupations, the collective occupations, and the hierarchical occupations.

The educator concerned with continuing education cannot make his greatest contribution unless he understands the nature of the work environment of the professional group he is serving.

In making comparisons between professions it is also important to realize that different professions are in different stages of development. Roughly three stages seem to be identifiable:

1. the stage in which continuing education is just beginning to be recognized as necessary to proficient practice (librarianship would be included in this category);

2. the stage in which continuing education has been joined to formal pre-service education to form a continuum where one leads naturally into the other and is not thought of as something that may or may not be added on; and

3. the stage in which the stated goal is the availability of continuing education to every professional who wishes it, wherever he may be, made possible by full use of the new technology.

Factors Affecting the Design of a Continuing Education System

Those designing continuing education systems for a profession should keep in mind certain criteria which, from a survey of the literature, seem to be necessary components in order to have an effective system. These are:

1. Adoption of a systems approach to education which looks upon education as a life-long process for the continuing development of the whole person. The systems approach calls for patterns that are cumulative—formal education is joined with continuing education as a continuous process.

2. Recognition of certain basic factors about adult learning that are quite different from the learning patterns of the young.

3. Adequate determination of the practitioner's learning needs, recognizing that content of the continuing education opportunity which can be related to the individual's actual job is the most influential factor in motivating participation in continuing education.

4. Continuing professional education programming must meet highly personalized and practical criteria of the individual: a) personal satisfaction; b) freedom of choice; c) continuity; d) accessibility; and e) convenience.

5. As continuing education is a free enterprise system, it must be built on a learning needs analysis of those to be served.

6. For all continuing education programs learning objectives should be stated in specific enough terms so that the individual participant knows or can demonstrate what he is able to do as a result of the learning experience.

7. All continuing education programs should be subjected to systematic continuous evaluation. Broad goals must be translated into specific objectives which can be observed and measured; specific objectives are a necessary condition for effective evaluation.

8. Continuing education programs should make provision for self-evaluation by each participant in terms of his particular goals and objectives.

9. Those responsible for continuing education programs should be able to account for past actions by answering questions concerning both the ends and the means of their programs.

10. For maximum effectiveness, continuing professional education and curricula must incorporate multidisciplinary concepts, knowledge and skills.

11. Continuing professional education must make imaginative use of the tools offered by instructional technology; drab

formats and uninspired presentations will not produce widespread participation.

12. Because of their resources and expertise, universities should take the lead in developing standards and evaluative criteria for continuing education formats and modes of instruction.

13. The provision of recognition for continuing professional education activities increases the probability of active participation in these activities.

14. Professional continuing education must locate and utilize the special expertise of practitioners.

The problems involved in providing continuing library education are nation-wide; hence continuing library education will benefit from national planning which builds an administrative partnership of the profession's best available individual-learning resources. A nationwide university without walls, available to all and meeting the criteria for excellence in continuing education, requires the formation of an educational partnership of all relevant groups, (including library associations, library schools, employing libraries, state library agencies, government agencies with responsibility for continuing education, and the individual practitioner) to build a coordinating structure which will provide administrative continuity for policy formulation, planning, program budgeting, evaluation and distribution.

Summary of Recommendations

This section recapitulates the suggestions made throughout this review of the literature, but chiefly made at the conclusion of each of the chapters. These suggestions are listed randomly; no attempt has been made to indicate any priority or ranking order.

The Role of the Professional Association

Several suggestions are made that would seem to merit special attention by those planning for continuing library education, based on what has been and is being accomplished in professional associations.

1. Focus on what the chief continuing educational needs are within the profession, and then design organizational structures that will produce new skills, new information, and new distribution patterns to meet those needs.

208

2. Establish a uniform recognition system for continuing education within the profession. Special attention is called to the use of the "continuing education unit" as adopted recently by the American Nursing Association and the American Medical Association's "Physician's Recognition Award." Seek a variety of ways of honoring those who lead and those who participate in continuing education endeavors.

3. Experiment with a training laboratory concept in which people can, through simulation, try library practices without commitment.

4. Encourage groups from the same library to attend continuing education experiences. A single individual who has been motivated by a continuing education experience finds it very frustrating to go back and find out that no one else understands what he is talking about.

5. Develop a computerized system, similar to that developed by the American Institute of Architects, for inventorying all live programs (those that must be attended) and packaged courses. Until a computerized system can be worked out, a central clearinghouse type of listing of continuing education activities should be published regularly. Another alternative would be a central switching center to which all requests for information on live and packaged courses would come and would then be redirected to the sources of these materials. Some type of effective clearinghouse of continuing education activities would seem to be the natural function of professional societies.

6. Local, state, and regional professional associations which are not now active in continuing education should review their programs to determine what more they could be doing. Reaction from practicing librarians gives the impression that in many communities local chapters often primarily fulfill social functions or make continuing education a once-in-a-while activity. National associations should provide materials and guidelines to local chapters interested in intensifying their continuing education activities.

7. Consider ways of increasing the number of preprints and of review articles and papers. There does not seem to be much emphasis placed on publication of original research findings. This type of publication should be balanced with comprehensive statements of emerging trends in theory and practice, based on application of research findings covering a wide range of topics and including trends and practices in other disciplines that have application to library and information science.

8. Issue a regular publication, jointly financed and sponsored by the various professional associations, featuring continuing education, which would cover what all of the associations are doing and have to offer. Excellent examples can be found in the Journal of Continuing Education in Nursing, published bimonthly, and in the American Dental Association's quarterly, Continuing Education.

9. Experiment with types of correspondence opportunities, using packaged materials or games, but differing from usual correspondence courses because individuals using the materials in one location are urged to take the courses together and use mini-lab techniques as practiced by the American Institute of Architects.

10. Issue a cassette a month which would review not only information from library science and information science, but information from related disciplines that can affect the practicing librarian and the library which he or she serves. Coverage of subjects would be proportionate to needs expressed by practicing librarians based on survey techniques.

11. Prepare for distribution on demand in-depth subject cassettes which would be supplemented with written material, slides, graphs, charts, etc. The preparation of these would be governed by current needs expressed by practicing librarians based on survey techniques.

12. Give consideration to four components in all planning and programming for continuing education: 1) content that is job-oriented; 2) constant search for modes that meet the personalized criteria of individual librarians; 3) expertise used in preparation of the medium; 4) smooth and continuing distribution system.

13. Develop a dissemination of information service for librarians. This would constitute the development of a professional data bank, which would offer decentralized distribution of information by use of the telephone. This reference service for librarians would contain data on such topics as: the latest information on networks and their availability; legislation; employment information; status of unionization in libraries, etc.

14. Use marketing techniques for production and distribution of materials and services. If these are based on real needs from the field, they can be self-supporting as demonstrated by other professional groups in their production of materials.

15. Exploit the new technology in continuing education programming; formats such as preprints, cassette tapes, cassette-based packaged programs, talk-back TV programs, and Cable TV need to be used more widely.

16. Develop a "Standard Condition of Employment" based on the statement in the ALA Library Education and Manpower Policy Statement (A-42), to be used by employers guaranteeing that time and funds for continuing education will be provided by the employing institution. An excellent example can be found in the engineering profession.

17. Build quality control into materials and programs produced through the use of ongoing user evaluations and through a national review structure consisting of experts drawn from different professional associations, as well as from library schools and from practitioners in the field.

18. Develop and use consistently a comprehensive model for managing and evaluating short-term institutes and workshops.

19. Re-examine the type of continuing education programming offered by other professional associations in terms of the increased emphasis on competencies demanded by the public and in accordance with current insistence on accountability.

20. Formulate guidelines and position papers endorsed jointly by the various library associations. Examples from nursing,

medicine and banking suggest the types of such statements
that would prove useful: "Landmark Statement on Continuing
Education," "Guidelines for Continuing Education Programming,"
"Evaluative Model for Managing and Evaluating Short-Term
Institutes and Workshops," "Recognition System for Continuing
Education," etc. The statements that are adopted should be
printed in full in major library and information science journals
and given visibility for the benefit of the whole profession.

21. Establish a master planning committee for continuing education
in each state and region.

22. Assign   one individual to be responsible for coordinating
continuing education programming within each association and
with other relevant groups outside the profession.

23. Engage in inter-disciplinary and inter-professional cooperation
in the planning and implementation of continuing education
programs, as well as joint planning among the various professional associations within the profession.

Continuing Education in the Work Environment

In the interest of the organization as well as for the benefit of the
individual practitioner, management should encourage participation in continuing education activities.

1. Administrators should take the initiative and responsibility
for defining and providing support opportunities for the continuing education of their staffs.

2. The continuing education and/or professional development
program of the library should be conceptualized as a sub-
system of the total organizational system.

3. Management should recognize the need for establishing a long-
range educational program with definite objectives to parallel
long-range library goals. There is evidence that continuing
education on an if-and-when basis is not sufficient to cope
with the requirements of a library actively responding to
societal changes.

4. Continuing education programs require strong support and encouragement by supervisory personnel. Top administration should make it explicit that one of the functions of supervision is stimulating subordinates to continuing education and reviewing with them their plans for development. Conscious recognition of what an "innovator" type of supervisor is and does relative to continuing education helps make plain what top administration can expect of supervisors.

5. In the work environment a philosophy should predominate in which it is assumed: 1) that most individuals have a natural inclination toward growth and development and that the individual will accept his share of responsibility for development; 2) that each person is considered a unique individual and his or her special talents are recognized, encouraged to develop, and utilized, 3) that each individual is allowed to identify his personal career goals and match those against the library's goals, and 4) that management's function is to supply the opportunity, guidance, and stimulation.

6. Continuing education programs require the personal motivation of the individual employee. There is evidence that for an individual to be personally motivated toward continuing education, he must see the results of the learning as being related and necessary to the performance of his job.

7. Individual jobs should be organized and enriched so that the nature of the work will provide individual motivation for growth and development.

8. Policy statements should recognize updating personnel as part of the daily work.

9. Employee appraisal should be recognized as closely related to development. To serve as a motivating factor toward continuing education, there is evidence that appraisal needs to be a continuous, cumulative process, using a management by objectives approach.

10. An active continuing education committee, representing the views and needs of all levels of the organization, should be established. The function of such a committee is to initiate,

213

review, and recommend action programs in continuing education. The committee should also suggest priorities based on the conduct and evaluation of "reviews of need" in the work force as related to organizational goals and needs. A professional development committee can create and sustain enthusiasm for continuing education because its very existence demonstrates the administration's support and reliance on continuing education as a professional development technique.

11. It should be recognized that individual and group needs are so varied that short courses, degree programs, formal courses, institutes, etc., will not meet all continuing education needs. The organization should provide a sufficient number of alternatives in order for each professional to select and integrate what is useful and needed by him.

12. Deterring environmental factors relating to continuing education, such as lack of time, inconvenient location, poor working conditions, should be eliminated insofar as possible.

13. Ways and means should be developed to overcome the physical and psychological barriers of individuals participating in continuing education opportunities outside the work place. Management should set up   some central place in the library where information on outside continuing eduction is collected, kept up to date, and made easily available to those considering or in need of outside continuing education opportunities.

14. A system should be operative which periodically and systematically evaluates the need for continuing education opportunities.

15. An ongoing evaluation system should continuously feed back information on ways and means by which the continuing education program can be improved.

16. Management should maintain an accurate record-keeping system which reflects the number and types of personnel engaged in employer-sponsored modes of continuing education and the cost per participant. Ways should be found to measure and assess the modes of continuing education in terms of their value to the organization and to the individual.

17. Participation in decision-making should be viewed as one way of stimulating employees toward engaging in continuing education opportunities.

18. The organization should continuously maintain a climate for learning. Elements in such a climate include: 1) the concept of professional group practice should pervade the library in which stimulation for continuing learning is inherent; 2) the learner shares in the plan for his learning; 3) research as a method of continuing learning is recognized; 4) a developmental style of leadership exists throughout the organization; 5) management continually seeks ways of helping employees keep up with the literature explosion.

Role of the Academic Institution in Continuing Education

Based on a review of the literature and recent surveys in library schools, the most important overall recommendation is that ways and means be found to make continuing education an important component of the program of each school of library and information science. As society continually looks to universities to set quality standards for education and as universities are uniquely qualified to serve this role because of special expertise present on university campuses, the following specific suggestions are made which emerge from a review of the literature.

1. A clear distinction should be made between the objectives for doctoral study which is oriented toward research and the objectives of "advanced specialist" and other continuing education programs, which are functionally oriented toward the participant's professional objectives, even as has been done in other professions, such as engineering.

2. Closer relationships should be developed with libraries and professional associations so that continuing education needs may be more clearly defined.

3. In addition to offering programs to practicing librarians on campus, collaborative arrangements should be worked out with libraries. On their side, libraries should provide released time to employees to participate in university-sponsored programs.

4. To insure the success of collective activity between the university and the employing institution four conditions must be met satisfactorily from the university's point of view: 1) adequate financing, 2) academic merit, 3) mutual benefit, and 4) adequate staffing.

5. Continuing education should be given equal status with degree programs and research-oriented activity.

6. The reward system in the university should include recognition for continuing library education activity on a par with degree and research-oriented programs.

7. Research needs to be sponsored in the following areas:
   a. The standards that should be applied to continuing education programs, especially non-credit programs.
   b. The relative efficiency of different modes of continuing education, especially non-credit programs, and correspondence programs.
   c. The effectiveness of new instructional methods as they can be applied to continuing education, especially television, Cable TV, programmed instruction.
   d. The factors involved in motivating librarians to participate in continuing education.
   e. Ways and means of building a nationwide system of continuing education that will service effectively the continuing education needs of every professional, regardless of his or her geographical location.

The Modes of Continuing Education

This paper reviews seventeen modes of continuing education: four course-work and related modes; four interaction modes; seven self-teaching modes; and two specialized modes -- the continuing education center concept and the staff college.

In general the university credit courses seem well suited for in-depth learning of fundamentals in areas not previously studied, but they present certain disadvantages, such as lack of emphasis on the frontiers of knowledge, geographical and scheduling problems, and certain inbuilt psychological barriers for the practitioner. A mode that overcomes some of the disadvantages inherent in university courses within degree programs is the post-Master's course especially designed to meet the needs of the practitioner. This mode seems to be gaining in favor in library schools and is recommended, although it, too, has certain disadvantages, chief of which appear to be the amount of promotion necessary to get a sufficient number of registrants to make the

216

courses economically feasible for the university to offer, and travel time for those located away from universities.

Non-credit employer-sponsored courses present another mode which holds potential especially in meeting the refresher and updating needs of practitioners, if suitable standards are set and met and if continuing effort is given to their planning and evaluation.

A popular format is the short intensive course which in this review includes workshops and institutes -- because specific definitions are not consistently used in announcing these programs. Short-term programs are especially valuable in meeting specific on-the-job needs covered by the courses and because they provide, away from the work environment, an opportunity to obtain a perspective which is difficult to acquire on the job. Such opportunities also provide a valuable exchange of ideas with other practitioners, an opportunity to engage in problem-solving in a non-threatening atmosphere, and often stimulate a great deal more reading than is done regularly. Overall they have high potential as vehicles for continuing education. To overcome the difficulty of absorbing such large amounts of material in a short period of time, many variants are being experimented with currently, such as short courses meeting periodically with assignments in between, rather than concentrating all the course work in one block of time. An accurate, up-to-date, easy-access clearinghouse of short courses, workshops, and institutes, well in advance of when they are offered, should be continually maintained.

One of the interaction modes -- attending professional meetings -- is one of the most popular modes of continuing education for librarians (ranked as the second most important for their professional development in one study -- S-72:135). Studies in other disciplines show that one of the chief values of the professional meeting is the opportunity provided for interaction on an informal face to face basis with others. Professional meetings are particularly valuable for keeping up-to-date in one's field; they are of maximum value to those who have not allowed themselves to get completely out of touch with the topics discussed or presented.

Two other interaction modes -- the invited conference and leaves with pay -- are important means of continuing education sponsored by employers, but major weaknesses are: the number of people that can be reached by these two modes is small and each is costly to the employer. Nonetheless, in spite of these two disadvantages, the value to those reached is so great that it would seem that they should be encouraged to the greatest extent possible.

217

Another mode of employer continuing education is the in-house lecture and/or seminar. These would seem to hold great potential if systematic efforts to evaluate these programs were made and if the participants are involved in planning and programming as well as the evaluation of these efforts. In spite of the potential value of the programs there appear to be few systematic records of the number, costs, and benefits of these programs as they currently exist in libraries.

Of the seven self-teaching modes, reading is regarded as the most important mode in keeping up-to-date. The amount of literature to be covered, however, is so vast as to be frustrating to the individual practitioner, and it is suggested that library managers continually seek ways of helping the individual in keeping up with the literature produced, even as librarians do for the users of their libraries.

The continuing education role that is being played by "information men", who attend course modes and participate in interaction modes, in communicating knowledge to their associates is being recognized as being of considerable magnitude.

A mode that has great potential for continuing education is that identified in the literature by various names -- invisible colleges, journal clubs, grass root seminars. These voluntary groups are generally started by concerned individual professionals. It is suggested that management and individual professionals who are concerned about continuing education should take the initiative in finding ways and means to stimulate the formulation of such groups. It would also seem that many library committees might use this mode by means of correspondence to make their assignments more meaningful and productive.

Other types of voluntary activity indicated by the individual's own efforts which have been found to be valuable means of continuing education are teaching, writing and publication, and research. Each of these is considered by the individuals engaging in them as a very important part of their continuing education efforts, but overall the number engaged in these activities in any profession represents a small percentage of the total number of professionals.

The literature indicates that a major trend in continuing professional education is the use of home study combined with the new concepts and methodologies of instructional technology. Home study courses reinforced by the provision of media centers (which could be located in libraries across the land) provide at least one means by which every professional could engage in systematic continuing education throughout his or her life. It is one model that is being experimented with -- especially in Europe -- that could lead to the fulfillment of the university without walls concept. The rapidity with which this mode is gaining supporters is proving that learning does not have to be confined by space-time limitations and that continuing education efforts can flourish if indeed they cater to the personalized criteria of individual professionals.

The renewal center or teacher center in a setting adjacent to schools where the education of teachers takes place simultaneously with the education of children is a related mode to the media centers that would be supportive of home study programs. In the case of the teacher renewal centers, leadership at NEA is insistent that the teachers be given a central role in governance of such centers and specific guidelines are being established to insure this concept. Flexibility regarding use of the center and continuous and easy access to all resources provided by the new technology are characteristics of all renewal centers.

The staff college concept has been promoted as an important mode of continuing education, especially in the area of public administration. As conceived by writers in this discipline, attendance at a staff college is considered as the capstone of educational experience for leadership in public service. Philosophically such a mode is considered necessary because it is believed that no other type of educational or training facility or current programs in continuing education provide curricula in sufficient depth to prepare public administrators for the type of imaginative and informed leadership necessary to plan and develop public policy. The staff college concept usually demands the full attention of the participants, requiring complete separation of participants from their normal activity for the duration of the various programs offered. The staff college is usually envisioned as an institutional arrangement which is innovative in its approaches and not bound by traditional or already existing limitations or policies.

Regardless of the mode of continuing education chosen, those responsible for planning and programming must think in terms of using and keeping pace with the new technology. No one method can be relied on for continuing education; available knowledge and methodologies from the combined fields of library and information science education, the behavioral sciences, and instructional technology must be integrated into practical applications to meet the needs of the individual librarian. In addition to experimenting with different modes of continuing education and the wide utilization of imaginative tools made possible by the new technology, there is need to know the effects of the various forms of participation on each other.

Interpretive Summary

Throughout professional literature today there is increasing emphasis on the necessity of providing the kind of education that will help the individual practitioner adapt to new developments by continuous self-education throughout his or her career. Also, continuing education is seen as something beyond the self-development of the individual and viewed as something that is a national necessity. The following comment of Calkins (C-2:18) of the Brookings Institution is pertinent:

> Continuing education is no longer merely a good and worthy
> thing for self-development; it has become a national necessity....
> it has become indispensable to the effective operation of our
> free society... and the management of the multifarious public
> affairs of the country... no one in these times can go far on the
> intellectual capital he acquires in his youth. Unless he keeps
> his knowledge or skill up to date, revises it, adds to it, enriches
> it with new experience and supplements it with new ideas as they
> displace the old, he is soon handicapped for the duties of the day.

As the problems of continuing education are nationwide, it is recommended that only a nationwide coordinating structure which articulates and reinforces existing personal, local, state, regional, and national education resources will be able to provide the objective sought -- provision of equal, coordinated educational opportunities throughout the country for librarians and information scientists who need and want to pursue a lifetime of learning. A partnership of all relevant groups will provide learning resources which none can provide alone. To succeed, such a partnership will require a structure that will provide for continuity of policy, planning, coordination, administration, evaluation, and the development of a distribution system that will make a reality of the concept of a nationwide university without walls.

APPENDICES

HELPING

OURSELVES

OUT

OF

THE

MAZE

PROGRAM ON CONTINUING EDUCATION IN PROFESSIONAL ASSOCIATIONS*

JANUARY 28, 1973, 1:55 - 6:00 P.M. SHOREHAM HOTEL
WASHINGTON, D. C.

A mini-workshop
sponsored by
the
Association of
American
Library
Schools
Committee on
Continuing
Library
Education
for the
Continuing
Library
Education
Network.

1:55 - 2:00 p.m. Opening Remarks
Dr. Elizabeth W. Stone, Chairman, AALS Committee
and Chairman, Department of Library Science
The Catholic University of America

2:00 - 2:20   AMERICAN INSTITUTE OF ARCHITECTS:
Dr. Stuart W. Rose, Director of Continuing Education

2:20 - 2:30   Questions from participants

2:30 - 2:50   AMERICAN INSTITUTE OF BANKING:
Dr. Robert P. Cavalier, Director of Education

2:50 - 3:00   Questions from participants

3:00 - 3:20   NATIONAL EDUCATION ASSOCIATION:*
Dr. Roy A. Edelfelt, Division of Instruction and
Professional Development; Associate Editor,
The Journal of Teacher Education.

3:20 - 3:30   Questions from participants

3:30 - 3:45   Coffee break

* As noted in the attached "Who's Who" statement, Dr. Robert A. Luke
made the presentation for NEA, as Dr. Cavalier was unexpectedly called
out of the city the day of the program.

ˇ5 – 4:05 p. m.	AMERICAN SOCIETY FOR MECHANICAL ENGINEERS: Dr. Donald E. Marlowe, Past President of the Society and Vice-President for Administration, The Catholic University of America
4:05 – 4:15	Questions from the participants
4:15 – 4:35	SOCIETY FOR THE ADVANCEMENT OF CONTINUING EDUCATION FOR MINISTRY (SACEM): Dr. Connolly C. Gamble, Jr., Founder and first President of the Society, and Director of Continuing Education, Union Theological Seminary, Richmond, Virginia
4:35 – 4:45	Questions from participants
4:45 – 4:55	Remarks or Questions to whole panel.
4:55 – 5:05	Break
5:05 – 5:25	Idea Groups
5:25 – 5:40	Idea group reports
ʻ0 – 6:00	Recommendations for action.

****

The representatives from other professions have been asked to be prepared to discuss the following topics on the national level:

(a) Function, objectives, and scope of their programs
(b) Guides and criteria established for program development
(c) Clientele served (professional and/or others)
(d) Organizational structure (regional, state, etc.)
(e) Sources of funding
(f) Program formats (workshops, correspondence, cassettes, etc.)
(g) Methods of distribution
(h) Personnel (faculty)
(i) Guides and criteria developed for evaluations methods
(j) Rewards or recognition given to individuals for participating in continuing education programs.
(k) Programs and prospects for the future.

WHO'S WHO

PARTICIPANTS IN THE MINI-WORKSHOP ON
CONTINUING PROFESSIONAL EDUCATION

DR. ROBERT P. CAVALIER, Director of Education, American Institute of Banking

Dr. Cavalier brings a background on industrial and academic psychology to the field of Continuing Education. Before he joined the American Institute of Banking as National Education Administrator in 1967, he served on the faculty of Fairlie Dickenson University as Assistant Professor of Psychology and Director of Educational and Vocational Counseling. There he also acted as consultant to the Reading and Study Institute.

Dr. Cavalier received an AB degree in psychology and philosophy from Fordham University, an MS in Industrial Psychology from North Carolina State University, and a Ph.D. in Psychology from Columbia University. He is the author of several articles on teaching and education, and the member of several professional associations including the American Psychological Association, the American Association for the Advancement of Science, the American Academy of Political and Social Science, the American Educational Research Association, and the American Association of University Professors.

Some of the innovative publications that Dr. Cavalier has designed are on display outside our room today, such as The Instructor Performance Inventory, The Learning Methods Laboratory, Toward Becoming a Better Teacher, A Proposal for Continuing Career Education in Banking Through a National Consortium of Colleges and Universities, in Cooperation with The American Institute of Banking..., Continuing Career Education.

DR. CONNOLLY C. GAMBLE, JR., Society for the Advancement of Continuing Education for Ministry (SACEM)

Dr. Gamble is currently Director of Continuing Education and Morgan Foundation Associate Professor of Bibliography at Union Theological Seminary in Richmond, Virginia. Before assuming that position he served as assistant librarian at the Seminary. Prior to that he served as pastor of the Presbyterian Church at Whitmire, South Carolina. He served as President of SACEM from 1967-1969 and as Executive Secretary from 1969 to the present.

Dr. Gamble received his A.B. degree from Lenoir Rhyne College, a B.S. in Library Science from the University of North Carolina at Chapel Hill, and a B.D., Th.M. and Th.D. from Union Theological Seminary.

Publications of SACEM that Dr. Gamble has brought with him for distribution include: SACEM: Society for the Advancement of Continuing Education for Ministry, Tower Room Scholars, Continuing Education Resource Guide (New England, Mid-Atlantic, South, North Central, West).

ROBERT LUKE, Professional Associate of the National Education Association
Division of Instruction and Professional Development.

Mr. Robert Luke is currently in the National Education Association's Division of Instruction
and Professional Development.* In addition he is a member of the IPD Project team on
Teachers' Centers. Before joining NEA, Mr. Luke served as Director of Adult Education
for the Lincoln Library at Springfield, Illinois. Prior to that he was Director of the WPA
State Library Project. His other positions include that of Assistant State Librarian of the
Colorado State Library.

Mr. Luke received his B.S. in Library Science from the University of Denver. His articles
have been widely published in education periodicals.

Some of the recent publications of the Division of Instruction and Professional
Development on display are: Remaking the World of the Career Teacher;
The Teacher and His Staff; Differentiating Teaching Roles; The Real World
of the Beginning Teacher, and 3 articles by Dr. Roy A. Edelfelt: "Redesigning
the Education Profession," which focuses on the arguments for the idea of
differentiated staffing; "The Reform of Education and Teacher Education: A
Complex Task," and "Inservice Training of Teachers." The latter states:

"More and more, continuing education is coming to be seen as
on-the-job or job-related training. Teachers are beginning to
recognize that inservice education is a career-long endeavor,
and are exerting greater individual effort in self-education. Most
important is the fact that teacher education beyond the initial degree
is being seen more as improved professional performance."

DR. DONALD E. MARLOWE, Past President of the American Society for Mechanical
Engineers and Vice-President for Administration,
The Catholic University of America

Dr. Marlowe became Vice-President for Administration of Catholic University in 1970 after
serving as Professor of Mechanical Engineering and Dean of the School of Engineering and
Architecture. Prior to joining the faculty at Catholic University, Dr. Marlowe was
Associate Professor of the U. S. Naval Ordinance Laboratory at White Oak, Maryland. He
holds degrees from the University of Detroit and the University of Michigan. During World
War II he worked in naval research, specializing in weapons development for undersea warfare.

In addition to serving as President of the American Society for Mechanical Engineers, Dr.
Marlowe was President of the National Council of Engineering Examiners during 1966.

---

* The Division of Instruction and Professional Development (DIPD) is a new division of
NEA created on September 1, 1971, as a merger of the National Commission on Teacher
Education and Professional Standards, Center for Study of Instruction, Adult Education, and
Educational Technology Division.

DR. STUART W. ROSE, Director of Continuing Education, American Institute of
Architects

Dr. Rose brings a background of architecture and structural engineering to the field of
continuing education. Since he joined the AIA in 1971, he has been pioneering programs in
continuing education for architects and engineers. Among his programs are training
laboratories, computer centers, tapes and cassettes and correspondence courses, many of
which can be used by other professions. His research work has been published in architectural
journals and in the proceedings of several professional associations. His educational background includes a B.A. in architecture and a B.S. in structural engineering from Kansas
State University, an M.A. in architecture from the University of Washington, and a Ph.D.
in administration and higher education from the University of Michigan.

Dr. Rose conceives of continuing education as falling in two major categories:
(1) activities leading to behavioral change, such as the 26 training laboratories
he has developed; formation of clinics where professionals can come for help
in problem solving; development of a series of games which wi ll elicit the kind
of behavior sought   to successfully carry out activities, and (2) activities
and services providing information, such as RAP (Review of Architectural
Periodicals) on audio tape cassettes; in depth reports, which include slides, wo rk
sheets and syllabus type information; reference services centering in national
data bank of information; and continuing education reference data, focusing
chiefly on sources of packaged materials in various media. Examples of the
announcements of RAP and the training laboratories are on display.

APPENDIX B

DATA SHEET ON CONTINUING EDUCATION AS IT EXISTS IN
LIBRARY ASSOCIATIONS

I. Please list the specific programs, courses, or activities in the area of library continuing
education that are being carried out or being planned by your library association. Please use
additional sheets if necessary.

	Offered or Developed		Nature of Programs
Before 1971-72	During 1971-72	Planned 1972-73	
1. ( )	( )	( )	Workshops: (Specify content) At national conferences
2. ( )	( )	( )	At regional conferences
3. ( )	( )	( )	At state level
4. ( )	( )	( )	At local level
5. ( )	( )	( )	In cooperation with other library associations
6. ( )	( )	( )	In cooperation with other professional groups
7. ( )	( )	( )	In cooperation with library school(s)
8. ( )	( )	( )	In cooperation with employing institutions

227

Offered or Developed			
Before 1971-72	During 1971-72	Planned 1972-73	Nature of Program
			Institutes or Seminars:
9. ( )	( )	( )	At national conferences
10. ( )	( )	( )	At regional conferences
11. ( )	( )	( )	At state level
12. ( )	( )	( )	At local level
13. ( )	( )	( )	In cooperation with other library associations
14. ( )	( )	( )	In cooperation with other professional groups
15. ( )	( )	( )	In cooperation with library school(s)
16. ( )	( )	( )	In cooperation with employing institutions

228

Offered or Developed			Nature of Program
Before 1971-72	During 1971-72	Planned 1972-73	
17. ( )	( )	( )	Development of packaged printed programs
18. ( )	( )	( )	Development of cassettes for distribution
19. ( )	( )	( )	Development and distribution of bibliographies
20. ( )	( )	( )	Publishing of articles in journals
21. ( )	( )	( )	Publishing of books specifically designed for continuing education
22. ( )	( )	( )	Development of programs which have travelled from one geographical location to another
23. ( )	( )	( )	Development of programmed texts (printed)
24. ( )	( )	( )	Development of programmed learning (computer)
25. ( )	( )	( )	Development of tutorial centers
26. ( )	( )	( )	Use of cable TV
27. ( )	( )	( )	Use of talk-back TV

229

Offered or Developed			Nature of Program
Before 1971-72	During 1971-72	Planned 1972-73	

Other:
28. ( )   ( )   ( )

29. ( )   ( )   ( )

30. ( )   ( )   ( )

31. ( )   ( )   ( )

32. ( )   ( )   ( )   Research projects in the area of continuing library education (specify). Include brief description of proposals submitted even though they may not have been funded or implemented.

33. ( )   ( )   ( )   Hold an annual conference on continuing education?

34. II.   What are the continuing education objectives and concerns of your association?

35. III.   How high a priority does continuing education have in your association in relation to its other objectives?

36. IV. In your library association, how is it determined what programs will be developed and implemented?

37. What is the relation to needs of practicing librarians to programs offered?

38. How are needs determined?

39. V. What is the clientele toward which your programs are directed?

40. ( ) All members of the association

41. ( ) Only professional librarians

42. ( ) Professionals, technicians, clerical

43. ( ) Professionals and library technicians

44. ( ) All employees in the library

45. ( ) Other patterns:

VI. What is the relation of your organizational structure to continuing educational programming? (Is it by regions, states, type of interest group, etc.)

46. ( ) By regions

47. ( ) By states

48. ( ) In local areas where chapters are organized

49. ( ) By type of interest group

50. ( ) Other:

VII. How are continuing education programs funded?

51.   ( )   By dues

52.   ( )   By special grants

53.   ( )   By registration fees

54.   ( )   By   combination of a, b, and c

55.   ( ))   By combination of a and c

56.   ( )   By combination of a and b

57.   ( )   Other

58. VIII. What are your methods of distribution for materials developed?

59. IX. How are the "experts" chosen or identified who develop programs?

60. X.   What ways are provided for evaluation of materials and programs produced?

61.   Has a set of evaluative criteria been developed?

    XI. Does your association provide any type of reward or recognition to individuals who
         participate in continuing education programs?

62.   ( )   Yes
63.   ( )   No

What specific form does recognition take:

51.   (   )   Certificate

52.   (   )   Special recognition at annual meetings

53.   (   )   Certification

54.   (   )   Other

XII.   Does your association have one specific person or group that has special responsibility in the area of continuing education?

55.   (   )   Yes
56.   (   )   No

57.   What is the title of this person?

58.   What is the scope of their job?

Is it volunteered or paid effort?

59.   (   )   Volunteer
60.   (   )   Paid

61.   What is the name of the person or persons who has this responsibility in your organization at the present time?

62.   What type or training or orientation is given to the person or persons responsible for this function?

XIII. Does your association serve as a clearing house for:

63.   (   )   Bibliographies
64.   (   )   Model programs
65.   (   )   Approved projects
66   (   )   Disapproved applications
67.   (   )   Reports of utilization of research in continuing education

233

XIV. Does your association provide support for:

68.   (   )   Training in administrative concepts and practices for top administrators?

69.   (   )   Training   in administrative and management concepts for middle managers.

70.   (   )   Training for first line supervisors for the role as a developer of the human
resources assigned to him or her?

71.   (   )   Training that has as its objective updating the practitioner in his subject specialty

72.   (   )   Planning for continuing education program development

73.   (   )   Training key personnel to optimally   utilize nonprofessionals

74.   (   )   Provide consultation in continuing education program development for groups
in your association wishing to plan continuing education programs?

75. XV.   Has your association developed guides and criteria for program development?

76. XVI. Developed evaluative criteria by which a library can determine its needs and those of its
employees in the area of continuing education?

77. XVII. Does your association establish experimental programs intended to discover new
methods and solutions of persistent problems in the field. (This refers to actual
experimental programs, not just a review of existing activity.)

78. XVIII. Does your association search for new and effective educational techniques and modes in
order to maximize the content presented in continuing education programs?
[ ] yes [ ] No.
79.   If yes, how is this done?

234

MEMORANDUM   January 1972

To: Continuing Library Education Network Members

From: Elizabeth W. Stone, Chairman
        AALS Committee on Continuing Library Education

        Chairman, Dept. of Library Science, The Catholic University of America

Re: Summary of data received from library associations in response to questionnaire mailed
        out entitled, "Data Sheet on Continuing Education as it Exists in Library Associations."

In August, 1972, questionnaires were mailed to twenty-six library associations. This total
includes the thirteen divisions of the American Library Association.

The Committee wishes to thank the representatives of the six associations which had send back
the completed questionnaire by the middle of December. In reviewing the data contained in the
attached summary sheet, it should be realized that the response of six out of twenty-six represents
only a 23% response by the library associations. Therefore, the report is only a sampling of what
is being done, and not a comprehensive survey of all twenty-six library associations to which
the questionnaire was sent.

Associations answering the questionnaire, and their Continuing Library Education Network
representatives are:

American Association of Law Libraries   Association of Jewish Libraries
Mr. Jack Ellenberger   Mrs. Edith Degani

ALA -- Reference and Adult Services Division   Medical Library Association
Mrs. Martha L. Reynolds (completed by   Miss Julie A. Virgo
    Andy Hansen, Executive Secretary, RASD)

ALA - Resources and Technical Services   Special Libraries Association
          Division   Mr. H. Robert Malinowsky
Mr. Robin Downes (completed by Carol Kelm,
    Executive Secretary, RTSD)

I. Please list the specific programs, courses, or activities in the area of library continuing education that are being carried out or being planned by your library association.

| | Didn't Answer | Offered or Developed | | | Nature of Programs |
		Before 1971-72	During 1971-72	Planned 1972-73	
1.	4	2	2	2	Workshops: (Specify content) At national conferences 1. Divisions of SLA regularly sponsor workshops at the annual conference. Content varies according to divisional needs. 2. Cataloging clincs, discussions of new publications or concepts in the fields of specialization of the association. At regional conferences
2.	5	1	1	1	1. Dealing with various aspects of hospital and medical library practice. At state level
3.	5	1	1	1	1. Dealing with various aspects of hospital and medical library practice. At local level
4.	3	3	3	1	1. Workshops on library technique. 2. Local SLA chapters have had many workshops. No list available in my files. 3. Generally in connection with or in lieu of programs at the AALL chapter level, i.e., workshop, "Law Library and Automation." In cooperation with other library associations
5.	4	1	1	1	1. Occasionally, in support by joint sponsorship; i.e. April 1972 DCLA/LL Sic,/SLA continuing education workshop, Mayflower Hotel, Washington, D.C. 2. A workshop on Government Documents planned for March 1973 -- SLA local chapter, state associations, and others.

| | Offered or Developed | | | |
Didn't Answer	Before 1971-72	During 1971-72	Planned 1972-73	Nature of Programs
6.				**In cooperation with other professional groups**
5	0	1	1	1. Some local chapters of SLA holding workshops with ASIS.
7.				**In cooperation with library school(s)**
5	1	1	1	1. To the extent that library school facilities are used.
8.				**In cooperation with employing institutions**
6	0	0	0	
9.				**Institutes or Seminars:**
1	5	4	2	**At national conferences**

At national conferences
1. Offer one day long courses on 20 topics
2. Preconference institutes: LC Classification (1966); Subject Analysis (1969), Acquisitions (1969 & 1972).
3. Preconferences: Orientation of the Out of School Adult to the Use of the Public Library (1967), Computer-Based Reference Service (1971).
4. Four rotating AALS Continuing Education Institutes offering four special subject area curricula, preconventions since 1964. Enrollment usually in excess of 100. For details, consult AALL headquarters, 53 West Jackson Boulevard., Chicago, Illinois.
5. San Francisco Conference - Continuing Education Seminars: (1971)
   1. Participation and persuasion techniques.
   2. Library publications, in house and out.
   3. Reference update.
   4. People and jobs.
Boston Conference -- Continuing Education Seminars: (1972)
   1. Technical report literature update.
   2. Environmental and ecological literature, where does it all come from.
   3. Making and living with a budget.
Pittsburgh Conference -- Continuing Educat Education Seminars: (1973)
   1. Cataloging of unconventional library material.
   2. Unity of information science in theory and practice.

	Offered or Developed			
Didn't Answer	Before 1971-72	During 1971-72	Planned 1972-73	Nature of Programs

9. (Continued)

3. How to train the special librarians.
4. Interpersonal communication.
5. Personnel management and administration.

10.

4	1	1	2

At regional conferences
1. Offer 1-3 courses from (above) 20 topics.
2. Possible seminars on time, cost and methodology of technical services.

11.

4	1	2	2

At state level
1. Offer 1-3 courses from (above) 20 topics.
2. Possible seminars on time, cost and methodology of technical services.

12.

4	1	2	1

At local level
1. Offer 1-3 courses from (above) 20 topics.
2. San Francisco Bay Chapter held a seminar on Personnel Management.

13.

5	0	0	1

In cooperation with other library associations
1. Possible co-sponsorship with state and regional groups of technical service librarians on possible seminars on time, cost and methodology of technical services.

14.

3	2	2	2

In cooperation with other professional groups
1. Blank
2. Conference on the future of the general adult reading.
3. Indexing seminars co-sponsored with the National Federation of Science Abstracting and Indexing Services.

15.

5	(	0	1

In cooperation with library school(s)
1. The 1973 Pittsburgh Conference Seminars are being presented by University of Pittsburgh Library School Institute on How to Teach Special Librarianship at University of Michigan, May 1972.

16.

8	0	0	0

In cooperation with employing institutions

	Offered or Developed			
Didn't Answer	Before 1971-72	During 1971-72	Planned 1972-73	Nature of Programs

17.

| 3 | 2 | 2 | 2 | Development of packaged printed programs |

1. Have talked about this but no concrete plans
2. Blank
3. Blank

18.

| 5 | | 1 | 1 | Development of cassettes for distribution |

1. Collect and disseminate, act as a clearing house for these materials.

19.

| 0 | 5 | 5 | 3 | Development and distribution of bibliographies |

1. One bibliography being prepared on environmental and ecological literature, result of conference seminar.
2. At the rotating institutes, since 1964.
3. Blank
4. In RQ and Adult Services as separate leaflets e.g., Helping Minority Businessmen.
5. Relevant to medical library practice.
6. RTSD Office and Division and Section Committees develop bibliographies for distribution at ALA conferences and with letters from people asking for assistance.

20.

| 1 | 5 | 4 | 4 | Publishing of articles in journals. |

1. Especially the Resources & Technical Services Division journal, Library Resources & Technical Services.
2. Blank.
3. Blank.
4. Special Libraries.
5. Chicago Law Library Society Proceedings, 64 LLP #2 (1971).

21.

| 4 | 1 | 0 | 1 | Publishing of books specifically designed for continuing education. |

1. Have talked briefly of this.
2. Reading for an Age of Change.

22.

| 2 | 2 | 3 | 3 | Development of programs which have travelled from one geographical location to another |

1. Blank
2. Possible seminar on time, cost and methodology of technical services.
3. Reference Book Exhibit.
4. Attempted to take some local chapter workshops to other areas, but unable to bring it about.

239

	Offered or Developed			
Didn't Answer	Before 1971-2	During 1971-2	Planned 1972-73	Nature of Program

23.

Development of programmed text (printed)
     5   0   0   0
1. One school did not check a corresponding year, but indicated, "Some of our members have."

24.

Development of programmed learning (computer)
     6   0   0   0

25.

Development of tutorial centers
     6   0   0   0

26.

Use of Cable TV
     5   0   1   0
1. Division program during 1972 annual ALA conference.

27.

Use of talk-back TV
     6   0   0   0

28-31.

     4   1   1   1
Other:
1. Guidelines and criteria for practitioners in specific areas of concern, e.g. "Library's Responsibility to the Aging."
2. No dates given.
   a. Acting as a clearinghouse for continuing education activities of related organizations and associations.
   b. Conducting research.

32.

Research projects in the area of continuing library education.
     5   0   1   1
1. Two projects.
   a. Continuing education needs for medical librarians.
   b. Continuing education needs for medical librarianship.

33.

Hold an annual conference on continuing education?
     5   1   1   1
1. Blank

240

34.

II.   What are the continuing education objectives and concerns of your association?

    1.   a.   To upgrade the library service our members can offer in their libraries, by developing new skills and upgrading existing skills.
           b.   To design and implement a total plan for continuing education for all levels of health science library personnel.

    2.   To: "Stimulate the continuing professional growth of library personnel presently and potentially engaged in public service."

    3.   Provide continuing education opportunities through programs and publications to librarians working in the field of acquisitions, cataloging, and the development and coordination of the country's library resources.

    4.   To offer professional training and guidance to librarians, professional and otherwise, in small, often isolated, libraries.

    5.   The association's major concern is to continue to hold seminars at the annual con-conferences. Seminars should be of interest to all groups of special librarians, interested in updating and alerting new and old libraries to new techniques in the profession.

    6.   Continuing education of presently employed law librarians who are employed both at advanced and intermediate levels of professional responsibility. For details, see attachment, "AALL Recruitment Checklist," 1969 ed., pp. 22-28.

35. III.   How high a priority does continuing education have in your association in relation to its other objectives?

    1.   A very high priority, given resources and faculty for the rotating annual AALL Institutes, especially.

    2.   High priority with SLA Education Committee is supported and watched at all times. Increased interest has been shown in the past two years.

    3.   It has a high priority in the Synagogue, School and Center Division of the Association in which there are many non-professional librarians.

    4.   Continuing education, particularly through programs, publications, and opportunities for informal discussion, is an important part of the division's activities.

    5.   One of the budget.

    6.   Objectives not ranked.

241

36. IV.   In your library association, how is it determined what programs will be developed and implemented ?

    1.   By the Education Committee.
    2.   By recommendation of the Director of Medical Library Education and/or the Committee on Continuing Education with approval of the Board of Directors.
    3.   The staff liaison can suggest programs but the membership units (Committee and Governing Bodies) of the Division decide which programs to undertake.
    4.   By Executive Committee of each of the two divisions of the Association.
    5.   An Education Committee appointed by the President suggests and implements all programs at the Association level. Local chapters carry out their own.
    6.   Board of Directors decides on basis of input from committees, members, and other groups.

37.   What is the relation to needs of practicing librarians to programs offered ?

    1.   The needs of practicing librarians are given priority insofar as they are identified.
    2.   Various, from course to course, but most courses are practically oriented.
    3.   Hopefully all the programs are tailored to the needs of practicing librarians, especially technical service librarians.
    4.   The programs are designed to meet the needs of practicing librarians.
    5.   Blank
    6.   Programs offered at conferences are based somewhat directly on what the practicing librarians request of the Education Committee. The Committee takes suggestions from all members and decides which are the most important.

38.   How are needs determined ?

    1.   Through questionnaires, personal contact, bulletins.
    2.   Board of Directors decides on basis of input from committees, membership, and other groups.
    3.   By the Education Committee.
    4.   From surveys and questionnaires.
    5.   By requests made by members, informal observations of officers of the Association.
    6.   Concerns expressed in journal articles, letters to the editor, and informal conversations at meetings suggest appropriate programs.

39. V.   What is the clientele toward which your programs are directed?

	No. of Responses	No. of Assoc. Responding *	
40.	4	3.33	All members of the association
			1. Primarily library personnel engaged in Public Service
41.	0		Only professional librarians
42.	1	.5	Professionals, technicians, clerical

	No. of Responses	No. of Assoc. Responding *	
43.	1	.33	Professionals and library technicians
44.	0		All employees in the library
45.	3	1.83	Other patterns: 1. Anyone assuming professional responsibility. 2. Technical Service Librarian and publishers, jobbers, booksellers 3. Librarians, professionals, and others who are sole staff members in small, often isolated, libraries.

VI. What is the relation of your organizational structure to continuing educational programming (Is it by regions, states, type of interest group, etc.)?

46.	1	.5	By Association
47.	0		By states
48.	3	1.5	In local areas where chapters are organized 1. Occasionally 2. Blank 3. Blank
49.	4	3.0	By type of interest group 1. Within states and regions as well as nationally. 2. Blank 3. Blank 4. Blank
50.	1	1.0	Other: 1. Twenty courses are available. These may be sponsored by any regional medical library, regional medical program, regional medical group, or any other interested group on a local, state, or regional basis.

VII. How are continuing education programs funded?

51.	0		By dues
52.	0		By special grants
53.	2	2.0	By registration fees
54.	2	1.5	By combination of a, b, and c
55.	1	1.0	By combination of a and c

No. of   No. of Assoc.
Responses   Responding *

56.   0   By combination of a and b.

57.   2   1.5   Other
                                 1.   Sale of materials
                                 2.   By the Association, whose income may come from
                                       a, b, c, or some other source, e. g. publishers.

58. VIII.   What are your methods of distribution for materials developed ?

    1.   Through Headquarters and advertised in Special Libraries.
    2.   Pre-institute and at the institute.
    3.   Via articles in professional journals and published books which developed from ALA
          pre-conference institutes.
    4.   Membership lists.
    5.   Given as part of course package. Info is mailed or telephoned upon request.
    6.   a. RC to membership
                  b. at conferences
                  c. sales
                  d. Other organization's meetings

59. IX.   How are the "experts" chosen or identified who develop programs ?

    1.   Through personal contacts with librarians in the field and through library schools.
    2.   By a Special Committee on Annual AALL Educational Institutes.
    3.   By a Committee on Continuing Education or the Director of Medical Library Education.
    4.   Volunteers are chosen from membership with known expertise on the program's subject.
    5.   By Executive Committees of each Division of the Association. "Experts" are those
          members with professional degrees plus experience in their special fields.
    6.   Through recommendations of Board members, membership, and existing committees.

60.X.   What ways are provided for evaluation of materials and programs produced ?

    1.   Self review and student response at the institutes.
    2.   a. Questionnaire
                  b. An extensive grant application has been made which will do this in a number of
                     different ways.
    3.   Annual conference seminars are evaluated by the people who attend.
    4.   Planning committees generally review and evaluate the seminars or institutes. Readers
          or editors evaluate manuscripts before publication.
    5.   The Executive Committees, or subcommittees thereof, evaluate the materials
          and programs.

61.   Has a set of evaluative criteria been developed ?

          No   3   1. ALA reviewed preconferences and continues to scrutinize the
          Yes   2   format. (No)
      Somewhat   1   2. See 55 LLJ 190-99 (1962) and 65 LLJ 130 (1972) (Yes)
                            3. Not as good as it could be. (Somewhat)

XI. Does your association provide any type of recognition to individuals who participate in continuing education programs?

62. 3 responses Yes 1. A certificate of comparative literature from the prescribed 4 annual institutes as 1 body of   study.
2. Is now going to be offering a Certificate of Attendance.

63. 3 responses No

What specific form does recognition take:

64. 3 Didn't Answer

65. 2 Certificate

66. Special recognition at annual meetings

67. Certification

68. 1 Other
1. Certificate of attendance.

XII. Does your association have one specific person or group that has special responsibility in the area of continuing education?

69. 3 responses Yes

70. 3 responses No

71. What is the title of this person?
1. Chairman of Education Committee
2. Director of Medical Library Education Committee on Continuing Education
3. Committee appointed annually by AALL President.

72. What is the scope of their job?
1. To direct and coordinate the educational activities of the Association.
To advise, provide guidelines, establish standards, conditions.
2. Develop Continuing Education seminars at annual conferences.
Attempt to coordinate local seminars and workshops.
Survey and recommend ways to strengthen the educational programs, for career in special librarianship and information science. Select John Cotton Dana lecturers and administer the John Cotton Dana program.

Is it volunteer or paid effort?

73. 2 Volunteer

74. 1 Paid
1. Full-time with subsidiary staff.

245

75.   What is the name of the person or persons who has this responsibility in your organization at the present time ?
         1.   Julie A. VIRGO, Medical Library Association
         2.   H. Robert MALINOWSKY, Assistant Director of Libraries, University of Kansas, 66044, Special Libraries Association
         3.   Ms. WILDMAN, Yale Law Library, Mr. ELLENBERGER American Association of Law Libraries

76.   What type of training or orientation is given to the person or persons responsible for this function ?
         1.   Senior educational standing in the AALL.
         2.   Background in research, library education and medical librarianship, i.e., academic qualifications and experience.
         3.   None.

XIII.   Does your association serve as a clearing house for:

	No. of Responses	No. of Assoc. Responding *	
77.	3	2.5	Bibliographies Two indicated this to "some extent."
78.	0		Model Programs
79.	1	.5	Approved projects
80.	0		Disapproved applications
81.	0		Reports of utilization of research in continuing education
82.	2	2.0	Didn't answer No Not at present

8 XIV.   Does your association provide support for:

83.	1	.17	Training in administrative concepts and practices for top administrators ? 1. Planned for 1973.
84.	2	.67	Training in administrative and management concepts for middle managers ? 1. Primarily 2. Planned for 1973
85.	1	.17	Training for first line supervisors for the role as a developer of the human resources assigned to him or her ?
86.	3	1.5	Training that has as its objective updating the practitioner in his subject specialty.
87.	2	.5	Planning for continuing education program development
88.	1	.5	Training key personnel to optimally utilize nonprofessionals
89.	2	.5	Provide consultation in continuing education program development for groups in your association wishing to plan continuing education programs ?
90.	1	1.0	No.
91.	1	1.0	Didn't answer.

92. **XV.**   Has your association developed guides and criteria for program development?

  No.   4   1. See 55 LLJ 190-199 and 65 LLJ 130 (1972). (Yes)
  Yes   1
  No answer 1

93. **XVI.**   Developed evaluative criteria by which a library can determine its needs and those of its employees in the area of continuing education?

  No   6

94. **XVII**   Does your association establish experimental programs intended to discover new methods and solutions of persistent problems in the field. (This refers to actual experimental programs, not just a review of existing activity.)

  No.   4
  Yes   2

95. **XVIII**   Does your association search for new and effective educational techniques and modes in order to maximize the content presented in continuing education programs?

  Yes   4
  No   2

96.   If yes, how is this done?

  1.   The Division through its sub-units continually reviews its programs to make it more helpful to Division membership and technical service librarians in general.
  2.   When program content is agreed upon, a conscientious attempt is made to seek the best vehicle for conveying the content to the participants. There is no outgoing search for new methodology unrelated to the content of specific programs, however.
  3.   Contact with other professional educators, participation in professional associations. , e. g. American Society for Hospital Education and Training. Conducting research in this area, progressively seeking out literature and information on the topic.

---

* PROCEDURAL NOTE: For several questions there are two columns of figures. The first column gives the number of times a particular item was indicated. Often associations listed more than one item or activity in which they were engaged. The last column, "No. of Associations responding," endeavors to reflect this by giving a weighted response.
For example, if an association lists more than one item, each one counts equally so that the total will be one. The total, therefore, of the last column will always add up to the number of library associations upon which the data for that particular question is based.

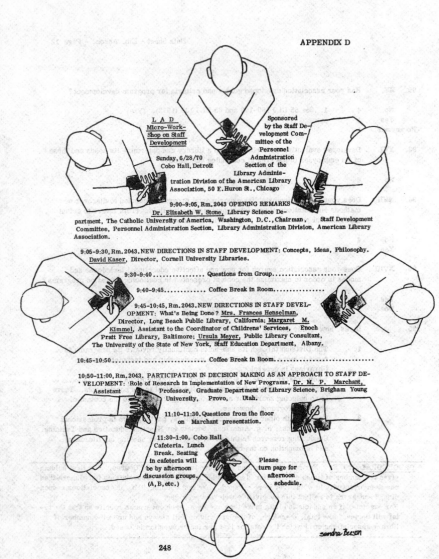

L A D
Micro-Work-
Shop on Staff
Development

Sunday, 6/28/70
Cobo Hall, Detroit

Sponsored
by the Staff De-
velopment Com-
mittee of the
Personnel
Administration
Section of the
Library Adminis-
tration Division of the American Library
Association, 50 E. Huron St., Chicago

9:00-9:05, Rm. 2043 OPENING REMARKS
Dr. Elizabeth W. Stone, Library Science De-
partment, The Catholic University of America, Washington, D.C., Chairman, Staff Development
Committee, Personnel Administration Section, Library Administration Division, American Library
Association.

9:05-9:30, Rm. 2043. NEW DIRECTIONS IN STAFF DEVELOPMENT: Concepts, Ideas, Philosophy.
David Kaser, Director, Cornell University Libraries.

9:30-9:40 . . . . Questions from Group . . . .

9:40-9:45 . . . . Coffee Break in Room . . . .

9:45-10:45, Rm. 2043. NEW DIRECTIONS IN STAFF DEVEL-
OPMENT: What's Being Done? Mrs. Frances Henselman,
Director, Long Beach Public Library, California; Margaret M.
Kimmel, Assistant to the Coordinator of Childrens' Services, Enoch
Pratt Free Library, Baltimore; Ursula Meyer, Public Library Consultant,
The University of the State of New York, Staff Education Department, Albany.

10:45-10:50 . . . . Coffee Break in Room . . . .

10:50-11:00, Rm. 2043. PARTICIPATION IN DECISION MAKING AS AN APPROACH TO STAFF DE-
VELOPMENT: Role of Research in Implementation of New Programs. Dr. M. P. Marchant,
Assistant Professor, Graduate Department of Library Science, Brigham Young
University, Provo, Utah.

11:10-11:30. Questions from the floor
on Marchant presentation.

11:30-1:00. Cobo Hall
Cafeteria. Lunch
Break. Seating
in cafeteria will
be by afternoon
discussion groups.
(A, B, etc.)

Please
turn page for
afternoon
schedule.

sandra Beeson

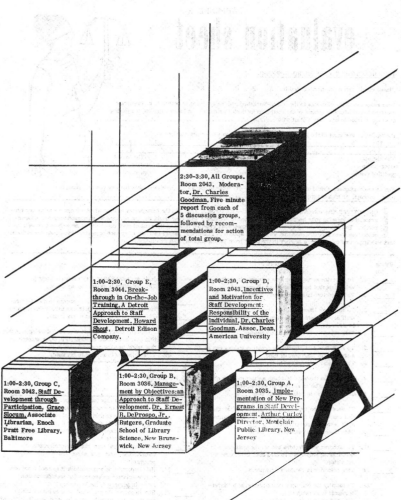

2:30-3:30, All Groups, Room 2043. Moderator, Dr. Charles Goodman. Five minute report from each of 5 discussion groups, followed by recommendations for action of total group.

1:00-2:30, Group E, Room 3044. Breakthrough in On-the-Job Training, A Detroit Approach to Staff Development, Howard Shout, Detroit Edison Company.

1:00-2:30, Group D, Room 2043. Incentives and Motivation for Staff Development: Responsibility of the Individual, Dr. Charles Goodman, Assoc. Dean, American University

1:00-2:30, Group C, Room 3042. Staff Development through Participation, Grace Slocum, Associate Librarian, Enoch Pratt Free Library, Baltimore

1:00-2:30, Group B, Room 3036. Management by Objectives; an Approach to Staff Development, Dr. Ernest R. DeProspo, Jr., Rutgers, Graduate School of Library Science, New Brunswick, New Jersey

1:00-2:30, Group A, Room 3035. Implementation of New Programs in Staff Development, Arthur Curley Director, Montclair Public Library, New Jersey

evaluation sheet

YOUR REACTIONS TO THE MICRO-WORKSHOP

Please circle group you participated in: A   B   C   D   E

Your response to the elements in the micro-workshop and the response of others is an important contribution to future programs of the Staff Development Committee. It helps complete the job that has been started today. Let's start with ....

Rating Scale: For most of the items a rating is asked for on a ten-point continuum:

```
10    9    8    7    6    5    4'    3    2    1    0
```

The highest   Average: The lowest
rating: an un-   sometimes;   rating: an unqualified yes   yes and no.   qualified no.

You as the evaluator, should use whatever number --from ten to one -- best describes the way you feel about the point, concept, or idea being judged. Let's look at..................

1 OBJECTIVES. Objectives are the destinations -- the targets. They are the components against which we can appraise our program. Not knowing your needs exactly, we tried to anticipate what they might be, but perhaps we surmised your needs incorrectly. For future planning we would like to know your greatest needs in the area of staff development as well as how well the objectives were accomplished that we tried to achieve. Therefore, please indicate after each objective if you considered it one that was important to you. Use number in the scale from 10 (the highest) to 0 (the lowest).

Rating 10)	Objectives

1. To describe some of the new concepts in staff development that have been found effective.
2. This objective is related to my needs.
3. To show how innovative and creative concepts in staff development can be successfully implemented in a library system.
4. This objective is related to my needs.
5. To show how participation in decision making can be a stimulus to staff development.
6. This objective is related to my needs.
7. To describe the ways in which management by objectives can be an aid to staff development.
8. This objective is related to my needs.
9. To describe the types of administrative strategies that can be used to motivate employees to engage in staff development activities.
10. This objective is related to my needs.
11. To discover what factors are strong motivators in encouraging employees toward staff development activities.
12. This objective is related to my needs.
13. To identify the characteristics typical of a "developmental leadership style."
14. This objective is related to my needs.
15. To provide some background reading suggestions to help participants go into more depth on the subjects presented after they return to their jobs.
16. This objective is related to my needs.
17. To motivate participants to engage in a self-learning agenda adapted to their own career development.
18. This objective is related to my needs.
19. To specify concepts relative to staff development that that have been found successful in other disciplines that might be experimented with in libraries.
20. This objective is related to my needs.

2 OVERALL PROGRAM RATINGS

21. How would you rate today's micro-shop in comparison with similar continuing education experiences in which you have participated of similar length?
22. How important do you consider it to send at least one prepared paper by one of the leaders in advance of the micro-shop?
23. How would you rate the pre-conference information sent you about the program?
24. How important do you consider it to send from one to five selected references for each discussion group in advance of the Workshop?
25. How important do you consider it to send a bibliography on the main theme of the workshop in advance?
26. How important do you consider it to distribute a bibliography on the main theme at the time of the workshop?

_____ 27. Did the size of the micro-sessions permit ample multilateral participation by everyone?

_____ 28. To what degree do you feel that the program will benefit the library which you represent?

_____ 29. Do you feel that you will be able to recognize staff development opportunities more readily and be able to handle them more effectively as a result of this micro-workshop?

_____ 30. Do you feel that you received enough background information and material to stimulate in you a desire to carry on your own self-development program even though no formal development programs may be available to you in your area?

_____ 31. Would you like to see a later Micro-Workshop concentrate on just one area of staff development in greater depth, rather than several areas as we did today: Yes ( )...Please specify.
No ( )...Skip to next question

_____ 32. Implications of Behavioral Sciences for Staff Development

_____ 33. Development of Human Resources in the Library

_____ 34. Individual Career Development

_____ 35. Employee Motivation

_____ 36. Environmental Conditions which Affect Staff Development.

_____ 37. Training Techniques and Educational Methods for Staff Development Programs

_____ 38. Management by Objectives as an Approach to Staff Development

_____ 39. Participatory Management as an Approach to Staff Development

_____ 40. Other:(Please specify) _____

_____ 41. For maximum participation, how important do you feel it is to try to continue to offer the micro-workshop without specific cost to the registrants?

_____ 42. How well informed on advanced staff development theory and practice do you consider yourself?

3 YOUR REACTIONS....TO OTHER TYPES OF PROGRAMS

CAN THE STAFF DEVELOPMENT COMMITTEE MEET YOUR NEEDS THROUGH OTHER PROGRAMS AND ACTIVITIES?
(Please use rating numbers to indicate the degree of importance you attach to each suggestion.)

_____ 43. By preparing guidelines to help the individual library manager or administrator to improve and expand his program for staff development and continuing education. Such a handbook would serve principally as a checklist to remind librarians of areas in which to proceed.

_____ 44. By designing a model for use by librarians for making decisions about the need and requirements for continuing education and for producing staff development programs in any size or type of library or library system. The model would provide for decision-making check points.

_____ 45. By providing guidance, counsel, or programming in the area of staff development for state or regional library programs. (Note: Members of the Staff Development Committee are located in all sections of the country and would be happy to help you implement programs similar to the one we had here today.)

_____ 46. By working for the development of a National Plan for Continuing Education in cooperation with all interested groups, associations and institutions, which would provide a conceptual and practical blueprint for the provision of equal, co-ordinated, educational and staff development opportunities throughout the country for those librarians who want, need and are willing to continue their lifetime of learning. Such a national plan should include definitive proposals as to how to proceed with a group of feasible programs which would take into account the use of new media of communication and instruction.

_____ 47. By bringing to practicing librarians the best of articles related to staff development in related disciplines. It might also include reporting on successful staff development programs in libraries, particularly at the state and regional level. (See "Clips and Quotes on Staff Development for Librarians" in your portfolio for a sample of the type of material such a publication might contain.)

_____ 48. By developing standards and evaluation procedures for workshops, institutes, and seminars on staff development.

_____ 49. By working for the preparation of packaged multi-media programs for professional updating that can be lent or rented to local libraries or librarians who wish to improve the currency of their expertise or gain new professional skills or understanding in support of the recommendations made in this area by the Committee on New Directions for ALA.

_____ 50. Would you take courses to update yourself if they were offered via the following media? (Please indicate your degree of interest in as many media as interest you.)

_____ a. Correspondence course (home study)
_____ b. Programmed instruction (step-by-step teaching units)
_____ c. Eductional TV(closed circuit TV beamed to specific locations)
_____ d. Radio courses utilizing two-way radio
_____ e. Courses recorded on tapes
_____ f. Courses recorded on records

_____ g. Tele-talk (telephone for two-way discussions)
_____ h. Electronic Video Recorder (television courses available by plugging into your own TV)
_____ i. Tutorial centers located in libraries which would include syllabi, visual aids, teacher guides, models for individual study of prescribed units of study.
_____ j. Other: _____

_____ 51. Engaging in an exploratory study which would determine ways and means of building closer reciprocal relationships between practicing library administrators and library science professors (especially library school deans and those teaching administration, personnel management, and human relations in library organizations).

_____ 52. Other:_____

evaluation sheet 2

AND LASTLY......

Here begins the first installment of a continuing activity of the Staff Development Committee --
an effort to discover the attitudes, opinions, and needs of practicing librarians in the area of
staff development. It's a small beginning, but it will help us in planning to meet your needs more
effectively.

Please circle the group in which you participated: A   B   C   D   E

FUTURE WORKSHOPS AND PROGRAMS WILL BE SHAPED BY YOUR RESPONSES..................

1. What, in your opinion, is the chief obstacle to library staff development and change?

2. How many hours per week, on an average, do you devote to your own professional self-development? _____ hours

3. How many hours per week, on an average, do you devote to the development of your subordinate staff members?
    _____ hours.

4. In your library, are supervisors asked to report in detail on their activities and accomplishments in creating an environment
    conducive to the growth of their subordinates -- or what they are doing to make it possible for their subordinates to further
    their own self development?   Yes ( );   No ( )

5. What recently published book, journal article, report, film, or other media on staff development, utilization, or recruitment
    would you especially recommend for nationwide promotion by the ALA Staff Development Committee?

6. In your opinion, what was the best feature of the Micro-Workshop?

7. In your opinion, what was the least favorable aspect of the Micro-Workshop?

> Because these questions take more than a quick rating, we thought you might prefer to
> answer them later, but we would like you to return this sheet before you depart for home.
> Please drop your response sheet into the box provided at the LAD desk in the ALA
> Headquarters Offices in Cobo Hall.

Page 2

8. In your opinion were the physical arrangements and provisions for your comfort adequate? Yes ( ); No ( ).
If no, what suggestions would you make for improvements next time?

9. Do you feel that at each workshop an effort should be made to have some of the leaders from outside the profession of librarianship? Yes ( ); No ( ).

10. Do you have any suggestions to make for future Micro-Workshops in regard to:
a. Choice of leaders?

b. Choice of methods?

c. Opportunities for participation?

d. Scheduling and pace of the program?

e. Bibliographies and their distribution?

f. Promotion of the workshop?

g. Size of audience to be accomodated?

h. Other?

11. In this Micro-Workshop you succeeded in meeting some of my needs, but in the future planning, I would like you to take into account the following needs in the area of staff development that were not developed today.
a.

b.

c.

12. Overall, did the products (discussions, insights, ideas for action, etc.) justify your time spent in attendance at the workshop?

13. On the basis of this experience, will you recommend the Staff Development Micro-Workshop to be held the first day of the Dallas ALA Convention, June 20, 1971, to others? Yes ( ); No ( ).

PS We're curious about what magazines you read. Would you please list here three periodicals **outside librarianship** that you read regularly, in order of their usefulness in your work (that part of it that is related to the development of human resources in libraries.

APPENDIX F

TENTATIVE DRAFT OF A POSITION PAPER

BY THE STUDY COMMITTEE ON

THE ROLE OF THE ASSOCIATION OF AMERICAN LIBRARY SCHOOLS

IN CONTINUING LIBRARY EDUCATION

Committee Members *

Dr. Lawrence A. Allen, Dean
School of Library Science
University of Kentucky
Lexington, Kentucky 40506

Mrs. Hallie B. Brooks, Professor
School of Library Service
Atlanta University
Atlanta, Georgia 30314

Dr. Irving M. Klempner, Professor
School of Library Science
State University of New York
Albany, New York 12203

Mrs. Allie Beth Martin, Director
Tulsa City-County Library
Tulsa, Oklahoma 74103
   and
Faculty Member
School of Library Science
University of Oklahoma
Norman, Oklahoma 73069

Dr. M. P. Marchant, Associate Professor
Graduate Department of Library and
   Information Sciences
Brigham Young University
Provo, Utah 84601

Miss Sarah Rebecca Reed,
Associate Director
Graduate Library School
Indiana University
Bloomington, Indiana 47401

Miss Peggy Sullivan, Assistant Professor
Graduate School of Library and
   Information Sciences
University of Pittsburgh
Pittsburgh, Pennsylvania 15213

Dr. Elizabeth W. Stone, Professor
Assistant to the Chairman of the
   Department of Library Science
The Catholic University of America
Washington, D.C. 20017 (Chairman)

* Committee members were appointed by Dr. Margaret E. Monroe, President
of the Association of American Library Schools, in the Spring of 1971 and
charged with the task of presenting a report at the January, 1972, annual
meeting of AALS.

TABLE OF CONTENTS

TENTATIVE DRAFT OF A POSITION PAPER

PART I

THE ROLE OF AALS IN CONTINUING LIBRARY EDUCATION

A. Introduction

The task which has been assigned to this Committee is that of

defining the role of the Association of American Library Schools in continu-

ing library education.

Recognition of the importance of the continuing education of the

librarian has been increasing in recent years. Because of societal changes,

acceleration of new knowledge, the impact of new technology, and increasing

demands for changing types of library[1] services, modern librarians are con-

fronted by an almost impossible task in attempting to keep themselves

abreast of new developments. Recognition of the need for continuing educa-

tion of the librarian has caused many library associations to accept responsi-

bility in the areas of continuing education. Within AALS, the fulfillment of

this responsibility requires a role definition in the area of continuing education

_____

[1] In this report the term "library" encompasses all kinds of
information facilities. Similarly, "librarian" includes the information
scientist and/or specialist; and "library school" includes the information
science or information service school.

The Role of AALS...page 2

for its membership as well as for practicing librarians who may benefit from AALS's roles.

On the one hand, the task requires willingness on the part of library school graduates to continue their learning and development in order to deepen and extend their technical, conceptual, and human relations competence as professionals in our society; on the other hand, it calls for increased responsibility by the library schools to be sensitive to changes in the continuing education needs of their graduates and a willingness to work cooperatively not only with other schools, but with other relevant groups to meet the needs for continuing library education.

The Committee, therefore, sees its primary mission as delineating the role of AALS in continuing library education and making recommendations for the implementation of this role.

The Committee also recognizes the need for concerted effort and coordination of all relevant groups in the continuing education of the librarian at the national level and has attached to this report an appendix dealing with goals, criteria and components relative to national planning for continuing library education. [1] To understand the full dimensions of a

program of continuing library education, the Committee feels that planning

within the Association of American Library Schools should consider the

advantages and potential of coordinated planning with other relevant groups

at the national level.

B. Basic Assumptions

    1. Continuing education is essential for all library personnel, whether

---

[1]For other material relative to national planning for continuing
education see: James J. Kortendick, "Research Needs in the Field of
Continuing Education for Librarians," in Harold Borko, ed. A Study of
the Needs for Research in Library and Information Science Education
(Los Angeles, Calif.: Institute of Library Research, University of
California, 1970). In addition to presenting eleven suggestions for research
proposals in the area of library continuing education, this paper gives a brief
historical review of continuing education research and an extensive bibliography in the area of continuing education covering material from many
related disciplines. See also: Peter Hiatt, "National Planning for Continuing
Education," Library Trends, 20: 169-183 , July, 1971. For a national
survey showing the job related and course needs of MLS librarians, see
James J. Kortendick and Elizabeth W. Stone. Post-Master's Education
for Middle and Upper-Level Personnel in Libraries and Information
Centers. Final Report, Phase I. (Washington, D.C.: Department of Library
Science, The Catholic University of America, 1970) (ED 038 985). Subsequently republished and revised as Job Dimensions and Educational Needs
of Middle and Upper-Level Library Personnel. (Chicago, Ill.: American
Library Association, 1971).

they remain within a position category or are preparing to move

into a higher one. The best library education can become

obsolete in a few years unless the librarian makes a very

determined effort to continue his or her education.

   a. Continuing education opportunities include both formal and

      informal learning situations, and need not be limited to

      library subjects offered in library schools.

   b. Library administrators are responsible for providing support,

      funding and opportunities in the form of in-service program-

      ming, including leaves, sabbaticals, and released time for

      the continuing education of their staffs. [1]

2. Most ALA accredited library schools state as one of the objectives

  of their fifth year programs that the student should establish essential

  habits of continuing self education throughout their professional

  careers. This implies that the accredited schools should:

   a. Assist alumni, former students and librarians in their geo-

      graphical area to achieve this objective;

   b. Develop programs (formal courses and curricula) which would

      attract enough students to make a major impact on problems

      faced by graduates in their work situations;

---

[1]Library Education and Manpower; A Statement of Policy Adopted
by the Council of the American Library Association, June 30, 1970. Chicago,
Ill.: ALA Office for Library Education, 1970, p. [8].

   c.   Sponsor workshops, institutes, and seminars which would have

       a strong impact because of:

       1.   Adequate funding and staffing

       2.   Long range planning

       3.   Cooperative planning by all relevant groups

       4.   Provision for an organized, comprehensive, and sequential

           patterning of opportunities for learning.

3.   The importance of continuing education demands an even distribution of

    continuing library education opportunities available throughout the

    country. In some regions of the country there is good coverage,

    but in other areas there is little.[1]

4.   Programs offered should use educational technology to full advantage.

5.   In planning and developing programs the continuing education experience

    and resources of other professions should be studied and adapted when

    feasible.

6.   The complexity of the problem demands that any vigorous national

    planning for continuing education of librarians will, at a minimum,

    call for   coordination and cooperation between five components:

    the individual librarians, the library schools, the libraries, the

    library associations, and the state library agencies.

---

[1]For an example of thorough planning for a region see: Robert E. Lee, Lawrence A. Allen, and Peter Hiatt, A Plan for Developing a Regional Program of Continuing Education for Library Personnel in the Western States (Boulder, Colorado: Western Interstate Commission for Higher Education (WICHE), 1969).

7. Continuing education is one of the most important problems facing library education today. Provision of continuing education for librarians would be a major factor contributing to the ability of librarians to satisfy newly emerging user demands for in-depth information.

C. Statement of Recommended Role of AALS in Continuing Library Education.

The Committee recommends that the AALS role in continuing library education be twofold. The Association's first responsibility is to encourage the development of continuing library education for its membership. An equally important role is that of cooperating with other agencies and groups responsible for continuing library education. Another way of expressing this would be that AALS has a role both "inside" the Association by working for its members and "outside" by working with other library agencies and groups to stimulate more continuing library education.

The AALS membership is thought to include:

1. Graduates of Graduate Library Schools (both accredited and non-accredited)

2. Faculty and administrators of Graduate Library schools.

Realizing its commitment on a national scale, AALS has a responsibility in working with other library agencies, as well as other professions, to

261

stimulate a plan of continuing library education for all library personnel. In this capacity, it would be working with such organizations as A. L. A., L. E. D., C. N. L. A., and library administrators.

More specifically, the role "inside" can be seen to consist of the following objectives:

1. To develop a positive and constructive attitude toward continuing library education programs on the part of library school faculties and administration.

2. To assist library school personnel in the process of planning and conducting quality continuing library education programs.

3. To stimulate more continuing library education programs for graduates of the Graduate Schools.

4. To develop a means of communications (i. e., network) for library educators and others interested in continuing library education.

5. To stimulate the development of research into continuing library education.

The "outside" role would have five specific objectives:

1. To assist in national planning for continuing library education.

2. To stimulate continuing library education programs in other library agencies.

3. To work with agencies, groups and professions outside of the library world to develop continuing library education programs.

4. To develop a positive attitude toward continuing library education on the part of all supervisory personnel in libraries.

5. To assist in developing ways and means for working librarians to take advantage of continuing library education programs, i.e., time and financial assistance.

PART II

AALS APPROACHES TOWARD IMPLEMENTATION OF THE
PROGRAM

A. Role Inside AALS

1. The establishment of a standing Committee on Continuing Education. A positive important action that the Board of AALS could take immediately would be the appointment of a standing Committee on Continuing Education, which could serve such functions as the following:

   a. Provide the leadership within AALS for working in close cooperation with other groups in national planning for continuing education.

   b. Provide stimulation from the Association to the individual library schools to encourage each school to have a planning

body for continuing education (including those for whom the
programs would be planned as well as those who would be
presenting the programs).

c. Develop standards and guidelines for library school programs
of continuing library education.

d. Develop a communications program to report on experimental
programs being tried in the various library schools as well
as to abstract articles and books on continuing education that
appear in other professions and other disciplines for distribution
to the library schools.

e. As need can be documented, conduct workshops on some phase
of continuing education for those responsible for continuing
education in the individual library schools.

f. Take the initiative in working with state and regional library
associations in developing continuing education programs needed
in a given area -- those best suited to the area's needs and
resources. Working toward this end, AALS might:

1. Start a series of regional conclaves on continuing education.

2. Assist states and regions with demonstration conferences
where the effectiveness of programs is being tested in
practice.

3. Work closely with state and regional associations in the
   development of experimental programs.

g. Serve as a clearing house for providing resource leaders and
   bibliographic data to individual library systems which want to
   develop continuing education programs in specialized areas.

2. Once schools are "encouraged" to have continuing education committees,
   there should be an "interest group" in AALS for continuous communication
   among them, leading to regional planning, sharing ideas at AALS meetings, etc

3. As new developments and changes emerge, AALS should take the
   lead in studying these to see what they should mean in terms of
   training and re-training. For example, education for networks
   should permeate the training of the librarian with a new outlook on
   the world of information -- its forms, its organization, its dissemination. Training of personnel to serve effectively in information networks must go beyond the definition and description of existing and
   emerging networks:

   a. It should redefine current notions of information in order to
      further understand how information is transferred, assimilated
      and used.

   b. It should utilize the newer instructional media.

   c. It should broaden the concept of the library to include the idea
      of an information center articulating with one or more networks.

   d. It should inculcate the principles of systems organizations and design.

  e. It should provide for first-hand bibliographic control of all

    kinds of materials.

  f. It should provide for first-hand observation of and practicum

    experience with existing networks.

  g. Proven concepts, practices, and instructional methods developed

    to train personnel for networks at the fifth-year level should be

    communicated to the national body responsible for a nationwide

    program of continuing education.[1]

4. As new developments and changes emerge, AALS should take the lead

  in calling working conferences to identify the necessary skills, know-

  ledge, and insights. For example, at the present time, a working

  conference is needed to identify the skills, knowledge and insights

  necessary or required in present and future network organization and

  administration. The scope of such working conferences should in-

  clude both basic professional continuing education and in-service

  education. The recommendations that emerge from such a working

  conference relative to continuing education should be submitted to

  the national body responsible for a nation-wide, regional, or state-

---

[1]These recommendations were among those suggested by participants
at the Interlibrary Communications and Information Networks Conference,
held at Airlie House, Warrenton, Virginia, September 28-October 2, 1970.
See: Joseph Becker, ed. Interlibrary Communications and Information Networks
(Chicago: American Library Association, 1971)

wide programs of continuing education to incorporate into the

curricula developed, the materials prepared for distribution, etc.

5. AALS should constantly be on the alert both to finding research that

needs to be undertaken and to acting on research that has been

accomplished.

6. AALS should study carefully the kind of feasible financing that it

needs to promote at the federal level -- and having made that

decision work politically to gain support for this decision. Examples

of possible objectives are:

a. To band together as an association and negotiate for loans for

post-MLS education to be paid back in full by a certain length

of time by the individual recipient after completion of a program.

b. To negotiate federal funding at a level sufficient to make

continuing education an asset rather than a liability to library

schools.

c. To promote the concept that federal funds for continuing library

education be granted not only directly to library schools, but

also be available to individual library systems, library associations,

state and regional associations, provided these organizations work

in cooperation with a library school. Such a policy would also

make it possible for funds to be granted for cooperative national

planning for continuing library education.

 d. To develop an attitude that federal funding for continuing library education
    should be established at some fair ratio, at least equal to that for formal
    pre-service education.

 e. To identify the research projects that it feels should have priority in the
    area of continuing library education and take steps to get these funded.[1]

B. Role in Cooperation with Other Relevant Groups

The AALS should lead the profession in an all-out effort to bring about
national planning for continuing library education.

 1. Work for the organization of a Joint Study Committee on Continuing
    Library Education to delineate the dimensions of a program of
    continuing library education and the type of national planning and
    organization structure necessary to further continuing library
    education. To have the greatest influence the Joint Study Committee
    should elicit the cooperation of other groups such as: The American
    Library Association and its various divisions, the Special Libraries
    Association, the American Society for Information Science, the
    Canadian Library Association, the Council of National Library

---

[1]For example, in the Kortendick section of the Borko report
there are recommended 11 research studies important to the continuing
education of librarians. These and others that might be suggested by the AALS
Committee on Continuing Education should be assigned priorities and active
search be made to find funding for them and funds for the implementation of
their recommendations. Kortendick, op. cit., pp. 205-217.

Associations, and other similar groups. It would be expected that
the report of the Joint Study Committee on Continuing Library
Education might cover, but not be limited to, such matters as the
following:

a. Outline a conceptual and practical blueprint for the provision
   of equal, coordinated, continuing library educational opportunities
   throughout the United States and Canada for those librarians who
   need, and are willing to continue, their lifetime of postgraduate
   learning.

b. Make provision for a nationwide organization of some type to
   create prototypes and advise and coordinate the type of functions
   it deemed necessary to further continuing library education.

c. Make definitive proposals as to how to proceed with feasible
   programs which would take into account fully such factors as
   content based on need, excellence, personal satisfaction, the
   opportunity for freedom of choice by the individual librarian, the
   necessity for continuity, accessibility, and convenience.

d. Take the initiative in promoting and planning regional working
   conferences to be held in six to eight sections of the country to
   identify the problems and issues in continuing library education
   and to gather together and consider the recommendations for

action emanating from these conferences.

e. Identify and analyze current continuing education programs and existing resources, human and material, which could be used in coherent national planning for continuing library education. This would include an identification of the gaps that exist in current continuing library education programming.

f. Concurrent with a survey of available continuing library education activities, potential resources, and gaps in present programming, examine the continuing education needs of library personnel. Some continuing education needs typically identified by research already completed include:

1. Administration and management, including the development of human resources in libraries.

2. Automation of library processes and information retrieval systems (especially for those librarians who have been out in the field for five or more years)

3. Changing patterns of library service, e.g., reaching the unreached.

4. Developing networks and network personnel.

270

It is possible that such a survey of needs could be accomplished through the working regional conferences (outlined in Item 1.d.of this section) and the incorporation of data thus obtained with the research that has already been done in discovering such needs.[1]

---

[1]Examples of such studies include:

Becker, Joseph, ed. Interlibrary Communications and Information Networks (Chicago: American Library Association, 1971).

Gaver, Mary V., "The Educational Third Dimension: I. Continuing Education to Meet the Personalized Criteria of Librarians," Library Trends, 20: 118-143, July, 1971.

Ginsberg, Eli and Carol A. Brown, Manpower for Library Service. (New York: Columbia University, Conservation of Human Resources Project, 1967). (ED 023 408)

Harlow, Neal and others, Administration and Change: Continuing Education in Library Administration (New Brunswick, New Jersey: Rutgers University Press, 1969).

Kortendick, James J., op. cit., pp. 205-217.

Kortendick, James J. and Elizabeth W. Stone, Job Dimensions and Educational Needs of Middle and Upper-Level Library Personnel (Chicago, Ill.: American Library Association, 1971).

Monroe, Margaret E., "Education in Librarianship for Serving the Disadvantaged," Library Trends, 20:445-462, October, 1971.

Presthus, Robert, Technological Change and Occupational Response: A Study of Librarians (Final Report. Project No. 07-1084). (Washington, D. C., Office of Education, Bureau of Research, 1970), pp, 69, 108. Part of: A Program of Research into the Identification of Manpower Requirements, the Educational Preparation and the Utilization of Manpower in the Library and Information Profession, an Overview. (Ontario, Canada, New York University, 1970).

271

School Library Manpower Project, <u>School Library Personnel Task Analysis Survey: A Report Prepared in Phase I of the School Library Manpower Project by the Research Division of the National Education Association in a National Study to Identify the Tasks Performed by School Library Personnel in Unified Service Programs at the Building Level</u>   (Chicago, Illinois: American Library Association, 1969).

Stone, Elizabeth W., <u>Factors Related to the Professional Development of Librarians</u> (Metuchen, New Jersey: The Scarecrow Press, 1969).

TENTATIVE DRAFT OF A POSITION PAPER

APPENDIX A

GOALS, CRITERIA, AND COMPONENTS OF

NATIONAL PLANNING FOR CONTINUING LIBRARY EDUCATION

I. Identification of some of the basic questions that must be answered in

the area of continuing library education.

A. What are the education needs of library school graduates and why ?

B. What is continuing library education ?

C. What are the objectives of continuing library education ?

1. To enable the professional librarian to "keep abreast" ?

2. To help him sharpen and extend his skills and concepts ?

3. How are the following needs to be met ?

a. For foundation learning

b. For remedial learning

c. For emergency education

d. For specialization[1]

D. What would constitute a conceptual and practical blueprint for the

provision of equal, coordinated, educational opportunities through-

out the country for those librarians who will continue their lifetime

_____

[1]For discussion of these points, see Margaret E. Monroe, "Variety
in Continuing Education," ALA Bulletin, 61:275-278, March, 1967.

postgraduate learning?

1.   What individual opportunities should be provided?

2.   What group learning opportunities should be provided?

E.   What are the dimensions of a program to implement such a national,

practical blueprint?

1.   What criteria should be met?

2.   What should be the pattern of organization?

3.   What should be the pattern of financing?

4.   How could good programs that have been and are being offered

by library schools, associations and information centers, and

by library systems, be integrated into the national planning and the

made more effective through meeting sound criteria and

through repetition and exchange of information about them?

5.   How and by whom will priorities for effort and support be

established?

6.   How will research and development on the use of new media

and suitable instructional methods and techniques at this level

be provided and by whom?

7.   Who will be responsible for the long range planning, the

correlation and coordination necessary to meet the objectives of a comprehensive national plan for continuing education?

8. How will provision be made for the interpretation and dis-
    semination of concepts and research findings from other
    disciplines that are relevant to the professional growth of
    librarians?

9. What standards and criteria for evaluating and measuring out-
    comes of programs are needed? How and by whom are they
    to be developed?

II. Objectives and Criteria of Continuing Library Education.

A. To develop a conceptual and practical blueprint for the provision
    of equal, coordinated, educational opportunities throughout the
    country for those librarians who need, want, and will continue
    their lifetime learning.

    1. Libraries designed to distribute knowledge will not serve
        society fully unless librarians first share and agree on some
        fundamental ideas as to what constitutes a practical and
        feasible plan of continuation for the profession.

    2. National planning should incorporate answers to the questions
        raised in this report.

B. To develop a plan that will meet certain personalized criteria of
    researchers and practicing librarians. Without meeting these

criteria, any plan is doomed to failure. The personalized

criteria that must be met are:

1. Content of high quality based on <u>actual needs of practicing</u>

    <u>librarians.</u>

    a. The entire plan has to be centered around the felt needs

        of the librarian as a lifetime student.

    b. In turn, the librarian will be influenced in his needs by

        the demands and needs of his clients -- the library users

        (and non-users).

    c. Research has shown that the chief factor that motivates

        librarians toward participating in continuing education is

        content that is related to their jobs -- the work itself.

2. Freedom of choice

    a. The capability for activating any plan of lifetime learning

        is poised only within the individual minds of freely choosing

        men and women.

    b. The individual should have the right to choose any or all

        of the curricula available -- whatever is most beneficial

        to him.

c. There should also be a choice of medium or presentation as well as a choice of content.

3. Continuity

a. The plan should provide an organized, sequential curriculum, comprehensive in scope, which is consistently available.

b. The curriculum materials developed should be available over a nationwide distribution system, on a continuous basis.

4. Accessibility.

a. No library school graduate should be denied the opportunity to participate in continuing library education because of his distance from an organized center of learning.

b. In order to meet the criterion of accessibility it would be necessary to use the most recent mass media of communication, such as TV, talk back TV, EVR, cassettes, etc.

5. Convenience:

Opportunity for continuing education should be available at a time, place, and pace convenient for each librarian.

a. Individual learning opportunities, at home or at place of employment, would be reinforced by interrelated self-instructional devices.

b. Provision of group learning opportunities, with active user-librarian orientation, centered in libraries.

c. Additional opportunities available through local, state, and regional library associations.

d. Although materials would be developed nationally, the curriculum would be available on a local or regional selective basis.

e. Methods exist to give the librarian frequently repeated opportunities to choose what he wants to learn in an orderly, sequential way -- at his own choice of time, place, and pace. Placing such "recorded instruction" in personal and institutional libraries would permit multiple repetition of whatever presentations are chosen for regional broadcast and ready access by individuals to the same materials. Varieties of emphasis and different levels of complexity should be offered.

6. Personal Satisfaction

a. Any program that receives acceptance will have to make sense to the librarian on his own terms.

b. To be rated successful any program will have to demonstrate that it meets the individual needs of librarians.

7. Evaluation

      a.   The content of programs developed must be carefully and continuously scrutinized.

      b.   A spectrum of evaluation should be designed ranging from self-appraisal on a voluntary and anonymous basis to traditional formal examinations chosen for set structured, predetermined objectives.

C.   To design a plan that will meet criteria of all relevant groups so that these will accept it:

    1.   Library schools themselves

    2.   The profession   generally -- its associations

    3.   Individual libraries

    4.   State library agencies

    5.   The U. S. Office of Education

D.   To develop a plan that will incorporate such concepts as: provision and use of a research data base; the use of systems design; the behavioral approach to learning; systematic evaluation; the use of multi-media; and the organized distribution and dissemination of program elements.

The Role of AALS...Appendix A
Page 8

III. Possible Ways in Which Established Criteria might be Met:

    A. An organization should be created (or designated) to plan, design, build and implement national planning for continuing library education.

        1. Although programming for continuing library education should be nationally coordinated, it may be developed and should be made available on a regional and local selective basis.

        2. Existing institutional and inter-institutional programs should be reinforced and augmented, and not disturbed or displaced by national planning.

    B. Production of curricular and course materials

        1. Development by specialists in a given field of organized, sequential curricula, comprehensive in scope

           a. Within each field of librarianship, develop courses which would be continuously available

           b. Individual librarians would have the right to choose from any or all of the courses developed in a particular area.

        2. Using the curriculum and course content developed by specialists, the national planning body would help in the development of teaching materials, such as:

           a. Syllabi

    b. Readings.

    c. Films

    d. Programmed instruction

    e. Slides and film strips

    f. Cassettes

    g. Transparencies

    h. Exercises, games, and role plays

    i. Video tape

    j. All other suitable modalities of instruction

3. In developing the curricula certain concepts should be used and integrated throughout. These would include:

    a. The use of a systems approach in developing materials

    b. Continued research which must identify the needs of practicing librarians.

    c. The broadening of the concept of the library to include the idea of an information center articulating within one or more networks.

    d. The use of instructional methods geared to the characteristics of the adult learner.

    e. Learning from the continuing education activities of other professions.

    f. Means of evaluation should be built into the programs developed for the librarian-learners and for the library educators.

The Role of AALS...Appendix A
Page 10

      g.   Changes in courses would be made whenever required
           by advancing knowledge and new technology.

C. Presentation and Distribution

    1. Responsibility for presentation and distribution of materials
       developed would be in the hands of the national planning body,
       thus providing maximum efficiency in utilization of the materials
       prepared by leading library educators.

    2. Possible distribution patterns:

       a.   Each regional or local distribution center might receive and
           distribute all or any part of the nationally developed presenta-
           tions, depending upon local needs.

       b.   Materials could be distributed to an individual library or
           group of libraries which could make use of materials for
           the purpose   of staff development.

       c.   Materials could be distributed to library schools for their
           continuing library education programs and adapted by them
           for different formats, such as regular course offerings,
           seminars, or workshops.

       d.   The organized, sequential curriculum for each area of
           librarianship could be presented over a nationwide

distribution system, using television on a continuous

basis. Under this plan the curriculum would be rotated

continuously, largely through the use of videotapes, with

the pattern starting over again as soon as it had been

completed.

e. Materials could be packaged in such a manner as to provide

individual "tutorial environment" modules which would be

available to local libraries.

D. Self Evaluation

With the help of self-test design specialists, a series of self-appraisal

examinations could be designed along with each course.

1. The librarian-learner could elect to take self-examinations on

any given segment of a program to determine only for himself

whether his progress was satisfactory.

2. If the librarian wished to receive formal recognition, or credit,

for what he had done, he could choose more formal examinations.

E. Related activities relevant to national planning for continuing library

education would be developed as demand arose, and might include:

1. Publication of a Continuing Education Bulletin

Concurrent with the development of the program it is proposed

The Role of AALS...Appendix A
Page 12

that bulletin announcements, likely enlarging into some sort of

reasonably regular Continuing Education Bulletin would be

developed to publicize, coordinate, and direct continuing

education opportunities.

2. Development and use of some means of recognition and reward

   for those in continuing education programs.

   a. Would make provision for recognition of other continuing

      education activities such as: developing significant in-service

      programs in individual libraries; engaging in research that

      should be brought to the attention of all; experimenting with

      research and reporting on it so that others could profit;

      making significant contributions to the literature.

3. Maintain a research and development unit that would:

   a. Continually do research on the use of new media in continuing

      education, which includes full utilization of: television,

      radio, teaching machines, memory storage machines,

      cassettes, tutorial centers, EVR, cable television, etc.

   b. Develop guidelines for experimental courses and curricula.

284

    c.   Design ways in which curricula and programs could be
evaluated based on feedback from users of the programs.

    d.   Determine priorities for the development of programs.

    e.   Encourage individuals and/or groups to engage in research
needed in the area of continuing education.

4.   Development of a center for consultative and/or clinical service.
Through such service, a local librarian with his close associates
would have an opportunity to meet with a leader or trainer who
would help a management team in a specific library think through
its problems.

5.   Development of a visible policy of career development.
This would be in keeping with other professions. This would
include the development of a rationale for the requirements
of different progressions in librarianship. The individual
librarian should be aware of the requirements for his advancement in the profession, whether he chooses to pursue his
career in bibliographic services and guidance, or whether he
chooses to advance in administrative positions.

6.   Promote interest throughout the profession in continuing education
and seek sources for its support and development. This would
include extensive coverage in library periodicals.

The Role of AALS...Appendix A
Page 14

E. Financing

Ideally a program of continuing education should be self-financing,
but experience shows that educational systems have rarely paid
their entire cost by direct charges to the learner. The preparatory
stages are usually paid for by a variety of contributory sources and
endowments, many of which carry over into the operational stages,
at which point the users add their fees. Realistically a large investment would be necessary to get such a national program underway.
A more detailed computation of the legal, engineering and technical
aspects of the system would provide a sharper focus on cost items.
Such computations represent an administrative stage and should follow
consideration of the report by the organizations involved in the plan.
These generalizations are applicable to the proposals of this report.

Libraries are going to be a power source in this country because
they will control knowledge, which is a type of energy. Any form
of energy equals power. As librarians gain expertise in their control
and dissemination of knowledge, many national level foundations and
commercial organizations will become increasingly interested in
library development and the development of the personnel to keep the
knowledge flowing to the user. Many of these organizations might

The Role of AALS...Appendix A
Page 15

prefer to achieve their knowledge objectives more efficiently --
although indirectly -- by contributing portions of their budgets to a
national body of major university stature. Even a fractional increase
in the efficiency of such knowledge expenditures by the improved
quality and comprehensiveness reasonably to be derived from a
nationwide continuing library educational system can add up --
depending upon one's views -- to a national necessity, or a bargain,
or both.

APPENDIX B

WHAT IS "CONTINUING EDUCATION" ? [*]

Cyril O. Houle

The question posed by the title will here be dealt with, though perhaps not answered, in three different contexts: the denotation of the term itself, its connotation in practice, and its usefulness for the future.

Denotation

A good place to begin is with the dictionary, which defines many subtly varying meanings for both "continuing" and "education." The present concern is chiefly with the first of these two words as it defines some segment of the second, however the latter may be considered: as process or the result of process; as the evocation of knowledge from within or the provision of it from without; as discovery or discipline; or as it is used in any other sense. Presumably there is education which is not continuing but is either initiatory or conclusive, but no typology thus based on placement or duration has become established, with the result that continuing education stands alone as a term whose parallels are implied but not formally stated.

The root word is "continue" which has many meanings of which the most relevant to the present case appears to be: "to carry onward or extend; to prolong; to add to or draw out in length, duration, or development; specif., to resume or carry on (discourse), esp. after intermission."[1] Thus continuing education might be defined as any kind of learning or teaching which extends or builds upon previous experience in the same general realm of knowledge and whose specific goals are not intended to terminate all study in that realm. It implies that the learner has studied some related body of content previously and is carrying on the process further; it implies that the program depends upon his having done so; and it implies that he proposes to continue such learning in the future. The term is broader in its formal definition than several others which are sometimes used as synonyms. Thus continual or continuous education is

---

[1]*Webster's Unabridged Dictionary*, Second edition.

[*]Discussion paper prepared for Seminar on Continuing Professional Education, University of Chicago, Autumn, 1969.

that which proceeds without interruption or cessation, continuation education
is some segment of study after the initiatory experience,and continued
education is that which is protracted in time.

Connotation

When a cluster of terms begins to be widely used and applied in various
settings, each one takes on a host of different meanings. Thus continuation
education means for many people the organized programs provided on a part-
time basis for young people who have been permitted to leave full-time study
but who are still below the compulsory attendance age. Sometimes, too, the
meanings acquire a generalized usage not inherent in their formal definitions.
In this case, the terms based on the word "continue" almost invariably connote
education in adulthood rather than in childhood, part-time rather than full-time
study, and individually-selected learning rather than compulsory instruction --
yet nothing in the terms themselves would seem to require such limitations
as these.

Such examples suggest that the term "continuing education" has already
acquired a wealth of nuances of application and usage though it has been widely
used for only about twenty years. Much of this proliferation has arisen not
from any clear-cut denotative analysis but by the independent discovery of the
term at different places and times (it has no one coiner) and by its borrowing
from one situation to use in another. It would be tedious to spell out all its
usages, but it may be useful to identify the three major thrusts of thought and
effort which have brought it to prominence.

1. The established professions have always either accepted or stressed
the need for their practitioners to engage in a lifelong learning program and,
as the members of other occupational groups have sought to gain the social
acceptance and legal protections afforded to professions, they have adopted this
value as their own. The traditional techniques for achieving it --such as
books, journals, conventions, lectures, and local societies - have existed
for a very long time without requiring a generic name. But as the pace of
knowledge-advancement quickened, the techniques of adult learning were
multiplied, new systems of communication developed, and the number of
practitioners grew, it became ever more clear that an old idea was achieving
a major new reinforcement and that some broad term was required to sum it
up so that multiple efforts could be seen in some kind of conceptual whole.
The term which came to predominate was "continuing education," often with
the word "professional" added to define it more specifically. In every

profession or semi-profession today, there has been a massive development
of efforts to help practitioners enlarge and extend their previous learning
in many ways, old and new, and this great surge forward on so many fronts
has brought the term itself into common usage.

It has also brought about many ambiguities. Each profession naturally
thinks about the term as applying to its unique program of services and may
restrict it to its innovative activities such as taped research digests, telephone
or radio lectures, or computer-assisted instruction. The members of a
single profession also often use the term to identify some single goal. In
nursing, for example, some authors adopt the broad usage of "continuing
education" while others restrict the term to designate the effort of an individual
to move upward from one recognized academic or performance level to
another one, as when the graduates of diploma programs seek to achieve the
baccalaureate.

2.   Since the end of World War II, the number of people attending
short-term residential conferences under various auspices has grown astro-
nomically and, chiefly because of the influence of the W. K. Kellogg Foundation,
this form of learning has come to be called "continuing education" by many
people. In this case, the evolutionary line of the term is clear. The first
building specifically designed for such conferences on a university campus
was the Center for Continuation Study of the University of Minnesota. When
Michigan State University and the Kellogg Foundation developed plans in the
late 1940s for a much larger and more complex center than that at Minnesota,
the term "continuing education" was used instead of "continuation study, "
partly because of the awkwardness of the latter expression and partly to
signify the larger dimensions of the proposed endeavor. The great success of
the program in Michigan led the Foundation to make grants for other similar
buildings and programs, and eventually other centers (financed in various ways)
were created at many other universities. These key institutions did much to
establish the idea of short-term residential conferences under countless
auspices and to give them the name by which most of them are generically known.

This broad development was reinforced by the fact that the major early
centers were located in universities which, in theory at least, deal with
advanced and not with introductory knowledge; hence the word "continuing"
appears to be particularly apt so far as their adult educational endeavors are
concerned, particularly in programs which are not part of a formal credit
offering. Furthermore most of the conferences were occupationally oriented

and the term received additional reinforcement in this application from its use by the professions. While these two considerations would apply to most forms of university extensions, the dramatic growth of buildings and programs in the post-World War II years led the new term to be distinctively applied to the offering of conferences.

3. The very term itself appeared to be attractive to many people and therefore achieved a momentum of its own, particularly in its application in institutions of higher education. As noted above, the attachment of the term to residential short-term conferences was historical rather than as a result of denotative analysis. Subsequently it became ever more widely realized that other forms of instruction could equally well fit within the term. As a result, a number of universities changed the names of their extension divisions to divisions of continuing education, other universities created units bearing the same name, and categories of institutions, most particularly the community colleges, established a generic usage of the new term.

Part of its attractiveness came from its contrast with more traditional expressions which seemed to many people to have lost their meaning or their luster. "Adult education" which logically appears to be a broadly and accurately descriptive term, had been given a number of specialized meanings by its embodiment in various programs -- most particularly literacy classes, non-intellectual personal improvement courses, or group dynamics --and therefore was rejected by those who disliked such programs. "Extension" is inherently meaningless, but long practice had given it two connotations: the traditional work of general extension with its off-campus courses, correspondence study, and other forms of teaching which, to some people, seem to embody a decayed academicism; or the traditional work of agricultural extension which seems, to its critics, to be bound up with the life of our agricultural past. For many who disliked such old terms as these, "continuing education" had a fresh new air.

No term can remain new very long, however, and, as this one became widely used and therefore more and more distended in meaning, it lost some of its earlier appeal and began to have its own body of critics who found it illogical, diffuse in application, pretentious, faddish, or, perhaps worst of all, cute.[1]

----

[1]A good example of this criticism is that contained in a paper by Professor Watson Dickerman entitled "What Is This 'Continuing Education'?" Adult Education, XV (Autumn, 1964), pp. 3-8.

While this criticism has not yet risen to any crescendo, it is increasingly clear that "continuing education" has lost something of its freshness and has taken on nuances of negative value which did not characterize it previously.

Future Usefulness

Any effort to establish standardized meanings for "continuing education" or its related key terms is not likely to succeed. None of them was coined by an individual or group who could now be consulted to provide an ultimate historic source of authority. More important, the attempt to distinguish between orthodox and unorthodox usage would prove to be an imposition upon a living language. But it may be useful to apply the test of denotative meaning to "continuing education" and its related terms to see where such an exercise might lead. The following effort to identify meanings therefore rests upon inherent and logical meaning as contrasted to general usage and is based on a desire to be clear, not to be persuasive.

A distinction must be made, first of all, between generic and specific names. A community may have a park district, a school playground program, a golf course, a lawn tennis association, a softball league, and a popular rental library. The people who know of these endeavors realize that each is a form of recreation and the relatively few who think of them collectively will consider them in this light. They do not need laboriously to carry the word "recreation" in their titles to establish their identity, either separately or in common. Nothing prevents the usage of that word; the park district may even be called "the recreation department"; but such unity among the various agencies as exists is defined by an awareness of their inherent purpose not by their adoption of a common title.

It is suggested here that "adult education" parallels "recreation" (or such other terms as "health" and "welfare") as defining a broad generic purpose. The attempts of men and women to learn and the efforts of individuals, groups, and institutions to teach them are numerous and protean in form, but their diverse purposes and forms can all be encompassed in the term "adult education."

"Continuing education" has already been formally defined -- and it is suggested here that this definition become the accepted operative one. The term would not then be parallel to "adult education" but would signify one part of it: that learning which clearly, in the mind of learner or teacher,

-38-

advances from some previously established base to extend and amplify
awareness or capacity -- and does so during the years of adulthood. A clear
example of such use is provided by the professions. Nobody would refer to
the M. D. program as continuing learning though its curriculum assumes the
whole process of knowledge- and skill-acquisition which begins in earliest
infancy. In continuing education, as here considered, it is always necessary
to look to the immediate situation. Somewhere earlier a base has been
established; now that base is being built upon.

"Short-term residential education" is an awkwardly long term but it is
aptly descriptive and should not be conceptually confused with either of the
two foregoing terms. A place where such education is conducted may
properly be called a center for continuing education, or, more broadly, a
center for adult education since it falls within both rubrics, yet the part
should never be confused with the whole and it should not be forgotten that
short-term residential education is but one manifestation of a broader
function.

As for other specific names, let them grow from local contexts and bear
the meaning of their history and lore. "Extension" means different things on
various parts of a university campus; yet each place where it is used, it means
something; and it may be a mistake to try to gain exact correspondence between
generic and specific names or otherwise to reduce richly diverse practice to
rigid categories. Both Cooper Union and the New School for Social Research
have adult education as their central function and that fact is widely recognized.
Would either one wax in significance if its name were changed?

So we come to the end of this semantic exercise with a renewed awareness
of the distinction between what things are and what they are called. However
the term "continuing education" may be applied in practice, it (and its allied
terms) have broad conceptual meaning in theory. Perhaps the wisest course
of action with respect to the term would be not to tidy up its application in
various institutional settings but to examine its nature. What does it really
mean to say that a form of learning is continuing rather than, say, initiatory
or conclusive? And, granted the distinction in essence, what should be the
difference in practice?

APPENDIX G

Summary of the Report of the Study Committee* on

THE ROLE OF THE ASSOCIATION OF AMERICAN LIBRARY SCHOOLS
IN CONTINUING LIBRARY EDUCATION

<u>Charge:</u>   The Committee to draw up a <u>tentative draft of a position paper</u> on
THE ROLE OF AALS IN CONTINUING LIBRARY EDUCATION[1] was appointed by Dr. Margaret
E. Monroe, 1971 President of the AALS, in the late Spring of 1971, and charged
with the task of presenting a report at the January 1972 annual meeting of
AALS.

<u>Mission:</u>   The Committee saw as its mission the delineating of the role of
AALS in continuing library education, and the making of recommendations for
the implementation of this role.

<u>Assumptions:</u>   The present report has been written against a background of
4 major assumptions: (1) that the continuing education of librarians is one
of the most important problems facing library education today; (2) that in
spite of the undeniably good job which is being done by some library schools,
there is a great need for coordination and expanded programming in postgraduate continuing library education in order to meet the needs of practicing
librarians; (3) that the library schools have a responsibility to develop
programs which will (a) enable graduate librarians to continue their lifelong
professional development and (b) meet the needs of the profession by lessening
the gap that exists between available knowledge, concepts, and technology and
their application in library practice; and (4) that continuing library education is a national problem for which the best solutions can only be found
through coordinated and vigorous national planning involving at a minimum
five cooperating components: the library schools, the library associations,
the libraries, the state and regional library agencies, and individual
librarians.

<u>Objectives:</u>   "Inside" AALS.   (1) To develop a positive and constructive
<u>attitude</u> toward continuing library education programs on the part of library
school faculties and administration. (2) To assist library school personnel
in the process of <u>planning</u> and <u>conducting</u> quality continuing library education
programs.   (3) To stimulate more continuing library education <u>programs</u> for
graduates of the Graduate Schools. (4) To develop a means of <u>communication</u>
(i.e., network) for library educators and others interested in continuing
library education.   (5) To stimulate the development of <u>research</u> into continuing library education.

————————
*The members of the Committee are: Dr. Lawrence A. Allen, Mrs.
Hallie B. Brooks, Dr. Irving M. Klempner, Mrs. Allie Beth Martin, Dr.
M. P. Marchant, Miss Sarah Rebecca Reed, Miss Peggy Sullivan, and Dr.
Elizabeth W. Stone, Chairman.
   [1]In this report the term "library" encompasses all kinds of
information facilities. Similarly, "librarian" includes the information
scientist and/or specialist; and "library school" includes the information
science or information service school.

   Distributed at the Annual Conference of the Association of American
Library Schools, January 21-23, 1972.

"Outside" AALS.   (1) To assist in national planning for continuing
library education. (2) To stimulate continuing library education programs
in other library agencies. (3) To work with agencies, groups and professions
outside of the library world to develop continuing library education programs.
(4) To develop a positive attitude toward continuing library education on
the part of all supervisory personnel in libraries. (5) To assist in developing
ways and means for working librarians to take advantage of continuing library
education programs, i.e., time and financial assistance.

Recommendations for Implementation:

"Inside" AALS: (1) Establish a Standing Committee on Continuing Library
Education, to serve such functions as: (a) Provide leadership within AALS
for working in close cooperation with other groups in national planning for
continuing library education; (b) Stimulate each school to have a planning
body for continuing library education; (c) Develop standards and/or guidelines
for continuing library education programs. (d) Establish a communications
program (1) to report on experimental programs within library schools and (2)
to report on continuing education activities in other professions. (e) As
need can be documented, conduct workshops for those responsible for planning
and leading continuing library education programs. (f) Take initiative in
working with state and regional associations, in the ways which best meet
the needs of a given area. (g) Serve as a clearing house for providing
resource leaders and bibliographic data to individual library systems wanting
to develop continuing library education programs.   (2) Form an "interest
group" in AALS for continuous communication among those responsible for continuing library education in the individual schools, leading to regional planning, sharing ideas at AALS meetings, etc.   (3) Take the lead in studying
new developments and trends, and determining what they should mean in terms
of training and retraining.   (4) Call working conferences to identify the
necessary skills, knowledge, and concepts related to new developments and
changes as they emerge. (5) Identify   research that needs to be undertaken; take action on research that has been accomplished.   (6) Study the
kinds of financing that need to be promoted at the federal, state, or regional
level and work politically to gain support for such financing.

"Outside" AALS: (1) Work for the organization of a Joint Study Committee
on Continuing Library Education to delineate the dimensions of a program of
continuing library education and the type of national planning and organization
structure necessary to further continuing education.   (2) It would be
expected that the report of the Joint Study Committee might cover, but not be
limited to, such recommendations as: (a) Outline a conceptual practical blueprint for the provision of equal, coordinated, continuing library education
opportunities. (b) Establish community, professional and personal criteria
to guide long-range planning and programming. (c) Make provision for some
type of national planning body to create prototypes, and advise and coordinate
the type of functions deemed necessary to further continuing library
education. (d) Make definite proposals as to how to proceed with feasible
programs which would take into account established criteria. (e) Identify and
analyze current continuing education programs and existing resources, human
and material, which could be used in coherent national planning for continuing
library education. (f) Examine the continuing library education needs of
library personnel.

Believing in the importance and necessity of national planning
for continuing library education, the Committee has appended to
its report APPENDIX A: GOALS, CRITERIA, AND COMPONENTS OF
NATIONAL PLANNING FOR CONTINUING LIBRARY EDUCATION. It includes
suggested areas of planning and action under the following
headings:

I.   Identification of basic questions that must be answered
     in the area of continuing library education.

II. Objectives and criteria of continuing library education

III. Possible ways in which established criteria might be met

A.   An organizational framework to implement national
     planning.

B.   Production of curricular, course and teaching
     materials.

C.   Presentation and distribution

D.   Provision for self evaluation

E.   Related activities relevant to national planning
     for continuing library education to be developed as
     demand arose.

REPORT OF THE STANDING COMMITTEE ON
CONTINUING LIBRARY EDUCATION
FOR THE YEAR 1972

During the year the Committee met on May 11 and 12 in Washington, D.C., and on June 24 and 25 in Chicago, and five meetings of the Committee are being held during the 1973 annual conference.

As a result of actions taken at these meetings, and in keeping with the position paper adopted by the AALS on Continuing Library Education, the Committee engaged in the following activities:

1. In May, a letter was sent to Dr. Frederick Burkhardt, Chairman of the National Commission on Libraries and Information Science, and to all members of the Commission, bringing to the attention of the Commission the "grave concern for the critical need for a nationwide effort for continuing library education" and urging the Commission to establish continuing library education as one of its top priorities.

2. Letters were sent to the presidents of 26 other library associations urging them to write similar letters to Dr. Burkhardt, stressing the importance of establishing continuing library education as one of the Commission's top priorities.

3. In order to open up a channel of communication between relevant groups concerned about continuing library education, the Committee decided to form a Continuing Library Education Network, initially to include two other groups, the library schools and other library associations. The Deans of the 57 library schools and the presidents of 26 library associations were invited to name a representative to this network. Fifty-seven library schools and 23 library associations responded by appointing representatives. The Network as it existed in November, 1972, was published in the Winter issue of the Journal of Education for Librarianship.

4. To engage in long range planning more effectively, it was decided that a data base was needed and accordingly the Committee designed a questionnaire which was sent to all of the members of the Network. Returns were received from 32 schools and six library associations, and the results have been summarized and will be distributed to members of the Network on January 28.

5. A need was expressed to learn how other professional associations have provided for continuing education at a national level. To meet this need a Mini-workshop on Continuing Education in other Professions was planned for January 28, 1973, at the annual meeting of AALS. Five professions which have developed continuing education programs at a national level, which have headquarters in the Washington area, were invited to participate in the Workshop, to be held from 1:55 to 4:55 p.m. Following this presentation an exchange of ideas is scheduled for members of the network until 6:00 p.m.

6. The Committee worked on preparing a position paper for a long-range plan for continuing education within AALS, including ways and means by which AALS might join with other relevant groups concerned about continuing library education. The conclusion was reached, however, that more uninterrupted time is needed for this project, and the Committee is planning a two or three day meeting to concentrate on just this activity, to be held during the first six months of 1973.

The Committee set priorities for its first year and these are represented by the projects just reported. However, the Committee has also discussed a wide range of other activities which it is considering, as outlined in the position paper adopted by AALS at its January 1972 meeting. For example, it had planned to send a newsletter to the members of the network reporting on surveys, model programs, packaged courses, research, etc., in the area of continuing education, but it is now recommending that such information be included in or combined with the "Innovation Clearing House Newsletter." Another example is a bibliography on continuing education being prepared by one member of the Committee.

Respectfully submitted,

Elizabeth W. Stone, Chairman, reporting for the
Standing Committee on Continuing Library Education

Lawrence A. Allen   Allie Beth Martin
Lois Bewley   Sarah Rebecca Reed
Frank Birmingham   Clayton Shepherd
Hallie B. Brooks   Peggy Sullivan
Jack Dalton   Rod Swartz
Dorothy Deininger   Kieth C. Wright
Thomas Galvin
Edward Holley
Irving M. Klempner
M. P. Marchant

TENTATIVE AALS POSITION PAPER ON CONTINUING LIBRARY
EDUCATION FOR SUBMISSION TO OTHER RELEVANT   AND
INTERESTED GROUPS

INTRODUCTION

Present day developments, including changes in our society, the accelerated
growth of new knowledge, the implications of new technology, and the increasing
demands for additional or changing types of library, information and communication
services support the assumption that continuing library education in one of the
most important problems facing librarianship today. In recognition of these
societal changes and increased demands for professional services, the library
and information science professions should adopt a vigorous role in providing
opportunities for continuing education for all their profession. Libraries
designed to serve the information needs of the citizenry will not service fully
unless librarians first share and agree on some fundamental ideas as to what
constitutes a practical and feasible plan of continuing library education.

BASIC ASSUMPTIONS

1. Need for Continuing Education

   A. Continuing education is essential for all library personnel, whether
   they remain within a position category or are preparing to move into
   a higher one. The best library education can become obsolete in a
   few years, unless the librarian makes a very determined effort to continue
   his or her education.

   B. The gap between knowledge and application grows wider for several
   reasons: rapid advances in research; unequal distribution of opportunities
   for continuing library education; patterns of educational opportunities and of
   dissemination of knowledge which are not efficient in terms of the librarian-
   student's needs.

2. Objectives of Continuing Education

   A. Any continuing education program in librarianship should aim toward the
   total improvement of the individual with specific attention to his development in the following categories: personal growth, improvement of basic
   professional skills, acquisition of new skills in other fields, attitudinal
   changes, etc.

3. Content of Continuing Education

   A. Programs that are developed should be based on educational needs as
   expressed by the profession and take in consideration societal, professional
   and individual requirements:

      (1) Diversity of job and career related programs--program should be
      developed in enough breadth and depth to meet all career needs.

      (2) Continuity of programs--librarian-student should be able to build
      an individualized program from various sources in which each learning
      experience builds upon the previous one.

(3) Convenience and accessibility--any and all programs should be accessible to all librarians, regardless of geographic location, type of library, or position within the library.

(4) Personal satisfaction.

B. Techniques and methods exist to meet the individual librarian's requirements for continuing professional education through his or her career. Existing knowledge and tools from the combined fields of library education, information science, educational technology, and the behavioral and management sciences are available, and should be used to the fullest advantage.

C. In planning and developing programs the continuing education experience and re-sources of other professions should be studied and adopted and/or adapted when feasible.

D. Any national program developed should be based on an evaluation of what continuing education programs exist today in the field and how well they are meeting the needs.

E. Constant evaluation should be made and new research and developments in librarian-ship and related fields should be constantly incorporated into the overall program.

4. Organizational Structure for Continuing Education

A. The complexity of the problem demands that any vigorous planning for continuing education for librarians will, at a minimum, call for coordination and cooperation among five components; individual librarians, state, regional and national library and information associations, library schools, the libraries, and state, regional and national agencies.

These components have a financial responsibility to assure the development of their human resources. While financial support of continuing education opportunities will not insure staff development, the lack of support can cause its failure. Considering the great importance of competent staff in providing good library service and the speed of obsolescence in human expertise in modern society, there is an imperative need for acceptance of this responsibility in order to assure adequate service.

B. The problem is of national dimensions and the best solutions can only be found through coordinated and vigorous planning at the national level. A national organizational structure is needed which insures cohesion of efforts and insures a balance that can articulate effectively individual, local, state, regional, and national programs and educational resources.

School_____

DATA SHEET ON CONTINUING EDUCATION AS IT EXISTS IN ALA ACCREDITED GRADUATE
LIBRARY SCHOOLS AND THEIR PARENT INSTITUTIONS

I. Please list the specific programs, courses, or activities in the area of library continuing
   education that are being carried out or are being planned by your library school.

	Offered or Developed		Nature of Program
Before 1971-72	During 1971-72	Planned 1972-73	

1. ( )   ( )   ( )   Formal courses for credit (specify) :

2. ( )   ( )   ( )   Non–Credit courses (Specify):

3. ( )   ( )   ( )   Workshops (Specify):

4. ( )   ( )   ( )   Seminars or institutes (Specify):

5. ( )   ( )   ( )   Conferences (Specify if in cooperation   with other
                                  groups):

	Offered or Developed		Nature of Program
	Before 1971-72	During 1971-72	Planned 1972-73	

6. ( )   ( )   ( )   Professional enrichment programs for alumni
Specify:

7. ( )   ( )   ( )   Development of packaged courses (Specify):

8. ( )   ( )   ( )   Development of continuing education program which was developed in your school by one or more faculty members, but was implemented in another state (either by your faculty members or by leaders in the state using the program produced by your faculty).

9. ( )   ( )   ( )   Research in the area of continuing library education (Specify): Include proposals submitted even though they have not been funded or implemented.

10. ( )   ( )   ( )   Consultant services provided by your faculty for continuing library education programs

11. ( )   ( )   ( )   Role taken by members of your faculty in state or regional long-range planning for continuing education.

2. ( )   ( )   ( )   Other:

3. II. What are the continuing education objectives and concerns of your school?

14.   III. In your library school, how is it determined what programs will be developed and
        implemented?

15.   What is the relation to needs of practicing librarians to programs offered?

6.   How are needs determined?

17.   IV.   What provision is made by your school for the continuing   education of faculty members?

18.   What is the reward system for continuing education activity?

19.   Are there any specific requirements regarding the continuing education of faculty
           members?

V. Interface with other professional programs on your campus:

Do you discuss continuing education with those in other professional programs on your campus?

20. ( )   Yes
21. ( )   No

Do you attend planning sessions or programs of other professional groups on your campus?

22. ( )   Yes
23. ( )   No

Are you aware of what other professionally oriented groups are doing on your campus in the area of continuing education?

24. ( )   Yes
25. ( )   No.

26. In what ways do you interact or do you think it would be beneficial to interact with other professional continuing education programs on your campus?

VI. It was stated in a recent study by the National Science Foundation[1] relative to engineering continuing education, that generally continuing education has a second class status on university campuses. Do any of the following conditions noted in that study exist on your campus relative to continuing education programs?

Over-all on campus		In Library School		Unfavorable conditions relative to university continuing education programs
Agree	Disagree	Agree	Disagree	
26. ( )	( )	( )	( )	The university reward system does not acknowledge that continuing education is a respectable and reputable career line for faculty.
27. ( )	( )	( )	( )	Continuing education effort at present is contingent on individual faculty members sacrificing the rewards of the academic system (promotion, salary increases)
28. ( )	( )	( )	( )	Faculty members have to squeeze continuing education efforts into the myriad of other activities demanded of them

[1]Continuing Education for R & D Careers: An Exploratory Study of Employer-Sponsored and Self-Teaching Models of Continuing Education in Large Industrial and Federal Government Owned R & D Laboratories. Prepared for the National Science Foundation by Social Research, Inc., Chicago, 1969. ED 035 813.   304

	Overall on Campus		In Library School		Unfavorable conditions relative to university
	Agree	Disagree	Agree	Disagree	continuing education programs
29.	( )	( )	( )	( )	There is a general down-grading of non-credit activities in the spectrum of university teaching relative to courses in the regular degree curricula. Yet there is general agreement that continuing education must be non-credit (in large part) in order to develop formats which are more flexible in meeting the individual's needs for continuing education.
30.	( )	( )	( )	( )	Little attention is given to seeking new methods of developing, evaluating, and experimenting with new methods of instruction in order to explore their potential usefulness in the field of continuing education.
31.	( )	( )	( )	( )	There is an absence of long-range planning for continuing education in collaborative arrangements with professional associations, employing institutions, or other professional groups.

VII. Administratively how are continuing education programs on your campus:

32. Approved?

33. Patterned?

34. Continued?

35. Discontinued?

36. Financed?

305

37. VIII. .   Higher education design patterns are in the process of transition today on a
nationwide scale. On your campus do you observe indications of a change in
role or a trend toward loosening up in the offering of continuing education
opportunities to professional groups or individuals ?

APPENDIX L

MEMORANDUM

To: Continuing   Library Education Network

From: Elizabeth W. Stone, Chairman
           AALS Continuing Education Committee

Date: January 11, 1973

Re: Report on returns from questionnaire sent to ALA accredited library schools
           concerning Continuing Education Attitudes and Activities

Attached is a copy of the major portions of the report based on the questionnaires sent out to the
ALA accredited library schools on Continuing Education Attitudes and Activities.

I want to take this opportunity to thank the Continuing Library Education Network representatives
in each of the schools for their cooperation in returning the questionnaire.   Thirty-two of the
57 schools to which the report was sent (56%) returned the questionnaires and are included in the
following summary report. A list of the schools returning the questionnaire is given   in Appendix
A . along with the names of the continuing education representatives for each of these schools.

REPORT OF
AALS CONTINUING EDUCATION COMMITTEE ON
QUESTIONNAIRE RESPONSES RELATIVE TO

CONTINUING LIBRARY EDUCATION AS IT EXISTS IN ALA ACCREDITED
GRADUATE LIBRARY SCHOOLS AND THEIR PARENT INSTITUTIONS

December 1972

PURPOSE AND SCOPE OF THE SURVEY

The Continuing Library Education Committee of the Association of American Library Schools formulated and mailed out a questionnaire to review the present status of continuing library education in ALA accredited graduate library schools and their parent institutions in order to provide a partial data base on which to build long-range plans and future activities in cooperation with the Library Continuing Education Network.

The Library Continuing Education network was initiated during 1972 by the AALS Committee on Continuing Education. During 1972, those invited to join the network were representatives from ALA accredited Library Schools (one appointed by the Dean from each school) and representatives of library associations (one appointed by the president of each association). A list of the members of the Continuing Education Network as it existed in November 1972 is printed in the Winter issue of the Journal of Education for Librarianship. By the end of November, all of the 57 schools had reported a representative to the Continuing Education Network.

The questionnaire was formulated during the summer of 1972 and was mailed to the library school representatives in the Continuing Education Network in August of 1972. Of the 57 schools accredited by the American Library Association at that time, 32 questionnaires had been returned by mid-December 1972. The findings reported in this survey represent the data as recorded by the representative for each responding library school in the Continuing Education Network. There was a considerable amount of unevenness in the replies returned; some forms were filled out in great detail, others were minimally answered.

In examining the data in this survey it should be borne in mind that the findings represent only 56% of the library schools to whom the questionnaire was sent, and that there was a wide variation in the amount of data reported. Therefore, the report can be taken only as an indication of the current status of continuing education as it exists in the accredited library schools, not as a definitive picture of the total continuing education philosophy and activities in library schools today.

SUMMARY OF RESPONSES, QUESTIONS 1 THROUGH 5 OF THE QUESTIONNAIRE

Format of Continuing Education Opportunities

The breakdown of the types of formats used chiefly by the library schools in their offerings relative to continuing library education is presented in Table I. The number of formal courses for credit, the seemingly preferred manner of offering continuing education opportunities, has remained nearly constant over the past few years as reported by the 32 schools participating in the study. Perhaps the most encouraging conclusion that can be gained from the data presented in Table I is that in spite of heavy losses in Federal funding the number of workshops planned for the current academic year shows a distinct increase over the preceding year.

In examining Table I it should be noted, however, that there seemed to be considerable confusion on the part of some of the responding schools as to the distinction, if any, between an activity labelled "workshop" and an activity labelled "seminar or institute." In analyzing the responses, it seemed that one school may have called a "workshop" an event that might have been called an "institute" by another school.

TABLE I

BREAKDOWN OF CONTINUING LIBRARY EDUCATION OFFERINGS AS REPORTED BY
32 LIBRARY SCHOOL RESPONDENTS ACCORDING TO TYPE OF FORMAT: 1972

Item No.	Format	No. of Schools	No. Before 1971-72	No. During 1971-72	No. Planned 1972-73
1	Formal Courses for Credit	26	23	23	22
2	Non-credit Courses	7	4	4	5
3	Workshops	19	12	8	15
4	Seminars of Institutes	23	18	15	12
5	Conferences	19	10	12	12

The Scope of Offerings Reported in Library   Continuing Education

For purposes of analysis the highly diversified subjects covered in all types of formats listed for continuing library education opportunities were broken down into categories which were rather arbitrarily set as indicated in Table II. In this table, major fields have been assigned a number which ends in zero (Column 1); areas within fields have numbers not ending in zero (Column 2). Column 3 gives the number of the 32 reporting library schools which listed offerings in the major fields. Column 4 indicates the number of schools with offerings in specific areas within fields; Column 5 indicates the number of total offerings in a given area. For example:

                01   Administration   12   15

   This indicates that 12 library schools listed 15 offerings in this area.

From the data reported by the 32 responding library schools, 200 different offerings were reported, making an average of six continuing education opportunities reported from each school.

From Table II it can be noted that the highest area concentrations were:

                Multi media   17
                School/media librarianship   16
                Administration and
                   management   15

One of the surprising results of the survey was that there were relatively so few listings reported in the area of automation in spite of the fact that some surveys have indicated that this is a major need of practicing MLS librarians.

A breakdown by number of offerings reported in major fields shows the highest concentrations of offerings were:

                Types of librarianship   51
                User services   35
                Administration   27

The rank order of the number of offerings given by the library schools in the major fields is indicated in Table III.

TABLE II

BREAKDOWN OF CONTINUING LIBRARY EDUCATION OFFERINGS[1] AS REPORTED
BY 32 LIBRARY SCHOOL RESPONDENTS ACCORDING TO FIELDS AND AREAS: 1972

(Data from Questions 1 through 5 on Questionnaire)

Fields of Study (Col. 1)	Areas of Study (Col. 2)	No. of Library Schools Offering Programs in Field (Col. 3)	No. of Library Schools Reporting Offerings in Area (Col. 4)[2]	Total No. of Offerings Reported in Area (Col. 5)
00 Administration		15		
	01 Administration and Management		12	15
	02 Interlibrary Cooperation		1	1
	03 Library Systems Analysis		1	1
	03 Development of Human Resources		6	6
	07 Public Relations		2	2
	08 Housing and Buildings		2	2
				8
10 Communications		14		
	11 Communications		2	2
	12 Multi-media		14	17
	13 Microfilm		1	1
	14 Cable TV		1	
				23
20 History		3		
	21 Library History		1	1
	22 Oral History		1	1
	23 Book Arts		1	1
				3

[1] "Offerings" includes subjects reported for five formats covered in questions 1-5 of questionnaire -- formal courses, non-credit courses, workshops, seminars or institutes, conferences.

[2] Total of Column 4 does not equal total reported in Column 3 as some schools gave offerings in more than one "area" within a "field."

Fields of Study (Col. 1)	Areas of Study (Col. 2)	No. of Library Schools Offering Programs in Field (Col. 3)	No. of Library Schools Reporting Offerings in Area (Col. 4)[2]	Total No. of Offerings Reported in Area (Col. 5)
30 Organization and Distribution of Library Material and Data		15		
	31 Bibliography		3	3
	32 Circulation		1	1
	33 Classification and Cataloging		5	6
	34 Data Processing		6	6
	35 Indexing and Abstracting		2	3
	36 Information Retrieval		2	3
				22
40 Philosophy and Theory of Librarianship		13		
	41 Education for Librarians		4	5
	42 Contemporary Library Theory and Practice		4	6
	43 Comparative Librarianship		3	5
	44 Individuals in Library and other Organizations		1	1
	45 Intellectual Freedom		2	2
	46 Librarian Reading		1	1
	47 Curriculum		2	3
	48 Copyright		1	1
	49 Information Science		2	2
				26
50 Resources		7		
	51 Government Documents and Information Sources		4	5
	52 Reference		2	2
	53 Resource Sharing		1	1
	54 Census		1	1
				9
60 Selection and Acquisition		6		
	61 Selection and Acquisition		5	5
	65 Publishing		1	1
				6

[2] Total of column 4 does not equal total reported in Column 3 as some schools gave offerings in more than one "area" within a "field."

1-5

Fields of Study (Col. 1)	Areas of Study (Col. 2)	No. of Library Schools Offering Programs in Field (Col. 3)	No.of Library Schools Reporting Offerings in Area [2] (Col. 4)	Total No. of Offerings Reported in Area (Col. 5)
70 Types of Libraries				
	Special	8		
	Other	17		
	71 Special Libraries		2	2
	72 Archival Practices		1	2
	73 Law		1	1
	74 Map Librarianship		2	2
	75 Medical		4	4
	76 Music		2	2
	77 Prison Legal Libraries		1	1
				14
	81 Operation of Educational Information Service Center		1	1
	83 Public Libraries		9	13
	85 State Library sociations		3	3
	86 School/Media Libraries		12	16
	87 University and College Libraries		4	4
				37
				51
90 User Services		16		
	91 User Services		3	4
	92 Children and Young People		10	12
	93 Traditional Literature and Oral Narration		5	6
	94 Reading Interest		4	5
	96 Service to Disadvantaged and Minorities		6	8
				35

[2] Total of column 4 does not equal total reported in Column 3 as some schools gave offerings in more than one "area" within a "field."

TABLE III

RANK ORDER OF CONTINUING LIBRARY EDUCATION OFFERINGS AS REPORTED BY
32 LIBRARY SCHOOL RESPONDENTS ACCORDING TO MAJOR FIELDS: 1972

Fields of Study	Number of Library Schools Giving Offerings in Field
Types of Librarianship (other than Special)	17
User Services	16
Administration	15
Organization and Distribution of Library Materials and Data	15
Communications	14
Philosophy and Theory of Librarianship	13
Special Librarianship	8
Resources	7
Selection and Acquisition	6
History	3

The range in the number of offerings in continuing library education given by the library schools is summarized in Table IV.

TABLE IV

RANGE IN NUMBER OF CONTINUING LIBRARY EDUCATION OFFERINGS
AS REPORTED BY 32 LIBRARY SCHOOL RESPONDENTS: 1972

Total Number of Different Offerings Listed by a Single School in All Areas and in all Formats	Number of Schools in Category
15 – 17	2
12 – 14	3
9 – 11	5
6 – 8	6
3 – 5	5
0 – 2	11

RESPONSES TO QUESTIONS 9 THROUGH 12.

Summary of Responses

Item No.	Nature of Program	No. of Schools Indicating Programs or Activity	Number of Schools Checking:		
			Before 1971-72	During 1971-72	Planned for: 1972-73
6.	Alumni Enrichment Programs	12	8	8	8
7.	Packaged courses for Continuing Education	9	4	4	6
8.	Continuing Education Program Developed in School for another Program in another State	6	3	6	3
9.	Research in Continuing Education	10	5	3	5
10.	Consultant Service for Continuing Education Programs Outside School	15	8	14	11
11.	Role taken by Faculty in Long-Range Planning in Continuing Education at State or Regional Level	19	7	13	17
12.	Other	9	3	2	5

Breakdown by Individual Questions:

Question 6. Professional enrichment programs for alumni were specified by only 34.4% of responding library schools, and these appeared to be rather !imited in scope. A summary of the responses to Question 6 follows:

	No. of Schools Listing	
Mini-courses, workshops, 1 day programs	5	
Lectures 3	2	
Non-degree programs	2	
Welcome to attend specific courses	1	
Librarian in residence program	1	11
Not specific (under discussion)	3	3
Didn't answer	11	
None	7	:18
	315	32

In questions 7 through 37 there are often two columns of figures given.
For each question, Column 2 gives the number of schools that answered
affirmatively in regard to the specific category. Often, however, schools
listed more than one item or activity in which they engaged when responding
to a specific question. Column 3 endeavors to reflect this by giving a
weighted response.

For example, in Column 3 each school is given one point. If a school lists
more than one idea, each one counts equally so that the total will be one.
The total, therefore of Column 3 will always add up to the number of library
schools upon which the data for that particular question is based.

Looking at the data presented in Table V for question 7, the sub-total for
Column 2 is 13 courses, while the subtotal for Column 3 is 9 schools reporting.
This is explained by the fact that one   school listed packaged courses in three
areas -- cataloging, selection, and reference. Therefore, each of these
areas was given a score of one in Column 2 and a weight of one-third (.33)
in Column 3. Another school listed 3 packaged courses, one in automation
and two in administration; thus automation was given a score of one in .
Column 2 and administration was given a score of 2 in Column 2. However,
in Column 3 administration was given a weight of 0.67 and automation a weight
of 0.33. The total of Column 3 is 32, the number of questionnaires on which
the reporting on this question is based.

Question 7. Development of Packaged Courses.

Nine schools reported 13 packaged courses that had been developed. If the reporting schools
indicate the extent to which packaged courses have been experimented with by the total
number of library schools, it is clear that the development of such courses is minimal in
continuing library education. The average for the reporting 32 schools is 0.4 per school,
but this is even less per school as two schools account for six of the total of thirteen
courses reported. There was no indication on the questionnaire to what extent these 13
courses had been used by groups other than the developing school.

The specific answers given in response to this query are summarized in Table V.

TABLE V

NUMBER OF PACKAGED COURSES DEVELOPED
AS REPORTED BY
32 LIBRARY SCHOOL RESPONDENTS BY SUBJECTS: 1972

Type of Packaged Course Reported (Col. 1)	Total number of courses listed for 32 reporting schools (Col. 2)	Response by schools (Col. 3)[1]
Cataloging	3	2.33
Administration	2	.67
Courses on Videotape..........................	2	2.0
Automation	1	0.33
Basic Reference	1	0.33
Bibliography......................................	1	1.0
Book Selection...................................	1	0.33
Grantsmanship...................................	1	1.0
Hospital Librarianship..........................	1	1.0
Sub-total	13 courses reported from	9 schools
Didn't answer	0	13
None Total	0	10
	13	22

Question 8 stated: "Development of continuing education program which was developed in your school by one or more faculty members, but was implemented in another state (either by your faculty members or by leaders in the state using the program produced by your faculty)."

The response was as follows:

	Number of Schools
Indicated affirmative answer	6
Didn't answer	17
None	9

---

[1] See procedural note on page 9 for explanation of this column, which in each instances totals the number of questionnaires from schools on which data was based.

Of the six schools indicating an affirmative answer, three indicated types of programs: One school listed evaluation of reference service in a state; another listed workshops in participative management in other states; another listed workshops in 4 other states in the area of administration and management.

Question 9 stated: "Research in the area of continuing library education, including proposals submitted even though they have not been funded or implemented yet."

Ten schools indicated activity in research for continuing library education, and the number of projects listed for 1972-73 was two greater than that of the preceding year.

The specific data reported in answer to Question 9 is reported in Table VI.

TABLE VI

NUMBER OF RESEARCH PROJECTS IN CONTINUING LIBRARY EDUCATION AS REPORTED BY 32 LIBRARY SCHOOL RESPONDENTS: 1972

Type of Research Listed in Responses	Total number of Projects listed from 32 Schools	Responses by Schools[1]
Feasibility studies for continuing professional library education	3	2.33
Urban information program	2	1.33
Mathematical and special training for medical and special librarians	2	1.33
Preparation of texts for continuing education programs	2	0.67
Preparation for 6th year program	1	1.0
Southeast Asia library education program	1	1.0
Teaching selected courses by tape and telephone communication	1	1.0
Teaching methods for library continuing education programs	1	0.33
Indicated research, but did not indicate specific nature of it	1	1.0
Sub total	14 projects listed from	10 schools
Didn't answer	0	14.0
None	0	8.0
Total	14	32 schools

[1] See procedural note on page 9 for explanation of this column, which in each instance totals the number of questionnaires from schools on which data was based.

318

Question 10: Asked about consultant services provided by library school faculty for continuing library education programs. The answers are summarized in Table VII.

TABLE VII

TYPES OF CONSULTANT SERVICES PROVIDED BY FACULTY FOR CONTINUING LIBRARY EDUCATION PROGRAMS AS REPORTED BY 32 LIBRARY SCHOOL RESPONDENTS: 1972

Type of Consultant Services Reported	Total number of Services Reported from 32 Schools	Number of Responses by Schools[1]
Serve on university (faculty) continuing education committee	4	4.0
Work with local library systems	4	3.5
Consultant for workshops	2	2.0
Faculty acted as consultants for special continuing education projects	2	2.0
Indicated but did not specify nature of service	3	3.0
Serve in project to identify exemplary programs for school library media specialists	1	0.5
Sub total	16 types of service from	15.0 schools
Didn't answer	0	11.0
None	0	6.0
Total	16	32.0 schools

Question 11 asked what kind of role was played by members of library school faculty in state or regional long-range planning for continuing library education. Table VIII summarizes the responses from the 32 schools participating in the survey.

---

[1] See procedural note on page 9 for explanation of this column, which in each instance will total the number of schools participating in the survey.

TABLE VIII

TYPE OF ROLES PLAYED BY FACULTY IN STATE OR
REGIONAL LONG-RANGE PLANNING FOR CONTINUING LIBRARY EDUCATION
AS REPORTED BY 32 LIBRARY SCHOOL RESPONDENTS: 1972

Type of Roles Played	Number of Types of Roles from 32 Schools	Number of Responses by Schools [1]
Faculty on or closely connected with state library association on continuing education	6	5.0
Planning in conjunction with state libraries	4	3.0
Surveys	3	2.5
Consultant to director of state continuing education program	2	2.0
Faculty on ALA Committee on Continuing Education	2	1.5
Leadership in planning for center of adult education	1	1.0
Indicated role played, but did not specify nature	4	4.0
Sub total	22	19.0 schools
Didn't answer	0	10.0
None	0	2.0
"?"	0	1.0
Total	22	32.0 schools

Question 12 asked for other types of continuing education activities. The schools responded as follows:

No other activities............................ 5 schools
Didn't answer................................. 18 schools
Indicated other activities..................... 9 schools

Of the 9 schools that indicated other activities were carried out, six were specific and listed the following activities:

1. Workshop conducted by faculty member in reference resources for paraprofessional employees in a public library branch system.

---

[1] See procedural note on page 9 which explains this column, which in all instances will total the number of schools participating in the survey.

2.   Cooperation with East/West Center   Communication Institute Documentation Internship
     Program for Asian librarians.

3.   Monthly colloquium series, which although primarily for MLS students, is open to all
     librarians.

4.   One faculty member will assist in planning   an institute for Asian and African
     population librarians in connection with an International Population Conference.

5.   Plan and participate in a symposium with a guest speaker each night during one week.

6.   Writing books and articles on continuing education.

CONTINUING LIBRARY EDUCATION AND OBJECTIVES

Questions 13 through 19 in the instrument dealt with continuing library education and objectives.

Question 13 specifically asked: "What are the continuing education objectives and concerns of
your school ?"

There was a wide range of attitudes expressed by the schools , from those that said that
objectives and concepts were very nebulous or informal to two schools who submitted tentative
formal statements of the proposed role of the library school in continuing education, which were
in the process of being refined by the faculty.   The statements submitted in draft form were com
prehensive and showed that continuing education was a high priority item of these schools.

A summary of the answers given to Question 13 as listed on the questionnaire is
presented in Table IX.

Typical of responses categorized in Table IX as "informal" is the following statement: "Our
objectives regarding continuing education are pretty informal: We tend to feel we should do something consistently (every summer), but that's about as far as we have gone. "

Typical of responses categorized in Table IX as "nebulous" were answers such as, "Objectives
have never been made explicit, " or "Nebulous, not defined. "

Under the heading, "Meet needs of alumni and librarians by providing further study, " three schools
specified that their priority within this goal was to meet the needs within their particular state.

Another school expressed particular concern about helping librarians move into higher
administrative positions or to help librarians shift from one type of librarianship to another.

From an analysis of the answers, it would seem that in all but a few instances. objectives and
policies regarding continuing education were not based on any over-all range plan of development,
but tended to develop as specific needs were noticed. Perhaps the most encouraging observation
from the data presented in regard to this question was that generally schools seemed to be aware
of their need for formulating definite objectives. In addition to the two schools that submitted the
tentative policy statements noted earlier, three other schools indicated that committees had been

formed to work out comprehensive statements. Another school reported that the library school
was cooperating with the total university in working out a policy statement which would include a
statement of a philosophy of continuing education for the whole university and the development of
standards for programs.

TABLE IX

OBJECTIVES AND CONCERNS OF 32 REPORTING LIBRARY
SCHOOLS IN CONTINUING EDUCATION: 1972

Continuing education objectives and concerns	No. of objectives and concepts listed	No. of Schools[1]
Meet needs of alumni and librarians by providing further study	15	7.33
Informal	9	6.5
Widen the range of educational opportunity	10	5.17
Nebulous	6	2.0
Ph.D. and 6th year Post-MLS programs	4	1.83
Offer workshops	4	1.42
Indication and "regular-formal" programs failed; looking for other formats	2	1.0
Interdisciplinary with other academics	1	0.25
Sub total	51 items listed from	25.5 schools
Didn't answer	0	6.5[2]
Total	51 items	32.0 schools

[1] See procedural note on page 9 for explanation of this column, which is each instance
totals the number of questionnaires from schools on which data was based.

[2] The reason for .5 library schools occurring in column 3 is that although one school did
not answer the question, they indicated what their response would be in a previous question, so
"Didn't answer" was weighted .5 as was their "Indicated response."

Question 14 asked how it is determined what programs will be developed and implemented. The highest number of responese were: collective faculty action, committees, and individual faculty action. The total response to the question is presented in Table X.

TABLE X

METHODS FOR DETERMINING WHAT CONTINUING LIBRARY EDUCATION PROGRAMS WILL BE DEVELOPED AND IMPLEMENTED AS REPORTED BY 32 LIBRARY SCHOOL RESPONDENTS: 1972

Method of Determining Programs	No. of times Listed	Response by Schools[1]
Collective faculty action	20	11.08
Committees	9	3.83
Individual faculty action	9	3.67
Dean	6	2.58
Alumni	5	2.08
Practitioners	5	1.5
Informal	4	1.5
Professional groups	2	.75
Students	2	.75
Availability of resources and personnel	2	.5
Negotiate with other [university] groups	1	.50
School priorities	1	.25
Sub total	66 methods listed by	29.00 schools
Didn't answer	0	3.0
Total	66 methods	32.0 schools

[1] See procedural note on page 9 for explanation of this column, which in each instance totals the number of questionnaires from schools on which date was based.

Question 15 asked: "What is the relation of needs of practicing librarians to programs offered?"

The responses indicated that selected needs were considered, although not always before the program was developed.   Table XI reflects the total responses given to this question.

TABLE XI

RELATIONSHIP OF NEEDS OF PRACTICING LIBRARIANS TO CONTINUING
LIBRARY EDUCATION PROGRAMS OFFERED BY LIBRARY SCHOOLS
AS REPORTED BY 32 LIBRARY SCHOOL RESPONDENTS: 1972

Relation of needs to programs offered	No. of times Listed	Response by Schools[1]
Reflects selected needs	10	8.0
Librarians expressed need (Before)	6	4.5
Librarians acceptance (As indicated by participation)	5	5.0
Current issues and trends	4	2.5
Other	4	4.0
Not carefully considered	1	1.0
Sub total	30 listing from	25.0 schools
Didn't answer	0	6.0
Don't know	0	1.0
Total	30	32 schools

---
[1] See procedural note on page 9 for explanation of this column, which in each instance totals the number of questionnaires from schools on which data was based.

Question 16 attempted to discover how needs in the area of continuing education were determined. The respondents mentioned most frequently practitioners, alumni, and surveys. Other factors in termining needs are indicated in Table XII.

TABLE XII

FACTORS CONSIDERED IN DETERMINING NEEDS IN RELATION TO CONTINUING LIBRARY EDUCATION PROGRAMS AS REPORTED BY 32 LIBRARY SCHOOL RESPONDENTS: 1972

Factors considered in determining needs	No. of Factors Listed	Response by Schools [1]
Practitioners	15	6.58
Alumni	10	3.83
Surveys	10	4.67
Professional groups	7	2.17
Faculty observation	6	1.92
Literature	5	1.58
Informal	4	2.17
Council	4	1.75
State and federal	3	.83
Librarian acceptance	2	2.0
Sub total	66 factors	27.50 schools
Didn't answer	5	4.5
Total	71	32.0 schools

[1] See procedural note on page 9 for explanation of this column, which in each instance totals the number of questionnaires from schools on which data is based.

Question 17   asked what provisions are made for the continuing education of faculty members. The highest single listing was sabbatical leaves and released time, which was mentioned sixteen different times by the 32 responding schools. The next highest provision listed was travel funds which was mentioned by 8 schools. The complete tabulation of the responses received from the schools is shown in Table XIII.

TABLE XIII

PROVISIONS MADE FOR THE CONTINUING EDUCATION OF LIBRARY SCHOOL
FACULTY MEMBERS AS REPORTED BY 32 LIBRARY SCHOOL RESPONDENTS: 1972

Provisions for continuing education of faculty members	No. of Times Listed	Response by Schools[1]
Sabbatical leaves and release time	16	7.52
Travel funds	8	3.1
Free tuition and audits	6	2.73
Lightening teaching load	5	1.65
Encourage (funds) research	3	.7
Definitely expected	2	1.25
Changing around of teaching schedules	1	.5
Loans	1	.2
Other	19	9.6
Sub total	61 items	27.25 schools
Didn't answer	3	3.0
None	3	1.75
Total	67 items	32.0 schools

The category "other" included a motley of answers. Most were answers that laid stress on "encouraging" faculty to attend workshops, etc., or join, become active, in a professional group.

[1] See procedural note on page 9 for explanation of this column, which in each instance totals the number of questionnaires from schools on which data was based.

Question 18   asked the reward for continuing education activity in which the faculty might engage.
The response made most frequently was that continuing education by the faculty was "taken into
consideration." The next highest was "none", followed closely by the category labelled in the
chart "negative reinforcement." This term implies answers that stated that lack of continuing
education activity would be held against the person, and hence that continuing education by faculty
members is expected. The difference between "negative reinforcement" and "taken into consideration" is similar to plus and minus. "Taken into consideration", as asked in the chart, implies
that when salary, promotions, etc. are being considered, continuing education on the part of the
faculty member will help -- will be a plus value. Table XIV summarizes all the responses
that were made to the question.

Lessening of teaching hours here shows lessening of course load _after_   engaging in continuing
education, whereas in Question 17 it was to facilitate the taking of continuing education.

TABLE XIV

THE RELATION OF FACULTY CONTINUING EDUCATION TO THE REWARD
SYSTEM AS REPORTED BY 32 RESPONDING LIBRARY SCHOOLS: 1972

Rewards for faculty continuing education activity		No. of Times Listed	Response by Schools[1]
Taken into consideration		11	8.0
Negative reinforcement		9	6.0
Unknown		2	1.5
Reduction of teaching hours		2	1.5
Other		2	1.5
Brighter Halo		1	1.0
	Sub total	27 items	19.5 schools
Didn't answer		3	3.0
None		10	9.5
	Total	40 items	32.0 schools

[1]   See procedural note on page 9 for explanation of this column, which in each instance
totals the number of questionnaires from schools on which data was based.

327

Question 19 asked if there were any specific requirements regarding the continuing education of faculty members. The largest response here was "no." Other answers are indicated in Table XV.

TABLE XV

SPECIFIC REQUIREMENTS REGARDING THE CONTINUING EDUCATION OF LIBRARY SCIENCE FACULTY MEMBERS AS REPORTED BY 32 RESPONDING LIBRARY SCHOOLS: 1972

Specific Requirements	No. of times Listed	Response by Schools[1]
None	21	20.0
Relevant requirements (in broad sense)	4	3.5
Ph.D. for promotion	3	1.5
Sabbatical leave required	1	1.0
Sub total	29 listings	26.0 schools
Didn't answer	6	6.0
Total	35 listings	32.0 schools

INTERFACE WITH OTHER PROFESSIONAL GROUPS

Questions 20 through 26 dealt with the interface of library school programs with other professional programs on the same university campus.

Eighteen of the 32 library school respondees indicated that they did discuss continuing education with those in other professional programs on campus. The specific breakdown was as follows:

Yes, discuss continuing education with other professional programs	18
No	8
Sometimes, limited extent, occasionally	3
Not applicable	1
No answer	2
	32 schools

[1] See procedural note on page 9 for explanation of this column, which is each instance totals the number of questionnaires from schools on which data was based.

Thirteen of the schools indicated that they attended   planning sessions of other professional groups on campus, eleven said they did not, others gave varying answers as indicated below:

Yes, attend planning sessions of other professional groups on campus	13
No	11
Yes, to some extent	2
Rarely, not regularly	2
Not applicable	2
No answer	2
	32 schools

When asked the more general questions as to whether library school personnel was aware of what other professionally oriented groups were doing on campus in the area of continuing education, 24 answered yes. Other answers to this question are indicated below:

Yes, aware of what other professional oriented groups on campus are doing in area of continuing education	24
Somewhat	2
No	2
Not applicable	1
No answer	3
	32 schools

Three schools indicated that they were kept informed through newsletters, extension bulletins and other publications.

The last question relative to interface with other professional groups asked in what ways library school personnel interacted or thought it would be beneficial to interact with other professional continuing education programs on campus. The activity that was mentioned the most often in this regard was participation in campus continuing education advisory council. Mentioned next most frequently was increased awareness, pooling of resources, additional concern for bigger total program. Four schools, however, indicated that they could not see benefit from campus interaction; they thought it better to interact within the profession. In this regard one school stated, "Each college 'does its own thing' -- little related to our interests." The complete data obtained from this question is presented in Table XVI.

329

TABLE XVI

ACTIVITIES AND ATTITUDES TOWARD INTERACTION WITH OTHER PROFESSIONAL
CONTINUING EDUCATION PROGRAMS ON CAMPUS AS REPORTED BY 32 RESPONDING
LIBRARY SCHOOLS: 1972

Ways of Interaction	No. of Times Listed	Response by Schools[1]
Participate in campus continuing education advisory council	7	6
Increased awareness, pooling of resources, additional concerns for bigger total program	6	5.5
Benefit from other's expertise when we put on programs	5	4.5
Can't see benefit from campus interaction; better to interact within profession	4	4.0
Students from our department take courses elsewhere and students from other departments take our courses	2	2
Hope to be able to contact other schools within university	2	2
Rely on news media for knowledge of other programs	1	1
Teach at adult education center	1	1
Sub total	28 listings	26
No answer	0	5
Not applicable	0	1
Total	28 listings	32 schools

It should be noted that on the questionnaire that there were two questions labeled as number #26.

---

[1] See procedural note on page 9 for explanation of this column, which in each instance totals the number of questionnaires from schools on which data was based.

STATUS OF CONTINUING EDUCATION ON UNIVERSITY CAMPUSES

Questions 26 through 31 related to the status of continuing education on university campuses.

The statements to which the respondents were asked to react were conclusions that were reached regarding continuing education for research and development personnel in a study sponsored by the National Science Foundation.

The only statement with which the respondents seemed in near agreement with the engineering study was in #28, "Faculty members have to squeeze continuing education efforts into the myriad of other activities demanded of them." The respondents disagreed rather uniformly with the findings of the engineering study which stated that continuing education effort at present is contingent on individual faculty members sacrificing the rewards of the academic system (promotion, salary increases). One respondent, in disagreeing, as this question applies to the library school, stated that activity points are given which count towards promotion.

A summary of the answers to this section is presented in Table XVII.

TABLE XVII

THE STATUS OF CONTINUING EDUCATION ON UNIVERSITY CAMPUSES
AS REPORTED BY 32 LIBRARY SCHOOLS: 1972

Question Number	Unfavorable conditions relative to university continuing education programs	Over-all on campus Agree	Disagree	In Library School Agree	Disagree
26	The university reward system does not acknowledge that continuing education is a respectable and reputable career line for faculty.	10	16	5	21
27	Continuing education effort at present is contingent on individual faculty members sacrificing the rewards of the academic system (promotion, salary increases)	5	19	2	24
28	Faculty members have to squeeze continuing education efforts into the myriad of other activities demanded of them.	17	6	20	7

In comparing the answers between library science and over-all campus attitudes in the three questions, 26, 27, and 28, the answers tended to be the same in 19 instances, opposite in one, not applicable in 3, and markedly different in 9 instances.

TABLE XVII
(Continued)

Question Number	Unfavorable conditions relative to university continuing education programs	Over-all on campus		In Library School	
		Agree	Disagree	Agree	Disagree
29	There is a general down-grading of non-credit activities in the spectrum of university teaching relative to courses in the regular degree curricula. Yet there is general agreement that continuing education must be non-credit (in large part) in order to develop formats which are more flexible in meeting the individual's needs for continuing education.	12[1]	8	12[1]	10
30	Little attention is given to seeking new methods of developing, evaluating, and experimenting with new methods of instruction in order to explore their potential usefulness in the field of continuing education.	7	16	4	23
31	There is an absence of long-range planning for continuing education in collaborative arrangements with professional associations, employing institutions, or other professional groups.	15	6	13	15

In comparing the answers between library science attitudes and over-all campus attitudes in the three questions, 29, 30, and 31, the answers tended to be the same in 13 instances, opposite in one, not applicable in 7, and markedly different in 11 instances.

In relation to all the questions 26 through 31, the comment of one school seems significant and that is that answers were based on "arguments from silence and may be invalid." This statement was made in regard to over-all campus answers.

---

1. Three schools indicated that they agreed with the first part of question number 29, but disagreed with the second part, (to both over-all on campus and library school sections.) Two schools refrained from answering altogether, saying they had "no opinion as question is contradictory."

ADMINISTRATION OF CONTINUING EDUCATION

Questions 32 through 36 asked how continuing education was administered on the parent campuses of the library schools in regard to approval, patterning, continuation, discontinuation, and financing. The answers to each of these is summarized in the following data.

Question Number	Response	No. of times Listed	Response by Schools[1]
32.	Approved		
	School or Department level	11	8.5
	Center for Continuing Education	9	6.0
	Faculty	9	5.83
	Dean	8	5.50
	Curriculum Committed	2	.83
	Same as regular academic program	2	1.33
	Varies	1	1.00
	Sub total	42 listings	29.00 schools
	Didn't answer	2	2.0
	Not applicable	1	1.0
	Total	45	32.0 schools
33.	Patterned		
	Faculty	6	5.5
	To suit need of individual school or department	6	5.5
	Varies greatly	3	3.0
	Continuing Education Committee	3	2.0
	Special Courses	2	2.0
	Individual professors develop, faculty discuss collectively	2	2.0
	Individual professors	2	2.0
	Informally	2	2.0
	Sub total	26 listings	24.0 schools
	Didn't answer	7	7.0
	Not applicable	1	1.0
	Total	34 listings	32.0 schools

---

[1] See procedural note on page 9 for explanation of this column, which in each instance totals the number of questionnaires from schools on which data was based.

333

Question Number	Response	No. of Times Listed	Response by Schools[1]
34	**Continued**		
	At direction of School or Department	7	7.0
	Faculty	6	5.5
	Usually "1-shot" affair; predetermined period	3	2.5
	Based on enrollment	2	1.5
	At direction of Continuing Education Committee	2	1.5
	Same as regular	1	1.0
	Varies	1	1.0
	Sub total	22 listings	20.0 schools
	Didn't answer	10	10.0
	Not applicable	2	2.0
	Total	34 listings	32.0 schools
35.	**Discontinued**		
	At direction of school or program	8	7.0
	Enrollment	4	2.5
	Faculty action	4	4.0
	Automatically lapses, could be reinstated	3	2.5
	At direction of Continuing Education Committee	1	1.0
	Same as regularly	1	1.0
	Varies	1	1.0
	Sub total	22 listings	19 schools
	Didn't answer	11	11
	Not applicable	2	2
	Total	35 listings	32 schools
36.	**Financed**		
	Tuition	17	11.67
	Outside (Federal) grants	9	4.17
	Continuing Education Committee	6	4.50
	School or Department budget	5	2.67
	Same as regularly	2	2.0
	Varies greatly	1	1.0
	State Department of Libraries	1	1.0
	Sub total	41 listings	27 schools
	Didn't answer	4	4.0
	Aren't (i.e., Hence no program)	1	1.0
	Total	46	32.0 schools

ATTITUDES TOWARD LOOSENING UP IN THE OFFERINGS OF CONTINUING EDUCATION
OPPORTUNITIES TO PROFESSIONAL GROUPS OR INDIVIDUALS.

Question 37, the final one in the questionnaire, stated that higher education design patterns are
in the process of transition today on a nationwide scale. It asked: "On your campus do you
observe indications of a change in role or a trend toward loosening up in the offering of continuing education opportuniteis to professional groups or individuals?"

Answers to this question were quite varied. They are summarized in Table XVIII.

TABLE XVIII

ATTITUDES TOWARD LOOSENING UP THE OFFERINGS OF CONTINUING EDUCATION
OPPORTUNITIES TO PROFESSIONAL GROUPS OR INDIVIDUALS AS PERCEIVED
BY 32 LIBRARY SCHOOL RESPONDENTS: 1972

	No. of Responses	Response by Schools[1]
Yes.	10	10.0
Yes, particularly in other fields	3	2.5
Yes, we are making every effort to accommodate non-degree programs and students	3	2.5
Steady increase in number of offerings and emphasis	3	3.0
No drastic changes seen	3	2.5
Yes, broader programs and involvement of entire faculty	2	1.5
Yes, particularly in Library Science	1	1.0
Yes, more from without than within though	1	1.0
Increased interest (upgrade present library work force)	1	1.0
Yes, if it isn't a money loser	1	1.0
Unclear. There's a ____ program for part-time study but we're reluctant to participate as it is outside the University	1	1.0
Yes, university is willing to take courses to the people	1	1.0
Sub total	30 listings	28 schools
Didn't answer	3	3.0
Not applicable	1	1.0
Total	34	32.0 schools

Comments made by two of the respondents seem to have significance in relation to loosening up programs and reflect attitudes expressed by others.

1.   The major problem in regard to continuing education for librarians is the fact that librarians have little, if any, incentive, to continue their education. Unlike teachers, they seldom receive salary increases because they have taken additional courses. Libraries must not only provide salary increases, but they must also give librarians time off to take additional courses. Libraries as well as the librarians benefit from programs of continuing education.

In relation to this problem, it is encouraging to note that at least one ALA Committee is meeting during Midwinter 1973 to discuss a "rewards system for continuing education."

2.   We can offer 1-2 day institutes, workshops, clinics, etc., as we see fit. The administration favors them.... But where, oh, where, do you get typists, artists, stamp stickers, ticket designers, address finders, etc., etc. in a fully loaded semester? These facilities or aids do not exist in any great number -- and they are vital. We can find experts or do the program ourselves. It is everything else that kills the desire.

The conclusion would seem clear that except in a very few instances the respondents were in agreement that on their campuses there were observable indications of a change in role or a tendency toward loosening up in the offering of continuing education opportunities to professional groups or individuals. This would seem to be true in spite of the two problems just mentioned.

APPENDIX L (continued)

Continuing Education questionnaire
APPENDIX A

<u>List of Accredited Library Schools Returning Questionnaire and
Names of Continuing Education Network Representatives</u>

State University of New York, Albany
  Ms. Lucille Whalen,
Brigham Young University
  Dr. Maurice P. Marchant
University of California, Berkeley
  Dr. Patrick Wilson
University of California, Los Angeles
  Prof. Raymond F. Wood
The Catholic University of America
  Dr. Elizabeth W. Stone
Drexel University
  Miss Bridgitte Kenney,
Emory University
  Mr. John Clemons
Florida State University
  Dr. Martha Jane Zachert
University of Hawaii
  Dr. Josefa Abrera
University of Illinois
  Dr. Herbert Goldhor
Indiana University
  Sarah R. Reed
University of Iowa
  Dr. Frederick Wageman
Kent State University
  Mrs. Clara Jackson
University of Kentucky
  Dr. Lawrence A. Allen
Long Island University
  Prof. Kathryn S. Wilkins
McGill University
  Dr. Violet Coughlin
University of Maryland
  Mr. John Colson
University of Minnesota
  Mrs. Joan H. Leigh
University of North Carolina
  Dr. Fred Roper
University of Oklahoma
  Dr. Harry Clark
George Peabody College for Teachers
  Mrs. Virginia O. Harman
University of Pittsburgh
  Dr. Peggy Sullivan

Pratt Institute
  Mrs. Patricia Senn Brieivik
Rosary College
  Mr. Melvin J. Klatt
University of Southern California
  Dr. Raymond Kilpela
University of Texas at Austin
  Mr. Heartsill H. Young
Texas Woman's University
  Prof. John J. Miniter
University of Toronto
  Mrs. . Adele Fasick
Wayne State University
  Dr. Genevieve M. Casey
Western Michigan University
  Mr. Martin Cohen
University of Western Ontario
  Prof. Gloria M. Strathern
University of Wisconsin
  Dr. Muriel Fuller

337

-1. Abrahamson, Stephen, and others. Medical Information Project: A Study of an Audiovisual Device as a Technique for Continuing Education for General Practitioners. Final Report. Los Angeles: School of Education and School of Medicine, University of Southern California, 1970. (ED 051 846.)

The unique factor in the Medical Information Project is that working from nothing, it undertook to design and put into operation a communication system for general medical practitioners using an individualized, programmed, audiovisual medium. The development of this system involved three general phases. Phase I consisted of: 1) obtaining and reviewing literature pertaining to medical communication problems; 2) designing a means of sampling, drawing the sample, obtaining the physicians' participation; 3) laying out the general design for research and development; 4) developing and validating the instruments to be used to assess the physicians' cognitive and affective reactions; 5) testing and selecting the hardware to be used as the communication device; 6) developing the programming concepts; 7) developing the production process and 8) selecting the content areas and the medical consultants for the program topics. Phase II consisted of: 1) distributing the hardware to the participating physicians; 2) producing and distributing the training program on equipment utilization; 3) pre- and post-program questionnaires and interviews and 4) producing and distributing the fifteen content programs. Phase III consisted of: 1)collecting and processing raw data and 2) analyzing the data.

The system involved selected physicians receiving regular slide-record programs which they played on audiovisual projectors at their own convenience and later evaluated.

-2. Academic Instructor and Allied Officer School. AIAOS Additions to Principles and Techniques of Instruction. Maxwell Air Force Base, Ala.: Academic Instructor and Allied Officer School, Air University, November, 1967. (ED 024 876.)

A brief but comprehensive paper which summarizes and stresses the importance of every teacher knowing some of the basic principles of learning. Characteristics of the learning process that are emphasized: learning is purposeful; learning is multi-faceted; learning is partly a common process and partly an individual process; learning is a guiding process as described by Gagné in his hierarchy of learning capabilities; learning is a process of internalizing experience - the student can only learn from that which he experiences himself; learning is an active process - the student must be involved in the experience.

339

A-3.   Aceto, Vincent J. An Exploratory Study of the Occupation of
       Teacher of Librarianship. Cleveland: Western Reserve
       University, June, 1967 to June, 1968. (EP 010 851.)

A-4.   Ackerman, Leonard. "A Study of Selected Employee Development
       Specialists in the Federal Government: Their Background and
       Perceptions of Their Role and Organizational Location." (Un-
       published Doctor's dissertation, George Washington
       University, 1967.)

       In this study the author found that those responsible for
       employee development did not think that they had adequate
       access to top management; and that in order to influence manage-
       ment they must be in a position in the organizaticn close to
       those who are responsible for making decisions. In addition,
       there appeared to be some feeling that where employee develop-
       ment is part of the personnel function there was not only limited
       access to top management but that employee development was
       not considered one of the major functions of personnel. It was
       found that personnel specialists placed primary emphasis on
       knowledge of rules, regulations, and procedures while Employee
       Development Specialists were more concerned with teaching
       techniques, individual and group behavior, and current manage-
       ment theories. The conclusion of the researcher was that
       there was a need for: 1) role definition for Employee Develop-
       ment Specialists; 2) qualification standards for Employee
       Development Specialists and 3) review of the organizational
       location of Employee Development Specialists.

       This study has implications concerning the qualifications and
       placement of directors of staff development in libraries.

A-5.   "ACS Short Courses Applauded." Chemical and Engineering News
       43 (March, 1965) 56.

A-6.   "ACS Short Courses to Travel." Chemical and Engineering News
       43 (September 6, 1965) 135-39.

A-7.   Adams, Henry B., ed. Adult Learning Seminar, Proceedings.
       Syracuse, N.Y.: Syracuse University, Continuing Education
       Center for Public Service and the National Council of Churches
       of Christ, 1967. (ED 020 482.)

340

This seminar focused upon needs of ministers, objectives of programs of continuing education and processes by which programs are evaluated.

A-8.   Adams, Henry Babcock. <u>Continuous Education for Ministers.</u>
       December, 1966. (ED 015 365).

       The author outlines five main types of programs available for the
       continuing education of ministers, and urges continuous systematic
       education and a revision of the concept of theological education.

A-9.   Adams, Scott. "Operation Bootstrap: Medical Librarians and Continu-
       ing Education." <u>Kentucky Library Association Bulletin</u>, 32
       (April, 1968), 4-11.

A-10. Adelson, Marvin. "The System Approach--A Perspective." <u>SDC
       Magazine,</u> 9 (October, 1966), 1-3.

       The systems approach is able to produce "demonstrably good" or
       defensible solutions which may take many forms. In each case,
       the use of available techniques may be different; the systems
       approach is a creative process which includes arrangements for
       all appropriate sources to make relevant contributions. The systems
       approach is organized, creative, empirical, theoretical, and
       pragmatic. System analysis cannot or will not: provide a sim-
       plistic set of procedures to arrive at incontestable conclusions,
       accomplish everything at once, or guarantee the transferability of
       techniques developed in other subject areas.

A-11. Adult Education Association. "Common Concerns: The Position of the
       Adult Education Association of the U.S.A." <u>Adult Education,</u> 18
       (Spring, 1968), 197-213.

       Fifteen common but interrelated concerns have been identified and
       for each there is a brief statement of the present situation, a short
       list of goals, and a brief platform statement which suggests some
       ways to get from where adult education is today to where it hope-
       fully will be in the near future. They are: 1) agencies of adult
       education; 2) adult education and the process of social change;
       3) the American adult as a learner; 4) objectives of adult educa-
       tion programs; 5) learning experiences especially for adults;
       6) evaluation to improve program effectiveness; 7) public

understanding of adult education; 8) professionalization and staff development; 9) appropriate facilities; 10) relations among adult education agencies; 11) relations with other agencies; 12) financing adult education; 13) a body of professional knowledge; 14) research and 15) international adult education.

A-12. Allen, Dwight W. A Differentiated Staff: Putting Teaching Talent to Work. The Teacher and His Staff, Occasional Papers, No. 1. Washington, D.C.: National Commission on Teacher Education and Professional Standards, National Education Association, 1967.

A-13. Allen, Dwight W. Micro-Teaching: A Description. Stanford: School of Education, Stanford University, 1966. (ED 023 314.)

A-14. Allen, James E., Jr. "The Educational Third Dimension." Paper read to the Galaxy Conference on Adult and Continuing Education, Washington, D.C.: December 9, 1969. Mimeographed.

Allen terms continuing education "the educational third dimension." This is based on the proposition that education is a lifelong process, and that after basic elementary and secondary education, followed by post-secondary training, there must be concern with a third dimension -- the lifelong learning of adults. He envisions cooperative, community, inter-professional continuing education programs which would provide a whole new range of insights.

A-15. Allen, Lawrence A. An Evaluation of the Community Librarians' Training Courses, with Special Emphasis on the Entire Training Function in the Library Extension Division of the New York State Library. Albany: New York State Library, 1966. (ED 024 406.)

This study was designed to: 1) evaluate the Community Librarians' Training Courses which had been conducted for five years in New York State to train persons without professional library training who were serving as librarians and 2) appraise the entire training program of the Library Extension Division in order to provide guidelines for future development. Methodology for the study involved intensive evaluation of two courses and questionnaires administered to all System Directors, Consultants, and students. Recommendations were made for improvement of the course, the expansion of the program, and coordination with other agencies. The report also includes the questionnaire used, cost figures, a bibliography of on-the-job training, and course evaluation materials.

A-16. Allen, Lawrence A. and Conroy, Barbara. "Social Interaction Skills." Library Trends, 20 (July, 1971), 78-91.

This article in the Library Trends issue (edited by Stone), entitled Personnel Development and Continuing Education in Libraries, offers a systematic approach to one of the most fundamental concerns of the training subsystem -- the development of a library staff effectively interrelating with colleagues and clients and working toward organizational goals. The nature of the need for social interaction skills grows from the fact that the library is a human organization. Allen and Conroy have drawn from their extensive experience in conducting institutes, workshops. Findings from the behavioral sciences are explored, and a sample model of team building illustrates the methods found by the authors to be most effective in this area.

A-17. Allen, Lawrence A. "Education of the State Library Consultant," Southeastern Librarian, 18 (Spring, 1968), 43-48.

The consultant role requires competence in a number of different areas. In this article these needs are grouped into three general areas: 1) behavioral sciences (interpersonal relationships, communication theory, conference leadership, adult education methods; 2) management and administration theory (the process of change, management theory, management functions, public administration, organizational sociology and psychology, cultural change); 3) library specialization (current trends and problems, library speciality, library research, internship).

A-18. Allen, Wendell C. and others. "Performance criteria for educational personnel development: a state approach to standards." Journal of Teacher Education, 20 (Summer, 1969), 133-35.

The authors feel that progress in establishing programs has been slowed by the pressure toward standards and that college, state organizations, and professional associations must be aligned "in a mutually responsible relationship to the individual throughout his career." Input from the trainee is also required.

Washington State has tried to establish a process for developing performance criteria and tasks -- instead of across-the-board standards ending in the same sequence of study for all.

New standards were prepared in 1968, based on the ideas that 1) preparation should be continuous throughout one's career; 2) programs should be individualized; 3) preparation should be on performance and 4) professional associations and school organizations should share the responsibility with universities.

A-19. Alvarez, Robert S. "Continuing Education for the Public Librarian," California Librarian, 30 (July, 1969), 177-86.

What is needed are 1) the type of instruction that stimulates and moves people to ask questions and explore a subject further on their own; 2) instructors who are well qualified to teach the information that is needed in many fields and 3) library managers who really want to hear and use all this information.

A-20. Ambry, Edward J., and others. Evaluation for Environmental Education: A Systems Analysis Approach for Self-Evaluation. Mountain Lakes: The New Jersey State Council for Environmental Education, 1969.

A-21. American Association of Colleges for Teacher Education. Professional Teacher Education II: A Programmed Design Developed by the AACTE Teacher Education and Media Project. Washington, D.C.: The American Association of Colleges for Teacher Education, 1968.

If one of the purposes of continuing education is to keep the practitioner informed on research developments and how to implement them, then this study has value as a model. It could be used by any group which has as its task answering these questions: 1) Can "the gap be bridged between the 'producer' of educational innovation and the intended audience, the 'user'?" 2) Can "a system be designed which will present the results of educational research to the 'user' in a meaningful, knowledgeable, and understandable way?" 3) Can "the integrated and functional use of media in instruction be effectively demonstrated?"

The workshop was based on two assumptions: 1) that the dissemination of research results has been primarily by the "written report," which fewer and fewer people have the time or inclination to read; and 2) that conferences, workshops, seminars, institutes, meetings ignore or "do real violence" to what is known about how learning takes place. The tendency is to talk about material and talk at the audience; the result has been lack of sufficient understanding of the content to make any decisions concerning implementation of results of research.

The project took the position, in harmony with basic literature, "...that the phase of the cycle pattern in the human cybernetic system (namely: perception, concept formation, use of concepts in making decisions, the execution of decisions, and the perception of the consequences of one's action)" reveal real interdependencies that can prevent learning if they are ignored and not provided for. The project dealt with only the first two phases of this model, perceptual input and concept formation (concepts cannot be transmitted from one person to another...they must be perceived by each person from experiences with the real referents or good portrayals of them). Two remaining steps, Decision Making and Trial, were, as they should be, left to the workshop participants to carry out in their own programs at their own institutions.

Sessions of the workshop included interaction analysis, micro-teaching, non-verbal communication, simulation, and media analysis.

A-22. American Association of School Administrators. Committee for the Advancement of School Administration. Inservice Programs for School Administration. Washington, D.C.: American Association of School Administrators, 1966.

This brief booklet summarizes the essentials of a comprehensive program for inservice (continuing) education for school administration. It points out procedures to be followed in organizing and supporting programs in every state. "Any improvements made in education in this country during the 20 years immediately ahead will be made largely through leadership of people now employed in administrative positions." Emphasizing the importance of allowing time to grow professionally on the job, the book states that "no school superintendent will serve his school district well who does not allocate a minimum of six hours a week to his own professional improvement. Professional growth is a part of his regular job." Activities

345

for timeallotted included: reading; conferring with well-informed people; serving on professional committees, attending professional meetings; attending workshops or institutes; taking formal course work in a university program; participating in a research project; contributing to professional literature; working with staff in experimental projects and long-range planning. Each school board is urged to make specific budgetary allocations (an amount equal to 10 per cent of expenditures for administrative services is recommended as a minimum); establish policy for staff participation in professional meetings; employ consultants to work with staff members in dealing with special problems; establish policies that provide for leaves of absence and sabbaticals; meet the cost of tuition and living expenses incurred by staff members in participating in institutes and workshops. The book encourages support by universities, the state Department of Education, the state association of school administrators, and the American Association of School Administrators and steps for implementing these suggestions are outlined.

A-23. American Association of School Administrators. Professional Administrators for American Schools. Washington, D.C.: American Association of School Administrators, 1960.

A-24. American Association of School Librarians. School Library Personnel Task Analysis. A report prepared in Phase I of the School Library Manpower Project by the Research Division of National Education in a national study to identify the tasks performed by school library personnel in unified service programs at the building level. Funded by the Knapp Foundation as the School Library Manpower Project. Chicago, Illinois: American Library Association, 1969.

This report analyzes the tasks performed by all types of personnel in school library programs in order to determine knowledge and skills needed to perform them. Using the data collected profile descriptions of jobs based on combination of tasks requiring approximately the same level of preparation were prepared. The report has implications for library continuing education programs as it indicates new patterns of knowledge and skills needed in training and retraining of school library personnel.

A-25. American Association of School Librarians, Supervisors Section. "Summary Sheet of Responses Received from ' Questionnaire About Continuing Education for School-Library-Media Supervisors.'"

(Mimeographed). Response to a questionnaire printed in School
Libraries, 18 (Summer, 1969), 53.

A-26. American Bankers Association. American Institute of Banking. Catalog,
1972-1973. Washington, D.C.: American Bankers Association, 1972.

The American Institute of Banking is an educational division of the
American Banking Association. The AIB framework of learning has
been developed to provide a total learning system for bank employees.
Through its program for learning, AIB produces selected training
aids, publications, program formats, and lesson guides that utilize
all applicable and available training resources. The program offers
professional development to bank personnel at all levels: new,
clerical, supervisory, middle management, and senior management.
Training is offered by chapters, study groups, study teams, accelerated study, in-bank study, and by cooperating with colleges and universities. Courses can lead to a basic certificate, a standard certificate, an advanced certificate, a general certificate. There are
35 courses listed as currently being offered for national use. The
list of local courses is printed in the Register.

A-27. American Bankers Association. American Institute of Banking. Handbook of Chapter Administration. Washington, D.C.: American
Bankers Association, n.d.

The Handbook of Chapter Administration has been prepared to provide
the basic information necessary for each chapter leader. Under the
Education and Training Program section, the formal education program is described and instructions given for administering the local
educational program. Informal education activities are also described: public speaking, debate and form and seminar.

A-28. American Bankers Association. American Institute of Banking. Handbook
on AIB-College Relations. Washington D.C.: American Bankers
Association, 1972.

The American Institute of Banking has recently organized a new element in its program -- cooperative programs in association with
colleges and universities. "At its meeting in 1968 the AIB Executive
Council, aware of its obligation to the future and sensitive to the
emerging trend of continuing education, rejected the previous idea
of separation and endorsed active cooperation between AIB chapters

and other post-secondary educational institutions." As a result a
totally new educational format was developed to make AIB standards
of instruction compatible with college standards. A new unit credit
system was established to provide the flexibility necessary in con-
structing cooperative programs with colleges already employing that
system. A specimen letter of understanding sets forth terms and
conditions for cooperation between AIB chapters and study groups
and other post-secondary educational institutions. In less than two
years, 52 of these Letters of Understanding were drawn up with academic institutions.

A-29. American Bankers Association. American Institute of Banking. Learning
Methods Laboratory: Design and Operation. Washington, D.C.: American Bankers Association, 1972.

The American Institute of Banking has established the Learning
Methods Laboratory to provide AIB chapters with an opportunity to
employ creative and innovative methods for achieving specific learning objectives.

Through formal participation in the Laboratory, AIB chapters can
establish learning objectives and design local offerings based entirely
on qualitative criteria without regard for number of hours of instruction that may be involved. The chapter bears the responsibility for
establishing qualitative standards, measuring performance, evaluating results, and determining whether the qualitative standards have
been fully satisfied, and on submission of credentials, the National
Office grants appropriate credit.

The term "Laboratory" is used to describe a national experimental
approach to the development of new learning methods and techniques.
In order to participate in the Laboratory, the chapter must submit an
application for listing course specifications. If selected for participation, the chapter must submit an Evaluation Report after the completion of the course. Nine procedural steps are described for the
conduct of a laboratory.

A-30. American Bankers Association. American Institute of Banking. The
Register: Accredited Local Offerings Through January 31, 1972. No. 2.
Washington, D.C.: American Bankers Association, 1972.

The Register is published annually before the American Institute of
Banking national convention. Its purpose is to provide information

on all locally developed chapter offerings accredited by the National
Organization for the current academic year. It contains a listing of
offerings initiated and developed by AIB chapters and study groups,
then evaluated by the National Office and assigned appropriate credit
for AIB certificates. Courses produced at the national level are listed
in the Catalog.

A-31.　American Council on Education. Higher Education and National Affairs.
　　　　Washington, D.C. (November 13, 1970), 4.

Here is an announcement of the establishment of an office of library
management studies to assist libraries in meeting increasing demands
for service with limited funds. American Council on Education and
the Association of Research Libraries are jointly undertaking this
venture also with some support by the Council on Library Resources.
Establishment of the office follows recent publication of a study of
management problems of research libraries by the firm of Booz,
Allen and Hamilton.

A-32.　"American Hospital Association--Continuing Education in the Hospitals
　　　　Field." In W.K. Kellogg Foundation. Annual Report, 1967. pp. 21-25.

The importance attached by the Foundation to the need for continuing
education is illustrated by the fact that the commitment in continuing
education to Hospital Research and Education Trust is the largest
single grant ($1,869,520) ever made by the Foundation in the hospital
field. The breadth and diversity of the approach to the problem is indicated by selected program segments: 1) cooperating university centers; 2) study programs in nursing management; 3) study of **correspondence** education in the hospital field; 4) development of inservice
education in hospitals; 5) clearinghouse of information on training
programs; 6) correspondence programs for hospital administration
and 7) demonstration projects. The overall program is described
as a "Partnership for Progress," -- "symbolic of the effort to involve
many universities, state hospital associations, and others in a national dedication to the improvement of hospital care through continuing education."

The report outlines many different elements of the "Partnership for
Progress" centered in various universities. One activity featured in
the report is experimentation with various forms of correspondence
programs. For example, a "Correspondence-Residential Program"

349

is designed for administrators of small hospitals who have not had the advantage of graduate study in hospital administration. In general the programs follow a design of two-week on-campus sessions divided by a period of home study.

Another facet of "Partnership for Progress" is aid to develop more effective individual hospital inservice education efforts (see entry "Hospital Continuing Education Project"). "Very closely related to the employer-training objective is a 'clearinghouse' of information about training programs in and out of the hospitals field. The service, therefore, provides up-to-date information on the sources of data in the area of continuing education emanating from concerned agencies, hospitals and individuals.

A-33. American Hospital Association. "Landmark Statements from the American Hospital Association." The Journal of Continuing Education in Nursing, 1 (July, 1970), 32-35.

In the Statement on Functions of a Hospital Department of Nursing Service, approved by the American Hospital Association, May 25, 1962, one of the functions listed was: "To provide and implement a program of continuing education for all nursing personnel." In May, 1968, the American Hospital Association approved a Statement on the Role and Responsibility of the Hospital for Inservice Education. All of the statements in this presentation refer back to the 1968 statement and deals with that phase of continuing education of the staff within an institution -- often referred to as inservice education.

The 1968 document considered it essential that each hospital have an inservice program of staff education, with one individual specifically responsible for it. Other criteria suggested were: 1) the framework within which the program is organized delineates lines of administrative control, establishes inter- and intradepartmental relationships, and provides mechanisms for planning and decision making; 2) the functions assigned to the program are delineated; 3) the objectives of the program are defined; 4) program content is planned on the basis of an analysis of employee and hospital needs; 5) the program is oriented to group instruction and enhances, but does not replace, educational activities that are the responsibility of the supervisory staff; 6) a system of evaluation of the program is established; 7) an adequate budget is provided; 8) appropriate classroom, conference and office facilities are provided; 9) appropriate audiovisual equipment and teaching aids are provided; 11) appropriate library facilities and materials are provided and 12) policies are established concerning attendance, scheduling and follow-up.

A-34. American Institute of Certified Public Accountants. New Approaches to Professional Development: A Review of CPAUDIO and Other Study Materials. New York: American Institute of Certified Public Accountants, 1971.

In this brochure, Robert E. Schlosser, Director, Professional Development for the American Institute of Certified Public Accountants, urges members of the Institute to take advantage of the CPAUDIO listings on fine tightly packed pages. A new type of program just being released and listed is the audiovisual instructional programs, which provide four complete courses. Each of these 5-Unit programs complete is priced at $160; a single unit of a program is listed at $40. A new program -- the graduate self-study program, entitled the Management Education Portfolio, was developed by the Education for Management, Inc. -- is announced in the brochure. This folio includes courses in 4 areas of management -- General Management Skills; Managerial Finance and Control; Management and the Computer; and Marketing Management -- each with 5 study units. Each course has a text section, a practice case, an examination case, and provision for evaluation. The evaluation is provided by an expert who will evaluate and grade the individual's work and send you a critique on your approach, your solution to the problem, your writing style and your report construction. If the work is satisfactory, a Certificate of Completion is awarded.

A-35. American Institute of Certified Public Accountants. Professional Development 1971: Courses, Seminars, Workshops, Lecture Programs, Training Programs, Individual Study Programs. New York: American Institute of Certified Public Accountants, 1971

The Professional Development Division of the American Institute of Certified Public Accountants plans in advance continuing education programs for one year and prints these in a booklet for all members. It plans six types of programs using a wide assortment of educational methods in various combinations: seminars, courses, workshops, lecture programs, training programs (including a basic and advanced staff training program), individual study materials (not designed to serve as a substitute for active participation in professional development programs). The 1971 booklet lists 63 programs, which represents

351

a nearly 50% change in material from that offered in 1970.

The American Institute assumes the principal responsibility for the development of materials and overall administration of the programs; it is the state societies who assume the responsibility of offering the programs throughout the nation.

A-36. American Institute of Physics. <u>American Institute of Physics Annual Report</u>. New York: American Institute of Physics, 1955.

A-37. American Law Institute and the American Bar Association, Joint Committee on Continuing Legal Education. <u>Catalog of Continuing Legal Education Programs in the United States, March, 1967-October, 1967</u>. CLE Catalog 4. Philadelphia: Joint Committee on Continuing Legal Education of the American Law Institute and the American Bar Association, 1967.

The catalog issues list programs for the spring and summer of 1967 and new continuing legal education publications.

A-38. American Library Association. Activities Committee on New Directions for ALA. <u>The Final Report of the Activities Committee on New Directions for ALA</u>. Chicago: Ill.: American Library Association, 1970.

Excerpts from this report relative to ALA's responsibility in the area of continuing education include the following statements:

> Doubtless the area of library education wherein most remains to be done, however is in non-formal post-professional training. The nature of the library need and the means for meeting that need are changing so rapidly that a librarian who permits his expertise to languish at a particular level for as short a time as five years risks finding himself obsolete. Enormous efforts must be expended to assure that all members of the profession be ever receptive to the need for change and do all they can do to keep their professional skills honed constantly to greatest effectiveness. Commitment to the continuing education of the profession must be made by the individual librarian, by the managers of libraries, and by the professional association -- especially the ALA. The ALA can do little to gain commitment from librarians and library managers except by setting an example and exerting moral pressure upon them.

but it can do much more than it has done to align its own huge resources and programs behind this critically important activity.

In a sense, the Association need not be reminded of its leadership responsibility in this important matter of continuing education; because in actuality much of the Association's program has since its beginning been directed toward the continual upgrading and professional growth of its members. Its extensive conference programming, publishing activity, and task-oriented committees, combine to make the Association by far the most active agency for library personnel development in the world. Accusations of Association non-interest are justified only in the sense that it has not in the past seen fit to bring together all of its activities concerned with continuing education under a single administrative oversight, so as to give them uniform organization, coordination, and direction. Such a move seems now to be called for.

The following are examples of ways in which the ALA could do more than it has done for the continuing education and professional growth of its members:

1) sponsor a wide range of seminars and workshops, perhaps mounted regionally but outside of the annual conference, on issues of current or topical concern to librarians; the recent MARC II workshops and occasional joint programs with the regional associations might serve as prototypes;

2) prepare packaged multi-media programs for professional updating that can be lent or rented to local libraries and to library agencies for use by their personnel;

3) design and produce programmed instructional courses for sale to librarians who wish to improve the currency of their expertise or gain new professional skills or understanding; both these recommendations would seem to be natural extensions of ALA's existing publishing program;

4) gain much wider promulgation than there has been in the past of the work done by ALA's clearinghouse for opportunities outside of ALA for the continuing education and professional growth of librarians;

5) lend consultative and advisory, perhaps even support, services to local libraries and library agencies wishing to develop continuing education programs of their own;

6) coordinate, articulate, and rationalize all ALA activities concerned with the professional upgrading of librarians.

Although covered by what has already been said above, one particular aspect of post-professional training is so needful of attention that in the eyes of the Committee it deserves special mention in this report. That is the need for management training for librarians who find themselves assigned to positions of administrative responsibility. It is patently false to assume that a good librarian will necessarily be a good manager, yet hierarchical promotion in many libraries appears to rely heavily upon this criterion. It appears essential that special effort be expended by the ALA to help facilitate the transition of good librarians into good managers when their duties and responsibilities call for it.

A-39. American Library Association. American Association of School Librarians. School Library Personnel: Task Analysis Survey. School Library Manpower Project. Chicago: American Library Association, 1969.

Funded in 1968 and directed by Robert N. Case, the School Library Manpower Project focused on three parts of the problem of the development and effective use of school library manpower: task and job analysis, education for school librarianship, and recruitment.

The task analysis survey identifies tasks presently performed in over 600 outstanding building level programs in U.S. schools. It provides basic data relevant to the education of school library personnel and staffing patterns in building level programs.

A report on Phase I, which included the Task Analysis Survey, is presented by Robert N. Case and Anna Mary Lowrey in "School Library Manpower Project: A Report on Phase I, " American Libraries, 2 (January, 1971), 98-101.

A-40. American Library Association, Library Administration Division, Personnel Administration Section, Staff Development Committee, Guidelines Subcommittee. "Developing a Model for Continuing Education and Personnel Development in Libraries," Library Trends, 20 (July, 1971), 92-96.

The principal objective was to design a model for use by librarians in analyzing and defining the basic problems and in developing the framework for a program of continuing education or personnel development which would facilitate the application of management techniques. Flowchart is included.

A-41. American Library Association, Library Administration Division, Personnel Administration Section, Staff Development Committee, Guidelines Subcommittee. "Guidelines to the Development of Human Resources in Libraries: Rationale, Policies, Programs, and Recommendations," Library Trends, 20 (July, 1971), 97-117.

This paper by an ALA Committee presents some conditions that research in the behavioral sciences seems to indicate are necessary for the optimum effectiveness of the growth of the human resources that make up an organization. Essentials in planning for personnel development are outlined, including emphasis on the fact that the design of the program must be based on the nature of the adult as a learner, and the necessity of involving participants in the planning of the library's development program.

It is apparent that there are many roadblocks preventing the release of the human potential in our libraries. These guidelines take the position that a great deal can be done toward diagnosing and removing these roadblocks by establishing and developing a favorable climate for staff development in the library organization, including meaningful policies and programs.

The paper concludes with some recommendations to other relevant groups within the library profession which also have responsibility in the area of continuing education for librarians.

A-42. American Library Association. Library Education and Manpower: A Statement of Policy Adopted by the Council of the American Library Association, June 30, 1970. Chicago: Office of Library Education, American Library Association, 1970, p. [8], paragraphs 33-35.

The last three of the 35 policy statements contained in this document refer to continuing education:

> Continuing Education is essential for all library personnel, professional and supportive, whether they remain within a position category or are preparing to move into a higher one. Continuing education opportunities include both formal and informal learning situations, and need not be limited to library subjects or the   offerings of library schools.

> The "continuing education" which leads to eligibility for Senior Librarian or Specialist positions may take any of the forms suggested directly above so long as the additional education and experience are relevant to the responsibilities of the assignment.

> Library administrators must accept responsibility for providing support and opportunities (in the form of leaves, sabbaticals, and released time) for the continuing education of their staffs.

A-43. American Library Association. Library Education Division. "Con- "Continuing Education for Librarians -- Conferences, Workshops, Short Courses 1971, " LED News Letter, No. 75 (December, 1970), 12-19.

A-44. American Library Association. Library Education Division. "Continuing Education for Librarians -- Conferences, Workshops, Short Courses 1972. " American Libraries, 2 (December, 1971), 1217-19.

_____. First Supplement, 3 (February, 1972), 179-181.

_____. Second Supplement, 3 (April, 1972), 423-26.

_____. Third Supplement, 3 (June, 1972), 662-64.

This was the first time that the directory was published in
American Libraries, and it was announced that the schedule
would be updated on a bimonthly basis. The purposes for
Continuing Education Directory were listed as 1) to publicize
opportunities for continuing education, 2) to encourage librarians
to take advantage of these opportunities, 3) to supply library
administrators and personnel officers with information about
programs at a sufficiently early date to permit necessary budgetary and other arrangements, and 4) to provide an inventory of
continuing education programs for purposes of planning and
evaluating such programs.

Entries are arranged alphabetically by state. Within each state
grouping, entries are in chronological order. For each entry
the date, title of program and name of director or instructor,
place, sponsors, academic credit offered, tuition or registration
charge, and person to contact for further information. In the
column headed, "Audience" letters are used to indicate the
following: N=National; R=Regional; S=State; L=Local. Appended
to the Directory is a subject index.

A-45. American Library Association. Library Education Division.
"Institutes for Training in Librarianship, 1968-1969, Under
Title II-B, Higher Education Act of 1965." LED News Letter,
No. 64 (April,1968), 1-4.

The list of the U. S. Office of Education approved institutes for
training in librarianship to be held during the summer of 1968 and
the academic year 1968-69. Participants were eligible to
receive $75 per week for the period of attendance plus $15 per
week for each dependent. They were also exempt from tuition.
Each institute established its own criteria for admission.

A-46. American Library Association. Office of Library Education.
Continuing Education for Librarians - Conferences, Workshops,
and Short Courses 1967-68. Chicago: American Library
Association, 1967.

A-47. American Library Association. Office for Library Education.
Continuing Education for Librarians - Conferences, Workshops,
and Short Courses 1968-69. Chicago: American Library
Association, 1968.

A-48. American Library Association. Office for Library Education.
Continuing Education for Librarians - Conferences, Workshops,
and Short Courses 1969-70. Chicago: American Library
Association, 1969.

Since 1967-68, the American Library Association has published
annually a register of conferences, workshops, and short
courses. This annual listing was started in 1964 by Sarah R.
Reed, then of the Library Services Division of the U.S. Office
of Education.

A-49. American Management Association. "The Systems Approach to Personnel
Management," American Management Bulletin 62
New York: American Management Association, 1963.

In a series of four articles, the position is taken that current
trends in technology and centralization need not dehumanize an
organization's resources. "If the personnel managers keep up
to date, if they do the long, tedious, difficult job of retraining
themselves to be effective in personnel administration in this
age of technology and computers, they ought to be able to go
much further in humanizing their organizations than has been
possible before."

Ways and means, using a systems approach, are suggested to
achieve this feat.

A-50. American Nurses' Association and the American Academy of Pediatrics.
"Landmark Statement: Guidelines on Short-Term Continuing
Education Programs for Pediatric Nurse Associates, December,
1970." The Journal of Continuing Education in Nursing, 2
(March -April, 1971), 35-40.

The joint statement of guidelines, collaboratively developed by
these two associations, covers goals, planning, organization and
administration, services and facilities, faculty, course content,
length of program, and eval uation. Following the goal statement
for continuing education programs, eleven specific objectives are
listed in behavioral terms.

A-51. American Nurses' Association, Council on Continuing Education. "Landmark Statement from The Organizing Group for the American Nurses' Association Council on Continuing Education: The Continuing Education Unit." Journal of Continuing Education for Nursing, 4 (January-February, 1973), 28-31.

Conscious of the need in the nursing profession for a means to quantify and record the involvement of nurses in continuing education, the American Nurses' Association (ANA) Commission on Nursing Education endorsed the use of the continuing education unit (c e u) in December 1971. "The Commission views the c e u as a mean s of recognizing individual nurses' participation in non-credit continuing education activities in nursing." For the past four years the ANA has worked with a group of associations interested in the feasibility of a uniform unit of measurement for continuing education and has been jointly engaged in a process of development, field testing, and refining of such a unit. The associations providing the major thrust have been the National University Extension Association, the American Association of Collegiate Registrars and Admission Officers, the U. S. Civil Service Commission, and the U. S. Office of Education.

The Continuing Education Unit (c e u) is defined as follows: Ten contact hours of participation in an organized continuing education experience under responsible sponsorship, capable direction and qualified instruction.

The use of the c e u is specified. Included in the system are classes, lectures, workshops, symposia, institutes, short courses, organized independent study, etc. Types of study ordinarily not awarded continuing education units are:

1)   Any program carrying academic credit
2)   Programs leading to high school equivalency certificates or diploma
3)   Organizational orientation training programs
4)   Short duration programs only casually related to any specific upgrading purpose or goal

Activites carried on outside of organized channels without sponsorship or instruction do not lend themselves to uniform measurement and, therefore, useful as it may be to the individual, are outside the program. Examples of activities not included are: selective and general reading, exposure to the communications media, travel, films, discussion groups, attendance at meetings, organizational and committee membership, community and social activities.

The ANA endorses the concept of continuing education for registered
nurses as one means by which nurses can maintain competence and
meet standards of practice developed by the profession. In its
Guidelines for Certification, ANA has defined the term certification
as "recognition of excellence in clinical practice. To meet the
requirements for certification, the individual practitioner will have
to submit data to indicate currency of knowledge, among other
criteria. Evidence of c e u units for courses attended would be one
valid source of such data."

The statement concludes: "The acceptance of the continuing education
unit is just one example of finally arriving at a suitable means of
recognizing and rewarding individual and institutional efforts in the
pursuit of continuing education."

A-52. American Nurses' Association. "Landmark Statement from the
       American Nurses' Association on Continuation Education."
       Journal of Continuing Education in Nursing, 1 (September, 1970),
       21-25.

       Several basic assumptions and concepts are established in the
       opening section on "Techniques and Purposes," 1) continuation
       education programs are departing from traditional, formal
       classroom techniques and are experimenting with the use of new
       media; 2) the need for interdisciplinary conferences focusing
       on broad problems of continuing education related to professional
       groups is receiving more attention; 3) the adaptabilities, interests,
       motivations, and experiences of adult learners are different in
       many respects from the young student; 4) programming is often
       sequential in nature (the same group of enrollees returning at
       scheduled intervals for a series of programs varying in length
       from a few days to several weeks and planned around a central
       theme).

       Turning from opportunities related to institutions of higher
       education, the statement discusses, in turn, continuing education
       opportunities relative to the individual, the professional organi-
       zation, and the employing agency.

       "The objective of continuing education in nursing is to add

360

constantly to one's nursing knowledge and competence so that neither becomes obsolete. Any one of the several types of continuing education opportunities described here represents a valid and fruitful means to that end. Furthermore, the categories are not mutually exclusive. The last one, in particular -- independent learning -- cuts across all the others and is essential for any nurse concerned with the quality of nursing care she provides."

A-53. American Psychological Association. Reports of the American Psychological Association's Project on Scientific Information Exchange in Psychology. Vol. I and II. Washington, D.C.: American Psychological Association, 1963.

The American Psychological Association, under a grant from the National Science Foundation, made a two year study on scientific information exchange in psychology. "The communication and exchange of knowledge and the establishment of priorities of discovery have been fundamental to the work of scientists from the beginnings of 'little science' to the present emergence of 'big science.' A variety of social devices have been utilized including books, journals, 'meetings,' colloquia, and personal correspondence and conversation. However, it is of very recent date that scientists have begun to employ conceptual schemes and empirical methods to the description and analysis of the scientific communication processes, channels, and institutions."

Four general processes can be identified in any successful system of scientific information exchange: the origination of information, its transmission, its storage, and its use. There appear to be three roles in the system: the source, the user, and information conveyance devices that have both transmission and storage functions. In an effort to develop a description of the scientific information -exchange environment in psychology, the initial problem attacked was the identification of the persons and institutions associated with these three roles and the determination of the scope of their responsibilities in fulfilling them. The second step was that of developing a description of the time characteristics of each process and of the "filtering" that determines the amount and type of information which will be available to the user. Since the storage afforded by different channels of communication differs in permanence and ease of access, the third step was that of examining the storage properties, when present, of various information conveyances. Finally, the user was studied -- his access to the information he needs, his decisions with regard to relevance, the types of information he uses, and the ways in which he uses it.

A-54. American Society for Engineering Education, Advisory Committee for the Engineering Technology Education Study. "Final Report: Engineering Technology Education Study," Journal of Engineering Education, 63 (January, 1972), 327-390.

The central objective of engineering technology education is to support the practical side of the engineering achievement with emphasis upon the end product rather than the conceptual process. There are many overlapping areas, but, in broad outline, the engineering technologist may be said to help achieve what the engineer conceives.

The report makes the following statement about continuing education:

Technologists and technicians, as well as engineers, must continuously update their knowledge through formal continuing education or independent study. It is recommended that local groups representing education, technical societies and employers form continuing education committees. They should arrange wherever possible for planned sequences of math-science-technical courses and also management studies to be provided at convenient hours on a scheduled basis. New techniques, such as taped courses, are becoming available for use in isolated locations. It is recommended that industry and government, as majority employers of technical personnel accept greater responsibility in the future for providing means of updating and enhancing the capacities of their technical employees at all levels as an active program to counteract technological obsolescence.

A-55. American Society for Engineering Education. Continuing Engineering Studies series: Monograph no. 1. Washington, D.C.: American Society for Engineering Education, 1967.

This monograph presents a precis of the professional developmen of engineers as developed by an ASEE Continuing Engineering

362

Studies Division Workshop, held in December, 1966, which states that:

"Any definition of professional development must include, at the minimum, the following elements:

1. A steady growth of one's abilities in his chosen field.
2. Growth into other fields, such as management.
3. Contributions to one's profession by means of published papers and patents.
4. Increased activity in professional societies.
5. Contributions to society, such as civic activities or politics.
6. Developing skill in and an awareness of the value of personal appraisal."

A-56. *American Society for Engineering Education, Goals Committee. "Goals of Engineering Education," Journal of Engineering Education, 58 (January, 1968), 369-446.

This landmark, comprehensive report represents the cumulation of 5 years of intensive survey and analysis, and the accumulation of a large mass of data from other professions by the Goals of Engineering Education Committee of the American Society for Engineering Education. "The Goals Committee has in no sense interpreted its charge as that of arriving at a consensus -- of counting the pros and cons on the many controversial issues to be faced and then recording a series of majority opinions. Rather the aim has been to evaluate current programs, practices and proposals in the light of their applicability ten or twenty years hence, and, on the basis of considered judgment, to propose a few broad goals which appear to be of paramount importance in determining the direction which engineering education must take."

For the past few years the engineering profession has been broadening basic engineering education which has had to coexist with specialization. In addition the provision must be made for continuing education at every level.

In the area of continuing engineering studies, the Committee recommended "...that engineering schools recognize more fully the place of continuing studies as a distinct category in the

A-56 (cont.-1)

spectrum of engineering education, and that wherever possible they
provide additional leadership in the planning and offering of programs of continuing studies as part of normal institutional activity.
It is also recommended that engineering schools cooperate to a much
greater extent with industry, government, and the engineering
societies in programs of continuing engineering studies in order to
achieve maximum benefit for the students and optimum utilization of
teaching resources. Finally, it is recommended that employers
facilitate in every possible way employee participation in programs
of continuing engineering studies."

In discussing these recommendations the Committee stated that:
"This is not merely a matter of dealing with current obsolescence,
retreading, retraining, or any of the other popularized versions
which have been developed, sometimes almost frantically, to
satisfy urgent localized needs. It is rather a matter of establishing
and maintaining an entirely new dimension of personal development
throughout the engineer's career. It is a matter of taking a long-
range look at the ever increasing rate of technological change, and
then deciding what now needs to be done to assure the continual
effectiveness of the profession in the 1970's and beyond." The Committee found the activity of educational institutions in "continuing
education" inadequate for the needs and service being considered
today. "What is urgently needed for the future is a more direct provision for maintaining the currency of all members of the profession
no matter what the year of graduation and regardless of the degree
level at which the individual enters or re-enters engineering practice.
... The future of the engineering profession will depend to a considerable extent on the demonstrated competence of individual engineers to make optimum use of the latest scientific and technical
knowledge in dealing with current and future problems. Participation in programs of continuing engineering studies will ensure that
such competence can be maintained."

The objective of continuing engineering studies, as stated by the
Committee, "is the specific enhancement of the competence of the
individual as a practicing engineer, rather than the attainment of an
additional academic degree." The report makes a distinction between the traditional "academic ladder" of successive degree levels
in formal education. It suggests that for continuing education the
term "career ladder" be used, meaning a sequence of more individualized studies pursued at various times outside of degree programs,

364

and selected principally for the independent purpose of career extension and stimulation." A chart (Fig. 1   ) is used to illustrate this
"dual ladder" concept which shows on the left that the academic
institutions alone are responsible for the degree ladder, but are
partners with industry, government and the engineering societies in
the broader career ladder activities. Dual involvement of the educational institutions   is to be expected, because the
greatest amount of educational experience and teaching talent is to be
found in faculty groups. At the same time excellent teaching talent
will also be found among engineering practitioners. It is essential,
therefore, that all groups cooperate in providing the necessary
expertise wherever it resides."

In order to compare the purposes and patterns of advanced and continuing education, the report sets up four categories in relation to
the individual's particular educational needs, as distinct from a pattern to accomplish the purpose. The primary functions for the
individual are designated as:

1) upgrading a person's education (that is, pursuing an articulated
   formal program of study to raise the student's level of
   education);

2) updating a person's education (making an individual's formal
   education comparable to that of a person receiving a degree
   any given year);

3) diversifying to new fields (a person educated in one field may seek to
   obtain some formal education in another field, but not necessarily at a higher degree level);

4) broadening of a person's education (this refers to the addition
   of new and broader perspective in one's own field, such as
   the inclusion of financial, political, and social factors, but again
   without necessarily raising the academic level of education).

The Committee viewed "continuing education" as primarily including
items 2, 3, and 4 -- updating, diversifying, and broadening. It
viewed advanced degree education as chiefly concerned with item 1 --
upgrading. "Another   feature   of advanced-degree education is
that it usually is preparatory, and is undertaken prior to embarking
on a career at a new and higher level of performance. By contrast,
continuing studies involve a more or less continuous performance,

365

A-56 (cont. -4)

usually concurrent with employment....Continuing studies are
conducted   principally through part-time study, either on or off-
campus, with employment being off-campus. In the process of continuing studies the schools, industry, professional societies, and,
of course the individual himself, all have an important role."

The Committee listed what appeared to it to be dominant characteristics of successful offerings of continuing studies from the point of
view of educational institutions, such as:

-- related to an identified immediate, or foreseeable, occupational
   need;
-- keyed to have a stimulating effect on career development;
-- presented by instructors, either from academic instutitions
   or from the field of practice, whose most outstanding
   characteristic is command of a particular knowledge or skill;
-- offered under various patterns of group meeting schedules,
   usually involving substantial concentration on the selected
   subject;
-- given at locations and times generally selected to accommodate
   the practicing engineer.

Participation in such studies can occur between, or after, all degree
levels and often will continue well beyond the age when most men
would consider entering formal degree programs.

Emphasis was put on the need for the highest quality faculty
members to plan and present such programs. "Not all faculty
members will wish to accept such assignments, but for those who do,
a policy of full recognition of service as a part of regular institutional
responsibility is highly desirable."

Other sections of this extensive report particularly related to continuing education deal with the need for faculty continuing education
and improved teaching methods.

The Committee found that industry, government, academic institutions, and engineering societies have a substantially unfilled
obligation in meeting the critical technical need for an organized
and comprehensive system of continuing studies."

A-57. American Society for Engineering Education. Interim Report of the
     Goals Committee. Lafayette, Indiana: Committee on Goals
of Engineering Education, American Society for Engineering
Education, Purdue University, April, 1967.

The report breaks continuing education into four categories:

  1) Upgrading a person's education [work toward a
     graduate degree] ;
  2) Updating a person's education [make his education
     comparable to that of a person receiving like degree
     at present time];
  3) Diversification to new fields [seek some
     formal education in another field, but not necessarily
     at higher degree level];
  4) Maturing of a person's education [add new perspective
     to his own field, such as inclusion of financial,
     political, and social factors] .

This report also noted another characteristic of continuing
education: that it usually refers to training which
better equips a person for his contemporary work, for the
job he has now or aspires to in the near future.

A-58. American Society for Information Science. Evaluation of 32nd
     Annual Meeting of ASIS, San Francisco, October 1-4, 1969.

In order to improve future meetings, a questionnaire was
mailed by the Society to the membership to ascertain attitudes
about a number of meeting features.

A-59. American Society for Information Science. ASIS-EIS Curriculum
Committee. "Models for the Evaluation of Curriculum in
Information Science Programs." Prepared for a workshop,
1968. Washington, D.C.: American Society for Information
Science, 1968.

A-60. American Society of Mechanical Engineers. Committee on Continuing
Education. Annual Report of the Committee on Continuing
Education, July 1, 1964/June 30, 1965. New York: American
Society of Mechanical Engineers, Committee on Continuing
Education, 1965. (Mimeographed.)

A-61. American Society of Mechanical Engineers. Committee on Continuing Education. Annual Report of the Committee on Continuing Education, July 1, 1965–June 30, 1966. New York: American Society of Mechanical Engineers, Committee on Continuing Education, 1966. (Mimeographed.)

A-62. American Society of Mechanical Engineers. Committee on Continuing Education. ASME -- An Educational Institution. New York: American Society of Mechanical Engineers, Committee on Continuing Education, June 3, 1964. (Mimeographed.)

A-63. Anderson, Frederic. "Factors in Motivation to Work Across Three Occupational Levels." (Unpublished Doctor's dissertation, University of Utah, Provo, 1961).

A-64. Andrews, Kenneth R. The Effectiveness of University Management Development Programs. Boston, Mass.; Harvard Business School, 1966.

A-65. Andrews, Kenneth R. "Is Management Training Effective? I. Evaluation by Managers and Instructors," Harvard Business Review, 35 (January–February, 1957), 85–94.

A-66. Andrews, Kenneth R. "Is Management Training Effective? II. Measurement, Objectives, and Policy," Harvard Business Review, 35 (March–April, 1957), 63–72.

A-67. Andrews, Kenneth R. "Reaction to University Development Programs: As Reported by More Than 6,000 Executives Who Went Back to School," Harvard Business Review, 39 (May–June, 1961), 116–134.

A-68. Andrews, Marie Scherer and Hanron, Jane Bragdon. "A Professional Enrichment Series." The Journal of Continuing Education in Nursing, 2 (November–December, 1971), 21–28.

This is a complete description of the planning and implementation of a series of eight lectures and informal discussions designed to acquaint the Alumni of the Boston College School of Nursing with varied technological, cultural, and professional advances. Helpful as a model in planning the details for such a series.

A-69. Anshen, Melvin. "Better Use of Executive Development Programs," Harvard Business Review, 33 (November–December, 1955), 67–74.

368

A-70. Argyris, Chris. "Executive Development Programs: Some Unresolved Problems," Personnel, 33 (July, 1956), 33-41.

A-71. Argyris, Chris. Integrating the individual and the Organization. New York: John Wiley & Sons, Inc., 1964.

Based on his extensive research on organizations, Argyris builds a model for any type of organization which indicates the dimensions the organization must have in order to provide the greatest opportunity for the growth and development of the individual employee. He points out that the use of his model may call for redesigning of managerial controls, rewards, and penalties. This may be pretty strong medicine for many executives who feel that present organizations and practices work reasonably well.

Demonstrating how current organizations are more often oriented to the psychological make-up of a child rather than an adult, he shows how an adult can maximize his needs and how an organization can adapt and change in meeting its own needs in addition to the individual's needs.

A-72. Argyris, Chris. "Some Unintended Consequences of Rigorous Research," Psychological Bulletin, 70 (September, 1968), 185-197.

The significance of this article is probably best emphasized by quoting from a review of it by Campbell: "One of the most provocative methodological papers of recent years is the attack by Argyris on the scientific method as it is used in the social sciences. It should be read and reread by everyone who wants to do empirical research in organizations. The main thrust of his argument is that much of the research in social and organizational psychology creates a Theory X relationship between the researcher and the subjects, with predictable consequences for subject behavior." [John P. Campbell, "Personnel Training and Development," Annual Review of Psychology, 22 (Spring, 1971), 579] According to Argyris, research subjects are not passive, and the only way to get around the dilemma is to involve them as full participants in the research effort. Obviously this would rule out such techniques as deception research, many questionnaire studies, and many studies requiring control groups.

A-73. Argyris, Chris. "T-Groups for Organizational Effectiveness,"
       Harvard Business Review, 42 (March-April, 1964), 60-74.

A-74. Asheim, Lester E. "Education and Manpower for Librarianship:
       First Steps Toward a Statement of Policy," ALA Bulletin,
       62 (October, 1968), 1096-1106.

       Lester Asheim, Director of the Office of Education of the
       American Library Association, issued this working paper in the
       fall of 1968. It was not issued as an "official policy statement"
       but was used to generate discussion which led to the adoption
       of such an official statement by the ALA Council in June, 1970.
       It was built around a consideration of various levels of activity
       -- both in training and practice -- and reflects the judgment
       of many advisors, educators, and librarians.

       "It is a basic premise of this paper that the librarian's pre-
       paration must be seen as encompassing the entire five-year
       program of general and special education and not just the one-
       fifth devoted to professional content. "   A strong foundation
       in the liberal arts is urged for all librarians.

       The paper emphasized the importance of continual learning for
       all library manpower, but especially for the "professional
       specialist. "

       The section of Asheim's paper dealing with "the new technology"
       sees the new machines as new tools. He does not see them altering
       "the basic aims of library service, however much they may
       affect the storage and retrieval of data, " and points out that "the
       role of the new devices, the impact of new approaches upon
       traditional methods, the implications for new services or better
       performance of current functions should be assimilated into the
       entire curriculum, enriching every course where it is pertinent. "
       He says that since the new tools and theories will affect ser-
       vice at every level, "it seems desirable to integrate informa-
       tion science concepts into the library school curriculum
       wherever possible. "

A-75. Asheim, Lester. "Library Education and Manpower", American
       Libraries, 1 (April, 1970), 341-44.

       This proposal for ALA's official policy on library training,
       education and manpower utilization in libraries was printed on

the recommendation of the ALA Executive Board prior to its presentation to the ALA Council at its annual conference in Detroit, June, 1970. Asheim states the proposed policy statement was based on his earlier paper "Education and Manpower in Librarianship" (October, 1968, issue of the ALA Bulletin), many suggestions and critiques which were received from the Office of Library Education reacting to this 1968 paper, and a series of regional conferences specially held to discuss the 1968 paper.

A-76. Association for Educational Data Systems. The Relationship of ADP Training Curriculum and Methodology in the Federal Government. Final Report. Contract No. OEC-1-7-071059-3808. Washington, D.C.: Association for Educational Data Systems. Sponsoring Agency: Office of Education, Dept. of Health, Education and Welfare, May, 1968. (ED 023 909)

This comprehensive paper, based on a conference held in Washington, D.C., in May, 1967, develops the outlines for an effective training program in Automatic Data Processing, using the new instructional methodologies, for top managers in the government and for the systems analyst. The objective set for the pilot project for training managers was: "To provide the manager with the knowledge and skills necessary to identify, understand and evaluate the potential and performance of the computer system in the accomplishment of his operations and mission objectives." For the development of this pilot program a sequential and modular array of subject matter curriculum is set forth.

The paper contains a wealth of material on related important topics, such as the section on "Automation and Technology in Education." "Transformation of the classroom is inevitable in the face of the population explosion and the increasing demand for education."

Another topic discussed is the "Present and Future Use of Media in ADP Training." "The answer lies not in the development and marketing of specific items of hardware, but in the systems approach: the 'orchestration' of media, software, and educator's use and acceptance." Another problem dealt with was "software" (also referred to as "brainware") and the lag in the production of quality materials. "Hardware is basically not a problem, but 'software' is the intelligence of the system and therefore the critical item."

371

Specifications were also worked out for the Instructional Program. These included: a) instructional programs to be organized into modular units to permit independent selection of only those units in which the student is not proficient by reason of education or training; b) means of individualization to be devised which will indicate the choice and sequence of modules appropriate for students with various levels of knowledge at entry and various performance requirements of the student. A matrix of entry requirements might include IQ, mathematical aptitude, educational experience, etc. The program director can determine the participant's entry level in the modular program; c) instructional program development to include recommendations of methodology for each module, including media alternatives (PI, texts, film, CAO, etc.) and pedagogical techniques (case history, simulation, etc.) Specifications are also given for Media/Hardware.

A-77.   Association of American Library Schools. "A Position Paper by the Study Committee on The Role of the Association of American Library Schools in Continuing Library Education." Paper distributed at the 1972 annual meeting of the Association of American Library Schools, Chicago, Illinois, January , 1972. (Mimeographed)

The paper delineates the role of AALS in continuing professional library education, and makes recommendations for the implementation of this role. Objectives and recommendations are made for the Association's role "inside" the organization itself and for the Association's role "outside" the organization in cooperation with other relevant groups. The paper was accepted by the Executive Board of AALS and a Standing Committee on Library Continuing Education appointed to start implementation of its various recommendations.

Appendix A, entitled "Goals, Criteria, and Components of National Planning for Continuing Library Education," includes suggested areas of planning in three areas: 1) identification of basic questions that must be answered in the area of continuing library education; 2) objectives and criteria of continuing library education; 3) possible ways in which established criteria might be met.

A-78. Association of American Library Schools. "Standing Committee on Continuing Library Education," Journal of Education for Librarianship, 13 (Fall, 1972), 137-142.

At the 1972 annual conference of the Association of American Library Schools a position paper on continuing library education was adopted which included the appointment by the President of a Standing Committee on Continuing Library Education. In this report the members of the committee are listed and plans were announced for a mini-workshop during the 1973 annual conference in Washington, D.C. on ways in which continuing education is being implemented in other professional associations. One of the charges of the committee was to a library continuing education network made up of representatives from the library schools and the library associations. The list of these liaison representatives from the schools and associations is included in the report. The report closes with a report on activities of the Committee from the time of appointment in January, 1972, through the summer of 1972.

A-79. Association of American Library Schools. "Summary of the Report of the Study Committee on The Role of the Association of American Library Schools in Continuing Library Education." Paper distributed at the 1972 annual meeting of the Association of American Library Schools, Chicago, Illinois, January, 1972. (Mimeographed.) See also Journal of Education for Librarianship, 12 (Spring, 1972), 267-69.
This is a summary of the total position paper prepared by the Ad Hoc Committee on Continuing Library Education. The summary is presented under the five headings: Charge, Mission, Assumptions, Objectives ("inside" AALS and "outside" AALS), Recommendations for Implementation ("inside" AALS and "outside " AALS).

A-80. Association of Engineering Education, Research and Methods Division. Committee on Measurement of Teaching. "Dimensions for Measurement of Teaching," Journal of Engineering Education, 58 (October, 1967), 139-140.

The Committee determined that the major dimensions of teaching may be conveniently placed in three categories: objectives, achieving objectives, and research and development. Within each of these categories, two dimensions were identified, resulting in six dimensions which are discussed in the article:

Objectives:
    Dimension 1: The degree to which teaching goals are
        stated in clear, objective, behavioral, measurable
        terms.
    Dimension 2: The degree to which stated teaching goals
        are appropriate in terms of the mission of the school,
        the students' welfare, and the present and future of the
        subject matter area.

Achieving Objectives:
    Dimension 3: The degree to which the methods or acts of
        teaching are appropriate and flexible in achieving the
        stated goals optimally.
    Dimension 4: The degree to which stated goals are actually
        achieved; that is, the results.

Research and Development:
    Dimension 5: The quality and quantity of research into
        problems of education.
    Dimension 6: The quality and quantity of development of
        new courses and of textual, and laboratory materials.

Dimensions 1 and 2 deal respectively with what is taught and with
an evaluation of what is taught. Dimensions 3 and 4 deal respectively with how the subject is taught and with an evaluation of how
well it is taught. Dimensions 5 and 6 deal respectively with contributions to the knowledge of how to teach and with contributions
to the literature of what to teach.

The union of these dimensions can provide a framework for
continuing discussion on the problems of evaluating and
improving teaching.

A-81.   Association of Research Libraries. Office of University Library
        Management Studies. "Management Review and Analysis
        Program." Washington, D.C.: Association of Research
        Libraries, 1972.

A-82.   Association of Research Libraries. Office of University Library
        Management Studies. Plan for Development of the Office of
        University Library Management Studies: A Summary.
        Washington, D.C.: Association of Research Libraries,
        1972. 8 pp. (ED 063 002).

A-83.   Association of Research Libraries. Office of University Library
          Management Studies. Planning Aids for the University Library
          Director. OMS Occasional Paper Number One. Washington,
          D.C.: Association of Research Libraries, 1971. 27 pp.
          (ED 061 949).

A-84.   Association of Research Libraries. Office of University Library
          Management Studies. Problems in University Library Man-
          agement. Washington, D.C.: Association of Research
          Libraries, 1970. 63 pp. (ED 047 719).

A-85.   Association of Research Libraries. Office of University Library
          Management Studies. "Review of Planning Activities in
          Academic and Research Libraries," ARL Management
          Supplement, Number One. Washington, D.C.: Association
          of Research Libraries, 1972. 4 pp.

A-86.   Association of Research Libraries. Office of University Library
          Management Studies. Second Annual Report of the ARL Office
          of University Library Management Studies. Washington, D.C.:
          Association of Research Libraries, 1972. 11 pp.

A-87.   Association of Research Libraries. Office of University Library
          Management Studies. A Summary of the Results of the Office
          of Management Studies Survey of the Recruitment, Staff De-
          velopment, and Minority Employment Practices of ARL
          Libraries. Washington, D.C.: Association of Research
          Libraries, 1972. 17 pp.

A-88.   "ATAC Schedules Effort to Update Personnel," Army Research
          and Development Newsmagazine, 8 (June, 1967), 1, 8-9.

A-89.   American Dental Association. "Continuing Education: A General
          Review," Journal of Dental Education, 33 (1964), 297-359.

A-90. American Library Association. "Graduate Library School Programs Accredited by the American Library Association." Chicago: American Library Association, 1973.

B-1. Bakewell, K. G. B., ed. Library and Information Services for Management. Papers presented at a Short Course held at the School of
Librarianship and Information Work at Liverpool College of Commerce
in December 1967. Hamden, Conn.: Archon Books, 1968.

A detailed presentation of a course which aimed at educating practicing librarians with limited experience of commercial information
in the particular problems of this field, and at the same time
giving managers an insight into commercial information sources and
methods. The course followed a definite pattern: first a manager
of a large industrial firm outlined the sort of questions the information
service could expect, then successive speakers dealt with sources
used for the collection of this information and the problems of communicating this information.

B-2. Baldwin, L.V. "In-Plant Graduate Courses on Videotape: Project Colorado SURGE." Journal of Engineering Education, 58 (May 1969),
1055 - 58.

In 1967, Colorado State proposed a pilot program of videotaped instruction in graduate engineering to major industrial and government
employers of the state. The proposal was called Project Colorado
SURGE, and acronym for Colorado State University's Research in
Graduate Education. Video-tape is used as an inexpensive transmission method for classroom instruction. The in-plant courses
are scheduled a day after the regular campus class. Student-
instructor contact is encouraged through phone calls and several
telewriting devices, as well as through instructor visists to the plant.
The aim of the project is to determine the cost and teaching effectiveness
of videotaped instruction in remote classrooms.

The evaluation methods are discussed in detail as well as the methods
of administration and personal liaison with the students. During
1968 - 69, 15 locations were served. Total enrollment for the year
was 949 students who have taken 40 courses in 130 separate sections.

Under long-term benefits the author lists: 1) reaching large groups
of individuals never able to reach before; 2) economically viable
project; 3) motivation for improved teaching. On the last point the
author states: "Many faculty members believe (whether it is true or
not) that knowledge of the current literature and outstanding teaching
skill are not accorded proper recognition. What a pleasure it has

been to see some of these men tackle the challenge of remote classes linked by CCTV, and how their morale has soared when it was realized that many young engineers now engaged in advanced research and development activities demand today's fundamentals and that CCTV as a medium tolerates only the finest teachers!"

B-3. Barrett, Gerald V., and others. Combating Obsolescence Using Perceived Discrepancies in Job Expectations of Research Managers and Scientists. New York: Management Research Center, University of Rochester, July, 1970. (ED 047 250.).

This document suggests that merely to make training programs available to professionals or to submit them to various kinds of development programs is to court obsolesence. The need for individual commitment via participation in a plan for self development is of prime importance. Out of the 143 research to development personnel involved in the study, "roughly 75% expressed the desire to spend more time on training and development activities, but fewer than one-half of the respondents --44%-- actually expected to have sufficient time for self development." The study highlights the conflict between the need for development and the time pressures of short term activites. The reward structure in terms of promotions, salary increases, and professional reputation was seen as an important determinant of self development efforts. "If organization members do not perceive a link between their development activities and the organization's reward system, the probability of active efforts to update knowledge and skills is lessoned."

The study also emphasized the importance of the extent to which organizations requirements might complement or conflict with the individual's needs. Seventy percent of the respondents reported a desire for more freedom to follow their own interests in selecting new projects to work on. Assuming that an individual would choose a project requiring a moderate amount of development, it would seem that providing additional freedom in a project selection is one way in which the organization can act as a stimulus to self-motivated development.

B-4. Bass, Bernard M. "Combining Management Training and Research. Management Analysis Exercises to Building International Data Bank." Training and Development Journal, 21: (April, 1967), 2-7.

B-5. Becker, Howard, "The Nature of a Profession." In Nelson B. Henry, ed., <u>Education for the Professions</u>, Sixty-first Yearbook of the National Society for the Study of Education, Part II. Chicago: The University of Chicago Press, 1962.

Becker's article porvides numerous definitions of a profession including the one most frequently quoted by Flexner.

B-6. Belasco, James A. "Training as a Change Agent: A Constructive Evaluation." Unpublished Doctor's dissertation, Cornell University, Ithaca, 1967. (ED 024 888).

B-7. Belzer, Jack. "Information Science Education: Curriculum Development and Evaluation," <u>American Documentation</u>, 20 (October 1969), 323-376.

This is a group of papers, two of which were presented at the conference of the Curriculum Committee of the Special Interest Group on Education in Information Science of ASIS in September, 1968, and the remainder of which were generated as a result of the conference held at that time. The conference theme was on educational objectives in information science stating that they should focus on 1) theory concerning information, its environment and its relationship to information systems; 2) information systems; 3) information services and their administration. "The program must be sufficiently flexible to allow students to specialize in areas of their personal interest or in the choice of their career. A common core, if it exists, must transcend all professional interest in information science. Such a core would relate to those elements which are common to information irrespective of their environment." Information systems is defined as dealing with the design and testing of items for a specific purpose or use in handling information; information services is defined as providing service to many users of information centers. Papers in the series are by Belzer, Jahoda, C. W. Stone, Hillman, Artandi, Klempner, Giuliano, Debons and Otten, Slamecka, Hoyt, Hayes, Schlueter, and Yovits.

B-8. Bennett, H. H. "Continuing Education: A Survey of Staff Development Programs," <u>School Libraries</u>, 19 (Spring, 1970), 11-20.

This report analyzes a number of efforts to improve school library services through personnel advancement. Three essentials for a successful staff development program are financial support, released time, and commendation or a tangible benefit.

B-9. Bennis, Warren G. "The Leader of the Future," Public Management, 52 (March, 1970), 13-19.

Rather than thinking about the organization as a machine, as Weber conceptualized bureaucracy, Bennis conceptualizes the model of an organization in terms of an organic metaphor--a description of a process, not structural arrangements. The process must include such terms as: open, dynamic systems, developmental, organic adaptive. Such a model leads to a new concept of leadership, which he summarizes as: an active method for producing conditions where people and ideas and resources can be seeded, cultivated, and inter-grated to optimum effectiveness and growth.

Immediately following its publication in the March 1970 issue of Public Management, one mid-western library system used this article to initiate a highly successful series of informal luncheon discussions on staff development.

B-10. Bennis, Warren G., and Edgar H. Schein (eds.). Leadership and Motivation: Essays of Douglas McGregor. Cambridge: The M. I. T. Press, 1966.

B-11. Best, Robert. "What Engineers Want." Chemical Engineering Progress, 62 (May, 1966), 49-52.

B-12. Bewley, L. M. "To Educate Ourselves Continuously.: British Columbia Library Quarterly, 33 (July-October 1969), 23-25

B-13. Biel, William C. "Training Programs and Devices," in Gagne, Robert M., ed., Psychological Principles in System Development. New York: Holt, Rinehart and Winston, 1962, 348-386.

B-14. Bird, Jack (Aslib. London.). Some problems involved in the running of short courses in librarianship and information work. In proceeding of the International Conference on Education for Scientific Work, Queen Elizabeth College London, 3rd to 7th April, 1967. FID, The Hague. 91-94. Area II Paper 5, 1 ref. Discussion, 95-101.

The development of Aslib courses since the war are described. At present about sixteen courses per year are run ranging in length from 1 day to 2 weeks. (Orig. Publ.)

B-15. Blake, Robert R. and Jane Srygley Mouton. "Training Traps that Tempt Training Directors," Training and Development Journal, 21 (December, 1967), 2-8.

B-16. Blizzard, Samuel W. "The Minister's Dilemma." The Christian Century. 73 (April, 1956), 509-510.

Related Studies: Several studies in related disciplines include: Mee (1968), Dillman (1961, 1962), Lazarus (1968), and Blizzard (1956)

B-17. Bloom, Benjamin S. ed. Taxonomy of Educational Objectives, Handbook I: Cognitive Domain. Report of a Committee of College and University Examiners. New York: David McKay, 1956.

Educational goals in the cognitive domain, as opposed to the affective domain, include objectives which deal with the recall or recognition of knowledge and the development of intellectual abilities and skills. Objectives in both domains can be operationally described, but operational statements of cognitative objectives are easier to construct and more straight-forward. A revised edition of Handbooks II Affective Domain was published in 1964 by Krathwohl, Bloom and Masia.

B-18. Bloomquist, Harold and Kinney, Margaret M. "Continuing Education of Medical Librarians: Continuing Education in the Professions," Bulletin of the Medical Library Association, LI (July, 1963), 357-67.

The authors examine seven of the professions (architecture, clergy, education, law, librarianship, medicine and nursing) to determine their attitudes toward the problem of continuing education as have certain of the other professions. Although education has always been discussed, only rather recently did there appear to be signs of a deep and growing concern with this matter."

B-19. Boaz, Martha. "Continuing Education," Drexel Library Quarterly. 3 (April, 1967), 151-156.

This article points out that differences are great among programs for librarians--in level, content, purpose, duration, work re - quired of participants and cost. To be successful, continuing education must make clear to the groups involved the meaning and value of education and must give them effective assistance in providing study which is genuinely significant. It also lists some unresolved problems and research needed.

B-20 Boaz, Martha. "Education A-Go-Go! Continuing . . ." California Librarian, XXX (July, 1969), 187-90.

Boaz stresses the fact that no longer can a college degree or several degrees guarantee that a man is well educated or that he will even be informed for any length of time after graduation unless he continues continually and forever to seek learning--short term education, long term education, education of every sort and variety. The article urges the consideration of departures from traditional educational patterns.

B-21. Boaz, Martha, "More Than Deliberate Speed." ALA Bulletin 60 (March 1966), 286-288.

The author argues that to meet higher standards of service there must be better utilization of clerical and professional staff. Education for library staff should be brought up to date, including the newer developments in information retrieval. Professional staff should have a subject qualification as well as a librarianship qualification. One of the main emphases of the article is that library schools and the library organizations should plan to introduce certification at state and national levels, and that such

certification should be made compulsory. The author closes with
a summary of ten suggestions for improving the library profession.

B-22. Bone, Larry Earl, ed. Library education: an international survey.
Papers presented at the International Conference on Librarian-
ship conducted by the University of Illinois Graduate School of
Library Science, June 12-16, 1967, 1968. University of Illinois
Graduate School of Library Science .

Papers read at a five day conference co-sponsored by the University
of Illinois, on the occasion of its first centennial and by the Council
on Library Resources, Inc. Attention was directed primarily to
the Americas and Europe. Major topics were: History and Present Status of Education for Librarianship; Organization and Operation of Library Schools; Curriculum Principles and Practices;
Teaching Methods; and Research and Advanced Study.

B-23. Bone, Larry Earl, and Frederic Hartz. Taking the Full Ride: Library
Routes to Continuing Education. " Library Journal 95 (October,
1970), 3244-3247. The authors list required qualities for librarians:
1) Be skilled communication leaders, 2) Be informed about the
advantages and limitations of the new media, 3) Be aware of the
community--its social, political, financial and educational
aspects, 4) Be skilled in the principles of management and their
application. To fulfill these requirements they present some
possible options--extensive reading programs, graduate library
schools, institutes and workshops. Bibliographic references.

B-24. Booz, Allen and Hamilton, Inc. Organization and Staffing of the Libraries of Columbia University: A summary of the case study
sponsored by the Association of Research Libraries in cooperation
with the American Council on Education under a grant from the
Council on Library Resources. Washington D. C.: Association of
Research Libraries, 1972.

This summary report of the detailed case study of the organization
and staffing of the research libraries of Columbia University ,
to be published in the spring of 1973, has several recommendations
in it for staff development. The study discusses the need to
develop staff capabilities in library areas which can benefit from

application of specialized talents and new technology. "The ability of Columbia University's libraries to meet the challenges and demands of the future will depend largely on the quality and effectiveness of their human resources and the way in which they are organized to work together."

Five advisory groups or committees are recommended, one of which is a Staff Development Committee to be established to advise on and participate in the staff development activities. The report recommends that a formal staff development plan designed to help meet organization and staffing requirements and to assist staff members in achieving their career objectives. "Individualized plans specifying development steps should be prepared for each member of Columbia's library staff. Each plan should be in accordance with overall library policies, and be prepared by the individual with his immediate supervisor." The study recommends that professional staff members should be evaluated by the Staff Development Committee, which should collect information on the full range of professional activities for the individuals being reviewed and submit recommendations concerning eligibility for promotion steps that should be taken to further the individual's professional growth, and whether performance appears to warrant special salary consideration.

B-25. Borg, Walter R. Minicourse Rationale and Uses in the Inservice Education of Teachers. Berkeley, Calif.: West Laboratory for Educational Research and Development, 1968. (EDRS ED 024 647).

This collection of materials reports the research and development of a series of inservice training "minicourses," short courses (about 75 minutes per day for 15 days) designed to teach specific teacher behavior patterns with use of microteaching technique, self-evaluation of video tape feedback, instructional films, and filmed illustrations by model teachers. The main document reviews the instructional model on which the courses are constructed, defines and discusses the advantages of microteaching, and describes the scope and future plans for the minicourse program.

B-26. Borko, Harold. A Study of the Needs for Research in Library and Information Science Education. Final Report, O.E., Bureau of Research No. BR-ITD-L&IS, Contract No. BR-#9-0256. Washington, D.C.: Office of Education, 1970.

B-27. Bracken, Marilyn. Biological Sciences Communication Project Communique: Survey of Texts and Instructional Material Used in Information Science Programs. A report prepared for the Biological Sciences Communications Project of the George Washington University conducted as an on-the-job project under the National Library of Medicine Grant Number 1 T1 LM 101-01A1. Washington, D. C., November, 1967.

B-28. Bracken, Marilyn and Shilling, Charles W. Biological Sciences Communication Project Communique: Survey of Practical Training in Information Science. A report prepared for the Biological Sciences Communication Project of the George Washington University conducted as an on-the-job project under the National Library of Medicine Grant Number 1 T1 LM 101-01A1.

A report on practical training for information scientists which suplements the author's 1966 study. Of 41 responding schools, 35 were providing advanced training for about 4400 students; 15 teach information science as a separate discipline, and 17 include it as part of a library science curriculum. Three-fourths of the training is at the graduate level, with practical training provided at the computer center.

On-the-job training programs are sponsored by 24 of 49 responding organizations involved in information science work. Several firms handle training on a contract basis, while the balance conduct it for their own employees only. Programs range from one week to one year in length. A Bachelor's degree is the major prerequisite.

B-29. Brady, Eugene F. "A Continuous Engineering Education Program for the Computer Industry." Journal of Engineering Education, 58 (May, 1969), 1049-51.

The article starts with two basic assumptions based on the Goals of Engineering Education Report (1968), 1) continuing education is a different kind of educational activity, separate from either undergraduate or graduate education at the college level; 2) Education in continuing education courses should be conducted as a cooperative effort between academic, industrial, government and the engineering societies.

This article describes a continuing engineering education program developed in compliance with these two recommendations at the Sperry Rand Corporation's Univac Division.

The program consists of five elements: 1) new graduate orientation; 2) tuition reimbursement; 3) management courses; 4) continuing professional education; and 5) general courses. The combined curriculum consists of approximately 40 courses, each offered at least once every third year. The evaluation procedures and results are documented.

B-30. Briggs, Leslie J.; Campeau, Peggie L.; Gagne, Robert M.; and May, Mark A. Instructional Media: A procedure for the Design of Multi-Media Instruction, A Critical Review of Research and Suggestions for Future Research. A final report prepared by the Instructional Methods Program of the Center for Research and Evaluation in Applications of Technology in Education (CREATE) Pittsburgh, Pennsylvania: American Institutes for Research, 1967.

The problem faced by today's teachers and educators in selecting the right media for instruction is presented. Chapter II outlines a procedure for choosing media for instruction which is based essentially on the fact that behavioral objectives for each course are presented first in sequence and then for each objective the type of learning involved is identified. Using this data the type of media is selected which is best suited to the type of learning involved. Illustrations are given of sample programs in which this method has been followed. Chapter V presents a selective view of literature on audio-visual media of instruction.

B-31. Bringing the Campus to the Office," Business Week, 1895 (December 25, 1965). 72-73.

B-32. Brodman, Estelle. "Continuing Education for Medical Librarianship; A Symposium--Internship as Continuing Education," Bulletin of the Medical Library Association, 43 (October, 1960) 408-12.

Brodman stresses the importance of internship in continuing education. She believes it is useful for those who work in small libraries as well as for those in larger institutions, and that it is a higher qualification than mere theoretical study.

B-33. Brodman, Estelle, "Continuing Education of Medical Librarians: Introduction," Bulletin of the Medical Library Association, LI (July, 1963), 354-56.

This article gives the history of the Committee on Continuing Education of the Medical Library Association, of which the author is chairman. It makes the point that the mark of any learned society is that its members continue their studies during their entire careers.

B-34. Brodman, Estelle, "Internships as Continuing Education," Medical Library Association Bulletin, 48 (October, 1960) 412.

B-35. Brodman, Estelle, "A Philosophy of Continuing Education," Bulletin of the Medical Library Association, 56: (April, 1968), 145-146.

Continuing Education is important to the individual, to the library and to society as a whole, and therefore, every librarian should attempt to foster continued learning and the questioning mind.

B-36. Brodman, Estelle, "Why Continuing Education?" District of Columbia Libraries, XXXVII (Fall, 1966), 51-54.

For the present the overriding need in continuing education is probably a knowledge of the theory and practice of the newer machines which are so greatly changing library routines. The author believes librarians need to develop their critical faculties, and that the study of the new machine methods is only one among many where professional reflective thinking is required.

B-37. Brooks, Harvey, "Dilemmas of Engineering Education." Harvard Alumi Bulletin, 68 (No. 14, 1967), 20-23.

B-38. Browne, Duffe and Smith, Mary Howard, The Investigation, Development, and Dissemination of Procedures and Techniques Helpful
to Interinstitutional Use of Television and Related Media. Atlanta,
Georgia: Southern Regional Education Board, December 1967.
ERIC ED 021 443.

The faculty can and should play a vital role in the developing of
the media programs. A study by the Southern Regional Education
Board concluded that faculty committees could successfully plan
curriculum for media by supplementing its own competencies with
the utilization of consultants who were specialists in content or in
media.

This study suggests another point to consider. The universities
who belong to this regional board went together to plan and produce
recorded instructional materials to be used at the various institutions. This was found to be feasible and effective and allows a
school to share its strengths and supplement its weakest areas.
To be realistic, no faculty is ever truly balanced, and even an open-
end budget will not insure finding the right professor to fill all
the needs.

B-39. Bundy, Mary Lee and Wasserman, Paul. "Professionalism Reconsidered." College and Research Libraries 29: (January, 1968), 5-26
The question of librarianship is considered in terms of three key
relationships as a professional: client, organizational and professional. This critical assessment suggests that librarianship
falls short of the professional model. The contributions of professional associations and of library schools to the advancement of
the process of professionalization are also analyzed.

B-40. Bundy, Mary Lee, "Public Library Administrators View Their Professional Periodicals", Illinois Libraries, (June 1961). 43:
397-420.

B-41. Burke, John G., and Mary Lux. "Coming Through Your Front Door;
Prerecorded Video Cassettes,: American Libraries, 1:1069-1073,
December, 1970.

B-42. Burton, Howard, "Maximum Benefits from a Program for Staff Reading," College and Research Libraries, 15(July, 1954), 277-80.

B-43. Butt, J. L., "Continuing Education: What is the Society's Appropriate Role ?, Part I," Agricultural Engineering, (September, 1964), p. 508.

B-44. Butt, J. L., "Continuing Education: What is the Society's Appropriate Role ?, Part II," Agricultural Engineering, (October, 1964) p. 547.

B-45. Butt, J. L. "Continuing Education: What Others Are Saying, Part III," Agricultural Engineering (November, 1964), p.634.

B-46. Butz, Otto, and others. "College Forum: Problem 56--Upgrading Your Faculty." College Management, (July, 1966), 12-14.

The problem posed: "Many students and energetic faculty members have recently put their complaints in writing and have handed you 'concrete evidence' that there are nonproductive, sterile faculty members at your college. Most of them are on tenure and have been on the college's staff for at least 15 years. You have been asked to devise a "formula" solution, a policy statement, for this problem."

The four panelists were in agreement that this was one of the most pressing problems on the campus today. Their solutions varied.

C-1. Calkins, Robert D. "Education for Business--Changing Perspectives and Requirements." Paper read before the International Society of Business Education, New York University, New York, (August 25, 1965). (Mimeographed).

C-2. Calkins, Robert D. "New Tasks for Our Universities: An Occasional Paper on the Role of Colleges and Universities in the Continuing Education of Adults." National Institute of Public Affairs, Washington, D.C., 1967.

This brief (18 page), thought-provoking article by the President of the Brookings Institution discusses the thesis that continuing education is now a matter of national priority with the universities bearing the major responsibility for fulfillment.

> "Continuing education is no longer merely a good and worthy thing for self development; it has become a national necessity. . . it has become indispensable to the effective operation of our free society . . . and the management of the multifarious public affairs of the country . . . no one in these times can go far on the intellectual capital he acquires in his youth. Unless he keeps his knowledge or skill up to date, revises it, adds to it, enriches it with new experience and supplements it with new ideas as they displace the old, he is soon handicapped for the duties of the day."

C-3. Campbell, John P. and others. Managerial Behavior, Performance, and Effectiveness. New York: McGraw-Hill, 1970.

C-4. Campbell, John P. "Personnel Training and Development." Annual Review of Psychology, 22, (Spring, 1971), 565-602.

Dr. John P. Campbell, Associate Professor of Psychology at the University of Minnesota, and senior author of Managerial Behavior Performance and Effectiveness, (New York: McGraw-Hill, 1970), presents the first comprehensive review of literature on "Personnel Training and Development" to be published by the Annual Review of Psychology. After commenting on the sad state

390

of training and development literature in general--"voluminous, nontheoretical, poorly written, and dull, " as well as "foolish in the extreme"--Campbell reviews the recent literature in four general areas: theoretical and conceptual issues bearing on the training and development problem; recent developments in training techniques; fresh thoughts on the evaluation problem; and empirical literature in several specific topics.

If training and development are to be important in the area of behavior change, Campbell feels it will be necessary to :

"1. Devote considerable time to an empirical analysis, via the systems approach, of the training and development system and its interactions with other systems.
2. Take an intelligent plunge into the methods and concepts of behavior modification . . . as exemplified by Bandura .
3. Adopt the PI programmed instruction model for every training activity. That is, our task should be to specify terminal behaviors, decompose the learning task into its structural components, and seek an optimal sequence of these components. This is rational not mechanistic behavior.
4. Forget about the either/or approach to training evaluation. Instead, we should worry about measuring behavioral outcomes and their interaction with other subsystems in the organization. We should also worry about the differential effects of competing training strategies. Knowing these differential effects is the ultimate payoff. " (pp. 594-595).

C-5. Canada, John R. "Guidelines for Educational Television Instructors. " The Journal of Engineering Education. 58 (October, 1967), 149-50.

This article gives practical guidance for persons who plan to present an educational television lecture with little or no prior experience. The type of visual aids that can be used, the TV studio equipment, the technical constraints and tips on preparing instructional materials for TV are covered in the article.

C-6. "Career Opportunities. " Chemical and Engineering News 45 (March 13, 1967) 98-31A.

C-7. Carnegie Commission on Higher Education. Less Time, More Options. New York: McGraw-Hill Book Company, 1971.

The Carnegie Commission suggests that students of all ages should have more options regarding both the process and the content of their education. Flexibility and choice of options are two essentials of reforms being suggested in higher education. The Commission recommended "We favor more opportunities in lieu of formal college and more stages at which the college-going students can change direction, step out to obtain a non-college experience and drop out with formal recognition for work accomplished."

C-8. Carnegie Corporation of New York. 62d Annual Report. New York: Carnegie Corporation, 1967.

C-9. Cassata, Mary B. "Learning from Library Institutes." Wilson Library Bulletin, (December, 1968), 363-65.

So concerned is the federal government with a trained librarians shortage that it has been supporting continued education programs since July, 1967, under Title I I -B of the Higher Education Act. This is a report on a study made of the first 39 library training institutes approved for 1968 under H.E.A. The consensus was that as an intensive and concentrated learning experience, it holds immediate as well as delayed rewards that will bring much good to both the participant and the profession.

C-10. Cavalier, Robert P. "Continuing Education in Professional Associations: American Institute of Banking." Paper presented at a Mini-Workshop on Continuing Education sponsored by the Standing Committee of Continuing Library Education of the Association of American Library Schools during the Annual Meeting of the Association, Washington, D.C., (January 28, 1973). (transcription of tape of the presentation).

The American Institute of Banking (AIB) is a division of the American Bankers Association, but is distinct in the sense that AIB has individual memberships. There are about 240,000 bankers who are members of the Institute, which is roughly 25% of the total bank population, which is now just over a million. Founded 73 years ago, the AIB enrolls each year about 120,000 bankers in

C-10 (cont.)

courses which are conducted at 375 chapters throughout the country.
Every community in the land, regardless of size or density, has
some form of AIB study group. Beyond the formal chapter structure
there are 200 additional "study groups".

Cavalier pointed out that one of the unique things about the Institute
is that these various study units are conducted on a volunteer basis
by bankers. Each chapter has its own organization with elected
officers. The total structure is voluntary. The essence of the
Institute is its volunteer effort. In order to maintain quality control over such a huge volunteer structure, the study materials,
which provide the instructor with as much information as he may
need to conduct the course, are produced at AIB headquarters.

In addition to all this, the AIB also conducts a correspondance
program which is also very successful, reaching about 2,000 new
enrollments each year; currently there are 6,000 enrolled. At
the national level there are 300 on the staff of ABA and 40 staff
people on the AIB staff.

The chief materials used in the program are textbooks for the 35
courses now offered, with 17 more in the planning stage. The
courses are divided into four content areas: 1) Foundations
in Banking; 2) Banking Functions; 3) Management and Supervision;
4) Communication Courses; 5) General Electives (courses may
be taken from the local college, but no non-banking courses are
tied into the certificate procedures).

There are three levels of certificate procedures: 1) Basic Certificate (15 credits of work); 2) Standard Certificate (additional
21 credits); 3) Advanced Certificates (66 credits of AIB work).
Each year about 300 advanced certificates are issued as opposed
to 5,000 basic certificates. A further certificate, the General
Certificate, consists of 36 credits and the student can apply any
of the credits taken in any of the functional areas.

During the last three years, the AIB has developed 133 formal
cooperative programs between AIB chapters and local colleges.
At present, Cavalier explained, there is an attempt to coordinate
all of these college relations into a national consortium. "It
is our view that the AIB can serve as a catalyst with the community
college system for the purposes of a national relationship, whereby there would be reciprocal credit among the schools."

During the question and answer period one member of the audience
asked the speaker, "What has been your experience with video ?"
The answer: "We thought is would be a good idea to get into the
video business and we developed a 15 minute program on bank
hold-ups--very interesting show, professionally done.   We find
that this is a very expensive way to do things.   This particular
show cost about $35,000.   So what we did with the program was to
arrange with the Bureau of National Affairs to put it on 16mm film
and it is now being marketed by B.N.A. films."

C-11. Cavalier, Robert P.   Instructor Performance Inventory. American
Bankers Association, 1972.

The Instructor Performance Inventory (IPI) was designed by
Cavalier to provide a means for instructors in the American
Institute of Banking programs to understand and improve their
teaching performance.   It is not a method of faculty rating or
evaluation; rather it is a technique to be used voluntarily by the
instructor for his own self-development.   The form consists of
three parts.   The first part deals with the treatment of material
in class; the second part concerns teaching method and technique,
and part three offers student-instructor relations.

The IPI Instructor's form is paralleled by the IPI Student's form,
in which the students evaluate the teacher's performance.

The IPI for the instructor and the IPI for the student contain the
same items.   A third booklet is the instructor's score sheet providing the necessary forms for the teacher to compare his self-
evaluation of his own teaching with that of his students.   These
inventory booklets are handsomely printed and packaged.

C-12. Cavalier, Robert P.   Toward Becoming a Better Teacher. American
Banker's Association, Washington, D. C., 1972.

Cavalier has written this booklet to help upgrade the quality of
teaching in the courses sponsored by the American Institute of
Banking.   He states that the methods and techniques of effective
teaching are based on the psychology of communication and motivation.   He discusses course content (scope and depth of coverage),
and student-instructor relations.

C-13. Cavalier, Robert P. and Yates, Glen L. Continuing Career Education: An Opportunity for Cooperation Between Industry and Higher Education. American Bankers Association, Washington, D.C., 1971.

The authors present a rationale for a proposal which calls for the cooperation of the banking industry and higher education in establishing standards and procedures for the continuing career education of bankers. They point out that industry, by providing educational programs for their employees, has kindled the interest of the employees to enlist in formal programs for which there is more general recognition. "The growth of such employment practices as the giving of rebates for educational tuitions related to advancement in one's job, and altering work schedules to a four day week eliminate other obstacles which have historically made education impossible for most adults." Several examples of college credit now being given for non-traditional learning experiences are given, including the initiation of the College-Level Examination Program (C.L.L.P.) which was initiated by the College Entrance Examination Board in 1965 to provide an option whereby credit could be waived on the basis of performance on an equivalency test.

C-14. Chapman, Brian. The Profession of Government, 3rd ed, London: University Books, 1966.

Chapter 3, Training, contains a description of several national systems of in-service continuing education useful as background ideas for building continuing education programs.

C-15. Charters, Alexander N. Publications on Continuing Education. Syracuse, New York: Syracuse University, 1970.

C-16. Clark, Harold F. and Harold S. Sloan. Classrooms in the Factories: An Account of Educational Activities Conducted by American Industries. Rutherford, New Jersey: Institute of Research, Fairleigh-Dickenson College, 1958.

C-17. Clegg, Denzil. "The Motivation of County Administrators in the Cooperative
        Extension Service." Unpublished Doctor's dissertation,
        University of Wisconsin, 1963.

C-18. Cohen, David and Samuel S. Dubin. "A Systems Approach to Updating
        Professional Personnel." In: National Seminar on Adult Edu-
        cation Research, Toronto, February 9-11, 1969. Pennsylvania
        State University, February, 1969. (ED 025 718.)

        The authors visualize the professional updating process
        through a model which enables both the educator and the pro-
        fessional to deal with relevant factors to promote more
        individual competence. They feel that the mathematical
        model they present can provide a basis for its use as a decision-
        making tool f or continuing education.

C-19. Cohen, Morris. "Background to Law Library Education." Law Library
        Journal, 55 (August, 1962), 190-199.

        This is a description of the early efforts of the American
        Association of Law Libraries to organize its series of ro-
        tating, usually pre-convention, educational institutes.
        These proved highly successful and now constitute the
        largest part of the continuing education program of AALL.

C-20. Coleman, James, E. Katz, and H. Menzel. "The Diffusion of an
        Innovation Among Physicians." Sociometry. 20 (December,
        1957), 253-270.

C-21. Colley, D. I. "Training: The Theoretical Background." Library
        Association Record, 72 (November, 1970), 349-50.

        This concise article by the city Librarian of Manchester,
        England, relates current theories of motivation to training
        concepts. Colley presents the thesis, in keeping with the
        theories of Malsow, McGregor, and Herzberg, that em-
        ployees are motivated to work hard and to accept and
        seek responsibility and to show considerable initiative when
        they are employed by an organization which satisfies their

needs. At the Manchester public library, Colley has taken a "cross-bearing" on what these needs are, by asking employees what they expect from work. Return from employees show that top expectations are: 1) to have an interesting job; 2) to experience a feeling of achievement; 3) to be on good terms with colleagues; 4) to have chances of promotion and growth; 5) to receive full appreciation of work done. All but one of these (to be on good terms with colleagues) arise from job content and are related to Herzberg's satisfiers, i.e. if these expectations are fulfilled there is job satisfaction and motivation to work.

He concludes: "Today's manager is not content to train for increased efficiency or increased production. He appreciates that the greatest resource he has is the untapped potential of the individual men and women who constitute his work force. His training programme is designed to release this potential and is designed with the objectives, the needs of the individual employee in mind. With this reorientation there is no barrier to the achievement of the objectives of the organization." The expectation list referred to in the study is appended to the article.

C-22. Conley, Veronica L. and Carol M. Larson. "Among Regional Medical Programs--An Enduring Committment." Journal of Continuing Education in Nursing, 1 (November-December, 1970), 28-33.

In 1965 some 55 Regional Medical Programs were set up across the nation. Thus far emphases in the programs have been on continuing education with nurses and physicians most active. Most of the Programs have a Continuing Education Task Force, with some adding a continuing education director or coordinator on the core staff.

C-23. Conroy, Barbara, "A descriptive and evaluative report of the Washington Seminar Library Career Development Institute." Washington D. C. Department of Library Science, Catholic University of America, 1971.

The basic objective of the institute was to imporve the library effectiveness of the attendees and to develop their potential for future leadership. An intense and concentrated program of learning opportunities focused on increasing the personal and

professional competence of its nine participants. A model was
designed, implemented and evaluated which can serve as a basis
for attaining educational goals of library schools.

C-24. *Continuing Education for R and D Careers: An Exploratory Study of
Employer-Sponsored and Self-Teaching Models of Continu-
ing Education in Large Industrial and Federal Government
Owned R & D Laboratories. National Science Foundation
Chicago, 1969. (ED 035 813.).

In this comprehensive survey of the objectives and modes of
continuing education, technological obsolescence in an individual
means a deficiency of knowledge causing him to approach
problems with viewpoints, theories, and techniques less
effective than others currently used in his field of specialization. One of the chief goals of the Committee was the
planning of the academic curricula and structuring the employment situation similar to that of engineers who are
trained for a lifetime of continuing study as part of their normal careers. "When this goal is achieved, 'overcoming'
obsolescence will give way to 'preventing' obsolescence--
which is in turn synonymous with 'keeping up to date' with new
knowledge and maintaining useful skills and knowledge. "

All major modes of continuing education are reviewed and
their strengths, weaknesses, and most effective use analyzed.
In the research relative to the academic institutions and continuing education, one of the most basic changes recommended
is to incorporate into the university reward system acknowledgement that continuing education is a respectable and
reputable career line for academic faculty. "Academic
effort at present is contingent on individual faculty members
sacrificing the rewards of the academic system or squeezing
continuing education efforts into the myriad of other activities
demanded of them. This is one side of the coin. The other is
the general down-grading of non-credit activities in the spectrum of university teaching relative to courses in the regular
curricula. Yet there is general agreement that continuing
education must be non-credit (for the most part) in order to
develop formats which are more flexible than university
credit courses in meeting individual's needs. "

The study concludes that universities and colleges should accept leadership in developing, evaluating, and experimenting with new methods of instruction in order to explore their potential usefulness in the field of continuing education. "Employers must be prepared to increase the amount of released time of employees to engage in continuing education in order to take advantage of appropriate modes of continuing education which are available only or primarily at times other than evenings and weekends . . . . While released time is a matter of employer policy, its relevance to university efforts is that without it universities are effectively stymied in experimenting with varying-size blocks of time . . . . Special emphasis is placed on the need for long-range planning for continuing education in collaborative arrangements. We also recommend . . . that the search for new and different educational techniques and modes be continued in order to maximize alternatives available."

Other findings of particular interest: 1) There is evidence that continuing education on an if-and-when basis is insufficient to cope with the requirements of a R & D laboratory, and 2) for an individual to be personally motivated toward education or training, he must see the results of the learning as being real and necessary in the performance of his job.

C-25. Continuing Education in the Professions. Current Information Sources, No. 8. ERIC Clearing House on Adult Education, Syracuse University, 1967. (ED 014 026.)

C-26. Continuing Education in the Professions. Current Information sources, N. 24., Syracuse, N.Y. ERIC Clearinghouse on Adult Education, Syracuse University, 1969. (EDRS, ED 033 250.)

A 225 item annotated bibliography on professional continuing education in the following areas: engineering, sciences, medicine and health, education, library science, law, religion, public administration, military, and social work.

C-27. "Continuing Education Needs Pegged by Poll." Library Journal, 94
(November 15, 1969), 4092-93.

> A study based on a poll of library school graduates with an
> average of about ten years of work experience brought out
> a number of suggestions as to who ought to be doing what
> about continuing education for librarians.

C-28. "Continuing Education Plan Reports Success in New York." Library
Journal. 94 (January 15, 1969), 135-36.

> This article reports on the program to provide continuing
> education for librarians which was set up under the sponsor-
> ship of the Westchester Library Association and the New
> York University School of Continuing Education. The study
> tried to find out if benefits had been realized from the program.
> The results seem to indicate that continuing education can
> make librarians happier and able to take on more responsi-
> bility.

C-29. "Continuing Education Plan Slated for Western States," Library Journal. 93 (December 15, 1968), 4605-06.

> An effective continuing education program for the library
> personnel of thirteen western states was the aim of a study
> by the Western Interstate Commission for Higher Education.
> The first phase of the nine-month study called for a team
> of experts in library science and adult education to visit
> each state to explore educational needs of library personnel.
> Three consultants then developed the basic plan. Actual pro-
> grams were begun in 1969.

C-30. Continuing Engineering Studies--A Report of the Joint Advisory Committee.
New York, Engineer's Council for Professional Development,
and others, April, 1965.

> In 1964 the Joint Advisory Committee in Continuing Engineering
> Studies was formed with two representatives each from the
> Engineer's Council for Professional Development, The
> American Society for Engineering Education, the Engineer's

Joint Council and the National Society for Professional
Engineers. In addition, two representatives from government agencies in Washington were added, in recognition of the
large number of engineers employed by the government.
The role of the Joint Committee was to study the extent of the
overall situation, consider possible methods of solution to
the problem, the respective roles that the universities,
societies, industries, and the government should play in the
solution, and finally, to make specific recommendations
to implement action toward achieving the desired goals.
Their first step was to form Industry, Academic Institution,
Engineering Society, and Government Task Force Groups.
The Committee's work led to the formation of a permanent
Committee on Continuing Education with a full time director.

C-31. Cook, Desmond L. Better Project Planning and Control Through the
Use of System Analysis and Management Techniques. Paper
presented at the Center for Educational Statistics, Washington, D.C., November 20-22, 1967. Washington, D.C.:
Symposium on Operations Analysis of Education, November
20, 1967. (ERIC ED 019 729.)

" . . . the typical research, development, or engineering
project in education can and should be fundamentally thought of
as being a system. . . . Under this definition or characteri-
zation the concepts of system analysis and management techniques assume validity and become useful tools for project
planning and control." (p. 8)

The steps in planning and controlling a project are:
1. Establish a goal or objective.
2. Define the project - (system analysis).
3. Develop a project plan - (using graphic representation of
    the order of the tasks).
4. Establish a time schedule.

Excellent definitions are presented of system analysis,
management techniques, project planning and control, and
their component parts. (pp. 2-6).

401

C-32. Cook, Desmond L. The Impact of Systems Analysis on Education.
Columbus, Ohio: Ohio State University, Educational Research Management Center, April 18, 1968. (ERIC ED 024
145.)

Defines the use of "system" in its educational context to be
a problem considered in its broadest context, placing emphasis
on the functional relations between the variables in the system;
investigation of the interactions between the variables along
with their main effects; and the placing of emphasis on the
study of models which are developed to represent the actual
system.

"To those of you who have concern over the representation
of systems by mathematical formulas, I would call your attention to the fact that an equally valuable way of representing
systems is through some type of descriptive flow-graph
procedure. " He summarizes the specific applications of
systems philosophy in the field of education as being:
1) instructional systems; 2) project management systems;
3) management information systems which establish a
"data base" which can be used not only for operational control of the school, but for long-range planning; 4) planning-
programming-budgeting system; 5) operations research.

He concludes that the systems concept has had and will continue
to have an impact on the field of education and urges that the
approach be implemented by more emphasis being given to the
development and understanding of processes and the creation
of attitudes favorable to their use.

"It would appear to me that more time is going to have to be
spent on such topics as management, management systems,
information management, systems concepts and related topics
if the educational administrator of both the present and the
future is to better understand the wide variety of systems
applications being made. "

C-33. Cook, Desmond L. An Overview of Management Science in Educational
Research. A paper presented as a part of a Symposium on
Management Science in Educational Research, 15th International
Meeting of the Institute of Management Science, Cleveland,

Ohio, September 11-13, 1968. Columbus, Ohio: Educational
Program Management Center, Educational Development
Faculty, College of Education, Ohio State University, Sept-
ember, 1968. (ERIC ED 025 002).

Management science is defined as the basic process or
function of rational decision making. The concept of educational research is expanded to include use of new management techniques developed by the private sector which are a-
daptable to decision making in the total educational context.
Four trends in the field of educational research are briefly
reviewed: 1) increasing use of scientific problem-solving
methods; 2) increasing use of management information systems; 3) increasing emphasis on long-range planning to
correlate the educational system with political, economic,
and social subsystems for   more effective human resource
development; and 4) increasing use of systems concepts.
Examples are cited for each with references given.

Five problem areas that have resulted from utilization of
those techniques and tools are discussed.

C-34. Cook, Desmond L. PERT Applications in Educational Planning.
Columbus, Ohio: School of Education, Ohio State
University. (EDRS ED 019 751.)

The author identifies two types of educational planning:
1) long-range planning represented by such activities as the
development of an educational program designed to meet the
anticipated needs of an established and/or newly emerging
nation for the next two or three decades or the establishment
of a master plan for the long-range development of an agency or institution; 2) planning related to activities which are
limited in scope and brief in duration, such as the construction
of a new building, the development of a new curriculum or the
installation of a closed circuit educational TV system.

The second type the author refers to is an educational project
which is a once-through activity and for this type of educational
activity he recommends the use of PERT techniques and cites
these advantages: 1) PERT often results in a clearer statement
of project objectives and goals; 2) PERT requires that those
involved in the project make explicit the means by which they

403

plan to reach the objective; 3) the use of PERT results in clearer definition of each actual task to be done; 4) the use of PERT enables the project manager to identify at an early stage the potential trouble spots in the project plan; 5) the use of PERT assists a project manager to know where to replan in the event that the original plan is inappropriate for some reason; and 6) the use of network techniques facilitates the communication process, since plans are portrayed in a graphic manner.

C-35. Cook, Desmond L. The Use of Systems Analysis and Management Techniques in Program Planning and Evaluation. Paper presented at the Symposium on the Application of Systems Analysis and Management Techniques to Educational Planning in California, Orange, California, June 12-13, 1967. Orange, California: Chapman College, 1967. (EDRS ED 019 752.)

Cook suggests combining systems analysis and management techniques by using the former to help establish objectives alternatives and tasks, and the latter for planning and control.

C-36. Cope, Oliver. "The Future of Medical Education." Harper's Magazine, 235 (October, 1967), 98-104.

C-37. Cope, Oliver, and Jerrold Zacharias. Medical Education Reconsidered: Blueprint for Reform. Endicott House Summer Study on Medical Education, 1965. New York: Lippincott, 1966.

C-38. Corcoran, Robert J. "Training for Department Heads." The Municipality, 63 (March, 1968), 61-71.

The program at Madison, Wisconsin, is built around the concept that training should start with top officials. The program is conducted by the Institute of Government Affairs, University of Wisconsin Extension. The article contains course content, methods used, and a summary of a followup survey of participants.

404

C-39. Cornell University Libraries. "Report on the Committee on Continuing
Education and Professional Growth." Ithaca, 1969. (Mimeographed).
(EDRS, ED 056 718.)

This report by a group of Cornell librarians examining the opportunities for continuing education for librarians showed special
concern for the areas of bibliographic control; library organization
structure; professionalism ("which must become common and
pervasive rather than unusual and suspect"); supporting staff;
management training ("which must become common and pervasive
rather than unusual and suspect"); computers; and programmed
instruction and emulation. The report contains a suggested program for continuing education. Useful references in the appendixes:
a survey of educational opportunities for personnel in colleges and
universities, a bibliography of university and industrial personnel
information, the educational plans of selected companies, and
selected labor union programs of continuing education. Excellent
example of what a library staff committee can do in the area of
continuing education.

C-40. Corrigon, Robert E. and Kaufman, Roger A. Why System Engineering?
Palo Alto, California: Fearon Publishers, 1965.

This programmed book was written "to provide a thorough overview of the need for applying system engineering and system
functional analysis methods as prerequisites to efficient total
system design." Drawings and flow charts illustrate the text
which includes specific discussion of steps in system design. A
self-test and a glossary of terms are included.

C-41. Corson, John J. "Equipping Men for Career Growth in the Public
Service," Public Administration Review, 23 (May, 1963), 1-9.

Corson argues that a joint re-evaluation by employers, training
officials, and university faculties of preservice and post-entry
training for professionals is needed to fit the progressive levels of
understanding required as the executive moves upward along his
career path. Using as a model Henri Fayol's matrix showing the
substantive knowledge and the understandings needed by an employee
at various levels in an organization, Corson insists that the career
executive not only needs an ever expanding grasp of the substantive

405

field in which he specialized in his education but an overlay made up
of 1) an acquaintanceship with the environment surrounding the
organization; 2) administrative and executive skills and processes.
To obtain the "overlay" he sees "an urgent need, after six to eight
years in the public service, for a rigorous stocktaking of what they
have learned as to work direction and as to the function of other
units of the agency and of the government. Simultaneously, this is
the time for them to begin to underpin their personal philosophy of
public service with clear thinking as to the role of the government in
relation to the individual, the society, and the economy." He
emphasizes that the higher the career executive rises, and the
more years that elapse after he commences on his career, the
greater is his need for replacing the obsolescent both in his understanding of the substantive field in which he works and in administrative technique. He suggests that those who need to "refresh their
spirits to make more flexible their reasoning processes, as well
as to acquaint them with the new that should replace the obsolete
in what they earlier learned...need detachment from the day to day
environment and the stimulation of new faces and new places." He
proposes an additional solution -- the Staff College -- so structured
as to provide the same detachment, simulation, and individualized
opportunity, or it will add little of consequence to the development
of public executives.

C-42. Corson, John J. and R. Shale Paul. Men Near the Top: Filling Key
       Posts in the Federal Service. Baltimore, Maryland: Johns Hopkins
       Press, 1966.

       "The need is for the establishment of a career-long process that
       will utilize all means (successive assignments, intra- and inter-
       agency training, and education at universities) to equip the individual
       with the variety of competencies required at the top in the program
       field he has chosen." In regard to university training, the authors
       warn that it can provide stimulation for learning only if the university
       recognized the individual's own need and does not force the individual
       into rigid programs reflecting the faculty's conception of the execu-
       tive's needs, or into courses and seminars designed for the training
       of Ph.D. candidates in teaching and research.

       The report is based on a study of top-level federal employees taken
       from a random sampling of those who served in early 1963 in Civil
       Service positions classified in GS 16-17-18. The selection of the
       817 to whom the questionnaire was sent was made by the Commission's

staff. The original was followed up by mail and phone. 443 replies were received of which 424 were usable.

Methodology involved a questionnaire (given in appendix C) which was designed to reveal (a) the nature of all activities that consumed time for a typical week; (b) individual's judgement as to which of these activities were "most significant" and which were "least significant;" (c) a summary of individual's education; and, (d) a step by step analysis of the individual's work experience since entry designed to illustrate how he reached present post and suggest the skills and experience he brought to it; and to provide a basis for speculation on adequacy of the experience he gained on the way up to cope with responsibilities he now bears.

From this randomly selected sample, some eighty were selected, also at random, to provide a representative subsample of the larger group and face to face interviews were conducted with these. The purpose of the interviews: to find full understanding of what inter- viewee included in questionnaire; to explore part the individual played in decision making; to show relations involved with other people and institutions of each individual; to discover satisfaction and dissatisfaction with job; to find how much of job is dependent on knowledge of substantial field in which he worked and how much dependent on general process of administration.

-43. Craig, Robert L. and Bittel, Lester R. Training and Development Handbook. Sponsored by the American Society for Training and Development. New York: McGraw Hill, 1967.

The comprehensive handbook is made up of 32 presentations from leading practitioner in the field of personnel training and develop- ment. It's purpose is to provide a broad reference source for those responsibile for developing human resources in any organization. In addition to chapters on specific teaching methods, the book has chapters on: The Evolution of Training, Determining Training Needs, Ther Learning Process, Testing for Training and Development, Evaluation of Training, Job Instruction Management Development, Vocational and Technical Education Training Facilities, Use of Consultants, Universities and their Extensions, Scientific and Technical Personnel Development, Organization of Training, Trainer Education and Training, Planning and Scheduling, Budgeting, Records, and Legal Aspects of Training.

C-44. Crawford, Meredith P. "Concepts of Training, in Gagne, Robert M., ed. Psychological Principles of System Development. New York: Holt, Rinehart, and Winston, 1962.

One of the most comprehensive single essays on the systems approach to training. Discusses the relation of the sub-training system to the parent system; major steps in development of projects for training; construction and evaluation of training programs; the management of the learning process, motivation for training. As an example, a case study is given of a military training development project.

C-45. Cross, K. Patricia, "When Will Research Improve Education?" Berkeley, Calif.: Center for Research and Development in Higher Education, University of California, 1967. Appeared in The Research Reporter, II(1967), 1-4. ERIC ED 025 206.

The author sees imporvement in education practice coming only when attention centers on two processes: research and development. She feels that improvement in education will take place when we study the right kinds of questions and when we learn how to apply research knowledge to the actual practice of education. The author contends that research problems should have both theoretical reference and practical relevance. The main thrust of the paper is that the transition from research to practice is not one leap, but a process, a flow, from basic through applied investigation, to invention and development, to innovation, and finally to evaluation. Evaluation must keep pace with research and development.

C-46. Cuadra, Carlos, and others. Technology and Libraries. Research and Technology Division Technical Memorandum TM-3722. Santa Monica, California: Systems Development Corporation, 1967. (EDRS ED 022 481).

The need to improve the readiness of library personnel to use applicable technologies effectively is emphasized. "A limiting factor in the exploitation of technology is the ability and preparation of library personnel to appraise and use technology. This report encourages intensive improvement in this area including curriculum improvement in library schools (including Post-MLS training) as well as on-the-job training.

408

C-47. Culbertson, Jack et al. The Design and Development of Prototype
       Instructional Materials for Preparing Educational Administrators.
       Final Report. Washington, D. C. : U. S. Office of Education,
       1968. ED 019 723.

C-48. Culbertson, Jack, "Differentiated Training for Professors and Educa-
       tional Administrators, : Paper presented to Annual Meeting of the
       American Educational Research Association. Chicago, Illinois. :
       February 8-10, 1968. (EDRS ED 021 309).

       In this paper, Culbertson suggests the development and organiza-
       tion of a differential training program at the post-graduate level
       for those educators preparing for educational administration in
       actual school situtations and those preparing for positions as
       researchers or teachers. This differentiation is based upon the
       assumption that the skills and values as well as the setting in which
       skills and values are to be applied by the two groups are substan-
       tially different. It is also based on the assumption that it is no
       longer possible for a given individual to acquire effectiveness in
       all aspects of knowledge utilization. Based on these assumptions,
       Culbertson describes programs which are different for the researchers
       and administrators and which are specifically related to differing
       skills, values and knowledge required by these two classes of
       personnel. He outlines in some detail the types of differences that
       will obtain in the areas of recruitment for admission to the programs,
       the curriculum content, the working relations with professors,
       the kinds of reality oriented learning situations provided each,
       internship experiences, and the differences in culminating program
       activities such as theses vs. projects.

C-49. Cummings, Martin M. The National Library of Medicine and Medical
       Education. Journal of Medical Education, 44 (September, 1969),
       739-744.

       The author describes the educational functions of the National
       Center for Biomedical Communication (Lister Hll Center), two
       of which are: 1) to offer new communications modalities for con-
       tinuing education of all health professionals and 2) to improve
       the teaching of medical students and graduate students. The
       components of the network designed to meet these and other
       objectives are: a library, specialized information services,

specialized education services, audio and audiovisual facilities, and data processing and data transmission.

In explaining the specialized education services component, Cummings pointed out that although there were many regional medical programs with significant activity, these efforts have resulted.". . . in somewhat disparate programs. Materials now being generated in one locale may have little utility in another area because of the differences in size, format, and types of equipment. As a result, a large investment may be jeopardized because materials produced in one environment cannot be used easily in another without costly conversion. As we are frank in expressing our concerns with total decentralization of communications systems, we are aware that others may be suspicious of a national effort. It is hoped, therefore, that through discussion and dialogue in the spirit of meeting national needs, some resolution of this important problem can be reached. This is necessary if for no other reason than that neither group now has sufficient funds to do significant work under present conditions."

C-50. Cummings, Roy J. "Removing Intuition from Course Development: Methods at FAA to Prevent Overtraining and Undertraining," Training and Development Journal, (January 1968), 18-27.

The author outlines the step-by step procedures in the development of a course based on training needs, job task analysis and the formulation of training requirements. Presents systems chart of total plan.

C-51. Curnow, Geoffrey Ross. "The Dimensions of Executive Work in the U.S. Federal Career Civil Service: A Factor Analytic Study." Unpublished Doctor's dissertation, Cornell University, Ithaca, 1967.

C-52. Conroy, Barbara. "Staff Development and Continuing Education Programs for Library Personnel: Guidelines and Criteria." Paper submitted to ERIC Clearinghouse on Library and Information Sciences for publication, September 30, 1972 (Mimeographed.)

D-1. Dabney, Walter H. and Williamson, Marritt A. "Effective Teaching Workshop for Developing Institutions." Journal of Engineering Education, 58 (October, 1957), 141-142.

The article reports on an Institute designed specifically to help improve the teaching of engineering in developing institutions. College teachers, Deans of participating schools, along with the project leaders at Vanderbilt University decided to concentrate on only four areas and treat them in depth. Three of the four topics, each presented in one day sessions, were: Course and Curriculum Planning; Productive Keys to Instructional Planning; and Tests and Examinations. The fourth area involved "learning by doing" by making use of "micro-teaching," a method developed at Stanford and presented by Dr. Bush of that University. This was the first experience with micro-teaching with college faculties. In the sessions each participant teacher taught before a live class of engineering students, followed by a critique of persons trained in teaching methods. Each teacher spent about 20 minutes in an actual class situation in front of the camera, on a subject of his choosing. After the presentation, the student, using score cards, graded six aspects of the teacher's performance and were then excused. The faculty member then saw a playback of himself teaching and was given a summary of the student criticisms of his performance. Educators also critiqued the performance and suggested one or two variations in stimuli and in teaching techniques that they would like to see applied during a second demonstration. The faculty member then took 10 to 20 minutes studying a leaflet learning for the first time the criteria on which he has been rated, and reappeared before the camera another time. After this different set of students left, a playback and critique followed again. Tapes were erased after each critique and a rule was made that no dean would be allowed to attend the sessions where members of his faculty were performing. Before the teachers left the Institute, they were each given a notebook containing papers by other authorities on improving teaching techniques. It was hoped that this would provide a stimulus for each participant to start a collection of teaching aids.

D-2. Dalton, Gene W. and Thompson, Paul H. "Accelerating Obsolescence of Older Engineers," Harvard Business Review, 49
(September-October, 1971), 57-67.

This article is based on research in six technology-based
companies which shows that, on the average, individual performance among technically trained men peaks at an early age
and declines steadily thereafter. It is the author's concern
that there appears to be neither adequate recognition of the
problem nor effective action to cope with it. He makes some
suggestions and urges that concentrated ways be found through
research to cope with obsolescence.

The author seriously questions whether courses alone are an
effective remedy to the problems of aging and obsolescence.
He suggests that companies use more creative approaches,
such as keeping employees up to date with TV classrooms on
company time. He also makes a case for sabbaticals, believing that they can serve both as a reward and important incentive. He especially suggests that organizations engage in better
management practices and look at those practices which waste
their most valuable and costly resource -- people. He points
particular attention at performance evaluation systems which
should be designed to stress positive reinforcement and job
assignments. He also suggests the value of portable pensions
so that professionals will be freer to move to other organizations. As a model he cites the Teachers Insurance and Annuity
Association (TIAA) as used in higher education. Finally he
suggests that older men may be given an assignment as a
coach or sponsor to younger men just out of school; this type
of assignment will meet his developmental and participatory
needs, even though he is not a supervisor.

D-3. Dalton, Jack. "Library Education and Research in Librarianship:
Some Current Problems and Trends in the United States."
Paper presented at the 35th Session of the IFLA General
Council, Copenhagen, Denmark, August 1969, Libri, 19
(No. 3, 1969), 157-174.

Dalton limited his presentation to four questions relative to
library education and research in the 1960's, none of which
dealt specifically with continuing library education, but his
remarks provide an excellent survey of developments in professional library education which should be taken into account
in planning continuing education policies and programs.

He pointed out, for example, that it is necessary to remember that under our system the school is accredited, not the man, and that for most of our graduates no general examination beyond the library school degree is likely to be required.

He raised the question of whether one can deal with _flow_ of information without knowing a great deal about what is flowing. "We must cover the full range of activities, as must every occupation/profession, and of course this is a difficult problem for every professional school....I wish merely to underscore the problem with which I think the schools have not grappled sufficiently. Are the programs now offered adequate to the needs of the people Weinberg had in mind? How does one educate the chiefs? Library school deans in my country are regularly asked if our programs are not designed to train too many men and women for top positions and not enough for the ordinary tasks. The opposite is true and is likely to remain true for a long time."

He concludes: "We are just about to enter a new decade, but we are considering here the education of a group who must be prepared for the problems of a new century. As we approach these problems, we share with all professions everywhere a duty to inquire more and more carefully whether we are meeting our responsibilities to the public, whether we are sufficiently involved in the most pressing problems of our time, and whether we are 'preparing future professionals to anticipate the long-range consequences of their actions.' Above all, their attention must be 'directed to the potential impact of the shaping and sharing of information on the shaping and sharing of every other valued outcome in human affairs.'"

D-4.   Dalton, Jack. "Observations on Advanced Study Programs in the Library Schools of the United States." In: Bone, Larry Earl, ed. Library Education: An International Survey. Champaign, Ill.: University of Illinois Graduate School of Library Science, 1968, pp. 317-328.

Defining "advanced study" programs as all those beyond the master's level offered by the ALA accredited library schools, Dalton makes his observations relative to admissions questions, programs, degrees, "where do the graduates go?", financial considerations, and recruiting. In the section on "Programs," he states that it is difficult, if not impossible, to make any

413

generalizations about those programs entitled post-master's or advanced study. They have grown out of the belief that many librarians consider that the one-year degree program does not provide enough time for an adequate introduction to the many areas that can best be handled by formal academic programs. If the librarian does not wish to continue his education via the route of a research oriented three-year doctoral program, there are a number of one-year, non-degree, post-master's programs which are being offered by an increasingly large number of schools from which he can choose.

It is obvious that these individually planned programs are not primarily concerned with research. It is possible to find programs ranging from those needed for certification purposes to those offering the possibility of becoming the library school counterpart of some of the better advanced study programs in other fields, such as those provided for the Niemann Fellows in Journalism at Harvard or the Mid-Career Fellows in Princeton's Woodrow Wilson School of Public and International Affairs. We need many more of the latter variety.

Dalton identifies the most pressing problem facing American librarianship as upgrading our "advanced study" programs to the stage where they will be able to produce and provide places for those who are "prepared to commit themselves deeply to the job of sifting, reviewing, and synthesizing information, i.e., to handling information with sophistication and meaning" as described in the Weinberg Report and in Overhage's article in the February 17, 1967, issue of Science.

Dalton concludes:

Our advanced study programs are, of course, not very far advanced. When they are, they will produce and provide places for the kind of people described above. These people are available and will be available in increasing numbers. We have before us a job of selective recruiting at a high level. We have done very little of this kind of recruiting and it will not be easy to persuade the people we need most. But we know we need them, even if our vision of the promised land we are offering them is still a little cloudy.

Here lies the most pressing problem facing American librarianship today.

D-5. Danton, J. Periam. <u>Between MLS and Ph.D.: Sixth-Year Specialist</u>
<u>Programs in Library Schools Accredited by the American</u>
<u>Library Association.</u> Chicago: American Library Association,
1971.

This study by Danton was a special project of the Committee on
Accreditation of the ALA, which was awarded a J. Morris Jones
--World Book Encyclopedia--ALA Goals Award for 1969-70.
The purpose of the survey was to study the post-master's
programs in the ALA accredited library schools and to determine their aims, content and methods. Danton, on the basis
of his survey, makes suggestions regarding the sixth year
programs for the future.

Danton found that all but four of the 20 schools offering (or
having offered) a sixth-year program awarded a certificate or
a degree -- thirteen certificates and four degrees. He found a
very wide variation in the title of the award, and states:
"There are, in fact, almost as many different designations as
there are awards, fourteen in all. This seems a distinctly
disadvantageous situation. Who, even in the library profession,
is likely to be aware of all of these different titles, and to
recognize that, despite their varied phraseology, they represent
the same amount, and frequently the same kind, of advanced
professional education. It would seem highly desirable that the
Association of American Library Schools, and, perhaps, the
C.O.A., attempt to secure agreement among the accredited
schools on a single certificate title, or, at most, upon not more
than two or three titles.   It would also seem desirable that
the schools which give no award do so. " Danton notes that the
specialist programs at the sixth-year level exist in numerous
other fields and that, as in library science, they are a recent
development. He cites as an example the conference held by
the American Association of State Colleges and Universities
on "The Specialist Degree" in 1969, in which it is stated:
"Specialist degree programs are intended for those preparing
for positions which call for a higher level of study than the
Master's degree but not the emphasis on research required
for the Doctor's degree. A major object of such programs
is to strengthen an individual's area of specialization. ...
Specialist degree programs are functionally oriented toward
the student's professional objectives. "

Overall, based on the findings from his survey, Danton makes observations and recommendations, including the following:

-- The basic concept of the sixth-year program is sound; the idea should be encouraged and supported.
-- A large majority of the programs will continue and probably improve qualitatively and expand quantitatively.
-- A majority of the programs are functioning reasonably well to excellently.
-- Most programs can be and a few need to be improved in one or more respects.
-- A year or two of professional experience should be generally required for admission.
-- The schools offering programs should spell out clearly and in detail the nature of their programs, what they want, what a student may expect to secure by enrolling, and what will be expected of him.
-- The schools should upgrade the educational attainment of their faculties to the end that, except under unusual and carefully evaluated circumstances, students at the sixth-year level will not be taught by instructors holding no degree higher than the B.L.S./M.L.S.

D-6. Danton, J. Periam. "Doctoral Study in Librarianship in the United States," College and Research Libraries, 20 (November, 1959), 435-453.

D-7. Davies, Don. "Professional Standards in Teaching: Moving from Ideas to Action," Journal of Teacher Education, 13 (June, 1962), 191 ff.

D-8. Davis, Richard A. "Continuing Education: Formal and Informal," Special Libraries, 58 (January, 1967), 27-30.

Whether formal or informal, continuing education requires that the librarian have a goal in mind and a plan of achieving it. Advice should be provided by local associations and by the library schools. Those interested in continuing education for librarianship need to consider new and imaginative avenues rather than depend on traditional, not always satisfactory, techniques.

D-9. Davis, Richard A. "Theses and Dissertations Accepted by Graduate Library Schools: 1966 through December 1967," Library Quarterly, 38 (October, 1968), 442-452.

D-10. Dean, J.F. "Senior Staff Training -- An Approach," Library
World, 70 (June, 1969), 339-41.

A report from a medium sized public library in England of
its decision that senior assistant librarians' posts would be
filled on an interchangeable rather than a permanent basis,
making job rotation part of their senior staff training scheme.
They feel that job rotation and training courses help by varying and increasing the professional content of the work.

D-11. DeProspo, Ernest R. "Management by Objectives: An Approach to
Staff Development." In: Stone, Elizabeth, ed. New Directions
in Staff Development: Moving from Ideas to Action. Paper
presented at Micro-Workshop on Staff Development at
American Library Association conference, June 28, 1970.
Sponsored by Staff Development Committee of the Personnel
Administration Section of the Library Administration Division
of ALA. Chicago: American Library Association, Library
Administration Division, 1971, pp. 39-47.

D-12. DeProspo, Ernest R. "Personnel Evaluation as an Impetus to
Growth," Library Trends, 20 (July, 1971), 69-70.

Ernest R. DeProspo, associate professor, Graduate School
of Library Science and Co-Director, Bureau of Library and
Information Science Research, Rutgers University, sums up
the suggestions found in library literature and in actual practice in the field of employee evaluation in libraries, and finds
that the philosophy, methods and techniques add up to a system
which is using a "traitist" approach to evaluation, which is
dehumanizing. He feels present practice falls far short of
the objective of appraisal, namely to serve as a motivator for
future performance. As a correction of present practice De
Prospro presents the case and offers practical suggestions for
libraries adapting some form of appraisal by objectives which
he states would, in addition to its humanizing effect on library
employees, provide great impetus to staff development and
growth.

D-13. DeProspo, Ernest R., and Huang, Theodore S. "Continuing Education for the Library Administrator: His Needs." In:
Harlow, Neal, and others. Administration and Change:
Continuing Education in Library Administration. New Brunswick, N.J.: Rutgers University Press, 1969, pp. 21-27.

417

D-14. De Solla Price, Derek J., and Beaver, Donald. "Collaboration in an Invisible College," American Psychologist, 21 (November, 1966), 1011-1018.

D-15. Dill, William R., and others. "How Aspiring Managers Promote Their Own Careers: Why do some young men in business progress rapidly to top management jobs while others, with the same educational background, reach a stalemate?" California Management Review, 2 (Summer, 1960), 9-15.

D-16. Dill, William R., and others. "Strategies for Self-Education," Harvard Business Review, 43 (November-December, 1965), 119-130.

    The authors base their study on the assumption that it is each individual's responsibility to pursue his or her own education. In making the survey, the authors asked the respondents if they had clearly thought through what they were preparing for, knew what they wanted to do, knew how they wanted to change, and what part of their self education had the highest priority, and finally if they had developed specific strategies for this agenda.

D-17. Dillman, Beryl R. "The Professional Growth of Teachers as Perceived by Members of Other Professions -- Physicians, Lawyers, Clergymen." (Unpublished research paper presented at the American Educational Research Association National Annual Convention, Atlantic City, New Jersey, February 21, 1962.) (Mimeographed)

    "This study is based upon the assumption that the teacher's professional growth is a matter of concern for members of all professions, and that teachers, as well as other educators, are interested in knowing how their perceptions of professional growth compare with those of persons of other professions. While teachers and other educators may consider certain activities extremely important for professional growth, influential persons in other important professions may perceive these activities as less important." The study brings to light those aspects of the profession which could upgrade the teaching profession in the eyes of other professional persons. The study reveals that in general physicians, lawyers, and clergymen do not vary to a statistically significant degree in their perceptions of importance of teachers activities relative to the teacher's professional growth. Out of 32 items listed, activities considered particularly important were reading professional literature, conducting parent teacher conferences, participating in faculty meetings. Participating in community service was not perceived as being extremely important for the teacher's professional growth, as viewed by the members of the other professions queried.

D-18. Dillman, Beryl R. "Teacher Perceptions and Practices in the Development of Responsibility for Professional Growth." (Unpublished research paper presented at the American Education Research Association National Annual Convention, Chicago, February 25, 1961.) (Mimeographed)

Dillman, using his findings in this pilot study, reaches certain conclusions from which he draws pertinent implications. A selection from these that have some implications for research related to the professional growth of librarians are quoted:

-- A significant inverse relationships exists between importance of activities for professional growth as perceived by teachers, and relative time and energy expended toward fulfillment of these activities. In fact, many of the activities teachers deem very important for professional growth merit relatively little teacher time and energy expended in their direction.

-- Teachers, in developing their own professional growth, should strive for more opportunity to read professional literature. Although most teachers consider this extremely important, very few (if any) of them devote sufficient time to satisfy this need.

-- Additional formal education for enrichment purposes and for an advanced degree is necessary for the teacher's personal development of professional growth.

-- For the best interests of professional growth, teachers should affiliate with related professional organizations rather than teacher unions, especially teacher unions affiliated with labor.

D-19. Dimmock, Mary Laverne. "Sixth Year Study and the Academic Libraries," _Library Journal_, 96 (September 15, 1971), 2731-33.

The author argues that it is imperative that library schools recognize their obligation to provide post-master's programs of study for their graduates which are structured, uniform in performance requirements, and culminate in a degree.

D-20. Dimock, Marshall E. "The Administrative Staff College: Executive Development in Government and Industry," _American Political Science Review_, 50 (March, 1956), 166-176.

D-21. Dimock, Marshall E. "Executive Development after Ten Years." In: Hawley, Claude E. and Weintraub, Ruth G., eds. _Administrative Questions and Political Answers_. New York: Van Nostrand, 1966.

Dimock examines critically the shaping of career development and the importance of positive programs for intensified continuing education after a decade of service.

D-22. Doherty, Victor W. "The Carnegie Professional Growth Program: An Experiment in the In-Service Education of Teachers," _Journal of Teacher Education_, 18, (Fall, 1967), 261-268.

D-23. Donahugh, Robert H., and others. _Report of the Commission on Continuing Education, Kent State University, School of Library Science_. Kent, Ohio: Kent State University, School of Library Science, 1971.

The committee started with the following assumptions: 1) the primary target of continuing education should be the professional librarian; 2) administrators should be tapped to learn specific anticipated needs; 3) continuing education should involve contact with a university unit; 4) the different kinds of libraries would require different approaches to continuing education. Following a survey of school librarians, media administrators, public library administrators, Kent graduates, and special librarians, the Commission came up with the following statement:

Continuing education for librarians is of prime importance. It should be the concern of all librarians, all administrators, the library schools, the professional associations, and the State Library. The chief target should be the professional librarian -- to improve, bring up-to-date and inspire. The professional librarian in her/his continuing education should emphasize leadership training and also teacher training. For the professional librarian must be prepared to lead, to train, to teach -- not only staff members but also patrons, whether individual or corporate. While non-professional staff members should be encouraged to continue their educations (through State Library workshops, college courses, etc.), the professional librarians should probably be required to continue theirs.

The report stated that although everyone was in favor of continuing education the presentations must be coordinated -- "too many brochures and flyers are being mailed out. Too many conflicting dates. Too much confusion, where there is plenty of communication." Recommendations made include the following: 1) Continuing education for librarians be coordinated by the State library in consultation with other institutions offering courses or workshops; 2) non-library courses be offered as well as advanced updating; 3) the letters and questionnaires collected by the Commission throughout be analyzed and turned into a springboard for planning [the raw data is included with the report].

Concerning levels of continuing education the Commission stated its position: 1) the thrust of continuing education should be post-MLS; 2) formal courses should be available in addition to workshops, seminars, etc.; 3) continuing education should be required for faculty members as well as for practicing librarians; 4) devices for allowing feedback and followup of conferences and institutes should be studied; 5) continuing education for professional librarians should emphasize inter-disciplinary activities -- it should cross all lines; 6) if no credits are allowed, a certificate of attendance should be issued; and 7) continuing education should eventually be required especially if certification of librarians is anticipated.

D-24.   Downs, Robert B. "Education for Librarianship in the United States and Canada." In: Bone, Larry Earl, ed. Library Education: An International Survey. Champaign, Ill.: University of Illinois Graduate School of Library Science, 1968, pp. 1-20.

421

Brief history of library education in the United States and discussion of current trends and major problems.

D-25. Drucker, Peter F. "Increasing Executive Effectiveness,"
Administrative Management, (April, 1967), 40-42.

Drucker develops the thesis that the manager must develop his own effectiveness. He concludes: "Organizations are not effective because they have better people. They have better people because they motivate them to self-development through their standards, through their habits, through their climate. And these, in turn, result from systematic, focused, purposeful self-training of the individuals in becoming effective executives."

D-26. Drucker, Peter F., and others. Oakland Papers: Symposium on Social Change and Educational Continuity. Notes and Essays on Education for Adults, 51. Brookline, Mass.: Center for the Study of Liberal Education for Adults, 1966. (ED 030 044.)

Sponsored by the Kellogg Foundation, the symposium was a result of the experimental alumni education program at Oakland University in Rochester, Michigan. Oakland is seeking a relationship with its alumni based on continuing education.

The four symposium papers included "The University in an Educated Society," by Peter Drucker, in which he discusses the learning patterns needed in a highly technical society; the competencies required by man as a builder of society are discussed by Max Lerner in "The University in an Age of Revolutions"; Rollo May, in "The University in an Age of Anxiety," explores man's drive for expanding consciousness and the needs this process generates, and "The University and Institutional Change," by Margaret Mead, asks how educational institutions can take their current practices and make suitable changes.

D-27. Drucker, Peter F. "Work and Worker in the Knowledge Society."
In: Drucker, Peter. The Age of Discontinuity: Guidelines to our Changing Society. New York: Harper and Row, 1969, pp. 287-310.

D-28.* Dryer, Bernard V., ed. "Lifetime Learning for Physicians:
Principles, Practices, Proposals, " Journal of Medical
Education, 37 (June, 1962), i-134.

This comprehensive "landmark" report emphasized the necessity of cooperative, long-range planning by all concerned professional groups if lifetime professional education is to be
achieved within a profession. Through full use of the new
technology, it advocated the concept of "universities without
walls". The study has three major parts: 1) Principles
(based on assumptions); 2) Practices (based on the criteria
considered necessary for continuing education programs:
excellence of content, personal satisfaction, freedom of choice,
continuity, accessibility, and convenience); 3) Proposals for
action. The necessity of a wide use of multi-media is
emphasized throughout as an imperative. Eight health related
national professional associations sponsored and joined in
developing the study. An 11 page bibliography on continuing
education emphasizing a multi-media approach is included.

D-29. Dryer, Bernard V. "Lifetime Learning for Physicians -- Principles,
Practices, Proposals: Summary of the Report of the Joint
Study Committee in Continuing Medical Education, Journal of
the American Medical Association, 37 (May 26, 1962), 676-79.

The Joint Study Committee in Continuing Medical Education was
organized in 1961 as a result of widespread recognition of the
need for coordination and leadership in the field of continuing
education for physicians. The American Medical Association
invited other major medical associations to send representatives to a meeting "to consider the formation, under the
sponsorship of major medical organizations, of a national
agency to further continuing medical education." A committee
was appointed which recommended that a "critical study be
conducted, with a full-time study director, in order that a detailed proposal might be submitted to the cooperating organizations for approval." Dr. Dryer was chosen the Study Director.
One year after the appointment, the commitee presented its
report, Lifetime Learning for Physicians, written by Dr. Dryer.

The summary covers the following topics: assumptions on which
the report was based; the objectives, curriculum and evulation
procedures of a "university without walls"; curriculum and
teaching materials; presentation and distribution system;

423

elective participation; self evaluation; international extension; and organizational structure.

D-30. Dubin, Robert and Taveggia, Thomas C. The Teaching-Learning Paradox: A Comparative Analysis of College Teaching Methods. Eugene, Oregon: Center for the Advanced Study of Educational Administration, University of Oregon, 1968.

Forty years of educational research has shown that there is no difference between various methods of instruction as measured by final exam scores (which measure course content mastery). Textbooks and reading materials may be the commonality between methods. Computer Assisted Instruction (CAI) may be cheaper in the long run and produce a better cost-benefit ratio than other methods. Fewer instructors are needed; there is no time or place limit. CAI courses can be available 24 hours a day at any location where there is a data transmission terminal hookup.

D-31. Dubin, Samuel S., and others. Educational Needs of Managers and Supervisors in Cities, Boroughs and Townships in Pennsylvania. University Park, Pa.: Pennsylvania State University, 1968.

This study was undertaken by the Department of Planning Studies, Continuing Education, the Pennsylvania State University 1) to determine the professional education needs of managers in municipalities and supervisors in cities in Pennsylvania, 2) to suggest methods meeting these needs, and 3) to indicate the role of colleges and universities in helping to meet these needs. Recommendations are made for educational institutions, supervisors, and for professional associations.

Fifty per cent of all the managers answering the questionnaire felt that they "should have" courses in: Management Development, Public Relations and Public Reporting; Effective Communication in the Organization; and Budget Administration. On the other hand, the managers thought that their supervisors should have training in subjects such as Effective Utilization of Manpower Resources, Improved Decision-Making with Individuals, Creativity and Innovation, Supervisory Training and Development. A detailed statement on the methodology and the construction of the questionnaire used as well as a sample of the questionnaire is included in the report. It would serve as a model for surveys for other professional groups regarding needs in continuing education.

D-32. Dubin, Samuel S., and others.   Highlights of a Study on Managerial
and Supervisory Educational Needs of Business and Industry
in Pennsylvania. University Park, Pa.: Pennsylvania State
University, 1968.

After outlining eight reasons for the need of continuing education in management and supervision, the authors report on the
needs of those answering the questionnaire in Top Management,
Middle Management, and First-Line Supervision. Communication in the Organization was indicated as most needed by top
management; second for middle management; and third for
first-line supervisors. Management Development was ranked
second by top management; first by middle management; and
third for those supervised by middle management. Effective
Speaking and Written Communication both ranked within the
first six courses for all three groups. Based on the study, the
authors make five curriculum recommendations for the
university; eight for business and industry, as well as suggestions for the individual manager and supervisor, and for professional associations.

D-33. Dubin, Samuel S., and others. "Keeping Managers and Supervisors
in Local Government Up-to-Date." Public Administration
Review, 29 (May-June, 1969), 294-298.

This is a summary article reporting on the findings of the
study entitled "Educational Needs of Managers and Supervisors
in Cities, Boroughs, and Townships in Pennsylvania." Their
major recommendation, based on the fact that managers and
supervisors do want to keep up-to-date in order to handle their
increasingly complex jobs, was that educational institt ions
should be encouraged to offer courses identified by managers
and supervisors in municipalities as most needed, at locations
convenient to municipal employees. As the respondents indicated a substantial willingness to enroll in noncredit courses
as well as credit courses, it was further recommended that
universities should offer noncredit courses, seminars, and
workshops designed specifically to meet the needs of the
managers and supervisors in local government.

D-34. Dubin, Samuel S., and others. Research Report of Managerial and
Supervisory Educational Needs of Business and Industry in
Pennsylvania. University Park, Pa.: Pennsylvania State
University, 1967.

D-35. Dubin, Samuel S., and others. Survey Report of Managerial and Supervisory Needs of Business and Industry in Pennsylvania. University Park, Pa.: Pennsylvania State University, 1967.

D-36. Dubin, Samuel S., and Marlow, H. LeRoy. Continuing Professional Educational Needs of Hospital Administrators: A Survey of Pennsylvania Hospitals. Hospital Educational Research Report H-54. University Park, Pa.: Pennsylvania State University, 1965.

D-37. Dubin, Samuel S., and Marlow, H. LeRoy. Continuing Professional Educational Needs of Supervisory Personnel in the Nursing Service and Nursing Education: A Survey of Pennsylvania Hospitals. Hospital Educational Research Report H-55. University Park, Pa: Pennsylvania State University, 1965.

D-38. Dubin, Samuel S., and Marlow, H. LeRoy. The Determination and Measurement of Supervisory Training Needs of Hospital Personnel: A Survey of Pennsylvania Hospitals. University Park, Pa.: Pennsylvania State University, 1965.

D-39. Dubin, Samuel S., and Marlow, H. LeRoy. Continuing Professional Education for Engineers in Pennsylvania. University Park, Pa.: Pennsylvania State University, 1965.

This report defines continuing education as that education which is needed by the professionally employed engineer as perceived by him or his employer to enhance his total job competence.

This series of studies by Dubin and his associates provide models that can be helpful for other professional groups. Many of them contain the actual instruments used to obtain the data.

D-40. Du Bois, Edward A. C. The Case for Employee Education. New York: American Management Association, 1967.

D-41. Duncan, Margaret. "Making the Special Librarian Special: The Case for Continuing Education," California Librarian, 30 (July, 1969), 191-198.

The forms continuing education may take are many, ranging from self-instruction to programs leading to a doctorate.

Instruction that is part of a well thought out program of
inservice education will be mo re effective in increasing the
value of a librarian to his library. A program of internship
could be adapted to almost any special library with excellent
results.

D-42. Dunnette, Marvin D. Managerial Effectiveness. New York: McGraw-
Hill Book Company, 1969.

This book is rated by Gellerman as "the keenest analysis of
what's wrong with current systems of managerial performance."

D-43. Dutton, Donnie. "Reception of the Interpersonal Relations Series of
the Continuing Education Project for Public Health Workers in
North Carolina." Birmingham, Ala.: American Public Health
Association, Southern Branch, 1968. (ED 044 640.)

D-44. Dutton, Donnie, and others. "Continuing Education in Alabama After
One Year. Montgomery, Ala.: Alabama State Department of
Public Health, 1968. (ED 044 646.)

D-45. Dutton, Donnie. An Evaluation of Leadership Training in Louisiana.
Birmingham, Ala.: American Public Health Association,
Southern Branch, 1968. (ED 044 647.)

D-46. Dutton, Donnie, and Hering, Frederick W. Reactions from Alabama
Public Health Workers on a Demonstration Continuing Education
Project. Birmingham, Ala.: American Public Health
Association, Southern Branch, 1968. (ED 045 895.)

D-47. Dutton, Donnie. Leadership Training for Public Health Workers
in North Carolina: An Evaluative Study. Birmingham, Ala.:
American Public Health Association, Southern Branch, 1968.
(ED 044 648.)

D-48. Dutton, Donnie. Effect of the Interpersonal Relations Series of the
Continuing Education Project on Inducing Attitudinal and
Behavioral Changes among Public Health Workers in North
Carolina. Birmingham, Ala.: American Public Health
Association, Southern Branch, 1969. (ED 044 650.)

D-49. Dutton, Donnie, and Hering, Frederick W. Assessment of Work-
shops on Principles of Public Health Law and Legal Tools for
Effective Health Administration. Birmingham, Ala.:
American Public Health Association, Southern Branch, 1969.
(ED 045 896.)

427

D-50. Dutton, Donnie and Edwards, Virgil. Group Dynamics and Public Health. Nashville: Tennessee State Department of Health, 1970. (ED 045 897.)

> These eight reports evaluate a series of continuing education workshops held for public health workers in Baltimore, Maryland, and in the states of North Carolina, Alabama, Tennessee, and Florida.

D-51. Dougherty, Nathan. "Foundation for Our Future, 75 Years of Progress: American Society for Engineering Education." Journal of Engineering Education, 58 (May 1968), 1019-1031.

428

E-1.   Edelfelt, Roy A. Redesigning the Education Profession. Washington,
        D.C.: National Education Association, 1969. 17 pp.

        The author discusses the current inadequacies of the education
        profession in providing for the kind and quality of services required
        in schools and for the growth and development of the profession.
        He speaks to the problems of educational manpower, organization
        of schools, and governance of the profession. His conclusion sug-
        gests questions concerning priority and strategy which still must
        be answered by teachers--before someone else answers for them.

E-2.   Edelfelt, Roy A. "The Reform of Education and Teacher Education:
        A Complex Task," Journal of Teacher Education,
        (Summer, 1972),

        Dr. Edelfelt, a member of the staff of the Division of Instruc-
        tion and Professional Development, National Education Associa-
        tion, states that if "renewal centers" ("the new panacea being
        proposed ...for inservice teacher education [by the U. S.
        Office of Education]) are to be effective, pervasive reforms in
        education and teacher education will need to accompany the
        establishment of such centers."

        The renewal center (or teacher center, or teacher education
        school) is pictured in a setting adjacent to schools where the
        education of teachers takes place concurrently with the education
        of children, schools in which the community, the school, and
        the college have reached some mutual agreements (contracts)
        about common and individual purposes. He argues that "renewal
        centers for teachers cannot succeed if they are not by the
        teacher, of the teacher, and with the teacher. Teachers are
        tired of being done to, of having innovation imposed, of being
        led or pushed into in-service training. They are suspicious
        and resentful from too many experiences with educational per-
        sonnel who don't teach, who devise schemes and content with
        little teacher input that teachers are expected to embrace and
        apply.... The time is right to emphasize intrinsic motivation,
        and this must begin with teachers working on their own problems,
        indicating their own needs.... The plans or guidelines developed
        for teacher renewal centers must provide for teachers a central
        role in the governance of such centers." He lists   six
        provisions that should be included in the governance of such
        centers.

                                    429

He closes with an Epilogue: "Whatever is done with teachers and students, whatever new roles are developed, our primary goal is to free and nurture the individual in his growth, our top priority is to foster self-fulfillment, our major dream is to help every man gain an awareness of himself. Teachers, though grounded in fact and based in science, must still lean hardest on that element of being we call artistry. That is the pivotal function in teaching, and I submit that any plan for teaching or learning which does not value artistry above mechanism and system will become humdrum and banal."

E-3. Egger, Rowland A. "Criteria that Should Inform a Doctrine of Mid-Career Education." (Paper prepared for a conference on university education for mid-career government officials, February 11-12, 1966.) Princeton, N.J.: Princeton University, Woodrow Wilson School of Public and International Affairs, 1966. (ED 016 898.)

As mid-career management and public affairs education for Federal civil servants require an accepted set of rules and standards for making judgments relating to the intellectual improvement of career civil servants who qualify for higher positions, criteria are needed which indicate changes achieved in individuals, purposes served by the educational experience, and the actual and potential suitability of a given educational setting. Considering the abilities and limitations of the average mid-career candidate and the liberal arts standard that dominates university graduate education, the author argues that the underlying issue is really this -- whether preparation for management and public affairs is to be organized as integral, professional graduate education with its own content and methodology, or whether there can be an instructional apparatus which is professional for some students, semiprofessional for others, and nonprofessional for still other students and for most of the faculty.

E-4. Eisele, C. Wesley. "The Medical Audit in Continuing Education," Journal of Medical Education, 44 (April, 1969), 263-265.

Eisele suggests the internal medical audit as a tool for meeting the criteria of continuing medical education. Its advantages are that it is continuous, community and hospital based, and directly related to the physician's day-to-day activities in the care of his patients.

E-5. Engineers' Council for Professional Development. 35th Annual
          Report--1966-1967. New York: Engineers' Council for
          Professional Development, 1967.

E-6. Evaluation and Measurement Newsletter, No. 11, May 1971. Toronto:
          Ontario Institute for Studies in Education, Department of Measure-
          ment and Evaluation, 1971.

          The topic of this issue is accountability. Included are articles
      by Henry S. Dyer, "Toward Objective Criteria for Accountability,"
      and D.W. Robinson, "Accountability for Whom? For What?"

E-7. Evans, Richard I. and Leppman, Peter K. Resistance to Innovation
          in Higher Education. San Francisco: Jossey-Bass, 1967.

          The authors include an extensive bibliography on the problems
      of introducing innovation.

E-8. Eyman, David H., comp. "A Checklist of Dissertation Titles for
          Doctorates Granted by Library Schools through December, 1972,"
          Ann Arbor, 1973. (Mimeographed.)

F-1. Faegre, Christopher L., and others. Analysis and Evaluation of
Present and Future Multi-Media Needs in Higher Education.
Silver Spring, Md.: Communication Research Program,
American Institutes for Research, 1968. (ED 024 351.)

A decision has to be reached as to: 1) whether proposed media
systems are justified in terms of potential benefits for the
investment required and 2) the degree to which presently
operating media systems should receive continued funding and
support. The purpose of this paper is to help the educator
develop a strategy for media evaluation and selection.

The evaluation of a proposed or presently operating media
system is a key phase of the media system planning process.
This evaluation requires a means for systematically and
objectively collecting data about the media system. FIELD
was developed and tested and revised to provide an instrument
for data collection which can be administered, summarized
and interpreted on-site by the institution performing the self-
evaluation. (FIELD=Field Instrument for Evaluation of
Learning Devices). The FIELD instrument is included.

F-2. Fahs, Ivan J., and Miller, Winston R. "Continuing Medical Education and Educational Television," Journal of Medical
Education, 45 (August, 1970), 578-587.

The authors describe progress that has been made in producing
programs which are televised over open-circuit channels to
aid physicians in becoming better practitioners.

F-3. Fancher, Evelyn P. and Hudson, Earline. "Continuing Education
Programs for Librarians in Tennessee -- A Survey,"
Tennessee Librarian, 24 (Summer, 1972), 125-126.

The authors, noting that the February, 1972, listing of continuing education programs published in American Libraries had no
entries from Tennessee, carried out a survey to find out the
unreported status of continuing education in that state. They
discovered that many institutions were providing opportunities
and that librarians were interested in further opportunities
in staff development and continuing education. Their recommendation was a clearing house of opportunities available in
the state.

432

F-4.   Fast, Elizabeth T. "The Supervisor's Section," School Libraries,
        19 (Spring, 1970), 47-48.

        Final results of the survey of school library media supervisors
        indicates that there is a real need for programs to train new
        supervisors and to update the knowledge of experienced super-
        visors. Most interest was shown in short term workshops,
        especially on administration.

F-5.   Felter, Jacqueline W. "Continuing Education for Medical Librarian-
        ship: A Symposium -- Informal Study," Bulletin of the Medical
        Library Association, 48, (October, 1960), 420-23.

        Planning and pursuing a solitary reading program takes a
        measure of self-discipline. Whatever the means of informal
        study, the important thing is that there must be a deeply felt
        need and desire for it, and time must be deliberately set aside
        for it.

F-6.   Ferguson, Lawrence L. "Better Management of Managers' Careers,"
        Harvard Business Review, 46 (March-April, 1966), 139-153.

        A plea for bringing scientific knowledge and methodology into
        the selection, development, and promotion programs of organi-
        zations. Gives documentation that major companies are collect-
        ing, analyzing, applying and testing new kinds of information
        and procedures which may help them to do a better job of pre-
        dicting the future growth of managers. It describes the follow-
        ing requirements for a system to develop scientific procedures
        for a long-range personnel research program: 1) need for date
        that will be predictive of further growth of an individual.
        Growth is defined as "being able to handle specific responsi-
        bilities of greater scope and accountability"; 2) knowledge in
        behavioral terms of what permanent demands will be in the
        future in terms of organizational plans; 3) a system for storing
        and processing comprehensive data on personal attributes and
        nature of tasks, and 4) a feedback-and-research system for
        analysis and evaluatiom of the managerial growth process.

F-7.   Ferretti, Fred. "Educational Television," American Libraries, 3
        (April, 1972), 336-384.

        The author examines educational television both for its pro-
        gramming in this past decade and its promise in the 1970's.
        A 110 item filmography with subject index is included.

F-8. Finn, Melvin. "Employment Service Management Development, "
      Employment Service Review, 3, (October, 1966), 19-22.

      "For the past several years the Bureau of Employment
      Security has sponsored both in-service and out-service train-
      ing for management personnel to bring a greater depth of
      understanding of the changing role of the Employment Service."
      Finn reports that this objective is achieved most effectively
      by involving persons from universities in their development
      programs at all levels. Details are given of present and past
      programs.

F-9. Fleisher, Eugene. "Systems for Individual Study: Decks, Cassettes,
      Dials or Buffers?" Library Journal, 96 (February, 1971),
      695-698.

F-10. Flexner, Abraham. "Is Social Work a Profession?" School and
      Society, 1 (June 26, 1915), 901-911.

      Probably the most comprehensive definition of a profession was
      given by Flexner at the National Conference of Charities and
      Correction in 1915. He characterized a profession as: 1)
      basically intellectual, carrying with it great personal responsi-
      bility; 2)learned, being based on great knowledge and not
      merely routine; 3) practical, rather than academic or theoret-
      ical; 4) technical in that its technique can be taught, which is the
      basis of professional education; 5) well organized internally;
      6) altruistic, professional viewing himself as working for some
      aspect of the good of society.

      Flexner also pointed out that every profession must have a
      journal which provides more than just news, propaganda, and
      agitation:

          ...it is important to remember that we do not thus rise
          above the journalistic to the scientific or professional level.
          A profession must find a dignified and critical means of
          expressing itself in the form of a periodical which shall
          describe in careful terms whatever work is in progress;
          and it must from time to time register its more impressive
          performances in a literature of growing solidity and variety.
          To some extent the evolution...towards professional status
          can be measured by the quality of publication put forth in
          its name.

F-11. Florida State University. Urban Research Center. An Annual
Report of the Urban Internship Program–Urban Extension
Service conducted by Florida State University's Urban Research
Center during the 1966–67 Fiscal Year. Titusville, Fla.:
Florida State University, 1968. (ED 030 020.)

Florida State University's Urban Research Center serves a
rapidly growing seven county area in east Central Florida.
Under Title I of the Higher Education Act, the Center increased
its service through a uniquely designed research–education
program for public administrators. The purpose was to
identify and alleviate community problems. The 2,000 participants included mayors, county and city commissioners, fire
chiefs, businessmen, and educators. A major objective was to
stimulate thinking and action about the desirability of continuing
education of political leaders. A survey was made of educational interest among public officials. Information was spread
through the mass media and a newsletter, and conferences on
urban exploration, communications, and recreational facilities
were held.

F-12. Foecke, Harold A. "Effective Teaching and the Educational System,"
The Journal of Engineering Education, 58 (October, 1967),
117–121.

Foecke, Dean of Engineering at Gonzaga University, discusses
effective teaching in relation to the entire educational enterprise.
The first section describes the interaction of the essential
elements of any education system. The author then narrows
the discussion to roles of the engineering teacher within the
system of engineering education in this country. Next he
focuses attention on modes and criteria of effective teaching.
In this latter section he discusses the art of facilitating learning;
knowledge and technology of evaluation; effectiveness in minor
roles. "As the various roles of the teacher are distinct, so
too there are distinct ways of developing effectiveness in the
discharge of these roles. And, in each case, not only do the
methods of discerning effectiveness differ, but distressingly
little progress has been made in devising the procedures and
criteria for determining their effectiveness." The concluding
section of the article deals with relevant educational research
and development.

F-13. Ford, Robert N. Motivation Through the Work Itself. New York: American Management Association, 1969.

> The author presents a description of AT&T's experience with job enrichment.

F-14. Foulkes, F. K. Creating More Meaningful Work. New York: American Management Association, 1969.

> The author, a professor at Harvard, demonstrates the capability of motivated groups of workers to set their own goals. When members of a group are ready to establish their own criteria and goals, they often exceed the goals that have previously been selected by their supervisors.

F-15. Fox, Marian L. "A Nursing Inservice Education Program: Policy of Operation," The Journal of Continuing Education in Nursing, 1 (November-December, 1970), 11-15.

> The author stresses the importance of a written "Policy of Operation," giving statement of purpose and objectives of the Inservice Education Program, and spelling out clearly defined policies to guide, direct, and control the range of program activities and responsibilities. It should, she continues, be formulated by the Director of Nursing Service and approved by the Hospital Administrator.
>
> A Policy of Operation is defined as a statement of intent directing the course of action to be followed in achieving the Inservice Education Program goals (which need to be achievable and realistic). The policy should specify why an inservice education program has been established; what courses and programs will be offered; who is to receive pre- and post-employment orientation, on the job training and continuing education instruction; and what instructional theories and principles will be applied. The author sets up some criteria to use in formulation of the policy statement. The article concludes with a discussion of evaluation -- its purpose, methods, and expected results.

F-16. Frasher, Richard D. "An Appraisal of the Status and Future of the Continuing Education (Non-Credit) for Engineers in the United States." (Unpublished Master's thesis, Ohio State University, Columbus, 1969)

This Master's thesis gives a history of the Joint Advisory Committee on Continuing Engineering studies and concludes that continuing education for engineers must reach out to the individual at his location; it must answer his and his employer's needs and be at a level comparable to those needs. Any continuing engineering educational program needs to be flexible enough to meet and answer the needs of graduate engineers and their employers. He recommends that the associations and societies in the engineering profession assume responsibility for coordinating activities between the educational institutions and the employers. The universities would serve as centers of expertise (advisers and consultants) ready to supply knowledge, teachers, teaching aids and facilities. Industry would support the joint continuing education developed and minimize the further development of in-house programs. Programs from associations, universities, and industries should be planned jointly to produce quality programs and criteria of evaluation for the programs developed should be provided.

F-17. Frasure, Kenneth. "In-Service Role of Professors of Educational Administration -- A National View." Paper presented to an interest group at the National Conference of Professors of Educational Administration in August, 1966. (Mimeographed)

The author, Professor of Education, School of Education, State University of New York, describes in some detail a national study he had conducted to answer the question of how professors might best serve practicing administrators. A postcard questionnaire was sent to administrators and professors. "In general, such items as reading the literature, professors taking over administrative posts, studying theory and having administrators teach courses did not have strong appeal for respondents. On the other hand cooperative endeavors including the direct discussion of administrative practices, problems and organization rated high priority in total scores among both professors and superintendents in the national study."

F-18. Frasure, Kenneth. Maturing Opportunities for In-Service Education of Educational Administrators. Albany, New York: Council for Administrative Leadership, 1967.

The author is alarmed that the continuing needs of educational administrators are largely ignored. From earlier surveys

the author feels that less traditional forms of inservice education should be used with administrators. He advocates and
describes two: 1) use of simulation in continuing education
programs, and 2) a staff college for education leaders in each
state or section of the United States. He outlines these essential
elements of the staff college concept: objectives, participants,
program, procedures, staff, finance, and facilities.

F-19. Frasure, Kenneth. "Perspectives Concerning In-Service Education
for Educational Administrators." Albany, N.Y.: Council for
Administrative Leadership, 1966. (Mimeographed)

The author conducted a study in New York State of ways of helping educational administrators by having both administrators
and education professors respond to the question "How professors
might best serve practicing administrators?" Both the professors and asministrators were in general agreement as to the
rank order of twenty items submitted to them. In the total
ratings, the items that included conferences and the exchange
of ideas were more favored than were items based upon research and theory.

"The professors tended to rate as more important than did
the superintendents such items as meetings of administrators
from the same school system, involving practicing administrators in research, problems of a practical nature, studying the
application of administratory theory to situations, and work
with theoretical constructs based on administrative theory. On
the other hand, the superintendents placed a higher rating than
did the professors on issuing bulletins of information, providing
a personnel file of employable young administrators, developing
an area administrative resource and consultant list and on
individual consultant services for administrators. Items
dealing with reading and information for the superintendents
were given a low rating by superintendents."

F-20. Frasure, Kenneth. Your Leadership Development Program. Paper
presented at the Annual Conference at the American Association
of School Administrators. Atlantic City, N. J.: February,
1968. (ED 021 330.)

Dr. Frasure reports on a national study which compared the
agreement and disagreement found through a national survey of
the activities that administrators believed would be helpful to

them as provided by professors of education in universities.
Upon this background study he now summarizes the understandings, knowledge, and skills that should be emphasized in
programs of leadership development and suggests that a possible organization form for meeting the needs of practicing
administrators might be a staff college in each state. He
concludes his address with emphasis upon the fact that no
single agency can make the thorough massive frontal attack
necessary for marshalling the resources available in the
area of continuing education today. A fast approach based
on coordination of national, state and local forces is needed
to consider and develop the continuing education of administrators. As a background for such effort he states that
agreement must be reached on: 1) the group or groups to be
served; 2) the nature of the needs of these groups; 3) the
kinds of curriculum that are needed; 4) the methods that
should be used; 5) the resources that are available; 6) the
organizational forms and patterns that would serve best;
7) the means of evaluating the success of the effort.

F-21. Frenckner, T. Paulsson, "Development of Operational Manage-
        ment Methods: What Does it Mean for the Education of
        Managers?" International Social Science Journal, 20
        (1968), 29-34.

        The development of management training should include
        coordination so that common goals of specialists with different
        educational backgrounds can be utilized. It is also important
        to develop a common operational language; a managerial dis-
        cipline based on decision-theory approach; a systems
        approach.

        The author states the belief that for the continuous improvement
        of management it seems necessary for a large part of all
        management education to be devoted to the learning process
        itself.

F-22. Fry, Ray M. "Commitment to Change," Missouri Library Associa-
        tion Quarterly, 30 (March, 1969), 58-64.

        Significant change in the library profession is necessary and
        inevitable. This article discusses a few of the federal programs
        which have the greatest potential for change: the training and
        retraining programs under Title II-B of the Higher Education

Act of 1965, the research program under the same Act, and
the interlibrary cooperation programs under the Library
Services and Construction Act.

F-23. Fryden, F. N. "Post-Master's Degree Programs in the Accredited
U. S. Library Schools," Library Quarterly, 39 (July, 1969),
233-244.

The library schools' formal Post-MLS programs for continuing
education as they existed in 11 accredited library schools in
1968 were surveyed by Fryden. On the basis of his research,
he raised some pertinent and troubling questions, and concluded with the practical suggestion that other occupational
groups be examined to see what they did to promote continuing
education beyond the first professional degree.

G-1. Gagné, Robert M. "The Analysis of Instructional Objectives for the Design of Instruction," In: <u>Teaching Machines and Programmed Learning II</u>. Washington, D. C.: National Education Association, 1965.

G-2. Gagné, Robert M. <u>The Conditions of Learning</u>. New York: Holt, Rinehart and Winston, 1965.

According to research done by Briggs and others (1967) for each behavioral objective stated for a course or unit of a course, the next step is to classify the objective in terms of the type of learning involved. Gagné offers ways of categorizing the types of learning involved. The categories outlined by Gagné in this work appear to be the most promising of possible alternatives. The eight types of learning specified by the author would seem to offer the best set of categories which are defined in terms of different sets of conditions of learning. These are: signal learning, stimulus-response learning, chaining verbal association, multiple discrimination, concepts, principles, and problem solving.

G-3. Gagné, Robert M. "Learning Decisions in Education." in <u>Conditions of Learning</u>. New York: Holt, Rinehart and Winston, 1965, 237-266.

The concept of an educational system as an arrangement of people and conditions whose purpose is to bring about learning is introduced. The following areas of decisions which affect the function of an educational system are discussed: learning objectives; the structure of knowledge to be learned; motivation; conditions for learning; the transferability of knowledge and assessment. There are 12 references.

G-4. Gagné, Robert M. "Learning Theory, Educational Media, and Individualized Instruction." A paper presented at a Faculty Seminar, Bucknell University, November 16-17, 1967. (Mimeographed.)

Gagné concluded his presentation by making the following generalizations concerning the use of media for instruction. "They are not 'the answers,' but merely the basis for further investigation of the uses of media."

441

1) No single medium is likely to have properties that make it best for all purposes. There is, so far as we know, no special magic in any particular medium.

2) The most important signal criterion for a choice of medium is often the nature of the learning task itself--that is, the objective of instruction. . . .

3) When one considers the six functions of instruction (gaining and controlling attention, stimulating recall, guiding the learning, providing feedback, arranging for remembering, and assessing outcomes) it is evident that any given medium may perform one of these functions best . . . . That is to say, the precise answer to the question of "which medium" is not to be found by matching courses with media, or even topics with media, but rather in matching specific instructional functions with media.

4) It may be that the most striking effects of instructional planning are to be sought in various combinations of media, where each may perform a particular function best. . . . What it means . . . is that any given medium might be used alternately with others over relatively short periods of instructional time.

G-5. Gagné, Robert M. "Military Training and Principles of Learning," American Psychologist, 17 (February, 1962), 83-91.

This is the now classic paper in which Gagné first made the reasonable assumption that total performance can be analyzed into a set of component tasks that are relatively distinct from each other and that proficiency of task components is what determines total performance. Based on these assumptions Gagné formulates the basic concepts of training design to be: a) identifying the task components that make up the desired performance; b) incorporating these component tasks into a training program; c) arranging the learning of the components in an optimal sequence for transfer to total performance. He places primary emphasis on what is to be learned and the substantive content of training or development experience. After these important components have been met, then attention can be turned to other matters such as specific techniques to be used. He considered so-called "learning principles" as secondary in importance to the considerations cited above.

In summing up his case for the position that task analysis has everything to do with training, he states: "If I were faced with the problem of improving training, I should not look for much help from the well-known learning principles like reinforcement, distribution of practice, response familiarity, and so on. I should look instead at the technique of task analysis, and at the principles of component task achievement, intratask transfer, and the sequency of subtask learning to find those ideas of greatest usefulness in the design of effective training. Someday I hope that even the laboratory learning psychologist will know more about these principles.

In reviewing this paper, Campbell states: "Unfortunately Gagné's statement has stimulated very little activity among people interested in organizational training and development. It stands in a state of suspended animation. What follows is a mere pittance of what there should be. " [John P. Campbell, "Personnel Training and Development, " Annual Review of Psychology, 20 (April, 1971) 567.]

G-6. Gagné, Robert M. (ed.) Psychological Principles in System Development. New York: Holt, Rinehart and Winston, 1962.

The procedures for developing systems and psychological principles of these procedures are described and explained. Each chapter describes techniques employed at a stage of development, gives examples, and discusses the relationships between the techniques and their psychology. Each chapter has a reference list; the entire book is indexed.

This book marks the first which systematically deals with the conception of the application of psychological principles to the invention, development, and use of complex man-machine systems. In many ways the presentation might be called a theory of psychotechnology.

G-7. Gagné, Robert M. "A System Approach to Adult Learning. " In: Wientge, K. W. and others (eds.). Psychological Research in Classroom Learning. St. Louis: Washington University, 1967, 6-21.

G-8. Gagné, Robert M., Bolles, R. C. "A Review of Factors in Learning Efficiency. " In: Galanter, E. (ed.). Automated Teaching. New York: John Wiley & Sons, Inc. 1959.

G-9. Gagné, Robert M. and Paradise, Noel E. "Abilities and Learning Sets in Knowledge Acquisition," Psychological Monographs: General and Applied. 75:14. Washington, D. C.: American Psychological Association, 1961.

G-10. Gamble, Connolly C. Continuing Education and the Church's Ministry: A Bibiliographic Survey. Richmond, Virginia, Union Theological Seminary, 1967. (ED 029 258.)

> A review of books, articles, papers, and brochures from the period 1948-67 that deal with, or are relavant to, the continuing education of clergymen. In the first section, problems with personal faith, the Ministry of the Church, Ministerial Roles and tasks, and professional growth and learning are considered, together with pressures on the laity more fully in mission and to understand technological and social change, relationships of religion and the Churches to society, and the changing requirements of mission. Student decision and motivation, student recruitment and selection, personnel practices, clergy income, and issues and innovation in seminary training and subsequent continuing education are also examined. Conclusions and recommendations are set forth with particular reference to the United Presbyterian Church. The document includes 21 references and a list of residential programs.

G-11. Gamble, Connolly C. Continuing Education for Ministry and Personnel, and Evaluation. Richmond, Virginia, Union Theological Seminary, 1968. (ED 029 247.)

> This 1968 national survey on ministerial continuing education dealt with educational leadership in the United States, analyzed participation, and assembled information on evaluation. Educators were asked about role concepts, years of service, training and prior experience, proportion of time devoted to continuing education, numbers of persons devoting major time to ministerial continuing education, chief problems, and their own continuing education. Fiscal policies, criteria for selecting participants and developing programs, provisi ons for educational counseling, denominational strategies, and extradenominational participation were investigated. Respondents also indicated specific objectives, evaluation techniques, personal preferences among programs, programs with the most educational value, popular types of programs, and lessons gained from experience. (Twelve references are included.)

444

G-12. Gamble, Connolly C., Jr. "Continuing Education in Professional
Associations: Society for the Advancement of Continuing Educa-
tion for Ministry." Paper presented at a Mini-Workshop on
Continuing Education sponsored by the Standing Committee on
Continuing Library Education of the Association of American
Library Schools during the Annual Meeting of the Association,
Shoreham Hotel, Washington, D.C., January 28, 1973.
(Transcription of tape of the presentation.)

Society for the Advancement of Continuing Education for
Ministry (SACEM) came into being as a result of four years of
national meetings of people engaged in continuing education for
ministry. Gamble pointed particular attention to the last word,
"ministry"; the organization is not restricted to an ordained
clerical group; rather it is a resource for helping the people
of the churches, Protestant, Catholic, Jewish, to find the
resources for lifelong learning that will enable them to become
more competent for life whether they are mechanical engineers,
clergymen, or people engaged in other forms of the ministry.

In SACEM, unlike some other continuing education efforts,
people in this movement are concerned about the person of
the learner as well as the information and updating and other
forms of learning with which the persons are involved. The
organization came into being in 1967 and is deliberately
broader than people who are professionally engaged in continuing education.

The organization has a membership of 300, and for most of
the people involved continuing education represents a second
assignment. This means that continuing education for ministry
across this country and Canada is a sideline operation. Out of
300 theological seminaries across the country there are only
10 persons who have continuing education as a primary
assignment.

During its 6 years of existence, SACEM has held an annual conference each year, four days in length. Gamble said in this
regard: "We regard this as a form of training in continuing
education for our members. We expose our own programs as
based in colleges, conference centers, to the scrutiny and
critique of our peers in order to share information and gain
insight into better ways to operate our programs of continuing
education. We draw on people from a number of different

G-12 (cont.)
professions to see what common features of continuing education
exist, and what the particular concerns of people engaged in
continuing education for ministry are. "

Gamble reported that the most enthusiastic supporters of continuing education for ministry are the laymen. SACEM, he explained, is not at the grass roots level. Rather it seeks to
work with those preparing and planning programs of continuing
education, helping them to become more skillful, in the design
and operation of those programs.

"The fulfillments that come with continuing education are inferior to the individual, difficult to identify, and seldom
expressed in terms of financial reward or better career
opportunities. "

Gamble reported that there is another group -- the Academy of
Parish Clergy, now 4 years old -- which was also spun off by
the National Council of Churches, Department of Ministry.
This group is an academy of people who are engaged in leader-
ship of congregations in the religious groups of the United
States.

Gamble saw that one of the most encouraging signs was the
recognition on the part of congregations as the primary funding
agencies for the minister's continuing education. More and
more churches when a call is issued to a pastor include a provision for the continuing education of the pastor as a part of
the call. Dollars are designated as part of the church budget,
and time is alloted to be available for only continuing professional development. "This is generating possibilities that did
not exist two or three years ago. "

In the discussion that followed on how money for continuing
education is funded, Gamble answered: "It is not a personal
expenditure on the part of the minister, it is a professional
expense in the same way the car allowances are a professional
expense. But many churches find it difficult to distinguish
these differences. "

G-13. Gardner, John W. "Agenda for the Colleges and Universities,"
In: Eurich, Alvin, ed. Campus: 1980. New York: Delacorte
1968.

One item that Gardner puts on the agenda is that academic
institutions must give more thought to continuing education and
off-campus instruction. "We have abandoned the idea that
education is something which takes place in a block of time
between six and eighteen (or twenty-two) years of age. It is
lifelong. We have abandoned the idea that education is something that can occur only in a classroom. A system of education suited to modern needs and aspirations could not come
into being until these two notions were finally done away with."

He predicts that the continuing education movement will develop
at a rapid pace regardless of what colleges and universities do
about it, but he asserts his belief that the colleges and universities should provide intellectual leadership with respect to
such education, "and that depends on their own creative activity
in this field. If they ignore it, the movement will pass them by
and the leadership will go out of their hands. If that happens,
I think they will have reason to regret it."

He predicts that by 1980 it may well become the national pattern
for millions of people whose skills need to be updated and expanded to enroll part-time in higher education while holding
full-time jobs in business, industry and government.

G-14. Gardner, John W. Excellence: Can We be Equal and Excellent, Too?
New York: Harper and Row, 1961.

G-15. Gardner, John W. "Participant Training" and "Personnel and
Training," In: AID and the Universities. New York: Education and World Affairs Council, 1963, Chapters 3 and 6.

Guidelines used by universities in continuing education for
foreign government personnel are presented. These are useful for academic personnel considering continuing education
for public administrators.

G-16. Gardner, John. Self-Renewal: The Individual and the Innovative Society. New York: Harper and Row, 1964.

This book has become a recent classic, which although not primarily written for a management audience, has much in it of value for them. Managers and personnel administrators are too often preoccupied with policies, procedures and rules which may stifle the creative and the innovative opportunities for self-renewal which an innovative society or organization requires. Gardner observes: "Someone has said that the last act of a dying organization is to get out a new and enlarged edition of the rule book." He warns against managerial techniques becoming the means of "processing" human beings. He believes firmly that the impact of the organization on the individual requires continued study and research. If the individual has a commitment to self-renewal, Gardner believes the organization can remove some of the obstacles and even provide the opportunities, but the emphasis remains on the self. "The ultimate goal is to shift to the individual the burden of pursuing his own education." Further: "In a society capable of renewal, men not only welcome the future and the changes that it may bring but believe that they will have a hand in shaping that future." Not all people are creative, but there are many kinds of creativity, and many more individuals could realize creative potential which would contribute to the success of an organization if the roadblocks were removed. In summary, if the educational system prepares the individual for an accelerating rate of change, and the business organization gives him opportunities to gain versatility and responsibility in a variety of jobs and assignment situations, that individual will not be dragged screaming into the future. He will welcome it.

G-17. Garrison, Guy, ed. Changing Role of State Library Consultants: Report of a Conference Held at Allerton House, Monticello, Illinois, November 26-29, 1967. University of Illinois Graduate School of Library Science, Monograph Series no. 9. Champaign, Ill.: University of Illinois, 1968.

Library consultants attending the conference noted the following special areas in which state agencies should be able to provide consulting services: technical processing, library automation, library laws, personnel administration, budgeting and financial administration, communication techniques, planning assistance

448

G-17 (cont.)
for aid programs, library building planning, collection development, public relations, and interlibrary cooperation.

The discussion groups made six recommendations relating to
the education of State Library personnel:

XI. We recommend that appropriate divisions of the
American Library Association (Library Education
Division and Association of State Libraries) communicate to the U.S. Office of Education and to library
schools the urgent need for institutes for state library
consultants under Title II-B of the Higher Education Act;
we further urge that the U.S. Office of Education give
high priority to funding such programs, particularly
those developed cooperatively to meet the needs of more
than one state.

XII. We recommend formation of a committee (ad hoc if
necessary) to propose topics for, and offer assistance
in, institutes or seminars for state library consultants
under Title II-B of the Higher Education Act.

XIII. We commend and encourage the establishment in
accredited library schools of formal advanced programs
beyond the master's degree which provide opportunity
for specialized preparation for state library consultant
work.

XIV. We urge that state library agencies develop and fund
programs which will allow agency personnel to take advantage of opportunities for continuing education in their
fields of specialization through attendance at short
courses, institutes, and regular academic courses.

XV. We recommend that all state library agencies establish
and maintain lines of communication with library education agencies in their state and region through such
means as joint appointments, dual sponsorship of continuing education programs, and cooperative service
and research projects.

XVI. We recommend that state library agencies and library
schools in geographical areas where suitable organizations already exist (such as the Midwest with its

449

"Midwest State Library Agencies" and its "Library
School Conference Group" under the Committee on
Institutional Cooperation) should jointly formulate long-
range plans for educational programs for library consultants. Such programs should: 1) explore changing
training needs of consultants, 2) plan training programs
for different activities and levels of experience, 3)
include both formal and informal learning experiences,
and 4) suggest ways of recruiting consultants into the
program, 5) identify problems in released time, funding,
and civil service requirements, 6) determine costs of
such programs and find funding methods, and 7) provide
procedures for periodic evaluation and reporting to the
profession.

G-18. Garrison, Lloyd N., and others. "Developing a Model for In-Service
        Education," In: Operation PEP. Symposium on the Application
        of Systems Analysis and Management Techniques to Educational
        Planning in California. (Chapman College, Orange, California,
        June 12-13, 1967.) Burlingame, California: 1967, pp. 101-106.
        (ED 023 181.)

G-19. Gatzke, Herbert K. and Schechter, Daniel S. "The American Hospital
        Association," The Journal of Continuing Education in Nursing,
        2 (March-April, 1971), 32-33.

        The authors describe the continuing education activities of the
        Association and the manner in which a W. K. Kellogg Foundation
        grant of $1.9 million funded the Hospital Continuing Education
        Project. One of the products is Training and Continuing
        Education... which was distributed to each registered hospital
        in the United States and Canada.

G-20. Gaver, Mary V. "The Educational Third Dimension: I. Continuing
        Education to Meet Personalized Criteria of Librarians,"
        Library Trends, 20 (July, 1971), 118-143.

        Gaver reports on her questionnaire to a non-random sample of
        "librarian achievers" to discover what motivates them toward
        continuing education activities; to find out the kinds of continuing
        education that had been most effective with them; and to learn
        what strategies they would recommend to the young professional

450

just starting his or her career. In addition to a thorough analysis of the returns to these questions, the author concludes that
"current efforts of the associations are fragmented, lacking in
continuity, with no culmination but rather a tapering off, and
little of sequential learning result in many cases." Strong
recommendation to the American Library Association to take
a more structured approach, which the author notes, has been
made before by Rothstein and Stone, and is almost made by
Hiatt in the last article of this Library Trends issue on Personnel Development and Continuing Education in Libraries.

G-21. Gaver, Mary. "Is Anyone Listening? Significant Research Studies
for Practicing Librarians," Wilson Library Bulletin, 43
(April, 1969), 764-772.

G-22. Gaver, Mary V. "Library Supervisors and Manpower," ALA
Bulletin, 62 (February, 1968), 141-5.

Library administrators concerned with professional growth
should 1) upgrade the competence of present employees by a
program of continuing education, 2) develop job definitions
and classifications in order to make full use of the professional
staff, 3) restructure the total staff to fit the kind of manpower
available, 4) give attention to self-education in the demanding
administrative task of being a supervisor, 5) work with other
agencies and library groups to gather regular data on the
states' manpower situation.

G-23. Geis, George L. "Premature Instruction," Educational Technology,
(April, 1970), 24-30.

The paper proposes that a decision to design and develop any
instructional system be deferred until six steps are carried out:
1) establishing the need for a consequence; 2) defining the components necessary to produce the consequences; 3) defining the
human "job"; 4) specifying performance criteria; 5) reexamining
the performance environment; 6) considering resources and
constraints. The author suggests that when and what to teach
should be considered before how to teach. "The first concern
of the instructional designer ought to be the definition and
demonstration of goals and needs of the societal level.

451

Solutions to problems that the needs present may, but do not necessarily, involve changing human behaviors. Furthermore, only some of these elements of the solution which do involve behavior change are likely to require instructional systems. Finally, no such system should be developed until an inventory of relevant constraints and available resources is constructed and a plan for maintaining learned behavior is devised."

G-24. Gellerman, Saul W. <u>Management by Motivation.</u> New York: American Management Association, 1968.

A followup to his earlier book, <u>Motivation and Productivity,</u> in which he explained motivational theory. Here he applies these theories to actual management problems. The objective is to try to help managers to look at problems the way the behavioral scientist does. The position of the behavioral scientist is that conventional rewards and punishments do not offer a practical motivational strategy. "To achieve such a strategy, we must identify motivational levels which management is not only in a position to operate, but whose effects produce a favorable long-term balance of advantages over drawbacks."

Of particular interest is a section in which Gellerman concentrates on one "of the most powerful and yet most misunderstood sources of leverage upon the motivation that actually becomes available to an organization: the selection of the people who will belong to it and of those who will manage it."

G-25. Ginzberg, Eli and Brown, Carol A. <u>Manpower for Library Services.</u> New York: University Conservation of Human Resources Project, 1967.

This thought-provoking report by Ginzberg (one of the foremost manpower experts in the United States) and Brown, covers many aspects of library manpower. The authors present several findings that are related to continuing education.

-- Librarians need to have more understanding of personnel management as more and more supporting personnel are being added.
-- As more and more libraries join systems, it is increasingly necessary for the library to understand the management of a large organization. "If graduate library schools

452

are to educate leaders rather than technicians, they must stress many hitherto neglected aspects of management."

— "No matter how much increased attention is paid to strengthening programs of formal education at the library school, more attention must be devoted to in-service training."

— "Our final finding and recommendation is that the field of librarianship broaden and deepen its knowledge about itself. There are too few facts, and the facts that are available are frequently of such questionable quality that a responsible leadership cannot formulate action programs and press for solutions. If leaders are to lead and not be pushed by events they must devote more time and energy to encouraging systematic research into their profession. Only with sound knowledge of the past and present will it be possible to formulate plans for the future."

G-26. Gladmon, William T. "A Report to the House Interstate and Foreign Commerce Committee on Educational Television Legislation." (ED 013 418.)

Educational television stations WQEX and WQED, in Pittsburgh, have been providing specialized adult education courses for managers and supervisors in business and for physicians and nurses. Other educational television stations throughout the country are active not only in these areas, but also in fire and police training, and in providing credit and noncredit courses at the college and professional levels. Televised courses have greatly improved access to top-level instruction. They encourage company-sponsored training, save time and money, make the community more training-minded, and stimulate active discussion and the exchange of group or departmental ideas.

G-27. Goheen, Robert F. "The Teacher in the University," American Scientist, 54 (2), (1966).

G-28. Goldstein, Harold, ed. <u>Implications of the New Media for the Teach-</u>
<u>ing of Library Science.</u> Monograph series, no. 1. Urbana,
Illinois: University of Illinois, 1963.

This publication resulted from a three day conference origin-
ated by the Media Research and Development Committee of the
Library Education Division of ALA and sponsored by the New
Media Branch of the U.S. Office of Education.

One of the most important papers in this collection is the first
on "Strategies of Learning" in which C.R. Carpenter stresses
the importance of the library educator's being more aware
of the conditions and processes of human learning. "How
many library educators understand the main groups of determinants which operate to result in desired learning and how
many apply what they know in the conduct of the education
activities for which they are responsible?" Throughout the
work, an attempt is made to show how media models can be
used for more effective learning on the part of the student.

G-29. Goldstein, Harold. "The Importance of Newer Media in Library
Training and the Education of Professional Personnel." <u>Library</u>
<u>Trends,</u> 16 (October, 1967), 259-65.

Pre-service and continuing education courses in library schools
and libraries pay far too little attention to audiovisual materials
beyond concentration on the machines themselves. A study
initiated in 1965 by ALA's Audio-Visual Committee on the use
of non-print materials and equipment in libraries showed a
general lack of involvement with the new media. The capabilities of AV aids should be brought to the attention of
practicing librarians through continuing education opportunities.
There is an urgent need for professional recognition of the
problem.

G-30. Gomersall, Earl R. and M. Scott Myers. "Breakthrough in On-
The-Job Training." <u>Harvard Business Review,</u> 44, (July -
August, 1966), 62-72.

A valuable article from several points of view. First, it
stresses the importance of experimenting with new theories
developed in the behavioral sciences in the work place.

"The manager should look to behavioral scientists not to solve his problems, but only to provide needed information about them. To ask the scientists to do more robs the manager of his charter and violates the very principle which he is expected to implement through job enlargement." (p. 71)

Secondly, it provides concrete research in an extremely critical area of an organization's activities (and one seldom subjected to research)--the initial orientation period of the employee in which the employee defines his activities, and learns what is expected of him by the organization, and how he is to learn his job. The orientation training period provided at the Texas Instruments Company, as described in this study, was designed to reduce the anxiety of new employees by explaining exactly what the company expected, the hazing they would probably get from experienced employees, and the type of behavior to expect from their own immediate supervisor. The experiment showed that, compared to a control group, those receiving such orientation reached high production levels much sooner.

Other important emphases brought out in the study are the importance of an atmosphere of approval, genuine respect, and interest in the work place, and the value of job enlargement (enrichment) as a means of making the employee in a real sense a manager himself.

G-31. Goodlad, John I. The Future of Learning and Teaching. Washington, D.C., National Education Association, 1968.

Several important emphases relative to the educational system are made by the author: the importance of individual concern, the changes needed in education to make it a much more intense experience. To what extent is each individual being provided with opportunities to develop his unique potentials to the maximum? To what extent is each individual developing a deep sense of personal worth — the sense of selfhood? To what extent are our people developing mankind values - values that transcend all men in all times and places? What kinds of human beings do we want to produce?

455

G-32. Goodman, Charles H. "Employee Motivation." Library Trends, 20 (July, 1971), 39-47.

Goodman, Associate Dean of the School of Government and Public Administration of American University, stresses the uniqueness of the individual in the organization, especially his "needs system" as defined by Maslow. Factors and conditions that tend to motivate an individual are discussed: involvement through participation, job enrichment, target setting conferences, and high performance goals set by the supervisor and the employees.

G-33. Goodman, Charles H. "Incentives and Motivation for Staff Development." In: Stone, Elizabeth W., New Directions in Staff Development: Moving from Ideas to Action. Chicago: ALA, Library Administration Division, 1971. pp. 51-57.

Paper presented at Micro-workshop on Staff Development at American Library Association Conference on June 28, 1970. Sponsored by Staff Development Committee of the Personnel Administration Section of the Library Administration Division of ALA.

G-34. Goodman, Lillian Rachel. A Model of Objectives for a Program of Continuing Education for Psychiatric Nurses in Community Mental Health Work in Massachusetts. Boston University, Massachusetts School of Education, 1969. (ED 047 196.)

The purpose of this study was: 1) to develop a model of required functions and effective behaviors of psychiatric nurses in mental health programs in Massachusetts and 2) to construct a model of objectives of a continuing education program for them. Perceptual data concerning functions of nurses were gathered by interviews with authorities, supervisors, and nurses concerning effective and ineffective behaviors. Additional Data were gathered from non-participant observation in two state hospitals and two mental health centers. Data analysis led to the formulation of two categories of functions: direct nursing care, and collateral nursing care (including administration, staff development and training, consultation and research). Authorities felt the ideal function of the psychiatric nurse was individual therapy but perceived that they actually were performing collateral functions, particularly administration. Supervisors and nurses perceived the most important ideal function to be that of general nursing care but they both saw their real functions about equally divided between direct and collateral nursing care. The work of psychiatric nurses in community mental health programs was seen to be the same in state hospitals and in mental health centers.

G-35. Gosling, Robert, and others. The Use of Small Groups in Training. Codicote Press, Hitchin, Hertfordshire, England, 1967. (ED 030 837.)

These three British Studies illustrate the use of small group methods to impart human relations knowledge and skills to professionals in medical and social services. The first paper deals with general practitioners who meet weekly over extended periods of time for case discussions. The second describes experiences of the family discussion bureau in setting up short residential courses for social case workers, with a blend ing of training group methods, course work, and case study seminars built around the theme of marital interaction. The last paper points to ways in which a change agent, a psychiatrist trained in group dynamics as well as psychotherapy, used small group methods to help personnel in boys' penal institutions become receptive to new ideas. Two substantive issues appear throughout: 1) The widespread anxiety generated by the prospect of having to make changes in one's professional role in order to use new insights gained through training; 2) the nature of unconscious regressive forces or 'pathology' in group behavior.

G-36. Gossage, Loyce Clyde. The Qualifications and Educational Needs of Industrial Training Directors. Unpublished Doctor's dissertation, University of California, Los Angeles, 1967. [EDRS ED 024 903.]

The author verified his hypothesis that training directors are required to perform educational duties for which they have not received appropriate, organized instruction. Because of his duties the training director should know how to teach, how to organize an education program, and how to evaluate the results of teaching. The training directors surveyed said that

457

the most important competencies and knowledges that can be
acquired in formal university courses are: 1) ability to develop
and supervise training programs; 2) knowledge of education
theories and practices; and 3) ability to communicate. The
respondents thought preparation for the position of training
director should include both general and specialized courses in
education, business, communications, and psychology.

This paper, with its 17 principle findings, has implications for
the qualifications and education needs of directors of staff
development programs in libraries.

G-37. Grabowski, Stanley M. "Continuing Education in the Professions."
Adult Leadership, 19 (May, 1970), 34-35.

The author reports on the great upsurge in literature dealing
with continuing education in the professions. A 1962 survey
showed a million professional persons (excluding teachers)
engaged in formal or independent study related to professional
development. Since that time the literature shows an increase
in university involvement on professional continuing education, sponsorship by government, business and industry,
and in research programs.

Out of the hundreds of documents that have entered the ERIC
system in the area of continuing education, the author has
chosen a few representative examples in general studies,
public administration, medicine and health, education, law,
and religion.

G-38. Grabowski, Stanley M. "ERIC Special Degree Programs for
Adults." Adult Leadership. (June, 1971), 75-76.

An annotated bibliography.

G-39. Grabowski, Stanley. "Motivational Patterns of Adult Participants
in Independent Study Programs." Continuing Education for Adults.
179 (December, 1972), 1-5.

The author, in conjunction with his doctoral dissertation
studied the motivational factors of adult learners enrolled in

the independent study program at University College, Syracuse University. The author identified seven clusters in the analysis of the motivational data. These were: 1) desire to know; 2) desire to reach a personal goal; 3) desire to take part in social activities; 4) desire to reach a social goal; 5) desire to escape; 6) desire to study alone; 7) desire for intellectual

G-40. Granger, Charles H. "The Hierarchy of Objectives." Harvard Business Review, 42 (May-June, 1964), 63-74.

Granger defines an objective as an aim or end of action and as a guide to intermediate decisions and actions. An organizational model which assumes broad participatory input in objective achievement is assumed in his approach.

G-41. Greenfield, Lois B. and Page, Raymond J. "Evaluating Teaching Methods in Continuing Engineering Studies." Journal of Engineering Education, 60 (October, 1969), 123-34.

The authors completed a survey to see what evaluation of methodology had been done in continuing engineering studies. They found much interest, but little results. Manufacturers had done little experimentation on their teaching devices; universities had made only limited efforts to study educational methodology in the continuing engineering studies area (methodology in the medical field seemed to have progressed much further).

The conclusions reached from the survey were: 1) either their survey had reached the wrong people, or little was being done; 2) interest was high and therefore the Continuing Engineering Studies Division of the American Society for Engineering Education could make a contribution; 3) computer assisted instruction,   electrowriter, closed-circuit TV, and programmed instruction were all in use; no preponderance of any one methodology; 4) closed-circuit TV is discarded sometimes because of the cost.

The recommendation of the authors: evaluation must be made a part of continuing engineering studies -- not follow current fads without reason.

459

G-42. Greenwood, James W., Jr., "Nature and Importance of Systems
Education." International Associations, 1 (1970), 3-5.

The author, Federal Executive Fellow, the Bookings Institute,
argues that it is necessary to reorient our total thinking about
education so as to "look upon education as a life-long process
for the continuing development of the individual. In planning
the education program, we will have to learn to consider
the whole person—not merely one or two aspects of his existence. In short we will have to adopt a systems approach
to education."

He states that the managers and the administrators of the future
(as well as those today) need, in addition to technical and
human relations skills, conceptual skills which will enable
them to:

--communicate with other disciplines
--intelligently apply the findings of science technology for
   the benefit to society
--mentally relate the significant factors in a situation as
   a basis for decision making
--visualize the interactions of complex structures and reliably
   predict the probable effects of alternative courses of action.

These are the conceptual skills that are characteristic of
the systems approach to problem solving.

Interrelatedness is the emphasis in the systems approach --
the interrelatedness of the elements and processes with a
sub-system, the interrelatedness of sub-systems, the interrelatedness of systems with their environment and on the
holistic viewpoint, the recognition that the whole is something
more than or different from the mere sum of the part.

He closes with a warning: "The managers of today and of
the future—in industry, government, and education—must
be prepared to apply the systems approach or perish."

G-43. Gregory, Carl. "Management of Creative Personnel." Journal of
Creative Behavior. 3 (Fall, 1969), 271-6.

The author considers it a necessity for managers to "demoth"
their conceptual thinking about organizational theory based
on unverified concepts. He believes that to a large degree
the success of an organization during the next decade will
positively correlate with management's ability to reappraise
the corporate beliefs and "thereby separate reality from
fiction".

His concern is with "Intelligence Engineering" which he defines as the "maximum utilization of individual and collective
minds to achieve preconceived objectives."   One of the
emphases he makes is the importance of management seeking
closer cooperation with faculty in institutions of higher
education. "Valuable exchanges of ideas can be accomplished
through: 1) Cooperative planning; 2) joint conferences and
seminars; 3) use of academic consultants; 4) part-time
academic teaching by professionals; 5) encouragement and
financial support for researching management problems;
and 6) joint re-evaluation of business school programs."

G-44. Grinter, L.E. "The President's Report to Engineers' Council
for Professional Development." In: 35th Annual Report for
the Year Ending September 30, 1967 of the Engineer's Council
for Professional Development. New York: Engineer's
Council for Professional Development, 1967.

The Engineer's Council for Professional Development decided to direct its energies toward stimulating the interest of
engineers, particularly young engineers, in programs of
Continuing Education for Engineers. Following an earlier
recommendation of a study entitled Continuing Engineering
Studies, the societies in the council have encouraged non-
degree post-graduate study. Recognition of an engineer's
achievement in continuing education is a function of the ECPD.
The recognition program being developed envisions acceptance
as units of a continuing education program for engineers
of a large number of courses. Upon submission by the student
of transcripts covering twenty or perhaps thirty credit hours,
or equivalent, of continuing education studies that formed
a coordinated program, ECPD would award a national certificate with appropriate congratulations. The author views the
program as providing an intellectual opportunity for many

461

engineers whose interests or perhaps capacities are not
entirely fitted to completion of another academic degree.

Another recent development reported by Grinter was the
formation of a Joint Engineering Societies Forum to discuss
ways and means of encouraging greater cooperation and joint
activity between the technical and non-technical engineering
societies. "It appears . . . that the time is near at hand when
some more formal organization for broad cooperations
address the entire profession for engineering might be accepted
with relief if not universal enthusiasm. Hence, the usefulness
of a possible federation of engineering societies seems worthy
of our serious consideration now. "

G-45. Gropper, George L. "Does 'Programmed' Television Need Active
Responding ?" AV Communication Review. , 15 (Spring, 1967),
5-21.

G-46. Guba, Egon G. and Daniel Shufflebeam. Evaluation: The Process of
Stimulating, Aiding and Abetting Insightful Action.
Bloomington, Indiana: Indiana University, 1970.

The authors define evaluation as follows: "Evaluation is
the process of obtaining and providing useful information for
making educational decisions. "

Within the definition are six key terms that they discuss:
process, obtaining, providing, useful, information, educational
decisions. The part of the book that has been discussed the
most is that dealing with types of evaluation. These four
processes are: context, input, process, and product (CIPP).
Context evaluation services planning decisions; input evaluation services structuring decisions; process evaluation
services implementing decisions; product evaluation services
results of decisions. This CIPP model was used to train a
number of trainers during the early part of 1972 by the
Bureau of Libraries and Learning Resources, USOE. These
leaders inturn were resource people for a more general
conference in New Orleans in the fall of 1973 to which librarians
and educators were invited to learn the meaning of the model
and how to use it.

462

G-47. Gutzman, Stanley D. "Career-long Sabbatical." <u>Library Journal</u>,
94 (October 1, 1969), 3411-15

Gutzman argues that intellectual reinvigoration is a strong
rationale for study at any age and level. One way to insure
continued discussion and action is for academic departments
to establish traditions of discussion and action. The librarian's
job should be one long intellectual exercise, involving projects
that can be formal and organized or informal, non-directed
efforts.

H-1. Hall, Anna C. Selected Educational Objectives for Public Service Librarians: A Taxonomic Approach. Pittsburgh: University of Pittsburgh, 1968.

Includes analysis of curricular content in selected library schools in order to determine the relationship between educational outcomes and the instruction offered.

H-2. Hamreus, Dale G. Self Instructional Materials for Research Training. Supporting Documents to a Final Report. Monmouth, Oregon. Oregon State System of Higher Education, Teacher Research Division, 1967. (ED 021 778.)

H-3. Hanan, Mack, "Make Way for the New Organization Man." Harvard Business Review, 49 (July-August, 1971), 128-138.

In this article, Mack Hanan, Managing Director of Hanan & Son, New York management consultants who specialize in long range planning for organizational growth, outlines three ways organizations can respond to the need patterns of the "new organization man."

The author perceives the new organization man's needs structure to place a far greater emphasis on self-fulfillment from his work than did the past generation's organization man. "Another major difference concerns the ways in which the new man wants to maximize his rewards from participation. He wants to share in the personal benefits of leadership." (p. 129) Many of these men have found that consistent dialogue can accelerate institutional change and they want to set up a sort of running dialogue with their companies a) to find out how the organizations are being operated and b) to gain opportunities to "sit in the seats of power themselves and put their own views into practice on issues of corporate policy." (p. 129) Because they have been in the forefront of change, "their time frame for waiting it out in the corporate environment has been considerably reduced. So, accordingly, has their satisfaction with receiving token offerings." (p. 129)

The author's suggestions for a minimal system of accommodating the organization to the needs of the new organization man center in three categories: 1) personal involvement--new ways of getting these men involved; 2) collaborative leadership--emphasizing the joint exercise of authority and innovative approaches to

goal setting achievement; 3) self fulfillment options--"centering
on the invigoration of individual rights within the corporate
framework and on the setting of fast-track recognition for excellence."
(p. 131)

H-4. Hanford, W. E., and others. "Chemical News Via Audio Tapes:
Chemical Industry News." Journal of Chemical Documentation,
12 (February, 1972), 3-4.

H-5. Harlow, Neal, and others. Administration and Change: Continuing
Education in Library Administration. New Brunswick, New
Jersey: Rutgers University Press, 1969. pp. 1-8.

Dr. Harlow in his introduction to five excellent papers which
show what several academic disciplines have to offer the
library administrator, states the authors' conviction that the
continuing education of library administrators is the "most
critical 'new need' in the education of librarians." The solution
suggested: "Only the discipline of formal education--systematic,
questioning, interpretive, open-ended, and demanding--can hope
to keep up to date with today's growth and change." (p. 6)
"Continuing Education for the Library Administrator: His Needs,"
by Ernest R. DeProspo, Jr., and Theodore S. Huang (pp. 21-8)
reports on a survey of library administrators. It was found that
the administrators most urgently needed continuing education
in three areas: 1) application of machines; 2) personnel administration; and 3) evaluation of library problems.

H-6. Harrison, J. Clement. "Advanced Study: A Mid-Atlantic Point
of View." In: Bone, Larry Earl, ed. Library Education:
An International Survey. Champaign, Illinois: University of
Illinois Graduate School of Library Science, 1968. pp. 329-336.

Harrison notes the curious situation that exists in the United
States with a system of education for librarianship based on
graduate study at the university. However, for the past 20
years there has been very little opportunity for "advanced study."
The concentration has been on the master's degree (which he
considers far from "advanced study"). Until recently doctoral
study has provided the only opportunity for advanced work, and
has only been offered by a small number of institutions. He

H-6 (cont.)

discusses a new dimension of advanced study between the master's and the doctorate, the "Advanced Certificate" program. Harrison sees two purposes for these "intermediate" programs: 1) they afford an opportunity for some sort of specialization not now provided at the basic mater's level; 2) they afford the practical librarian who has been in the field for a while an opportunity for updating. These programs are misused, however, if they are "allowed to deteriorate into 'green stamp' operations, designed to give the practicing librarian 'promotion credit'."

Harrison argues that if "these 'advanced' programs are to have any real validity they should have a life of their own, properly organized and directed towards some clearly indicated objective. My own view is that, given these conditions, they have a tremendously important part to play in 'advanced study in librarianship'." Harrison opts for "advanced certificate" programs with specialization as their prime objective. He states that this would also serve the needs of the librarians in the field who are returning for refresher work in a special area.

Harrison concludes:

It seems, therefore, that there is a strong case for "advanced study in librarianship," quite apart from doctoral study (with "research" as a necessary concomitant). It may be the only solution to the problem of specialization. It surely has a tremendous potential in "continuing" and professional education. It will only play its proper part, however, if its real purposes are determined beforehand, if it is coordinated with the basic programs, and if the schools recognize that they must have adequate resources in terms of faculty, materials and accommodation before they decide to embark upon such programs. In the United States there are ominous signs of advanced non-doctoral programs becoming the poor relation within the household. . . .

All degrees, one eminent British authority has advocated, should be like passports, i.e., renewable every so often and, if not renewed, declared invalid. Obviously this will never happen (people like us will see to that). As the next best thing, however, well-organized "advanced study" could be the answer on both sides of the Atlantic.

466

H-7. Harrison, K. C. "INTAMEL, International Meeting, Gothenburg, 1969; Staff Training in Large City Libraries," International Library Review, 1 (October, 1969), 475-78.

Staff training is essential because of the increasing complexity of services, expanding as they are in quantity, quality and variety. It cannot be stressed too much that all staff training programs should be adaptable and flexible, taking into full consideration the changing background and conditions in the profession.

H-8. Hartman, G. W. "The Field Theory of Learning and Its Educational Consequence." In: National Society for the Study of Education. Forty-First Year Book, Part II: The Psychology of Learning. Chicago: University of Chicago Press, 1942.

H-9. Harvard University. "The School's Executive Development Programs: The advanced Management Program; Objectives of Training for Top and Middle Managers and What Makes Program Tick." Harvard Business School Bulletin, 41 (May-June, 1965), 7-9.

H-10. Harvey, John F. The Librarian's Career: A Study in Mobility. ACRL Microcard Series No. 85. Rochester, New York: University of Rochester Press, 1957.

H-11. Harvey, John F. and Lambert, Bettina. "The Educational Third Dimension: II Programs for Continuing Library Education." Library Trends, 20 (July, 1971) 144-168.

Some aspects of the problems inherent in keeping librarians up-to-date and educating them after library school are discussed and approaches toward solving these problems are suggested.

H-12. Hendrix, Vernon L. and Oosting, Kenneth W. A Professional Library for Junior Colleges. Minneapolis: Minnesota University, 1967. (ED 017 236.)

Because of its role in our society, the junior college must not become dated in the information to which it has access. The professional library is a means of providing new and/or contrasting ideas, and it serves as a valuable inservice education tool. An 86-item bibliography is included in the groupings of 1) higher education, 2) junior colleges, general, 3) administration, 4) facilities, 5) students, 6) curriculum, 6) faculty, 8) finance and public relations, 9) instruction and library, 10) research studies and methods, 11) periodicals, 12) student personnel, and 13) references.

H-13. Henselman, Frances. "What's Being Done?" In: Stone, Elizabeth W. New Directions in Staff Development; Moving from Ideas to Action. Chicago: ALA, Library Administration Division, 1971.

Paper presented at Micro-workshop on Staff Development at American Library Association Conference, June 28, 1970. Sponsored by Staff Development Committee of the Personnel Administration Section of the Library Administration Division of ALA.

H-14. Herzberg, Frederick. "One More Time: How Do You Motivate Employees?" Harvard Business Review, 46 (January–February, 1968), 53–62.

Frederick Herzberg, an American psychologist on the faculty at Case-Western Reserve University, has produced a theory of motivation that has received a wide amount of attention. In his first book on the subject, Work and the Nature of Man, Herzberg stated two basic and fundamental propositions of his now famous Motivation-Hygiene theory: 1) the factors producing job satisfaction are separate and distinct from those that lead to job dissatisfaction; and 2) the dissatisfiers (Hygiene factors) such as organization policy, administration, supervision, inter-personal relations, working conditions, salary, contribute very little to job satisfaction. As described in this article, "the stimuli for the growth needs are tasks that induce growth . . . they are the job content." (p. 57) He suggests that work be enriched to bring about effective utlization of personnel. He sums up the argument for job enrichment quite simply: "If you have someone on the job, use him. If you can't use him get rid of him, either via automation, or by selecting someone with lesser ability. If you can't use him and you can't get rid of him, you will have a motivation problem." (p. 62)

H-15. Herzberg, Frederick. Work and the Nature of Man. New York: World Publishing Company, 1966.

Herzberg asserts that man has two different sets of needs: factors in the environment and factors that are inherent in the work itself. Herzberg's assertion that work can be a motivator in itself is an important behavioral science breakthrough. When a job provides an opportunity for personal satisfaction or growth, it is a strong motivating force--the strongest motivating force, according to Herzberg. He believes, however, that there is no conflict between the environmental approach to motivation and the approach through the job, or work, it self. Both are important. He refers to the environmental approach as hygiene, and this has a limited capacity to influence employee behavior; the approach through the job he refers to as "motivation", and this is capable of lasting effects. Herzberg uses the term motivation to describe feelings of accomplishment, of professional growth and professional recognition, that are experienced in a job that sufficiently challenges the worker's capabilities. Therefore, Herzberg sees job design as a very important motivating factor, and he uses the term "job enrichme nt" as a means of introducing more effective motivation into jobs.

H-16. Herzberg, Frederick, and others. The Motivation to Work. 2d ed. New York: John Wiley & Sons, Inc., 1959.

H-17. Hewitt, Gordon B. Continuing Education in Pharmacy: A Report. British Columbia, Pharmaceutical Association Province of British Columbia, March, 1965. (ED 019 545.)

This comprehensive report examines the educational needs in the technical, social, and economic aspects of a pharmacist's career. The aims and objectives and proposed program of a system of professional, managerial, and general education of pharmacists is presented. Outlines next steps needed in continuing education.

H-18. Hiatt, Peter. "The Educational Third Dimension, III. Toward the Development of a National Program of Continuing Education for Library Personnel." Library Trends, 20 (July, 1971), 169-183.

Hiatt, Director of the Continuing Education Program for Library
Personnel for the Western Interstate Commission for Higher
Education (WICHE), opens this concluding article of this issue
of Library Trends featuring Personnel Development and
continuing education in libraries with several important assumptions: 1) the continuing education of librarians is one of the
most important problems facing the profession today; 2) the task
of continuing education is not only passing on the wisdom; experience, and knowledge of the past, but it is also preparing
librarians for change in themselves and their institutions; 3)
ultimately the individual is himself primarily responsible for
his own education and most of his learning efforts must be
self-directed; 4) continuing education--formal and informal--is
essential for all people employed in libraries, not just the
"librarians" who constitute the professional segment of the
library community; and 5) the fragmented elements of present
continuing education programs have not been put together in
any pattern.

Hiatt's thesis is that the pieces should be put together in an
organized whole through the development of a practical, well
organized national plan so that continuing education, utilizing
all available methods and technologies, would efficiently meet
the life-long learning needs of all library personnel. He
suggests that "such experimentation is most likely to occur
when a broad, regional view is taken, and seems even mo re
probable on the national level. " As a basis for building up to
national planning, he describes the work being done in WICHE
on a regional basis. Not everyone may agree with his particular
version of what national planning should be or with his suggestion
that the location of the profession's national program for continuing
education should be within the American Library Association
structure, but most would probably agree with his position that
"professional associations and library schools must share
responsibility for continuing education. "

H-19. Hiatt, Peter, and others. Education of State Library Personnel:
A Report With Recommendations Relating to the Continuing
Education of State Library Agency Professional Personnel.
Prepared by the Associaton of State Library Agencies and the
Library Education Division, Interdivisional Committee on
Education of State Library Personnel, under a grant from the
H. W. Wilson Foundation. Chicago, Ill.: American Library
Association, 1971.

This significant report has implications for continuing education far beyond the group for which it was specifically designed, namely, State Library Agency Professional Personnel. In fact most of the report can be applied equally well to all levels of library personnel and in all types of libraries. In addition to serving as a model for other planning and designing programs to meet continuing education needs, the appendixes contain valuable concise data on such topics as: The Adult as a Learner; Program Guidelines; Human Relations Laboratory Training; examples of programs conducted by State Library Agencies; and examples of other professional association continuing education programs; and sample workshop and institute programs.

Selected conclusions and recommendations from the report include: 1) Within the state library agency, the greatest immediate need is for continuing education of "consultants."
2) Although important content to meet the needs of state library personnel can be identified, of greatest importance seems to be the need for consultant techniques, especially an understanding of group processes and interpersonal communication skills.
3) The best method of learning for consultants and administrators is the participative, laboratory method of adult learning.
4) To implement educational activity, it was decided to adopt a "Training The Teacher (Triple T or TTT) program, with a multiplying effect resulting when each of the state library trainers returned home to design and carry out a continuing education program for his colleagues.
5) It was recommended that a National Advisory and Action Committee for Continuing Education of State Library Personnel be established. "It is hoped that this National Committee could serve as the prototype for a national committee for continuing education of all library personnel." Seven specific functions for the National Committee, composed of eleven members, meeting twice yearly, are presented.
6) A long range recommendation was to develop and test materials to aid in the continuing education of state library personnel, such as tapes, programmed learning texts, audio-visual and other educational equipment, and packaged programs for use in libraries in remote areas.

H-20. Hinchliff, William Emerson. "Staff Development--Key to Library Progress." Wisconsin Library Bulletin, 63 (January, 1967), 30-32.

A description of the Milwaukee Public Library staff development program.

H-21. Hines, Theodore C. Programed Learning and In-Service Training in Libraries. New York: Columbia University, School of Library Service, n.d. (Mimeographed)

The author points out the advantages of programmed instruction as a method for in-service training. However, he did not believe that it was adaptable to the type of instruction on procedures and routines which make up the bulk of library in-service instruction. "This is due to the cost of producing programs and the lack of uniformity in detailed procedures among libraries. "On the other hand, he thought programs relative to library purposes might prove useful as orientation or background training. "Programs designed for library school classes, if they are produced, should be valuable for training sub-professional staff, and their development should be encouraged." He considered it of major importance to encourage the development and publication of programs teaching the use of the library; these programs would also be valuable in staff training.

H-22. Hintz, Carl W. E. "The Librarian's Continuing Education." Pacific Northwest Library Association Quarterly, 29 (January, 1965), 120-22.

A survey of the situation indicates that the elements for a program of continuing education are already in existence. The greatest need is to organize the program on a more formal basis and to secure its acceptance as a normal part of the activities of the professional librarian.

H-23. Hodges, J. B. "Continuing Education: Why and How." Education Leadership, 17 (March, 1960), 330-346.

H-24. Hoehn, Arthur J. A Program for Providing Maintenance Capability. Lowry Air Force Base, Colorado: Maintenance Laboratory, Air Force Personnel and Training Research Center, Air Research and Development Command, 1957. (Mimeographed)

H-25. Hollister, James Elliott. The Minister's Time, Leisure, and Continuing Education and a Study of Time Use, Participation in Leisure Activities and Continuing Education. Berkeley: University of California, 1968. (ED 035 832.)

472

This document surveys the work and leisure time, participation in leisure activities and participation in informal continuing education of some Protestant ministers serving urban congregations in California. It emphasized differences in life styles.

H-26. Holton, Gerald, and others. Harvard Project Physics Report. Three speeches delivered to the American Association of Physics Teachers (AAPT) Meeting, February, 1967, prepared by Harvard Project Physics, Cambridge, Mass.: Harvard Project Physics, 1967. (EDRS ED 020 117.)

Although this Harvard project aims at the development of a physics course to be used on a national scale at the high school level, many of the philosophical concepts any many of the methods used are applicable to the development of packaged courses for continuing education. For example: 1) The importance of feedback from classes using course materi als for continuous testing and rewriting of course materials.
2) Use of people from other disciplines to help in the development of course materials, building the broadest possible base of knowledge and skills.
3) The importance of developing a wide range of ma terials to use in the teaching of a given course. For example, a) student guides (texts); b) teacher's guides including extensive discussion of all materials; c) transparencies with multi-color overlays; d) 16 mm sound films; 3) 8 mm film loops (silent); f) programmed instruction booklets; g) collections of readings in course areas; and h) achievement tests.
4) Division of course into a fixed number of basic units with the provision of optional units from which the teacher can choose to meet individual needs of students.
5) All materials and programs reflect aims and objectives of the curriculum as a whole.
6) Use of the multi-media approach in teaching all courses.
7) The teacher should be a collaborator in curriculum developme nt.
8) Provision of enough flexibility in model course so that there is adequate provision for dealing with diversity in student needs.
9) The quantity and diversity of instructional materials for each unit of a course must far exceed needs of any one student so that the teacher can select to meet his needs and those of his students.
10) To guard against unlimited flexibility, each course should have a basic number of units that are studied by all.
11) The approach should progressively shift from "teaching" to

"learning."

12) The importance of teacher training is a major facet of the program (recommendations would be applicable to teachers of any type of experimental course development).

H-27. Honey, John C. "A Report: Higher Education for Public Service." Public Administration Review, 27, (November, 1967), 294-321.

H-28. Horn, Francis. Tomorrow's Targets for University Adult Education. Paper presented at 10th Annual Seminar on Leadership in University Adult Education. Lansing: Michigan State University, Continuing Education Service, 1967. (ED 019 536.)

Horn uses the term "continuing education" broadly to include those studying for degrees as well as those who are not. He predicts that in 10 to 20 years 10 per cent of the nation's working force will be on some kind of sabbatical leave for continuing education--full time. He also argues that every university has responsiblity for continuing education courses to retool professional people; this responsiblity cannot be shifted to other agencies.

H-29. Horwitz, Milton J. Research in Professional Education, with Special Reference to Medical Education. New Dimensions in Higher Education, Number 22. Washington, D.C.: U. S. Office of Education, 1967. (ED 013 347.)

The growth of research in medical education was reviewed as an outstanding example of research in professional education. Successive developments in research in medical education are described in relation to the pattern of accelerating change that followed World War II. In addition, an overview is presented that summarizes the role of professional organizations in educational research, the trends in research studies, and a list of questions concerning professional education that are relevant to all areas of professional education.

H-30. Hospital Continuing Education Project. Training and Continuing Education: A Handbook for Health Care Institutions. Chicago: Hospital Research and Educational Trust, 1970.

Sponsored by the W. K. Kellogg Foundation, this book describes
techniques involved in the process of developing continuing
education programs. The objective was to improve and expand
continuing education opportunities for hospital personnel through
a "Partnership for Progress" between hospitals, hospital
associations, and universities. As the chapters were prepared
they were made available to all 50 states through conferences.
Chapters cover: training as a management strategy; learning
needs--basis for programming; conducting learning needs analysis;
setting learning objectives; designing learning situations; developing
the instructor's guide; various teaching tools; the case study, the
role play, and the in-basket exercise; incorporating audio-visual
media; selecting instructional methods; evaluating results. Feedback
from the conferences was evaluated and used in revising chapters
before final pub lication.

H-31.*Houle, Cyril O. "The Comparative Study of Continuing Professional
Education." Convergence, 3 (no. 4, 1970), 3-12.

Professor Houle of the University of Chicago considers the value
of comparative analyses of the professions in the area of continuing
education. Points of comparison that he thinks would be worthy
of a study include: methods used in professional continuing education;
new innovative techniques, instead of reliance on the traditional
practices of journal readings, short courses, or conventions;
comparison of the patterns of opportunities offered by relevant
groups such as universities, industry, government agencies.

He centers particular attention on what he considers the most
worrisome group which is common to all professions--the laggards,
whose performance is so poor they are a menace to their clients
and source of embarrassment to their colleagues. What causes
each profession to have recruits of this type? Houle suggests
that one reason may be that the student is often given a poor model
to follow during his formative stage in the profession; later he
becomes dissatisfied with the thought of having to engage in either
life-long learning and/or research. Motivation toward continuing
education he views as a major problem in all the professions.

Houle also faces up to that most difficult area--definition of the
term Profession. He submits the thesis that much of the difficulty
over definition might be resolved if a profession were striving
toward an ideal state toward which many occupational groups could

be striving. Some of the aims such a group might seek are as follows:

1) To master the rudiments of fundamental and complex bodies of knowledge and theory that have been derived for theoretical and descriptive rather than practical reasons.

2) To use these bodies of knowledge to deal with a category of specific problems and concerns that arise in the vital practical affairs of mankind.

3) To create a body of knowledge and technique that is broadly concerned with the nature, history, dimensions, and processes of its field of practical application.

4) To transmit this body of knowledge and technique to all recognized practioners both before they enter service and throughout their careers.

5) To test the capacity of individual practioners to perform their duties at an acceptable level of accomplishment and license those who are qualified to do so.

6) To maintain associations that will advance . . . practitioners and maintain their standards of performance.

7) To secure legal recognition of the special rights and privileges of the vocation.

8) To foster the general public's awareness of itself as an entity by a broadly conceived public relations program explaining the functions of the professionalizing group and its position on relevant issues.

9) To establish a tradition of ethical practice, sometimes reinforced by a formal code or by legislation.

10) To establish and enforce penalties for those who fail to act in terms of accepted standards of practice.

11) To establish formal relationships between the profession's practitioners and the people who use their services.

12) To establish formal relationships between the profession's practioners and those of allied occupations.

13) To nurture a subculture for the members of the profession, with lore, folkways, mores, traditions, role differentiations and relationships, variations in authority and power, meaningful and random clusterings of people, and other social attributes.

Houle crystallizes another important concept when he warns professions engaged in comparative analyses should take into account that there are three essentially different pattern of work. To avoid comparisons that distort it must be constantly kept in mind that every professionalizing occupation has its dominant way of working (though in no case is it universal to all persons engaged in the practice of that occupation). Three patterns are identified by Houle: The ENTREPRENEURIAL, the COLLECTIVE, and the HIERARCHICAL.

Houle cautions at the end of his article that it is much easier to editorialize about comparative study of the profession than to study it scientifically by means of solid research. Research of the type he suggests is being done by some of the professions, but it will take time to find results that will be valid. He feels, however, that that the effort would be well worth the good that would result from it.

H-32. Houle, Cyril O. "Education for Adult Leadership." Adult Education, 8 (Autumn, 1957), 3-17.

H-33. Houle, Cyril O. "A Firstling of His Heart and Hand." Perspectives in Biology and Medicine, 12 (Summer, 1969), 561-583.

This is a delightful essay featuring one of the characteristics of Sir William Osler--his constant preoccupation with what is now termed "continuing medical education." The paper was presented at Oxford University on the fiftieth anniversary of Osler's death. In closing Houle said: "To survey his career, observing its patterns and consistencies through all its transplantations and concerns, is to see how steadfastly he held to the idea that the physician must be a lifelong student and that the medical profession must be organized to foster his learning. All professions and the people they serve have reason to be grateful that, throughout Osler's career, continuing education was a firstling of his heart and hand."

It is interesting to note, as Houle did in his paper, that the only two other professions that deeply interested Houle were nursing and librarianship. He worked out a curriculum for a library school at Oxford, but it never materialized.

H-34. Houle, Cyril O. The Inquiring Mind. Madison: The University of Wisconsin Press, 1961.

H-35. Houle, Cyril O. "The Lengthened Line." Perspectives in Biology and Medicine, 11 (Autumn, 1967), 37-51.

This is a later version of the paper that Professor Houle
presented to the 1967 Midwinter Conference of the American
Library Association.

H-36. *Houle, Cyril O. "The Role of Continuing Education in Current
Professional Development." ALA Bulletin, 61 (March, 1967),
259-267.

Houle asserted that continuing education will not cure all problems,
without it no cure is possible. Just reading is not enough. A
broad objective must be analyzed into specific goals and the
means to reach them must be perfected and adopted. The
practicing professional needs:
1) To keep up with the new knowledge related to his profession.
2) To establish his mastery of the new conceptions of his
own profession.
3) To continue his study of the basic disciplines which support
his profession.
4) To grow as a person as well as a professional.

Houle presented the content of this article at the 1967 ALA
Midwinter Meeting in New Orleans on January 11, 1967. Following
his opening address papers were presented by a panel of four
librarians (Kortendick, McJenkin, Monroe, and Stevenson).

H-37. Houle, Cyril O. "To Learn the Future." Medical Clinics of North
America, 54 (January, 1970), 5-18.

Emphasizing the concept of inter-professional cooperation, Houle
recommends that members of each profession should not act as
though they alone had any need of continuing education and should
drop the assumption that their processes are wholly unique. Such
inter-professional efforts to learn would, according to Houle, lead
to important consequences for our society.

H-38. Houle, Cyril O. "What is Continuing Education." Discussion Paper
for Seminar on Continuing Professional Education. University
of Chicago, August, 1969. (Mimeographed)

Continuing Education is defined by Houle as "any kind
of learning or teaching which extends or builds upon previous experience in the same general realm of knowledge and
whose specific goals are not intended to terminate all
study in that realm. It implies that the learner has studied
some related body of content previously and is carrying on
the process further; it implies that the program depends
upon his having done so and it implies that he proposes to
continue such learning in the future. The term is broader
in its formal definition than several others which are
sometimes used as synonyms. Thus continual or continuous
education is that which proceeds without interruption or
cessation, continuation education is some segment of study
after the initiatory experience, and continued education is
that which is protracted in time."

H-39. Houston, George C. Manager Development: Principles and Per-
      spectives. Homewood, Illinois: Richard D. Irwin, 1961.

H-40. Howard University, Washington, D.C. College of Medicine. Second
      Annual Report for Training Program for Neighborhood
      Physicians. Final Report. Washington, D C., January 20,
      1971. [ED 052 723]

      The purpose of the Howard University Training Program
      for Neighborhood Physicians is to engage these physicians
      in services stressing ambulatory patient care, while at the
      same time creating in them a sense of responsibility. One
      of the major reasons for initiating this program was the
      realization that until a few years ago many of the black
      physicians in Washington, D.C. had little or no affiliations
      with the local hospitals and thus had no opportunity to con-
      tinue their medical education and practice pattern im-
      provement. The Howard University program used exist-
      ing community and university health services and para-
      medical agencies to form an educational comprehensive
      medical care service. The neighborhood physician became
      part of the university staff. This report presents the
      information on: 1) the development of the department of
      family practice; 2) the educational activities engaged in;
      3) the application of findings on the continuing medical
      program; 4) the objectives and accomplishments of the

contract; 5) the satellite program in Baltimore; and 6) a prototype model kit. The appendix includes samples of participant and faculty correspondence and a schedule of activities in June and July.

H-41. Hughes, Everett C. Men and Their Work. Glencoe, Illinois: The Free Press, 1958, p. 137.

Hughes, in raising the question of "for what are the people being trained?" answered with an illustration from librarianship in the following manner:

"A recent study of librarians gives the impression that the most successful librarian is no longer a librarian, but an administrator . . . an acute problem in a number of occupations . . . . It might be that the advanced library schools are merely institutions where people get themselves groomed to stop being librarians and become administrators . . . . And if the professional school becomes a graduate school culminating in a Ph.D. -- for which a piece of research is required--must one not ask whether this is either the best way to get research done or the best way to train administrators? A piece of research done as training for promotion to a position where one will no longer have to do research may probably have some of the faults of a diagnosis done with an eye on what diagnostic procedures the patient can pay for. But we are now talking of problems which may arise in any profession, new or old, when the practice becomes involved in complicated institutional settings. The new profession, being so involved from the beginning, may give us some of our best clues for analyzing the problems of the old."

H-42. Hunervager, S.G. "Re-Education for Executives: Many Organizations Are Sending Their Executives Back to School." Personnel Administration, 24 (January-February, 1961), 5-9.

H-43. Hurt, Peyton. "Staff Specialization: A Possible Substitute for Departmentalization." American Library Association Bulletin. 29(July, 1935), 417-421.

H-44. Husband, David P. "The Auto-Tutorial System." Audiovisual
      Instruction. 15 (February, 1970), 34-5.

H-45. Hutchison, Dorothy H. Editorial: "Some Thoughts on Structuring
      for Continuing Education in Nursing." The Journal of
      Continuing Education in Nursing. 1 (July, 1970), 5-7.

The author notes that in spite of the great flurry of activity
in developing continuing education programs, generally
continuing education is not the major thrust of the agency
in which it occurs and that it generally has a relatively
low priority. Faculties put degree programs first; nursing
service may give it less support than to the management arm;
government agencies see it as useful, but marginal; professional organizations state they believe in it, but infrequently
committ the staff and dollars to it that it does for other
program components. On the basis of all of these conditions
Hutchinson makes a plea to examine structures within the
universities, within hospitals, within the professional
organization, within voluntary agencies, within regional
and governmental structures.

The article concludes: "Surely there is wide structural
variation among programs of continuing education, and
nursing contributes to this variety. Probably no one way
is right, but some structures are probably better than
others. Until continuing education in nursing emerges as
an entity, drawing upon the theory and technology of
adult education . . .until the philosophical committment is
backed by well prepared administrators, competent faculty
and an adequate financial base, it will continue to grow
'like Topsy.' Those in the field have a responsibility to
thoroughly examine the accrued experience and contribute
their knowledge so that the structure does in fact enable,
facilitate, support and encourage the vital function of
continuing education in nursing."

I-1. Immelman, R. F. M. "Continuing Education of Library Personnel,"
      South African Libraries, 37, (December, 1969), 128-43.

      This excellent and very helpful article covers the whole subject
      of continuing education. It covers those developments which
      are peripheral to the subject, such as work-study schemes,
      in-service training, internship, and librarian-trainees. Also
      discussed are the need for developing the professional caliber
      and intellectual standing of professional librarians if they are
      to cope with the vast increase in the volume of knowledge, the
      growth of subject specialization, and rapid technological
      changes.

I-2. Indiana University, Graduate Library School, and Indiana State
      Library. "Public Library Service for the Inner-City Disadvan-
      taged: A Title II-B Institute." In: Hiatt, Peter, and others,
      Education of State Library Personnel: A Report with Recom-
      mendations Relating to the Continuing Education of State
      Library Agency Professional Personnel. Chicago: American
      Library Association, 1971, pp. 37-45.

      As part of their institute, "Public Library Service for the
      Inner-City Disadvantaged," the Indiana University Graduate
      Library School and the Indiana State Library included an experi-
      mental consultant-development intensive training in group
      processes and the consultant role, and then developed their
      expertise in the role of resource   and reactor team for the
      institute as a whole.

      As specific objectives, content, methodology, detailed
      schedule, and a narrative report of the institute are included,
      the paper has value as a model for other continuing education
      seminars.

I-3. "In-Service Training and Intramural Communication for Supervisors:
      An Institute Sponsored by the School of Library Science, U.S.C."
      News Notes of California Libraries, 56 (Fall, 1961), 377-399.

I-4.   Institute for Local Self Government. Continuing Continuing Education for the Public Service: A Design for Action for Education and Training for the Public Service. Berkeley, Calif.: Institute for Local Self Government, 1971.

This report was prepared to assist the University of California to consider its continuing education role for community development/public administrators.

Chapter Two deals with specific "Continuing Education Needs: The View From the Field." It lists essential conditions for a successful continuing education program for the public service: 1) the continuing education program should begin with what the public servant has already experienced and act as a gate to what he has yet to discover; 2) the program should follow the most successful modern pedagogical models; 3) it should provide state and local government executives with as much insight into organizational and extra-organizational human relationships as possible;"...continuing education should be aimed at achieving the goals of the government executive; to be most effective they should be his goals." The report points out additional guides for continuing education programs based on research by Professor Howard McCluskey, School of Education, University of Michigan, concerning the differences between adult learning and childhood learning relative to the time dimension, authority relationships, and reality potentials. As they would equally apply to any library continuing education program they are quoted:

The Time Dimension: Few adults have access to the large blocks of time that are available to young people. Instead the adult must look to few and scattered periods such as evenings, weekends, vacation or released time from regular obligations. The adult's use of time is competitive. When engaged in learning, some other activity must give way.

Authority Relationships: The authority of the teacher of the young is established by law and reinforced by many factors. In adult education , the superiority possessed by the teacher is based only on the competence with which he performs his instructional tasks. The fact that both students and teachers are adults has significant implications for the climate of interaction in the learning process. It suggests the desirability of shared responsibility for the success of learning in

483

which the teacher helps the learner to learn and the learner helps the teacher to teach.

Reality Potentials: For the young, schooling is largely pre-paratory for a world of experience yet to come. For adults, learning arises from and becomes part of the here-and-now world of life itself. There is often a one-to-one relation between the item learned and the presence of that item in daily work experience. In no other area of education is the ratio of input to impact potentially so favorable and impressive.

Chapter Three makes the report's major recommendation -- "A California Staff College for State and Local Government to provide continuing education for the public service, under the sponsorship of the University of California." This proposal is presented in great detail, including curriculum guidelines, major budget features, and physical facilities. In concluding their case for the Staff College the following Harvard comment is cited as pertinent:

There is surely one lesson at least, that the schools of public administration can learn from the older professional schools in American universities; the better ones have moved steadily away from applied training that is designed to help a man gain admittance to his profession, and towards the new fundamental kinds of education that help him adapt to new developments by continuous self education throughout his career.

Chapter Four gives a comprehensive review of "Technology: The New Resource for Continuing Education."

Chapter Five presents 100 annotated bibliographical references on the role of academic institutions in community development/ public administration continuing education. Appendix A pre-sents 31 pages of sample models for continuing education in the public service. Appendix C summarizes an International Seminar on Training of Senior Local Government Officers held in Berlin in March, 1970.

I-5.   "Institutes for Training in Librarianship," School Libraries, 18
          (Spring, 1969), 65-72.

          An announcement of institutes for training in librarianship, held
          in the summer of 1969 and the academic year 1969-70. The
          program upgraded and updated the competencies of persons
          serving all types of libraries and information centers.

I-6.   International City Managers Association. The Municipal Yearbook:
          An authoritative resume of activities and statistical data of
          American cities. Chicago: International City Managers
          Association, 1934-

          Each yearbook includes a chapter on personnel administration
          in which trends and new or significant training problems are
          mentioned briefly. References to specific university programs
          are frequently included.

I-7.   International City Managers Association. Program of Professional
          Development for Urban Management: A Policy Statement.
          Chicago: International City Managers Association, 1964.

          This is a policy statement of the Association calling for in-
          creased attention to continuing education for city managers.
          Attention is called to unmet needs and the emerging necessities
          for career development.

I-8.   Isaacs, Julian M. "In-Service Training for Reference Work,"
          Library Association Record, 71 (October, 1969), 301-302.

          The article describes a training method used in the commercial
          and technical reference department of a public library which
          could be applied to other libraries. The method involves per-
          sonally supervised training, assessment and the use of question
          papers dealing with different kinds of reference queries.

I-9.   Issue Committee and Lindeman, Edward C. "Evaluating Your Program."
          Adult Leadership, 1 (April, 1953), 18-19.

J-1.   Janaske, Paul C. "OE's Institutes Program," Library Journal,
        93 (September 1, 1968), 2972-74.

        A summary report on the current program of institutes for
        training in librarianship under Title II-B of the Higher Educa-
        tion Act and on the plans for fiscal 1969.

J-2.   Jensen, Barry T. "Taped Lectures in Management Team Training:
        A Review of Several Group Experiences," Training and
        Development Journal, 21 (January, 1967), 6-9.

J-3.   Jerkedal, Ake. Top Management Education: An Evaluation Study.
        Stockholm, Sweden: Svenska Tryckeri Bolagen, 1967.

        This thoughtful study concentrates on three areas of manage-
        ment training: 1) relationships between training objectives and
        training evaluation; 2) relationship between background factors
        and initial standing -- change; and 3) attitude change.

        The author found that the tendency to change was most closely
        related to two variables: 1) the degree of motivation which
        impels participants to take training, and 2) whether or not the
        organization which sends the staff members to courses has
        impressed upon every participant why he should undergo the
        training and how the course will meet his training needs in his
        present job. The emphasis throughout is that those engaged
        in management training should be more generally aware that if
        training is to be more effective it must not be primarily seen
        as an exercise in instruction, but provision must be made for
        an analysis of training objectives and the necessary evaluation
        to see if the objectives have been attained. The research
        evaluation tools used in the four courses are included.

        The author concludes by questioning seriously whether manage-
        ment training without evaluating results is worth the effort
        involved.

J-4.   Jesse, William H., and Mitchell, Ann E. "Professional Staff
        Opportunities for Study and Research," College and Research
        Libraries, 29 (March, 1968), 87-100.

        This study examines the opportunities available to academic
        librarians to spend part of their working time in study and
        research, The information was obtained from questionnaires
        returned from 52 libraries, and 15 college libraries. Among
        the opportunities considered are time released from ordinary
        schedules for course work and research, sabbatical and special
        leaves for these purposes, and financial assistance.

J-5.   Jessup, F. W., ed. Lifelong Learning: A Symposium on Continuing
        Education. Oxford, England: Pergamon Press, 1969.

        Beginning with an assessment of the need for educational
        change in Great Britain, the papers in this anthology underline
        the relationship of continuous learning to both work and leisure.
        Consideration is given to the idea of lifelong learning and its
        implications for British institutions of formal education.

J-6.   Jones, Charles E. "Report of the Committee on Recognition of Con-
        tinuing Engineering Studies." In: 35th Annual Report for the
        Year Ending September 30, 1967 of the Engineers' Council for
        Professional Development. New York: Engineers' Council for
        Professional Development, 1967.

        The Committee on Recognition of Continuing Engineering
        Studies was appointed by the Engineers' Council for Profes-
        sional Development because it was felt a new approach was
        needed to stimulate the participation of engineers in continuing
        education courses aimed at improving their technical and non-
        technical capability and understanding in order to improve their
        effectiveness as employees and their own satisfaction as pro-
        fessionals. The new approach decided upon was a well-
        organized recognition system in addition to the academic degree
        system of education. This report describes the system in
        detail. A few of the more salient features are summarized
        here. The system is based on 1) a mechanism to evaluate and
        record continuing engineering studies and courses in accordance
        with course evaluation criteria; 2) a system of accumulation of
        credit and the evaluation of the composite for recognition of
        awarding national Achievement Certificates. Criteria were
        established in the areas of content, extent, instruction

competence, student performance, and sponsorship. For the award of an Achievement Certificate, criteria were established on the basis of units of study. For example, an ECPD certificate will be awarded upon the accumulation of a minimum of 20 units of study together with the submission of a short essay outlining the plan of the student in his pursuit of continuing education, and the way he considers the 20 units to fit into his plan. Additional certificates will be granted for each additional 20 units of study recognized by ECPD accompanied by an essay. Course certificates will be issued in triplicate, the original and one copy to be given to the student by the organization conducting the course. The third copy will be sent to ECPD headquarters. The essay shall be read to determine whether the student has given proper consideration to an integrated program of continuing education in selecting his courses. When the ECPD considers that the selection has been too random or opportunistic, additional units beyond the 20 submitted may be required before a certificate is issued. A time limit will be established beyond which credits will become obsolete.

J-7.   Jones, W. H., and Booth, Alan. "Decisions by Scientists and Engineers to Participate in Educational Programs Designed to Increase Scientific Competence." Unpublished nondegree study, National Science Foundation, 1966.

J-8.   Josey, E. J., and Blake, Fay M. "Educating the Academic Librarian," Library Journal, 95 (January 15, 1970), 125-130.

Education for academic librarians must turn to subject specialization and prepataion for meeting the faculty standards. Opportunities for continuing education must be provided.

J-9.   Journal of Continuing Education in Nursing.

Launched at a national convention of the American Nurses' Association in 1970, the journal's objectives are: 1) to bring together a body of literature pertinent to continuing education in nursing; 2) to scan the horizon for developing trends in education and health care, which will have impact on continuing education in nursing; 3) to report program designs and educational approaches which have proved effective in meeting some of the learning needs of the nurse practitioner and those significant others under nursing supervision who assist in providing care to patients; 4) to present experimental and innovative

J-9 (cont.)

approaches which offer new and more promising routes to the adult nurse learner; 5) to explore problem areas of major concern to those in continuing education; 6) to offer an additional outlet for those who are motivated to write and add to the developing theory, methodology, and body of information relating to continuing education in nursing.

K-1. Kanun, Clara. Evaluation of a Graduate Professional Improve-
      ment Program, 1965-1966. St. Paul, Minnesota: University
      of Minnesota, General Extension Division, 1966. (ED 010 856.)

      The purpose of the study was to evaluate the Graduate Profes-
      sional Improvement Program, jointly sponsored by the General
      Extension Division and The Institute of Agriculture of the
      University of Minnesota. To achieve this objective a survey
      questionnaire was administered to participants, their employers,
      and the faculty. Participants were surveyed both before and
      after their courses, which included graduate degree credit
      courses, certificate credit courses, and noncredit seminars.
      The participants were professional workers in the fields of
      agriculture and agricultural education. A consensus was
      reached that the courses fulfilled the student's expectations
      and education needs. The study is chiefly valuable as suggest-
      ing possible design techniques that might be used to evaluate
      other continuing professional education programs.

K-2. Kaser, David. "Continuing Education in the Library Profession."
      In: Louisiana University, Baton Rouge, Libraries. Libraries
      Lectures, numbers 1-4. Baton Rouge, La.: The Library,
      1967, pp. 1-9.

      The author, Director of the Cornell University Libraries,
      recognizes that there are opportunities in the literature which
      facilitate the self-education of the individual librarian, and
      which can help him overcome the resistance to change. He
      finds that it is library management which is doing the least to
      overcome resistance to change. Very few libraries have effec-
      tive programs of staff development, according to Kaser. But
      he feels that many things can be done "to counter-effect pro-
      fessional dry rot." He lists some of these activities and ad-
      knowledges that they take time, but he believes that the time
      invested "returns the time invested many times over in bene-
      fits to the individuals involved, to the libraries with which they
      are associated and certainly to the profession at large. Further-
      more, it costs management only inconvenience to have a staff
      member on leave without pay. I would like to see a library
      frankly carry on its staff 10 to 15 per cent more librarians
      than it can afford to pay at any given time, on the assumption
      that at least that many people would always be on foreign

490

assignment, on sabbatical leave, working on sponsored research or on a grant, or in some other way on leave without pay."

He insists the best way to accomplish needed change in the profession must come from the library management. "Library management must now, I believe, assume its proper leadership role in making librarianship that kind of profession by concerning itself with the constant and continuing education of our best people. By helping them fulfill themselves individually, we help the profession fulfill itself collectively, and society cannot afford to support us unless we return a full measure for its investment in us."

K-3.   Kaser, David. "Making the Effort." In: Stone, Elizabeth W.
        New Directions in Staff Development: Moving from Ideas to
        Action. Chicago: American Library Association, Library
        Administration Division, 1971, pp. 6-10.

        Paper presented at a Micro-Workshop on Staff Development at
        the American Library Association Conference, June 28, 1970.
        sponsored by the Staff Development Committee of the Personnel
        Administration Division of ALA.

K-4.   Kaser, David. "The Training Subsystem." Library Trends, 20
        (July, 1971), 71-77.

        The author offers a general view of the training subsystem and
        its elements, the degree to which training is systematically
        provided for in library systems, and the extent of library re-
        sources that are being regularly budgeted for training. His dis-
        cussion is based on a survey that he conducted of 145 of the
        largest libraries in the nation late in 1970. He concludes that
        although the American library community is becoming increas-
        ingly aware of the need for training programs and for the con-
        tinuing education of personnel, and that although substantial
        resources are being devoted to the effort, there is no systematic
        approach being made to the problem; managers are playing an
        essentially passive role in the area of personnel development.

K-5. Katz, Saul M. Education for Development Administrators: Character, Form, Content and Curriculum. Pittsburgh, Pa.: Graduate School of Public and International Affairs, University of Pittsburgh, 1967.

This article presents a model curriculum with four themes deemed necessary for the development of administrators of development programs. The themes discussed and developed are a substantive knowledge of the development process; a grounding in purposeful methodology; a thorough understanding of the principles and practices of administration; and preparation for a professional career. The content of these four themes is sketched by characteriz'ng the courses in blocks of work that comprise them. The courses are then combined to

K-6. Kelley, Alden D. The Continuing Education for the Ministry Movement. 1969. (ED 042 081.)

The continuing education of the clergy includes, in addition to theological education, sociocultural disciplines, training in professional skills, and personal development. Institutional structures for providing continuing education are many and varied -- theological schools, universities and colleges, conference and study center, institutes, interseminary centers, denominational boards, and interdenominational organizations. The question of who has the responsibility for providing continuing education is debatable. A strong case can be made for seminaries, but it might be a peripheral interest and a financial strain. It has been suggested that an interseminary approach -- already undertaken with some success -- seems the best approach.

The residential study approach has some advantages over other programs, as shown by the "Tower Room Scholars" (Union Theological Seminary in Richmond), the "Seabury Fellows" (Seabury-Western Theological Seminary, Evanston), and others. There should be some association with, or in the setting of, a good University.

A minister may be motivated by a career or identity crisis or by the authority of hierarchical jurisdictions. The author urges

492

denominational or interdenominational boards to publicize evaluative criteria for judging programs, to provide financial support, and to act as the intermediary between the agencies and the ministers.

K-7.   Kellogg Foundation. Continuing Education: An Evolving Form of Adult Education. Battle Creek, Michigan: W.K. Kellogg Foundation, 1959.

K-8.   Kellogg Foundation. Toward Improved School Administration: A Decade of Professional Effort to Heighten Administrative Understanding and Skills. Battle Creek, Michigan: The W.K. Kellogg Foundation, 1961.

K-9.   Kelly, Burnham. Preparatory Study Toward the Improvement of Education in Collegiate Schools of Architecture. Final Report. Washington, D.C.: Association of Collegiate Schools of Architecture, 1968. (ED 042 081)

The Committee in Graduate Study and Research of the Association of Collegiate Schools of Architecture held a conference in Chicago in April 1968 to study possible innovations in architecture and architectural education. Drawing upon the experiences of educators in the areas of medicine, engineering, and research design, the conferees studied the problems and opportunities in developing graduate study. From the conference, four resolutions were formed and presented to the annual meeting of the association of collegiate schools of architecture, which were approved.

K-10.   Kendall, Patricia L. Continuing Education for Medical Practitioners. Evanston, Illinois: The Association of American Medical Colleges, 1965. (ED 021 193)

A survey was made of the provision for continuing education for physicians as provided by medical schools. Courses were found in most communities studied, but it was not thought that they were an effective means of improving the quality of medical care. They were seen, however, as means of maintaining good relations with local practitioners, the state medical society, and legislators.

493

K-11.   Kenney, Louis A.   "Continuing Education for Academic Librarians."
        California Librarian, 30 (July 1969), 199-202.

        Continuing education courses offer about the only means whereby
        librarians already in the field may prepare themselves to deal
        with the communications explosion and the applications of com-
        puter technology in the university library. If the library fails
        to keep up, it will soon find itself in an inferior position when
        it comes to providing adequate high quality information ser-
        vice. Kenney also urges library schools to give two or three
        more years of graduate training to persons entering the upper
        levels of the profession.

K-12.   Keren, C. "Guidelines for Development of a Training Program for
        Special Librarians." In: The Proceedings of the International
        Conference on Education for Scientific Work, Queen Elizabeth
        College, London, 3rd to 7th April, 1967, 1967.
        The Hague, FID, Area IIIb, Page 2, 1104-1109.

K-13.   Kimberly-Clark Corporation. Research and Engineering. "Bank-
        Account" Policy for Continuing Education: Environment for
        Growth. Up-dating and Refresher Study, Graduate and Post-
        Graduate Fellowships, Career Development by Objective.
        Neenah, Wisc.: Kimberly-Clark Corporation, 1968.

        Kimberly-Clark is an industry which believes in the unique cap-
        acity and growth potential of the individual, and offers a plan
        providing time and money for continuing education in the form
        of up-dating refresher study, and graduate and post-graduate
        fellowships. The plan also provides for career development
        by objective.   Three objectives are given for the program:
        1) providing an environment for individual growth; 2) stimula-
        ting in all employees a positive attitude toward the need for a
        high level of professional and technical competencies which
        is continuously up-dated and extended; 3) supplying an op por-
        tunity for each person to carry out self-development activities
        which meet his own needs and objectives for future growth.

K-14. Klapper, Margaret S. The MIST Program. Birmingham, Ala.:
University of Alabama, School of Medicine, 1970.

MIST is a telephone medical information service by which a
physician receives consultation by calling a special operator
who routes calls to the proper on-call faculty member. Each
call is taped and analyzed for future information. The service
is in operation 24 hours a day, seven days a week.

K-15. Klassen, Robert. "Institutes for Training in Librarianship:
Summer 1969 and Academic Year 1969/1970," Special
Libraries,60 (March, 1969), 185-189.

K-16. Klausmeier, Herbert J. and O'Hearn, George T. Research and
Development Toward the Improvement of Education. Madison,
Wisconsin: Dembar Educational Research Service, Inc., 1968.
Reprinted as an issue of The Journal of Experimental Education,
37, (Fall, 1968), 1-163.

K-17. Klempner, Irving M. "Information Centers and Continuing Education for Librarianship," Special Libraries, 59 (November,
1968), 729-732.

The lack of continuing education for librarians is a major
factor contributing to the inability of libraries to satisfy the
newly emerging user demand for in-depth information. Failure
to recognize the new information demands and failure to update
training and education to meet and satisfy this new demand are
largely responsible for the increasing of activities of information centers. Klempner urges all librarians to take the
initiative and to exert influence on all who are capable of providing and support the formal courses, meetings, seminars,
and workshops essential to keep them abreast of current developments.

K-18. Klotsche, J. M. The Urban University and the Future of Our Cities.
New York: Harper and Row, 1966.

The educational and continuing education responsibilities of urban
universities are presented. The author sees unlimited

possibilities for the recreation of American cities through
using the resources of research, teaching, and professional
services of universities. Special responsibilities of faculty
members of urban universities are delineated.

K-19.*Knezevich, S. J. "Systems Analysis and Its Relationship to Educa-
tional Planning." In: Oliva, Frank D. and Koch, E. L., eds.
Designs for the Seventies: An Administrative Perspective.
Calgary, Alberta: University of Calgary, Department of
Educational Administration, 1970.

The author, Director of the National Academy for School
Executives of the American Association of School Administrators, presents a brief but comprehensive explanation of the
"systems approach," its demands on an organization, and its
implications for a systems oriented administrator. The educational enterprise is conceptualized as a unified systematic
vehicle for translating resources in the form of money and
people into outcomes or outputs related to the goals of society.
The school system is viewed as a conversion system made up
of seven inter-related subsystems, which he identifies as:
a goals and priorities setting subsystem, a resources sub-
system, a control subsystem, a client service subsystem, an
educational manpower subsystem, an environment relations
subsystem, and a student manpower reentry and retraining sub-
system. A model showing the school as a conversion system
and its related systems is discussed. Two other dimensions
of the systems approach, PERT (program evaluation and
review techniques) and PPBS (planning programming budgeting
system) are described as major tools that can be used by the
systems oriented administrator. He concludes this unusually
helpful description of the systems approach with this
statement:

There must be literally a systems effort to move beyond
the confusion and limited awareness of systems approach
in school administration that presently characterizes the
state of the art. It must be a task force effort of local
school administrators acting in concert with specialized
representatives of institutions of higher learning, federal
agencies, and professional activities.

This excellent paper offers insights that could be used by a profession in building its continuing education subsystem.

K-20. Knezevich, S. J. The Systems Approach to School Administration: Some Perceptions of the State of the Art in 1967. Paper presented at the U. S. Office of Education Symposium on Operations Analysis of Education, November, 1967. (ED 025 853.)

Knezevich maintains that in order for systems approach to flourish in education, it is necessary to:

1) prepare more definitive educational objectives.
2) recognize the needs for the generation and use of models for educational operations.
3) develop quantitative reasoning and analysis capabilities.
4) put greater emphasis on generating alternative means to use resources to attain objectives.
5) increase administrative staff strength for planning and systems analysis.
6) have better dissemination of systems concepts and techniques. A massive effort is necessary to spread the systems concepts among administrators.

K-21. Knowles, Malcolm. Higher Adult Education in the United States. Washington, D.C.: American Council on Education, 1969.

Knowles argues that as the desire of adults for education increases, there will have to follow a proportional change in attitude by educators toward the education of adults. In this regard, Knowles has stated that the pressures being introduced by adults' needs have already begun to show themselves on the changed face of educational policies.

"Considered only a few decades ago to be a peripheral activity of the University, concerned primarily with the administration of educational programs for farmers and housewives at the high school level, adult education has emerged since the war as one of the significant and urgent missions of the modern university. "

K-22. *Knowles, Malcolm S. The Modern Practice of Adult Education: Andragogy versus Pedagogy. New York, Association Press, 1970.

The author is the Director of the Graduate Program of Adult Education at Boston University, which started in 1960. Its goals include the dual objectives of extending knowledge about adult education through research and equipping adult education practitioners with the ability to manage adult learning experiences. In this program, Knowles has been developing and testing his theory of learning, which he has named andragogy -- the art and science of teaching adults. (Andragogy is based on the Greek words, andros, meaning man, and agogos, meaning leader, which he sees as more appropriate to adult education than the word pedagogy, based on the Greek word for child, paidos.)

In practice, his theory involves shifting from transmittal techniques toward experimental techniques in the adult learning process. Thus there is a shift away from such transmittal techniques as lectures, assigned reading, and canned audio-visual presentations to experimental techniques that can make use of the learner's own experience. These include simulating, exercises, case method, critical incident process, community action project , and a wide variety of small group discussion techniques. In andragogy, "action learning" and "participative learning" are printed in bold face.

Knowles emphasizes that the reason an adult enters into education at all is to be able "to better deal with some of life's problems about which he feels inadequate now." Thus, an adult's approach to education is problem centered and Knowles contends that the organizing principle for the curriculum of adult education should involve problem areas rather than subject categories. Another difference in the approach to andragogy, as opposed to pedagogy, is the importance of starting adult learning with the problems and concerns that the adult learners bring with them. "The first thing that adult educators typically do in a classroom situation is to take a problem census. They have their adult students identify what it is that they are curious about or worried about or concerned about. Then they build a learning program around these curiosities and concerns.

Accordingly, andragogy is a student-centered, problem-oriented technology.

K-23. Knox, Alan B. "Continuing Legal Education of Nebraska Lawyers." Nebraska State Bar Journal, 13 (October, 1964), 121-36.

Through questionnaire and interview it was found that the continuing education needs of lawyers in Nebraska were quite similar to those of the American Bar Association as a whole. Because of these similarities, it seems warranted to generalize the most marked findings to the total membership.

K-24. Knox, Margaret E. "For Every Reference Librarian -- A Development Program." Southeastern Librarian, 11 (Winter, 1961), 303-10, 320.

K-25. Knox, Margaret E. "Professional Development of Reference Librarians in a University Library: A Case Study." Unpublished Doctor's dissertation, University of Illinois, Urbana, 1957.

K-26. Kohn, Robert D. "The Significance of the Professional Ideal." The Annals, 101 (May, 1922), 1-5.

K-27. Koontz, Elizabeth O. A Consumer's Hopes and Dreams for Teacher Education. The Tenth Charles W. Hunt Lecture. Washington, D.C.: The American Association of Colleges for Teacher Education, [n.d.] (ED 027 273.)

The author mentions four distinct hopes, all interrelated: 1) teacher education should become a joint endeavor between in-service teachers and teacher educators, possibly through the implementation of standards; 2) teacher education should become an educational continuum in selection, initial preparation, induction into the profession, and graduate and continuing education, by encouraging local boards to contract with teacher

499

institutions of new career programs for the disadvantaged, and
by a reorganization of the certification process; 3) teacher
education should be individualized and should emphasize sensitivity; 4) systematic orientation and induction of prospective
teachers into teaching should be developed through the study
of the sociology of the teaching profession in terms of essential
teaching tasks or abilities.

K-28. Kortendick, James J. "Continuing Education and Library Adminis-
        tration," ALA Bulletin, 61 (March, 1967), 268-272.

        This article describes an interdisciplinary seminar on middle
        management development held at Catholic University in the
        summer of 1964. It was a pilot project to determine the effec-
        tiveness of the workshop or seminar aimed specifically at pro-
        fessional librarians on middle management levels. Its purpose
        was to increase the effectiveness of present performances and
        to heighten the capacity for acceptance of added responsibilities.

K-29. Kortendick, James J. "Guid e to Library Education. Part I:
        Curriculum: Administration." Drexel Library Quarterly,
        3 (January 1967), 92-103.

        After covering content, scope of courses, and teaching techniques
        as used in the master's curriculum, the author discusses the
        role of continuing education in upgrading library administration,
        especially the role of the university in this regard. A concen-
        trated, cooperative and coordinated effort is necessary by
        those in positions of power to make continuing education and
        career development their continuing responsibility.

K-30. Kortendick, James J. "Research Needs in the Field of Continuing
        Education for Librarians, " In: Borko, Harold, ed. A Study of
        the Needs for Research in Library and Information Science
        Education. Final Report. Washington, D.C.: U. S. Office of
        Education, Bureau of Research; Los Angeles: Institute of
        Library Research, University of California, 1970, pp. 194-233.

This article reports on a research study developed to find out if federal librarians were interested in continuing education. The majority of those participating indicated that they felt a need and a desire for further study and would avail themselves of opportunities if they were available and appropriate to their needs.

K-31. Kortendick, James J. and Stone, Elizabeth W. Job Dimensions and Educational Needs in Librarianship. Chicago, Ill.: American Library Association, 1971.

This book reports on a study that was undertaken to meet more fully the continuing education demands for practicing librarians, especially at the upper and middle levels. The purpose of the research was to provide a data base for curriculum development at the post-MLS level that would equip library personnel to meet the changes confronting them.

The research centered on a study of job dimensions of practicing librarians and the educational needs of these librarians. Findings are translated into recommendations for action in the area of continuing library education. The data collected and included in the work has potential value for planning continuing library education programs at the post-MLS level.

K-32. Kortendick, James J. and Stone, Elizabeth W. Post-Master's Education for Middle and Upper-Level Personnel in Libraries and Information Centers. Final Report. Phase I. Washington, D.C.: The Catholic University of America, Department of Library Science, 1970. (ED 038 985.)

A major way of upgrading the profession of librarianship is through the provision of post-MLS educational programs. The data base collected for use in curriculum development of such programs utilized two data-gathering instruments: 1) a questionnaire to MLS practicing librarians; and 2) interviews with top-level library administrators. The data collected are presented under three headings: 1) questionnaire results; 2) interview results; and 3) summary, conclusions and recommendations for further study.

The data collected provides an information base for developing
specifications for courses responsive to knowledge and skill
requirements, especially through the analysis of the job
inventory findings and the analysis of needed competencies.
Based on the findings from the study, three priority courses
will be developed and packaged: Human Resources in the
Library System, Administration of the Special Federal Library,
and Application of Computer Technology to Library Processes.

Summarized the conclusions were: 1) the programs developed
should use an interdisciplinary approach; 2) a systems approach
should be used in planning and implementing programs; 3) the
approach should be practical and based in the library school;
4) multi-media approach to instruction should be used; 5)
motivational factors should be taken into account in order to
reach a substantial number of librarians; and 6) the program
should be offered on a part-time basis because of financial
reasons.

K-33. Kortendick, James J. and Stone, Elizabeth W. Post-Master's
Education for Middle and Upper-Level Personnel in
Libraries and Information Centers. Final Report, Phase II.
Washington, D.C.: The Catholic University of America,
Department of Library Science, 1972.

Included with the final report are its three main products --
three packaged Post-MLS courses edited by James J.
Kortendick and Elizabeth W. Stone. These are:

Becker, Joseph and Pulsifer, Josephine S. Application of
Computer Technology to Library Processes: Teacher's
Guide and Syllabus. Washington, D.C.: The Catholic
University of America, Dept. of Library Science, 1971.

Goodman, Charles H. and Stone, Elizabeth W. Human Resources in the Library System. Study Guide; Leader's
Handbook: Designs for Learning; Leader's Handbook: Aids.
3 vols. Washington, D.C.: The Catholic University of
America, Dept. of Library Science, 1972.

Zachert, Martha Jane K. The Governmental Library Simulation for the Study of Administration in a Special Library:
The Federal Library Model; Participant's Resource-Log;

<u>Director's Guide</u>. 3 vols. Washington, D. C.: The
Catholic University of America, Dept. of Library Science,
1971.

K-34. Krathwohl, David R., Bloom, B. S., and Masia, B.B. <u>Taxonomy</u>
<u>of Educational Objectives. Handbook II: Affective Domain.</u>
New York: David McKay, 1964.

This book concentrates on educational goals in the affective
domain, whereas Handbook I concentrated on the Cognitive Domain (1956). The affective domain includes objectives which
describe changes in interest, attitudes, and values, as well as
the development of appreciations and adequate adjustment.
Objectives in both the cognitive and affective domains can be
operationally described, but operation statements of objectives
in the cognitive domain are considerably more straightforward.

K-35. Kraybill, E. K. "Evaluation of a Summer Institute on Effective
Teaching," <u>Journal of Engineering Education</u>, 58 (October,
1967), 135-38. (See also Kraybill, E.K. "Evaluative Study
of Summer Institute on Effective Teaching for Engineering
Teachers." Unpublished Doctor's dissertation, University of
Michigan, 1966.)

The object of this research was the evaluation of measurable
changes in teaching effectiveness of engineering instructors as
a result of attending a two week summer Institute on Effective
Teaching for Engineering Teachers.

Although the usual evaluations and judgments by participants and
staff were obtained for all the Institutes, a more objective and
systematic evaluation of any changes of teaching effectiveness
was sought in the study.

Four methods were selected for implementing the evaluation
effort: student ratings of instructors before and after the
Institute; instructor self-ratings before and after the Institute;
inventory of partipants' knowledge, skills, and attitudes relative
to effective teaching before and after the Institute; and assessment of degree of "rigidity" of participants relative to
conceptual change and patterns of behavior. The author reached

the following conclusion: "The Institute can be viewed as successful in providing preparation deemed requisite to changes in classroom behavior that can be considered increased teaching effectiveness."

Study is valuable as a model of program evaluation designed to increase teaching effectiveness and to influence those making decisions as to whether or not teachers should receive formal training directed toward improving their effectiveness.

K-36. Kraybill, Edward K. "Evolution of Quality Teaching Programs in Engineering," Journal of Engineering Education, (October, 1967), 122-126. (ED 023 314.)

Kraybill, of the School of Engineering, Duke University, traces the history of developing more effective teaching by means of association programs, surveys, self-studies, summer programs, etc. He notes particularly the formation of the Committee for Young Engineering Teachers within the American Society for Engineering Education in 1950, which "provided a major step in the direction of enabling engineering teachers to obtain some training in pedagogy." This group was open to A.S.E.E. members who were under 36 or below associate professor in rank. Their objectives were: 1) an understanding of the general goals and responsibilities of the two professions which every teacher of engineering follows, engineering and education; 2) orientation into the history, lore, and the 'unwritten laws' of the dual profession of engineering education; 3) an acquaintance with the most effective instructional materials and methods, with methods of evaluating student achievement, and with the elements of counseling and student guidance; 4) guidance in his personal professional development both as engineer and as teacher.

The formation of this committee stimulated the holding of program meetings at ASEE for young teachers, considering such topics as determining teaching objectives, how people learn, effective evaluation practices, and the like. The influence of this group led to some institutional inservice programs, in which voluntary participants, aided by the College of Education, might meet once per week throughout a full semester.

Probably the most thorough analysis of the teaching-learning process ever undertaken by engineering education, according to

504

Kraybill, was the report of the Committee on Improvement
of Teaching, released in 1952 by its Chairman, L. E. Grinter.
That report recommended: "...that special schools or post
graduate training programs for the specific purpose of aiding
teachers to improve their methods of instruction be established
in strategically located institutions."

More recent activities included short workshops before the
Annual meeting of ASEE sponsored by the Committee for
Young Engineering Teachers, and "perhaps the most significant
activity to date," the holding of a series of four summer
Institutes on Effective Teaching for Engineering Teachers.
Two-thirds of the attendees were young engineering teachers
and one-third were more experienced ones who promised
before coming to conduct an appropriate inservice program
for their own faculty on returning to the home institution.
Recently there have been supplanted by regional Institutes of
the same nature in an attempt to reach more teachers.

K-37. Kreitlow, Burton W. Educating the Adult Educator. Part I:
Concepts for the Curriculum. Madison, Wisc.: Experiment
Station, College of Agriculture, University of Wisconsin,
1965. (ED 023 969.)

The author looks forward to the time when continuing education
and retraining is the positive alternative to unemployment; to
the time when the adult response to questions about his
employment will elicit but three alternative responses: 1) " I
have a job, "; 2) "I'm in retraining," and 3) "I'm retired."
Within this framework there can be no unemployment. "It is
then that the narrow walls of thinking about education must
crumble, and there will no longer exist the myth about higher
education being a terminal educational goal. "

K-38. Kreitlow, Burton W. Educating the Adult Educator, Part II:
Taxonomy of Needed Research. Report from the Adult Re-
Education Project. Madison, Wisc.: Research Development
Center for Cognitive Learning, University of Wisconsin,
1968. (ED 023 031.)

Kreitlow establishes a framework for research in adult education and identifies the research areas needing attention.

K-39. Kronick, David A. "Continuing Education for Medical Librarianship: A Symposium — Refresher Courses," Bulletin of the Medical Library Association, 48 (October, 1960), 415-19.

Refresher courses should help us to identify the gaps in our knowledge, to review advances in the profession, and to identify new areas of interest which are relevant to our work. However, he objects to the rigidity of many such courses and feels they should provide an organized means to discuss mutual problems in medical librarianship.

K-40. Kronick, David A., and Rees, Alan M. Educational Needs in Medical Librarianship and Mental Health Information. Cleveland: Case Western Reserve University, 1969.

K-41. Kronus, Carl L. "Inducing Attitudinal Change Among Librarians." Journal of Education for Librarianship, 12 (February, 1971), 104-115.

The paper deals with the relative importance of the social context versus ideational content as change agents in conference situations.

K-42. Kunztown State College, Department of Library Science. Educational Trends: Innovations, Technology, Multi-Media, Taxonomies of Learning, Librarianship: A Bibliographical Checklist, 1965-1971. Kutztown, Pa.: Kutztown State College, 1971.

A 122 item bibliography which was designed to serve as a bibliographical aid for administrations, library science educators, librarians, teachers, curriculum coordinators, researchers, and others who are interested in 1)planning and conducting research in educational media curriculum and instruction; 2) planning and producing an improved instructional program; 3) interested in educational trends, innovations, and forecasts. Fourteen chapters cover such topics as: Background Readings; Educational Research; Bibliographies — Theory and Methods; Educational Aims and Objectives, Philosophy, Curriculum Innovations; Computer Assisted Instruction; System Analysis,

506

K-42 (cont.)

Programmed Instruction and Simulation; Libraries Media
Centers and Multi-Media; Checklist of Nonprint Materials.

L-1. Lancaster, Otis E. "ASEE-Pen State Summer Institutes on Effective Teaching for Engineering Teachers." The Journal of Engineering Education, 58 (October, 1967), 127-131.

A report on four unique, two-week, eight-hour-a-day (plus reading assignments), summer institutes devoted exclusively to discussion of the "teaching-learning" process, at the Pennsylvania State University, 1960 through 1963, under the sponsorship of the Educational Methods Division, ASSEE, and the Ford Foundation. Over a four-year period, there were 247 participants -171 Young Engineering Teachers (YETS) and 76 more experienced teachers (METS) - who acquired knowledge, skills, and attitudes which would be condusive to conditions considered essential for effective learning.

The institutes consisted of three kinds of activities: daily reading assignments, lecturers, and discussions directed by authorities on the subject, and practicums in which the participants gave their interpretations of the principles.

There were nine practicums: four demonstrations of teaching and five of related preparations for teaching. In the demonstrations, each participant gave a 10-minute lecture, conducted a 20-minute discussion class, taught a 40-minute class, and made a 5-minute presentation over closed-circuit television. In these simulated classes, each participant alternately assumed the role of student and of teacher. All of the teaching and speaking demonstrations were recorded on audio tape, and the television classes were recorded on video tape. The recordings were played back immediately after each presentation for criticism, first by the participant and then by other members of the group and by the workshop leaders.

L-2. Landau, Robert M, Personal Information Acquisition, Storage and Retrieval, Washington, D. C.

"A recent survey of 200 scientists in a variety of disciplines revealed that: less than 15% maintain over 100 files of professional interest; less than 50% maintain indexes to their files; and 75% consult personal files less than 25% of the time to answer professional questions. This, together with other data collected, suggests that personal files are ineffective sources of information required for professional activities. The lack of use of personal files is not because other sources are adequate, but rather because present arrangements can not be more usefully employed. Information is proliferating at an ever increasing rate. The road to improvement is not clear. Some help on published material is being provided by abstract services. Maintenance of personal files is becoming more difficult. Neither coordinate indexing schemes (with or without mechanical aids) nor SDI systems have been widely accepted. We limp along, making decisions on a small fraction of the information we know should be available. Some hope for improvement may lie in the recent convergence of technologies which will allow the dream to become a reality. Significant experimentation in this area is now taking place.

L-3. Landis, Frederick. Continuing Engineering Education: Who Really Needs It? New York University (NASA Grant NGL-33-016-067).

In a study of 1146 engineers in 12 major companies, it was found that continuing education is frequently hindered by the attitude of the immediate supervisor, by the absence of easily identified pay-out function, by haphazard regional planning and by the anti-intellectual attitudes that persist in many organizations. In part, the study concluded that" . . . most engineers are not interested in continuing education, they are interested in doing their current job better. They will respond to training rather than to education and they will demand an almost immediate payoff in terms of recognition or salary," and that even though top management may have expressed a real interest in continuing education, the immediate supervisor must encourage and adjust to continuing education needs, in spite of possible interference with work schedules.

L-4. "Landmark Statement from California: Assembly Bill No. 449." The Journal of Continuing Education in Nursing. 2 (September-October, 1971), 2831.

This bill, passed by the Assembly of the California legislature, is the proposed addition to the Business and Professions Code, relating to health occupations. It represents a history-making attempt to legislate for continuing education. The bill provides for the establishment of a Council on Continuing Education for the Health Occupations, consisting of a director, who shall serve as the chairman of the council, and four additional members appointed by the director;

one administrator of a licensed hospital; one registered nurse; one licensed vocational nurse, one public member.

The duties of the Council are "To establish standards for continuing education which will assure reasonable currency of knowledge as a basis for safe practice." The standards "shall be established in a manner to assure that a variety of alternatives is available," including, but not limited to, academic studies, in-service education insitutes, seminars, lectures, conferences, workshops, extension studies, and home-study programs.

L-5. Lange, Carl J. Developing Programs for Teachers. Professional Paper 20-69. Alexandria, Virginia: Human Resources Research Office, George Washington University, 1969. (ED 033 902).

L-6. Lange, Carl J. and others. Training Leaders with Sound Films and Group Discussion Techniques. Alexandria: Human Resources Research Office, George Washington University, 1969. (ED 030 081.).

L-7. Larimer, George S., and W. Ward Sinclair. "Some Effects of Two-Way Television on Social Interaction," AV Communication Review, 17 (Spring, 1969), 52-62.

L-8. Lassiter, Robert T. G., Danclovic, Joseph, and Andes, C.R. "Sandia Laboratories Tests Another Model: Continuing Professional Development." IEE Transactions on Education, E-15 (May 1972), 114-118.

This is a description of Sandia Laboratories' experiment with a formal program for individualized continuing education through "development of human resources so that a person can be effective in his job throughout his career." Their continuing professional development (CDP) approach was developed by their Education Committee, composed of a cross section of technical and administrative managers.

Although the first model used for experimentation (which is described in detail) proved disappointing in some respects, criteria for a successful plan evolved: 1) A careful analysis of the educational needs that must be fulfilled to meet individual and organizational goals. 2) A broader range of activities than has been available to meet those needs, and 3) Mutual committment on the part of management and staff to pursue those activities on a long term basis.

At the moment the Laboratories are considering the use of a
decision tree or logic flow diagram which would 1) identify those
factors which infuence the individual's and organization's need for,
and willingness to undertake long term development, 2) depict
the interrelationship of those factors in manageable pieces, and
3) specify alternatives for the employee, the supervisor and the
organization.

L-9.   Lauwerys, J.A. "Definition and Goals of Professional Reading,"
       Phi Delta Kappan, 38 (June, 1957), 365-368.

L-10. Lazarus, Charles Y. "Quest for Excellence - a Businessman's Responsi-
       bility," Bulletin of Business Research, Ohio State University,
       43 (May, 1968), 1-5.

L-11. Leadership for Change: A Report of the Outreach LeadershipNetwork.
       Part I: Administrative Report by Barbara Conroy; Part 2: Eval-
       uation Report by John Bardwell and others. Durham, New Hampshire:
       Outreach Leadership Network, New England Center for Continuing
       Education, University of New Hampshire, 1972.

       The authors present a complete and thoroughly documented report
       of an institute which sought through "planned change" to extend
       library service to the "presently unserved" in New England.
       The project moved beyond traditional patterns and through the
       traditional barriers by using new methods of media and new
       strategies (or old ones new ways). The program consisted of
       three components: 1) preliminary activities intended to aid parti-
       cipants in becoming aware of community needs and attitudes;
       2) a concentrated sequence of workshops involving the partici-
       pants in a step-by-step development of individual action programs,
       and 3) follow up activities designed to facilitate the action programs
       by the participants. A team of outside evaluators, using a model
       developed at Ohio State University, known as CIPP (standing for
       four types of evaluation: context, input, process, and product),
       was responsible for the design and implementation of the evaluation
       plan to measure the effect of the project's training program exper-
       iences on the participants involved.

This 174-page report of this continuing education program for librarians is valuable as a model based on the principles and concepts of participatory management, of planned organizational development and of educational technology.

L-12. Leaf, Alexander, "The Harvard Medical Curriculum," The Harvard Medical Alumni Bulletin, (May/June, 1970), 4-11.

L-13. Lee, Robert and Charlene Swarthout Lee, "Personnel Planning for a Library Manpower System," Library Trends, 20 (July, 1971) 19-38.

Dr. Robert Lee, University Chief Librarian, and Professor, School of Library and Information Science, Western Ontario University, and his wife, Dr. Charlene S. Lee, provide in this article and overview of the major aspects of personnel planning for a library system.

The authors describe personnel planning, which is concerned with the management of human resources, in the following terms: "It is explicit planning; it is planning with such clarity and distinctness that all the elements in a library manpower system are apparent. Since it is planning for human resources, it must place particular emphasis on assisting each individual, according to his background, to achieve his career values, desires and expectations. Since it is planning for the use of human resources for effective organizational operation, personnel planning must include a statement of what kinds of qualities are desired, at what places, and at what times. It is planning which includes all personnel within the system. It is planning with emphasis on both preparing for the future and providing knowledge necessary for effective day-to-day utilization of manpower."

After identifying the initial step in personnel planning as the determination of organizational objectives which are needed in every area of activity, the succeeding component parts of personnel planning are identified and described. These are 1) the manpower plan, concerned with a forecast of organizational needs, as well as an inventory of the skills and abilities of existing personnel; 2) the personnel development plan, which is concerned with effective utilization of existing staff; and 3) the recruiting plan which is concerned with locating personnel to fill unmet and specific needs.

L-14. Lee, Robert E. , Allen, Lawrence A. , Hiatt, Peter. A Plan for Developing a Regional Program of Continuing Education for Library Personnel in the Western States. Boulder, Colorado: Western Interstate Commission for Higher Education, 1969. (ED 047 767.).

The Western Interstate Commission for Higher Education (WICHE) has provided a helpful model for other regional planners of continuing education programs in the development and publication of this paper. The plan described includes: purpose; program objectives; needs surveys; and programming, a specific regional four-year plan, including organization structure, program tasks and evaluation. "The intent of this plan is to improve the professional services of library personnel in the western states, with particular emphasis on developing a long-range program for continuing education. " The plan was designed to assist each of the participating WICHE states (Alaska, Arizona, Colorado, Idaho, Nevada, New Mexico, Washington, and Wyoming) in developing a long-range continuing education program for library personnel. Program activities are directed to personnel at all levels in all types of libraries. Typically, the education planned is of a continuing nature to provide for the individual's professional growth after his formal program of education has been completed. The four-year plan (July 1969–June 1973) provides for four periods: an organizational stage; two implementation phases, and an evaluation stage.

Complementing the levels of personnel outlined in the plan are various advisory committees, each involving library leadership in all phases of the program's development.

The continuing education needs most often identified for library personnel were listed as: administrative and managerial skills and abilities; role of libraries and their relevance to contemporary social issure and concerns; changing patterns of library service, and current library developments; and basic library skills.

L-15. Leonard, Alvin and Parlette, G. Nicholas. Partnership in Learning, an Historical Report. American Public Health Association, San Francisco, California, 1960 through 1966. (ED 015 402.).

The history (1960 - 1966) of the continuing education program of the Western Branch of the American Public Health Association is reviewed, together with the professional educational needs and the federal support that brought it into being. Of particular note are the seminars and courses developed on such topics as chronic disease, health services, administration, mental health, and environmental health during this period. An account is also given fo the current (1967) organizational structure (including the committees representing the 13 member states), sources of funds (mainly tuitions, grants, and contracts), responsibility for curriculum development and course presentation, methods of study and instruction, program evaluation (notable the use of PERT procedures), and practical applications in state public health program administration. (The document includes education qualifications of 1966-67 registrants, and eight figures and tables.)

L-16. Lewin, Kurt. "Field Theory and Learning." In: National Society for the Study of Education. The Psychology of Learning. 41st Yearbook, Part II. Chicago: University of Chicago Press, 1942, 215-242.

L-17. Lieberman, Irving. "Library Executive Development Institue -April 1969," Noted for the Alumni, 26 (Fall, 1969) 12-13.

L-18. Likert, Rensis. The Human Organization: Its Management and Value. New York: McGraw-Hill 1967.

The management system of an organization must have compatible component parts if it is to function effectively. Experiments in organizations must involve internally consistent changes. Because the organic integrity of each system must be maintained while experimental variations are being made a systems approach must be used. A planned change should start by altering first the most influential causual variable then there should be systematic plans to modify in coordinated steps all of the operating procedures which now anchor the organization to its present management system. The systems principle must also be applied to development activities

to insure 1)consistency between the system of management of a company
and the content of development programs for its managers, and
2) the internal consistency of content of management development
courses. Successful organizations are characterized by internally
consistent principles and procedures. The need for consistency and
the systems approach must be considered in all 1) organizational
research; 2) attempts to improve organizations by applying
research findings and 3) management development programs.

L-19. Lilley, Dorothy. "Graduate Education Needed by Information Special-
ists and the Extent to Which it is Offered in Accredited Library
Schools. " Unpublished Doctor's dessertation, Columbia University,
New York, 1969.

L-20. Lippitt, Ronald. "Dimensions of the Consultant's Job. " Journal of
Social Issues, 15 (No. 2, 1959) 5-12.

Recent literature in the progessions gives an important place to the
consultant in staff development and continuing education. Lippitt
defines the consultation relationship as "a voluntary relationship
between a professional helper (consultant) and help-needing system
(client) in which the consultant is attempting to give help to the
client in the solving of some current or potential problem, and the
relationship is perceived as temporary by both parties. Also,
the consultant is an outsider, i.e., is not a part of any hierarchical power system in which the client is located. " Lippitt gives
typical questions and problems faced by the consultant in the application of his role: 1) What seems to be the difficulty ? Where does
it come from ? What maintains it ? 2) What are my motives as
a consultant for becoming involved in this helping relationship ?
What are the bases of my desire to promote change ? 3) What seem
to be the present, or potential, motivations of the client toward
change or against change ? 4) What are my resources, as a consultant,
for giving the kind of help that seems to be needed now, or that may
develop ? 5) What preliminary steps of action are needed to explore
and establish a consulting relationship ? 6) How do I as a consultant
guide, adapt to the different   phases of the process of changing ?
7) How do I help promote a continuity of creative changeability ?

L-21. Liveright, A.A. "Learning Never Ends: A Plan for Continuing
Education." In Eurich, Alvin C., ed. Campus 1980: The
Shape of the Future in American Higher Education. New York:
Delacorte Press, 1968.

Liver predicts a new institutional form--a College of Continuing
Education--in each urban university. The student body is the
entire community; the faculty is drawn from all facets of the
community; the Alumni Association includes the key leaders in
the community. "By process of this total community involvement,
the university and the idea of education and lifelong learning have
become accepted by all persons and classes in the community."
Problem solving for the city will center in the Metropolis University
and the College of Continuing Education. The College of Continuing
Education will design its curriculum to meet the needs of adults
by establishing four institutes, each with its own planning committee
composed of community members with relevant experience together
with the faculty of the College of Continuing Education. These
are identified as: 1) The Institute for Occupational and Professional
Development, to answer the needs of the adult as a worker;
2) The Institute for Personal and Family Development, to assist the
adult to achieve maximum effectiveness in family and personal
relations; 3) the Institute for Civic and Social Development, to prepare
him for participating in community, national, and world affairs; 4)
the Institute for Humanistic and Liberal Development, to encourage
self-realization and personal fulfillment. In addition to the Institutes,
three centers are projected: 1) a Center for Counseling and Community Referral: 2) a Center for Problem-Solving. According to
plan, the centers are an integral part of the College of Continuing
Education. They cut across the four institutes and provide services
and research to all of them. The use of the most up-to-date
information storage and retrieval systems in the Learning Center
(physical core of the campus) will make maximum use of the new
technology; it will tie in with networks of information and also
have tie ins with home learning carrels.

L-22. Liveright, A.A. and DeCrow, Roger. New Directions in Degree
Programs Especially for Adults. Chicago: Center for the Study
of Liberal Education for Adults, 1963.

The authors cite three reasons behind the growing demand for
continuing adult education. One is that adults need to return to

516

education to update and expand their intellectual horizons.
Another is that the demand has changed because of the expanded
use of multi-media devices which make access to education
difficult. The third is the growing practice of giving credit
based on examination alone, that is without such requirements
as classroom attendance or weekly papers.

L-23. Livingston, J. Sterling. "Pygmalion in Management," Harvard Business
Review, 47 (July-August, 1969) 81-9.

Emphasizes the importance of managerial expectations for individual
and group performance. From his research it is revealed that:
1) What a manager expects of his subordinates and the way he
treats them largely determines their performance and career
progress: 2) a unique characteristic of superior managers is
their ability to create high performance expectations that subordinates fulfill; 3) subordinates, more often than not, apprear
to do what they believe they are expected to do.

L-24. Long Huey B. Continuing Education Interests of Municipal Officials
in East Central Florida. Titusville, Florida: Florida State University,
Urban Research Center, 1967. (EDRS ED 011 639.).

This study investigated continuing education activities and attitudes
of 71 city officials (mostly male and middle-aged) in seven counties
of East Central Florida. A questionnaire obtained data on regularity
of educational activities, preferred methods, interest in education
related to the official's duties, desired subject areas, organizations
and institutions considered responsible, attitudes toward residential
short courses, and perceived adequacy of the educational preparation
for public office. Findings indicated that appointed city officials
attach greater value to such activities than elected officials, but
interest in general is strong, particularly in courses on fiscal
policy and management. However, limited programs and travel
requirements with attendant loss of time make courses unattractive.
Officials prefer that the Florida Leaque of Municipalities and the
Florida State University system assume responsibility for education.
Regional education centers might provide a connection between the
local region and the campus. A longitudinal study of these respondents and an indepth study of characteristics of participants and
nonparticipants would be valuable, as would provision of experimental
programs. The questionnaire used in the study is included.

L-25. Lorenz, John G. "The Challenge of Change," PNLA Quarterly, 29 (October, 1964) 7-15.

> Speaking at a conference of the PNLA, Lorenz said that the library profession recognizes the need for continuing education and has made a beginning; but, he emphasized that it still has a long way to go to achieve adequacy by any standard.
>
> Lorenz sensed the urgent need for a dynamic program of continuing education to assist the profession in understanding, even anticipating, the stresses of rapid and radical change. "The development of strong programs for the coming decades demands from professional associations, library schools, and librarians a committment to the ideas of self-renewal and excellence in professional education." He put forth the thesis that society has a right to look to the various professions themselves for effective planning and action in developing opportunities for continuing education. He emphasized that successful programs are too important to be left to chance planning and chance sponsorship. Only as all appropriate agencies coordinate their efforts can such programs be developed and maintained.

L-26. Lowrie, Jean E. "Sixth-Year Degree," Library Journal, 92 (January 1967), 170.

L-27. Luke, Robert. "Continuing Education in Professional Associations: The National Education Association." Paper presented at the Mini-workshop sponsored by the Standing Committee of Continuing Library Education of the Association of American Library Schools at the Annual Conference, at the Shoreham Hotel, Washington, D. C., Jaunuary 28, 1973.

> Mr. Luke of the Division of Instruction and Professional Development of the National Education Association, prefaced his remarks by noting how radically theories of learning have changed since the second world war. Increasingly, the emphasis is on learning functions, on inservice or continuing professional development as far as teachers are concerned. Another factor is a demonstrated lack of confidence in public education and this has led to new forces which may be called "accountability." "What this boils down to is states are going to set up certain standards as to what youngsters should attain as a group, and measure the youngsters at some point to

see if they meet that standard, and the teacher will be held accountable for any variance in that scale" Another changing factor is an
increased emphasis on competency, rather than on serving time, or
meeting requirements--this is reflected in competency-based
teacher education. "Recognition of achievement is going to be
based on demonstratable skills, rather than on clock hours in
classes." Finally, Luke explained that boards of education have
been moving increasingly into the field of inservice education;
previously it was almost entirely centered in the institutions
of higher education. Now boards of education are themselves
setting up inservice education programs. "The reasons that these
boards are doing such programs is precisely the same reasons that
business likes to train its own people; the superintendents and
boards have pressures on them from the federal government,
Congress, state legislature--everywhere. To respond to these
pressures, the boards are offering their own programs of inservice
education.

Luke explained that NEA was doing basically three things in continuing
professional development: 1) "Our basic philosophical position
unlike the other two groups you already heard, is teacher's dues
will not be used for inservice professional development. Rather
teacher's dues will be used to put pressure on boards of education
and colleges of education to provide the kind of inservice education
that is relevant. 2) We are currently developing a program of
teacher centers. The basic idea of the teacher center is an inservice
educational development process, which involves a wide range of
learning experiences, including constant evaluation. We are concerned that the governance of the teacher center should be made up
of teachers. 3) We are also working for a needs assessment
program. "This is a tricky business because of the variety of
responses that you receive. Local associations are trying to find
the kinds of procedures for need identification that take into account
all of the kinds of influences that work on teachers. We want local
associations to work collaboratively with students, faculty, administration so that needs represent a comprehensive picture of the
situation.

In closing, Mr. Luke made three predictions about inservice education in the future so far as NEA's role in that operation: 1) The
staff of an organization like NEA is going to become increasingly
involved in a consultative role in process planning of inservice
education programs and what they ought to do. This consultation

will be both at the needs assessment level, and at the negotiating
level. 2) Increasingly, the teachers of other teachers in inservice
education are going to be teachers themselves. There is a tremendous amount of knowledge and experience in that group.
Furthermore, they have an enormous amount of credibility.
3) Training is going to become increasingly behaviorally measured.
The assessment of a training program will depend on whether or
not there is changed teacher behavior.

L-28. Lynch, Patric and Blackstone, Peggy L., eds. Institutional Roles for
Inservice Education of School Administrators. Columbus, Ohio:
University Council for Educational Administration, 1966.

A report of a task-force seminar of the University Council for
Education Administration reviews the status and problems of inservice
and continuing education of Alburquerque, New Mexico, school
administrators.

L-29. Lysaught, Jerome P. "Continuing Education: Necessity and Opportunity."
Journal of Continuing Education in Nursing 1 (September, 1970) 5-10.

The author explains that in 1968, the independent National Commission
on the Study of Nursing and Nursing Education became operational.
This body was the outgrowth of a recommendation made 5 years
earlier by the Surgeon General's Consultant Group on Nursing. He
states that three documents have been produced which "describe
one of the broadest examinations ever conducted of any profession."
They are 1) A summary report and recommendations of the Commission
were made in February 1970 after two years of intensive study.
2) The final report, An Abstract for Action, also in 1970. 3) A
final volume of appendices to an Abstract for Action which provides more detailed information on the conduct, preliminary findings and evolving outcomes of the investigation.

From the Commissions's intensive study, "it is significant, then,
that one of the most salient problems in all nursing soon emerged
as that of continuing education." In the report the following definitions were adopted and used:

L-29 (cont. -1)

Preparatory Education: initial sequences of professional
content, combined with requried elements of other
disciplines, which enable the graduate to pursue basic
nursing practice with safety and skill while providing
a foundation for the pursuit of increased competency
and advanced learning.

Continuing Education: a formalized learning experience or sequence designed to enlarge the knowledge
or skills of practitioners who have completed preparatory sequences. As distinct from Advanced Education,
continuing education courses tend to be more specific,
of generally shorter duration, and may result in
certificates or completion or specialization, but not
in formal academic degrees.

Advanced Education is sequences of professional courses
aimed at developing specialized qualifications and
characterized by formal academic recognition of
completion, such as the doctoral degree.

Inservice Education: a program administered by an
employer designed to upgrade the knowledge or skills of
the agency's own employees.

Because of the "chaos and lack of articulation" of these programs,
The Commission identified its primary recommendation in nursing
education that:

Each state have, or create, a master planning committee that
will take nursing under its purview, such committee to
include representatives of nursing, education, other
health professions and the public, to recommend specific guidelines, means for implementation, and deadlines
to ensure that nursing education is positioned in the
mainstream of American educational patterns with its
preparatory programs located in collegiate institutions.

The Commission was concerned with "the paradoxical need for
increased graduate education in nursing balanced by a need for
assurance of institutional and faculty quality. Too sudden a
proliferation of graduate programs, perhaps in place of the
enlargement of existing programs, could threaten the entire

Advanced Education area of the nursing profession. Accordingly, the Commission recommended that:

> The state master planning committee for nursing education be particularly concerned that the number of graduate programs be consistent with human and economic resources, and that the inauguration or expansion of weak programs not be permitted.

The committee felt it important to deal with continuing and in-service education as an intergral part of a "spectrum of educational activities that were required for professional competence and growth.

The state master planning committee for nursing education was also asked to identify one or more institutions to be responsible for regional coverage of continuing education programs for nurses within that area.

It also state that:

> --Federal and state funds be utilized to plan and implement conintuing education programs for nursing on either a statewide or border basis (as suggested by the current interstate compacts for higher education); and
> --In the face of changing health roles and functions, and the interdependence of the health professions, vigorous efforts be taken to have continuing education programs jointly planned and conducted by interdisciplinary teams.

The basic philosophy of the Commission's action program for continuing education is summarized as follows:

> 1) Continuing education should be an essential element on the agenda of the master planning committee-- on an equal plane with preparatory and advanced education.
> 2) There must be designated responsibility for the planning accomplishment of the program . . . The institutions of higher learning and the interstate commissions for higher education must become more involved and must be

L-29 (cont. -3)
given responsibility and support in far greater
measure for the lifelong growth of professional
learning.
3) The importance that we have placed in the Commission report on the growth of nursing practice
through the joint planning of congruent roles in
health care demands--among other things--that
continuing education be run on congruent and
interdisciplimary bases.

The Commission further recommended that:

Health care facilities, including hospitals, nursing homes, and other institutions, either individually or collectively through joint councils,
provide professional training and staff to supervise and conduct inservice training and provide
released time, facilities, and organizational
support for the presentation of inservice nursing
education as well as that for other occupations.

This recommendation, also, had three important elements:

1) Through cooperative and joint approaches,
better means can be built, rather than be
bounded by the limited funding and human
resources of one institution.
2) There must be professional inservice
faculty for the students.
3) Adequate time and conditions must be provided for these educational efforts or else
they will be shunned by those for whom they
were intended to positive opportunities.

Lysaught concludes his paper by stating:

No amount of institutional or financial aid,
however, can servive to deflect the absolute
pinpointing of responsibility for development
on the individual nurse. As Florence Night-
ingale emphasized, not to progress is to fall
back. In our technological world of today with
its commonplace miracles of health care and

523

distribution can, in the last analysis, make
nursing an unambiguous profession. The
National Commission, the master planning
committees, the joint practice boards, the
growth of support bodies, all these can place
tools at nursing's disposal. But in a world
in which knowledge is the surest power,
nursing will ultimately choose to wield power
or to cast it away. Continuing education
is an intergral portion of the long path
upward for nursing.

L-30. Lysaught, Jerome. "Research on the Use of Programmed Instruction
Among Adult Learners in Professional Health Fields." Paper
presented at the National Seminar on Adult Education Research,
(Chicago, February 11-13, 1968). New York State University
of Rochester. (ED 017 879.).

M-1. McClelland, David C. The Achieving Society. Princeton, New Jersey: Van Nostrand, 1961.

M-2. McClelland, David C. "Business Drive and National Achievement," Harvard Business Review, 40 (July-August, 1962), 99.

M-3. McClelland, David C. "That Urge to Achieve," Think, 32 (November-December, 1966), 19-23.

David C. McClelland, Chairman of the Department of Social Relations at Harvard, has produced one of the popular modern theories on motivation which he calls the "Need for Achievement" theory. This theory states that a person's desire to do things better is due to a very specific motive, namely the need for achievement or n-Ach motive, and further that the n-Ach motive is an acquired motive.

McClelland has found from his research that those possessing the achievement motive have the following characteristics: 1) they "set moderately difficult, but potentially achievable goals for themselves" (p. 19); 2) they "prefer to work at a problem rather than leave the outcome to chance or to others." That is, "they are concerned with personal achievement rather than with the rewards for success per se" (p. 30); 3) they have "a strong preference for work situations in which they get concrete feedback on how well they are doing." (p. 20).

In his research McClelland measures the strength of the n-Ach motive by "taking samples of a man's spontaneous thought (such as making up a story about a picture they have been shown) and counting the frequency with which he mentions doing things better." (p. 20)

One of the significant findings that McClelland has discovered is that the n-Ach motive can be acquired through training by teaching a person to think and behave in n-Ach terms. Such training has been given to American, Mexican, and Indian business executives as well as to under achieving high school boys. "In every instance save one (the Mexican case), it was possible to demonstrate statistically, some two years later, that the men who took the course had done better (made more money, got promoted faster, expanded their businesses faster) than comparable men who did not take the course or who took some other management course." (p. 22)

M-4. McClelland, David C. "Toward a Theory of Motive Acquisition,"
American Psychologist, 20 (May, 1965), 321-33.

M-5. McConnell, T.R. Research or Development: A Reconciliation: A Monograph. AERA-PDK Ward Lecture, Annual Meeting American Educational Research Association, New York, February 17, 1967. Bloomington, Indiana: Phi Delta Kappa International, 1967.

There is much debate whether research should be "basic" or "applied,"
whether it should be long-range and seeking to enlarge on basic understanding of learning and motivation or if the research should be geared
toward practical solutions to the educational problems of the moment.
The author says that reconciliation is to be found in the selection of
educational problems which have both theoretical reference and practical relevance. The production of knowledge about education is only
a partial answer to improved practice; the appropriate utilization of
knowledge is also essential. "The transition from research to practice is not one leap. It is a process, a flow, from basic through
applied investigation, to invention and development, to innovation or
production, and finally to evaluation." There is some feeling that
development may outrun research in an overenthusiastic rush to inno-
vate for innovation's sake. McConnell warns, "Without evaluation,
development may easily become quackery."

M-6. McConnell, T.R., and others. "The University and Professional Educa-
tion," National Society for the Study of Education. Sixty-First Year
Book: Education for the Professions. Chicago : University of Chicago
Press, 1962, 254-78.

M-7. McCune, Shirley D. and Mills, Edgar W. Continuing Education for Ministers: A Pilot Evaluation of Three Programs. Washington, D.C.:
National Council of Churches, 1968. (ED 024 870.)

Three continuing education programs for Protestant clergymen were
studied to assess program impact, gain further understanding of occupational roles and education needs of ministers, and develop hypotheses
and improved evaluation techniques.

The study revealed that educational needs pertained mainly to perspective on one's ministry, stronger occupational identity, and study of
rapid social change. It was also found that regional, age, and program

format variations were more significant than denominational differences. It was recommended that such programs incorporate evaluation research, sponsor research and make their goals more specific.

M-8. McCurdy, Patrick P. "Compulsory Continuing Education," Chemical and Engineering News, 36 (February 14, 1972), 1.

McCurdy editorializes: "We must formalize continuing education programs, making their availability compulsory with employee participation voluntary. Adult education programs, continuing education such as those sponsored by The American Chemical Society, company-sponsored training are all fine as far as they go, but they don't go far enough. Under a compulsory system, organizations would be required to set up definite and formal programs whereby employees could devote a given portion of their time acquiring new knowledge. Cost could be handled much the same as depreciation allowances for capital equipment. After all, we've worked out a system that compensates for equipment obsolescence, we've established another to compensate raw material suppliers for depletion -- how about our most precious raw material, human talent?

"As it is, our base educational system trains people for 12 or 16 or more years, then turns them out and says: OK, you're on your own. Then we line up a whole system against them. It's a gross mismatch. Our educational system is too geared to a lifetime cycle. But more and more people are obsolescing well within their lifetimes. They need after-service."

M-9. McDaniel, Keith K and others. Continuing Education of Professional Engineers. Professional Engineers in Industry Survey Report. Washington, D.C.: National Society of Professional Engineers, 1966.

In this 1965 study of continuing education participation, 5000 professional engineers were contacted, and slightly over half completed the questionaires. Of the respondents, 55 per cent had successfully pursued continuing education between 1960 and 1965 and had borne the major expense themselves. The average respondent had earned 21 credits toward an advanced degree. As for attendance: programs lasting 12 weeks or longer ranked highest when offered by academic institutions; while programs lasting 1-3 weeks ranked highest when offered by companies or professional societies. Technical programs ranked highest, regardless of sponsor, but managerial programs were also well received.

The main reasons for attendance were: 1) broaden technological
background; 2) increase specialized expertise; 3) improve
prospects for a raise or promotion. Major reasons for non-
participation were; 1) subject matter held no interest; 2) advanced degree not needed; 3) course not seen as potentially
useful in advancement; 4) attendance would have been incon-
vient. The findings suggest that employers must provide
more time, together with other assistance and incentive.

M-10. McGlothin, William J. "Continuing Education in the Professions."
The Journal of Education for Librarianship, 13 (Summer, 1972),
3-16.

The author participated in a conference on Continuing Library
Education held by the Association of American Library Schools
at which a position paper was adopted entitled, "The Role of
AALS in Continuing Library Education." As the banquet
speaker at the close of the conference, he gave this speech and
reacted to some of the concepts he had heard during the meetings
which he had attended, stating: "A capsule review of the concepts and practices of other professions may confirm your
decisions or suggest modifications." He examined the two
most distinguishing characteristics of a profession: 1) its
special competence, based on long training, and 2) its ethical
or moral component, which determines the way in which the
special competence of the profession is to be used.

In discussing the content of continuing education he accepted the
definition of needs which Houle made in a presentation at the
Midwinter ALA meeting in 1967, namely needs for: new knowledge, new roles, basic disciplines, and personal growth. Turning to the conduct of continuing education, he suggested in addition to established practices (periodicals on continuing education,
directors of continuing education, seminars, courses, etc.) the
importance of thinking of an agency as a "learning community"
rather than just an "administrative community."

He urged that whatever decision was reached by the profession
-- to modify the programs of established associations and
agencies or to organize new ones -- that there should be a joint
effort between the schools and the professional associations.
In closing he emphasized the importance of organizational
structure and financial support, but that they could not

substitute "for vision that sees the possibilities of the future
in the difficulties of the present. Unless we have vision we
have no sense of direction. Unless we have vision we cannot
choose people to work on programs to undertake. It is this
belief that makes what you are undertaking at this conference
so compelling. For, it seems to me, you have been outlining
the vision of a profession whose members have accepted their
responsibility to increase professional competence at the rate
and to the extent that the dizzying changes of the world around
them now require."

M-11. McGrath, Earl J. "The Ideal Education for the Professional Man,"
National Society for the Study of Education. Education for the
Professions, 61st Yearbook. Chicago: University of Chicago Press,
1962, 281-301.

M-12. McGregor, Douglas. The Human Side of Enterprise. New York: McGraw-
Hill Book Company, 1960.

McGregor presents his popular theory distinguishing between two
basic management styles. His Theory X represents the traditional,
standard bureaucratic and authoritarian attitudes of direction and
control of employees. His Theory Y presents the integration of
individual and organizational goals which represents a democratic
approach that allows the employee opportunity for creativity, innovation, and responsibility.

His philosophy of staff development goes far beyond the "manufacturing approach" which relies chiefly on mechanical approaches and
in which the employee is a "passive agent being rotated or sent to
school or promoted, or otherwise manipulated." In Chapter 14 he
develops an environmental framework in which the individual will
"grow to what he is capable of becoming." In turn, McGregor
examines some environmental conditions that affect staff development; economic and technological characteristics of the organization
policies and practices; the behavior of the immediate supervisor;
the role of the management development staff.

Also of special interest to those concerned with staff development is
Chapter 15 on "Acquiring Managerial Skills in the Classroom" in

which he states that managerial competence is created on the job, not in the classroom, but that "classroom education can be used as a powerful aid to the process of management development, providing there is sufficient understanding of the different kinds of learning which are involved and of the different methods of strategies that are appropriate to these."

In commenting on this book, Warren G. Bennis states: "His famous Human Side probably did more to educate managers...than any other book written in this decade." Charles A. Myers states: "Few approach the readability and provocativeness of McGregor's book, which has become something of a classic in the recent literature of management."

All of McGregor's writings present a strong case for a humanistic-democratic approach in all human groups and organizations.

M-13. McGregor, Douglas. The Professional Manager. Edited by Caroline McGregor and Warren G. Bennis. New York: McGraw-Hill Book Company, 1967.

Four themes recur throughout this volume. The first is the importance of theory; the second, that man is a rational being and must come to terms with his emotional and human side; third, he places the idea of "integration" within the framework of transactional concept of power and influence; and finally, concern for the managing of differences and the ways in which management could cope with diversity.

M-14. McJenkin, Virginia. "Continuing Education for School Librarians," ALA Bulletin, 61 (March, 1967), 272-75.

Continuing education requires identification of needs, leadership to plan for these needs, and financing to implement programs to meet these needs. This means cooperative involvement of school library employers, school librarians, and library educators to review and evaluate present programs and to develop long range plans of continuing education.

M-15. McKeachie, Wilbert N. The Learning Process as Applied to Short-Term Learning Situations, Preconference Workshop, Conference Proceedings. West Lafayette, Indiana, National University Extension

Association, Conference and Institute Division, Purdue University, April 23-27, 1965. (ED 019 532.)

Starting with the premise that the basic problem is not planning whether learning will take place, but rather "what kind of learning will take place . . . learning is going on all the time," McKeachie offers helpful suggestions to every workshop, institute, or conference planner on how learning can be effected.

Concepts set forth include: 1) describing objectives specifically and using the techniques which are most effective for that particular kind of learning.; 2) learning is facilitated by some kind of feedback; 3) motivation affects the kind of learning that takes place; 4) all those involved in an educational situation should have some role in objective formation (sponsors, participants, leaders, resource persons should all be involved); 5) objectives should be reshaped by group effort if it is discovered during the progress of the program that objectives are not being met. As to methods he states, "if you're really concerned about efficiency, it's very hard to beat reading . . . but it does not have the advantage of providing very frequent checks upon learning." He suggests that lectures are better for motivation than for learning; he questions the value of non-directive discussions in which people express opinions, but nobody knows whether his opinion is any better than anybody else's. Role playing is evaluated as a fairly powerful technique for doing something in the attitudinal motivational area. "I think we have a good deal of evidence that this is one of the best ways to open up a person to the other persons's point of view." The author concludes with emphasis on taking individual differences into account by providing differing kinds of learning experiences--learning experiences that fit one person and his motives best may not fit another at all.

M-16. MacKenzie, Ossian, and others. Correspondence Instruction in the United States. New York: McGraw-Hill Book Company, 1968.

M-17. McKnight, Philip C. and Baral, David P., comp. Microteaching and the Technical Skills of Teaching: A Bibliography of Research and Development at Stanford University, 1963-1969. Stanford, Calif.: Stanford University, 1969. (ED 030 621.)

66 items, including published and mimeographed materials, doctoral dissertations, and 3 films developed at the Stanford School of Education.

531

and 3 films developed at Stanford School of Education.

M-18. McLeish, John A.B. "Continuing Professional Education in Canada," Convergence, 3 (November 4, 1970), 76-88.

The author singles out new and immensely varied strategies of continuing education as being the chief continuing education needs in Canada, particularly strategies that are sophisticated and supple enough to deal with complex clusters of professions and with the semi-isolated rural professionals. The accounting profession is one that has taken the lead in meeting the problems of distance, loss of time, and lack of funds. In addition to traditional methods they are developing the systematic "travel subsidy" as a device to remove the excuse that they cannot get to renewal projects. They are also experimenting with the lengthy in-residence type of program to provide more depth to continuing education and to provide an opportunity to experiment with strategies of teaching. The Anglican Church is also experimenting with in-residence renewal programs. The United Church of Canada bases its program mainly on the faculty of theology at Winnipeg. It is made up of several major components: 1) the resources of the seminary go to the man throughout his career, rather than the man coming to the seminary; 2) topics for study are determined from the "ministering situation" rather than from the course of study at the seminary; 3) it is ecumenical; 4) attention is paid to the "therapeutic, supportive function;" 5) short, monthly residential meetings of a local professional group are integrated through a "facilitator" from the theology faculty, who sees that the necessary books and outside participants are made available. The university levies a fee of $25 on each participant from September to April, regardless of the frequency or duration of the meetings. Conclusions reached from the United Church of Canada experience are that both "content" and "process" are indispensable; busy field professionals are willing to read in preparation for the local seminars; the ecumenical mix is proving a strength.

The medical profession provides for geographical distances in quite a different way by the use of dial access and information retrieval, which makes available over 350 tape-recorded messages dealing with advice on the latest data in treating a wide variety of diseases. All Saskatchewan physicians have been provided with a booklet listing, classifying and indexing the tapes. To hear a tape, the doctor need only dial a number. The tapes are continually renewed and updated. For conferences in a specific center, slides are provided to accompany tapes.

A motivation device that is being experimented with on a Conference on Continuing Education in Toronto, modeled on a California experiment, provides opportunity for professionals to take periodic examinations on new data and techniques, the result of the tests being made known only to participants. An interesting new development in engineering at the University of Saskatchewan is a "postgressional certificate" in further engineering studies, which makes available to the professional field-oriented learning without the obligation to take on the more research-oriented traditional graduate program. Motivation for continuing education is being studied by Professor Allan Tough of the Department of Adult Education in Toronto.

One of the most encouraging signs is the unique new development in inter-professional continuing education, called the Professional Education Project. It is subsidized by the Kellogg Foundation and the Ontario Institute for Studies in Education. The chief objective is to assist in the process of initiating new directions in professional education through interprofessional dialogue and exchange. In two national meetings to date there have been representatives of a dozen professions. The Project also pbulishes a newsletter (available from the Department of Adult Education) which inventories the resources in professional (including continuing) education. A central document of the Project is entitled "Professional Education: Some Critical Points," of which 23 deal specifically with aspects and needs of continuing professional education in Canada.

M-19. McLenna, Kenneth. "The Manager and His Job Skills," Academy of Management Journal, 10 (September, 1967), 235-45.

M-20. McMahon, Ernest E., ed. "Common Concerns: The Position of the Adult Education Association of the U.S.A." Adult Education Journal, 18 (Spring, 1968), 197-213.

A desire to focus attention on the education of the adult; to meet his needs; and to replace chance with planning led to the founding of the Adult Education Association of the United States. Its present platform is: to make adult education a primary concern rather than a secondary concern within many of the organizations and institutions which maintain adult education divisions; to help those agencies for which adult education is appropriately a secondary concern to perform their tasks better; to offer the services of the Association to emerging adult agencies and to help them establish patterns of organization and programming.

Fifteen interrelated concerns of adult education are identified. They are: 1) agencies of adult education; 2) adult education and the process of social change; 3) the American adult as a learner; 4) objectives of adult education programs; 5) learning experiences especially for adults; 6) evaluation to improve program effectiveness; 7) public understanding of adult education 8) professionalization and staff development; 9) appropriate facilities; 10) relations among adult education agencies; 11) relations with other agencies; 12) financing adult education; 13) a body of professional knowledge; 14) research; 15) international adult education. For each concern a statement of the present situation, a list of goals and a platform statement of the Adult Education Association of the U.S.A. is given.

M-21. McMahon, Ernest E. Needs of People and their Communities and the Adult Educator: A Review of the Literature of Need Determination. Washington, D.C.: Adult Education Association of the U.S.A., 1970. (ED 038 551.).

McMahon maintains that the educational needs of the professions, despite seminars and conferences of professional societies and universities, go unsatisfied. Among his suggestions for learning common needs are: listening posts, power structure, business, government, civic associations, society activities, surveys. In planning educational programs, it is necessary to look directly to the individual and what he needs and wants from education. An 88 item bibliography includes professional continuing education, training design, and other pertinent concerns.

M-22. McMahon, Ernest E., Robert H. Coates and Alan B. Knox. "Common Concerns: The Position of the Adult Education Association of the U.S.A.," Adult Education Journal, 18 (Spring, 1968), 197-213.

M-23. McNamara, Walter J. "Pretraining of Industrial Personnel," Personnel Psychology, 16 (August, 1963), 233-48.

This article has some important implications regarding the fight against loss of competence in an organization. It was found in many cases workers thought unpromising for retraining were not really unpromising, but rather had never received basic training on certain necessary skills in order to take the courses offered. When basics were offered in a special precourse training program, these "unpromising" workers were brought up to the same educational starting line as those who had the missing skills and did just as well as those who had the skills before the precourse. In other words, a good deal of what on the surface may seem like irreparable competence loss may be largely a matter of supplying a few missing but easily supplied prerequisites. The article has implications for admission to programs.

M-24. Mager, Robert F. Developing Attitude Toward Learning. Palo Alto, California: Fearon Publishers, 1968.

A positive and inspirational book to aid the teacher in sending students away from instruction anxious to use what you have taught them - and eager to learn more. Stress throughout is to prepare the student to use the skills and knowledge he has learned and to prepare him to learn more about the subjects he has been taught. One way, and the way that is stressed throughout the book, is to send the student away with a tendency to approach rather than avoid the subject of study. An important method stressed by the author is to learn to state useful objectives - ones that help us to see where we are heading and tell us how to know when we have arrived. Ways of improving approach responses are identified as: 1) making sure that there are as few adverse conditions present as possible while the student is in the presence of the subject we are teaching him; 2) by making sure that the student's contact with the subject is followed by positive rather than adverse consequences; 3) by modeling the very kind of behavior we would like to see exhibited by our students. "To be a professional means to accept responsibility...responsibility for actions and results. It is to act in the best interest of those served...to help them grow rather than shrivel. When we accept the responsibility for professionally influencing the lives and actions of other people, we must do all we can to make that influence positive rather than negative.

"When we accept the money and the trust of the community, we must accept not only the responsibility for sending our students away with as much knowledge and skill as is within our power to give them, but also for sending them away with the ability and the inclination to use those skills to help themselves and others."

M-25. Mager, Robert F. Preparing Instructional Objectives. Palo Alto, Calif.: Fearon Publishers, 1962.

This is one of the most frequently quoted and helpful books on the formulation of objectives in performance terms. In order to describe terminal behavior (what the learner will be doing) the author suggests: a) identifying and naming the over-all behavior act; b) defining the important conditions under which the behavior is to occur; c) defining the criterion of acceptable performance. He recommends that a separate statement be written for each objective: "the more statements you have, the better change you have of making clear your intent." If each learner is given a copy of the objectives, Mager states "you may not have to do much else."

Summarized briefly, operational goals are observable and objectively measurable. They state explicitly and precisely what the student should be able to do and under what circumstances. They are not to be confused with typical course descriptions that list subject matter to be covered by the teacher. Operational goals do not use such nonobjective terms as "appreciate" or "understanding."

M-26. Marchant, Maurice P. "Participative Management as Related to Personnel Development." Library Trends, 20 (July, 1971), 48-59.

Participative management is not the abdication of responsibility by top management and allowing staff members to do whatever they wish; rather it is the enforcement of decisions down to the level best suited to determine them by virtue of availability of relevant information and the effect of the decision on the operation. An important by-product of participative management is the professional growth of personnel.

M-27. Marchant, Maurice P. "Participative Management in Libraries." In: Stone, Elizabeth W., ed. New Directions in Staff Development: Moving from Ideas to Action. Chicago: American Library Association, 1971, pp. 28-38.

The elements of participative management as interpreted by the author in his research include: high degree of confidence and

536

trust between superiors and subordinates; free moving communications; decisions made by those who are intimate with the problem and involved in the consequences of their decisions; group goal setting; review and evaluation at all levels primarily for problem-solving rather than punitive purposes. Marchant tested the extent to which participative management is applied in 22 academic libraries, all members of the Association of Research Libraries. Twenty-one measured between authoratative and consultative, with only one measuring participative.

In regard to the professional members of the libraries studies, Marchant found that the staff's job satisfaction seemed to be highly affected by managerial style and the opportunity to participate in the decision-making process. "Moreover, the group interaction associated with participative management helps the staff unify its value system regarding both the relative importance of various aspects of the library and the quality of those aspects in a given library." (p. 35.) Although Marchant does not see participative management's main contribution in the area of staff development, he does see it as an opportunity for staff to apply learning acquired elsewhere. The relationship between participative management and staff development is dealt with in more detail in the author's article in the issue of Library Trends for July, 1971, entitled "Participative Management as Related to Personnel Development."

M-28. Marco, Guy. "Doctoral Study in Librarianship in the United States." College and Research Libraries, 20 (November, 1959), 435-453+.

M-29. Markham, Arleigh. "Residencies in Engineering Practice," Journal of Engineering Education, 59 (May, 1949), 1032.

The author, Program administrator for the ASEE-Ford Foundation Program of Residencies in Engineering Practice, explains a program designed to increase the industry-education interface. The object of the Residencies Program is to offer young engineering professors the opportunity to gain experience in the practice of the engineering profession for which he is teaching -- "to see first hand, how the realities of engineering practice demand that engineering decisions be based on many factors other than the technical and often on incomplete technical information."

For those selected for an award, the Program pays employment interview costs and moving costs. The Resident occupies a position as paid employee of the company, working for a continuous period of about 12 to 15 months in close association with a senior engineering decision-maker, who has significant responsibility and impact on the company's business. The program was proving so successful that plans are being made to expand it.

M-30. Marlowe, Donald E. "Continuing Education in Professional Associations: American Society for Mechanical Engineers." Paper presented at a Mini-Workshop on Continuing Education sponsored by the Standing Committee on Continuing Library Education of the Association of American Library Schools during the Annual Meeting of the Association, Shoreham Hotel, Washington, D.C., January 28, 1973. (Transcription of tape of presentation.)

Dr. Marlowe, Vice President for Administration of The Catholic University of America and Past President of the Society for Mechanical Engineers, explained that the term "continuing education" is rather narrowly restricted to "continuing technical education." An engineer assumes that he will need to recharge himself technologically in a major way at least three times during his career.

In engineering, motivation for continuing education is very simple -- it is a matter of professional life or death. We have the term technical obsolescence, and this simply means that technology has proceeded at a rate such that if the individual has not kept up with it he becomes useless to his employers in a very short time.

He explained that the matter about continuing education as a "fringe benefit" has been fought out in the engineering profession "over the last 20 years; we have established that educational costs are part of the costs of the employer doing business. Most of our continuing education programs are financed either in the form of the employer directly running the educational program or subsidizing the individual who embarks on it."

Just as there is no centralization in other affairs, Dr. Marlowe explained that there was no centralization in continuing education. Nevertheless, continuing education is the principal reason for the existence of professional engineering societies.

538

Like the bankers, the engineers depend heavily on regional and sectional organizations. In the mechanical engineers, there are eleven regions and 95 local sections -- most are based in large cities. Their continuing education programs are financed by dues and by sales of educational materials.

Dr. Marlowe brought with him one example of a modern program -- a cassette lecture on air pollution. The course consists of 12 lectures over eight and one-half hours, a notebook of all the slides, one reprint volume, and one reference volume. Total cost: $165.00. He enumerated other self-taught materials for study. The journals which are available as part of the dues of the society will print 7 to 8 articles a month as preprints (usually four to six page offset prints, available for 75¢ or $1.00). The journals also contain abstracts of papers, and the individual can write in for the papers desired. Everyone gets a certain number free with dues, and everyone pays for each one over that number. Books are also published, from seminars and symposiums, which sell for $11 or $12. "A couple of odd things: if you talk to engineers about how they learn about new things, the advertising in our journals is extremely important. Not only is it a way to support the journals, but they are also heavily read for new information. Particularly if you want to know about equipment. A totally free form of education results from the efforts of salesmen. Everyone who is active in engineering spends a certain portion of his day talking to salesmen to find the latest equipment. I have had practicing engineers tell me that fifty per cent of their input for new information comes from salesmen."

Dr. Marlowe explained that most of the continuing education efforts are used by the younger members of the profession, people 45 and under. When someone is graduated at 23 years of age from the university, he is almost continually registered in a short course or some form of continuing education. "The reason for the drop in educational participation seems to be that about 40-45 years of age, about half of the engineers go into management, and then cease the technical practice of engineering. As managers, all undergo crash courses in management skills that their technical careers did not prepare them for, but this is not supplied by the engineering societies themselves."

"We don't depend on certification as a reward for continuing education; if word gets around that a journal or course is not any good, it dies. People don't care about the money, it is the investment or their time that has to be worthwhile."

Dr. Marlowe predicted great changes coming in the continuing education field. Standard journals, preprints, audio tapes, etc., will continue. Already the inhouse TV course is here. In many states there are state networks where a university course is transmitted by microwave to a local large employer and the employees take time from work to take the course. The students have audio connection with the instructor so that they can ask questions.

"In regard to program success, I think we have followed the free free enterprise system of the architects. We take surveys, determine the needs, offer the courses. If people come and the program goes, fine — if not, we cut its throat. We find that people and employers are willing to pay very substantial sums for good programs. The short course of a week costing $1,000 is not uncommon."

Question: The employer is interested in paying for the education of the engineers, but aren't there potential areas of conflict here? I mean in a tight money economy the employee himself is competing for positions and is interested in continuing education, the employer would feel less interested when many candidates are available.

Answer: There are certain feedbacks that take place. It is true that continuing education is a company overhead; the first thing the employer wants to do is cut his overhead. At the same time, when he is in a tough competitive situation he wants his best engineering done so that his next line of products will command more than their share of the market. The other thing is that the young engineer has come, in the last 15 years, **to** look for it as a condition of employment. When a recruiter comes to campus now, the young candidate, especially the good one, will not ask what the retirement system is, rather he will say "What is the opportunity for continuing education?" The poor student will ask about the retirement system. So the employer who wants to get the top graduate has got to make a very serious commitment to continuing education. You asked if there was a time when this was not so -- and there surely was.

But over the past few years, the concept has developed and it held up through the recent recession.

Question: Why was the idea of employer funding for continuing education accepted?

Answer: The thing that made it possible was the war years with the sudden advent of things like radar that no one knew anything about. If you were manufacturing TV sets and wanted to get into the radar business, you could not hire for any price a group of engineers to do the job. You had to let them educate themselves.

During the question period at the end of the panel, another question was asked about the cost of continuing education. Dr. Marlowe replied:

Continuing education has to be a cost of doing business item and I think that is the direction in which librarians should think. You need to articulate why this is a necessity in the library business as one of the costs of doing business. Until you can articulate that, you are going to always have the tension about how to allocate monies. Even among the "more affluent professions" the small town is a problem. How do you carry out a program with only three engineers? Individualized self study is a most difficult thing, and some form of a small groups seems almost essential.

In answer to another related question, Dr. Marlowe said:

Half your enemies are in your own profession. Remember that continuing education is a very disturbing thing to the person who does not want, or feel able, to take part in it. We have some of those in engineering who say -- "all that _____ theory, kids running around to school, what they need is good practical experience." That's the worm in our apple and I am sure that you have some in yours, too.

M-31. Martin, Allie Beth. "Out of the Ivory Tower." Library Journal, 96 (June 15, 1971), 2060.

M-32. Martin, Warren Bryan. The Development of Innovation: Making Reality Change. Berkeley, Calif.: Center for Research and Development in Higher Education, University of California at Berkeley, 1968. (ED 026 004).

In the traditional U.S. higher education system, there is need for intensive study of hierarchical administration organization, course content, and updating of conservative faculty attitudes. If the university is to survive this era of rapid social change, new educational alternatives must be considered.

Much faculty resistance to change stems from a lack of data on innovative developments. Their work load could be reduced and time spent in creative activities if students were taught by the tutorial method and allowed to study independently. Workshops on educational change would provide opportunities for specialists to utilize research data for improving the local university situation and research and development centers could test concepts of significance to a particular institution.

College administration should adopt industry's system approach, in which decentralized leadership is emphasized and status is determined more by achievement than by position.

M-33. Maslow, Abraham H. "A Theory of Human Motivation." Psychological Review, 50 (May, 1943), 370-96.

In 1943 the late Dr. A. H. Maslow, then of Brooklyn College, presented a statement of his theory of human motivation which has become the most widely taught view of motivation in North American business schools, and provides the theoretical framework for much organization theory. Maslow explained that motivation theory is "not synonymous with behavior theory. The motivations are only one class of determinants of behavior. While behavior is almost always motivated, it is also almost always biologically, culturally, and situationally determined as well."

In this early paper Maslow stated that he was attempting to formulate a positive theory of motivation which would satisfy all the criteria necessary for any theory of motivation and at the same time conform to known facts, clinical and observational as well as experimental.

542

In his motivation theory, Maslow has five sets of goals, which
he terms basic needs: 1) psychological needs (thirst, hunger,
etc.); 2) safety needs (security and order); 3) love needs
(belongingness); 4)esteem needs (success, self-respect; need
for confidence and for independence and freedom); 5) need for
self-actualization (desire for self-fulfillment).

He took the view that "man is a perpetually wanting animal."
Thus when a lower need is fairly well satisfied, the next higher
need emerges, and dominates man's conscious life, and serves
as the center of organization of behavior, since "gratified needs
are not active motivators."

M-34. Maslow, Abraham H. _Motivation and Personality_. 2d ed. New
York: Harper and Row, 1970.

M-35. Mathison, David E. "Correspondence Study in Multimedia Learning Systems." _Continuing Education for Adults_, No. 154, 1970.

M-36. Mead, Margaret. "Thinking Ahead: Why is Education Obsolete?"
Harvard Business Review, 36 (November-December, 1956),
23-27, 164-70.

In this essay Margaret Mead states one of the most vivid truths
of the new age: "No one will live all his life in the world into
which he was born, and no one will die in the world in which he
worked in his maturity." This is an age in which continuous
change makes it impossible to succeed in one's career on the
basis of only that learning achieved during childhood and early
adulthood.

M-37. Mead, Margaret. "Redefinition of Education," _National Education
Association Journal_, 48 (October, 1959), 15-17.

M-38. Meaney, John W., and Carpenter, C. Ray, eds. "Telecommunications: Toward National Policies for Education." The report of
the National Conference on Telecommunications Policy in
Education, Georgia Center for Continuing Education, Athens,

543

Georgia, December 4-6, 1968. Washington, D.C.: Joint
Council on Educational Telecommunication, 1970.
(ED 044 917.)

Papers from a conference on telecommunications are presented
in this report, as well as the discussion and recommendations
of the five conference commissions. The papers are concerned
with education and telecommunications, the corporation of
public broadcasting, information systems for the future, cable
television, satellite systems, the President's Task Force on
Communications Policy, and systems applications. The work
and reports of the conference commissions centered around the
relationships of telecommunication with universities, schools,
preschool education, continuing education, and urban education.
The recommendations of the conference commissions were
that 1) the Joint Council on Educational Telecommunications
(JCET) should insure the recognition of education's stake in the
new technologies, 2) that JCET should emphasize the importance
of the opportunity that now exists to bring two-way cable communications into the American home, 3) that JCET should help
with strategy to use communications media in attacking social
problems, 4) that JCET should join with other agencies to
bring about cooperative production of instructional materials,
and 5) that JCET should urge the United States Office of Education to expand its programs for training faculty and technicians
in the use of telecommunications.

M-39. Mee, John. "Participation in Community Affairs -- The Role of
Business and Business Schools." Unpublished research paper,
Indiana University, 1968.

Interviews with 140 M.B.A.'s holding middle management
positions with retailers or large companies from all sections
of the country, showed that 90% were in agreement on the
importance of the business executive's being involved in
community and government activities yet performance was far
short of their stated opinion about active participation (19%
were engaged in one activity; 22% in 2 activities; 29% in two or
more activities; 30% were not active). The fault appeared to
lie in two areas: 1) business organizations did very little to
communicate what their view of community participation was;
only one-third of the respondents felt their companies

544

considered it essential that executives participate; 2) business schools failed to give any training to help graduates participate effectively in community affairs. Those interviewed suggested that companies make it understood that the need for involvement cannot be cynically self-serving and that business schools instill deeper appreciation of executives' potential influence in community life through curriculum emphasis on the role of business in government committees; group dynamics — how to be effective in multi-person meetings; local politics and the businessman; and social responsibility of the corporation.

M-40. Melching, William H., Ammerman, Harry L., Whitmore, Paul G., and Cox, John A. Deriving, Specifying, and Using Instructional Objectives. Alexandria, Va.: The Human Resources Research Office, George Washington University, 1966.

Four papers are presented emphasizing the importance of stating instructional goals in terms of the performance expected of the student on completion of instruction. It is pointed out that performance or behavioral goals contrast sharply with the practice of stating instructional goals in terms of instructional content or subject matter. While the former emphasizes what the student must do, the latter tends to be concerned with topics to be covered, saying little if anything about what the student must learn. One procedure is focused directly on the student; the other, in contrast, is focused on the subject matter covered in the course. The criteria of a behaviorally stated objective are listed as:

1) To describe what the learner will be doing when he demonstrates that he has attained the objective.
2) To describe the important conditions (if any) which the learner must demonstrate his competence.
3) To state the standards of performance expected of the student.

M-41. Meng, Mabel. "Report from North Dakota — Recognition for Continuing Education." The Journal of Continuing Education in Nursing, 2 (November-December, 1971), 21-41.

This is an example of how one professional organization sought to encourage continuing education and give recognition to the

545

continuing learner. The Plan for Recognition for Continuing Education is based on "recognition points" which may be acquired under three categories of continuing education: 1) short-term courses or programs; 2) independent and informal study (2-5 recognition points for every one hour or presentation; limit of 15 points for publication of scholarly articles); 3) formal academic study relevant to nursing or fulfilling a requirement for a degree (1 semester credit = 15 points; audit of courses, 1/3 the recognition points of a course taken for credit). Each member of the Association is encouraged to strive for the acquisition of 50 recognition points in each 2-year period. Recognition will be given in the following ways: 1) a certificate for each person achieving 50 points; 2) a letter of recommendation will be sent to each individual's employer upon the award of recognition. A Continuing Education Approval Committee determines criteria for approving continuing education activities, approves activities for recognition points, approves application from members for these recognition points. Sample application forms for receiving points toward certificate are included.

M-42. Menne, John W., and others. "Use of Taped Lectures to Replace Class Attendance," AV Communication Review, 17 (Spring, 1969), 42-6.

M-43. Menzel, Herbert, and others. "The Effectiveness of the Televised Clinical Seminars of the New York Academy of Medicine." (ED 020 457.) See New York Academy of Medicine, Second series, 42, no. 8.

In 1963 the New York Academy of Medicine, with the New York City Municipal Broadcasting System, inaugurated an experimental program of weekly one-hour televised clinical science seminars to explore the acceptability and effectiveness of open-circuit TV as an additional medium of continuing medical education in a large metropolitan area. This report presents the findings and the audience surveys and text of the test questions. Surveys showed that there was a steadily growing audience for the weekly broadcast -- 408 in private practice alone estimated as an average in January, 1964. [This article appeared in the Bulletin of the New York Academy of Medicine, 2nd Series, vol. 42, no. 8.]

M-44. Menzel, Herbert. <u>Physicians' Local Advisory System. Final</u>
<u>Report and Appendices.</u> New York: New York University, 1969.

Realizing the importance of colleague communication in
increasing the physician's medical knowledge, this study
attempted to determine what variables affect the success of
local colleague networks (invisible college) in raising the
individual level of information and awareness of current
developments in medicine. The Appendix describes in full the
methods used and the information test used. The author has
studied and reported in other places the role played by informal,
unplanned, person-to-person communication in professional
relationships.

M-45. Merrell, V. Dallas. <u>An Analysis of University Sponsored Execu-</u>
<u>tive Development Programs.</u> Los Angeles: University of
Southern California, 1965. (ED 019 531.)

M-46. Merrill, Irving R. and Yaryan, Ruby B. <u>Broadcast TV as an Aid</u>
<u>to Continuing Education.</u> Terminal Progress Report.
San Francisco, Calif.: California University Medical Center,
1968. (ED 027 447.)

The effect of massed versus distributed television presentations
on attendance and learning in a voluntary situation were compared in a field experiment involving 114 physicians in general
practice. The factorial design was based on four experimental
groups, each located in a different community. Physicians
viewed videotape presentations in a local hospital over a period
of four weeks, with three one-hour sessions (distributed viewing) and a single three hour session (massed viewing). On the
fifth week they completed a learning achievement test over
televised instruction. The results indicated that attendance
was significantly greater under massed than under distributed
viewing, especially when the sessions took place in the evening
rather than the morning. The presentations produced gains in
learning achievement, and there was no statistically significant
difference in learning achievement between massed and distributed viewing.

M-47. Merritt, Leroy C. "Doctoral Study in Librarianship -- A Supplement." College and Research Libraries, 23 (November, 1962), 539-40.

M-48. Metropolitan Fund, Inc., Detroit Area. Regional Mid-Career Education: A Proposed Educational Program for Mid-Career Local and State Government Officials in the Metropolitan Detroit Region. Detroit, Michigan: Metropolitan Fund, Inc., 1966.

The report includes: 1) the feasibility of a mid-career educational program; 2) the nature of the "knowledges" required of public executives in today's complex society; 3) the means of imparting these "knowledges" and 4) the experiences of universities around the nation in executive development education. Data is based on interviews with selected decision-makers, questionnaires completed by potential program participants, followup interviews, and a limited inventory of university sponsored executive development programs conducted in 1965.

M-49. Meyer, Herbert H., and others. "Split Roles in Performance Appraisal," Harvard Business Review, 43 (January-February, 1965), 123-9.

Within the process of employee appraisal lies the potential for motivation of the employee, but usually the process has been used critically and destructively. Using a constructive, developmental approach, the authors show how appraisal can be used to allow the employee to set objectives and goals for himself and how appraisal can become a motivating process.

M-50. Meyer, Thomas C., and others. "Communications: Report of an Experiment in the Use of Telelectures for the Continuing Education of Physicians and Allied Health Personnel." The Journal of Medical Education, 43 (January, 1968), 73-77.

A telelecture is a lecture presented in one location which is transmitted by telephone lines to other stations. Related slides and the outline of the lecture are provided for each station. After the lecture is heard, listeners may ask questions over the telephone and hear their answers over a loudspeaker connected to the incoming telephone line.

M-51. Meyer, Thomas C. Establishing a Telephone Dial Access Medical Tape Recording Library. Madison, Wisc.: Medical Center, University of Wisconsin, [n.d.] (ED 021 160.)

Modern communications methods make it possible to provide post graduate education for physicians at a time and place convenient to them, and at a time when they are most receptive to new information. This project involves a library of tape recordings of 4-6 minutes duration, available by telephone dial access to practicing physicians. The recordings contain information of an emergency nature or present current recommended procedures. A list of available topics is circulated to physicians and they may call at any time of the day or night, request a recording, and it is played for them over the telephone line. A feasibility study, involving 88 tapes, has been conducted. This project will expand the library to 200 tapes, establish a duplicate library elsewhere in the state, continue exploration of transmission methods, explore increased automation, and evaluate the value and effectiveness of the system. The document includes sample budget, summary of utilizations, and evaluation forms.

M-52. Meyer, Thomas. A Feasibility Study in Determining Individual Practice Profiles of Physicians as a Basis for Continuing Education of these Physicians Utilizing a Postgraduate Perceptor Technique. Final Report. Madison, Wisc.: University of Wisconsin, 1970. (ED 052 299.)

The purposes of this project were to develop a profile of the individual physician's practice, test the physician in the major areas of his practice, and provide educational consultation according to practice profile and test results. A test bank of 1,800 5-option multiple choice questions was classified into 18 categories based on classification of diseases, with three levels of sophistication represented in each category. Questions from about five categories were randomly selected for each of 37 participating physicians. Each physician's categories were determined from his practice profile, which was

549

determined in a week of observation by a medical secretary.
The resulting data were used by educational consultants, who
met with the individual physicians to plan educational programs
to meet their needs. The project found that the procedure holds
potential as an aid in educational planning by highly motivated
physicians, but cautions that it is too narrow to be useful in
evaluating physician performance. Also, the test bank,
although useful in principle, will require modification before it
will succeed in practice.

M-53. Meyer, Ursula. "New York's Statewide Continuing Professional
Education Program: The Early Stages of Development."
Paper presented at the First Annual Staff Development Micro-
Workshop, American Library Association Convention, Detroit,
Michigan, June 28, 1970. In: Stone, Elizabeth W., ed. New
Directions in Staff Development: Moving from Ideas to Action.
Chicago: American Library Association, 1971.

The author, Public Library Consultant, New York State Department of Education, reports on the new approach toward continuing professional education in New York State. Still in the
development stage, the objective of the plan is to create a staff
development program on a statewide basis. Meyer reports on
the progress that has been made in the area of librarianship.
The objectives for the total program are outlined. The ten
questions asked in 98 interviews with 221 public libraries are
given with the answers received. From the survey it was found
that of the proposed topics for study the top ranking topic was
group dynamics, communication, leadership; second highest
topic was personnel development, communication guidance.
Questionnaires used are presented in the Appendix.

M-54. Meyerhoff, Erich. "Continuing Education of Medical Librarians:
Evaluation of the Association's Past Performance and Suggestions for the Future," Bulletin of the Medical Library Association, 51 (July, 1963), 376-83.

Meyerhoff evaluates the Association's programs and activities
for continuing education which have been conducted in connection with its annual meetings. He states that the most important single element in the success of this program is the quality
of instruction. The problem is not to stimulate interest, since

librarians have demonstrated their interest over and over
again, but to channel it into the most fruitful course.

M-55. Meyrick, R. L. "Medicine Today" -- A Small Scale Trial of Subjec-
tive Responses of Doctors Viewing Television in Groups."
Association for the Study of Medical Education (England),
Television Section, 1969. (ED 028 646.)

The intent of this admittedly small scale and unsophisticated
trial was to test the response of general practitioners to being
given a form to fill out following a television broadcast, to
test the semantic differential method for testing subjective
responses to the programs, and to see if some means of testing
by multiple-choice questions could be used to assess knowledge
gain immediately following the broadcast. Three programs of
the BBC 2 production "Medicine Today" were selected as the
subject matter for these tests. Clinical tutors and other or-
ganizers in ten areas were sent 270 forms on each of the three
months to distribute to groups of doctors who met in hospitals
and elsewhere to watch the lunchtime transmission of the programs. Replies from the general practitioners numbered 104,
95, and 107 respectively for each of the three programs. The
semantic differential provided the most valuable assessment of
subjective responses so far obtained for these programs and
was easily understood by the doctors. Multiple-choice questions
following the second program proved to be confusing and were
replaced by factual questions for the third program. A section
including copies of the questionnaires and compilation of the
responses is appended.

M-56. Miles, Matthew B. Learning to Work in Groups; A Program Guide
for Educational Leaders. New York: Teachers College Press,
Columbia University, 1959.

M-57. Miller, Ebert L. Research and Evaluation Techniques: Preparing Designated Public School Personnel to Evaluate Present
and Future Title I Projects (June 20 - August 12, 1966).
Muncie, Indiana: Ball State University, 1966. (ED 021 814.)

This is a report of an 8-week summer institute conducted to
train 27 public school persons to better evaluate Title I,

Title III, and other curriculum improvement programs, with
a focus on improving the planning measurement and educational
research competence of participants.

M-58. Miller, Howard M. "Career Development of Engineers in Industry,"
Journal of Engineering Education, 59 (June, 1969), 1113-1116.

The author points out that for the engineer to be deeply involved
in continuing development, he "must feel assured that he will
have opportunities to use his talents and skills to the maximum
extent of willingness and ability, and that his progression,
whether in administrative or technical channels, will be com-
mensurate with his value to the company." There must be provision for this "dual" ladder or pathway of advancement in an
organization.

Real development does not necessarily involve job change by
vertical promotion; it can involve an entirely new experience
or simply the realignment of responsibility, carrying with it
the big motivational values in job change; the challenge of doing
something new and worthwhile. "To assure optimum career
development, each job assignment must be made with two
thoughts in mind: What will the man contribute to the job, and
what will the job contribute to the man?" To assure a return on
employment development programs, they "must be based on
the philosophy that each person is an individual and that his
special talents should be recognized, encouraged to develop,
and utilized; that his development must be continuous; that
he must accept his share of responsibility for development; and
that management's function is to supply the opportunity, guidance, and stimulation."

Stating his belief that the primary aim of engineering education
should be that of learning to adapt to changes in knowledge and
human needs, he concludes that it is the individual's academic
training that will produce engineers prepared to cope with
change and that industry must see that development opportunities continue. "The individual must be induced to reach, and
continuing education must be within his reach. Career development -- indeed, individual development -- is a continuum which
largely depends on momentum. This momentum is a function
of the attitude of the individual, and this attitude depends on
the incentive he receives in his environment -- from educators,

from employers, and from professional societies among others."

Miller emphasizes that individual and group needs are so varied that formal courses "simply will not fill them." He lists other ways to induce the development of engineers: membership and active participation in technical and professional engineering societies; payment by the employer of the expense of attendance at non-local meetings (engineers seem to feel this is solid evidence of support); the availability of an adequate information retrieval system service (formal and informal); and formal communication: either a speech or technical report about one's work. "The listener or reader learns, and nothing is more effective in forcing the organization and consolidation of one's thoughts than having to prepare a presentation." Of similar value is the utilization by engineering educators of industrially employed engineers for special lectures to students, as well as the converse; the organization by employers of meetings of engineers for visiting lecturers, usually from universities.

He concludes by urging mutual cooperation between engineers, employers, educators, and societies to produce an environment in which the engineer will keep current with technology and in which he can make his maximum contribution.

M-59. Miller, Richard I. A Comprehensive Model for Managing an ESEA Title III Project from Conception to Culmination. Fairfax, Va.: Center for Effecting Educational Change, Fairfax County Public Schools, 1968. (ED 024 842.)

This paper is much broader than its title sounds; it can serve as a model for managing other kinds of projects, from their inception to their termination. As such it could be useful for those who write projects, those who operate projects, and those who evaluate projects, both in terms of improvement and in terms of continuation.

M-60. Monroe, Margaret E. "Variety in Continuing Education," ALA Bulletin, 61 (March, 1967), 275-78.

"The first task of continuing education should be that of reducing the resistance to change. There is no aspect of librarianship which cannot profit from such reduction, and for all types of libraries, all types of services, our educational objective should be to reduce the half-life of professional knowledge to match the pace of change in our society." After outlining the contributions of different types of library agencies involved in continuing library education, she cites the unique contributions of library schools to continuing education: 1) stress on theory and its usefulness in enabling better understanding of problems and promising better solutions to them than experience alone might permit; 2) attention sustained on a problem long enough to see it from all angles; and 3) borrowing of insights, concepts, and skills from other disciplines and professional fields. She recommends statewide cooperative planning for continuing education incorporating four aspects of continuing education: foundation, remedial, emergency and specialization in training, each of which is described.

Monroe asserts that if the need for continuing education in these areas is met the librarians themselves must sustain the climate for such learning.

Elements in maintaining such a climate as that mentioned by Monroe are: 1) administration of libraries built on a concept of professional group practice in which librarians would find stimulation for continued learning inherent; 2) the professional learner sharing in the plan for his own learning; 3) the potential of research activity as a method for continuing learning by the professional.

M-61. Montana Medical Association. A Symposium on Continuing Medical Education in Montana. Boulder, Colo.: Western Interstate Commission for Higher Education, WICHE Mountain States Regional Medical Program, Montana Medical Association, 1969. (ED 033 306.)

The distinguishing thing about this symposium was that a significant part of the program centered around interprofessional program development and the strategy needed for such development. Also a plan for continuing medical education was discussed, and some priorities were set.

M-62. Moon, Harold L. <u>The Systems Approach to Training: A Model.</u>
New York: F. W. Dodge Division of McGraw-Hill, Information
and Training Services, 1964. (Mimeographed)

The author does a remarkably comprehensive job of explaining
by charts, graphs, and texts, in only 8 pages, the application
of the systems approach in solving training problems. He
breaks the process down into five major phases: 1) definition
of the input, output, and subject matter; 2) identification of the
operating conditions and constraints; 3) design and production
of the components; 4) evaluation and refinement of the system;
5) operational monitoring of the output for quality control.

M-63. Moriarty, John L. "A Community Effort in Continuing Education
for the Development of Engineers." <u>Journal of Engineering
Education,</u> 59 (May, 1969), 1046-48.

The author, Coordinator of Professional Activities, Engineering
Department, Bendix Corporation, built interdependent relationships in the area of mid-career continuing education on three
premises: 1) the engineer must develop a greater sense of professional responsibility and a willingness to take the initiative
for his own continuing education; 2) the employer must be willing to provide incentive and guidance to engineers willing to
grow; 3) the educator must be willing to work with both the
engineer and the employer to prevent technological obsoles-
cense and thereby promote technological advance.

Moriarty describes a variety of programs. One involves a
Technical Advisory Council which is dedicated to fostering
advanced education through off-campus programming. Another
is a guided self-study program with the University of Iowa and
help from the Carnegie Corporation by which the students make
on-campus contact with professors on a weekly basis. Students
have to take the burden of the initiative in arrangement of
courses, agreements concerning sequences of study, etc. A
third approach is a "multiphase approach" consisting of intra-
community classes, home study programs, and in-house activities. A fourth approach consists of special topics seminars
-- an in-house project on a high level. Each subject discussed
has a three-point rationale in mind for professional development:
1) a broad overview of a subject area to extend basic understanding; 2) thinking is stimulated to the point where the

utilization of a particular tool, technique, or approach may
appear feasible; 3) a review is offered of current applications
and questions encouraged regarding implementation for special
problems.

A fifth type of updating is provided by videotape instruction for
graduate credit. The lecture is given before a live class on
campus and two days later the tapes are viewed on a large
television monitor in a room equipped with comfortable seating
and enough lighting for note-taking. Video sessions are held
three times a week and the instructor is available after class
for consultation via long-distance telephone.

Still another special program involves special in-house credit
courses. In this instance the instructor came from the university once a week to the company for a two-hour lecture.

A final program described is a special ten-session orientation
program for new employees, in which all new engineers were
exposed as a group for one hour once a week to various working aspects of the company. One byproduct of these sessions
was in encouraging and stimulating young engineers toward
their career objectives.

M-64. Morris, Lloyd P. "Teleduction: Networks for Knowledge."
        Library Trends, 19 (April, 1971), 482-492.

        Nothing on the educational horizon has such great potential to
        help our education system as the application of the already
        known communication technology techniques of two-way informa-
        tion handling and dissemination.

M-65. Morrison, Perry David. The Career of the Academic Librarian:
        A Study of the Social Origins, Educational Attainments, Voca-
        tional Experience, and Personality Characteristics of a Group
        of American Academic Librarians. ACRL Monograph no. 29.
        Chicago: American Library Association, 1969.

        Morrison investigated the demographic, social and economic
        origins, education, career patterns and psychological attributes
        of librarians in various specializations and at varying levels
        of responsibility. His approach included the use of

questionnaires, and Ghiselli's self-perception inventory. His study also has curriculum implications for continuing education programs. For example, in his study of 676 academic librarians, he found that the supervisory qualities among librarians were very low -- the most disturbing part of his whole study. He found that the outlook of library supervisors was entirely different from supervisors in other occupations and believed that this had a direct influence on the recruitment of new librarians. This book is based on his 1961 Ph.D. thesis at the University of California.

M-66. Morse, Gerry E. "The Swinging Pendulum of Management Control." In: The Systems Approach to Personnel Management. New York: American Management Association, 1965, pp. 3-8.

Gerry E. Morse, Vice President, Employee Relations, Honeywell, Inc., Minneapolis, Minnesota, takes the position that current trends in technology and centralization need not dehumanize an organization's resources. "If personnel managers keep up to date, if they do the long, tedious, difficult job of retraining themselves to be effective in personnel administration, in this age of technology and computers, they ought to be able to go much further in humanizing their companies than has been possible in large organizations in the past. These new tools will give management a better understanding of the individual, of his skills and potential, plus a far better measure of his progress and his job satisfaction." (p. 7)

M-67. Morton, Florrinell F. "Library Education for the Seventies," Catholic Library World, 41 (January, 1970), 285-92.

The author gives a brief, over-all picture of library education, with a section on "in-service programs." She predicts expansion of programs at every level.

M-68. Morton, J. A. "Educating and Developing Leaders in Technology." Journal of Engineering Education, 59 (May, 1969), 1043-45.

The author, of the Bell Telephone Laboratories, tells of their programs to provide for more specialization. One is in connection with three years of part time study at local universities

(LUPT program); the other new method is OYOC (One year on campus). One year is spent full time on campus at a university which may not be close to home; the second year is spent at home in specialized technology courses and interdisciplinary internships. Other plans are being developed for the future. Morton's thesis is that whereas in the past learning and practice have been viewed as separate and distinct, now a "new synthesis" must be developed in which "learning and practice are combined into a unified system, with interactions mutually re-enforcing throughout life. We in practice must make possible a life process of learning-practice. We cannot expect the universities to turn out the universal specialist fitted once and for all for a creative life in innovation."

He argues that "renewal of people through learning is a process -- and the two are coupled parts of a life process. Just as we generate and couple science and technology into new systems for service, so must we join with the education world to develop learning-practice systems for continuous renewal of our people. Indeed, if we do not do our part in the on-going education of our people, they cannot do their part in on-going innovation of technology. In such a learning-practice system, growth in capability to see and solve larger problems forges on for life. What used to be major goals -- marks, degrees, papers, patents, and promotions -- become not destinations, but milestones that go whizzing by in our quest for greater understanding and capability."

M-69. Moses, Stanley. The "New" Domain of Post-Secondary Education. Syracuse, N.Y.: New York Educational Policy Research Center, Syracuse University Research Corporation, 1971. (ED 053 642.)

This paper argues that government agencies have traditionally been concerned with recording and reporting only the dimensions of the formal "core" of educational activity -- the sequential ladder ranging from kindergarten through graduate and professional schools. Missing is a similar recording of participation in the "educational periphery" -- vocationally oriented programs in business, government, the military, proprietary schools, and anti-poverty programs as well as culture and leisure oriented programs in core institutions such as religious education, television, correspondence courses and private associations. According to data drawn from various sources, the total learning force, in terms of 1970 head count participation, is about evenly divided between the core and the periphery. Public and governmental acknowledgement of the periphery's size and significance should lead to a re-evaluation of educational priorities, to innovation within core institutions, and to a new understanding of the variety of alternative possibilities for individual learning and for public policy.

M-70. Mosher, Harold A. and Ackoff, Albert K. "The Interdependent Roles of University and Industry." Journal of Engineering Education, 59 (May, 1969) 102 3-28.

M-71. Mosher, Frederick T. "Background Paper." In: Jones, Victor, ed. Proceedings, Conference on Continuing Education for Public Administrators in State, County and City Governments in California, Davis, November, 1963. Berkeley, Calif.: Institute on Governmental Studies, University of California, 1965.

Mosher describes the universal need for professional continuing education in these terms:

A well-educated college graduate has just begun his education upon graduation. He reads, discusses, assimilates knowledge throughout his life. But it is becoming increasingly difficult for a well-educated man to stay well-educated, however motivated and however brilliant he may be. If he is in a moderately specialized professional field -- as most of us are -- it is a difficult job just to keep up with his own field without some formalized off-the-job instruction.

The meager, but traditional, picture of continuing education for public administrators in relation to the university is described by Mosher:

It is the paradoxical, unhappy and potentially tragic fact that most of the great universities have not addressed themselves to the responsibility of continuing education of government executives in any fashion comparable to their undertakings on behalf of business administrators, doctors,

engineers, architects and a host of others in private
professions. They have demonstrated less concern for the
broad and vitally important education of top public administrators than for professionals in a variety of governmental
specialities.

M-72.* Mosher, Frederick. Professional Education and the Public Service:
An Exploratory Study. Final Report. Berkeley, Calif:
University of California at Berkeley, Center for Research and
Development in Higher Education, 1968. (ED 023 971.)

The study was designed to assess major links between professionalism and professional education and public service, to
highlight some of the resulting problems among professions,
and to set forth hypotheses to guide a more intensive future
research. Results indicate that professionalism is rapidly
rising in American society, government at all levels leads
in the employment of professionals, and administrative leadership is growing mo re and more professional in terms of education and experience.

Four major underlying problems facing professional educ ation
are outlines: 1) Professional boundaries and spillover problems
occur when a profession uses the strategy of widening the
boundaries of its own activities by taking in a broader foundation
of knowledge. "The process of assimilation in competing with
other professions may be difficult and highly competitive....
The ensuing digesting can be most disruptive, even destructive
of the unity and integrity of the profession itself." 2) Intro-
professional fission -- to what extent should subspecialization
be encouraged in the educational process? The process of
specialization forces subdivision into professional segments
which weaken the profession's identity with the parent profession. Mosher warns that professionals can only continue to
exercise social and political influence as long as they can maintain the appearance of internal unity; 3) Obsolescence -- how
to cope with the accelerating growth of knowledge relevant to
the individual profession? How much emphasis should the
profession as a whole give to continuing education? A practitioner may be at his peak between 25 and 35; by the time he
reaches 50, he may be totally obsolete unless the profession
has taken positive steps to cope with obsolescence. The educational process by which the professional is refreshed should be

560

studied and changed to cope with this problem. The
question is: How can they gain the skills that are essential
for the successful fulfillment of their jobs? 4) Organization and management --To what extent should professional
education prepare student for managerial responsibilities
which a large percentage of them will subsequently assume ?
It has been found that a growing proportion of administrative
positions in all professions are filled by those who have received little, if any, training for their roles as administrators
and managers.

With the "upgrading" of a profession, two by-products e-
merge: 1) necessity for increased development of subprofessionals; and 2) as the standards and qualifications
rise within a profession, there is an increasing obligation
on older practitioners to keep up through some form of
continuing education, or they will become unqualified for
positions of leadership. "Unless the older professional
engages in continual professional development, experience
can become positively disqualifying."

According to Mosher, as professionalization increases and
professional standards rise, it will become increasingly
difficult for any individual to change his occupation once
his initial decision has been made. As "upgrading" of the
profession increases, it will be increasingly difficult for
those from other professions to enter because of the number
of years and number of skills that will be necessary for
them to qualify as professionals.

M-73. Mosher, Frederick C. A Proposed Program of Mid-Career Education for Public Administrators in Metropolitan Areas.
A report of an Ad Hoc Faculty Planning Committee at the
University of California, Berkley, California: Institute
of Governmental Studies, University of California, 1965.

The Committee proposed a six-month program which would
consist of a regular course on Metropolitan Problems and
Development studied from various perspectives, and group
and individual research on selected problems. The participants would be young public administrators from various
governmental jurisdictions.

Part I sets forth the basic considerations leading to the development of the plan; Part II is a concise statement of the proposal itself. In the appendix are supporting materials, including preliminary syllabuses of each topic in the basic course, reports on feasibility and a statistical table of characteristics of public career executives.

M-74. Myers, M. Scott. "Conditions for Manager Motivation." Harvard Business Review. 44 (January-February, 1966), 58-71.

An outstanding article which shows the advantages and characteristics of managers who display a "developmental style" of leadership. These conditions are the type that also motivate employers to engage in developmental activities.

M-75. Myers, M. Scott. Every Employee A Manager. New York, McGraw-Hill Book Company, 1970.

Myers, on leave from Texas Instruments to serve as visiting professor at M.I.T., bases his work on recent behavioral theories (such as Maslow, McGregor, Herzberg, Likert, McClelland). His book describes the conditions that are necessary for people to work responsibly and creatively. The title, Every Employee a Manager, refers to the opportunities present for every employee to manage his own job if the concept of job enrichment is utilized in the work situation.

The author states that people's attitudes and perceptions are the primary causes of all systems' successes and failures, enabling poorly designed systems to succeed and causing well designed systems to fail. He summarizes the vital considerations affecting the effectiveness of organizational systems as follows: " . . . A system is considered effective when the people whose job performance is influenced by it; 1) understand its purpose; 2) agree with its purpose; 3) know how to use it; 4) are in control of it; 5) can influence its revision; 6) receive timely feedback from it. In discussing user participation in the design of systems, Myers said, "A system user can no more divest himself of responsibility for system design than the foreman

562

can delegate the handling of grievances and job instruction
to the personnel department. When system designers and
personnel managers permit this type of disengagement, the
results almost always are ineffective systems and inept
foremen."

See also the author's article by the same title in California
Management Review, 10 (Spring, 1968), 9-20.

M-76. Myers, M. Scott. "Who Are Your Motivated Workers?" Harvard
Business Review. 42 (January-February, 1964), 73-88.

Since its publication, this article has obtained the status
of a "classic", and is frequently referred to in management
literature.

N-1.   Nakamoto, June and Verner, Coolie. Continuing Education in the
       Health Professions: A Review of the Literature Pertinent to
       North America. Washington, D.C.: Education Resources
       Division, Capitol Publications, Inc., 1973.

       This comprehensive review of continuing education in four
       major health professions from 1960-1970 was prepared for
       the ERIC Clearinghouse on Adult Education. Following a
       general overview, there are six chapters on continuing edu-
       cation in medicine, four on dentistry, four on nursing, and
       four on continuing education in pharmacy. After the data
       presented on each of the four professions, there is a sum-
       mary and bibliography. The work concludes with a section
       drawing major conclusions from the study discussed under
       two main topics, participation and programs.

N-2.   National Commission for the Study of Nursing and Nursing Education.
       An Abstract for Action: Continuing Education in Nursing:
       Necessity and Opportunity. An essential step toward the
       reconstruction of our health care system. Rochester, New
       York: The National Commission for the Study of Nursing and
       Nursing Education, 1971.

       This is a pamphlet summary of the 1970 report of the National
       Commission for the Study of Nursing and Nursing Education -
       An Abstract for Action.

       The statement gives continuing education a coequal impor-
       tance with preparatory education. It is a "constant" factor
       in the provision of the finest kind of patient care.

       The "Proposal for Action" takes the position that if continu-
       ing education is to be soundly planned and conducted, there
       must be some more systematic approach taken in the future
       than there has been in the past. The report recommends
       that each state form a master planning committee for nurs-
       ing education to identify one or more institutions to be res-
       ponsible for regional coverage of continuing education pro-
       grams for nurses within that area. The report also suggests
       that more attention be given to health care teams and to
       inter-professional efforts in continuing education, and that
       planning be done on interdisciplinary bases.

N-3.　National Consultation on Continuing Education for the Ministry, 1st, Newton Centre, Mass., 1964.

> In an effort to state the problems of continuing education for the ministry, describe its aims, delineate an adequate program, define the roles of sponsors, evaluate the concepts emerging from other fields of continuing education, and advice on coordination of programs, consultation speakers discussed the task of the minister in the changing world, in military service, in psychiatry, in the local parish, and in rural churches.

N-4.　National Consultation on Continuing Education for the Ministry, 2nd, Chicago, 1965. (ED 015 408.)

> Among the points of consensus emerging from this consultation was the decision that final responsibility for education programming rests within the denominations, although ecumenical aid may stimulate it.

N-5.　National Council of Churches of Christ, Department of Ministry. Study Opportunities for Ministers, January 1968 to January 1969. New York: National Council of Churches, 1968. (ED 029 244.)

> This alphabetical directory presents continuing education opportunities for ministers as offered by 111 seminaries, councils of churches, and other agencies in the United States, Canada, and several overseas countries.

N-6.　National Council of Churches of Christ, Department of Ministry. Study Opportunities for Professional Church Workers, January 1969 to January 1970. New York: National Council of Churches, 1968. (ED 031 646.)

> This alphabetical directory of educational resources in many geographic areas (United States and overseas) is intended to assist the minister in uncovering further educational possibilities for professional church workers.

N-7.   National Education Association. National Commission on Teacher
       Education and Professional Standards. The Development
       of the Career Teacher: Professional Responsibility for
       Continuing Education: Report of the 1963-64 Regional
       TEPS Conference. Washington, D.C.: National Education
       Association of the United States, 1964.

       This report on eight regional conferences on continuing
       education and the summary of the recommendations for
       next steps in continuing education gives special attention
       to furthering cooperative and individual actions to
       improve continuing education. The report also serves as
       a bench mark against which progress in continuing education
       can be measured.

N-8.   National Education Association, National Commission on Teacher
       Education and Professional Standards. New Horizons for
       the Teaching Profession. A report of the Task Force on
       New Horizons in Teacher Education and Professional
       Standards, 1961, edited by Margaret Lindsey. Washington,
       D.C.: National Education Association, 1961.

       The importance of continuing (inservice) education is
       stressed throughout the volume. The report views
       pre- and inservice education as a continuous process, and
       accordingly principles regarding inservice education are
       centered in Chapter 4, entitled "Preparation of Professional
       Personnel." A sampling of the concepts presented includes:

           --A wide range of inservice opportunities should be
             available to h lp individuals obtain their goals.
           --Not all continuing education should apply to ad-
             vanced college degrees.
           --Inservice education under the aegis of the school
             system, as well as graduate study, is characterized
             by the same principles as preservice preparation,
             with emphasis on continuing liberal education and
             upon work in the field of speci ization, and in
             professional education that goes beyond keeping
             abreast of developments to concern for new insights
             and relationships, to willingness and ability to ex-
             plore the unknown.

The report identifies the following factors as those that
qualify an individual as a professional:
  --is a liberally educated person.
  --possesses a liberal education related to and essential
    for the performance of a function.
  --is able to make rational judgements and to take appro-
    priate action within the scope of his activities, and
    responsibility for the consequences of judgements
    and actions.
  --Places primary emphasis upon his service to society
    rather than upon his personal gain.
  --actively participates with his colleagues in developing
    and enforcing standards fundamental to continuous
    improvement of his profession and abides by those
    standards in his own practice.
  --practices his profession on a full-time basis.
  --is engaged in a continuing search for new knowledge
    and skill.

N-9.   National Education Association, National Commission on Teacher
        Education. "New Horizons in Teacher Education and
        Professional Standards." NEA Journal, 50 (January,
        1961), 55-68.

        This is a report about one of the major attempts to consider
        professional standards and growth of the teacher. It was
        sponsored by the National Education Association. The
        Commission identified new goals for professional standards
        and defined action proposals for implementing these goals.

N-10.   National Education Association. National Commission on Teacher
        Education and Professional Standards. Remaking the World
        of the Career Teacher. Washington, D.C.: National
        Education Association, 1966.

        As preparation for the 1965-66 Regional TEPS Conference
        (Teacher Education and Professional Standards), teachers
        were asked to submit proposals for discussion by conference
        participants in study groups. The proposals were to be
        a concise specific description of a hypothetical plan or
        program related to one or more of the following topics:
          1. New kinds of internship-residency programs for

567

beginning teachers.
2. New approaches to individualized professional growth programs for teachers .
3. New ways to differentiate assignments within a school--the "team of specialists" idea.
4. New ways to encourage status for teachers.
5. New ways to provide for the interrupted career or late choice of career.

The purpose was to stretch the thinking of those participating in the eight regional conferences past present stereotypes and boundaries. It was intended as a way to get with way-out ideas. Two sample ideas follow: One suggested that the requirement for college credit following a teacher's full certification be eliminated and that in its place be substituted brief statements in writing signed by both teacher and principal describing a teacher's proposed plan for professional growth and later a report on the accomplishment of the plan. This plan also included a proposal for a teacher's library "that should be one of the most significant rooms in every school building; it should contain the best and latest books in education as well as all important professional journals."

Another plan suggested "fixed-role therapy". This approach was designed to increase efficiency in producing realistic behavior changes. Participants would role play a fixed role for a two-week period. It was suggested that through this intensive role-playing experience, teachers would assume the desired new behaviors as a part of their permanent pattern of activities.

N-11. National Education Association. National Commission on Teacher Education and Professional Standards. What You Should Know About New Horizons. (A condensation of New Horizons in Teacher Education and Professional Standards. Washington, D.C.: National Education Association, 1962.

This is a pamphlet which summarizes effectively all of the main points made in the full New Horizons report.

568

N-12. National Education Association. Research Division. "School Library Personnel, Task Analysis Survey." *American Libraries* 1 (February, 1970), 176-177.

> For reference to full report see entry under American Association of School Librarians.

N-13. National Institute of Adult Education. Adult Education in 1968: The Year Book of the National Institute of Adult Education (England and Wales) and the Scottish Institute of Adult Education. London, 1968. [ED 028 323]

> This annual 1968 yearbook of adult education in Great Britain contains the following: 1) an annual review of activities; 2) a directory of the National Institute of Adult Education, the Department of Education and Science, and Organizations in Residential Education, Labor Education, Armed Forces Education, Educational Broadcasting, Industrial Training, and other phases of adult education in England and Wales; 3) A list of 134 studies in adult education (publications from April 1, 1967 to March 31, 1968); 4) Abstracts of relevant legislation and regulations; 5) education authority provisions, colleges and universities, conferences and courses, principal adult education organizations and publications, and local education committee offices in Scotland; and 6) overseas contacts with international organizations and with Africa, Austrailia and New Zealand, Asia, Europe and North America.

N-14. National League of Nursing. Statement on Nursing Education. New York: National League of Nursing, 1967. [ED 020 399.]

N-15. National Seminar On Adult Education Research. Abstracts of Papers Presented to the National Seminar On Adult Education Research. ERIC Clearinghouse on Adult Education, Syracuse University, February 9-11, 1969.

> Thirty-four abstracts of papers on adult education are presented in this document in addition to two historical reviews of adult education in the Confederacy and lyceums.

N-16.   National Society for the Study of Education, Committee on Education
        for the Professions. Education for the Professions: The
        Sixty-First Yearbook of the National Society for the Study
        of Education. 61, Part II edited by Nelson B. Henry.
        Chicago, Illinois: The University of Chicago Press, 1962.

        The object of this yearbook was to present current trends in
        professional education; it covers case studies in medicine,
        engineering, teaching, business. In the concluding chapter,
        entitled, "The Ideal Education for the Professional Man,"
        Earl H. McGrath states:

        "An education preparatory for practice ought to also culti-
        vate the idea that the completion of such a program of train-
        ing is but the cornerstone of professional competence. Only
        those conscious of the geometrical increase in knowledge
        relevant to their work and the changing circumstances of
        practice can avoid beginning to become professionally mori-
        bund on the day of graduation. Institutions have the respon-
        sibility to make continuing opportunities for professional
        and general education available to their graduates and others
        of similar interests in the community." (p. 301)

N-17.   Nattress, LeRoy William, Jr. "Continuing Education for the Profes-
        sions in the United States," Convergence, 3 (1970) 42-50.
        [See also: Nattress, LeRoy William, ed. Continuing Educa-
        tion for the Professions. Chicago, Illinois: Natresources,
        Inc., 1970. This work contains 16 papers drawn from the
        proceedings of the Sections on Continuing Education for the
        Professions of the Adult Education Association of the U.S.A.,
        the National University Extension Association, and the
        Galaxy Conference on Adult Education, held in Washington,
        D.C., December 8-10, 1969)]

        Nattress defines continuing education as "a process whereby
        a person who has completed his formal education [in his dis-
        cussions he only includes those who have received profes-
        sional training beyond the baccalaureate] is provided with a
        means for meeting his needs for further personal development.
        The learning, or how well the objectives are met, must be
        evaluated." He presents a model which gives a system ap-
        proach to his definition. He argues that the role of the edu-
        cators must be more than that of an educational agent or a
        facilitator of learning prescribed subject matter. "The edu-
        cator must be willing and able to interact with the student
        in each segment of the model."

Taking the three classic professions—the clergy, law, and
medicine—he explains that each illustrates a state of development of continuing education programs. The ministry
is an example of a profession in which continuing education
is just beginning to be recognized for "proficient practice";
in law, formal education has been joined with continuing
education in a continuous process; in medicine (the most
advanced) "There is an ultimate criterion by which effectiveness
can be measured, and a broadly based activity approach
to reduce morbidity and morality in the population has been
attempted. "

Continuing education for the clergy has thus far centered
in a wide variety of programs in the hope that individual
clergymen will be able to meet their individual needs at a
given time; however, clergymen themselves cite their own
reading and self-selected study groups as the primary modes
because of lack of continuing education and the expense in
time and money of the courses that have been offered. "At
present, therefore, we must conclude that continuing education
for the clergy is coming into existence and that a great deal
of change interms of content, methods, and techniques can
be anticipated. "

In spite of the fact that law is client based and the client
serves as the motivator and the initiator of learning, and
that the judge and jury serve to evaluate how much the
lawyer has benefited from the education experience, it
has become recognized that experience and self-study alone
cannot meet the need for continuing legal education. Therefore, at a national level, the Committee on Legal Education
and Admissions to the Bar of the American Bar Association
recommended in 1947 that the American Law Institute, in
cooperation with the American Bar Association, assume the
task of providing continuing legal education. Since 1965 the
Institute has published, annually, the Catalog of Continuing
Legal Education Programs and Publications in the United
States. (Current issue contains about 1000 entries.) However,
in common with programs for the clergy, programs often
pay little attention to statements of objectives and effectiveness
is measured by "popularity rather than the quality of learning."
Continuing legal education is unique in that almost all the
programs are carried on outside the law schools through

571

institutes sponsored by the American Bar Association.

Since the passage of Public Law 89-239 in 1965 and the
subsequent establishment of 55 regional medical programs
to combat more effectively certain diseases, medical
continuing education has increased at a rapid rate. Programs have been directed not only at physicians and sur-
geons, but to public health personnel, related professionals
and the general public. Largely because of the heavy
pouring of federal funds, there have been more innovations
in methods of techniques than in any other field. Examples
of these are: medical single concept films, telelectures;
slow scan television programs, educational television;
dial access libraries; telephone conferences; radio conferences; self-instructional materials; MIST, a telephone
consultation service which provides direct contact, on a
24 hour basis, with a faculty member of a university;
individual physicial profile, designed to gather data about
his practice, test the physician on the major areas of his
practice, and provide consultation relative to his practice;
educational resource index--a computerized index of educational
resources and events (classified by disease entity and type
of programming) to assist physicians in planning their
continuing education program. On the whole medical continuing education experiences are evaluated and thus,
according to the author, they show the way to future
continuing professional education.

Recognizing the need for better communication among those
professionals involved in continuing education, the Adult
Education Association (AEA) of the U.S.A. formed a Section
on Continuing Education for Professions in 1966, in order
to provide a forum where educators working with professionals
could discuss problems and solutions. The National University Extension Association (NUEA) formed a similar
section in 1969 for similar purposes, but limited membership to university extension representatives. As a result,
AEA has dealt more with the problems of the learner; NUEA
with the problem of administration. As yet the interdisciplinary approach made possible by these associations has
not attracted a large number of participants. "The professions seem to be moving separately down the same path."

Nattress believes the prospects for future development in
professional continuing education are excellent and that
they will be forwarded to the extent that 1) preconditions
for learning are identified and managed; 2) objectives
are stated , meaningfully and specifically; 3) ultimate
criteria are established, with the resulting identification
of a variety of learning experiences; 4) results are evaluated by sophisticated techniques that do not interfere
with the learning-teaching process are unobtrusive.

N-18.   New Jersey State Council for Environmental Education. Evaluation
        for Environmental Education. Mountain Lakes, New Jersey:
        New Jersey State Council for Environmental Education, 1969.

N-19.   "New Western Reserve Program Plans Continuing Education."
        Library Journal. 92 (June 15, 1967), 2341.

        This article describes an experimental program in
        continuing education for medical librarians. It's goal
        is to identify elements of library practice most subject
        to obsolescence and provide a methodology for evaluating
        the effectiveness of alternate approaches to providing
        continuing education.

N-20.   Nicholas, Robert A. A Study of Continuing Education Needs of Selected
        Professional Groups and University Extension Contract Pro-
        grams in Wyoming. University of Wyoming, June, 1966.
        [ED 017 749.]

        This study aims at developing principles for a model pro-
        gram of continuing education for the professions at the
        University of Wyoming. The author reviews the literature
        on the growth of the professions and on continuing education
        in the professions   generally with special reference to
        architecture, dentistry, law, medicine and pharmacy.

N-21.   Nixon, Alan. "Plan for More Professionalism by ACS." ACS
        News, 50 (February 14, 1972), 23.

        Nixon, President-elect of the American Chemical Society,
        proposed a $10 assessment against members for the year

573

in order to get a continuing education program going. The chief objective of ACS, according to Nixon, should be to act more directly in the support of its members--"establishing and maintaining a high-level, dynamic, economic, and professional environment in which they can work productively in not only their own but also their employers' and the public's interest."

N-22.   Nursing Update, 1970.

This magazine is intended to be a continuing education aid for the nurse, and provides the nurse-reader with practical, useful and up-to-date clinical and nursing information. It is designed both for quick reading and handy reference. Special feature include: "express stops" (marginal summaries of articles); quiz covering each article; capsule information (insert charts and summaries of key information); resource files (lists of supplementary reading); 3-hole punched for easy notebook filing.

O-1. Odiorne, George S. "A Systems Approach to Training," Training Directors, 19 (October 1965), 11-19.

   After defining the system concept as primarily a way of thinking about the job of managing in which inputs, processes, and outputs are dealt with, the author identifies eight kinds of training systems and recommends the cybernetic training system as the most effective and appropriate. He warns that unless a training system is endorsed by the top personnel in an organization the training may be wasted or harmful. "Where he sees conflict, the trainer must either change that environment and its messages, or forego the training as being harmful."

O-2. Odiorne, George S. "Yardsticks for Measuring Personnel Departments," The Personnel Administrator, (July-August, 1967).

   The author lists five major yardsticks to audit and evaluate personnel departments, but he states his preference and recommendation for managing the personnel department by objectives and the use of a systems type audit.

O-3. O'Donnell, Cyril J. "Managerial Training: A System Approach." Training and Development Journal, 22 (January, 1968), 2-11.

   The author explains the management process as a system so that those who are involved in management training can understand its real purpose. He discusses problems in managerial appraisal and management by results and declares that the end of the management training must be improvement or the manager's ability to achieve his goals.

O-4. Off, Charles B. and Loren D. Boutin. "Training Program Design. An Exercise in Developing Training Objectives by Specification of Terminal Behaviors." Training and Development Journal, 21 (August, 1967), 20-33.

O-5. Ofiesh, Gabriel D. "The New Education and the Learning Industry," Educational Leadership, 26 (May, 1969), 760-763.

"Gathering a variety of media and tacking them together does not provide us with a multi-media learning system. The 'systems approach to education' in brief, involved the specification of behavioral objectives, the assessment of student repetoires, the development of instructional strategies, testing and revision of instructional unit (validation), and finally packaging and administering a validated learning system." Such an approach Ofiesh maintains results in the development of learning experiences for the individual which are designed to meet his needs, and learning modes. "The learning experiences, however, are designed to produce the behaviors specified; in other words, the specified behavioral objectives are the constant in the system."

O-6. Ofiesh, Gabriel D. Programmed Instruction: A Guide for Management. New York: American Management Association, 1965.

O-7. Ohio State Department of Education, Trade and Industrial Education Services. Human Relations Training for Supervisory Personnel, Leader's Manual. Columbus, Ohio: Ohio State University, Trade and Industrial Education Service, Instructional Materials Laboratory, 1969.

This course has been prepared for industrial and business supervision and was developed by a statewide group of industrial leadership personnel and tested prior to publication. It is recommended that the course be taught in 5 two-hour sessions.

A learner portfolio of 15 handout sheets, a series of flannel board cutouts, and a tape recording of human relations cases are available separately to use with the course.

O-8. Ohio State University, College of Administrative Science. "Library Consultant's Seminar for the State Library of Ohio," In: Peter Hiatt and others, ed., Education of State Library Personnel: A Report with Recommendations Relating to the Continuing Education of State Library Agency Professional Personnel. Chicago, Ill.: American Library Association, 1971, 29-31.

The stated purpose of the seminar was: "To provide participants
with an opportunity for increased knowledge and understanding
of the objectives and role of the library consultants within the
State of Ohio library system and to provide the participants
with increased administrative skills to improve their ability
to perform their library consultant functions or tasks." As
outline of the specific objectives, content, methodology, and
scheduling are included, the paper has value as a model for
other continuing education seminars.

O-9. Ohio State University, Division of Continuing Education. Annual Re-
port of Continuing Education at the Ohio State University,
(July 1, 1967 through June 30, 1968.) Columbus, Ohio: Ohio
State University, Division of Continuing Education, 1968.

A report of the Ohio State University Continuing Education
program and its major areas of emphasis, by individual administration units, is presented. This is an example of one university's comprehensive programming. Sources of funds are
indicated for each program.

O-10. Ohliger, John. The Mass Media in Adult Education: A Review of
Recent Literature. Syracuse University, New York Eric
Clearinghouse on Adult Education. (November 1968.)

This review of recent literature in the Mass Media in Adult
Education is based on the assumption that the literature reflects
actual practices and trends. It explains the difficulties in
arriving at definitions, outlines the general trends in the uses
of the mass media, and examines individual media as well
as their use in the various area of adult education. References
in the text comprise the bibliography consisting of 120 titles,
most of which have abstracts appended to them.

O-11. Olean, Sally J. Changing Patterns in Continuing Education for Business.
Center for the Study of Liberal Education for Adults, Brookline,
Massachusettes. 1967.

577

After World War II, business and industry moved into the
adult education field, and are now spending a reported $20 billion
annually in higher education for their scientific personnel
and management. Large industries, like IBM, have complete
educational programs and facilities for their personnel. Ford
and General Motors use outside educational groups for executive
development programs. Such companies as Continental C
have a small headquarters educational staff administering
decentralized programs, either using their own programs or participating in programs available locally at colleges or universities. The American Bankers Association and the American
College of Life Underwriters have their own programs. Some
Companies use such unaffiliated educational organizations as
the American Management Association or the National Industrial
Conference Board. With better communication between universities and business, the universities could 1) set the conceptual
framework for long-duration education, 2) provide short-range
immediate pay-off education, 3) evaluate company-sponsored
programs, and 4) investigate new technology and methods
for teaching adults. This document is available from the center
for the study of Liberal Education.

O-12. Oliva, Frank D. and Koch, E.L. (eds.) <u>Designs for the Seventies;</u>
<u>An Administrative Perspective.</u> A collection of the papers
delivered at The Western Canada Educational Administrators'
Conference sponsored by the Council on School Administration,
Alberta Teacher's Association. (Seminar series for School
Administrators, Vol. 4.) Calgary, Alberta, The University
of Calgary, Department of Educational Administration, 1970.

O-13. Ontario Institute for Studies in Education, Department of Evaluation
and Measurement. <u>Evaluation and Measurement Newsletter.</u>
Toronto, Canada: The Ontario Institute for Studies in Education,
1970.

The Evaluation and Measurement Newsletter is issued inter-
mittently by the Department of Measurement and Evaluation of
the Ontario Institute for Studies in Education. Its purpose is
to provide information for school administrators, teachers,
and guidance workers. Issues contain articles, tests, measures,
and related publications and services related to evaluation and

evaluation and measurement. For example, the May 1971 issue
(No. 11) features an article by Henry S. Dyer, "Toward Objective
Criteria for Accountability, which features the controversial
issue of accountability, or cost-benefit analysis as applied
to schools.

O-14. O'Toole, John F., Jr. "Systems Analysis: A Rational Approach to
Decision-Making in Education," SDC Magazine, 8(July, 1965)
1-16.

This article recognizes a need for a systems analysis approach
in designing and developing more effective educational enterprise. The central idea of the systems approach to educational
system design is that functional components are inter-related
and that a complex process can be understood best if it is
related as a whole. This approach views a system in the broadest
possible perspective, including the system's surrounding social
and economic environment, and it pays close attention to the
information network binding the interacting elements of the
system together. No single educational problem or organizational level of the system can be porperly assessed or changed
independently without consideration of the impact such modifications may have on other functions and levels of the system.

O-15. Oregon, "A Study of the Continuing Education Needs and Interests of
Managers and Professional People in South-Central Oregon."
Oregon State System of Higher Education, Corvallis. Division
of Continuing Education. November, 1968.

O-16. Overhage, Carl F.J. "Science Libraries: Prospects and Problems."
Science, 155 (February, 1967), 802-806.

The author, professor of engineering and then Director of
Project Intrex, at the Massachusettes Institute of Technology
makes a strong appeal "to first-rate minds to divert to the
problems of our university libraries some of the effort that now
goes into research and teaching. He reviews the critical condition in large universities libraries and points out some new
technology that can be used to provide relief. According to
Overhage, the library crisis has three main areas:

1) the physical crisis produced by sheer bulk of material;
2) operational crisis (it takes too long to get materials to users);
3) the intellectual crisis : making materials easily retrieveable.

Calling scholars and administrators to face the challenges that are beyond the reach of librarians and information transfer engineers, Overage suggests ways to improve the situation.

He states that strong incentives will have to be provided for the practice of neglected areas. "A new kind of respectability and prestige must be attached to the writing of critical reviews, progress reports, bibliographies, monographs and textbooks. He asserts that it will be necessary for universities to enter into partnership with outside sponsors. He mentions the creation of review centers, located at large universities or research institutions, where a permanent staff of competent writers would provide assistance to the outstanding scientists who would accept responsibility for review articles.

He points out that if progress is to be made, there will have to be a system of incentives. Incentives will be an understanding of quality. "The publication of inferior material will have to be ruthlessly discouraged, lest such material appear in print and block access to good material, bringing discredit to the entire scheme. As always, the crucial task will be the selection of the individuals to whom the stipends are awarded. One of the major objectives will be endowment of the supported activities with great prestige, and this can be achieved only through selection of individuals by a jury with outstanding qualifications."

He concludes by pointing out that a new attitude on the part of universities toward these forgotten aspects of scholarship will have a strong implication for the future of research libraries.

O-17. The Open University: Report of the Planning Committee to the Secretary of State for Education and Science. London: Open University Planning Committee, Department of Education and Science, Her Majesty's Stationery Office, 1969.

P-1. "Pacereport, April, 1968. Owensboro City Schools, Kentucky.
(ED 023 620.).

Pacereport, established under terms of an ESEA Title III
Grant from the U. S. Office of Education to the Owensboro
City Schools, Owensboro, Kentucky, is published to provide
Title III project directors with a continuing source of news and
information on educational innovation. This issue concentrates
on eight specific inservice case studies including the following:
'A Self-Perpetuating System, ; San Bernardino, California:
'An Opportunity For Professional Growth,' Atlanta Georgia:
'Training Teachers To Train Themselves,' Marion, Illinois:
'An Area Pilot Program, ; Cedar Rapids, Iowa: 'The Key
To Improving Education Is The Teacher, ; Stillwater, Minnesota:
'Inservice Training--Audio Visual Media,' Durant, Oklahoma:
'Mobilab: Teacher Training,' Eugene, Oregon: 'Individualization
of Inservice Program,' Stevens Point, Wisconsin. Included
also are notes of particular importance to Title III projects.

P-2. Parker, Edvin B. and others. Communication and Research in an
Interdisciplinary Behavioral Science Research Area.
Stanford University, Institute for Communication Research,
July, 1968. Clearinghouse #PB 179 569 .

The introduction to this study states: "One of the reasons--
perhaps the major reason--for research agencies to sponsor
studies of the communication behavior of scientists is to learn
the nature of the relationship between communication behavior
and research productivity. The apparent hope is that funds
invested in improved scientific communication will lead to a
more efficient over-all use of funds invested in science. If
this hope is to be realized, we need to know, first, whether,
there is a demonstrable relationship between scientific
communication and scientific research productivity, and second,
what kinds of communication should be supported to achieve
increased productivity. "

"The major implication of these findings is that professional
societies, employers, and relevant government agencies concerned with increasing research productivity should concern themselves more with the facilitation of interpersonal
contact among researchers. Several innovations along these
lines have appeared recently, for example, in listing of papers

581

accepted for publication in American Psychological Association journals (so those interested can write the author for a reprint). Perhaps more attention should be paid to directories of researchers, particularly if they could be indexed by research interest categories.

These data provide support for the argument that costs of travel to meetings, of visits to other research facilities, and of telephone calls can be justified as likely to increase research productivity."

P-3. Parlette, Nicholas, and others. "Public Health Professionals and Continuing Education: A Study of Interests and Needs in Continuing Education in the West." Summary Report. (June 1968). (ED 023 041).

Service to public health and allied professionals has long been the concern and major function of the Program for Continuing Education in Public Health, sponsored by the Four Schools of Public Health in the West, and by the Western Regional Office of the American Public Health Association (APHA). To assess the effectiveness of this program, a study of continuing education and training, experience, heirarchical position, type of employing agency, and other relevant characteristics of 1,355 professional public health workers in the western states, as well as on preferences for 78 course types and for newly proposed methods and techniques of instruction. Nineteen topics were selected by 20 or more of the respondents. Eleven of these were already available or being developed. General problem areas and skills in community and organizational problem solving were the major concerns. Multidisciplinary courses were widely favored over single discipline courses; and television and videotapes were widely supported, but not teaching machines. Typically, participants were older, had more experience and higher positions, more often had advanced degrees, and were more likely to belong to the APHA or a state association, than nonparticipants. However, 66 of full-time professionals lacked a degree in public health.

P-4. Paton, W. B. "Staff Training in Libraries," Library Association Record, 60 (August, 1958), 243-48.

The ability to inspire and train staff constitutes one of the major attributes for success in a chief librarian. The author suggests various ways in which enlightened staff training can be furthered.

P-5. Paul, William J., Keith B. Robertson, and Frederick Herzberg. "Job Enrichment Pays Off," Harvard Business Review, 47 (March-April, 1969).

P-5. Paullin, Alyce Klussman. Participation, Learning Achievement and Perceived Benefit in a Televised Continuing Medical Education Program. Unpublished doctoral dessertation, The Catholic University of America, 1971.

The purpose of this study was to investigate the relationships of certain characteristics of practicing physicians who participated in a series of televised cardiology programs. The study was undertaken because developing programs of postgraduate medical education which will meet the needs of practicing physicians has become critical to medical educations because of such factors as: 1) decreased real-time available for busy doctors to engage in continuing education activities. 2) the rapidly expanding body of medical knowledge. 3) the increasing number of foreign medical graduates who are practicing in the United States. 4) modification of medical school curriculum. 5) the increased demand for health care services at all levels of American society.

The major findings included the following: 1) there was a significant positive correlation between level of participation and learning gain. 2) the level of participation in this study was considered high. 3) active participation can be sustained in a single medical speciality area, such as cardiology, for periods of 14 to 28 weeks. 4) television can be utilized as an effective and efficient tool in meeting the continuing education needs of practicing physicans, 5) open circuit broadcast television can be utilized for continuing medical education without apparent adverse reaction from the lay public, even when live patient demonstrations are integral components of the presentation.

P-6. Paulson, Casper F., Jr. <u>An Examination of the Structure and Effective-ness of Slide-Tapes Produced by Rational Analysis and Self-Sequencing Techniques.</u> Final Report, Office of Education Grant No. 7-27-000-238, Project No. 5-0952. Monmouth, Oregon: Teaching Research Division, Oregon State System of Higher Education, June 1967.

Two techniques for developing slide-tape presentation, from which teachers may learn to identify and construct behavioral objectives, were compared with respect to the structural characteristics, particularly sequencing of the product each technique produced and the effectiveness of each in terms of achievement. The two techniques were rational analysis (RA) and self-sequencing (SS).

Treatment effects were similar to the two treatments. Treatment effects approached significance in favor of the SS technique, but this variation was attributed to variations in sequence rather than the superiority of the SS technique.

P-7. Payne, John G. "Videotape Recording for Management Training: A Report from Western Electric on How to Use Television," <u>Training and Development Journal,</u> 21 (April, 1967), 18-25.

P-8. Peck, Janice R. Management Seminar Series I and II for Nursing Home Administrators, March-July 1969. Maryland University, College Park. Conferences and Institutes Division, November, 1969. (ED 041 238.).

Developed by the University of Maryland for the Maryland-D. C. Nursing Home Association, these two series, each containing 84 hours of instruction in four three-day seminars, were designed to meet nursing home administrators' need for managerial skills and to prepare them for licensing. (Based on experiences with the first series, course materials and faculty were changed slightly in the second). Preliminary conferences with 15 administrators showed favorable reactions to experience-based learning materials and discussion rather than passive learning. Seminars dealt, respectively, with planning and general concepts, leading and directing, measuring and controlling, and practical integration of knowledge and skills gained in the other seminars. One textbook (Leavitt's

Managerial Psychology) and a manual of 15 readings, were used. Tuition per series was $460 for association members, $560 for nonmembers. Certificates of participation went to 58 persons in all. The seminars were largely rated good or excellent. However, two of the seminars (mainly informational lectures) were not so well received, and participants would have like more time spent on presentation. Based on findings, it was proposed that the curriculum be revised to include 112 hours of instruction, possibly in four seminars of 3 1/2 days each during each semester. [ERIC].

P-10. Peck, Theodore P. "Continuing Education and the Academic Librarian." MnU Bulletin. 3(October, 1972) 111-116.

In order to meet many new developments (specified by the author) that are reshaping library services, it is imperative for academic librarians "to come to grips with the matter of continuing their education." This will be increasingly important as the trend enlarges to involve the librarian as a full working partner in course development (as at Hamline in Minnesota and Hampshire in New England).

The author suggests four approaches to continuing education: 1) enrolling in courses; 2) developing a wider acquaintance with periodical literature in new areas (he suggests Audio-visual Instruction, Educational Media, Information Records Management, Today's Education, Education Digest, and regular reference of ERIC indexes); 3) joining professional associations covering new fields, such as the National Education Association, Association for Education Communications and Technology, the American Society for Information Science; 4) on-site visits where first-rate applications of new trends can be seen in operation.

He concludes: "Continuing education of academic librarians should be a flexible program molded to fit the needs and interests of the individual . . . The essential thing is to begin now to avail oneself of the opportunities for broadening perspectives."

P-11. Penland, Patrick R. Advisory Counseling for Librarians. Pittsburgh, Pa.: Graduate School of Library and Information Sciences,

Pittsburgh University, 1970.

The papers in the first section of this publication develop an
understanding of the background, purpose and functions of
advisory counseling in libraries. The purpose of the papers
in the second section is to delineate the interrelationships of
information transfer and meaning transfer and to lay out a
background where flexibility can be developed in moving
from one frame of reference and orientation to another with the
same patron. The third section explores the principles and
functions of counseling and of guiding the healthy, self-actualizing
adult towards human development organized around life states,
social role and various coping behaviors. Papers in the fourth
section consider a variety of principles and methods of evaluation and research of advisory counseling for librarians. The
appendix contains items that have been developed for the teaching
of interpersonal communications.

P-12. Penland, Patrick R., (ed.) "Floating Librarians in the Community."
Papers presented at The Institute on the Floating Librarian
in the Emerging Community held July 13-31, 1970 at the Graduate
School of Library and Information Science, University of Pittsburgh.

One of the weakest areas of professional preparation, and professional in-service training and development is that of community
development education. Each year, many professionally trained
recruits go into the field of library service with only the most
rudimentary notion of , and training for community, group, and
power-structure analyses. Library educational services,
historically, have given little formal attention to any training
for the "floating" community librarian nor to developing the
ability to use the methods of community development education
for the broad informational and educational purposes of actual
and potential patrons in the community neighborhoods. Four
models of community communication services are the "outreach
project" for reaching users outside of the main building community
involvement, community work beyond regular library hours and
the role of the independent information specialist who works
outside of the confines of institutional support. The role of the
professional person is to stimulate the articulation of community
needs and interests and involve citizens in decision-making
processes, for which a major method is provided. The appendix
contains a number of measurements and a bibliography of pertinent
references.

586

P-13. Penland, Patrick R. "Media Designed Programs for Librarians."
       Pittsburgh, Pa.: Graduate School of Library and Information
       Science, University of Pittsburgh, 1970.

      Media materials and services may be used for two different
      but closely related purposes; motivating people to participate
      in informational and educational experiences, and motivating
      them to learn. This manual is an attempt ot overcome the reader's
      initial reluctance to use a variety of media.

P-14. Perlberg, Arye and O'Bryan, David C. The Use of Video-Tape Recording
       and Micro-Teaching Techniques to Improve Instruction on the
       Higher Education Level. University of Illinois, Department of
       General Engineering, 1968. (ERIC ED 023 314.).

P-15. "Personnel: New Duties, New Training." Wisconsin Library Bulletin,
       64 (September-October, 1969).

      This issue describes new state programs for human resources
      development. Some topics considered are: the personnel implications
      of the new media; the training of media support people; the program
      of training of library technical assistants; and a new graduate
      degree program for training librarians and media personnel for
      new aspects of library service.

P-16. Pfeiffer, John. New Look at Education: Systems Analysis in Our
       Schools and Colleges. Poughkeepsie, New York: Odyssey Press,
       1968.

      A clearly written survey for laymen and educators, concentrating
      primarily on administration. It includes a definition of the
      "Delphi Method" and relates it to systems development.

P-17. Phillips, Kathleen. "Training for Federal Librarians," Federal Library
       Committee Newsletter, No. 22 (June 1968), 7-13.

The salient findings that emerge from 97 (out of 150 questionnaires sent) replies received from federal librarians whose
average grade was GS 9.5 and whose average years in the
federal library was 10.75 years were: (Rank order of most
pressing training needs for federal librarians:)

1. Keeping up to date with new developments in library science.
2. Staff development and motivation.
3. Application of Automatic Data Processing to library science.
4. Management practices and problems in federal libraries.
5. Human relations and supervisory practices.
6. Special procurement problems in federal libraries.
7. Work planning, simplification and productivity analysis.
8. Communication techniques in federal libraries.
9. Orientation to major federal libraries.
10. Statistics on systematic record keeping.
11. Ideas and authors in field of librarianship.
12. Literature survey in specialized fields; state of the art review.

P-18. Physician's Recognition Award. Chicago, Illinois: American Medical
Association Department of Continuing Medical Education, 1970.

"At its Clinical Convention in December, 1968, the American
Medical Association House of Delegates established the Physician's
Recognition Award for participation in Continuing Medical
Education.

The Award was first offered during 1969. It was based on the
continuing medical education activities carried out by physicians
during the three year period beginning July 1, 1966, and ending
June 30, 1969. Over 16,000 physicians applied for the Award
at this first offering, and about 75% of the applicants were
found to be qualified.

The purpose of the Physician's Recognition Award is to accord
recognition to physicians who participate regularly in continuing
medical education and to encourage other physicians to engage
in this important activity. The AMA strongly believes that all
physicians should continue their education on a regular basis
throughout their professional careers.

Since a lifetime of learning is an obligation of those in our profession, the Award is planned in such a way that a physician engaged in any field or fields of medicine can qualify for the Award. Thus, physicians in medical administration, academic medicine, medical research, etc., can qualify for the Award as well as the generalist or specialist in clinical practice.

Application for the Award is voluntary and open to all doctors of medicine in the United States without regard to citizenship or AMA membership. An applicant with a medical degree from a foreign medical school may be considered if he is fully licensed to practice medicine in a state, or is certified by the Educational Council for Foreign Medical Graduates.

For recent graduates, AMA approved intern and residency training may be used for qualification. Some physicians will qualify on the basis of inter-residency training alone; others will use intern and residency training in combination with other continiuing medical education activities. Unless they are recent graduates, most practicing physicians will rely heavily on continuing medical education courses to qualify for the Award.

The Award is granted for a minimum total of 150 credit hours of continuing medical education that are earned over a continuous three year qualifying period.

For the purpose of the Award, a credit hour is one hour of participation in a continuing medical education activity. Of the 150 credit hours needed to qualify for the Award, a minimum of 60 credit hours must come from any combination of Required Education categories. Required Education includes those activities grouped together as the first six categories listed on the application form.

P-19. Piele, Philip, Annotated Bibliography on Educational Administrator Preparation Programs. Eugene, Oregon: Oregon University ERIC Clearinghouse on Educational Administration, October, 1968. (ERIC ED 023 198.).

A comprehensive annotated bibliography of the more significant recent (since 1962) literature describing or proposing programs for the inservice or preservice preparation of educational administrators. Thirty-six documents are included.

P-20. Pings, Vern M. and Cruzat, Gwendolyn S. An Assessment of a
Post Masters Internship in Biomedical Librarianship. Wayne
State University, Detroit, Michigan. Biomedical Information
Center. December 1970. (ED 046 426).

This paper attempts to assess the post masters training program
given at Wayne State University Medical Library between
1967 - 1970. Probabilistic conclusions suggest certain educational activities be undertaken: 1) There is no justification to
create a post masters program to teach basic library techniques,
and library schools must incorporate skill development within the curriculum or on-the-job training will have to be continued.
2) Two justifications for internship programs require establishment
of programs either to teach students the application of theoretical
knowledge in a working envoronment aimed toward a speciality.
3) Management and planning tasks for libraries cannot be
adequately taught in a one-year post masters educational program,
and 4) The distinctive feature of medical librarianship is its
environment and the librarian must comprehend how biomedical
information is generated and used, and should attend conferences
and seminars to gain this knowledge. The report concludes all
'experimental' education undertaken in the program, including
skill development, planning, management and investigative work
should rightly be started in library schools. An addendum
covers proposed educational objectives of the program. [ERIC].

P-21. Pletsch, Douglas H. "Communication Concepts for Adult Educators:"
Paper presented at the National Seminar on Adult Education
Research at Toronto, Canada, February 9-11. 1969.
(ED 025 727.)

P-22. Pluckhan, Maragaret L. and others. "Meeting the Challenge: Coordination
and Facilitation of Statewide Continuing Education for Nurses
Through Interdisciplinary and Interagency Action." The Journal of
Continuing Education in Nursing, 4 (January-February 1973), 22-27.

The paper tells of the work of a Task Force on Continuing
Education in Kansas and describes its interdisciplinary and
interagency composition. The Committee feels that its program
"is not only unique but essential to the nature of the mission of
coordinating and facilitating quality programs in sufficient

number to meet the expressed and identified needs for continuing
education for nurses in the state." All types of health services,
as well as nursing programs at universities, and nursing associations and clients are presented at the meetings which have
never had less that 20 in attendance (at their own expense and
coming from distances up to 210 miles).

At the first meeting four areas of concern were identified: dialogue,
assessment of needs, resources and funding, and objectives and
evaluation. To date, the group's chief document prepared by
the Objectives and Evaluation group states a need for a set of
basic standards on which to develop more specific criteria for
program objectives and evaluation tools. Accordingly, the
Guidelines for Continuing Education Programs for Nurses in Kansas
were developed and approved for statewide distribution:

1) Program content should be readily identified as being
   concerned with the improvement of nursing care.
2) Programs should be planned based on the expressed needs
   of potential participants, needs identified for the staff by
   employers and supervisors, needs of the professional nurse
   which he may not be aware of but may reduce his ability
   to provide effective health care services.
3) Statewide needs of practicing nurses in all types of health
   care agencies and all nursing specialities should be considered
   in program planning.
4) Consumers, as active members of the health team, should be
   considered in program planning to help them gain knowledge of
   health practices and understanding and acceptance of the
   changing role of the professional nurse.
5) Resource personnel should be qualified to present the material
   assigned.
6) Program objectives should be developed for each conference,
   continuing education course or workshop and corresponding
   tools be utilized to evaluate the program (one to two-week
   post-conference evaluation by the conferee and employer
   is also suggested.)
7) Principles and theories used in program development should
   be geared to the adult learner.
8) When a team approach to health care is presented, efforts
   should be made to have members of corresponding health
   disciplines represented in the audience as well as on the
   program.

9) Consideration should be given to previously scheduled programs to prevent unnecessary duplication of content in the same geographical area and overlapping of dates.

10) Program planners should be encouraged to consider their offerings in relation to other state programs. Advertisement of the program should include the number of C. E. U.'s (continuing education units) accepted. Contact hours for the programs should be stipulated on the program and/ or on a certificate of attendance.

P-23. The Pony Express: News from the SMU Institute of Technology. 2 (January 15, 1969), 1 (June 1, 1968), 1 (May 10, 1968). Dallas, Texas: Southern Methodist University, 1968/69.

P-24. Poorman, Lawrence Eugene. "A Comparative Study of the Effectiveness of a Multi-Media Systems Approach to Harvard Project Physics with Traditional Approaches to Harvard Project Physics." Unpublished dissertation, Indiana University, School of Education, 1967.

The author states philosophy behind multi-media approach and gives specific samples of evaluative tools used with students and teachers in the Harvard Physics Project.

P-25. Pope, Herman G. The Immediate Need to Educate Middle Managers. Public Administration Review, 27 (November 1967), 331-34.

The author points out that little attention has been given to the continuing education needs of persons who move from work involving substantive professional training to managerial positions. Courses to meet this need should range from one week to one month; appropriate methods of instruction are specified. The author feels that the community college is particularly suitable for providing such programs.

P-26. A Position Paper on Teacher Education and Professional Standards: Axioms and Goals; Selected Recommendations; Questions and Issues. Washington, D. C. National Education Association, National Commission on Teacher Education and Professional Standards, 1963.

592

The paper introduces its discussion with a group of premises, the first of which is: "Teaching is a profession to a degree that its members are professional."

Positions are stated on six areas: selection, preparation, continuing education, regulation of standards, theory and research, and invitation. For each of these areas there is a section on axioms and goals; another on selected recommendations, a third on questions and issues.

In the section on Continuing Education, eight goals are stated; starting with "Continuing Education is a career-long process of professional growth." Selected recommendations are given, starting with "An environment condusive to personal and professional growth is essential for teachers. Such an environment should include a high level of academic freedom, a reasonable work load, appropriate assignment, opportunity for intellectually stimulating relationships with colleagues, adequate facilities and materials for good teaching, a democratic atmosphere and recognit ion of diversity among individuals."

P-27. The Post-Doctoral Training Program in Education. Final Report, Eugene, Oregon: University of Oregon, 1967.

Experimentation with a post-doctoral research training program in education is described. The program had four participants from higher education and two were public school administrators. The unique feature of the program was its flexibility; trainees were able to pursue their individual major interests.

P-28. Porter, Elias H. Manpower Development: A System Training Concept. New York: Harper and Row, 1964.

The procedures in the "system training" are identified as:
1) the system program first sets up a simulated, meaningful task to be dealt with by the team as a whole; 2) the task is presented in a real-life setting (or as realistic facsimile);
3) the system provides an objective knowledge of results at the end of the exercise, and this permits team members to reconstruct the situation with which they were faced, the actions they took, and the consequences of their actions upon the task system; 4) team members have opportunity to discuss the situation-response-consequence data in the absence of outside evaluation of goodness or badness and in the absence of outside didactics.

593

P-29. Postell, William D. "Continuing Education for Medical Librarianship;
A Symposium--Some Practical Thoughts on an Internship Program,"
Bulletin of the Medical Library Association, 48 (October, 1960),
413-414.

Postell dissents from the view that internship be tried in medical
libraries. He claims it is too expensive a program and that
it takes too much time to do a good teaching job. No library
can afford to spare a staff member from his normal duties to
devote himself to such a program. In his opinion, the only way
an internship program could be established would be to obtain
outside funds.

P-30. Postell, William D. "Some Practical Thoughts on an Internship Program."
Medical Library Association Bulletin, 48 (October, 1960), 413.

P-31. Powell, Reed M. "Two Approaches to University Management Education,"
California Management Review, 5 (Spring, 1963), 87-104.

P-32. Prescott, Suzanne. "The Impact of Workshops on Practitioners: A Current
Evaluation." American Psychological Association, Washington, D. C.

For the mental health practitioner to keep abreast of his rapidly
changing field requires that adequate, up-to-date information
be sufficiently available to meet professional needs. This
study attempted to identify the ways in which such information is
gathered at workshops. The characteristics of participants in
a series of 1969 post doctoral institutes is described--their
clinical experience, professional affiliations, and previous experience with material in the area of their workshops. The
formats used in workshops are rated according to importance or
utility. The impact of the workshops on the participants is
surveyed. Some suggestions are offered for improvements in
workshops. Seven workshops are described in capsule form
to illustrate the general points made previously. Included in the
appendices are lists of workshop participants, samples of information gathering material, a list of suggestions for workshop
planners, and a suggested planning sequence. [ERIC].

P-33. Presidential Task Force on Career Advancement. Investment for Tomorrow. Washington, D. C. U. S. Civil Service Commission, 1967.

The report lists the most pressing employee development problems in the federal government and discusses ways of dealing with them, including continuing education in academic institutions.

P-34. Presthus, Robert. "Technological Change and Occupational Response: A Study of Librarians." Final Report. Project No. 07-1084. Office of Education, Bureau of Research. Part of: A Program of Research into the Identification of Manpower Requirements, the Educational Preparation and the Utilization of Manpower in the Library and Information Profession. Donaview, Ontario, Canada, York University, 1970.

P-35. Preston, James M. "Characteristics of Continuing and Non-continuing Adult Students." Unpublished Doctor's dissertation, University of California, 1957.

P-36. Problems in University Library Management. A Study Conducted by Booz, Allen & Hamilton, Inc., for the Association of Research Libraries and the American Council on Education. Washington, D. C. : Association of Research Libraries, 1970.

P-37. Proceedings: Conference on the Use of Computers in Medical Education. Reprint from Proceedings of Conference, Oklahoma City, Oklahoma, April 3, 4, and 5, 1968. Oklahoma University Oklahoma City Medical Center. (ED 046 229).

At a conference concerned with the role of computers in medical education, papers were given on the use of computers in continuing education, in clinical medical education, and in undergraduate medical education. Other subjects discussed were: medical technology and social change, criterion models of medical practice, faculty selection, EDUCOM (University Communications Council), automation in the medical library, MEDLARS, funding and costs, evaluation of computer use, and proper goals for medical education. [ERIC].

P-38. Professional Development Committee, National Association for Public School Adult Education. Washington, D.C. National Association for Public School Adult Education, 1969. (ED 042 084.)

From national, regional and state associations, colleges, and universities the National Association for Public School Adult Education (NAPSAE) Professional Development Committee requested policy statements relevant to professional development activities and procedures used to improve adult educators. A limited number of what might be defined as policy statements relating to professional improvement were returned: Associations tended to provide generalized statements. The sequential procedures provided in graduate programs by the institutions of higher education which sponsored either master's and/or doctoral programs for adult and continuing education were the most definitive. From study and collation of the information, the committee produced two interrelated policy statements and fourteen points of procedure for adoption by the board of NAPSAE. It recommended professional development through collegiate study, and affirmed its dedication to the professionalization of the field. Procedures include the development of: a nationwide program of fellowships, loans, and internships; a public information system; citizenship leadership teams. [ERIC].

P-39. Professional Growth Requirements, 1965-66. Washington, D. C. National Education Association, July, 1966. (ED 024 150).

This report on professional growth requirements for classroom teachers in the United States presents data showing the amount of professional growth required for salary increments in the 307 reporting school systems. The survey includes data on 1) semester-hour requirements and time limits specified, 2) activities required in each system, 3) provisions for time off from regular duties, 4) practices in requireing prior approval of activities, 5) whether sabbatical leave activities are counted, and 6) who evaluates the activities. In addition to the tables listing information by state and school district, summary tables giving an overview of professional growth practices are included.

P-40. Program of Continuing Education in Public Health, Policies and Procedures. San Francisco, California Western Regional Office American Public Health Association, 1967. (ED 012 865.).

This interdisciplinary, university-level program unique in that it
is presented in the field, is primarily designed for full-time
public health professionals in the 13 western states, sponsored
by the Schools of Public Health of the University of California
(Berkeley and Los Angeles) and the University of Hawaii, and
administered by the Western Regional Office of the American
Public Health Association. State public health association
continuing education committees and their subcommittees assess
state interests and needs, examine working drafts of current
course offerings and long-range curriculums, and help evaluate
the courses. The Continuing Education Committee of the
Confederation of Western Affiliates makes regional surveys
and policy recommendations. The Faculty Advisory Committee
composed of faculty members from participating schools of
public health, adopts long-range curriculums based on recommendations by the state continuing education committees and approves
proposed courses. Its subject area subcommittees develop
their own programs and plan individual courses. The course
coordinator works with staff, advisory committees, and
liaison persons on staffing, courses, and publications. [ERIC].

P-41. Proctor, Vilma. "MLA Certification: Its Present Problems and
Future Development," Medical Library Association Bulletin,
55 (January, 1967), 9-12.

P-42. Pulley, Jerry L. "At Last! An AV Kit for Correspondence Students,"
Audiovisual Instruction, 15 (February, 1970), 23-24.

Q-1.   Questionaire About Continuing Education for School-Library-
Media Supervisors." <u>School Libraries.</u> 18 (Summer,
1969), 53.

Q-2.   Quint, Mary D., ed. "Report of Committee on Continuing Education
at the Mid-West States Library Meeting, October 16 and
17, 1972." (mimeographed)

The report gives a perspective on the type of continu g
education activities currently being engaged in at the state
level in one geographical area. Activities reported include: emphasis on the enforcement of certification
requirements for personnel of all public libraries (Indiana);
surveys of library personnel, including continuing education needs; research studies related to continuing education; development of internship programs; experimentation with use of tapes of workshops ; plans for interstate
activities; collection of statistical information on the extent of current unemployed among librarians and the
number and type of positions currently vacant in response
to a request from the ALA Council. Documents are
attached to the report, including questionnaire forms
u sed, personnel statistics, statistics on number and
type of topics covered in education and training sessions;
evaluation of programs offered, with recommendations for
future action.

R-1. Randall, Raymond L. and Simpson, Dick W. Science Administration
      Education and Career Mobility. Summary of Proceedings
      and Working Papers of the University Federal Agency
      Conference (November 7-9, 1968), Bloomington,
      Indiana, Indiana University Institute of Public Administration,
      May 1, 1966.   [ED 019 563].

R-2. Ranta, Raymond L. "The Professional Status of the Michigan
      Cooperative Extension Service." Unpublished Doctor's
      dissertation, National Agricultural Extension Center for
      Advanced Study, University of Wisconsin, 1960.

R-3. Ready, William B. "The Rutgers Seminar for Library Administrators,"
      College and Research Libraries. 18 (July, 1957), 281-83.

R-4. Rebel, Karlheinz. "The Necessity of Further Education in the Pro-
      fession and Home Study as a Means of Realization."
      Convergence . 3(1970), 66-75.

Rebel, of the University of Tubingen, West Germany, proposes that the way for educational systems to get out of the
dilemna of lagging behind what is expected of them and of
having too much expected of them in the way of new tasks
is to find new forms for displaying knowledge and information.
His solution—home study. He points out that the most
striking difference between new teaching methods and use
of new media in education, and the more conventional forms
of teaching is the withdrawal of the teacher or lecturer, on
whose knowledge learning success is largely dependent.
"The teacher is replaced in modern teaching methods by a
team of experts, who share what have been the functions of the
teacher."

Rebel puts forward the thesis that home study provides a
type of teaching that is independent of the number of pupils;
that allows the greatest measure of individual teaching;
that can be adapted, because of its great flexibility, to the
most varied tasks and curricula; and that offers real chances
for the realization of the concept of an education and opportunities to learn that may last a lifetime."

He points out that home study could not fulfill great expectations if it were identical with correspondence courses
of the past. But he points out that they were vastly different in their structure from the direct methods of teaching.

Essential characteristics of modern home study are enumerated.
1) The teachers and the students are permanently separated.
   (this can be solved temporarily only when special
   arrangements are made for study groups, seminars, etc.).
2) The assignment of various people, who provide information
   to bridge the wide distance and to stimulate the student's
   capacities by the use of the various sense organs in the
   media compound.
3) Methods follow methodical objectives. It is based on a
   previously conducted analysis of the aims of learning, of
   the groups of addresses and of the steps of learning that
   follow one another logically.
4) It is characterized by "methodics" used to foster studies,
   study instruction and control--which makes it different
   from study taken purely on one's own. These means
   include correcting service, tests, reports on experiences,
   consultation service, annotated bibliographies, graphic
   presentations of study materials--all of which facilitate
   learning.
5) Dependence on cooperation with educational agencies,
   such as adult education centers and with organizations
   that have technical apparatus, libraries, and technical
   knowledge at their disposal. "To integrate home study
   into the education system, media centers should be
   established throughout the country, where films, videotapes, other audiovisual materials, books, scripts, and
   so on are available."

Rebel estimates that in the field of university home study
about 2.35 million students are studying in 15 countries
surveyed. Of this number engineers, teachers, managers
and economists form the largest groups. Of those studying
in Germany, 80 per cent wished to improve their professional
qualifications. "Consequently, the hope that home study
can give to overcoming problems of professional mobility
is decisive."

As an example of the development of home study at the University level, he cites the German Institute for Home Study at the University of Tubingen which has the following objectives: 1) the development of home study for teachers as a model for further educational study; 2) working out models for home study courses into basic, accumulatives, and contact study; 3) research tasks in the field of didactics and methodics of home study; and 4) coordination of the various attempts at introducing home study inthe Federal Republic of Germany.

Generally home study follows a basic pattern: course coverage extends over two years; study letters and other teaching materials are sent monthly or more often; direct courses from fixed parts of every program; the possibility of organizing voluntary study groups for participants living in the same area are explored; radio, TV, films, tapes, records, and programmed course sections are put into the media compound; at the end of the course the successful participants receive either a certificate or register to take examinations before state boards.

Along with the development of the home study concept the author sees the necessity for building media centers which would serve the following purposes: 1) be pools for machines, books, or printed materials, audio visual media, teaching programs, experiment kits, and for building up a documentation; 2) serve as laboratory centers where experiments and practical work are undertaken and all practical skills are taught; 3) be crystallization points for work and study groups; 4) possibly take over the task of advising and guiding people interested in the educational programs, including test centers open to all who want to be informed on his own interests and the possibilities for study.

In conclusion, Rebel states that "for the first time in the history of mankind, they [modern technologically oriented teaching methods] make possible a planned, directed, and systematic program of further education for everyone for their entire life. Scientific investigation has disposed of the old idea that learning is limited to childhood and youth and that adults are less suited to learning. . . . Because of this, learning takes on real meaning for the existence of every adult. Nevertheless there is one necessary prerequisite. The adult must be in a position to determine his own learning tempo and to fit the learning process into his own

routine. This means that the most suitably planned learning
process is the one that allows for a high percentage of
individualization. Home study, in its modern form, can
fulfill these demands better than conventional methods of
teaching."

R-5.   Reed, Sarah R., ed. Continuing Education for Librarians--Conferences,
       Workships and Short Courses, 1964-65. Washington: Office
       of Education, U.S. Department of Health, Education, and
       Welfare, 1964.

R-6.   Reed, Sarah R., ed. Continuing Education for Librarians--Conferences,
       Workshops, and Short Courses, 1966-67. Washington, D.C.:
       Office of Education, U.S. Department of Health, Education
       and Welfare, 1966.

R-7.   Reed, Sarah R., ed. Problems of Library School Administration;
       Report of an Institute, April 14-15, 1965, Washington, D.C.
       Washington: U.S. Department of Health, Education, and
       Welfare, 1965.

R-8.   Reed, Sarah R., and Toye, Willie P. Continuing Education for
       Librarians--Conferences, Workshops and Short Courses,
       1965-66. Washington: Office of Education, U.S. De-
       partment of Health, Education and Welfare, 1965.

       Beginning in 1964, Sarah Reed, then of the Library Services
       Division of the U.S. Office of Education, started an annual
       register listing continuing library education opportunities.
       Starting in 1967-68, the list has been continued by the
       American Library Association. Since 1971 the annual
       listing has been published in American Libraries.

R-9.   Reed, Sarah R. Education Activities of Library Associations. Paper
       read at the Drexal Institute of Technology Library Association
       Administration Workshop, Philadelphia, Pennsylvania.
       November 10, 1966. (mimeographed)

       At this one day institute Reed noted a pattern of cooperation of state associations with state agencies and library schools. She stated:

"In a state in which there is no graduate library school and in which the state agency does not have sufficient professional staff to undertake a program of continuing education, the Association's library education committee has major responsibility for immediate and long-range library education needs of its state. "

She emphasized the important role of library associations in continuing education by stating:

"Only as associations make the soundest possible provision for the education of its most precious resource-- its membership--will they have fulfilled one of their primary obligations as professional library associations. "

R-10.   Reed, Sarah R. "The Federal Government and Professional Library Education. " ALA Bulletin. 60 (February, 1966), 163-66.

R-11.   Reed, Sarah. "Guide to Library Education. Part 1: Trends in Professional Education. " Drexal Library Quarterly. 3 (January, 1967), 1-24.

The author surveys the entire field of professional education in the United States, showing the relationships to graduate library education. She discusses trends in eight areas: administrative organization, admissions, student affairs, faculty, curriculum, research, finance, accreditation.

As a part of her concluding remarks, she states: Continuing education . . . will become increasingly important. So far as the professions are concerned, not only their professional well-being but also actual survival may depend in large part upon their programs of continuing education. In no profession is this more true than in librarianship. The needs of the people served, the materials used to meet those needs, the patterns of library organization, and library technology--the entire library world is marked by change. Only through programs of

continuing education can the librarians of this nation keep
abreast of new knowledge and practices."

R-12.   Reed, Sarah R. "Library Manpower--Realism, Relevancy, and
         Requirements." Journal of Education for Librarianship.
         7 (Summer, 1966), 43-47.

R-13.   Reed, Sarah R., ed. Problems of Library School Administration:
         Report of an Institute, April 14-15, 1965, Washington, D.C.
         Washington, D.C.: U.S. Office of Education, 1965.

R-14.   Reemers, H.H. "Rating Methods in Research on Teaching." In"
         Gage, N.L. Handbook of Research on Teaching. Chicago,
         Illinois: Rand, McNally, 1963, chapter 7.

         Reemers provides a good overview of rating methods used
         in research on teaching, along with a large bibliography.

R-15.   Reemers, H.H., and Manual, Elliot. The Purdue Rating Scale
         for Instruction (rev. ed.). Purdue University, 1960.

         This scale can be used for student ratings and as a self-
         rating instrument for the teacher, who is charged to
         respond to the instrument "as he perceives himself."

R-16.   Rees, Alan. Education for Hospital Library Personnel: Continuation
         of Feasibility Study for Continuing Education of Medical
         Librarians. Interim Report no. 2. Cleveland, Ohio: Case
         Western Reserve University, 1968.

         The survey of all Ohio hospitals and hospital libraries de-
         scribed in this report constituted a preliminary task in the
         design, implementation, and evaluation of a comprehensive
         program of continuing education for hospital library personnel.
         The research methodology involved the formal conceptuali-
         zation and the construction of data banks of information re-
         lating to three basic hospital functions—patient care, training
         and research; and the gathering of data concerning facilities
         and resources of hospital libraries and personnel. The

program is sponsored by the Public Health Service, Washington, D.C., and the National Library of Medicine, Washington, D.C.

Subsequent reports give curriculum design and alternative modes for presenting courses. [Report No. 3 is available as EDRS ED 023 425.]

R-17.   Rees, Alan M. "Training Program in Medical Librarianship and Health Sciences Information." Annual Report. July 1, 1967-June 30, 1968, Cleveland, Ohio: Case Western Reserve University, Center for Documentation and Communication Research, 1968. [EDRS ED 027 035.]

The training program consists of three specialized courses in medical librarianship, a four-week orientation to medical librarianship, field trips and a seminar series on related topics. Resources of the local medical and academic communities were used and an internship program for librarians in the two Veterans Administration hospitals in the Cleveland area was established.

R-18.   Reinbold, John Clifford. "An Analysis of Changes in Attitudes of Participants in Selected Clergy Economic Education Programs." Doctoral thesis from Indiana University, 1965. Ann Arbor, Mich.: University Microfilms. (Xerox copy)

An assessment was made of clerymen's attitude changes toward American agriculture, business, and labor as a result of participation in educational programs sponsored by the Clergy Economic Education Foundation. Attitude tests were taken before and after the program. It was concluded that these programs do not accomplish the desired attitude changes, and that most participants enter with such positive attitudes that little further change can occur.

R-19.   Reisman, Arnold, ed. Engineering: A Look Inward and a Reach Outward. Proceedings of the Symposium, Milwaukee, University of Wisconsin at Milwaukee, College of Applied Science and Engineering, 1967.

R-20.   Reitz, J. Wayne.   Education Professions Development Act of 1967.
        Part E.   1969.   (ED 028 718.)

        The first funding of fellowships, institutes, and special pro-
        jects under Part E of the Education Professions Develop-
        ment Act of 1967 was announced in January, 1967. The Act
        is designed to help train "persons who are serving or prepar-
        ing to serve as teachers, administrators, or educational
        specialists in institutions of higher education." The actual
        amount made available was $6,900,000, of which $2,000,000
        was for fellowships and $4,700,000 for institutes and special
        projects. A large amount of the funds will train personnel
        for community colleges and support training directed to the
        needs of the disadvantaged.

R-21.   Retraining Programs for Women Chemists. Washington, D.C.:
        American Chemical Society, 1971. (ED 043 851.)

        Information is presented on existing retraining programs
        for women in chemistry, listed alphabetically by state.
        Data are included on a few institutions that do not have
        special programs in chemistry but do stress retraining for
        women. Included are 11 colleges and universities, with a
        brief description of the program offered, information on
        scheduling, costs, residence requirements, financial aid,
        and provision for part time as well as full time study,
        and sources for further information.

R-22.   Rhode Island University, Graduate Library School. Consultants
        Workshop, New England State Library Extension Agencies,
        September 709, 1967. Kingston, Rhode Island: Graduate
        Library School, Rhode Island University, 1967.

        The workshop for library consultants was prompted by the
        serious need of training for performance of consultant
        services. Work sessions were planned to insure participa-
        tien and also to demonstrate all the techniques available to
        a consultant who hopes to develop leadership in working
        with groups of people. It is believed that this was the first
        institute or workshop to be held specifically for state
        library consultants. This was followed by three others.

one in Wyoming for the Western States Conference in
September, 1969; one in November, 1969, at Ohio State
University for a two-week period; and a three-day Labora-
tory Learning Workshop in Sacramento, California, for
State Library and State Education Department consultants
in February, 1970.

R-23.   Richards, John R. and others. "Continuing Education Programs
in California Higher Education--Delineation of Functions,
Coordination, Finance, General Extension Centers." California: California State Coordination Council for Higher
Education, 1963. [ED 015 713.]

R-24.   Rindt, Kenneth E. Handbook for Coordinators of Management and
Other Adult Education Programs. Madison, Wisconsin:
University of Wisconsin Extension, Department of Business
and Management, 1968.

A handbook for implementing continuing education programs
and helping a coordinator accomplish the objectives of the
program. Divided into three parts, the Handbook covers:
1) philosophies and perspectives; 2) planning and organizing; and 3) conducting and follow-up. It includes an
Appendix of questionnaires, classroom diagrams, evaluation forms, promotional copy, and checklists that give
hints of proven worth, in such areas as need determination,
staffing, facilities, planning, program publicity and evaluation. The handbook also suggests some useful guidelines
for selecting the proper methods of techniques for instruction.
Emphasis is put on determining the approach that gets results in terms of participation, integration with previous
experience, and development of new insights. Suggestions
are given on the use and make-up of advisory committees
to assure educational content that meets real needs of the
participants.

R-25.   Ripley, Kathryn Jane. PERT as a Management Tool for Educators.
Paper presented at the Management Training Program for
Educational Research Leaders, Ohio State University,

April 24, 1968. Columbus , Ohio: Ohio State University , Educational Research Management Center, 1968. [EDRS ED 023 368.]

PERT helped greatly in the successful establishment of the Northern Virginia Community College in less than a year's time. The value of PERT in educational planning is force-fully presented. "PERT does not make the decisions, but it assists the director by presenting the basic facts needed for intelligent decision making." Once the total staff accepts PERT's built-in safeguards concerning time, resources, and responsibilities, and if they accept their unit's responsi-bility as diagrammed on the charts, the complex problems of planning, controlling, expediting, recycling etc., are clearly visible. In this particular instance there were nine major work packages: facilities, equipment and furniture, students, personnel, budget, library and textbooks, curriculum and catalog, contractual services, policies and operating procedures.

R-26.   Rising, Jesse D., ed. Proceedings of the Conference on Evaluation in Continuing Medical Education, August 25-26, 1970. Kansas City: Kansas University Medical Center, August, 1970. [ED 051 434.]

The sole objective of the conference was to assemble experts in the various fields of continuing education for health to discuss the evaluation of their programs. Included were different types of producers of various kinds of courses or programs, adult educationalists, professional evaluators, financers of programs, etc. Particular attention was given to defining the problems encountered in evaluation and to out-line possible solutions to them, with the goal of recording these deliberations for the benefit of newcomers to the field. No effort was made to arrive at any resolutions, conclusions or formal recommendations. Instead, an attempt was made to indicate the complexities of the field of evaluation of continuing medical education efforts and to help those with less experience or with a more restricted point of view. [ERIC].

R-27.   Roberts, Ellis W., and others. <u>Data Processing Curriculum for</u>
        <u>Educators. Final Report.</u> Harrisburgh, Pennsylvania:
        Commonwealth Development Association, September, 1967.
        [ED 020 451].

        This curriculum design could be used (quite possibly with
        inservice training sessions) by an instructor experienced
        in data processing to familiarize educators with the com-
        puter, and to teach them a systems approach to its use in
        the field of education. The curriculum consists of an out-
        line of the points to be covered in each lesson, supplemented
        by a statement of objectives, audio-visual aid suggestions,
        and practical classroom exercises. Topics include--
        a history of data processing, data preparation, computer
        hardware and capabilities, teaching use of cobol (a computer
        language), problem-solving techniques, applications, cri-
        teria for computer selection, and solution of a problem
        that is individual in nature. Classroom and laboratory
        time required to teach each of the phases of the study of
        voting behavior is used to demonstrate the integration of
        systems analysis and programing and to give experience
        in their use. A briefly annotated bibliography is given
        but is not correlated by page or volume to any particular
        lesson or part of a lesson. Additional references in the
        appendices indicate professional and industrial sources for
        course information and audio-visual aids. [ERIC].

R-28.   Roberts, T.J. <u>Developing Effective Managers.</u> London: Institute
        of Personnel Management, 1967.

        The first section of this book is devoted to the development
        of a system of staff development within organizations. The
        second part is on training--ways and means with special em-
        phasis on media. Third part highlights some important
        issues, such as the impact of organization structure, the
        organizational climate and managerial obsolescence.

        In discussing managerial obsolescence, Roberts states:
        "Companies will have to look at the problem in the round
        and accept as a basic premise the notion of management edu-
        cation as a continuous process that goes on throughout the
        manager's career. Given a sound basic education and a
        scheme of continuous management education, the problem

                                    609

of managerial obsolescence will be kept to manageable pro-
portions. Implicit in this is the responsibility of managers
themselves to accept the need and work out their own strategy
for self education. It is a prerequisite of managerial survival . . . . Management development is concerned with
discovering and realizing the full potential of a company's
human resources. The middle-aged manager who has
given good service and is still capable of a valuable contribution
but who, if nothing is done to help him, will be overtaken by
events, is as worthy an object of management development as
a bright young executive.

R-29.   Robertson, William O., and Dohner, Charles W. Study of Continuing
        Medical Education for the Purpose of Establishing a Demon-
        stration Center for Continuing Education in the Pacific
        Northwest. Final Report. Seattle; University of Washington
        School of Medicine, 1970. (ED 052 323.)

        In modern society, lifelong learning by the physician is
        essential. This study was conceived to: 1) define the
        educational needs of practitioners in the Pacific Northwest;
        2) assess the resources available to meet these needs;
        3) determine what educational programs are needed;
        4) develop evaluation methods for these programs; 5) identify
        physician participation factors; 6) develop evaluation tech-
        niques for clinical communication systems; 7) evaluate
        recent continuing education programs; and 8) develop a
        comprehensive plan for a continuing education center.
        The report describes in detail the techniques used to accomplish
        these objectives, with questionnaires and survey results con-
        tained in the appendixes. Ideally, medical education should
        continue in a lifelong pattern developed during undergraduate
        study. With imporvements in program content, promotional
        efforts, information networks, and program offerings in
        individual hospitals, continuing education can be made an
        integral part of physicians' careers. (ERIC).

R-30.   Roche, William J., and MacKinnon, Neil L. "Motivating People
        With Meaningful Work." Harvard Business Review.
        48 (May-June, 1970), 97-110.

The authors do not claim to present any new theories, but
using a broad foundation of motivational theory and research
by such men as Maslow, Hersberg, McGregor and Myers,
they show how the meaningful-work approach to motivation
has been used at Texas Instruments, Inc. Their thesis is
that " the motivated worker characteristically can assume
a part of the managerial functions associated with his job;
he can share in the planning, organizing and controlling of
the work he does. " (p. 98) The reason this article is particularly valuable is that it tells step by step just how this
process was actually used at Texas Instruments--and in
enough detail to be of help to any administrator wishing to
implement group decision making.

The formula described, which has proved itself repeatedly
in practice, has certain prerequisites: the line managers
must adopt a new style of managing, one that is quite foreign
to the traditional style; the workers must be convinced that
management is committed to making the program work; and
top management must give the program whole-hearted
support and encouragement. The purpose of this particular
company program is to induce its workers to participate
in a continuing cycle of management activity that makes
their work increasingly meaningful in their own eyes.
Once an employee has caught the concept, he is ready to
work with his supervisor to set realistic, but ambitious,
production goals. In the author's experience these goals
have usually been achieved.

R-31.   Rochester University, New York, Management Research Center.
        Combatting Obsolescence Using Perceived Discrepancies
        in Job Expectations of Research Managers and Scientists.
        Rochester, New York: Rochester University, July, 1970.
        (ED 047 250.)

        The "Exercise Future" questionnaire, which covers individual
        preferences and expectations about conditions in one's future
        sphere of work, was completed by 143 research and develop-
        ment scientists, engineers, and managers as part of an ex-
        periment to test effects on subsequent self-development
        activities. Three fourths saw the importance of educational
        upgrading and desired it, but only 44 expected to have time
        allocated for their own development. Positive attitudes were

revealed toward the expected increasing impact of computers on research and development, but the reward structure was expected to be consistent with needs for self-development to avoid obsolescence. Freedom from organizational constraints was important to most, few expected to exert any influence on the rules. (A table and 20 references are included.) (ERIC).

R-32. Rockwood, Ruth H., Personnel Utilization in Libraries, Selected Papers. Tallahassee, Florida: Florida State University School of Library Science, 1970. (ED 046 464.)

An institute on the utilization of personnel in libraries was conducted by the Florida State University School of Library Science in October, 1969. Papers presented are grouped into the following three broad categories: 1) changing attitudes toward personnel administration, 2) procedures for selecting middle management and 3) ways and means of developing effective leadership. The premise is that shortages in library personnel at all levels, but especially in the middle management positions, and inefficient use of personnel have kept libraries from providing the best possible services to individuals and communities. This publication is directed to professional librarians with management experience to show them how to better use their staffs to improve the library. The papers presented include: 1) leadership, 2) democratic administration and morale; 3) communications; 4) policy of selection; 5) selection devices; 6) civil service; 7) opportunities for growth; 8) decision making and the delegation of authority; 9) the management team; 10) inservice training: a panel discussion; and 11) a model plan for utilization of personnel. (ERIC).

R-33. Roemmich, Otto. Policies of Junior Colleges in California for Instructors' Attendance at Professional Conferences. Fullerton, California, North Orange County Junior College District, January 23, 1967. (ED 015 717.)

In a questionnaire survey to determine the policies of California Junior Colleges for attendance at professional meetings, 63 of the 78 colleges responded. While all districts

permitted instructors to attend conferences, only 31 had
relevant written policies. Out-of-state conference attendance was commonly subject to local district limitations.
Procedures for determining who might attend varied among
the colleges, and in most cases several prople were involved
in the decision. Policies or plans to determine frequency
of attendance were generally lacking, although funds were
budgeted in all but four colleges. The range of budget
allotments was $700 to $13,640, with little relationship between college size and budget provision for this purpose.
Generally, districts paid conference expenses, even when
overnight lodging was not required. Variations existed
in class coverage for teachers attending conferences,
with most using other faculty members as substitutes.
Post-conference reporting practices varied. Responses and
comments to specific survey items are summarized. (ERIC).

R-34.   Rogers, A. Robert. "What's Your Score: Assessing Library's
        Potential for Change." Ohio Library Association Bulletin,
        40 (January, 1970), 11-12.

        According to the writer, the answer to the title's question
        may lurk in the attitudes toward change held by the library's
        key personnel. He then provides a continuum attitude scale
        of radical liberal, moderate, conservative and reactionary,
        and a method for using this scale to predict change.

R-35.   Rogers, Carl R. "The Facilitation of Significant Learning." In:
        Siegel, Lawrence (ed.) Instruction: Some Contemporary
        Viewpoints. San Francisco: Chandler Publishing Company,
        1967.

R-36.   Rogers, Carl R. Freedom to Learn. Columbus, Ohio: Charles E.
        Merrill Publishing Company, 1969.

R-37.   Rogers, Carl R. "A Revolutionary Program for Graduate Edu-
        cation." The Library-College Journal. 3 (Spring, 1970),
        16-26.

R-38.   Romani, John H. "Perspectives on Post-entry Training f or the
        Local Public Service." Public Management. 45 (July, 1963),
        146-151.

        The urgent need for post-entry training, the status of
        present programs, and suggestions for motivating such
        training are discussed. The author considers colleges and
        universities a major, and relatively, untapped resource
        for providing such training.

R-39.   Rose, Stuart W. "Continuing Education in Professional Associations:
        The American Institute of Architects." Paper presented at a
        Mini-workshop sponsored by the Committee on Continuing
        Library Education of the Association of American Library
        Schools at the Association's Annual Meeting, Shoreham Hotel,
        Washington, D.C., January 28, 1973. (Transcription of tape).

        Dr. Rose, Director of Continuing Education of the American
        Institute of Architects, explained the structure of the system
        of continuing education established within the AIA. There are
        two divisions: one side is those activities that deal with be-
        havior, skills, how we do things, process-verb-oriented and
        action-oriented. On the other side is information, the kinds
        of things that are needed to plug into the process side in
        order to bring the whole thing together.

        On the behavioral side are a series of training labs. These
        are short impact, one, two, three and one-half day training
        programs at the national level and are made available to
        groups all over the country. Nationally we handle the
        scheduling charge, and registrations. The majority of
        people attending are high level employees of architectural
        firms. In trying to get training programs going for those
        employees who cannot take time away from their work, we
        have developed a whole series of local labs (architectural
        training laboratories) which use local resources and are
        a series of programs that can occur during lunch hours,
        evenings, i.e. at times that have no conflict. These local
        labs are much less expensive. Typical training labs
        might cost fifty dollars a day for a two day program. The
        locally based labs might only cost twenty dollars. The
        objective of the labs are to help the individual to change
        behavior by doing activities himself. Each lab has a number

of tasks that each participant must engage in. For each
lab there are two evaluation sheets; one filled out at the
close of the lab; one is sent out as a follow-up about three
months later. These sheets are used constantly to improve
the labs. In a sense the aim is cultural diffusion to change
behavioral patterns.

Also on the behavior side of the continuing education system
are "architectural service centers." Dr. Rose explained
"What happens here is this: architects in their training
education get very high kinds of competitive training, much
higher than is real in fact, and they are not too good at
sharing. So, for some kinds of services an architect could
provide what would require equipment (as physicians share
X-ray equipment, or a blook lab) we are trying to get similar
kinds of equipment sharing provisions of better service
things set up for architects. A consortium might be able to
keep such expensive equipment busy, as none could afford
it alone. "

Another are in behavioral development is the "Game seminar."
These seminars are like the training labs, but they are
correspondence oriented. They are not like the usual correspondence courses, because they are essentially training
laboratories. "We use a lot of mini-lab techniques in the
program. "You lose some of the live interaction, although
not all of it because sometimes around the country those who
started a course at the same time might be studying together
in some course. But we take advantage of the fact that
they are back home and there is better chance to cause fusion
of new behaviors in the back home setting. In the training
lab we always ask how much they will start changing when
they get back home to the office on Monday morning. For
example, in the architectural 'land development' lab, the
architect would come in and actually learn to put a whole
project together. In the short lab there is no chance to have
him actually contact the kinds of people he would normally.
In the correspondence course, which means now we can get
a whole firm or a group of three to six to take, by the end
of the course he has an actual deal put together with his investors, his loan and everything is assembled step by step. "

Turning to the information side of the continuing education
system, Dr. Rose explained that there are a couple of

"artifacts." There are monthly cassettes. Once a month a
cassette comes out that is called "Review of Architectural
Periodicals." (RAP). In the production of RAP fifty journals
and newsletters are reviewed; if the information can effect
an architect in his office, it is flagged; next items are ranked
on priority of importance for the subject; the article is condensed (usually to about a fourth of the flagged information
can go onto an hour tape). The tape is a digest of the hottest
items found that month. The price for a yearly subscription
is $54 to AIA members; $72 to nonmembers. Currently
about 4,000 are subscribing; in some instances 8 to 10
share the use of a tape.

The second information program is also cassette based.
In this case, each tape goes into depth on a subject. Sometimes a tape is supplemented with written matter. "For
instance, in the 'land development' area, numbers are terri-
ble to listen to on the cassette, so we have a printed work
sheet for the person to use with the cassette. Other cases
such as the one on 'Housing systems' have 67 slides keyed
to the cassette.

A third information reference service is a computerized
system of inventorying all of the programs   universities
and associations sponsor that could have relevance to what
architects want. This listing is categorized in two ways; live
programs that must be attended, or packaged courses, which
they can use at home.

The fourth information service is AIA AIDS, which is scheduled to begin in the summer of 1973. AIDS stands for
Architects Information Disseminating Service. "We have
centralized the development of a professional data bank, but
decentralized the distribution by use of the telephone.
Architects will be able to call from anywhere in the country
toll free. In this system the question will be to create information, in the other systems some one will buy a cassette
because he has an interest in that information, but he may
not apply that information right away. In this system he has
a specific problem on hand to deal with; he calls to get some
verbal information, and something in the mail in a day or two."

Dr. Rose commented that within these two domains --
behavior and information -- "we are having to search for

different ways to engage people. Some are principals --
they like to be engaged in a certain way. People have certain
habits, and styles of learning that must be engaged in
different ways. So, I am looking for opportunities that are
diverse to meet the needs of different people based on their
context and background. The subjects that could occur may
be the same, but the media contact can be made in a variety
of ways."

Each one of the programs has three components : 1) knowledge
or content of the subject -- some resource that has information; 2) expertise in a medium (thus in producing the tapes
there are production writers that look at the material from
a listening viewpoint and there are professional actors and
actresses and sound crews to make the production); 3)
mechanics -- matters of operation and delivery, which must
operate smoothly if anything is to happen at all.

The way the subjects to be covered are determined is a
simple marketing procedure. Basic components within the
profession are determined and then sampling is done with
a large array of subjects to determine demand. In producing what has been done to date, about 140 subjects were
generated and each individual expressed no interest to high
interest in stages. Anything that is done follows the priorities of subjects discovered.

In conclusion, Dr. Rose pointed out that "it is a free enterprise continuing education system. At this point in time there
is no requirement for an architect to engage in continuing
education, although some laws are coming into effect that
may require continuing education or re-registration. It
looks like it will take the form of so many hours or professional development activity a year. Now I am having to find
out what kinds of real problems they have, and how they
really do feel, and what ways I can viably make contact with
them."

In answering a question from the floor about the data base
for the AIDS program, Dr. Rose said: "We have the subject
priorities, so that we have some initial linkage into the
kinds of information that architects put a priority on. We
have a time lag in which we are going to develop the information base before we open up the 800 line. The papers

themselves will be stored as hard copy; we will be getting
a mini-computer to store retrieval terms so that on the
telephone we can do quick retrieval which will tell us how
much information we can send. There is a second part of
that service, which is a search capability starting with two
people. If we have a limited amount of information, I can
write out a sheet to someone who will get that information
so that we can mail it out. We are building the data base
dynamically. We will start with our best guess, and build
from there."

Question: "How do you train your training lab leaders?"

Answer: "For the training labs we find someone who really
knows how to do a certain thing, so we sent that instructor
up to Michigan State to work with two trainers, and they
spend a day and a half together. The two trainers are
basically educating this person on how to be a laboratory
instructor -- how to use group methods. One of the two
people from Michigan State always goes on the first presentation to give any assistance they need."

Question: "Who funds your program?"

Answer: "AIA is a trade association, and I am paid for by
dues -- anything beyond me is from the fees. When I came,
I got an $8,000 seed money to start the program. I invest
that in programs and set up recovery rates. So if a lab
costs $1,000 to prepare, then if the lab is presented six to
eight times I have another $1,000 to recycle for another
program. In 1972 I asked for only $4,000, and this year I
am asking for nothing."

Dr. Rose suggested to the librarians: "If you've got needs
-- needs that you feel strongly about -- I think you can design
organizational structures that will begin to give you new
skills and new information to meet those needs. I think first
you should focus on what the needs are, and then design the
organizational structure to carry it out. If that is done, the
money will fall into place."

R-40.   Rossman, Parker. The Clergyman's Needs for Continuing
        Education. New Haven, Conn.: Yale Divinity School, n.d.
        (ED 014 651.)

        Questionnaires on perceived needs for continuing education
        were sent in February, 1964, to all Yale Divinity School
        graduates of the classes of 1943, 1948, 1953, and 1958.
        Almost every respondent had been pursuing some sort of
        continuing education, largely in seminary credit courses,
        urban church institutes, missions or overseas study tours,
        clinical pastoral training, group dynamics workshops, and
        secular courses in such fields as sociology and psychology.
        A third of the 1948 and 1953 graduates, but less than a fourth
        of the 1958 class, reported continuing personal study in
        biblical, theological, and other areas. Most respondents
        were uncertain about continuing their education in the near
        future, mainly because of a lack of time and money. The
        expressed need for biblical and theological study was almost
        universal, but actual interest was strongest in refresher
        courses aimed at improving organizational and program work.
        Findings also suggest that interest in continuing education
        declines according to the length of time out of the seminary.
        (Statistical data and verbatim comments are included.)

R-41.   Rothenberg, Lesliebeth; Rees, Alan M., and Kronick, David A.
        "An Investigation of the Educational Needs of Health Sciences
        Library Manpower: IV. Characteristics of Manpower in Health
        Sciences Libraries." Bulletin of the Medical Library Associa-
        tion, 59:31-40, January 1971).

        In a statistical survey based on a mail survey of personnel in
        2,099 health sciences libraries located outside of the hospital
        setting, it was found that professionals (those possessing gradu-
        ate library degree) tended to request courses dealing with the
        organization of libraries, health sciences institutions and their
        relationships, while nonprofessionals (those not possessing a
        graduate library degree) inclined towards courses in technical
        processing. It was found that there was a significant difference
        in frequency of attendance of continuing education programs
        between professional and nonprofessional respondents.
        Seventy-five per cent of the professionals contrasted with 43
        per cent of the nonprofessionals, had attended one or more
        continuing education programs during the past five years.
        "The generally lower attendance record of nonprofessionals
        may be attributed to a number of factors, such as lack of pro-
        fessional motivation, in appropriateness of course offerings,
        and failure of libraries to provide release time and/or tuition
        waivers." Age did not seem to be a major factor in determin-

ing attendance patterns, but geographic location had a marked
effect on attendance patterns for professionals, but not for
nonprofessionals.

R-42. Rothstein, Samuel. "Nobody's Baby." Library Journal, 90
(May 15, 1965), 2226-27.

Finding that "continuing professional education is essentially
a peripheral activity with librarianship," Rothstein makes a
brief but vigorous plea for someone to adopt library continuing education as its "baby." He nominates ALA. He urges
that association to "move to establish offices for continuing
professional education with paid secretaries and field
workers," and suggests many appropriate activities for
such an office.

Rothstein points out that librarianship has reasons for continuing education that go beyond the requirements of the profession. "Our period of formal training -- the year in library
school -- is briefer than in most comparable callings. It is
deliberately conceived as a port of entry, not a terminus ...
What is more, this brief period of formal education commonly stresses range (generalism) rather than depth
(specialization); library schools seek to produce good librarians in posse rather than good cataloguers in esse. Finally,
with the whole world of knowledge for our ken, which field
can find wider horizons for study than librarianship ? Or,
if logic will not move us, how about shame ? Surely as
people who make their living from promoting and facilitating
continuing education for others, are not we obliged to take a
little of our own medicine ?"

He acknowledges the variety of ways librarians seek to continue their education (conferences, workshops, institutes);
however, he comments, "Effectiveness is something else
again. The duplication of programming is evident and yet
the coverage of subjects is scrappy. Worse, there is no
pattern or progression in the subjects that are covered.... "

R-43. Rouch, Mark A., ed. Toward a Strategy in Continuing Education:
Proceedings of the Consultation on Continuing Education for
Ministers of the United Methodist Church (University of
Chicago, October 20-23, 1968.) New York: United
Methodist Church, 1969. (ED 030 036.)

A plea was made for systematic career planning and careful research on career development. A partial report was given of a national survey made in 1968 to obtain a profile of leadership in continuing education for ministers...and to gather data on evaluation. A review was made of major categories of programs...and several innovations. A final paper discussed cybernation as responsible for heightening the anxiety of loss of meaning of the human role. A panel discussion on the minister's needs led to formulations of objectives for the minister's continuing education and recommendations for United Methodist strategy development in continuing education.

R–44. Royce, Marion. Continuing Education for Women in Canada: Trends and Opportunities. Monographs in adult education, 4. Toronto, Ontario: Ontario Institute for Studies in Education, Department of Adult Education, 1969. (ED 036 722.)

This report describes a number of innovative continuing education programs for Canadian women under the auspices of universities, local educational authorities, and other organizations. It covers daytime (largely part time) classes at Mount St. Vincent University, the Thomas More Institute, and the universities of British Columbia, Calgary, Guelph, and Manitoba. Offerings by extension departments and continuing education centers at McGill, the University of Toronto, and the universities of Alberta, British Columbia, Calgary, Guelph. and Manitoba, and activities of the Adult Education Division of the Calgary School Board, including those in cooperation with the University of Calgary. It also deals with a public affairs education program in Toronto, training of volunteers by and for the National Council of Jewish Women, discussion groups sponsored by the Young Women's Christian Association, career seminars at Centennial College, professional courses of the Quo Vadis School of of Nursing, as well as a federal work orientation program, correspondence study, English for new Canadians, and educational television in Quebec.

R–45. Ryan, Kevin A. A Plan for a New Type of Professional Training for a New Type of Teaching Staff. The Teacher and his Staff: Occasional Papers no. 2. Washington, D.C.: National

Commission on Teacher Education and Professional
Standards, National Education Association, 1968.

R-46. Ryans, David G. "A Model of Instruction Based on Information
System Concepts." In: Curriculum Research Institute.
Theories of Instruction. Washington, D.C.: Association
for Supervision and Curriculum Development, 1965.

Ryans views the teacher and pupil as information systems.
Several flow charts are included representing the teacher
as an information processing system, the pupil as an information processing system, the interaction of teacher-pupil-
situation in the teaching-learning process, and the systemic
integration of resources and media in conveying information
to the pupil.

S-1. Sabor, Josefa E. Methods of Teaching Librarianship. Paris: UNESCO, 1969.

Sabor, in the introduction, laments the fact that since J. Periam Danton's Education for Librarianship, "there is very little more to be said on methods for teaching librarianship. Even the country most active in this field, the United States of America, has not advanced much further, as may be seen from its constant reversion to the ideas of Charles C. Williamson."

Among the methodologies included in the book are: expository method, demonstration, commentary, interrogation, conversation and discussion, from observation to investigation, direct experience and analysis, research, and written work.

S-2. Schalock, H. Del, and Hale, James R., eds. A Competency Based, Field Centered, Systems Approach to Elementary Teacher Education. Volume I: Overview and Specifications. Northwest Regional Educational Laboratory, 1968. (ED 026 305.)

This main volume explains the ComField (competency based, field centered) Model - a systems approach to the education of elementary school teachers which entails specifications 1) for instruction and 2) for management of the instructional program.

In an overview, the ComField Model is described as a process; the conceptual frameworks on which it is based are detailed; and specifications for instruction and management are outlined.

Part I provides specifications for the instructional program in terms of:
1) Entry behaviors
2) Instructional competencies (three phases include foundations, laboratory, and practicum)
3) Noninstructional competencies
4) Facilitating competencies, and
5) The personalization of professional competencies

Part 2 details specifications for program management, including explanations of the nature of the management system--instruction, policy, adaptation, program execution, supply, personnel, research and development, costing, information transmission, and evaluation.

Factors involved in implementation of a ComField Based Program, including commitment, resources, adaptability, and time, are considered in Part 3.

ERIC ED 018 677 is a related document.

S-3. Schechter, Daniel S. "Innovations in Training and Education." Hospitals, 41 (June 1, 1967), 55-8.

One of the problems highlighted in this article is also applicable to library education and continuing education:

> The dividing line between technological activities and professional activities is not static and is constantly shifting. One might determine, for example, the line between the responsibilities of the physician and the nurse as it exists in 1967, but by 1970 such a dividing line might no longer be valid. During this period, a number of functions now performed by physicians will most likely be transferred to the nurse. The consequence is that the task of defining the role of the paramedical worker and then formulating an appropriate education experience is much more difficult than is usually conceived. This fact forces one to think much harder about the future in order to forecast the proper educational program for the nurse. This is most difficult to do, but it must be done. Otherwise, we will have made no permanent improvement in our current unsatisfactory situation.

Regarding the importance of continuing education in relation to upward mobility, the author quotes Eli Ginzberg of Columbia University:

> Initial training can be important in helping you to recruit, but people are concerned about what happens to them after they get their first job. All first jobs have somewhat questionable quality and yield questionable satisfaction. . . . Nobody is really interested in his first job. He is interested in what will happen over time. Unless you develop training systems that are geared to systems of promotion, that are geared to significant increases in wages and fringe benefits, you don't have a true training program. Your

624

efforts will be largely wasted.

The author directs attention on steps to take in the area of
continuing education. These are important because he sees
the school of tomorrow "blurring the traditional distinction
between teacher and learner, both because of the increasing
importance and practicability of self-instruction and the
increasing use of a variety of instructors." There are, he
believes, three major approaches to use of individual instructional
and self-instruction materials: 1) Television (open and closed
circuit, 2) Programmed instruction (in book form or machine
form), and 3) Correspondence education, which has the potential
to provide the knowledge needed, since employees may not
readily be spared for extended periods of outside study, and
is particularly applicable for institutions and individuals distant
from colleges and universities. "Correspondence instruction
may be undertaken while a person continues to hold his position,
and it may be undertaken at the learner's convenience . . .
Experimentation is needed in combining correspondence
education with other instructional media, such as programmed
instruction, films, and tapes." He concludes that such
continuing education programs as the Kellogg Foundation funded
Hospital Continuing Education Project (HCEP) focusing on
improving management skills of hospital personnel, and smaller
hospitals use of newer teaching methods and devices, are all
means of improving the manpower situation in these institutions
that contribute so significantly to the health care of the American
public.

S-4. Schick, Frank L. and Frantz, John C. "Library Science Research Needs."
Journal of Education for Librarianship, 3 (Spring, 1963), 280-91.

S-5. Schiffhauer, Joseph A. "Developing Human Resources Through an
Employee Upgrading Program." Personnel Journal, 51 (March,
1972), 199-203.

The author presents guidelines for setting up a meaningful and
continuing employee upgrading program. Upgrading is defined
as advancing to a higher level of skill, especially as part of
a training program.

S-6. Schiller, Anita R. Characterisitcs of Profesional Personnel in College and University Libraries. Urbana, Ill.: Library Research Center, Graduate School of Library Science, University of Illinois, 1968.

This is the first national survey describing the basic characteristics of all academic librarians. From this study of 2,282 individual college and university librarians, it is now possible to have a profile of the academic librarian regarding age, sex, marital status, degrees held, number of years of experience, salaries, rank, and present position. Considering the size and scope of the study, it is significant that there was a 93 per cent return to the questionnaire sent out--which in itself might be considered a model for framers of questionnaires. Data on all the variables considered is presented precisely in the text and in an array of clearly designated tables which makes for easy comparison of data about academic libraries with similar data based on surveys from other types of libraries.

S-7. Schilling, Charles W. and Berman, Bruce. Biological Sciences Communication Project Communique: Science Information Specialist Training Program: A Progress Report. A report prepared for the Biological Project of the George Washington University, Washington, D.C., March, 1968.

Description of a program to train graduate-level students to become information specialist administrators in the biological and medical sciences. Objectives of the training program are to impart to participants: 1) administrative skills; 2) professional information science education and experience; 3) knowledge of non-traditional systems and instrumentation; and, 4) foreign language proficiency. The course requirements and course descriptions that comprise the training program are given in some detail.

S-8. Schwartz, F. C., and others. "Effects of Management Development on Manager Behavior and Subordinate Perception." Training and Development Journal, pt. I, 22 (April, 1968), 38-50; pt. II, 22 (May, 1968), 24-30.
This study of a university sponsored management development program is distinctive and worthy of study because of its sound methodology, which used a feasible experimental research design

worth using in other research studies. The study provdied
information to the effect that there did seem to be important
interactions between the development program in which
participants took part and parts of the organization.

S-9. School Library Manpower Project. School Library Manpower Project:
　　　Phase I--Final Report. Chicago, American Library Association,
　　　1970.

S-10. "The School's Executive Development Programs: The Advanced Manage-
　　　ment Program; Objectives of Training for Top and Middle
　　　Managers and What Makes Programs Tick." Harvard Business
　　　School Bulletin, 41 (May-June, 1965), 7-9.

S-11. Schramm, Wilbur. "Instructional Television: Promise and Opportunity."
　　　Monographic Service, 4 (January, 1967), 1-23. (ED 019 848.)

S-12. Schramm, Wilbur. The Research on Programmed Instruction: An
　　　Annotated Bibliography. U. S. Department of Health,
　　　Education, and Welfare Bulletin No. 35. Washington, D.C.:
　　　Government Printing Office, 1964.

S-13. Schramm, Wilbur, and others. The New Media: Memo to Educational
　　　Planners. Paris: UNESCO, 1967.

S-14. Schur, H. 'Education and Training for Science Information Work:
　　　Co-operation Between University and Industry." Proceedings
　　　of the International Conference on Education for Scientific
　　　Work, Queen Elizabeth College, London, 3rd to 7th April, 1967.
　　　The Hague, FID, 1967, 223-226.

　　　In the Postgraduate School of Librarianship at the University
　　　of Sheffield co-operation between the School and industry takes
　　　place in four areas; 1) planning and execution of courses, where
　　　industry can be of help in formulating objectives of courses
　　　especially with their experience as employers of students 2)
　　　the practical training of students either in visiting or working
　　　in operating libraries or information services 3) in the area
　　　of research and development where industrial research

establishments may contract out work to independent research workers attached to the school, and 4) in staff and equipment, for example, the interchange of staff for limited periods and the access to specialized pieces of equipment e. g. computers.

S-15. Science, Government and Information: The Responsibilities of the Technical Community and the Government in the Transfer of Information. President's Science Advisory Committee, The White House, January 10, 1963.

S-16. Scientific American. The Big Business Executive/1964: A Study of His Social and Educational Backgrounds. Study conducted for Scientific American, Inc., by Market Statistics, Inc., of New York City in Collaboration with Dr. Mabel Newcomer. New York: Scientific American, 1965.

This study used a simple two-page questionnaire to gather data from 1000 top officers of 600 of the largest U. S. non-financial corporations. It serves as an excellent model of the way profile information about members of a profession can be presented in a format that invites study and that is easily understood by all who view it. All tables are converted into eye-catching color charts showing specific answers to each question posed in the questionnaire.

S-17. Seaman, Don F., and Wayne L. Schroeder. "The Relationship Between Extent of Educative Behavior by Adults and Their Attitudes Toward Continuing Education." Adult Education 20 (Spring, 1970), 99-105.

S-18. Seiler, John A. Systems Analysis in Organizational Behavior. Homewood, Illinois: Richard D. Irwin, Inc., and the Dorsey Press, 1967.

Organizational behavior occurs in a system of interdependent forces. These forces can be analyzed and each set in the perspective of the others. The book is the basis for courses at Harvard and has as its purpose the development of intellectual skill in learning how to study and analyze organized human behavior. Organization system: human technological, organizational, and social inputs.

S-19. Seminar on Middle Manager Development in Libraries. (Evaluation of event by participant.) Washington, D.C.: The Catholic University of America, (June 15-20) 1964. (Mimeographed.)

S-20. Shank, Russell. "Administration Training in Graduate Library Schools." Special Libraries, 58 (January, 1967), 30-32.

> The author suggests that library schools may more usefully contribute to the education of librarians already committed to special environments through the provision of post-graduate institutes and workshops on special administrative problems and through sponsorship of research on special library problems.

S-21. Shapiro, David S., and others. The Mental Health Counselor in the Community and Training of Physicians and Ministers. Springfield, Illinois: Charles C. Thomas, 1968. (ED 041 219.)

> This three year demonstration of a mental health program developed by the Bradley Center in Columbus, Georgia, centered on the training of physicians and ministers in standardized methods of managing emotional and social problems of patients and parishioners seeking help. Involved was the challenge of entering two Georgia communities and obtaining the endorsement and active support of key professional groups and engaging a significantly high percentage of physicians and clergymen in the training program and demonstrating, by sound evaluation techniques, that affirmative changes actually would occur in practice, perception, knowledge, and attitudes. The authors have also provided accounts of daily staff experiences in planning, decision making, and responding to successes and failures. (An index, forms and questionnaires, reports of research design, and 37 tables are included.)

S-22. Shea, William J. "Improving Your Executive Competence." Hospital Administration, 14 (Summer, 1969), 95-114.

> A plea is made for greater skillfulness and purposefulness in the task of self-development. The major responsiblity for development lies with the individual. Each individual needs to analyze what competencies (technological, organizationa,

behavioral) he needs to improve; what programming is required; what are the requisite conditions for success; what priorities need to be set to accomplish objectives. The author suggests the building of individual learning agendas consisting of goal setting; strategy to acquire learning; finding the resources of time, money, and energy to carry out the agenda. A method described for getting adequate support to assist each individual in his personal growth is the use of "contract negotiations" in which work objectvies are used as the criteria on which judgment of performance will be based. Feedback on performance is essential in order to know what progress is being made toward goals.

S-23. Shellaberger, Donna J.   Manual for CLE Lecturers.   Philadelphia, Pa.:
Joint Committee on Continuing Legal Education, 1969.
(ED 042 120.)

This manual is designed to help lawyers develop the skills needed to present effective, stimulating, continuing legal education (CLE) lectures. It focuses on the particular purpose and nature of CLE lecturing, relationships and interplay of personalities in CLE, commitments and constraints which lecturers should observe, program structure and format, study materials, lecture preparation, and guidelines on the use of phrasing, intonation, timing, humor, body movement, and other techniques. The appendix contains a lecture outline and five hypothetical problems.

S-24. Shera, Jesse H.   "The Self-Destructing Diploma." Ohio Library Association
Bulletin, 42 (October, 1972), 4-8.

Citing example of an upsurge of concern and activity in the area of continuing education in librarianship, Shera concludes that "good as these activities have been, and many have been conspicuously successful, they suffer from lack of coordination and a unified formalized structure that would establish them as an important part of the practicing librarian's professional life."

Ten conditions are identified in which library continuing education has flourished: 1) in periods of crisis, change, and professional stress; 2) in formats which emphasize interdisciplinary approaches by those outside of librarianship--"the degree of 'outside' participation offered"; 3) in patterns which are cumulative, "each building upon and being more advanced than that which precedes it";

630

4) in programming that demands more than passive
listening--"ideally exercises, reports, even tests or
examinations, should be required to give the participants a
goal toward which to work and a sense of accomplishment
when the program is ended"; 5) in allocation of time for
participants to talk informally with staff and other program
participants; 6) in cooperative planning and implementation
involving the libraries, the library schools, the state library
and the state library association ("with the state library
in the strongest position to assume leadership"); 7) in
application of the system concept; 8) in demanding sacrifices
on the part of all involved--participants and the employing
library; 9) in providing adequate financing; and, 10) finally,
in recognizing that continuing education is an integrated
whole, not a cluster of sporadic and isolated instances--"the
state library, the state library association, and the libraries
of the state must stop playing around the edges of the problem."

S-25. Shera, Jesse H. "Theory and Technique in Library Education."
Library Journal, 85 (May, 1960), 1736-1739.

S-26. Shilen, Ronald. Able People Well Prepared and the Adult Education and
the Mass Media Fellowship Programs--1952-61 of the Fund for
Adult Education. White Plains, New York: Fund for Adult
Education, 1961. (ED 028 370.)

The fund for adult education (FAE) was established by the Ford
Foundation as an independent organization in 1951 and existed
for a decade. Its purpose was to support programs of liberal
adult education which contribute to the development of wise
and responsible citizens for a free society. In the first year,
the fund began a program of study and training awards and
grants to individuals in the fields of adult education and mass
communications. This volume confines itself to the development
and growth of these fellowships.

S-27. Shorey, Leonard L. Some Factors Affecting the Personal and Professionnal
Growth of Teachers. Paper presented at the Adult Education
Research Conference, Minneapolis, Minnesota, February 27-28,
1970. (ED 036 769.)

The purpose of this study was to investigate the continuing
education activities in which teachers engaged and to determine
where possible, what factors influenced their participation in
courses; the kinds of help teachers received from selected
continuing education activities; the kinds of help they received
from colleagues; and the changes teachers perceived as
needed to facilitate their personal and professional growth.
Data were collected by means of a questionnaire sent to all
Public School teachers employed by the Windsor Board of
Education in Ontario. Returns were received to 61.9 per cent
of the questionnaires distributed. Five independent variables--
sex, age, academic qualifications, length of teaching experience,
and grade level taught--were selected, and all were found to
be signficant in influencing participation in the activities
investigated.

S-28. Shout, Howard F. Guide to Management Development. Detroit,
Michigan: Detroit Edicson Company, 1965.

The author, Director, Education and Management Development,
Detroit Edicson Company, used this guide as basis for his
presentation at the 1970 Staff Development (PAS/LAD/ALA)
Mini-workshop in Detroit. The book is based on the assumption
that staff development depends upon two conditions: group
relationships and climate.

S-29. Shout, Howard F. "On-the-job Staff Development at the Detroit Edicson
Company." In: Stone, Elizabeth W. New Directions in Staff
Development; Moving from Ideas to Action. Chicago: ALA,
Library Administration Division, 1971, 58-63.

Paper presented at Micro-workshop on Staff Development at
American Library Association Conference on June 28, 1970.
Sponsored by Staff Development Committee on the Personnel
Administration Section of the Library Administration Division
of ALA.

S-30. Silvertson, S. E., and others. "Medical Single Concept Films."
Medical and Biological Illustration, 19 (October, 1960).

Describes progress made in the development of medical single concept films. These are short films concentrating on specific subject matter that may be seen at the viewer's convenience.

S-31. Simmons, Beatrice. "Professional Development." Catholic Library World, 43 (October, 1971), 79-82.

Librarians have a special need for continuous education because their period of formal training is relatively brief and frequently stresses range or generalism rather than depth or specialization.

S-32. Simpson, Antholy F. "Graduate Study Benefits for the Library Employee in Manhattan." Journal of Education for Librarianship, 12 (Summer, 1971), 40-47.

On the basis of a survey, the author determined that only academic libraries and business libraries encouraged professional staff to improve their levels of competence and subject knowledge by obtaining additional qualifications.

S-33. Singer, Henry A. "ECL--A Dynamic Approach to Group Executive Training." Personnel Journal, 48 (May, 1969), 372-374.

S-34. Slager, Fred C. "What are the Characteristics of an Effective, Professional Growth Program?" Proceedings of the 38th Annual Convention, National Association of Secondary School Principals Bulletin, 38 (April, 1954), 206-209.

S-35. Slavens, T. P. "Opinions of Library Science Ph.D's About Requirements for the Ph.D. Degree in Library Science." College and Research Libraries, 30 (November, 1969), 525-32.

Opinions were sought from holders of Ph.D. degrees in library science concerning the most desirable elements of the doctoral programs in the library schools. Replies of the 96 Ph.D's. responding included comments on entrance requirements, course requirements and content, language requirements, examination practices and dissertation topics. All seemed to favor programs with thorough instruction in research methods, seminars and opportunities to study outside the library school. At the same time, they favored individualized, flexible requirements.

S-36. Sloane, Margaret N. Continuing Education for Special Librarianship. Where Do We Go From Here? New York: Special Libraries Association, 1968. (Mimeographed)

This report is a transcription of a planning session of over 100 members from 20 SLA chapters that met to discuss 1) the need for continuing education; 2) the structure of continuing education and 3) the concept of continuing education. As a result, seminars directed toward continuing education, beginning with the 1969 SLA conference, were planned. The details of the plans include a minimum of four seminars, conducted by leaders with demonstrated experience, and a basis of suggested topics as systems analysis, personnel management, materials, and automation.

S-37. Slocum, Grace P. "Participation by Committee." In: Stone, Elizabeth W., ed. New Directions in Staff Development: Moving from Ideas to Action. Chicago: American Library Association, Library Administration Division, 1971, pp. 48-50.

Paper presented at Micro-Workshop on Staff Development at the American Library Association Conference on June 28, 1970. Sponsored by Staff Development Committee of the Personnel Administration Section of the Library Administration Division of ALA.

S-38. Smith, B. Othanel, and others. Teachers for the Real World. Washington, D.C.: American Association of Colleges for Teacher Education, 1969. (ED 027 267.)

This broad outline for a teacher education program aimed at creating teachers capable of dealing with children of all races and backgrounds stresses the need for systematized instruction of teacher trainees. After a brief discussion of the importance of differentiated staffing and common schools, the report specifies the need for and uses of extensive theoretical preparation of the teacher trainee prior to field experience, and cooperation of local schools, community, and college to produce training complexes (attended before internship) where teaching situations are first video-taped, analyzed, classified, and indexed by educators according to situational categories

and theoretical concepts and then analyzed by teacher trainees
to improve behavioral insight and teaching techniques. Also
specified are: types of subject matter knowledge and how these
relate and should relate to college courses and teaching; preparation of teachers in governing themselves as a professional
group; and the goals and content of perennial teacher education.
A memo on financial implementation is included. [ERIC]

S-39.　Smith, Bardwell L. "Educational Trends and the Seventies,"
American Association of University Professors Bulletin, 56
(June, 1970), 130-36.

The author argues for a decline of separation between education
and business:

> The movement of continuing education has been around
> for some time. At the present, however, it is seriously
> in operation only within nonacademic corporations which
> routinely employ it as a standard operating procedure in
> a rapidly changing technological society where knowledge
> acquired years ago becomes obsolescent in due time. For
> many kinds of knowledge it is only proper that retraining
> be afforded within the precincts of business or industry.
> For other kinds there is cause for intellectual commerce
> between academically oriented communities, including
> its undergraduate members, and persons from various
> levels of leadership within other sectors of society.

> Indeed, one of the most natural rhythms beginning to
> characterize undergraduate education is between time
> spent on campus (away from the so-called real world)
> and time spent away from the campus in contexts of a
> vastly different sort. This very rhythm of time spent
> in both situations tends to make each seem more alive
> than either would be without the other.

S-40.　Smith, L. L. "Mid-Career Education for Urban Administrators:
Patterns and Potential." A paper prepared for the 1969
National Conference of the American Society for Public
Administration, 1968. (ED 029 219.)

A mid-career education of local city administrators is

necessary to meet complex and changing urban needs, and to
make intelligent use of available technicians and specialists.
A brief description of a proposed year-long mid-career
program for government officials and key private citizens is
presented along with comments on appropriate mid-career
curriculum, instructional methods, participants, and
financing.

Characteristics of successful mid-career programming
included: 1) the weaving together of the program ideas in an
interdisciplinary manner (not presented as traditional courses);
2) academic insights should be combined in a focus on the
nature of community and its problems; 3) a variety of approach
was emphasized, including involvement techniques related to
the examination of value assumptions and personal perspectives;
4) incorporation of interim-back-home assignments, requiring
the practical application of classroom learning; 5) residential
experience not to exceed two weeks which is extended through
"back-home" assignments and short regular once-a-week
sessions.

S-41. Smith, Robert G., Jr. Controlling the Quality of Training. Technical
Report 65-6. Alexandria, Virginia: Human Resources Research
Office, George Washington University, 1965.

The purpose of a quality control system in training programs
is stated as follows: "to ensure that only those students who
meet the training objectives to a satisfactory degree graduate
from the course" and, to provide a means for continuously
monitoring training and improving training where deficient.
The author outlines the essential elements of a quality system
in training as: 1) a detailed statement of training objectives
based on job requirements; 2) accurate and appropriate
proficiency measures; 3) effective communication concerning
test performance of students; 4) effective procedures for
corrective action, if necessary; 5) supervisory support.
Valuable information and conclusions on the specific methods
found most effective in quality control of training.

S-42.   Smith, Robert G., Jr. The Design of Instructional Systems.
        Technical Report 66-18. Alexandria, Va.: Human Resources
        Research Office, George Washington University, 1966.

        Describes the steps on which an instructional system should
        be built: 1) development of training objectives based on the
        job for which the student is being trained; 2) practice of task
        performance until the student has attained the objective; 3)
        practice of the knowledges and skills that are components of
        the task; 4) presentation of knowledge to the student; 5) control
        of student activity to maximally direct it to learning; 6) control
        of the training quality by means of a system developed for
        this specific purpose.

        "An efficient instructional system is conceived as one in
        which the components form an integrated whole, achieving
        maximum effectiveness at the least cost possible." Elements
        considered in this report include the presentation of media,
        student management, techniques for practicing knowledge and
        performance, knowledge of results, directing student activities
        toward the goals of training program, and testing and evalua-
        ting the system in terms of   efficiency and cost.

S-43.   Smith, Robert G., Jr. The Development of Training Objectives.
        Alexandria, Va.: Human Resources Research Office, George
        Washington University, 1964.

        A valuable resource which describes modern concepts and
        techniques used in determining training objectives. Emphasis
        is on the importance of training objectives that are relevant to
        jobs performed. In curriculum and course planning of primary
        importance to have answer to key question: "What must this
        person be able to do in order to do his job well?" The author
        outlines six major steps in process of developing clearly de-
        fined job-relevant objectives necessary for building courses:
        1) specialized form of system analysis is conducted to provide
        context for study of occupational specialty; 2) task inventory is
        prepared; 3) decision-making regarding tasks to be taught and
        the level of proficiency needed; 4) a detailed task description
        is prepared for those tasks to be taught; 5) task descriptions
        are revised to identify knowledge and skill components; 6) each
        specific objective is reviewed and revised to make certain that
        it describes a) the performance expected of the student, b) the

637

conditions under which the performance will be observed or
measured, and c) a standard of accuracy or speed to be
achieved.

S-44. Sollenberger, Judith K. In-Service Training: A Bibliographic Essay.
Rev. ed. Chicago, Ill.: American Library Association, 1965.
(Mimeographed)

S-45. Southern Methodist University Institute of Technology. Talkback Television at the SMU Institute of Technology. A brochure
published by the SMU Institute of Technology, 1968.

S-46. Southwestern Library Interstate Cooperative Endeavor (SLICE).
Quarterly Report, I (No. 1), 1972. Dallas, Texas: Southwestern Library Association, 1972.

The Southwestern Library Interstate Cooperative Endeavor
(SLICE) is a project of the Southwestern Library Association,
with an objective of promoting all library interests in the
southwest and Mexico. Appended to this first quarterly report
was Attachment D, which described a SLICE project entitled
Continuing Education for Librarians in the Southwest (CELS).
Funded during the summer of 1972, one of the first activities
of CELS was a preconference in New Orleans (October 31-
November 1) in which the CIPP process of Planning and
Evaluation was presented. Staff from the Ohio State University
Evaluation Center served as resource faculty for the New
Orleans Conference.

S-47. Spector, Audrey F. "The American Nurses' Association and Continuing Education." The Journal of Continuing Education in Nursing,
2 (March-April, 1971), 41-45.

The author tells of measures which are currently strengthening
the association's continuing education program, such as the
recent appointment of a Coordinator of Continuing Education,
with responsibility for unifying and strengthening the Association's
total activity in furthering the professional growth and development of nurses.

Another method which has been important in stimulating
interest in continuing education is the presentation of clinical
programs based on clinical papers at meetings, and their
effect in stimulation of nursing studies. A clinical paper is
defined as one "which describes a clinical problem and provides implications or suggestions for improvement of
nursing practice which can be shared with other practitioners."
This emphasis has greatly increased the amount of clinical
nursing literature. Another innovation used in connection
with clinical conferences was the "Guidelines for Speakers"
prepared by the ANA Public Relations Staff to assist clinical
speakers in making the presentation of their papers more
interesting to the audience.

The author states that the major concern of the ANA "is to
perform those leadership functions that can best be done by the
national association in a way that complements and does not
duplicate state and district nurses' associations' functions....
The ANA has constant contact with its 54 state and territorial
nurses' associations and the 870 district associations which provide
a vital communication network through which the association
can plan, coordinate, and implement its continuing programs."

S-48. Spencer, Howard C. "Continuing Liberal Education Through Independent
        Independent Study," Adult Education, 15 (Winter, 1965), 91-95.

S-49. "Spotlight on the Supervisor's Section," School Libraries, 19
        (Fall, 1969), 59-60.

        This article contains the results of a survey of school library
        media supervisors concerning their preferences in continuing
        education. Most favored more courses, institutes and pro-
        grams for school library media supervisors. The enthusiastic
        response indicates that many supervisors feel a real need for
        continuing education programs.

S-50. Spurr, Stephen H. "New Degrees for College Teachers." In: Current
        Issues in Higher Education, 1967: In Search of Leaders.
        Washington, D.C.: American Association for Higher Education,
        1967. (ED 020 200.)

S-51. Statement on Nursing Education. New York:National League for
          Nursing, 1967.

                    Statement is divided into the following sections: factors
          affecting nursing; beliefs; action; and community involvement.

S-52. State University of New York at Buffalo, School of Information and
          Library Studies, Continuing Education Committee. Report of
          Continuing Education Committee of SILS. Reported presented
          to the School of Information and Library Studies, December 22,
          1972. (Mimeographed)

                    Of the 241 SILS Alumni and librarian respondents in the geo-
          graphical area of Buffalo, New York, 195 indicated that they
          were interested in continuing their education in ways other
          than by joining professional societies, reading their journals,
          and attending their meetings. Out of 50 possible areas of
          study, highest interest was Administration (265 points);
          Media Uses (202 points); Media Creativity (180 points); Media
          Centers (156-1/2 points); Non-Book Materials (127 points);
          Collection Policies and Management (122 points); Government
          Documents (115 points); Library Systems Analysis (115
          points); Automation (107 points). Of the respondents saying
          they were interested in Career Update Program, 168 said
          they would be willing to pay for it; favorite time - evenings;
          favorite days - Wednesday, Tuesday, Thursday; 46 were
          interested in no credit study; 31 in academic credit; 78 in
          either (as it might be set up); 52 in both credit and no credit.
          The Committee regarded the survey as a mandate for action
          and plans are underway for starting promptly in a small way.

S-53. Stead, Eugene A. "The Role of the University in Graduate Training."
          Journal of Medical Education, 44 (September, 1965),
          739-745.

                    The author, Professor of Medicine, State University School of
          Medicine, Durham, South Carolina, insists that the most in-
          telligent use of university resources will never be possible
          until a continuum exists and college, undergraduate medical
          school, internship, residencey, service in the armed forces,
          and continuing education are considered as a whole system.
          The student should be enrolled in the university on a lifetime

basis and be able to return to further work at any time.

The author outlines the purposes of medical education as follows: 1) general education to make him a useful citizen; 2) language preparation to allow him to read the wide variety of books pertinent to biology and medicine; 3) problem-solving training; 4) apprentice training to teach the best use of present knowledge to improve health.

S-54. Stecklein, John E. Pilot Training Program with a Post-Doctoral Internship in Institutional Research (1966-67). University of Minnesota, 1967. (ED 021 810.)

This is a report of a program of 9 month post-doctoral institutional research internships established to provide on-the-job experience in well-established institutional research units in selected institutions.

S-55. Stein, Leonard S. "Adult Learning Principles: The Individual Curriculum and Nursing Leadership." The Journal of Continuing Education in Nursing, 2 (November-December, 1971), 7-13.

Concepts of adult learning with particular application to continuing education are identified and discussed:

1. "Learning depends on the learner's awareness of his own capacities" -- counseling (most often nondirective) is necessary to help the learner see clearly how much he or she can achieve.

2. "Previous adult learning tends to affect new learning" -- continuing education needs to take advantage of existing knowledge, skills, and understandings.

3. "Adult learners need motivation" -- an understanding of how new learnings will produce new satisfactions or ease present dissonance.

4. "Adult learning depends on the effective use of learning skills" -- part of the continuing education process is the need to redevelop the specific techniques of learning: how to analyze complex material; how to use aids such as multi-media.

641

5. "Adults experience a decline in physical powers" -- learning ability does not decline with age, but from 25 on physical powers do; this calls for attention to such things as adequate lighting and pacing of activities in continuing education programs.

6. "Stress reduces the learning performance of adults" -- in the adult learner there are sources of stress not related to the specific learning situation which have to be understood, such as fear or loss of job if new skills and knowledge are not gained.

7. "As people grow older they tend to become more rigid in their viewpoints" -- to the extent that 'rigidity' represents a well-functioning pattern of habitual competence, rather than an authoritarian personality, the skillful educator can take advantage of the fact.

8. "The learning process must contribute to social and organizational goals" -- personal satisfaction from learning is more easily achieved when that learning makes the individual happier in his relations with his or her fellow-workers, and other associates.

The author argues for continuing education as a crucial part of professional life, by which he implies that each professional must seek his or her own individual curriculum in the successful fulfillment of his leadership task.

S-56. Stein, Leonard S. Continuing Education for Priests: The First Year, 1968-69. St. Louis, Mo.: St. Louis University, 1969. (ED 042 088.)

For the 1968-69 school year, the School of Divinity at Metropolitan College of the St. Louis University initiated a systematic continuing education program for priests consisting of four courses: Current Moral Problems, Modern Priestly Spirituality, Institutionalism and Conscience, and Liturgical Celebration. In autumn, 30 priests provided 35 registrations. Eleven of these enrolled in the spring along with another 30 for a total of 41 priests and 44 registrations. The majority of the priests (73%) were parish priests, the remainder were diocesan officials, seminary or academy teachers, hospital chaplains, etc.

The most popular course was Institutionalism and Conscience
-- indicating local clergy confidence in the University's School
of Divinity as an important intellectual resource in the fulfillment of religious duties. No strong correlation appeared
between status, location, age, and course choice or number of
registrations. On the basis of the limited analysis the School
of Divinity has laid a foundation for a successful continuing
education program. [ERIC]

S-57. Sterner, Frank M. "Motivate -- Don't Manipulate," Personnel
      Journal, 48 (August, 1969), 623-7.

      The author urges every manager to review his approaches in
      dealing with people -- "Have I been motivating or manipula-
      ting?" In this article, manipulation involves "an intent on the
      part of a manager to deceive, take advantage of, control or
      use people to his own advantage." On the other hand, motiva-
      tion "refers to the opposite of this: that is, a constructive
      managerial approach which involves working with people for
      their own and the organization's benefit." After reviewing
      recent research findings in motivation theory, the author
      suggests ways and means of motivation open to the manager.

S-58. Stevenson, Grace T. "Training for Growth -- the Future for
      Librarians." ALA Bulletin, 61 (March, 1967), 278-86.

      Although there is much concern about continuing education
      and much activity, it needs focus and direction, coordination
      and cooperation to achieve maximum results. The plethora of
      conferences, workshops, institutes, and short courses offered
      by library schools, state extension agencies and library
      associations offer no pattern of progression. They do not build
      one on the other. Little or no coordination exists between
      these informal learning experiences or with formal education.

S-59. Stewart, Charles W. A Study of the Results of a Program of Continuing
      Education for Parish Clergy. Bloomfield Hills, Mich.: Institute
      for Advanced Pastoral Studies, 1969. (ED 021 190.)

      Data on the program of the Institute for Advanced Pastoral
      Studies were gathered through content analysis of 100
      unsolicited letters from conferees, analysis of before and after

643

questionnaires used with a conference and a control group
and given to four spring conferences in 1964, and analysis of
the Theological Studies Inventory used before the 1964
Spring Conference and four months later. It was concluded
that temporary changes in role perception and behavior as a
result of conference attendance may enable a minister to
change in his relationship with laymen from a prima donna or
laisez-faire style of leadership to one of "coach-player,"
changes varying somewhat with age and greatly with demonina-
tion. An orientation course can guide the conferee to learn
certain principles and sensitize him to his mistakes in preach-
ing, group counseling, or administration, but for lasting
learning, additional training and work with laymen outside the
church are needed. Parish ministers do a great deal of
attitudinal and perceptual learning in a short, intensive
experience, but there is need for follow up conferences six
months to a year later. [Document includes six tables and a
glossary.]

S-60. Stewart, J. D. "Managerial Training in Local Government: Experience
       in England and Wales," Studies in Comparative Local Govern-
       ment, 2 (Summer, 1968), 36-50.

       This is one of the best brief summaries of managerial and
       executive training in England and Wales, with special emphasis
       on recent developments, course content, format, and
       references to continental literature.

S-61. Stewart, Ward and Honey, John C. University-Sponsored Executive
       Development Programs in the Public Service. Washington,
       D.C.: U. S. Office of Education, 1966.

       The authors present comprehensive information based on a
       nation-wide survey of development programs. Some trends
       are noted. Criteria for inclusion of programs: 1) must run at
       least 5 full days or equivalent; 2) are non-degree, but more
       than ad hoc; 3) are not skill-oriented or purely technical; 4)
       are intended to provide a broadening of the educational experi-
       ence of middle-and/or upper-level government administrators.
       A six page "Selected Bibliography on Executive Development"
       is included.

S-62. Stock, Gary, and Cranford, George. Attitudes toward Educational Television. Project Report No. 4. Plattsburgh, New York: Office of Institutional Research, State University College, 1967.

S-63. Stogdill, Ralph and Shartle, Carroll L. Methods in the Study of Administrative Leadership. Columbus: Ohio State University, 1955.

S-64. Stogdill, Ralph and others. Patterns of Administrative Performance. Columbus: Ohio State University, 1956.

S-65. Stogdill, Ralph. A Predictive Study of Administrative Work Patterns. Columbus: Ohio State University, 1956.

Leadership was the main concern of these studies which are part of the Ohio State Leadership Studies. Of particular interest are the work analysis forms constructed from information gained by researchers during interviews. These included: time spent in contact with others; time spent in individual effort, and time spent in major responsibilities. Within each category the interviewee was asked to estimate percentage of time spent in these activities. Fourteen classifications were used to define "major responsibilities" as follows: inspection of the organization, inventigation and research; planning; preparation of procedures and methods; coordination; evaluation; interpretation of plans and procedures; supervision of technical operations; personnel activities; public relations; professional consultation; negotiations; scheduling; routing and dispatching; technical and professional operations.

S-66. Stolurow, Lawrence M. Some Educational Problems and Prospects of a Systems Approach to Instruction. Technical Report no. 2. Urbana, Illinois: University of Illinois, Training Research Laboratory, March, 1954.

The implications of media for the concept of instructional systems are discussed. Teaching by media implies a model of the instructional process. Media permit the analysis of instruction by being objective and repeatable. The computer is an especially promising tool.

645

S-67. Stolz, Robert K. "Executive Development – New Perspective."
Harvard Business Review, 44 (May–June, 1966), 133-143.

Stolz explains that staff development in major organizations
is far from dead, but in the most successful companies it
is carried on by the "use of individualized plans for the development of particular men." This he considers the most important characteristic of successful staff development in this
country. The process follows a basic pattern: a man's progress is periodically reviewed; consultations with the man
himself are made as to what might be done to advance his
development; the resulting plan is reviewed at a higher level
(where it may be challenged, changed, or added to); an
individualized development plan emerges tailored to the
individual's unique needs.

Other characteristics of successful companies in the area of
staff development: a commitment from top executives of the
importance of staff development, including an investment of
their time in development decisions; the primary purpose of
development action is to test the man by giving him tough
assignments that will test his decision-making ability;
courses are used to retool executives to meet new job demands;
courses are selected in which the participant is expected to
assimilate a body of knowledge, homework is expected, tests
may be given, evaluations by the faculty are made and sent
back to the organization; development activity is used as a
basis for promotion.

S-68. Stone, Donald C., ed. Education in Public Administration: A
Symposium on Teaching Methods and Materials. Brussels:
International Institute of Administrative Sciences, 1963.

The IIAS has collected a group of outstanding articles and
seminar papers presented at an international seminar
sponsored by the Institute. The papers point out differences
in philosophies and methods of continuing education for public
administrators in various countries.

S-69. Stone, Elizabeth W. "Administrators Fiddle While Employees Burn
-- Or Flee," ALA Bulletin, 43 (February, 1969), 181-7.

The author comments on the general apathy on the part of

library administrators toward staff development and
continuing education. The article points out the importance of
library administrators taking an active role in the development
of the human resources now recruited for the profession.
The main emphasis is that encouragement of professional
growth is good management. The author states: "Libraries
will probably lose their most talented professional staff at
an increasing rate unless they encourage opportunities for
career development that will enable the individual librarian to
experience a sense of achievement through the development of
his unique talents."

S-70. Stone, Elizabeth W. "Continuing Education: Avenue to Adventure,"
School Libraries, 18 (Summer, 1969), 37-46.

Formally or informally, a career school librarian must expect
to continue his education for the duration of his professional
life. Lifelong professional development is not only imperative
for obtaining excellence in school libraries, but it is an excit-
ing experience for the individual librarian himself. This was
a study focusing attention on the school librarian's perceptions
concerning his own responsibility for professional growth.

S-71. Stone, Elizabeth W. "Continuing Education for Librarianship: Ideas
for Action." American Libraries, 1 (June, 1970), 543-553.

The article demonstrates, based on responses to a questionnaire, the need for the cooperative efforts of seven relevant
groups in providing favorable conditions for the professional
growth of librarians. Continuing education is a nationwide
problem for which a cooperative nationwide plan based on the
best thinking and planning of all relevant groups within the
library profession is needed. Until recently continuing education has been essentially a periphery activity in librarianship;
this article emphasizes that the continuing education of
librarians is one of the most important problems facing
library education today.

Immediate actions recommended include the following:

1) the formation of an administrative partnership of all
concerned groups who, using multidisciplinary knowledge

647

and skills, would provide continuity of policy, planning, coordination, implementation, and administration for a nationwide continuing education program; 2) a thorough reexamination of what constitutes a truly effective program of continuing education; and 3) the use of system design techniques in planning and implementing opportunities which would make use of the new and imaginative tools now available through modern technology to reinforce the learning process."

S-72. Stone, Elizabeth W. Factors Related to the Professional Development of Librarians. Metuchen, N.J.: Scarecrow Press, 1969.

The primary purpose of this book was to answer the questions: "What motivates librarians to participate in professional development activities? What factors deter librarians from participation in professional development activities?" Its content also identifies the activities that the librarians themselves consider the most important for their professional growth as well as presents a profile showing what librarians are actually doing in this area. The book is unique in that it is the first research study in librarianship to deal specifically with the relation of motivation to professional development and continuing education.

The content of the book is based on data collected from a pool of library school graduates. The questionnaire used is included in the Appendix.

S-73. Stone, Elizabeth W. "Librarians and Continuing Education." Journal of Education for Librarianship, 11 (Summer, 1970), 64-71.

Based on research findings, the article deals with the type of factors that motivate librarians to participate in professional development activities. Eleven suggestions are offered to library educators to help them in their long-range planning for the continuing education of professional librarians in order to meet the actual needs of practicing librarians and to fulfill their criteria for participation.

S-74.   Stone, Elizabeth W., (ed.). New Directions in Staff Development:
        Moving from Ideas to Action. The papers of a one-day con-
        ference held in Detroit, Michigan, June 28, 1970, sponsored
        by the Staff Development Committee, Personnel Administration
        Section/LAD, American Library Association. Chicago:
        American Library Association, 1971.

        The editor of this book explains in the introduction that the
        first Micro-workshop on Staff Development was organized
        and operated by the Staff Development Committee of the
        Personnel Administration Section of the Library Administration
        Division of ALA. The papers emphasized new directions
        in staff development and continuing education in libraries, with
        special emphasis on approaching staff development through
        participation in decision-making, management by objectives,
        motivation of library personnel, and on-the-job training

        The assumption shared by the Staff Development Committee
        which led it to plan and implement the Workshop were three:

        1) That continuing personnel development is an important
        committment librarians must face today.
        2) That in librarianship we are a long way from realizing
        the potential represented by the human resources now em-
        ployed in libraries.
        3) That the American Library Association has a role in personnel
        development and as our leading professional body, it should
        emphatically foster continuing education of its membership.

S-75.   Stone, Elizabeth W. "Quest for Expertise: A Librarian's Re-
        sponsibility." College and Research Libraries. 32 (November,
        1971), 432-441.

        Much has been written concerning the need for the continuing
        professional growth of college and university librarians, but
        the ideas expressed have generally been the feelings and
        suppositions of library administrators or library school
        professors. This study is concerned directly with the per-
        ceptions of practicing academic librarians toward their
        own responsibility for professional growth, and their
        practices concerning these activities. The paper analyzes
        the gaps existing between "perceived importance" and "acutal
        involvement" in the academic librarian's professional development.

        649

S-76. Stone, Elizabeth W. Report of AALS Continuing Education Committee on Questionnaire Responses Relative to Continuing Library Education as It Exists in ALA Accredited Graduate Library Schools and Their Parent Institutions. Washington, D.C.: The Catholic University of America, Department of Library Science, 1972. (Mimoegraphed).

The Continuing Library Education Committee of the Association of American Library Schools formulated and mailed out a questionnaire to review the present status of continuing library education in ALA accredited graduate library schools and their parent institutions inorder to provide a partial data base on which to build long-range plans and future activities in cooperation with the Library Continuing Education Network.

The questionnaire was formulated during the summer of 1972 and was mailed to the library school representatives in the Continuing Education Network in August, 1972. Of the 57 schools accredited by ALA at that time, 32 questionnaires had been returned by December. Stone warns that in examining the data from this survey it should be borne in mind that the findings represent only 56% of the library schools to whom the questionnaire was sent, and that there was a wide variation in the amount of data reported. Therefore, the report can be taken only as an indication of the surrent status of continuing education as it exists in the accredited library schools, not as a definite picture of the total continuing education philosophy and activities in the library schools today.

The survey showed that the seemingly preferred manner of offering continuing education opportunities at the library schools is and has been formal courses for credit. Institutes and workshops were the second most popular. The least popular was the non-credit course.

From the data reported by the responding schools, it was found that 200 different offerings were reported, making an average of six continuing education opportunities reported from each school. The highest areas of concentration were Multi-media (17 responses); School/media librarianship (16 responses) and Administration and Management (15 responses). If the returns are examined by major field the highest concentrations of offerings were in Types of Librarianship (51); User Services (35); and Administration (27).

This article is a comment on the reaction to the Report of the
St udy Committee on "The Role of the Association of American
Library Schools in Continuing Library Education" as voiced
at the AALS Annual Meeting in January, 1972, in Chicago.
The Study Committee was organized by the AALS Executive
Board who saw the need for expansion, coordination, and
leadership in the continuing education of the graduate MLS
librarian.

The article focuses attention on particular items and issues
that were raised at the small group meetings in which the
document was discussed during the 1972 annual meeting.
These included: definition of continuing education; the assumptions
on which the Committee had worked; the emphasis on national
planning. During the conference a tally was taken of the participants to learn what they, as library educators, felt were the most
important activities in the area of continuing education in which
the library school should engage. They were:

1) Plan cooperatively with other library schools in the region;
2) Workshops, seminars, or institutes among librarians
    in a statewide area;
3) Develop long-term plans for and with the state library;
4) Group conferences among librarians of similar responsi-
    bilities from various libraries;
5) Credit courses offered outside degree programs.

It is also interesting to note what the educators present thought
were the least important for the library schools to engage in.
They are listed here with the number of people who checked these
items out of a possible 21 items: correspondence study (35);
radio-telephone network (26); Ph. D. programs (19); programs of
directed reading (18); and televised courses (17).

During the conference, two librarians who were not library
educators gave reactions to the position paper on "The Role of
AALS in Continuing Library Education." The remarks by Robert
N. Case, Director, School Library Manpower Project, are
printed in this issue of the Journal of Education for Librarianship
[12 (Spring, 1972), 269-272]. Some of the remarks of the other
reactor, Dale Canelas, Associate Librarian, Northwestern
University Library, are quoted in this article by Stone.

A selection of some of of the other findings include:
--34.4 per cent of the responding schools offered enrichment
programs for alumni
--9 schools reported that packaged courses had been developed; from the response to this question it seems apparent
that the development of such courses is minimal in continuing
library education.

S-77.   Stone, Elizabeth W. Report of AALS Continuing Education Committee
        on Questionnaire Responses Relative to Continuing Library
        Education as it Exists in Library Associations. Washington,
        D.C.: The Catholic University of America, 1972. (Mimeographed).

        The Continuing Library Education Committee of the Association
        of American Library Schools formulated and mailed out a
        questionnaire to review the present status of continuing library
        education in various library associations in order to provide
        a partial data base on which to build long-range plans and
        future activities in cooperation with the Library Continuing
        Education Network.

        The questionnaire was formulated during the summer of 1972
        and was mailed to Library Association representatives
        in the Continuing Education Network in August, 1972. Of the
        26 associations to whom questionnaires were sent, six had
        been returned by December, 1972. Stone warns that in examin-
        ing the data it must be borne in mind that the response of six
        out of 26 represents only 23% response by the library associa-
        tions. Therefore, the report is only a sampling of what is
        being done, and not a comprehensive survey of all twenty-six
        library associations to which the questionnaire was sent.

        The associations answering the questionnaire were: The
        American Association of Law Libraries, The Reference and
        Adult Services Division of ALA; the Resources and Technical
        Services Division of ALA; the Association of Jewish Libraries;
        the Medical Library Association; and the Special Libraries
        Association.

S-78.   Stone, Elizabeth W. "Role of AALS in Lifetime Learning for
        Librarians." Journal of Education for Librarianship.
        12 (Spring, 1972), 254-66.

S-79.   Stone, Elizabeth W., ed. "Personnel Development and Continuing Edu-
        cation in Libraries." Library Trends. 20 (July, 1971), 1-183.

        The editor of the issue also authored the introduction in which
        it is explained that the whole issue of Library Trends addresses
        itself to the following dilemna: "How can we optimally inte-
        grate the technical and human resources that we manage toward
        achieving the library's service mission and, at the same time,
        manage working arrangements and role relationships so that
        people's needs for self-worth, growth, and development are
        significantly met in our libraries?"

        The point of view throughout the issue is that courses, orient-
        ation programs, institutes, workshops, do not constitute the
        total means of staff development and continuing education. This
        is reflected in the table of contents which has articles by
        leading librarians on personnel planning, employee motivation,
        participative management, personnel evaluation, the training
        subsystem, social interaction, skills, continuing education to
        meet the personalized criteria of libraries, programs for
        continuing library education, national planning for continuing
        library education. The Staff Development Committee of the
        Personnel Section of the Library Administration Division
        of the American Library Association, which was responsible
        for the planning and implementation of such an issue, prepared
        two additional chapters for the issue, one on a model for continu-
        ing education and personnel development in libraries and the
        other, guidelines to the development of human resources in
        libraries. This is the first issue of Library Trends to be
        devoted exclusively to staff development and continuing edu-
        cation.

S-80.   Stone, Elizabeth W. Training for the Improvement of Library
        Administration. University of Illinois Graduate School of
        Library Science Monograph Series, Number 2. Ann Arbor,
        Michigan: Edwards Brothers, Inc., 1967.

        The introductory chapter summarizes the chief efforts that
        have been made in the continuing education of library ad-
        ministrators. The central part of the work is devoted to
        the development of course content to meeting administrative
        training needs. The final chapter on conclusions and recom-
        mendations suggests a long range plan for continuing education
        for library administrators. Author outlines six approaches.

S-81. Stone, James C. and Robinson, Clark N. The Graduate Internship Program in Teacher Education: The First Six Years. Berkely, California: The University of California Press, 1965.

The authors report on this internship program which differed in several ways from the "regular" program then in operation. The internship was a full year in length and was the principal means of acquainting students with classroom and with problems of instruction. The program made a serious effort to associate closely theory and practice and it made almost no use of the lecture as a method of instruction, rather seminars and conferences were used. The experiment had two stated objectives: 1) to increase the supply of secondary school teachers; and 2) to identify ways in which the regular program might be improved from experience with quite a different program. The authors reported both objectives were achieved.

S-82. Stout, Ronald M., (ed.) Local Government In-Service Training: An Annotated Bibliography. Albany, New York: State University of New York, Albany, 1968.

This bibliography is divided into four major categories: 1) Local Government Training in General; 2) Training Generalists Officials and Administrators; 3) Training Personnel in Functional Fields; and 4) Bibliographies.

S-83. Stover, Carl F. "To Improve the People Who Govern Our Cities." Western City. 42 (March, 1966), 17-43.

The former Executive director of the National Institute of Public Affairs argues that "One of our most urgent needs is to provide opportunities for the continuing education of those involved in local government . . . . We should establish in every major metropolitan area a college or university center for continuing education for the public service."

S-84. Stuart, Allan. Survey of Business Education for Adults in the Universities of Metropolitan New York. New York: New York University, 1966. [ED 014 040.]

654

A survey was made of professional business education courses
for adults, provided by 14 universities in New York City. Yearly
enrollments varied from 350 to 9,000. Teaching methods
varied according to the needs of the institution, and classes
were mostly held at night in school classrooms. More men
than women participated, the ages ranged from 17 to 72,
and the percentage of college graduates ranged from none to
60%. The majority of the institutions had a prescribed
method to formulate grades. Student fees varied from
nothing to $65, depending on how much financial aid was
available from industry, government, or educational institutions.
A trend was found toward cooperative educational efforts
among professional organizations, institutions, and government, but few inter-university programs existed. Professional
counseling and job placement services were provided. Programs
were blicized by mailing lists, bulletins, and public media.
Little had been done in research and development in business
education and there was a need for more publicity on adult
programs, clarification of faculty status, and study on degrees
and certificates. [ERIC.]

S-85. Stumpf, Felix F. "Continuing Legal Education: Its Role." American
Bar Association Journal. 49 (March, 1963), 248-250.

S-86. Sullivan, Peggy, ed. "Staff Development: A Continuing Theme with
Variations." School Media Quarterly. 1 (Spring, 1973), 179-200.

This issue of the School Media Quarterly features an editorial
and four articles relating to the importance of school media
personnel being involved in continuing education activities.
All edited by Sullivan, the four articles which make up the
series are "Beyond the Formalities," by Patrick R. Penland,
p. 182-190; "The First Step of the MILE," by Elinor Gay
Metcalf, p. 191-193; "The Short-Term Institute: A Vehicle
for Continuing Education," by Jane A. Hannigan, p. 193-197;
and "Teachers Need Choices, Too," by Anna M. Beachner,
p. 197-200.

S-87. Suppes, Patrick, "On Using Computers to Individualize Instruction."
In: Busnell, Don D. and Allen, Dwight E., eds. The Computer in American Education. New York: J. Wiley, 1967.

The availability of both the hardware and the software (of such tools as film projectors, overhead projectors, tape recorders, EVR, computer-assisted instruction, and computer programmed texts) makes this concept of teaching to meet the individual learner's needs within the grasp of the university. Suppes ends his essay on individualized instruction on this optimistic note: . . . "individualized instruction at a genuinely deep level is now a feasible goal."

S-88. Surace, Cecily J. The Human Side of Libraries. Santa Monica: Rand Corporation, 1968. [ED 025 297.]

This paper (originally given as a short course on "Fundamentals of Company Library Management" for the American Management Association) puts special emphasis on performance standards and employee evaluation. Advances in personnel management from the scientific management theory to the application of "human side of enterprise" approach should be reflected in the way library managers review performance and operate their libraries.

Surace notes that work measurement and job description methods for establishing standards and evaluating employees are being discarded in favor of management by objectives. Closely allied to management by objectives is performance appraisal by results, a method of evaluation which involves the employee in a self-motivating and dynamic environment of committment. Discussion and examples show that this performance appraisal technique is well suited for both personnel and departmental management in special libraries.

S-89. Swank, Raynard C. "Sixth-Year Curricula and the Education of Library School Faculties." Journal of Education for Librarianship. 8 (Summer, 1967), 14-19.

656

Swank's scholarly discussion is best summed up by his concluding paragraph:

"In summary, I conclude that sixth-year curricula are desirable, and perhaps necessary, for specializations in library service beyond what can be offered in the fifth year, whether taken by students who continue directly from the M.L.S. or by practitioners who return later from the field. I suggest, moreover, that if a clear distinction were drawn between education for service and education for teaching and research, and if options for both were available at all levels of library education, from the masters to the doctoral, the sixth-year could be used explicitly for advanced theoretical studies as well as for specializations of practice. It would become a staging period both for practitioners who later want to enter teaching and research and for researchers from other disciplines who do not want to enter library practice. I say a staging period because a sixth-year program cannot be accepted in the long run as adequate for the education of faculty in graduate schools. Similarly, the M.Ph., the D.Arts, and the Certificate of Candidacy are not substitutes for the Ph.D. in the education of faculty, although they might comprise a useful interim step to ward the D.L.S. in the education of practitioners."

S-90. Swanson, Harold B. "Factors Associated with Motivation Toward Professional Development of County Agricultural Extension Agents in Minnesota." Unpublished Doctor's dissertation, University of Wisconsin, Madison, 1965.

S-91. Sweeny, S.B. and Charlesworth, J.C., eds. Achieving Excellence in Public Service. Report of a Symposium. Philadelphia, Pennsylvania: American Academy of Political and Social Science, 1963.

This is an excellent source of ideas from some of the outstanding public administration educators and practitioners, (including John D. Millet, James E. Webb, O. Glenn Stahl, John W. Macy, and others) on relationships of education and continuing education to achieving excellence in public service.

S-92. Symposium on Continuing Education in Montana . Boulder, Colorado: Montana Medical Association, WICHE Mountain States Regional Medical Program, Western Interstate Commission for Higher Education, 1969. [ED 033 306]

The symposium centers on the objectives and methods of developing an "interprofessional" program of continuing education to meet the health needs of the area.

S-93. Symposium on the Application of System Analysis and Management Techniques to Education Planning in California. (Chapman College, Orange, California, June 12-13, 1967). Operation PEP, Burlingame, California, etc., June, 1967.

This is a collection of 21 reports presented at the two-day symposium which ended the 18 month planning phase for Operation PEP. The symposium served as a culminating activity in a training program for 100 California educators in the application of systems analysis and management planning techniques. The focus is on the evaluation of management science as a fundamental mode of performance for educational planners in California.

S-94. Syracuse University, Maxwell School of Citizen and Public Affairs. Continuing Education Center for the Public Service. Mid-career Seminar for the Local Public Service. Syracuse, New York: Syracuse University, 1966.

This pamphlet describes an experimental and innovative program for local officials and key private citizens. Participants reside at the Center for one week and then return to their home communities for two to three months of research. A final week in residence provides the opportunity to present, evaluate, and discuss the results of the independent study.

95. "The Systems Approach." <u>Audiovisual Instruction</u>. 10 (May, 1965).

 This entire issue of <u>Audiovisual Instruction</u> is devoted to
an examination of the "Systems Approach" to instruction.
The articles included are 1) Systems: An Approach to Im-
proving Instruction; 2) On the Design of Educational Systems;
3) Reply to Questions About Systems; 4) Educational
Escalation Through Systems Analysis; 5) Standard Operating
Procedures for a Learning Resources Center: A System
for Producing Systems; 6) The Articulated Instructional
Media Program at the University of Wisconsin; 7) First
Steps in the Systems Approach; 8) Systems Analysis and
Computer Simulation in the Implementation of Media; 9)
An Experimental Program in Educational Adaptation (case one);
10) An Experimental Program in Educational Adaptation
(case two); 11) Multi-media Systems of Instruction; 12) Media
Development: A Past of Instructional Change; 13) Afterthoughts on a
Systems Conference; and 14) Not the Last Word on Systems.

S-96. System Development Corporation. "Grooming Tomorrow's
Managers." <u>SDC Magazine.</u> 13 (January, 1970) 3-16.

 The entire issue reviews current trends in manager education
at the graduate level and emphasizes the urgent necessity
of making management training more interdisciplinary. The
leaders of the schools covered in the report found that behavioral and motivational factors were the areas in which
graduates of the past found they had the greatest need after
they were out on the job. Curricula are now being designed
so that more emphasis will be put on these aspects while
the future manager is still at the university.

S-97. Stufflebeam, D.L. "Toward a Science of Educational Evaluation."
<u>Educational Technology</u>, 8 (July 30, 1968), 5-13. (See also
Guba and Stufflebeam, G-46; other articles by Stufflebeam
are included in the work by Thomson. T-9).

T-1. Taft, Martin I. "Design for Education: A Systems Approach."
In: Reisman, Arnold, ed. Engineering: Proceedings of the
Symposium, A Look Inward and a Reach Outward. Milwaukee,
Wisconsin: University of Wisconsin-Milwaukee, 1967.

The author defines a system as "a set of resources (people, materials, facilities and information) organized to perform designate
functions in order to achieve desired results." The most difficul
thing to do in designing a system is to set the objectives--these
are quite often bypassed.

Next he defines the systems analysis approach: "The systems
analysis approach requires that we view the system under study
from the point of view of its inputs from and the outputs to the
universe in which it operates and consider the feedback interrelationships along informational channels between the outputs and
the inputs."

Taft's thesis is that many of the techniques that have been developed
in systems technology are applicable in the field of education in
administrative and curriculum areas as well as in other areas.

> The operations of an educational institution are
> determined by its educational objectives. From
> the managerial standpoint, the major objective
> of a school is to allocate available resources in
> such a way that the difference in educational
> potential between entering and leaving students
> is maximized. Students enter a school system
> with a given level of educational potential and,
> hopefully, leave with a much higher level. The
> central task of administrators is to allocate
> faculty, staff, material, facilities, and informa-
> tion at such times and places and in such pro-
> portions that the objectives of the school will
> be achieved in a most efficient manner.

> . . . . It's now merely a question of getting ef-
> ficient cooperation between the engineer and the
> sociologist, psychologist, economics people,
> and educationists, so that we can translate some
> of the major known relationships into practice
> and develop systems far more optimal than they
> are today.

S- T-2. Tagiuri, Renato. "The Concept of Organizational Climate." In:
Tagiuri, Renato and Litwin, George H., eds. Organizational
Climate: Explorations of a Concept. Boston: Division of
Research, Graduate School of Business Administration, Harvard
University, 1968.

In a period of special concern with our environment, it is natural
that recent studies have turned to a consideration of the environment within the organization. Renato Tagiuri, Professor of Social
Science in Business Administration at Harvard University and a
pioneer in the field of person perception and interpersonal behavior,
traces the history and development of the concept of organizational
climate. He offers as his definition for the term organizational
climate: "a relatively enduring quality of the internal environment
of an organization that a) is experienced by its members, b) influences their behavior, and c) can be described in terms of the
values of a particular set of characteristics (or attributes) of the
organization." (p. 27) Five dimensions that are suggested for
determining the quality of organizational climate are: 1)responsi-
bility--the degree of delegation experienced by employees; 2)
standards--expectations about the quality of one's work; 3)reward--
recognition and reward for good work vs. disapproval for poor
performance; 4)organizational clarity--orderliness (vs. disorder-
liness); 5)friendly, team spirit--good fellowship, trust.

T-3. Taholro, Edward B. "An Analysis of the Educational Needs of
Nebraska Lawyers in Relation to Career Cycle." Unpublished
Doctor's dissertation, University of Nebraska, Lincoln, 1966.

Although this study is based on information obtained within the
state of Nebraska, the recommendations are geared to the profession
at large regarding next steps in continuing legal education.

T-4. Tannenbaum, Robert and Schmidt, Warren H. Leadership and Organization: A Behavioral Science Approach. New York: McGraw-
Hill Book Company, 1961.

Outstanding work on patterns of leadership, emphasizing the situational approach to leadership. Material based on extensive
research at the Institute for Social Research, the University of
Michigan.

T-5.   Taylor, Edward Bunker. "Relationship Between the Career Changes
        of Lawyers and their Participation in Continuing Legal Education."
        Unpublished Doctor's dissertation, University of Nebraska Depart-
        ment of Adult Education, 1967.

        The two major national bar associations, the American Law Institute
        and the American Bar Association, have formed "The Joint Com-
        mittee on Continuing Legal Education" and charged its members
        to explore and emphasize the need for life-long legal instruction.
        Subsequently, the Committee has held several conferences and
        issued comprehensive reports on the subject, and has spearheaded
        the growth of continuing legal education.

        This particular study concluded that periods of job change and
        participation in adult education coincided significantly only during
        the first ten years of legal practice. The relationship between
        the number of lawyers who experienced special life events and
        their participation in adult education was most significant up to
        the age of 39 and between the ages of 45 and 49.

T-6.   Taylor, Robert S. Curriculum for the Information Sciences. Report
        No. 12. Final Report. National Science Foundation Grant No. GE-
        2569. Bethlehem, Pa.: Lehigh University, Center for the Infor-
        mation Sciences, 1967.

        The report brings together the work and thought of four years at
        the Center for Information Sciences, which was established in 1962.
        The conclusion reached was that there is a need for an upgrading
        of current curriculum to more effective levels of performance.
        "While there is a real need to develop continuing educational
        programs in this systems area, the new curricula should also be
        reflected in course design in library schools, to provide the capa-
        bility by librarians to analyze their systems critically." The in-
        formation system concept should recognize and accommodate all
        types of library collections and inter-relationships in the informa-
        tion transfer process. The main recommendation for the next
        few years is curriculum development in the areas of systems design,
        analysis, evaluation, and development

T-7.   The Teacher and His Staff: Differentiating Teaching Roles. Report
of the 1968 Regional TEPS Conferences. Washington, D.C.:
National Education Association, National Commission on Teacher
and Professional Standards, 1969.

The 1968 series of regional conferences from which the material
in this book is drawn culminated 18 months of effort called "The
Year of the Non-Conference." One important project of the Non-
Conference was the identification of 220 demonstration centers--
operational school and college programs which illustrate the
concept of "The Teacher and His Staff."

The concept of "the teacher and his staff" has grown and expanded
and in turn has developed new terminology, such as differentiated
staffing or differentiating staff.

> Educators in the future will perform a variety of
> tasks, some of which exist in schools today and
> many of which will be newly defined as teacher
> roles are differentiated. Roles will be identi-
> fied and classified in terms of degrees of diffi-
> culty, responsibility, and needed artistry and in
> terms of background of the people who assume
> specific kinds of tasks. Role identification and
> assignment will be supported by a thorough,
> sensitive guidance program for the professional
> development of educators. There will be a
> specially trained staff for teacher evaluation,
> analysis, and guidance.

> The term "teacher" will describe only some of
> the people who work with youngsters in learning.
> The concept of "classroom teacher" will refer to
> only one of the many kinds of teachers. The
> notion that teaching takes place in a room desig-
> nated as a classroom with a specified number
> of youngsters will no longer provide a valid
> definition of the teacher. Teachers will per-
> form in many roles which may not take place
> in classrooms as we have known them.

T-9.   Thiede, Wilson B. "Measurement and Evaluation in Adult Education."
         In: Goldhor, Herbert, ed. Research Methods in Librarianship:
         Measurement and Evaluation. Champaign, Illinois: University
         of Illinois Graduate School of Library Science, 1968, pp. 88-94.

         Measurement is defined as the process that provides data used in
         evaluation. Two other words which have the same meaning as
         evaluation are assessment and appraisal. Education is defined
         as the process concerned with changing behavior in the desired
         directions. Three broad types of evaluation are currently used
         in adult education programs: 1)assessment by participants,
         leaders, and administrators; 2)measurement of knowledge and
         attitudes and skills acquired; and 3)adoption of practices. The
         author outlines the five steps in the process of evaluation: 1)de-
         termining objectives; 2)defining the behavior desired; 3)determining
         acceptable evidence of behavior; 4)collecting evidence; and 5)sum-
         marizing and evaluating the evidence. The author believes that
         the most common failure in adult education programs is failure
         to arrive at objectives which are agreed upon, understood by, and
         accepted by both leaders and participants. Library education is
         discussed within the framework of the context outlined above.

T-10.   Thomson, David D. Planning and Evaluation for Statewide Library
         Development: New Directions. Columbus, Ohio: Ohio State Uni-
         versity Evaluation Center, 1972.

T-11.   Thornton, James W. and Brown, James W., eds. New Media and
         College Teaching. Washington, D.C.: National Education
         Association, Department of Audiovisual Instruction in collaboration
         with the American Association for Higher Education, 1968.

         Thornton emphasizes the fact that within the last few years an im-
         portant change has come about in the attitude toward the use of
         machines . . . "machines in themselves are the least important
         aspect of technology. . . the primary concern must be new rela-
         tionships between men and machines to accomplish clearly thought-
         out objectives."

         Opening with an illuminating article on the instructional functions
         of new media, by C. Ray Carpenter, it is stated that "the whole
         educational job is to provide appropriate opportunities and conditions

in our society for each person to learn what he has the assured
right and the abilities to learn wherever he lives in this nation
and whatever the time and condition of his life."

The body of the work contains 11 descriptions of new media, each
followed by case studies showing actual use in a learning situation;
after a chapter on the management of media services, the authors
conclude with this observation: "The future for anyone who believes
that new media can encourage better teaching is bright. One caution
only: The new media possess no magic. They must be directed by
humans to human ends. It is a perversion of their promise to use
them only to facilitate outmoded purposes. The key to better
teaching, now as ever, rests in the will of the teacher."

T-12.   Toronto Library Board. Continuing Education Directory for Metro-
          politan Toronto: 1970. Toronto, Ontario, Canada: Metropolitan
          Toronto Library Board, 1970.

This Metro Doc Continuing Education Directory was compiled
to inform the citizens of Metropolitan Toronto about some of the
opportunities abailable to them to continue their education. In
the preface it is stated that over 300,00 0 persons in the metropolitan area engaged in some kind of continuing study. This is
the second year that such a resource has been available to the
citizens of Toronto.

"In addition to publishing the Directory, Metro Doc (Metro
Directory Data Bank of Courses for Adults), in cooperation with
the Education Data Processing Branch of the Ontario Department
of Education, is designing a computer system to develop the
directory information into a data bank for use by administrators
and researchers. MetroDoc, therefore, is a prototype that
other communities in Ontario may wish to consult in setting up
similar information projects."

Published by the Metropolitan Toronto Library Board, the Directory is available in all public libraries and counselling centers.
Individual copies may be purchased for $10.00.

The format of the book is attractive with a color coding used
to distinguish the various sections. Fall, 1970, course listings
are on white and a preview of 1971 spring courses are listed on

665

blue in section 2. The courses are listed by subject category and for each, the days, times, length of course, fees, other costs prerequisites, and diplomas or certificates offered are shown. There is also a guide to subjects at the back in which all the subject headings and cross-references used in the directory are listed (green sheets). Registration dates and phone numbers, addresses, are given for all institutions listing courses (yellow sheets). Another section has maps showing location of public transit routes.

T-13. Toronto Library Board. Continuing Education Directory for Metropolitan Toronto: 1969. Index of course offerings arranged by subject; List of Institutions and Organizations; List of Counselling Services. Toronto, Ontario, Canada: Metropolitan Toronto Library Board, 1970.

John T. Parkhill, Director, Metropolitan Toronto Library Board, states in the foreward that libraries, counselling services and other agencies, are finding their task increasingly difficult as the volume of their task expands. This directly presents the first effort to organize and list information on Continuing Education in Metropolitan Toronto.

T-14. Toward a Better Utilization of Scientific and Engineering Talent-- A program for Action. Publication No. 1191. Washington, D.C.: National Academy of Science, 1964.

T-15. Trow, William Clark. Teacher and Technology: New Designs for Learning. New York: Appleton-Century-Crofts, 1968.

Dr. Trow emphasizes the importance of the learning environment, which he calls "life space." He state s that sufficient control is necessary to enable people of any age to learn what they need and want to learn more effectively than has been hitherto possible. He suggests looking at the learner's contacts with the environment in terms of how learning occurs to find areas where the environment needs to be managed and ways of controlling it. He goes on to state that here "complacency with the old is out of place as is disinterest in the new . . . . The new technology has the potentiality for improvement that does not reside in the old." (p. 17)

The approach he suggests involves more than an educator deciding which of the instructional media available should be
used, but rather how they can all be best fitted together along
with the school personnel - all to become not aides or adjuncts
but components in an educational system. (p. 116)

Rather than being a cause for alarm, Dr. Trow feels the spread
of the multi-media approach should bring satisfaction in the
awareness that needs are being met. He puts it this way: " . . .
the learner, like the customer, is always right in the sense that
it is his abilities, interests, and needs that largely determine
what he can and will do - not the ideas of scholars or even of
curriculum committees. Programming for the new media takes
this principle seriously." (p. 19)

T-16. Troxel, Wilma. "Continuing Education for Medical Librarianship: A
Symposium--Formal University Courses." Bulletin of the
Medical Library Association, 48 (October, 1960), 404-407.

Troxel discusses the courses now offered in library schools on
medical librarianship. She covers the purpose, content, and
benefits derived by the participants from these courses.

T-17. "'Tutorial Environment' at NLM." National Library of Medicine News.
24 (September, 1969), 5, 7, 8.

This article includes a photograph and description of an example
of compact, specialized, automated classroom providing a tutorial
environment for the individual medical student or practitioner
to sit at a console and have an entire study plan unfold before
him, utilizing his senses of sight, hearing, an d touch. Not intended to supplant "medical faculty with technological gadgetry, "
the system will rather "reinforce and perhaps compress the learning
experience, and must be seen in the perspective of an adjunct to the
efforts of an excellent faculty working with . . . students."
The center includes tapes, film-loaded cassettes, play-back
videotape showing a dissection recorded earlier, back-projecting
viewing screens, an oscilloscope to view a motion picture of
a brain being dissected, microscopic and projected slides,
drawings, models, a fixed brain for direct examination, and a
book-shelf containing standard texts for easy quick reference.

U-1.   Underwood, Willis O. "A Hospital Director's Administrative
        Profile," Hospital Administration, 8 (Fall, 1963), 6-24.

        This study was one of the main sources used by Corson in
        developing his research design for Men Near the Top (C-42.)
        The work is of importance because, based on a scientifically
        conducted investigation of the actual activities that were per-
        formed by a hospital director, it was concluded: "It is not
        enough for a hospital director to be skilled in the general
        aspects of communication....As the study indicated, while
        less than 20 per cent of the duties performed represent
        specialized hospital functions, over half of the knowledge re-
        quired to perform the overall hospital director's job is
        'specialized.'"

        The work has implications for those concerned with continuing
        education, for, if Underwood's finding is found to be generally
        the case in administrative positions in other professions, it
        would imply that certain considerations of balance should be
        taken into consideration when planning for continuing education
        programs in the field of management and administration.

U-2.   The United Presbyterian Church in the United States of America.
        Temporary Commission on Continuing Education. Report to
        the 181st General Assembly, San Antonio, Texas, May 1969.
        Philadelphia, Pa.: Temporary Commission on Continuing
        Education, 1969.

        This article recommends to the church at large ways and
        means of providing for the continuing education of ministers.

U-3.   U. S. Bureau of Labor Statistics. Technician Manpower Require-
        ments, Resources, and Training Needs. Bulletin no. 1512.
        Washington, D.C.: U.S.Govt. Print. Off.,1966.

U-4.   U.S. Civil Service Commission. Bureau of Training. Employee
        Training in the Federal Service, Fiscal year 1969.
        Washington, D.C.: U. S. Civil Service Commission, 1970.
        (ED 042 966.)

        This fiscal year 1969 report presents new developments

affecting training in the federal service, followed by training data and analysi s, and a statistical review. Special interest areas include interagency training centers, contributions of training as related to current performance, new missions and programs, and avoidance of technological obsolescence.

U-5. U.S. Civil Service Commission. Bureau of Training. Interagency Training Programs Bulletin, 1968-1969. Washington, D.C.: U.S. Civil Service Commission, 1969. (ED 023 053.)

This bulletin, published annually, lists training available for interagency use. It gives names of agencies offering inter-agency programs, general course descriptions, enrollment requirements, fees, addresses of office offering course, etc.

U-6. U.S. Civil Service Commission. Bureau of Training. Off-Campus Study Centers for Federal Employees. Pamphlet T-4. Washington, D.C.: U. S. Civil Service Commission, Bureau of Training, 1969. (ED 029 197.)

A directory of 129 off-campus study centers sponsored in 1968 by 14 Federal agencies in cooperation with schools and universities. Descriptions of the centers are grouped by sponsoring agency and include information on cooperating universities, programs offered, who may attend, general facts, and the office to contact.

U-7. U. S. Civil Service Commission. Bureau of Training. Studies and Reports Relating to Training and Education. Washington, D.C.: U. S. Civil Service Commission, Bureau of Training, 1968. (ED 028 341.)

The Bureau of Training tries to encourage wider use of this publication by other agencies. It helps to avoid duplication of research efforts and to stimulate experimentation needed to keep pace with technological progress. Each of the 95 studies reported in this issue includes a brief description of the study.

U-8. U. S. Civil Service Commission. Library. Personnel Literature.
Washington, D.C.: U. S. Govt. Print. Off.

> This is an annotated bibliography published monthly, which
> includes selected books, pamphlets, and other publications
> received in the Library of the Civil Service Commission
> during the previous month; periodical articles, unpublished
> dissertations, and microfilms are also listed. Typical sub-
> ject headings under which materials are listed that relate
> to continuing education include: career planning, internship,
> job enlargement, management improvement, motivation,
> training, training – evaluation, and training– methods.

U-9. U.S. Civil Service Commission. Library. Self Development Aids
for Supervisors and Middle Managers. Personnel Bibliography Series Number 34. Compiled by the Library Staff of
the Civil Service Commission and reviewed by J. Kenneth
Mulligan, Director, Bureau of Training. Washington, D.C.:
U. S. Govt. Print. Off., 1970.

> This bibliography brings together and updates through 1969
> a number of shorter reading lists which the Library has pre-
> pared on request during the last five years. Seventeen
> topics are covered, including career planning, conference
> leadership and participation, reading improvement, identifica-
> tion and development of managerial skills.

U-10. U.S. Civil Service Commission. Library. Training Methods and
Techniques. Personnel Bibliography Series Number 19.
Compiled by the Library Staff of the Civil Service Commission
and reviewed by W. Wayne Cobb. Washington, D.C.: U.S.
Civil Service Commission, 1966.

> This publication contains helpful annotations of major articles
> and books. It covers the following methods: case method,
> coaching, incident process, in-basket, job rotation, manage-
> ment games (simulation) role-playing, sensitivity training,
> team training, selecting and using visual aids. This material
> is updated each month by listings published in the regularly
> issued bibliographies of the Civil Service Commission library.

U-11. U.S. Congress. <u>Government Employee Training Act.</u> Public Law 507. 85th Congress, 1958. Washington, D.C.: U. S. Govt. Print. Off., 1958.

U-12. U.S. Congress. <u>Higher Education Act of 1965.</u> Public Law 329. 89th Congress, 1965. Washington, D.C.: U. S. Govt. Print. Off., 1965.

U-13. U.S. Congress. <u>Higher Education Act of 1966.</u> Public Law 752. 89th Congress, 1966. Washington, D.C.: U. S. Govt. Print. Off., 1966.

U-14. U.S. Congress. House. <u>Commission on Instructional Technology. A Report to the President and the Congress of the United States.</u> Washington, D.C.: U.S. Govt. Print. Off., 1970.

U-15. U.S. Department of Agriculture. Graduate School. <u>Faculty Handbook, Part II: Improving Teaching.</u> Washington, D.C.: U.S. Dept. of Agriculture Graduate Schools, 1967. (ED 024 854.)

This excellent faculty handbook for the Graduate School of the Department of Agriculture emphasizes the impor tance of the teacher's understanding of the factors related to the learning process. Included briefly, but comprehensively, are such topics as characteristics of adult learners; the influence of group structure on learning ; planning an adult course to make effective use of the laws of learning; stating objectives in keeping with the laws of learning.

Considerable attention is given to outlining the conditions in which learning is encouraged: 1) the student must be adequately motivated to change his behavior; 2) the student must be aware of the inadequacy of his behavior; 3) the student must have a clear picture of the behavior which he is attempting to adopt; 4) the student must have opportunities to practice what he is learning; 5) the student must have available a sequence of appropriate materials; 6) the student must gain satisfaction in learning.

671

In addition there are instructions and characteristics listed
for the principal methods of instruction: lectures, group
discussion, seminars, field trips, case method.

Lastly, the subject of evaluation of student performance is
dealt with. Three general types of tests are discussed, as
teaching, mastering and measurement.

U-16. U.S. National Advisory Council on Extension and Continuing Education. Message from the President of the United States Trans-
mitting the Fifth Annual Report of the National Advisory
Council on Extension and Continuing Education. Washington,
D.C.: U.S. Govt. Print. Off., 1971.

The report includes the Council's recommendations for
coordination and consolidation of programs which emphasize
the post-secondary continuing education of adult citizens and
for the establishment of a National Foundation on Higher
Education.

U-17. U.S. National Institute of Mental Health. An Annotated Bibliography
on Inservice Training for Allied Professionals and Nonprofessionals in Community Mental Health. Bethesda, Md.:
National Institute of Mental Health, 1968. (ED 023 991.)

U-18. U.S. National Institute of Mental Health. Annotated Bibliography on
Inservice Training for Key Professionals in Community Mental
Health. Public Health Service Publication no. 1900. Washington,
D.C.: U.S.Govt. Print. Off., 1969. (ED 037 355.)

One hundred eighty nine documents published between 1960 and
1967 were abstracted. Documents are classified under the
headings: "Background," "Legislation," "Planning," "Services,"
"Grants," "Manpower," "Roles of Organizations and Key
Professionals," "Training - Inservice, Postgraduate, Staff
Development," "Training - Residency and Academic Credit,"
and "Brochures and Curriculum Outlines." There is also
a subject index.

U-19. U.S. National Institute of Mental Health. Annotated Bibliography on Training in Mental Health for Staff in Residential Institutions. Bethesda, Md.: National Institute of Mental Health, 1968. (ED 023 990.)

An annotated bibliography of periodical literature through August 1968, pertaining to inservice mental health training for personnel in residential institutions, and including materials on training in mental hospitals, institutions for the mentally retarded, child care residential institutions, and nursing homes.

U-20. *U.S. National Institute of Mental Health. Continuing Education: Agent of Change. Proceedings of the National Conference on Continuing Education in Mental Health. Washington, D.C.: U.S. Govt. Print. Off., 1971.

This book of proceedings is a gold mine for anyone concerned with the planning and implementation of continuing education programs. Part I contains the speeches and discussions of four plenary sessions. Part II reports on 8 group meetings. Part III gives a digest of recommendations to the NIMH and discusses conference evaluation and follow up. Part IV contains supplementary materials, including preconference materials distributed (such as one paper on the definition of continuing education), evaluation questionnaires, and a roster of participants.

Dr. Thomas G. Webster, Chief, Continuing Education Branch, Division of Manpower and Training Programs, National Institute of Mental Health, opens the introduction by pointing out the problem of definition regarding continuing education. "Continuing education has many meanings, and questions of definition arise early in most discussions of the subject. For purposes of this national conference, continuing education was explicitly and broadly defined to include postgraduate education, staff development, inservice training, and adult education."

The conference was unique in the wide range of participants which cut across disciplines and professions. Throughout the conference the involvement of the adult learner in the processes

673

of assessing needs, planning, conducting and evaluating continuing education programs was emphasized repeatedly in
plenary and small group sessions. A related theme was the
involvement of employers, consumers of health services,
citizen groups, and other representatives with vested interests
in determining the relevance and priorities for continuing
education programs. "The involvement of such interest
groups was seen as useful mutual education and as a significant
part of the decision making process."

The conference emphasized throughout the individual needs,
motivation, learning process, identity development, and
behavioral change of learners, which were discussed from a
variety of adult educational and psychological perspectives.
"Probably the strongest area of consensus between adult educators, mental health educators, administrators, and practitioners was the importance of affective learning, experiential
learning, and behavioral change as compared to the over-
emphasis on cognitive learning which still characterizes many
educational programs."

Advances in educational technology were noted, and in a few
instances demonstrated, but this was not a main emphasis of
the conference. Finally the conference served as a demonstration in the use of conferences as a variety of continuing
education.

Dr. Webster in an address filled with valuable insights for
every professional concerned with the development of continuing education programs, stressed one lesson, in particular,
that academic persons should learn from the marketing
experts -- a lesson that is especially relevant to continuing
education, that is "the importance of understanding the consumer and involving his motivation in the program planning
rather than to assume that one is marketing pure gold and that
those who do not partake of it are 'poorly motivated' or in
some other ways not up to snuff."

The fourth, and last, plenary session closed with a summary
impression of the conference and the future by William J.
McGlothlin, Vice President, University of Louisville.

One of the several preconference materials that was distributed to the participants was a paper by Malcolm S. Knowles,

Professor of Education, Boston University, on "Some Key
Theoretical Issues in Inservice Training." In that paper, he
gave the following definition of inservice education: "...all
those experiences in a work situation that are designed to influence the growth of employees. Specifically, we would include
supervision as a part of inservice education. In fact, in industry
the role of the supervisor is shifting away from definition as a
controller of human behavior to definition as a developer of
human competency. And the training of supervisors is getting
to be less concerned with the mastery of techniques of control
and more concerned with the mastery of the techniques of
education."

U-21. U.S. National Institute of Mental Health. A Community Project in
Religion and Mental Health. Bloomington, Ind.: Indiana
University, Medical Center, 1967. (ED 042 080.)

Supported by the National Institute of Mental Health and the Lilly
Endowment, Inc., a demonstration program in continuing education for clergy and related professions in the field of mental
health was conducted. The purpose was to provide clinical
pastoral education within the clergyman's home community,
where he could learn to work cooperatively with the mental
health resources. A week spent at Indiana University provided
a core curriculum. It was followed by a series of tri-weekly
seminars at which current pastoral cases were discussed,
followed by a second week at the Medical Center, which
focused on material in the community. A followup was scheduled
6 months afterwards. It was concluded that the clinical method
was adaptable to continuing education for the clergy but it was
recommended that a residential training center was necessary
for continuity.

U-22. U.S. National Institute of Mental Health. Training Methodology:
Part I: Background Theory and Research, An Annotated Biblio-
graphy. Public Health Service Publication No. 1862, Part I.
Washington, D.C.: U.S. Govt. Print. Off., 1969.

This bibliography pertains to research and theory on individual
behavior, group behavior, and educational and training philosophy. It is the first of a group of four on training methodology.

The references are arranged in classified order, annotated, and indexed. The material is listed under 15 headings, including Human Factors Engineering, Human Behavior and Behavioral Change (General), Motivation, Sociology of Education and Training, The Adult Learning, Learning Theory and Research, Programmed Learning, Systems Theory and Applications, Role Theory, Educational and Training Philosophies.

U-23. U.S. National Institute of Mental Health. Training Methodology: Part II: Planning and Administration, An Annotated Bibliography. Public Health Service Publication no. 1862, Part II. Washington, D.C.: U. S. Govt. Print. Off., 1969.

This bibliography pertains to research and theory on planning and administration. It is the second of a group of four on training methodology. The references are arranged in classified order, annotated, and indexed.

U-24. U.S. National Institute of Mental Health. Training Methodology: Part III: Instructional Methods and Techniques, An Annotated Bibliography. Public Health Service Publication no. 1862, Part III. Washington, D.C.: U. S. Govt. Print. Off., 1969. (ED 024 880.)

This is one of the most comprehensive bibliographies available on training concepts, in 7 parts. In the series on training methodology there are four parts: Part I: Background Theory and Research; Part II: Planning and Administration; Part III: Instructional Methods and Techniques; Part IV: Audiovisual Theory, Aids and Equipment.

The related group consists of three bibliographies on mental health inservice training: Training for Key Professionals in Community Mental Health; In-Service Training for Allied Professionals in Community Mental Health; and In-Service Training in Mental Health for Staff in Residential Institutions.

It is planned that these excellently annotated, classified, and indexed bibliographies will be kept up to date at periodic intervals. Other abstracting services whose material has been included are ASTD, AAW, ERIC, HUMBRO, USCSC, and special bibliographies.

U-25. U.S. National Institute of Mental Health.   Training
Methodology, Part IV: Audiovisual Theory, Aids and
Equipment: An Annotated Bibliography. Public Health
Service Publication no. 1862, Part IV. Washington, D.C.:
U.S. Govt. Print. Off., 1969. (ED 023 981.)

This is the fourth title in a series of bibliographies on mental
health inservice training produced as 7 publications. Part IV
on Audiovisual Theory, Aids, and Equipment consists of
332 abstracts, resumes, and annotations of selected documents.
Television instruction and equipment, film instruction and
equipment, graphic aids, videotape and sound recordings,
multimedia instruction, programmed instruction, computer
assisted instruction, methodological research, and program
administration and evaluation are among the subjects and
categories represented in this bibliography.

U-26. U.S. National Institute of Mental Health. Whither WICHE in Continuing Psychiatric Education of Physicians: Training Institute
for Psychiatrist-Teachers of Practicing Physicians. Boulder,
Colorado: Western Interstate Commission for Higher Education,
1970. (ED 044 069.)

This report of the WICHE (Western Interstate Commission for
Higher Education)Training Institute on Continuing Education
for Physicians includes the following papers: "Historical Per-
spectives on WICHE's Continuing Psychiatric Education Program
for Physicians," by Raymond Feldman, which examines how
WICHE got started in the program, what it has done, and what
it should try to accomplish in the future; "Use of the Physician
Assistant," by Robert A. Senescu; "Psychiatric Problems of
Physicians in Rural Areas," by John H. Waterman; "Long
Range Planning in Continuing Education," by Howard Kern;
"Patient-Centered Teaching with Video t ape," by Robert T.
Daugherty; "Patient-Centered Teaching without Video Tape,"
by Donald Naftulin; "Teaching and Learning Techniques," by
Carl Pollock; two arguments each on the pros and cons of continuing psychiatric education for physicians; and a discussion
summary by C. H. Hardin Branch. The volume concludes with
an enumeration of unresolved issues, and plans for future training institutes. A li st of the Institute participants is included.

677

U-27. U.S. Office of Education. Bureau of Adult, Vocational and
Library Programs. Division of Library Programs.
<u>Institutes for Training in Librarianship: Summer 1969 and
Academic Year 1969-70.</u> Washington, D.C.: U.S. Office
of Education, January, 1969. (Mimeographed)

A list of the institutes, granted under the Higher Education Act
of 1965, Title II-B, which authorized institutes for a program
of education designed to offer opportunities for an intensive
training experience which meets the needs of the participant.
The programs upgrade and update the competencies of persons
serving all types of libraries, information centers, or instructional materials centers offering library type services, and
those serving as library educators. Institute program content
supplements existing library training programs.

U-28. "UC Extension Keeps the Pros up to Date." <u>Business Week</u>
(March 12, 1967), 196-202.

U-29. University of California, Los Angeles, Graduate School of Library
Service. <u>Certificate of Specialization in Library Science.</u>
Information Circular No. 50. Los Angeles, California: UCLA
University of California, Los Angeles, Graduate School of
Library Service, 1972.

The Certificate of Specialization in Library Science at UCLA
is one example of a Post-MLS specialization program that is
offered by an increasing number of library schools.

"In 1968 the Academic Senate and the Regents of the University
of California authorized the UCLA School of Library Service to
award post-MLS certificates of specialization. The program
recognizes the need for specialized training in various fields of
librarianship, and the growing importance to librarians of
research competence, especially in their specialized fields of
professional practice."

The admission requirements vary slightly for each field of
specialization; but the basic requirements are a bachelor's
(or higher) degree in letters and science, a one-year professional
degree awarded by a school or department accredited by the
American Library Association, and unconditional admission to
graduate status by the UCLA Graduate Division.

The requirements for the certificate:

1) Three or four academic quarters of full-time study, or the number of quarters depending upon the student's qualifications and stated professional objective.

2) Completion of a minimum of nine courses in the School of Library Service and other departments of the University.

3) A research paper, bibliographical study, or literature survey appropriate for publication in a professional or scholarly journal, or as a separate paper prepared for Direct Individual Study or Research.

4) Maintenance of a grade point average of 3.0 (i.e. B). Courses graded "C" or below may not be counted in the minimum number of nine required courses.

Eventually the program will provide about 20 fields of specialization, but all fields will not be offered every academic year. The following fields of specialization have already been authorized: Music Librarianship; Library Systems Analysis and Automation; Rare Books and Manuscripts; Science and Engineering Librarianship; Medical Librarianship; Library Development for African and Afro-American Studies. Other fields approved by the Faculty of the School of Library Service, but waiting for authorization for certification are: Law Librarianship; Archives and Oral History, Junior College Library Administration; and Cataloging and Classification.

U-30. University of Pittsburgh. Graduate School of Library and Information Sciences. The Professional Education of Media Service Personnel: Recommendations for Training Media Service Personnel for Schools and Colleges. Preliminary edition. Pittsburgh: University of Pittsburgh Graduate Library School, Center for Library and Educational Media Studies, 1964.

This excellent study presents detailed plans for developing new curriculum programs on the graduate level which will help the individuals prepare for acceptance of professional careers in educational media services: the audiovisual specialist; school librarianship; broadcasting; and instructional technology. For each program for each year (5th year, 6th year, and Ph.D.)

of each program, certain basic information is presented:
a) information to be acquired; b) application skills; c) production skills; d) research skills.

U-31. University of Wisconsin. University Extension Division. Center for
Programs in Government Administration. Summer Institute
in Executive Development for Federal Administrators, 1963.
Madison, Wisconsin: University of Wisconsin, 1963.

U-32. "Unplanned Obsolescence: The Bane of Executives," Los Angeles
Times, July 26, 1967, p. 12.

U-33. The Urban Institute. University Urban Research Centers.
Washington, D.C.: The Urban Institute, 1969.

Urban research centers associated with academic institutions
are described. Continuing education programs are noted when
included in a center's activities. Four centers using "New
Approaches" are described in detail as prototypes for such
centers. Appendices include indexes by states of university
urban research centers.

U-34. Uris, Auren. "Mogy's Work Simplification is Working New Miracles,"
Factory,   (September, 1965)

Work simplification is presented as a personnel development and
motivating activity, in which individual employees are trained
to apply industrial engineering techniques to their own jobs.

U-35. Utz, Alan P.   "Objectives for Extension Staff Training and Development Derived from Sociological Concepts." Paper presented
at the Annual Meeting of the Rural Sociology Society, San
Francisco, August, 1969. New York: Sociological Abstracts,
1969.   (ED 037 656.)

In this paper, an attempt has been made to treat sociological
concepts,and those from other disciplines, as tools for deriving
objectives for staff training and development. The cooperative
extension educator's job was considered as one in which he uses

these concepts in achieving change in individual and group by performing the functions of teaching, linking systems, maintaining and developing the organization, and conditioning the public for acceptance and support of educational programs. The behavioral components of objectives were described as appropriate only inasmuch as they are derived from staff members' needs relating to their job and its inherent functions. Determination of objectives was treated as a process that provides for continuous development and training. Some criteria were set forth for deriving and rank ordering objectives in a way conducive to the active, meaningful learning essential to staff development.

V-1. Vainstein, Rose. "What the Library Schools Can Do in the
       Training and Upgrading of Consultants." In: Garrison, Guy,
       ed. The Changing Role of State Library Consultants.
       Champaign, Illinois: The University of Illinois Graduate
       School of Library Science, 1968, 83-95.

       After examining library school catalogs, the author con-
       cludes that there is nowhere one could enroll in an existing
       sixth-year specialist program for consultants, whether for
       credit or non-credit. Some of the author's suggestions for
       improved approaches to consulting include: the combination
       of teaching research and consultant work; larger library
       science collections in state library agencies; methods for
       enhancing the ability to communicate; establishment of an
       Institute of Advanced Library Studies; the participation of
       teams on visits or consulting trips; more research on team
       efforts. Consultants should develop from experienced
       librarians; specialized study should be restricted to sixth-
       year post-graduate level programs.

V-2. Veblen, John. "Continuing Library and Legal Education--A
       Comparison." Pacific Northwest Library Quarterly, 29
       (January, 1965), 112-19.

       An attorney stresses the importance of continuing education
       to the library profession as well as to his own. He urges
       the study of continuing education programs of all other
       professions, choosing the best and discarding the rest.
       Insists that complacency should never find a home in this
       profession.

V-3. Venn, Grant. "Educational Implications of Technological
       Change." A report to the Annual Convention of the Depart-
       ment of Rural Education, Detroit, Michigan, October 6-9,
       1963. (ED 020 060.)

V-4. Villanueva, A. B. "Intergovernmental Employee Development,
       Through University Extension and State College Cooperation."
       Training and Development Journal, 22 (October 1968), 27-35.

       Describes a cooperative program between Moorhead State
       College and the University of Minnesota to provide Federal
       government administrators in the area with public admin-
       istration courses. The program allows the student to earn
       a certificate in public administration on the completion of
       45 credits. The variety of courses offered is wide, with
       five basic "core" courses, five "spread" courses in practical
       aspects of public administration, and subject matter courses
       in various social sciences.